C000296757

THE ROMAN ARMY

PATRICIA SOUTHERN

AMBERLEY

First published 2014

Amberley Publishing
The Hill, Stroud
Gloucestershire, GL5 4EP

www.amberley-books.com

Copyright © Patricia Southern, 2014

The right of Patricia Southern to be identified as the Author of this
work has been asserted in accordance with the Copyrights, Designs
and Patents Act 1988.

All rights reserved. No part of this book may be reprinted or
reproduced or utilised in any form or by any electronic, mechanical
or other means, now known or hereafter invented, including
photocopying and recording, or in any information storage or
retrieval system, without the permission in writing from the
Publishers.

British Library Cataloguing in Publication Data.
A catalogue record for this book is available from the British Library.

ISBN 978 1 4456 2089 3 (print)
ISBN 978 1 4456 3723 5 (ebook)

Typesetting and Origination by Amberley Publishing.
Printed in the UK.

Contents

Part I The Roman Army of the Kings and the Republic   13
 1 Historical Overview 753–30 BC   15
 2 The Army of the Kings 753–509 BC   33
 3 The Army of the Early Republic 509–400 BC   45
 4 The Army of the Fourth Century BC   54
 5 The Latins and Other Allies   71
 6 The Army of the Middle Republic from the Third to the Second Century BC   81
 7 The Army of the Second Century BC   98
 8 Marius and His Mules: The Emergence of the Professional Roman Army   118
 9 The Rise of the Great Generals 100–60 BC   125
10 Caesar 58–49 BC   142
11 The Civil Wars and the End of the Republic 49–30 BC   162

Part II The Imperial Roman Army   183
 1 Historical Overview 30 BC–AD 260   185
 2 Augustus and the Establishment of the Standing Army   205
 3 The Legions from the First to the Third Century AD   214
 4 Auxiliary Infantry Cohorts   239
 5 Auxiliary Cavalry *Alae*   254
 6 Special and Military Elite Units   274
 7 Officers and Men   288
 8 Administration of the Army   300
 9 Camps, Forts and Fortresses   317
10 Artillery and Sieges   336
11 Frontiers   347
12 The Army in Action: Peace and War   368
13 Life in the Army   390
14 The Army and Civilians   410
15 Naval Forces   421

Part III The Army of the Late Empire   429
 1 Historical Overview, Third to Fifth Centuries AD   431
 2 Army Reorganisation of the Late Third Century AD   447
 3 Field Armies and Frontier Armies   462

4 Forts and Fortifications   476
5 Officers and Men   498
6 The End of the Roman Army   508

   Timeline 753 BC–AD 476   512
   Glossary   520
   Bibliography   526
   Index   542

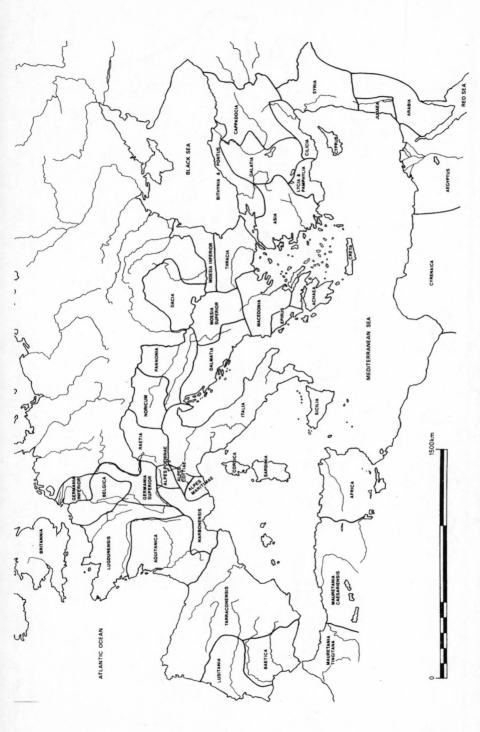

The Roman Empire reached its greatest extent under the Emperor Trajan in the early second century AD. This map shows the provinces at roughly that period, but provincial names and boundaries did not remain static thereafter. Trajan's successor Hadrian abandoned some of his predecessor's conquests on the Danube and in the east, and later emperors subdivided or amalgamated the provinces and gave them different names. Drawn by Graeme Stobbs.

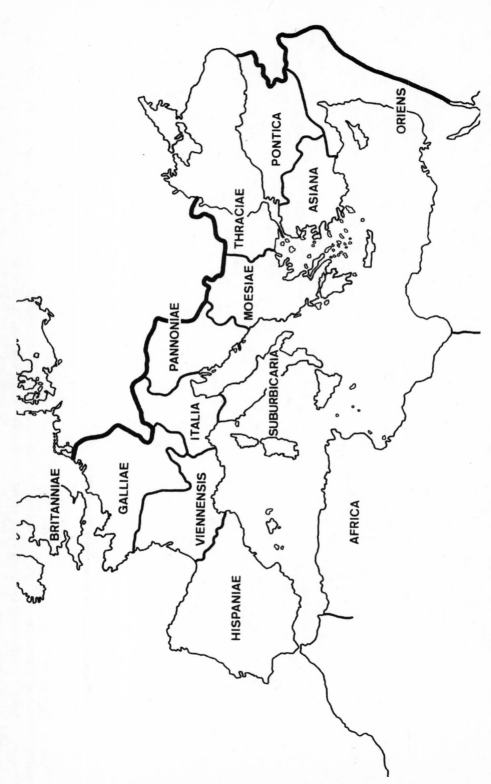

Diocletian reformed provincial government by grouping the provinces together in dioceses, and installing an extra tier of officials to govern them. Each diocese was governed by a *vicarius* answerable to the Praetorian Prefects, but the system is not fully attested until Constantine's reign. Drawn by Graeme Stobbs.

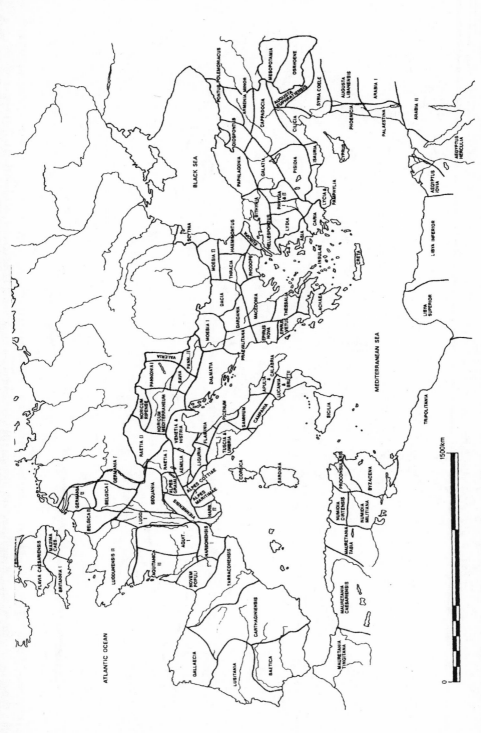

Within the dioceses, the provinces were split into much smaller units, so more officials were required to govern them. From now onwards, with some exceptions, civil and military affairs began to be separated, provincial affairs under the civil governors or *praesides* and the military command given to *duces*. Drawn by Graeme Stobbs.

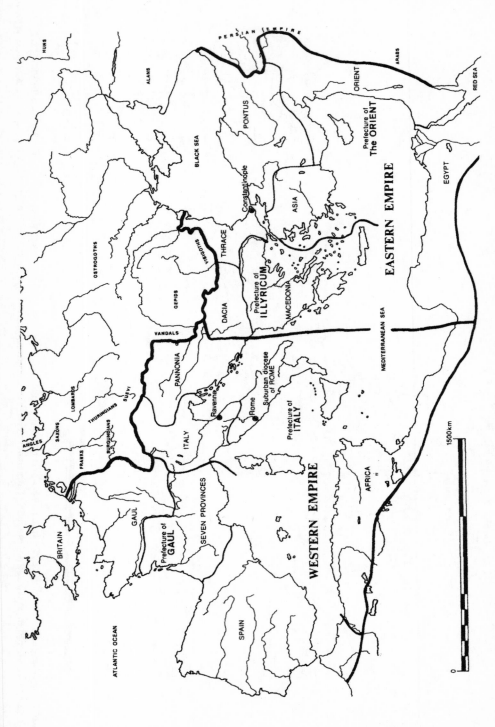

When Theodosius I died in AD 395 his sons Arcadius and Honorius became Emperors in the eastern and western sections of the Empire. There was no formal division into two halves until much later, but the east and west experienced different fortunes from the fifth century onwards. Drawn by Graeme Stobbs.

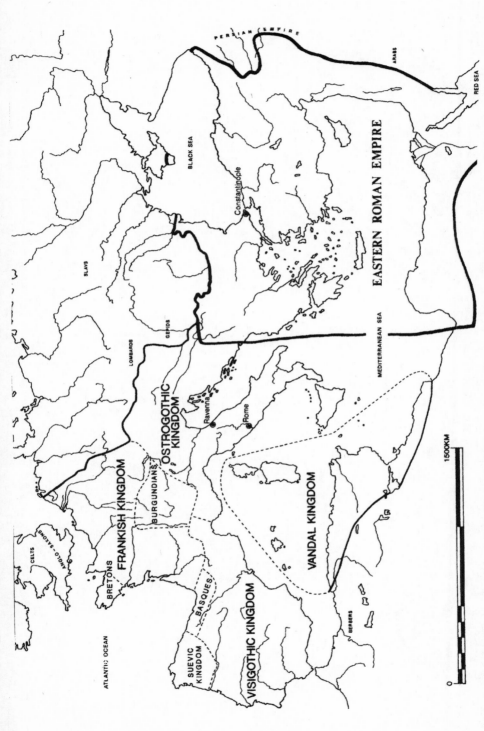

The western provinces were gradually transformed into separate kingdoms during the fifth and sixth centuries, but the eastern Empire preserved Roman forms of government for several centuries under the Byzantine rulers. Drawn by Graeme Stobbs.

Introduction

The Roman army endured for nearly a thousand years, through the era of the kings, the Republic and the Empire, and survived in much altered form in the Byzantine east. In the ten centuries of its existence it changed a great deal, so studying the Roman army from the traditional dates of 753 BC–AD 476 is equivalent to covering the history of the armies of Britain from the troops of William the Conqueror at the battle of Hastings to at least the First World War and beyond, or the armies of France from Charlemagne to Napoleon.

The division of historical events into manageable portions is at best artificial, but the Roman army falls naturally into three main groupings, which are followed in this book: the army of the kings and the early Republic, the Imperial army from the reign of Augustus to the third century AD, and the army of the later Roman Empire. In all these periods the army never ceased to develop and evolve, but though the armies in all three periods were different, the changes were progressive, without sharp and sudden divisions between them. The roots of the Imperial army are discernible during the Republic, and the Imperial army evolved into the later Roman army.

One of the main problems in organising the material in a history of the Roman army is that for the army of the kings and the Republic information is much less abundant than for the Imperial army, and in the late Roman Empire documentation for the army begins to disappear, ranging from sparse to nil. Many books on the Roman army concentrate on the first and second centuries AD because the whole panoply of archaeological, epigraphic, numismatic and literary evidence is available for its study, whereas for the Republican and later Roman armies these tools are less abundant. For the Republican army, archaeological finds and illustrative material are in short supply, so information that belongs to one particular context and time period often has to be used in wider contexts. There is more emphasis on what the army did, and less evidence for how it was organised during the five centuries of its existence. This lack of evidence precludes the thematic approach that can be made with regard to the Imperial army, with chapters on different kinds of units, their appearance, equipment, weaponry and fighting methods. At the end of the first century BC the historian Livy documented the army in action from its earliest times as part of his history of Rome, so the question must be asked, how reliable is Livy's work on the army of the early Republic? There will have been gaps in his sources which he may have filled in by means of speculation, but he seems to have been a diligent and honest researcher, within the confines of the glorification of Rome of course; nevertheless, he documents Roman defeats as well as victories, and he acknowledges his sources, occasionally admitting that there are discrepancies in what he has read so that he is not certain of the truth. It is difficult, for the author of this book at least, not to warm to Livy, but this does not mean that everything that he wrote should be accepted without question.

For the later Roman army, there is a frustrating lack of sources for material for the third century AD, the exact period when the most important changes took place. The epigraphic habit declined in the third century so there are fewer inscriptions than for the previous centuries, and the work of the main historians Dio and Herodian covers only the first decades of the third century. Chronology of events is not fully established, just when the many civil wars and usurpations require a more precise documentation. Comparison of the Roman army of the second century with that of the fourth can show how much it had changed, but cannot elucidate how and when the changes occurred.

The source materials for the study of the Roman army are varied and vast, but not always coherent or cohesive. One of the main sources of information about the appearance of the soldiers, where and how they lived, and about the tools and artefacts they used, derives from archaeological investigations and finds from the many different countries that made up the Roman Empire. Archaeological data is supplemented by a corpus of other sources. The Romans left behind an array of archival records concerning the administration of their armies, and these are to be found on papyrus, stone slabs, and wooden writing tablets; there are even rough daily records written on potsherds, the Roman version of scrap paper, presumably for copying up later in the unit offices. These records, together with tombstones, altars, and inscriptions recording building work, provide valuable information about the Roman army and the context in which it operated. This information is far from complete, but more is emerging all the time, and older opinions are re-examined in the light of new evidence. The definitive book can never be written, and the writer of this one makes no such claim to perfection. The excuse for producing it, if one is needed, is that it has always been an obsession.

Part I

The Roman Army of the Kings and the Republic

1

Historical Overview 753–30 BC

A historical survey of the Roman army must not only document the evolution of military organisation and operations, but also take into account the political and social background against which this extremely long-lived military force was established and developed. The distinction between civilian and military life that is taken for granted in many modern countries did not develop in ancient Rome until comparatively late in the history of the Empire. There was no standing army during the era of the kings or the Republic, so there was no distinct military or civilian career path for anyone to follow. All male citizens of military age and of a sufficiently wealthy social standing were eligible for service in the army in times of war, and in times of peace the soldiers reverted to being citizens once again, and returned to their farms or their relative slots in urban and political life, with the exclusion of the poorest men who did not count for anything in politics and did not serve in the army until later in the Republic.

The Romans were down-to-earth, pragmatic people. They compensated for the lack of artistic skills by their excellence in administration and law. They were not brilliant innovators, but they learned rapidly from their enemies, and from their own mistakes. They were enthusiastic borrowers of other people's ideas, often improving upon them, especially where the army was concerned. Some of the changes in military organisation resulted from external forces, as Rome met new problems and new enemies, while other changes were driven by internal political and social developments. As time went on, especially during the later Republic, it was sometimes the army and its needs that drove politics in Rome, rather than the other way around.

The Regal Period 753–509 BC

The tradition that Rome was founded in 753 BC is so deeply embedded in ancient and modern consciousness that it would be difficult to eradicate it. The Romans reckoned this date as their first year, counting all subsequent years from this time forwards, and denoting them by the initials *a.u.c.*, standing for *ab urbe condita*, from the foundation of the city. From the foundation of the Republic onwards, the Romans also used the names of the two annually elected consuls to denote each year.

The ancient Romans knew full well, as do modern historians, that 753 BC is an artificial date, a product of myth and legend, combined with the historical research of the ancient Roman scholars. The first known historian was Fabius Pictor, whose work dates to about 200. It is not known whether the early Romans kept official records of their political and military history. According to Livy, all records were destroyed when the Gauls invaded and sacked the city at the beginning of the fourth century BC, though some of the religious records did survive, and were published later in the Republic. It was a learned Roman called Terentius Varro who did some meticulous research and opted for 753 as the foundation date.

There were two foundation myths to be reconciled with each other. The earlier story relates how Aeneas and his father escaped from the city of Troy as it fell at the end of a very long siege. Aeneas was said to have founded the city of Lanuvium, and his son Ascanius founded Alba Longa, some miles south-east of Rome. A few hundred years later, Romulus and Remus, descendants of the kings of Alba Longa, founded Rome. It was important to retain the connection with Alba Longa in the many-faceted foundation myth, because every year the Romans left their city, leaving behind only a few people to carry on the government, to celebrate the religious festival of the Feriae Latinae at the Alban Mount. They continued to do this long after there was anyone left to explain the origins of this festival. The site still serves a semi-religious purpose, being the location of Castel Gandolfo, the summer residence of the Pope.

According to legend, round about the middle of the eighth century BC, King Numitor of Alba Longa was deposed by his wicked brother Amulius, who forced Numitor's daughter Rhea Silvia to become a Vestal Virgin, which meant that Rhea could not marry and produce heirs who might one day make a bid for kingship. But the god Mars made love to Rhea and became the father of her twins Romulus and Remus. Instead of having them killed, Amulius cast the two babies adrift in the Tiber, but they were rescued and suckled by the famous she-wolf, before a shepherd found them and brought them up as his own sons. The boys went on to found the city of Rome on the banks of the Tiber. Allegedly, Remus kept leaping over the unfinished walls of the fortifications that Romulus was building on what would become the Palatine Hill, and was killed by Romulus, who was not punished for this fratricide, but became Rome's first king.

Archaeology shows that if Rome really was established by Romulus in the middle of the eighth century BC, it was not the first settlement in the area. Some three centuries earlier there were people utilising the site, perhaps originally as a temporary base, which gradually became permanent. No remains of dwellings have been discovered, but a significant number of cremation burials have been found, indicating that the people burying their dead were not doing so as they passed through, but were living somewhere in the vicinity. By the eighth century BC people were starting to build huts on the Palatine and in the area near the river that would become the Forum Boarium. The traditional foundation date of 753 is therefore supported by dated archaeological finds, but only within the broad spectrum of the eighth century, and only in the context of a gradual accretion and development of a long-established dwelling place. Archaeological evidence from the Capitol Hill and the area at its base, which later became the Forum Romanum, suggests that activity there predates that of the Palatine. On the other hand, stretches of a wall have been found on the Palatine, founded on the original ground level, dated from pottery and brooches to around 720. It is interpreted as a defensive wall, not a building, and it is tempting to imagine that it was a corporate enterprise possibly organised by one of the early kings.

A lot was happening in Italy in the eighth century. By the middle of the century the Greeks had established colonies on the coasts, predominantly in southern Italy. By 725 they had founded a settlement at Cumae in the Bay of Naples. There were several reasons behind the foundation of colonies, among them population pressure, shortage of agricultural land, and the need for trade. This last element prompted the development of coinage among the Greeks, long before the Romans. Archaeological finds show that the Etruscan city states were receiving Greek and Phoenician goods, probably in return for copper and iron from Etruria and Tuscany.

The first settlers near the banks of the Tiber enjoyed several geographical advantages, which were noted by Cicero, and the historian Livy. Geographically, the embryonic city of Rome was located in fertile lands to the west of the Apennines, and there were easily exploitable landing places on the western coast. The settlement was placed at an easy crossing point of the River Tiber, and there was a good supply of water. The famous seven hills made the settlement, or several settlements, more easily defensible. The settlers were far enough away from the west coast to avoid seaborne attacks, but they were still close enough to the sea to facilitate the transport of goods inwards and outwards. The early settlers could control and tax north–south traffic crossing the Tiber, and they could control the lucrative salt pans at the mouth of the river. In an age when consumption of salt is actively discouraged on health grounds, it is easy to underestimate the importance of this commodity.

The territorial advantages of the chosen site of Rome would not by themselves ensure the future success of the inhabitants, if those same inhabitants had not been practical, hard-headed, adaptable, and completely intransigent when faced with disasters.

The early communities in Italy were organised on a tribal basis. The people of early Rome belonged to the area called Latium, inhabited by Latins who all spoke the same language and shared the same culture and customs as the Romans. To the north were the Etruscans, whose origins are still not fully elucidated. Their art and sculpture seem to point to an Asian origin, but this is disputed. What little is known of their language and script does not conclusively prove any of the theories about their origins. The Etruscans were to influence the developing city of Rome, and some scholars have suggested that they may have controlled it for a short time.

Beyond the Etruscans, were several Celtic tribes, on both sides of the Alps. To the east there were fierce Samnites, Marsi, Picenes, Aequi and Volsci. These people were distinct from the Latins, speaking a language called Oscan, which was not entirely obliterated even by the first century AD. The coastal areas of Italy and much of the south were populated and controlled by Greek city states.

Although there were elements of cultural uniformity among the Italic peoples, there was no concept of Italia in the sense of political or social unity. The early Romans were allegedly a mixed group of people, because it was said that Romulus invited all kinds of men to join the new settlement, including people with dubious histories, but Rome was not alone, since archaeological finds show that several early settlements in Italy were multicultural. According to legend, not all of early Rome's settlers came of their own free will. The story goes that there was a shortage of womenfolk, so the Romans mounted an expedition to seize some eligible females from the neighbouring Sabines. Perhaps this is a graphic account of more orderly intermarriage.

In early tradition there were three different tribes in Rome: the Ramnes, probably the original Romans living on the Palatine; the Tities comprising Sabines under their leader Titus Tatius gathered on the Quirinal Hill; and the Luceres, thought to be mainly Etruscans on the Caelian Hill. No archaeological finds have yet come to light that can support a distinct tribal background in each of the separate dwelling places. The three communities of early Rome were ruled by kings, traditionally seven of them from the foundation in 753 to the establishment of the Republic in 509. The figure seven probably had magical significance, and probably relates to the famous Seven Hills of Rome. The number of the kings, their names, the dates ascribed to their reigns, and the lists of their various achievements simply cannot be verified by historical research or archaeological discoveries.

What can be discerned is the gradual process of urbanisation that was taking place in several cities of Latium and other areas of Italy, around the middle of the seventh century BC. In Rome in particular, there are signs that corporate decisions were being made. In the area that would later become the Forum Romanum, some primitive dwellings were destroyed, and then the ground level was built up over the remains, most likely to avoid flooding from the River Tiber.

Gravel paving was laid down. This suggests a corporate decision and co-operative action. The first public buildings were being erected towards the end of the seventh century.

In the Regal period, the three original tribes of the Ramnes, Tities and Luceres were each divided into ten smaller groupings called *curiae*. The thirty *curiae* formed the people's assemblies and provided the basis for political functions and for the organisation of the army. It is not clear how the assemblies operated, or how they interacted with the kings. The only certainty is that wealth and nobility were what counted in Rome. The kings were drawn from the aristocracy, and controlled all aspects of political, religious, and military life. The kings were supreme commanders of the armies, political leaders, chief justices and high priests. They held power for life, but could not bequeath power to their descendants. When a king died, an *interrex* was chosen from the aristocratic families, but his office was limited to five days, and then another man would take his place for another five days, and so on until the new king was chosen.

Romulus c. 753–716 BC

The first king of Rome is part man, part myth. He was transformed into the god Quirinus when he died. As the founder of the city, he directed its affairs, defended it, and allegedly increased its population by inviting foreigners to join the new community. He is said to have chosen 100 men as his advisers, who may have evolved into the aristocrats of the later city, possibly even forming the prototype Senate. He most likely surrounded himself with favourites from among his friends, and it may have been a group of such friends who finally despatched him. Mystery surrounds the demise of Romulus. He was officiating at a religious festival when a fierce thunderstorm dispersed most of the onlookers, and he disappeared. It was said that he had ascended to join the gods, but it was also murmured that his friends had killed him, cutting him into pieces and carrying them away to disguise the murder. Rome had been founded on a fratricide, so perhaps it developed after a regicide.

Numa Pompilius c. 716–673 BC

The new king was the choice of the Sabines. Numa was said to have been related by marriage to the Sabine King Titus Tatius. His talents lay in the sphere of administration and law, and he introduced calendar reforms, establishing a year of 360 days, which remained in force with adjustments for the next six centuries until Julius Caesar adopted the Egyptian calendar of 365 and a quarter days. The cult of the Vestal Virgins was removed from Alba Longa to Rome under Numa's rule.

Tullus Hostilius c. 673–641 BC

A war with Alba Longa was threatened, but it was avoided when Hostilius and King Mettius of Alba agreed to appoint champions to fight on their behalf. Three brothers of the Horatii clan were chosen to fight for Rome, and vanquished their opponents, with the result that Alba Longa came under Roman control, and its development ceased. Eventually it disappeared, although the site was revered by the Romans who trekked there every year to observe religious ceremonies. There may have been a prototype Senate by this time in Rome. Hostilius is credited with building the *Curia Hostilia*, supposedly the first Senate House. The presence of an official meeting house implies that there were gatherings and proclamations, perhaps even debates, but it is not known how the early Senate functioned.

Ancus Marcius c. 641–616 BC

The new king was the grandson of Numa Pompilius. He is credited with an energetic defence of the city when some of the Latins attempted to stop the expansion of the upstart community at Rome. Ancus is said to have destroyed some of the Latin settlements, but he brought the inhabitants to Rome, though with what status is debatable. Ancus is also said to have built the first port at Ostia at the mouth of the River Tiber, and although no trace of this early coastal establishment has come to light, it is unlikely that the kings and people of Rome would have failed to notice the importance of Ostia for the development of their city.

Tarquinius Priscus c. 616–579 BC

Tarquinius may have been an Etruscan, or possibly a Greek citizen who had settled in the city of Tarquinii in Etruria. As soon as Ancus Marcius was dead, he made himself king, probably illegally. He paid for his actions later, being assassinated by the sons of Ancus Marcius. Tarquinius increased the size of the Senate, and the numbers of the Roman cavalry, both of which bland statements raise many questions as to how and why, but if the story is true, it probably indicates an expanding population and a need for more elaborate defence.

Servius Tullius c. 579–535 BC

Although Tarquinius was killed instantly by assassins appointed by the sons of Ancus Marcius, his quick-thinking wife Tanaquil removed the body and gave out that he was badly wounded, but was recovering. She suggested that a member of her husband's household, Servius Tullius, could deputise for him. The ruse worked, and Servius became king without being legally appointed. More importantly he held onto his power after it was announced that Tarquinius was dead. The new king set about reforming the political and military organisation of Rome. The so-called Servian reforms laid the foundations for the later Republican organisation of the city, though it is difficult to distinguish between the original schemes of Servius Tullius and the later accretions and developments of the Republic.

By Servius' day it is probable that the population had increased, making the division into only three tribes somewhat unwieldy. Servius created four tribes, and divided them into centuries, theoretically containing 100 men, which formed the basis of the voting systems and the army. This simplistic statement conceals endless debate about the political and military organisation.

Servius is also credited with extending the boundary (*pomerium*) of Rome, and the building of defensive walls. The two are not necessarily contiguous. The so-called Servian walls actually date from the fourth century BC, but it is possible that Servius built earthwork defences consisting of a bank and ditch, perhaps with a palisade on top. Livy says that the *pomerium* had a religious significance. Generals commanding armies were forbidden to cross it under arms.

Tarquinius Superbus c. 535–509 BC

In 535 or possibly the following year, Servius Tullius was assassinated and Tarquinius Superbus seized power. Among some historians it was once taken for granted that Tarquinius was of ethnic Etruscan origin, and that his rule must have ushered in a period of Etruscan domination of Rome. This is now played down in favour of strong influence. The ancient Roman authors thought that much of the regalia and ceremonial of the kings was derived from Etruscan sources.

Although Tarquinius Superbus has gone down in history as a despot, it seems that Rome developed further and faster than ever during his reign. Public buildings were constructed, roads were laid out, the water supply and sewage disposal systems were started. Tarquinius may have been responsible for the establishment of the Cloaca Maxima, the famous sewer that still lurks underneath modern Rome. Modern historians have claimed that Etruscan engineers must have been responsible for the building work, but the only firm indications of Etruscan workmanship derive from an early version of the temple of Jupiter on the Capitoline Hill, where sculptors from Veii made the terracotta statues.

Perhaps more importantly for Rome's future development, the city eventually became the dominant force among the Latin city states. If this was what so-called Etruscan domination entailed, then it was not such a detrimental concept for Rome.

The end of the reign of Tarquinius Superbus was prolonged, complicated and bloody. It began when his son Sextus raped the virtuous Lucretia, who then killed herself. Personal tragedy led to political upheaval. Lucretia's husband and Tarquinius' own nephew, Lucius Junius Brutus, ejected Tarquinius, who rallied other Etruscan cities, gathered an army and met the Romans in battle in 509. He lost, but survived, and three years later another Etruscan, Lars Porsenna, tried to take Rome. According to the Roman historians Tacitus and Pliny, he may have occupied the city for a short time. By this time the Republic had been founded. It lurched through several low points and crises, and survived them all, for the next 500 years.

The Roman Republic 509–200 BC

The date 509, embedded in tradition like the birth of Rome in 753, probably does not signify the exact year when the Republic began. Purists opt for 507 instead. The foundation of the Republic was probably a continuous process involving considerable upheaval. There are some archaeological traces of destruction of buildings in Rome, dating to the end of the sixth century BC, which may be associated with the expulsion of the kings and the withdrawal of Lars Porsenna.

It is unlikely that the Republic, with the Senate, the annually elected magistrates, the voting systems and the organisation of the city, all sprang up fully fledged on the morning after the Etruscans left the city. Porsenna and Tarquinius Superbus were still at large, and beyond them there were other potential enemies among the tribes and city states around Rome, who might try to take advantage of the leaderless city. Someone, or a group of people, would have to take command quite rapidly.

Fortunately for Rome, several developing Italian city states were too preoccupied with their own internal problems to take much notice of what was happening elsewhere. Several cities ejected their royal rulers and formed a new government at the same time as Rome became a Republic. One of the results of the widespread political upheaval is an archaeologically detectable economic downturn in the early fifth century BC.

The Senate and People of Rome

The Republic was governed by the Senate and People of Rome, expressed in Latin as *Senatus Populusque Romanus*, abbreviated to SPQR on monuments and documents. These initials are still used today in modern Rome on mundane things like drain covers and lamp posts. The early development of Republican government is not clearly elucidated, so a description of the system in its later, evolved form must serve as an indication of what might have happened at the turn of the sixth and fifth centuries BC.

The supreme corporate body, controlling finance, the army, law and order, internal affairs and foreign relations, was the Senate. There may have been an embryo Senate surrounding the kings as advisers and companions, but whether the term Senate could be applied to it at this stage is uncertain. After the expulsion of the kings, there would be a collection of men with some experience of government, since a small number of individuals would have acted as *interrex* (plural *interreges*) between the death of a king and the election of his successor. Membership of the Senate always depended on wealth, usually in the form of landownership. It also depended on suitability, good behaviour, and loyalty to the state, and any lapses could mean ejection from the Senate. From at least the second half of the fifth century BC, two officials called censors were elected, every four years, later extended to five years. These men usually held office for eighteen months, and had the power to revise the list of senators, removing those considered unsuitable. They also carried out a census of Roman citizens.

The peoples' assemblies were the various *comitia*, a plural term derived from *comitium*, meaning the place of assembly rather than the assembly itself, but not necessarily applied to a building. The people could not gather at will, but had to be summoned by a magistrate. No members of the *comitia*, however it was constituted, could formulate policy on their own account, and there was no debate about proposals put to the assembly for approval. Action was limited to a vote for yes or no. The earliest assembly was the *comitia curiata*, based on the thirty *curiae* of the regal period. One of its most important functions was to confirm the appointments of magistrates by passing a law called a *lex curiata*. Adoptions and wills were also within its remit. It functioned all through the Republic, though some of its responsibilities were taken over by the *comitia centuriata*, which as its name suggests was formed from centuries, grouped into classes. Allegedly this organisation derived from the reforms of Servius Tullius. The consuls, praetors and censors were elected by the *comitia centuriata*, but the voting procedure was heavily weighted in favour of the rich. Elections were decided by the majority vote of each century. There were fewer rich men than poor, but within the wealthy classes there were many more centuries, while the poorer people were all crammed into the fifth class in only one century, which limited huge numbers of people to one majority vote. The *comitia centuriata* could enact laws put before the people by the magistrates, and could vote for or against going to war.

There were other *comitia* based on territorial tribes. The division into tribes still functioned throughout the Republic and during the Empire. New citizens were assigned to tribes, even though they did not live in Rome. This is revealed on tombstones, especially early military ones where the formula included the name of the deceased, that of his father, and also his voting tribe. The *comitia plebis tributa* based on tribal divisions started out as the council of the plebs. This body elected the tribunes of the plebs and the aediles, and could enact plebiscites which were eventually made legal enactments. The *comitia populi tributa* included not just plebeians but all the people, and elected the military tribunes and quaestors. Both bodies could conduct trials for minor offences.

The Magistrates of the Republic

The Republic was not directly governed by the Senate and the people's assemblies. The Senate had no executive functions. Senators could not meet unless summoned by a magistrate, and not all magistrates had the right to do so. Any resolution agreed upon by the senators had to be framed in a law and put before the people for approval.

The chief magistrates of the early Republic were the two consuls, and the praetors, who ranked below the consuls in the evolved form of government. The modern term 'magistrate' evokes jury courts and presiding judges, but in a Roman context it indicates the elected officials of the government.

The oldest of the lists of consuls, the *Fasti Capitolini*, began in 509, but this is not taken as absolute proof that the first consuls were elected in that year. There were other records which differed in their start dates, and Livy comments that there were too many discrepancies in the records to be certain about who followed whom as consuls. The early chief officials may not even have been consuls. In the early Republic the praetors may have been the most important officials. The term derives from Latin *prae ire*, meaning 'to go before'. There may have been only one praetor, but there are references to a *praetor maximus*, meaning greatest praetor. According to grammatical rules, if there were only two praetors, the more important one ought to have been called *maior,* so the terminology suggests the presence of an unknown number of other praetors who were somewhat less than *maximus*. This also implies a shared responsibility for a number of tasks.

At some unknown time, annually elected pairs of consuls replaced the praetor or praetors. Republican Romans, nurtured in their hatred of rule by a single individual, devised the principle of collegiality, probably in the mid-fifth century BC. With two consuls in office for one year, each was theoretically able to counter any overweening ambition on the part of his colleague. The consuls were responsible for all aspects of government, controlling the armed forces by means of their official power, or *imperium*, which had to be formally bestowed by the people.

As the daily business of the Republic increased, the praetor reappeared in the fourth century BC. Initially only one praetor was elected each year, subordinate to the consuls, but able to hold *imperium* which authorised him to command troops. About a century later, two praetors were needed, the *praetor urbanus* for internal affairs, and the *praetor peregrinus* for foreign affairs.

In times of crisis, a Dictator was appointed. Existing magistrates remained in office, but were subject to his supreme civil and military authority. He selected a subordinate commander, the *magister equitum*, or master of horse. These men were limited to a term of six months in case they developed a taste for power, which is exactly what happened with late Republican Dictators, such as Lucius Cornelius Sulla, and Gaius Julius Caesar, both of whom transcended the six-month term and held office for as long as it took to put all their programmes into effect. Sulla survived and retired to his estates, but Caesar paid with his life in 44.

Lesser magistrates were the aediles and quaestors, posts held by young aspiring politicians. The aediles were originally plebeian officials in charge of the temples or *aedes* on the Aventine hill, but eventually this magistracy included patricians and plebeians, and the responsibilities of the aediles embraced care of the streets and buildings of the city, the food supply, and putting on games and shows – the more splendid the games, the greater the popularity of the aedile responsible for them. Quaestors were elected annually by the people, and their responsibilities were mainly financial, concerned with the treasury at Rome. Provincial governors would usually appoint quaestors to look after the finances of their provinces. The number of quaestors gradually increased, and the office eventually became the first stepping stone to a senatorial career.

These were the main elements of Republican government, not necessarily instituted immediately after the expulsion of the kings, but developing gradually as the need arose. The Romans retained the same officials throughout the long history of the Republic and into the Empire, but continually adapted the nature and function of the magistracies, adding more praetors, aediles and quaestors when the workload increased.

The number of annually elected consuls remained at two per annum for a long time, but from the fourth century onwards the consulship could be extended. In 326 the consul Quintus Publilius Philo and his army were besieging Naples when his office was due to end. One of the new consuls ought to have been sent out to replace him, but to change the commander in the middle of a war was not the best way of encouraging the troops and ensuring success, so the people of Rome decided that Philo should be enabled to act on behalf of a consul, *pro consule* in Latin, and so the proconsulship was created. It was not used on a regular basis until later in the Republic, but the principle was established and the proconsulship proved its worth if there was a crisis, requiring several commanders at the same time. The proconsulship was eventually employed in the government of Rome's steadily growing number of provinces.

The Struggle of the Orders: Patricians and Plebeians 494–471 BC

The schism between plebs and patricians, characterised by the secession of the plebs in 494, is still not fully explained. It has been suggested that the patricians were true Romans, while the plebs belonged originally to other tribes, or vice versa: the plebs were the original settlers and the patricians were infiltrating aristocrats who took over the government.

The Romans detected differences between plebs and patricians which led to a relatively short-lived law against intermarriage between the two groups. Oppression of the plebs by the patricians was a constant theme, probably caused by chronic debt leading to imprisonment, or brutal assault on plebeian defaulters by patricians. Whatever their grievances, in 494 BC the plebs decamped to the Aventine hill, refusing to serve in the army. Some scholars doubt that this event occurred at all, because there were no detectable results until the plebs repeated the process in 471, when the *concilium plebis* was formed, and tribunes of the plebs, two of them originally, ten eventually, were elected. The powers of the tribunes were limited at first, and it took a long time and a series of stages before the tribunes of the plebs were allowed access to senatorial debates, and eventually the right to convoke the Senate. The most famous attribute of the tribunes of the plebs was their responsibility to protect the plebs from patrician oppression, with the right of *intercessio*, for which 'veto' is not quite an exact equivalent. If any proposals were put forward contrary to the interests of the plebs, tribunes could block them. All this took about two centuries to come to fruition, but at the end of the Republic and the beginning of the Empire, tribunician power was adopted by Augustus and succeeding emperors as a vital element of their rule.

The Twelve Tables of Law 451–450 BC

From about 462 onwards, the plebs began to agitate for better clarification of the law. The law was known only to a few privileged people, but not clearly stated for the benefit of everyone else, so how could people keep within its boundaries if they did not know what was legal or illegal? Ancient historians state that a committee was despatched to Athens to study the laws drawn up by Solon, and to other Greek cities where laws had been codified. Presumably the Romans also studied how these laws had evolved and the amendments that had been made since the initial compilations had been made. In 451 ten men, all patricians, were elected to write the laws, *Decemviri legibus scribundis*. The usual magistrates resigned from office, and the *Decemviri* took over all responsibility for the government, as well as codifying the law. It is debated whether the intention was to disband the ten men at the end of a year, or whether they were to form the government from then onwards. At the end of the first year, only ten tables or lists of laws had been produced. This did not embody all the laws, so another ten men were elected, this time including plebeians. One man, Appius Claudius, served on both sets of *Decemviri*, largely because he agitated very strongly for re-election. Another two tables of laws were produced, thus making the total Twelve Tables by which they are known.

The Twelve Tables were probably never intended to embody a complete corpus of Roman law in the fifth century BC. The purpose was more likely to have been to clarify those areas where there had been controversial issues, leaving established custom to cover everything else. Republican schoolboys were made to learn the contents of all Twelve Tables by heart, but in modern times much of the text of the tables is lost, making it difficult to assign specific laws to a specific table. Modern scholarship has established the majority of the laws, divided into categories.

The achievement of codifying the laws is overshadowed by the subsequent behaviour of the *Decemviri* in general, and Appius Claudius in particular. They refused to relinquish their powers, and Appius was involved in a scandal that sounds like a replay of the rape of Lucretia by the son of King Tarquinius. He raped a virtuous girl called Verginia, and then claimed that she was his slave, thus breaking a law that the Twelve Tables had established, concerning false enslavement. Appius Claudius came to a sticky end in prison. Normal government was allegedly re-established by the Valerio-Horatian laws, customarily named after the two consuls Valerius and Horatius who enacted them.

War with the Neighbours c. 509–400 BC

It has been said that Rome's expansion from a city state to an Empire was all down to a continual search for safe boundaries, which may contain an element of truth, but ignores the need for trade and the acquisition of natural resources, and the territorial control that is essential if these needs are to be satisfied. It must not be imagined that Rome was the only aggressive state in the Italian peninsula with an acquisitive urge for territory. There was great unrest among the Italic tribes and new settlers such as the Greeks, who colonised much of the south. Tribes and city states made raids on each other's territory, and then after these struggles they sometimes allied with each other to fight a common enemy. In 540, while Rome was still ruled by kings, the Etruscans fought the Carthaginians, but later these two erstwhile enemies allied against the Greeks of Syracuse, while fighting for control of Cumae. These wars were prompted largely by trading concerns.

The tribes and city states surrounding Rome were not necessarily peace-loving victims of Roman expansionism, but nor were the Romans averse to territorial gains after a war. Warfare in the early Republic was probably limited to small-scale skirmishes. Few battles can be documented in terms of strategy and tactics, though sometimes is it possible to determine why a particular struggle began. The finer details of the wars are reserved for the chapters on the army.

Rome was only one of the cities of Latium, where the various city states had devised a shared legal status, allowing citizens of each state to intermarry (*ius conubium*) and to conduct trading ventures (*ius commercium*) with other states. These legal systems were adopted by the Romans when their differences with the Latins had been ironed out. At the very beginning of the Republic, the Latins rebelled but were defeated by the Romans at the battle of Lake Regillus in 499, or possibly 496. A treaty was drawn up in 493, and the Romans and Latins allied to fight against the Volsci and Aequi. For about a century, the Latins and the Romans were at peace, but Roman expansion caused resentment around 341. The Latins formed a united front, described in modern terminology as the Latin League. The Romans defeated the Latins and dissolved the confederation in 338. Separate alliances were made with each Latin state, so they were bound to Rome and forbidden to ally with each other. In other respects the cities were self-governing, and they did not pay monetary taxes, but instead were obliged to contribute troops for a joint Roman and allied army whenever there was a need. Treaties of alliance on this model were extended eventually to most of the Italian tribes and states, enabling Rome to assemble large armies of her own citizens supplemented by the allies.

An alliance was drawn up in 504 between the Romans and the Sabine tribes in Italy, but the agreement did not stop the Sabines from making armed incursions into Latin territories. The struggle only ended when the Sabines were granted Roman citizenship, at first without voting rights, their state being termed a *civitas sine suffragio*. The Sabines became full citizens in 268 BC, but the concept of citizens without voting rights was extended to other communities as Rome continued to expand.

Etruscan neighbours of the Romans were eventually absorbed into the Roman sphere. There was a long-standing feud with the Etruscan city of Veii, only ten miles north of Rome, with territories extending to the right bank of the Tiber. The citizens of Veii dominated the east–west route along the right bank of the Tiber connecting the interior to the coast, and thereby controlled the Via Salaria, or the salt road. Control of routes and the trade passing along them was vital to the Romans too, so they squabbled with Veii for much of the fifth century BC, and finally captured the city and destroyed it in 396. The fertile lands of the city were taken over and settled by Romans.

The rise to power and dominance was not a smooth progression for the Romans. At the beginning of the fourth century BC, while the Romans were occupied in struggles with Etruscan cities, the Gauls erupted from northern Italy, inflicted a disastrous defeat on the Roman army at the battle of the River Allia, and then they attacked Rome itself. Tradition states that most citizens abandoned the city for a while. The setback may have been exaggerated by the ancient historians, but the ensuing decades were fairly uneventful, as though the Romans had to devote much attention to repairing the damage.

In the mid-fourth century the Romans went to war for the first time with the Samnites, whose territory was to the east of Rome, but the Samnites had seized the city of Capua in Campania, and made it their headquarters. In 354 the Romans made a treaty with the Samnites, defining the River Liris (the modern Garigliano) as the boundary between Latium and Samnium. The agreement held for a few years, but did not bring peace. In three successive and prolonged wars (341, 327–304, and 298–290) the Samnites defeated the Romans more than once, but also taught them a lot in the process, until they were finally subdued.

Rome in the Third Century BC

The first half of the third century BC was characterised by continual warfare among the peoples within the Italian peninsula, but by the end of the century Rome had emerged as the dominant power with most of Italy under her control. The Romans were then drawn into external wars in countries outside Italy, and also began to experience serious internal problems.

The Romans insisted that all their wars were fully justified. This sometimes involved manipulation of the truth. By accentuating perceived threat, and playing down their own acquisitive urge for military glory and accumulation of land and booty, Roman politicians and historians could make it seem that the first aggressive moves were always instigated by other people, so their wars were reactive rather than proactive. It was not as simple as that. Once they were committed to war, the Romans lost battles, but did not lose the wars, and it is a measure of Rome's reputation for military success that other states asked for assistance against their enemies.

In 284 the city of Thurii, a Greek colony founded on the site of the ancient city of Sybaris (modern Sibari) approached the Romans for aid against the raids of the Lucanian and Bruttian tribes. This brought Rome into conflict with Tarentum, the leading Greek city of all the colonies of southern Italy. The Tarentines called upon King Pyrrhus of Epirus, in Greece, for help. From 280 to 275, the Romans fought Pyrrhus and were defeated. There was a respite for a couple of years while Pyrrhus took his army to aid Syracuse against the Carthaginians, and when he turned his attention to Rome again, the Romans were ready for him, and defeated him at Beneventum in Samnite territory in 275.

From then until the 260s Romans fought Samnites and Lucanians, gradually gaining ground and planting colonies to control the territory, notably at Paestum and Beneventum. Just as Rome was emerging as the most dominant force in the Italian peninsula, governing via her alliances with states and tribes, and her newly established colonies, she was drawn into wars with a more formidable enemy, this time from outside Italy: Carthage.

The Carthaginians were originally Phoenician settlers who, according to legend, founded the city of Carthage by a ruse, agreeing to take no more land than could be covered by an ox hide, which they cut into narrow strips and stretched out to delineate their first settlement. The story highlights the scheming, untrustworthy nature of the Carthaginians as viewed by the Romans, who called them Phoenicians, or Poeni, from which the word *Punicus* is derived. Hence the title Punic Wars, given to the three prolonged and bloody conflicts between Romans and Carthaginians from 264 to 241, 218 to 201, and again from 149 to 146.

The Romans were already acquainted with the Carthaginians. The first treaty or agreement between the two states was traditionally dated to 509 BC, although there is some debate about this early date. The next more securely dated treaty between Rome and Carthage was drawn up in 348, and in 278 Carthage offered the Romans some assistance against Pyrrhus, largely because they were anxious to keep both the Romans and Pyrrhus out of Sicily.

Carthage had strong trading interests, by dint of which she was a major maritime power in the Mediterranean, with an experienced navy manned by citizens, but the Carthaginian army consisted mostly of hired mercenaries. Conversely, Rome was a land-based power with a citizen army ably assisted by allied troops, but no navy of her own. The first ships and crews were contributed by Rome's allies (*socii*) on the Italian coast, termed the *socii navales*.

The Punic Wars are described more fully in the chapters on the army, so only an outline is given here. The first war began in Sicily in 264, and then the focus turned to naval battles. In 260 the Romans won their first naval victory at Mylae off the coast of Sicily. Four years later they decided to attack Carthage itself, but were eventually soundly defeated. They raised new armies and built new fleets and in 241, in a naval battle off Lilybaeum (modern Marsala), the consul Gaius Lutatius Catulus captured or destroyed over a hundred Carthaginian ships. Thus ended the first war with Carthage.

The Romans were now supreme in Sicily, which they annexed as their first province. They made an alliance with Syracuse, which remained independent, until 211 when it was taken over after a rebellion. Sicily contained fertile agricultural land, and there was an efficient taxation system already in place which the Romans took over intact. The acquisition of the first province required some adjustment to the system of government. A praetor was appointed to take charge of the island, assisted by two quaestors, one in Syracuse and the other in Lilybaeum.

An indemnity was imposed on the Carthaginians, for whom the next few years were bleak. The loss of Sicily meant that they had to look elsewhere for trade and profit. They chose Spain. There was peace for over two decades. The Romans dealt with Gallic tribes in Cisalpine Gaul, which literally means 'Gaul this side of the Alps'. Abroad, the Romans embroiled themselves in a war in Illyria, against Queen Teuta and her tribesmen who constantly harassed the Greek cities nearby. Rome went to war to protect her allies. The war was ended in 219, and the Romans withdrew.

Although the urge for expansion was not a dominant feature in early Republican Roman politics, Sardinia was acquired when, incredibly, the Carthaginian garrison in the island, disillusioned with their treatment and lack of pay, appealed to Rome for help. In 237 the Romans took over in Sardinia, and ten years later they converted it into a province. The Carthaginians had now lost control of two important islands in the Mediterranean.

They also lost two of their generals in Spain. Hamilcar Barca was drowned in 229. His sons were not yet old enough to succeed him, so his son-in-law Hasdrubal was chosen, but he was assassinated in 221. The new commander in Spain was Hannibal, eldest son of Hamilcar Barca. He invaded Italy in 218 and remained there for seventeen years. For nearly two decades, the Romans fought on more than one front, against Hannibal in Italy and the Carthaginians in Spain, and in 215 they embarked on the first war with Macedon. At the end of the third century, the young commander Scipio took the war to Africa and defeated the Carthaginians. The prolonged struggle almost brought Rome to her knees, but the Romans kept on raising armies and fleets, refusing to give in.

The new provinces yielded taxes and grain for Rome, but they would probably have been taken over even if they had not been potentially profitable, because they had to be denied to the Carthaginians. Strategic safeguards against perceived threat came first, and the profit was a welcome but secondary motive. The imperialist ambitions of the Romans were not yet fully established. After the defeat of the Illyrians in 229, the Romans did not create a new province. When the Carthaginians were forced out of Spain in 206, the Romans did not embark on conquest of the whole of Spain for nearly another decade. Carthage itself surrendered in 201, but the Romans withdrew, waiting for another fifty years to create the province of Africa out of Carthaginian territory.

A system had to be devised for the administration of the new provinces, so from 227 two extra praetors were created to govern them, making a total of four praetors elected annually. From the 240s, as Rome was becoming acquainted with more city states and tribes, two praetors had been elected, one for internal affairs, the *praetor urbanus*, and one for dealing with non-Romans, the *praetor peregrinus*, or more correctly *praetor inter peregrinos*, literally meaning 'among foreigners'. Praetorian provincial governors were enabled to make war if necessary, and to arrange treaties, either after a war and the conclusion of peace, or to facilitate the governmental process without resorting to armed force. There was a growing predilection of governors to derive personal profit from governing rich provinces. In theory, provincials could bring their grievances to Rome and find someone to represent them at law, but it was expensive and success was not guaranteed. Eventually a permanent court was set up, the *quaestio de repetundis*, to deal with extortion cases. The composition of these courts was a recurring political problem. The juries were the preserve of senators, who were reluctant to condemn other senators. In the 120s the tribune of the plebs Gaius Gracchus replaced senators with non-senatorial middle classes, called equites in Latin, or equestrians in English, referring to their distant association with the cavalry. Only a couple of decades later in 106, senators and equestrians were mixed, then a new scheme ousted senators altogether. In 91 Livius Drusus proposed to give the courts back to senators, and Sulla actually did so, but soon afterwards Pompey restored the balance by readmitting equites.

The prestige of the Senate had grown during the Punic Wars. Many senators had been killed in the long struggle against Hannibal, so the gaps had to be filled by the censors.

Increasingly, senators were men of experience who had served as military tribunes, held a succession of magistracies, and had commanded armies. Gradually a career structure was established, combining civilian and military posts. There was no clear division between army and government in Rome, and no specialised training in either sphere. Experience was everything. Sons of senators were not automatically enrolled in the Senate as part of their inheritance, but had to earn their places by serving in the lower ranks of the administration. The most junior administrative post of any merit was that of quaestor, with largely financial responsibilities, usually followed by a term as military tribune in a legion.

The post of tribune of the plebs was open only to plebeians, and by the third century BC plebeians had gained access to most of the magistracies of the government. After the quaestorship, the next civilian post was that of aedile, keeping the city in good order and providing games and shows, hopefully rising to praetor and then consul. These last two high officials were the ones upon whom *imperium* was bestowed, or the power to command armies.

For senators, ancestry was all-important, especially if some of their ancestors had held the consulship. Any man who entered politics without such distinguished ancestry was labelled a *novus homo*, a new man, and usually suffered from the extreme snobbery of the most important families. Rivalry between patricians and plebeians was replaced by an alternative rivalry between consular and non-consular families. Ancestry alone did not make a successful senator. Great wealth, mostly in terms of landownership, was essential, and if senators fell below the property qualification they were usually ejected from the Senate. They were expected to expend much of their wealth on the city of Rome and its inhabitants, especially in the realm of entertainment. Providing games and shows at the festivals could attract much political support. Gladiators made their first appearance in the middle of the third century and were employed not just for the spectacles but for attracting votes.

From the first half of the third century, Rome came into contact with Greek culture. Literary talents began to develop, strongly influenced by Greece. In 240 the playwright Livius Andronicus of Tarentum produced the first tragedy in Latin. At the end of the third century, the first known historian, Fabius Pictor, wrote a history of Rome in Greek. Around the same time, the comedies of Titus Maccius Plautus were produced, in Latin, but derived from Greek originals. Only about twenty of the many works of Plautus have survived, but an essence of his comedies can be experienced in the film *A Funny Thing Happened on the Way to the Forum*.

Although senators were expected to undertake public works for the benefit of all, there was no permanent stone theatre until Gnaeus Pompeius Magnus returned from his eastern conquests in the 60s, intent on copying the Greek theatre he had seen at Mytilene. Until then theatres were temporary wooden structures. Wealthy men made an impression by building temples. The first temple on the Capitoline hill was started at the end of the sixth century, and the first versions of the temple of Saturn and the temple of Castor and Pollux, whose later remains are still visible in the Forum in Rome, were begun in the early fourth century.

Another prestigious project was road and bridge building. The earliest properly surveyed road, with a metalled surface for ease of marching, was the Via Appia, built by Appius Claudius at the end of the fourth century BC to link Rome with Capua. The repair of roads was a constant feature in Republican Rome, especially since not all roads were paved. The Via Appia is now called Via Appia Antica to distinguish it from the Via Appia Nuova, built on a different alignment to take modern traffic. On Sundays, traffic is prohibited on the Via Appia Antica, making for a pleasant stroll, but for the rest of the week, while it is still possible to walk down it to the Porta San Sebastiano and the catacombs beyond, walkers are assailed by regular spurts of manic one-way convoys as the traffic lights at the city end turn green. Returning traffic travels one-way up the Via Latina to the Porta Capena, where it joins the Via Appia.

The next routes to be built after Appius Claudius showed how it could be done were the Via Aurelia from Rome to Pisa, and the Via Flaminia, now the Via del Corso in its sections in central Rome, leading to Rimini (ancient Ariminum). Significantly these routes linked Rome with the west and east coasts. Communications throughout Italy became more important as Rome expanded her control over the whole peninsula.

As the network of roads expanded, so did the planting of colonies. Ostia and Antium (modern Anzio) on the west coast were among the earliest settlements, established in the fourth century BC. By the end of the third century there were several other maritime colonies, notably Brundisium, converted into a colony in 244. The role of the maritime colonies was once thought to be military, providing protective garrisons, but this is now disputed. Outside Roman territory self-governing colonies were established. These could be quite large, and did have a strategic function, protecting routes.

Rome developed her first coinage in the third century. Prior to this, the Romans reckoned wealth in terms of land and livestock, then started to use bronze ingots. The Greeks living and trading around the Mediterranean had been using coins for centuries, so if Rome wished to expand her trade and to interact with coin-using communities, a comparable system of currency had to be established. In 289 the first bronze coins appeared, and twenty years later, silver coins were minted, called the *didrachma* after Greek examples. By the end of the third century, the silver *denarius* was issued, worth ten bronze *asses* (plural of the term *as*, nothing to do with donkeys).

The Later Republic 200–30 BC

The later Republic experienced almost continual turmoil. Internal political squabbles sometimes escalated into serious fighting, punctuated by external wars that required armies to be in the field for many years at a time. Wars were fought outside Italy, against the kings of Macedon, against Antiochus III of Syria, against the Achaeans in Greece, against the tribes of Spain, and against Jugurtha, chief of the Numidians in Africa. At the end of the second century, the tribes of the Cimbri and Teutones threatened Italy and were defeated by the strenuous efforts of Gaius Marius. In the first half of the first century the Romans fought two wars with Mithradates, king of Pontus. There were serious slave revolts, two in Sicily from 136 to 132 and again from 104 to 100, and a more famous uprising in Italy under Spartacus from 73 to 71.

The third Punic war began in 149. The Carthaginians had been thoroughly subdued by the Romans at the end of the second war. Disarmed and powerless, they rebelled, but by 146 they had been defeated again. This time their city was completely destroyed. At the end of the war against the Achaeans, the city of Corinth was also destroyed in 146.

Civil wars began in Italy in 90 when the allies of Rome lost patience with the repeated failure of promises that they would be given Roman citizenship. Despite their contribution to the armies and therefore to Rome's victories, the allies were not treated as equals. Roman legions fought allies for two years, but then the Senate gave in and grudgingly offered citizenship to the Italians. As this war petered out, another conflict began over the command of the armies to be sent to the east against Mithradates. It was awarded to the consul Gaius Marius, the hero in the war against the Cimbri and Teutones, but Lucius Cornelius Sulla wanted the command too, and marched his troops to Rome to get it. While he was away in the east, there was continued turmoil and bloodshed in Rome as Marius and his fellow consul Cornelius Cinna took control by force. Marius fortuitously died, and an uneasy peace followed. When Sulla returned to Rome, fighting between rival factions broke out again. Two eminent Romans rose to fame under Sulla's government: Pompey the Great, who earned his title from the army in the aftermath of the fighting, and Marcus Licinius Crassus, who was to suppress the revolt of Spartacus and later to lose his life in a war against the Parthians.

Sulla was made Dictator, an office which he held for longer than the stipulated six months, and set about strengthening the Senate and the oligarchs at the expense of almost everyone else. When his work was done he abdicated. While Sulla was putting his programme into effect, the young Pompey, technically under age and not properly qualified, was given military commands to round up the followers of Marius and Cinna, eventually going to Spain after Sulla's death to assist Metellus against the self-exiled Marian sympathiser Quintus Sertorius. Pompey's reputation had already been made, but his work in Spain brought him even more fame. He was to become the foremost general and the most influential man in Rome, until Julius Caesar eclipsed him.

After an initial reluctance to take on the government of states and communities that they had defeated, often on behalf of another state, the Romans started to create provinces more frequently in the second century BC. Roman interests in Spain had begun during the wars with Carthage. In 198 two provinces were created, Hispania Citerior and Hispania Ulterior, or Nearer and Further Spain, though it was a long time before the two provinces were pacified. In 148 Macedon was finally defeated and annexed as a province, and two years later the province of Africa was created from the territory of Carthage. In 133 the kingdom of Pergamum was bequeathed to Rome, and was converted to the province of Asia in 129. Transalpine Gaul was created in 112. After Pompey's victories in 63, Syria, Bithynia-Pontus, and Cilicia were annexed. Cyprus followed in 57. During the succeeding years the Romans were too preoccupied in fighting each other to acquire more territory, until Octavian defeated Antony and Cleopatra and took over Egypt in 30.

As the Romans created more provinces, more revenues flowed into Rome, but more soldiers were required to pacify or hold the new territories. There was also more opportunity for exploitation by Roman governors. There was a scramble for office in the elections in Rome. Men began to borrow incredible amounts of money to bribe the voters, in the expectation that once having reached the praetorship or consulship, they could recoup what they owed and much more if they could gain a post as a provincial governor. Some governors achieved this without overstepping the rules, but others such as Verres, who governed Sicily as though it was his own personal domain, stripped their provinces of anything they could. Cicero prosecuted Verres, securing a conviction after making only one of his prepared speeches. Rather than let the other speeches go to waste, he published them, medieval monks copied them, and for generations schoolchildren translated them.

The later Republic was beset by problems of land distribution, and several politicians tried to solve these problems, which concerned the urban poor in Rome and the veteran soldiers who had fought in the various wars. The burden of military recruitment had always fallen mainly upon the rural population. In the mid-second century BC the disappearance of the farmers from the land became a serious political issue, because of the consequent reduction in the pool of Roman citizens and Italian allies eligible for army service. Resettlement on the land was a perennial feature in political agendas. Modern scholars have concluded that the scenario built up by the ancient authors is misleading, in that the perception of the Roman government about the problem did not match reality, but perceived truth often overrules real truth.

Tiberius Sempronius Gracchus, tribune of the plebs in 133, introduced a land bill designed to replace the small farmers on plots of public land which they could not give away or sublet, and for which they were to pay an affordable rent to the state. This scheme would thus reconstitute the class of smallholders who provided recruits for the Roman army. The main problem was that the public land had gradually been taken over by landowners who had come to regard the plots as their own, so they would have to be evicted to allow new people to settle. Gracchus' law was passed amid rioting in which he was killed, but the land commission was established and the reforms went ahead.

The political programme of Tiberius Gracchus was revived ten years after his death by his younger brother Gaius, who was twice elected tribune, for the years 123 and 122 BC. Gaius proposed laws designed to remedy a wide range of problems, including attempts to prevent the exploitation of the provincials, and to improve the efficiency of the courts. In 122 Gaius stood for election as tribune for the third time, but he had lost the confidence of the electorate, and in 121 he was killed.

The late Republic was characterised by the growth of wide-ranging military commands to deal with specific large-scale problems that necessitated massive resources and military expertise that not all the consuls possessed. Pompey's rapid campaign to round up the Mediterranean pirates provides an example. The seaborne grain supply of Rome was threatened, and piecemeal attempts to control the pirates had failed. Pompey's command gave him control of all provincial territory around the Mediterranean up to fifty miles inland, combining land and sea operations on a scale that had never been contemplated in Rome. The pirate problem highlights the dilemma of the late Republic. Rome was a world power with world-embracing problems, and required commanders with extensive powers to deal with them, but the political eminence and military supremacy that accrued to these few commanders created further problems in Rome. One of the aspects of military command that accentuated this supreme power was the creation of armies that were loyal to their commanders and not primarily to the state. Republican soldiers swore an oath to obey their generals, but since the generals were the annually elected consuls it was probably not foreseen that one day the oath would divert loyalty away from the state. The first use of Roman troops against Rome occurred when Lucius Cornelius Sulla decided to force the Senate into granting him the eastern command against Mithradates by marching on Rome, which set a dangerous precedent.

The bond between soldiers and commanders was considerably enhanced by the lack of provision for veterans when the troops returned to Rome. Inevitably the men looked to their generals to obtain allotments for them. In 62 Pompey the Great met with opposition in the Senate when he tried to settle his veterans from the victorious campaigns against Mithradates of Pontus. Endless senatorial delaying tactics dragged on for a few years until Pompey joined forces with Julius Caesar, who was consul in 59. The necessary legislation was pushed through, but it merely solved the problems of the moment, without establishing a permanent system for veteran settlement.

After his consulship Caesar was proconsular governor of Illyricum and Cisalpine and Transalpine Gaul. His appointment was for five years, but he was aiming for military glory in conquering all the Gauls, and his proconsulship was renewed for a second five-year term to enable him to achieve his conquest. Command of troops and success in foreign wars was the only way to achieve and maintain political pre-eminence during the Republic, as Pompey had done. At the end of his second term Caesar wanted to stand for the consular elections again, but without giving up his command and his army to come to Rome to canvass in person. The Senate refused permission for his candidacy *in absentia* and slowly the Roman world approached civil war. While Caesar was in Gaul, Pompey had built up a power base of his own, governing his provinces of Spain via his legates, without leaving Rome, which set an example for Augustus' system of provincial government.

The war started before Pompey was ready, and ended with his defeat at Pharsalus in 48. He escaped to Egypt, where Caesar followed him to prevent him from borrowing money and raising another army. When Caesar arrived in Alexandria, the young Ptolemy XIII and his sister Cleopatra VII were involved in a struggle for the throne of Egypt, and Caesar was drawn into the fighting, eventually installing Cleopatra as ruler of the country with Roman backing.

The battles against the remnants of the Pompeian armies took Caesar to Africa and Spain, and finally back to Rome, where he tried to set in motion many political reforms that were patently necessary, but he was impatient and his methods were autocratic. He was assassinated in 44, precipitating another round of civil war. The Liberators, as the assassins called themselves, were soon in conflict with Caesar's right-hand man, Mark Antony, and Caesar's teenage great-nephew and heir, Gaius Octavius, or Octavian as modern audiences know him. Antony and Octavian combined with Aemilius Lepidus to form the so-called second Triumvirate, infamous for the proscriptions of many leading Romans and the ruthless eradication of enemies of the Triumvirs. Together Antony and Octavian pursued the Liberators to Greece, defeating them at Philippi in 42. In the third act of the civil wars Antony and Octavian divided up the Roman world between them, Octavian eventually taking control of the west, and Antony of the east, including Egypt. Antony's famous association with Cleopatra gave Octavian all the excuse he needed to go to war, persuading the Roman people and Senate that the Egyptian queen represented a mortal danger to Rome. At the naval battle of Actium, Octavian's admiral Marcus Vipsanius Agrippa made short work of Antony's fleet, and Antony and Cleopatra sailed away to Alexandria, where they committed suicide as Octavian approached the city with his troops.

Some ancient authors chose the battle of Actium in 31 as the foundation date for the Roman Empire. When Octavian took personal command of Egypt, governing it through an equestrian deputy with the title of prefect, he obtained personal control of the vast wealth of the country. This wealth, combined with control of the armies, enabled Octavian to remain in power. There were about sixty legions at his disposal after Alexandria fell, and the soldiers looked to him for veteran settlement, or continued employment, promotion, and pay. He made certain that no one else should accommodate the army and attend to its needs, and slowly and patiently he created the Roman Empire out of the ruins of the Republic.

2

The Army of the Kings 753–509 BC

The armies of the Regal period in Rome are only sparsely documented, and as usual when facts are few, theories proliferate. Even the Roman and Greek historians had to resort to speculation now and then, and occasionally some of them were honest enough to admit that this was what they had done. The surviving sources for the early Roman army are the works of the historians Livy, or Titus Livius, and Dionysius of Halicarnassus. Livy wrote 142 chapters, referred to as books, but only thirty-five are extant, covering the history of Rome from the beginning to the third century BC. The literary works of Dionysius of Halicarnassus belong to the last quarter of the first century BC. In addition to his books on literature and his biographies of historical characters, he wrote a history of Rome from its beginnings to the outbreak of the First Punic War in 264. The first eleven books survive complete, but the last nine books are known only in various extracts. Dionysius wrote in Greek, and was well aware of the parallels between Roman and Greek history.

It is unlikely that either of these ancient historians set out to falsify or fabricate anything in their narratives. They probably reported in good faith what they had researched, but their sources may not have been entirely reliable. The nature of these sources can only be guessed. There may have been a stronger oral tradition than is indicated in historical works, concerning heroes and spectacular achievements of different families, but these are likely to have been embellished with the passage of time until they grew into legends like that of Romulus. The tales that were handed down have an identifiable Greek slant to them, with several parallels in myths and legends about Greek heroes. This perhaps indicates that the first literate people to write about Rome, or to influence what was written, were Greeks from southern Italy whose traditions were grafted on to Roman ones.

Most evolving societies develop a need to record significant events and prominent people, either in pictorial form accompanied by an oral tradition, or in writing. The Etruscans may have kept some records of early Rome, and the first Roman leaders and priests may have recorded religious ceremonies, political decisions, and military activities. These may be the kind of records that Livy tells us were destroyed when the Gauls captured the city of Rome in the fourth century BC. The destruction cannot have been total, because Publius Mucius Scaevola, consul in 133, published *Annales Maximi*, the records of the chief priests. Individual families may have maintained their own histories, but perhaps not originally in writing. Extant and long-lost inscriptions recording events featured in the source materials of the early historians. From scattered writings, official records and oral tradition, Livy and Dionysius may have derived their stories. It is not useful to accept without question everything that these historians say, nor is it profitable to reject everything as unreliable, so the task of the modern historian is to sift potential truth from unverifiable myth.

When Rome became a properly organised city instead of a collection of possibly independent villages, it can be assumed that a leader of some kind would have emerged, by common consent, or possibly by force. This leader most likely combined responsibility for civilian, military, legal and religious affairs. Whether or not the first of these was called Romulus does not really matter, and whether he went by the title chief, general, tyrant or king is more a matter of semantics than politics. In other states in Italy and Greece, the pattern was broadly similar, with a king at the head, surrounded by aristocrats, some of whom would act as his advisers, and the people, probably of varying grades. Each division of society had privileges and obligations directly proportionate to their status.

The king would be able to call on the adult male citizens to protect the state against raids, or to undertake raids on other cities. The king may have gathered a warrior band around him, acting as a bodyguard. These men may have served with the armed forces whenever necessary, but probably remained separate from the war band, being armed and ready at all times. Livy says that Romulus had a bodyguard of 300 men called the *Celeres*, which implies that they were always ready and fast (*celer*) to act. There may never have been a man called Romulus or a bodyguard called the *Celeres*, but something like this setup is entirely feasible, so the emerging city most likely had a ruler by whatever name he called himself, surrounded by a group of men who were sworn to protect him.

Whether or not the first war bands could be termed armies is debatable. It was said that the first Roman army consisted of 3,000 infantry and 300 cavalry, derived from the thirty *curiae* or divisions of the three tribes of Ramnes, Tities and Luceres, which are all Etruscan names. Although it has been suggested that these terms refer to Romans, Sabines and Etruscans, the tribal names do not necessarily denote three distinct ethnic groups, and though they were associated with settlements on different hills in early Rome, there are no signs of territorial distinction. The division of the populace into three tribes facilitated the assembly of an army, because it meant that an equal number of soldiers and horsemen could be summoned from each group.

The soldiers would be adult male citizens, seventeen years old to about sixty, usually described as farmer-soldiers. The basis of the economy was agriculture, so it is to be expected that the farmers either worked their own land or possessed a farm, or possibly more than one farm. The soldiers were responsible for equipping themselves and marching out when the king summoned them. It is not known if an army was called out every year on a regular basis, or whether troops were assembled only when necessary. It has been suggested, but not necessarily accepted, that the religious ceremonies held in March and October may have marked the beginning and the end of the campaigning season. Whether or not they were called out on an annual basis, the men would need to return to their farms for the harvest. There was most likely an upper and lower age limit for those who were called up, but on the other hand in times of emergency it is probable that everyone capable of bearing arms may have been gathered. It is not known if there was a surplus of men on occasions, or worse, a shortfall. The king would be in overall command, but there may have been officers in charge of sections of the army. Livy writes of centurions commanding sections of the army under the kings, but this is probably anachronistic.

The equipment, arms and armour of the early armies may be indicated by archaeological finds and in art works. Protection for the head most probably consisted of circular helmets rising to a conical point at the top, like the Etruscan so-called Villanovan type, which was worn up to the seventh century BC. These helmets had no cheek pieces or neck guards. Body armour was probably made from bronze, consisting of a round or square plaque suspended from the shoulders to protect the chest. There were probably back plates as well, evolving into the type of all-encircling body armour or cuirass. If bronze was lacking or too expensive, the early Romans may have used leather or stiffened linen as body armour, but these would not survive in the archaeological record. Iron slowly replaced bronze for weapons, mostly spears, swords and daggers. It is possible that archaeological finds, especially those from tombs, and depictions of soldiers, may represent ceremonial usage and not necessarily ordinary weapons and armour. It is only safe to say that soldiers protected themselves somehow and provided weapons to fight with, probably with no standardisation. Men probably wore and wielded whatever they possessed. The early Roman army may have looked like an ill-assorted rabble, but if so, it is highly likely that the armies of other states looked no better.

Alongside the foot soldiers the early Romans fielded a small cavalry force of 300 men, representing ten horsemen from each *curia*. Most probably each man had to provide, in addition to his own equipment, his horse or horses, their equipment, and fodder if grazing was not available. Since horses are expensive to maintain, and require pasture, stabling, and constant care and attention, the cavalrymen would have to be among the wealthiest men in the city, and would have had slaves to perform the menial tasks, involving more mouths to feed. The mounted men may have filled several roles, acting as cavalry in attacks and pursuits, or alternatively simply riding to battle and dismounting to fight. They may have been used as messengers, perhaps as scouts, but reconnaissance and intelligence gathering were never strong points in the early Roman army. There is unfortunately no evidence as to how the 300 cavalry operated. Livy refers to mounted troops several times under Romulus, and says that the cavalry was used for the first time on the wings of the army in the battles against the Sabines. This is the traditional place for the cavalry of the later Republican and Imperial armies, and the units were called *alae*, from *ala*, meaning wing. There had to have been a first time that the horsemen were deployed in this way, but it is not certain whether Livy's statement is true.

There are some common features in the narratives of Livy and Dionysius, concerning the protection of Latium from raids by the Volsci and Aequi, and continuing hostilities between Veii and the Romans, usually over control of Fidenae, which is now Fidene, lying only a short distance from Rome itself. This reveals the highly local nature of warfare under the kings of Rome. Although Fidenae was eventually taken over by the Romans the struggle with Veii was a perennial problem, until the beginning of the fourth century BC, when after a long siege, Veii was destroyed, its people killed or enslaved, and its lands divided up between the Roman farmers.

The ancient historians tell how the early army fought off raids on Roman territory, which provides an early indication of Rome's obsession with fighting just wars, always responding to attacks and not actively provoking them. There was a religious element to this obsession, in that a college of priests called *fetiales* was given the task of vetting Roman complaints against offending states, in order to decide if war could be declared against them on a justified basis. Three of the priests were sent to the community concerned to try to arrange for restitution, in a procedure called *rerum repetitio*, literally asking for things to be handed back, which primarily indicates stolen goods or livestock. A time limit was set for the delivery of a reply to Roman complaints, and for the return of the goods, but if there was no result, the *fetiales* were to go to the borders of the territory concerned and throw a spear into the land, signifying a declaration of a just war. This is the archaic ceremony that Augustus revived for declaration of war against Cleopatra. He chose a piece of ground in Rome to represent Egypt, and threw a spear into it. His real purpose was to make war on Mark Antony, but it was bad form to declare war on a fellow Roman citizen, especially as the Roman world only recently emerged from two civil wars.

In part it may be true that Rome only reacted instead of taking arbitrary action, but it is just as likely that the early kings of Rome led out their troops to raid other people without any provocation. This is implied by the fact that the *fetiales* were also charged with considering complaints from other communities against Rome, and arranging reparation if the Romans were found to be culpable. If the wronged city or state simply attacked without going through these procedures, then the *fetiales* could declare any Roman response a just war. These activities perhaps do not merit the description of warfare, at least not when compared to the numbers of men put into the field in the long drawn out struggles with the Carthaginians and the later opponents of the Romans. But as time went on, it was not simply a question of a quick and profitable raid and then back home for the harvest. As a result of warfare and possibly by negotiation, Rome absorbed more territory, and this may have triggered changes in the way their army was organised.

The Establishment of the Hoplite Army in Rome

It is generally agreed that there was an organisational overhaul of the Roman army in the mid-sixth century BC, but since almost nothing is known about the way in which the very early army was organised, it cannot be discerned how radical this change was. According to Roman tradition it was King Servius Tullius who introduced electoral and military reforms designed to field an army made up of citizens of Rome. This was most likely a hoplite army. The Romans said that they had adopted it from the Etruscans, but in reality the hoplite armies originated nearly two centuries earlier in Greece. The ideas spread through mainland Greece, then to the islands and colonies, including those of southern Italy and from there to Etruria. The Etruscans may well have influenced the early Romans but the hoplite army did not originate with them.

An examination of Greek hoplites may have relevance for the Roman army of the mid-sixth century BC, but analogy does not constitute proof. Archaeological finds have revealed that hoplite armour and weapons were in use in Greece at least as early as the second half of the eighth century BC. The characteristic elements consist of the large round wooden shield, called a *hoplon*, about three feet or one metre in diameter, and a long spear, measuring about eight feet, later extended to more than twenty feet, with a metal spearhead and a spike at the opposite end. These two core elements remained the most essential and distinctive items in the hoplite armies throughout their long history and subsequent evolution. Some hoplites also carried swords. Apart from the massive shield, additional protection was afforded by metal armour, a helmet to protect the head, with cheek guards for protection of the face, a corselet or cuirass to protect the upper torso, and greaves for the lower legs. A bronze cuirass and helmet, dating to the eighth century BC, were found at the city of Argos.

The round wooden shield was very heavy. It sometimes had a covering of thin metal which would make it still more burdensome in exchange for only limited extra protection. Soldiers would pick it up and place it into position only when battle was about to commence. On the inside, the shield had an armband in the centre through which the soldier would place his left arm, and his left hand would slot into a grip near the outer edge of the shield. As the shield was curved, its top edge could be rested on the left shoulder to relieve some of the weight. The soldiers would stand sideways on to their companions, holding the shield forward, slightly tilted out at the bottom. The long spear could be held underhand for thrusting forwards, aiming at the opponent's groin, or it could be held overhand for thrusting downwards into the enemy's thigh. In Greek art portraying hoplites, the soldiers are most often shown with the spear in this position, and where casualties are depicted, the most common form of wound is to the thighs.

It is a reasonable assumption that some form of padding was worn inside the helmet, and underneath the cuirass, possibly made of linen, perhaps even quilted for extra thickness, but this is to go beyond the evidence and such padding would make the wearer uncomfortably hot. On the other hand in a very hot climate the metal would become unbearable to the touch, so it would have been advisable to place something less heat-absorbent against the skin. A few examples of arm guards have been found, but in general there was no protection for the upper or lower arms, one reason for its absence being the fact that the men needed to be able to move their arms freely to use their spears and shields. Given that thigh wounds seem to have been the most common form of injury, it is perhaps surprising that there was no protection for the upper parts of the legs, but such equipment would make it difficult to move about, so the soldiers did without the encumbrance. Sculptures and paintings as well as actual finds show that the cuirass ended at or just below the waist, and soldiers are often shown in ancient art wearing short pleated skirts hitched up at the sides. In some artwork soldiers are depicted with what look like closely fitting bathing trunks, while others are shown with nothing at all below the waist; perhaps these were the bravest men in the army. The combined weight of the shield and the metal armour would have been formidable, and as time went on the weight was reduced, but lighter armour increased the risk of casualties.

The most common conception of the way in which the hoplite armies fought was in a closely packed formation called the phalanx, which means 'roller'. The phalanx was generally eight–twelve men deep, but there was no specified length for the front, which could presumably be adapted to circumstances, depending on the available manpower and the terrain. The men would advance with shields overlapping and spears at the ready, like the ancient equivalent of a tank. In battle the men in the front ranks would absorb the enemy onslaught and do most of the fighting while the men in the rear ranks could do little more than keep up the pressure from behind. Theoretically as front rank men fell, the soldiers in the rank behind them would step forward over the bodies to fill the gaps, though with shields locked with those of the neighbouring soldiers, and with the pressure from the men behind, this was probably easier said than done. The flanks of the hoplite phalanx would be vulnerable, especially on the right, since this side was unshielded. Thucydides describes how the whole formation tended to veer to one side as each man tried to press into the protection of his neighbour's shield.

Another disadvantage was that the phalanx ideally required level ground, since rough terrain made it more difficult to maintain the close formation. Nevertheless, the psychological impact of the phalanx should not be underestimated. At a later time during the Republic, the general Lucius Aemilius Paullus said that he broke into a cold sweat every time he remembered the approach of the Macedonian phalanx at the battle of Pydna in 168. By this time the phalanx had gone through various stages of evolution and had become larger, and the Romans had gained much experience in fighting battles without the tight formation that the phalanx demanded. Paullus won the battle of Pydna and ended the war with Macedon.

It has been argued by van Wees that hoplites were not necessarily always confined to the phalanx formation. The large round shield and the long spear could enable the hoplite soldiers to operate just as successfully in open order, interspersed with and supported by lighter armed troops. The Greeks used a variety of such light troops, such as archers, slingers, and peltasts. The latter were armed with throwing-spears and slashing swords, and protected by a crescent-shaped shield that weighed much less than the *hoplon*. Not carrying the enormous weight that the hoplites had to bear, the peltasts were able to move rapidly, striking at the enemy and escaping quickly. The best peltasts were Thracians, who were frequently hired as mercenaries by the Greek states. Archers were not quite as effective against heavy armed hoplites, but as hoplite armour became lighter with the passage of time, arrows could do more damage, and the archers proved their worth, especially in hilly country and over rough ground where the phalanx broke up and left gaps. The Cretans were the most effective archers and were often hired to support the Greek citizen armies. The effectiveness of slingers should not be scorned even though they were armed with nothing more than stones or lead sling bullets, but these could penetrate flesh. It is suggested that the poorer citizens of some Greek states, who could not afford the expensive hoplite armour and weapons, could accompany the army, throwing stones at the enemy. As offensive weapons, stones might be considered rather useless, but medieval English troops facing the stone-throwing Irish soon learned not to sneer at such primitive methods. The scenario of the fictional Crocodile Dundee felling a mugger with a tin of beans springs to mind.

The hoplite phalanx and perhaps its attendant light armed troops may be the sort of army that the early Romans began to employ in the middle of the sixth century BC, under the last kings. The soldiers used the spear and the round shield, which they called *clipeus*. Finds from tombs illustrate the type of hoplite armour that may have been used, although the splendid examples found in burials may represent ceremonial usage. A tomb at Vulci on the Etruscan coast yielded armour of hoplite type dated to around 530, and another tomb at Lanuvium in Latium was found to contain similar armour, dated to the early fifth century BC. The armour among the grave goods of greatly honoured soldiers and generals may have been much more elaborate than ordinary armour, but lesser mortals serving in the army probably looked similar, but rather drabber.

There was probably very little uniformity among the soldiers in the armour they wore or the weapons they carried, despite the portrayals in paintings where the soldiers all look identical. The state decreed that soldiers should provide specified arms and armour at their own expense, and as far as is known the government did not regulate the workshops that produced the items, unlike the later Roman Empire where control of factories was very highly organised and controlled, and most likely resulted in a high degree of standardisation, at least on a regional basis. Since each man serving in the armies of the kings of Rome and the early Republic was responsible for providing his own equipment, there could have been considerable variation in styles. Wealthier men would probably make sure that they looked the part in full battle array, while others would perhaps not bother too much about display preferring to concentrate on effective protection.

Like the Greek hoplite armies whose soldiers were all citizens of the state, the soldiers of the early Roman armies would be composed of citizens of Rome with sufficient wealth to provide their own kit, and to feed themselves on campaign. They would not form an army of professional soldiers, but would be summoned to arms, possibly every year, and definitely whenever there was need for protection of the city, or for punitive raids on various enemies. After the conclusion of the fighting the solders would disband and go home to their farms. If the Romans of the Regal period employed lighter-armed troops such as the Greek slingers and peltasts described above, such troops may have been made up of poorer citizens, but there is no evidence to support this.

The Servian Reforms, Sixth Century BC

The introduction of a new style of army in Rome in the middle of the sixth century BC is not in doubt, but the method by which it was brought about is disputed. It is suggested that the creation of an organised army is nearly always closely bound up with state formation, when political organisation reaches the point where corporate decisions can be made and the populace can be encouraged or coerced to carry out the decisions of the king or leader. Usually the people would also be allowed to gather in official assemblies, with some limited powers to agree or disagree with those decisions.

King Servius Tullius is credited with two administrative reforms in Rome in the sixth century BC. He divided up the people of the city in two different ways. He created four territorially based tribes, each of which included all the people of a particular region of the city, no matter what their status. Servius' other method of dividing up the people was to classify them into groups based on their property and wealth. Both kinds of division are fraught with modern debate.

The new tribal system that Servius introduced stood side by side with the *comitia curiata* that was drawn from the thirty *curiae* of the original three tribes. The creation of four territorial tribes in the city of Rome may indicate that the population had increased, so that the greater numbers of people to be divided into only three tribes would have made administration a little more unwieldy. The territory of the four new tribes was where each member of the tribe lived, and where he paid his taxes. It would simplify administration if the city was divided into blocks with clearly indicated boundaries. It also simplified mustering the army because the soldiers were assembled all together in one place on a tribal basis.

It is not known if each of the four urban tribes of the Servian reforms also incorporated a designated section of the rural areas lying outside the city, or whether Servius created an unknown number of separate rural tribes. During the Republic there were separate rural or 'rustic' tribes in the areas surrounding Rome, and much debate attaches to the date when the earliest of these tribes were formed and the dates when they were increased to the final total of thirty-one rural tribes during the Republic. Together with the four urban tribes, this gave a total of thirty-five tribes, a number that was never exceeded. Throughout the later Republic and early Empire all new Roman citizens, either created individually or in groups, were enrolled in one of the thirty-five voting tribes. The name of the tribe to which citizens belonged was obviously important to them, and was usually inscribed in abbreviated form on gravestones or career inscriptions, along with the information about the family of the person concerned. Even when the Empire had expanded so that new citizens were too far away from Rome to reside in the designated territorial area of their voting tribe, new citizens were still enrolled in one of the thirty-five tribes. One of the most famous legionary centurions in Roman Britain, Marcus Favonius Facilis, who died at Colchester in the first century AD, was a member of the tribe called Pollia, and the name appears on his tombstone abbreviated to POL.

The division of the people into property classes is more problematic. The discussion concerns the number of classes that Servius instituted. The final number was five, with additional groups for the very wealthy at the top of the scale and for the very poor at the bottom. The evidence for the five-class system as a whole derives from a much later period than the reign of Servius Tullius, so there can be no certainty that the arrangements during the Republic of the third century BC, when the fully evolved system is attested, also applied to the circumstances that pertained three hundred years earlier. Servius' main concern was probably to facilitate the process of assembling an effective army whenever it was necessary, while at the same time giving the farmer-soldiers who served in these armies some limited political powers. It is debatable whether that remained the prime concern of the Republican Romans, who used the so-called five Servian classes mainly for political and electoral ends rather than as a basis for drawing up an army.

In Servius' day, the embryonic Roman state, like many of the earlier Greek cities, was not in a position to fund a hoplite army, or any other body of troops. The kings or leaders were forced to rely upon the wealthier citizens to provide their own arms and armour, and also to feed themselves for the duration of the campaign. Although each adult male who was physically fit and possessed of sufficient wealth was obliged to serve in the army, such matters could not be left to chance or voluntary enthusiasm, so the king or leader needed to know who were the wealthy citizens upon whom he could legitimately call when the occasion arose. For this purpose, Servius Tullius is credited with conducting the first census. This required the drawing up of an initial list of citizens, presumably noting the property assessment of each individual. It would form the basis for updating the lists as time passed, deleting casualties of war, and inserting names of heirs who had succeeded to the property. One of the problems is that in an age prior to the use of coinage it is not clear how wealth would be assessed. In a mainly agricultural community it would most likely depend upon property and livestock. Was it measured in terms of acreage, types of crop and potential or actual yields, and on heads of cattle, sheep and pigs, converted into the weighed bronze currency bars that prefigured more conventional coinage? The Latin word *pecunia*, which came to mean money when coinage was introduced, derived originally from *pecus*, meaning flocks or herds. This root word survives in English, but being impecunious does not mean that you have no sheep or cattle.

Alternatively, if it was not agricultural produce or acreage that counted for the wealth assessment, was it calculated on actual ingots of bronze that acted as a rudimentary form of exchange before coins took their place? Or was it a combination of the value of farmland and possession of bronze ingots? It is unlikely that the census under Servius Tullius reached the level of sophistication of the procedure of the Republic, when censors were elected once every four years, later every five years, to count people and assess their status. This prestigious office was held for eighteen months, and these important men had the power to revise the list of senators, ejecting men they thought unsuitable.

If Servius did conduct a census, he would be aware of who were the wealthy citizens who could provide their own equipment and food for a campaign. What he did with this information becomes the major point at issue, concerning the five so-called Servian *classes* (plural of *classis*), or groups of citizens based on wealth. There is no doubt that this system was in operation during the Republic, but it is not known whether Servius created it fully fledged, or whether he instituted something more primitive that evolved into the more complex organisation as new problems faced the Romans of the Republic.

In the third century BC each of the five classes was divided into centuries containing in theory 100 men, but in practice a variable number. The political assembly made up of the centuries of the five classes was called the *comitia centuriata*, which elected the consuls, praetors and censors, and enacted laws, though it had no say in formulating them. This assembly voted yes or no for going to war, and if the *comitia centuriata* existed under the kings this may have been its chief function, obliging the men who were to serve in the army to act according to the majority vote. Each man of each century cast his vote, and the majority vote of each century counted as its corporate decision. Then the majority decision of all the centuries taken together decided the outcome.

The first class was divided into eighty centuries, plus two centuries of engineers whose military role encompassed the construction of anything that might come under the heading of engineering. The second, third and fourth classes each contained twenty centuries, and the fifth class had thirty centuries plus two of horn-blowers or trumpeters who sounded commands in the army. Some scholars have placed the two centuries of engineers and horn-blowers with different classes, because the ancient authors Livy and Dionysius of Halicarnassus assign them in two different ways, although they agree on most other points. The number of centuries within each class bears no relation to the numbers of men in that class. At first glance it might seem that the first class with eighty centuries contained the largest number of people, also giving the impression that there were more very rich men in Rome than there were successively less wealthy individuals. This is not how the system worked. In the wealthier classes there were fewer men in each century than there were in the centuries of the poorer men, so the system was very heavily weighted in favour of the rich.

The inequality of the voting procedure is illustrated by the two groups that were outside the five classes. The cavalry, or equites, the wealthiest men of all in Rome, ranked above the five classes, and were divided into eighteen centuries. The number of men eligible for the cavalry was comparatively small, but this small number gained a disproportionate eighteen votes in the *comitia centuriata*. At the other end of the scale the men with no wealth to speak of ranked below the five classes, and were grouped together under the heading of *capite censi*, because they were not assessed by wealth, but counted by heads, from *caput* (plural *capites*) meaning head. The *capite censi* were not even designated as a class, and however numerous they were, all of them were assigned to one century, which gave them only one vote in the assembly. The remaining 192 centuries of the assembly rendered the single vote of the poorest group irrelevant, unless by chance the opinion of the assembly inclined towards the same direction as that of the poorer citizens.

With regard to the Roman army, in the evolved system of the Republic the members of each century were divided into two groups, the *iuniores* or younger men from seventeen to forty-five years of age, and *seniores* from forty-six to sixty. The younger men served in the wars, while the older men were held in reserve. In emergencies everyone would fight. Theoretically the first class of eighty centuries would have forty centuries of younger men and forty of older men. The next three classes comprised ten centuries of younger and ten centuries of older men, and the fifth class fifteen centuries of each age group. Since the population would not remain at a stable figure, because of variations in the birth rate, and deaths from diseases, accidents, or warfare, it is highly unlikely that the centuries would each contain exactly one hundred men at any time.

There were regulations as to what the men of each class must provide for going to war in the early army of Rome. What follows here applies more suitably to the hoplite style 'legion'. By the third century BC when the five-class system had evolved, the arms and armour prescribed for each class, and the way in which the army was organised, would have changed, and the rigid definitions that have been preserved in the ancient sources may have been anachronistic or perhaps even fictitious. Nevertheless, it is worth repeating what has come down to us. The first class of the Republic were armed with a spear and sword, and protected by the shield, a bronze cuirass, and greaves. The other classes were progressively less well equipped. The second class did not need to provide the cuirass, the third class did without this and also the greaves, and the fourth class had only the shield and spear. The fifth class used slings or stones and did not have to provide the body armour. The *capite censi*, excluded from politics, were likewise excluded from service in the army.

There is some scholarly support for Servius Tullius as the originator of the five classes. John Rich has argued that Servius designed the system in order to utilise to best effect all the available manpower among the citizens of Rome, but graded them in different classes according to their ability to provide the equipment. An analogy with Greece, specifically Athens, may or may not have some bearing on sixth century Rome. In the same century Athenian society was divided into four property classes by the lawgiver and politician Solon. The most important officials and army commanders were elected by the whole assembly of the people, but candidates were drawn only from the first two classes. Command of the army would by this means be placed firmly in the hands of the wealthiest people. The creation of the four classes may have been undertaken when Solon was archon or chief magistrate in Athens in 594, or as some scholars have argued, two decades later in 574, which brings the reorganisation closer to the reign of Servius Tullius in the mid-sixth century.

Despite the fact that the Athenians of the sixth century BC were capable of organising themselves into property classes, some scholars have suggested that the five property classes of the Roman Republic were far too sophisticated to have been introduced by Servius Tullius at such an early date. It could be the case that such an elaborate system was not even necessary at that time, and it has been argued that Servius required only one class, made up of men who could afford to provide the equipment for service in the hoplite army, while everyone else would be in a group labelled *infra classem*, or below the class. The Latin word *classis* evolved with time, and could simply denote a group of people, or it could also denote the fleet, as in *Classis Britannica*, the title of the Roman naval forces operating in the English Channel. In English, use of the term class in its social context automatically brings to mind a grading system, based on wealth or social standing, as in working class, middle class and upper class. This is how the term was used when the five class system had been fully developed in the Roman Republic. In the context of Rome under the kings, the term *classis* derives from its earlier root *calare*, to call or summon, hence *classis* meant a call to arms, just as *legio* or legion originally meant 'the choosing', when men were selected for service in the army. The word *classis* in the days of Servius Tullius may have simply denoted the hoplite army, while the group labelled *infra classem* may have fought as light armed troops, possibly with no armour and possibly armed with slings and stones. The phalanx would not always be able to decide the issue in battle if unsupported by light troops, so this theory deserves consideration.

The Servian constitution, whenever it was formulated, and however it was organised, combined electoral privileges with an obligation to serve in the army. If citizens were entitled to vote in the assemblies for their state functionaries, whatever these may have been under the kings, and to have a say for or against various proposals, then they also had a duty to protect the state by serving in the armed forces. Conversely, if citizens served as soldiers then they ought to have the right to a limited share in the government. The trouble is, no-one can be certain that this is how it worked under Servius Tullius

The Hoplites and Cavalry of the Early Roman Army

The hoplite army of the later kings of Rome may have operated as a phalanx supported by light armed troops, but the ancient authors who wrote about it would have been influenced by the armies of more recent historical periods. It is not known how the army was commanded under the kings, except that when the state fielded an army, the supreme commander would have been the king himself. Wars with enemies would probably not have been much more than small scale engagements, and would have been fairly localised, at least in comparison with the more distant long term conflicts that the Romans were embroiled in by accident or deliberate choice during the Republic. In the early days, control of the Tiber banks and crossing points may have featured regularly, and control of routes, especially those of the salt trade, would have been another source of conflict. Seizure of livestock and crops may have been a seasonal occupation, and reparation for such raids may have occupied several successive campaigning seasons.

A perceived threat need not always concern another city or state. There may have been warrior bands extraneous to the state armies, who could join with the king, or fight against him on behalf of some other leader. This may be what happened when the Roman Coriolanus went over to the Volsci, and the Sabine Attus Clausus came over to Rome with his war band. His name was Romanised and he became Appius Claudius, the founder of a line of famous, or notorious, Roman politicians.

The decision to go to war would have originated with the king, but it is possible that in early Rome, the people who provided the troops would be given the chance to accept or refuse the suggestion. This was one of the functions of the *comitia centuriata*, but it is uncertain whether this assembly existed at all under the kings, despite the tradition that the system that produced it was established by Servius Tullius.

When war had been decided upon, an army would have to be drawn up for the occasion, and the command structure implemented, whatever that was at the end of the Regal period. Though the Greek analogies should not be pressed too far, the comparison might help to illustrate the way in which the Roman army of the sixth century operated. Comparison with the formidable Macedonian phalanx is not altogether relevant, because it had evolved in size and formation by the fourth century BC.

The generals (*strategoi*) who commanded the sixth-century Athenian army were drawn from the first two of Solon's four property classes, but elected by the whole assembly. By the fifth century BC there were ten annually elected *strategoi*, which relates to the ten territorial tribes of greater Athens created by Cleisthenes, comprising the city and its surrounding lands. The army contained ten *taxeis*, one from each tribe, each commanded by a *taxiarchos* from the same tribe, but elected by the assembly like the generals. The assembly also elected two *hipparchoi* to command the 1,000-strong cavalry.

The Spartans had a much more tightly structured organisation, with the king at the head and a hierarchy of officers through whom the king's commands were relayed to the sections of the army. From a young age, all Spartans were trained to be soldiers, whereas no such training systems were adopted in Athens until the fourth century BC. Individual teachers of hoplite warfare were known in the previous century in Athens, but there was no compulsion to attend classes.

The hoplite soldiers may not have required intensive training, but the cavalry did require practice, if not actual training sessions, even if this was limited to managing a horse. The Athenian government assisted the horsemen to maintain their mounts, and to replace them when necessary. If not at the very beginning, the cavalrymen of Rome were eventually assisted in providing mounts and in maintaining them in time of war. Livy says that Tarquinius Priscus preserved the organisation of the cavalry, but doubled the number to 1,800 men, which is clearly related to the eighteen centuries of cavalry in the fully developed Servian constitution, probably anachronistically. It is not even certain that the increase was due to Tarquinius Priscus. The number eighteen was arrived at by retaining the original six centuries of cavalry, the *sex suffragia*, as they were called, and adding twelve new ones. Some men were given a 'public horse' paid for by the state. These men were known as *equites equo publico*. The system endured until the end of the Republic. In the first century BC, the young Gnaeus Pompeius Magnus made great play of parading with his public horse when it suited his political aims.

The Size of the Roman Army

There are alternative theories about the Servian army reforms and how they worked in practice. In the 1930s it was suggested by Plinio Fraccaro that Servius Tullius doubled the size of the army of the early kings of Rome. The first armies originally consisted of 3,000 infantry, or 100 men from each of the thirty *curiae* derived from the three tribes of the Ramnes, Tities and Luceres. The probable increase in the population of Rome by Servius' day would have made it possible to create an army of 6,000 infantry. Fraccaro thought that Servius did indeed institute the five classes from the very beginning, but it has also been suggested that all the soldiers would have formed a hoplite army, with all the men armed with long spears and protected by the large shield and bronze armour, without the need for the superfine distinctions of the five classes of the Roman Republic. In addition there would have been a number of light armed troops, as suggested by the theory that these were provided by the rest of the populace who could not provide the armour. The figure of 6,000 men is attractive, because mathematically it would have provided sixty centuries, the number that still pertained in the later legions, even though a legionary century never did contain a full complement of 100 men. It is also suggested that when the Republic was formed and two consuls were elected, the army was split between them into two groups of 3,000 men, going back to the original number based on the thirty *curiae*. This theory has not been universally accepted.

There are several possible permutations of the facts about the size of the armies that the kings could call upon, but none are as yet capable of absolute proof. The four urban tribes that Servius Tullius created could each provide ten centuries, producing a total of 4,000 men, forming a single phalanx-legion. This approximates to the figure of 4,200 that Polybius gives for the size of the Republican legion, although T. J. Cornell points out that this may represent the original legion of 3,000 men together with 1,200 light armed troops. In practice, it is quite possible that the kings of Rome did not raise armies of a stipulated number of soldiers every time they needed to go to war, and it is probable that, like many other armies in the field before or since, the numbers of men on the ground never matched the paper strength, even when they were first assembled.

3

The Army of the Early Republic
509–400 BC

For a few years at the end of the sixth century BC and for the whole of the fifth, the early Roman Republic was developing and adapting itself to circumstances. A government had to be formed after the kings had finally been removed, and this may have been a long, drawn-out process. The traditional date of 509 for the foundation of the Republic is not necessarily accurate, and the first appearance of the two annual consuls may not have been so abrupt. The Romans themselves knew that it was not as simple as it sounds to date the end of monarchy and the beginning of the Republic to one single year. Livy says that there were discrepancies of detail in the various different records covering the early years, so he could not decide on the exact order in which the consuls succeeded each other, nor could he always discern which events belonged to which year. The *Fasti Capitolini*, the most complete list of consuls, begins in 509, but the first officials may have been praetors, either singly or in multiples, and the collegiate consulship may have been a later development.

The fifth century BC was notable for a general economic slow-down in the lands around the Mediterranean. Archaeology shows that for a few decades, trade seems to have diminished, imports lessened, and luxury goods declined in number. Athenian pottery once predominated on some Italian sites, but almost disappeared in the fifth century. One reason for this may have been the dominance of the Etruscans and the Carthaginians in the western Mediterranean, which forced the Greeks to turn northwards and to Gaul for trading purposes.

Political Developments of the Fifth Century BC

It is perhaps only to be expected that the new Republic should experience internal problems, such as 'the Struggle of the Orders' between the plebeians and patricians, which was only gradually resolved over the next centuries. The first secession of the plebs took place at the very beginning of the fifth century, probably owing much to the various debt crises, but not fully understood. Since Rome was only one among various states which were all trying to expand, there was endemic warfare with Latins, Sabines, Volsci and Aequi. The first colonies were founded during the fifth century, in territory around Rome. There were high points, if taken from the social and cultural point of view, such as the creation of the tribunes of the plebs in 471, and the formulation of the laws in the Twelve Tables two decades later.

At the end of the sixth century when the kings were expelled, Roman territory had expanded beyond the original seven hills. Opposite the city, the right bank of the Tiber and its crossing points were under Roman control, and the left bank was Roman all the way to the sea. Various attempts have been made to estimate the square mileage of Roman territory in the early fifth century, but the actual figure is perhaps not as important as the fact that Rome was already the largest city in Latium.

The treaty of 509 made with Carthage indicates how Rome conceived of her political standing in Latium and Campania. This treaty is not accepted by all scholars, because it seems precociously early, and it is pointed out that the better-documented treaty of 348 between Roman and Carthage reproduces most of the alleged late sixth-century version. Therefore there is room for suspicion that the early treaty may have been fabricated by using the fourth-century document as its base. However, the source for the first treaty is Polybius, generally respected for his research and accuracy. Polybius says that he had seen the text on a bronze plaque, and that it was written in archaic Latin that only a few of his contemporaries of the second century BC could understand. The treaty begins with declarations of friendship between Carthage and Rome and their respective allies. The dominance of Carthage at sea is indicated by the fact that the Romans were forbidden to sail beyond the Fair Promontory, and if their ships were forced to make a landing, they were to depart within five days taking only what they needed for repairs. The contested part of the text concerns the clause whereby Carthage was forbidden to do injury to the cities of Ardea, Antium, Larentium, Circei and Tarracina, which were Roman preserves. In 509 this is considered unlikely. Antium and Tarracina were cut off from Roman control by the warlike Volsci, and it took another century before this part of the treaty approximated to the truth. The inclusion of these named cities in the treaty may have been more a statement of intent than a true description of contemporary circumstances.

The Carthaginians may have begun to notice Rome and decided upon an alliance because the power of their Etruscan allies was in decline. The Carthaginians had co-operated with the Etruscans against the Greeks, but Etruscan influence was diminishing, and in only another three decades it was more or less eliminated when the Greeks defeated the Etruscans in a naval battle off Cumae in 474. Towards the end of the fifth century Cumae was colonised by the Greeks. Since there was no central state or chief political authority in Etruria, Carthage would ally with different Etruscan states, and may have had an alliance with the Tarquins of Rome. It would therefore make sense to ally with the new government that had replaced the Tarquins. From the point of view of the Romans, it was always wise to respect the neighbours, and the Carthaginians were now powerful, having established a trading presence about forty miles away at Caere. This is confirmed by an inscription on a sheet of gold, written in Etruscan and Punic, which was found in excavations in 1964 at Pyrgi, the port of Caere.

The Secession of the Plebs and the Effect on the Army 494 BC

Within a very short time after the establishment of the Republic a section of the Roman people withdrew from the city and refused to fight in the army, in 494. This episode is fraught with difficulty. It has even been doubted that the event occurred at all in 494, though it is accepted that similar episodes occurred at later times. There was obviously deep dissension among the populace, possibly related to the escalation of debts. Livy tells the tale of an old soldier in Rome, hardly recognisable, dressed in rags, oppressed by debts because after serving in one of the wars he had returned home to find his farm and crops destroyed by enemy raids, so he could not pay his taxes and was forced to borrow, without the means to pay back what he borrowed. In the absence of a three-metal coinage at the time, the Romans were using weighed bronze, fashioned as oblong bars stamped with various designs. The customary scenario in ancient Rome is one of oppressive nasty patricians holding the poor innocent plebs in thrall, a concept fuelled by the accounts of some ancient historians. In the second book of his history of Rome, Livy recounts in some detail the events that led up to the secession, and some of what he says may be correct, although it is not known what his sources were. In essence, Livy explains that service in the army could be detrimental to the livelihood of individual soldiers, especially if they fell into debt because their farms suffered in enemy raids, like the example quoted above. The edict of the consul Publius Servilius illustrates what may have been happening in Rome, in that it was made illegal to imprison debtors, which would prevent them from mustering for the army, and it was also forbidden to seize the property and farm of a debtor if he was absent on military service. If this is not complete fabrication, it may serve to explain how the debt crisis and the secession of the plebs were related. According to Livy, when Servilius' edict was published the debtors who had been imprisoned in the houses of the lenders were released, and they immediately signed up for service in the army that was being raised in some haste, in order to repel an imminent attack by the Volsci. The attack was averted and the army may have been disbanded, but then the Sabines started to mobilise and the troops were needed again. The problem was that in the meantime Appius Claudius had overturned Servilius' ruling and the debt problems immediately returned along with all the discontent. When the army was being raised to fight the Sabines, the men who had been promised some relief from the problems of debt, and then had their hopes dashed, now decided that since they gained very little from going to war they would refuse to serve. Livy says that the people refused to submit their names for enlistment, and he describes more than one episode of this nature some time before the plebs withdrew to their hill, the Aventine according to one tradition, or alternatively the Sacred Mount three miles from Rome on the other side of the River Anio. Livy favours the latter suggestion, and explains that this is where the first tribunes of the plebs were elected. He describes two versions of how many tribunes there were initially. One version says that two tribunes were elected at first and later increased to five, or according to another tradition the first two tribunes were to choose another three men, making five tribunes from the very first. The number was later increased to ten. Despite their purpose of protecting the plebs the new tribunes do not seem to have been able to eradicate the problems of debt, or resolve the threat of withdrawal from army service.

In Livy's opinion there is no doubt that the people who withdrew from Rome did actually serve in the army. He portrays the consul Servilius as conciliatory towards the people and invents a speech for him explaining that the senators wished to do their best for the populace, who formed the largest part, but still only a part, of the whole community. Despite this seemingly helpful information, it is too imprecise to clarify matters, because it does not necessarily relate to the plebs as a body. The word plebs probably started out as a derogatory term, in the same way that lower orders can be used today, but not all plebs were poor, and they cannot be wholly equated with the landless urban mob, who according to the classes of the Servian constitution, whenever that was established, belonged to the lowest group with no effective voice in the political scene. These men did not serve in the army anyway, so if the plebs as a body were all part of this lowly group, the potential threat in refusing to serve would be meaningless.

This problem has been discussed by modern scholars in all its aspects, but for the purposes of military history the most important debate concerns the effect that the withdrawal of the plebs from army service would have had in Rome. What military role did the plebs fulfil, and would their withdrawal have damaged Rome's ability to field an army? Widely divergent theories have been propounded. On the one hand it has been suggested that the plebs must have formed the backbone of the hoplite army, and therefore the majority of them would have been the farmers who could be called up with their equipment when an army was being assembled. A contradictory argument is that they were not hoplites at all but the light armed troops that accompanied the army. In this context the story told by Dionysius of Halicarnassus is brought in as evidence. He says that Appius Claudius dismissed the threat posed by the secession of the plebs as nonsense, because the patricians could have assembled an alternative army from their adherents, or clients. This presupposes, as Dionysius did, that clients fell into a category that was distinct from patricians and plebs alike.

The refusal of the plebs to serve in the army only makes sense if they were included in the Servian *classis*, or more likely a number of *classes* with graded property qualifications. This theory implies that the five Servian *classes*, or at least a number of them forming a prototype version of the system, were already established in the fifth century. This is an almost heretical assumption according to some scholars, but worthy of consideration, as John Rich has suggested. If the plebs comprised all the people who were not patricians, they would have embraced a wide spectrum of property, land and status. On this basis they could well have been divided into groups classified by their relative wealth, and thereby allocated to a place in the fifth-century army. The plebs may not have formed the backbone of the hoplite army as has been suggested, but they may have constituted a significant part of it. This remains speculation, but it answers the questions of why the plebs thought that they had a persuasive political lever by withdrawing from service in the military forces, and how badly Rome would have been affected if they did.

Military Developments of the Fifth Century BC

The development and use of the army of the fifth century BC is hard to trace, despite the fact that Livy and Dionysius document the various wars. Livy provides beguiling details, and he is plausible because he refers several times to the works of other authors, and to records that he consulted, without actually naming them. Although both Livy and Dionysius are sincere enough in recounting wars, battles, and exploits of various heroes, there are some dubious factors. Were the sources that they used contemporary with the events they document, and even if there were any contemporary documents, were the records themselves accurate, and did the compilers, or Livy, Dionysius, or any other ancient historian inadvertently incorporate some anachronisms from their own times?

The organisation of the army in the very early Republic is not documented, so scholars have to rely on conjecture derived from what is known from later times. In order to command an army, a Roman officer, by whatever title he was known in the early Republic, would need to have special powers bestowed on him by the *comitia curiata*. These powers were all collected under the heading of *imperium*. It is not possible to pinpoint exactly when this began, just as it is not possible to be pedantic about the enumeration of the first consuls with their dates. At some point the consuls did command the armies, and they held *imperium*, which they had to relinquish when they crossed the boundary of the city, or *pomerium*, when they returned to Rome. It was forbidden to enter Rome as a commanding general even without troops, and anathema to enter the city with an army in tow. In the first century BC, Lucius Cornelius Sulla infamously did exactly that, and was reviled for it, but the unpalatable reality was that if any general chose to ignore these laws as Sulla did, there was no defence against it. The taboo did not stop Sulla from gaining the military command he wanted and later becoming Dictator. The surprising element is that for nearly five centuries until Sulla's time, generals had not made a habit of it.

In the early fifth century BC each consul may have commanded 3,000 men and perhaps about 1,200 light armed troops, but this figure depends on acceptance of the theory that the army was 6,000 strong from the time of Servius Tullius, and was split into two when the two annual consuls were established. The soldiers would assemble according to the territorial tribal system, and once formed up as an army, each soldier would swear an oath to obey the consuls. There may have been a similar oath to the kings, newly modified to suit the new circumstances of the Republic.

In the middle of the fifth century BC, a new kind of magistrate and army commander was established, replacing the annual consuls in certain years, but not altogether removing them. These were groups of military tribunes, elected in groups varying from three to six, and in one year there were eight of them. Each military tribune had consular powers. No one knows why this system was adopted from 445 to 367. There were only a few occasions when consuls were elected during these years. A possible explanation, not borne out by the facts, is that there was a need for a greater number of armies to be raised in these years, and therefore a need for more commanders, but rather than compromise the rule that there should only ever be two consuls, the Romans invented another post with a different name. It is a good theory but it cannot be shown that when tribunes with consular power were appointed there were more armies in the field, and on some occasions when more than one army was needed, the Romans appointed a Dictator, and allowed him and his master of horse (*magister equitum*) as well as the consuls to command armies, therefore there was no pressing requirement to invent a new type of commander. Although some of the tribunes did command armies, not all of them did so. Another theory is that the new system was connected with the efforts of the plebeians to gain access to the higher offices, the consulship not being open to them. The post of military tribune was accessible to plebeians, but it cannot be demonstrated that the plebs rushed to compete for the office, or even that they stood as candidates but failed to be elected.

There are no verifiable sources to elucidate what the army did in the fifth century, but certain broad general themes can be discerned in the works of the ancient historians. Rome was just one town among several in Latium, all of them with ambitions and willing to fight for supremacy. It was by no means assured that the Romans of the early Republic would be able to dominate the other Latin states, but clearly they had made an impression among the cities of Latium, otherwise the Latins as a body would not have felt compelled to rebel at the beginning of the fifth century. In going to war against the Latins, the first military success for the new Republic occurred when the Latins were defeated at the battle of Lake Regillus. The battle was fought in 499 according to Livy, or in 496 according to Dionysius of Halicarnassus, and Livy knew that there were different traditions about the exact date. Livy gives an account of the battle, though it is not known how reliable it is. Aulus Postumius was appointed Dictator, with Titus Aebutius as master of horse (*magister equitum*). They led an army of infantry and cavalry to Lake Regillus and met the Latins on the march. It was said that the Tarquins were with the Latins, which encouraged the Romans to fight all the harder. When battle was joined the two Roman leaders engaged in personal combat, though the details may be exaggerated or even fictitious, especially since many battles of this period allegedly feature such incidents. Postumius was still in the front line making final dispositions, when Tarquinius rode straight for him, but was driven off, and Aebutius attacked the Latin leader Octavius Mamilius. Both were wounded, Aebutius retiring from the field and Mamilius moving to the rear of the Latins where he continued to direct operations. His army included a number of Roman exiles who attacked the Dictator's troops and drove them back. But Postumius ordered the picked troops of his bodyguard to cut down any Romans who were running away, which persuaded the others to return to the fighting. Postumius then committed his guard to the battle, and being still fresh they attacked the exiles and killed many of them. Next he urged the cavalry to dismount and fight on foot, so they moved up to the front line where the infantry was tiring, but the soldiers were encouraged by the presence of the young aristocrats, and rallied. From then on, the victory was assured.

While the details of prominent officers engaging in individual combat may be partly heroic myth, the details that emerge from Livy's account are interesting, such as the use of the Dictator's personal guard in the battle and the dismounted cavalry joining the front line, then mounting up again to pursue the Latins. There was a tradition that the gods Castor and Pollux, sons of Jupiter, assisted the Romans at the battle, and were later seen watering their horses in the Forum in Rome. A temple was dedicated to them in the Forum in 484 BC; the impressive ruins that can still be seen in the Forum date from the reign of Augustus and later.

According to Livy the Latins were so severely defeated and subdued after this battle that when envoys came to them from the Volsci, urging an alliance against the Romans, the Latin cities decided to bundle the Volscian emissaries off to Rome, and were rewarded for their loyalty with the release of 6,000 Latin prisoners captured at Lake Regillus. Livy was at pains to add that the prisoners had all been treated extremely well by the Romans.

After this significant battle, the consul Spurius Cassius was able to arrange, or impose, a treaty on the Latins in 493. The text was inscribed on a bronze column and displayed in the Forum in Rome, and it survived until at least the first century BC. Livy and Dionysius of Halicarnassus summarise the terms, but modern scholars are of the opinion that their information is nowhere near complete. What has survived is significant. There was a declaration of peace between the two communities, and each party agreed not to help enemies of the other. The alliance was reciprocal in that the Romans could call upon the allies (*socii*) for military aid, and the allies could call on Rome for protection against attacks. There was a clause that booty was to be shared equally between Latins and Romans. The Latins were vulnerable to raids by the neighbouring tribes, in particular the Aequi and Volsci, and it was in Rome's interests to help the Latins to keep the enemy at bay. The alliance of 493 was between the Romans and the Latins in general, and not with individual Latin cities or communities, possibly because the concept of the city state had not yet developed in Latium at the beginning of the fifth century. Settlement may have been largely rural, with dispersed villages that would later combine into rudimentary townships with a corporate government.

The terms of this first alliance did not preclude independent action on the part of the Latins. During the fifth century and later, the Latins went to war whenever they felt it necessary, either to defend their territory or sometimes to mount an aggressive attack on their neighbours. Livy reports that just before the Latin revolt against Rome broke out, the Latins united with the Campanians in 341 and led the combined army in an attack on the Samnites, who appealed to the Romans, with whom they had recently sought an alliance. Basically the Samnites were saying call off your dogs, but at this point the Latins were not subject to Rome. The Romans told the Samnites that there was nothing in the treaty with the Latins that gave Rome the authority to prevent them from going to war against whomever they pleased.

Within a few years, this freedom of action among the Latin allies would be completely reversed. The early fifth-century alliance with the Latins differed from later alliances. After 338 when the Romans had crushed the rebellious Latin city states once again, separate alliances were made with each city, not with the Latin community as a whole. Each state was obliged to furnish troops, and was forbidden to collaborate with any other state, or to make war independently of Rome.

The fifth-century treaty with the Latins endured for more than a hundred years, but not without some problems to trouble the relationship between Romans and Latins. The two parties did not see eye to eye at all times, especially after the threat from the Volsci and Aequi had been overcome. The need for a protective alliance diminished, so the Latins did not require help from Rome quite so urgently or constantly. In 486 the Romans were able to arrange another treaty with the Hernici, a tribe which had allied with the Volsci. It is doubtful if there was a mutual agreement between the Romans, the Latins and the Hernici, giving all three parties leave to collaborate with one of the others. This alliance would be organised so as to keep the Latins and Hernici separate, but both of them firmly attached to Rome.

The allied troops fought alongside the Romans, but little is known of how they were organised. Information about the allies ranges from sparse to nil until the Greek author Polybius wrote about the Roman army of the third century BC. It is probable that the Latin allied troops of the fifth century served under a Roman commander rather than their own Latin leaders. If the Latins could provide hoplites, they may have been amalgamated in the Roman forces, but although the soldiers may still have been equipped as hoplites with large round shields and long spears, it is not known whether they would always fight in phalanx formation. A contribution of light armed troops may have been likewise incorporated into the support troops. The Latins may also have been able to furnish cavalry, who may have ridden to battle and fought on foot with the infantry, but Livy implies that it was unusual when the Dictator Postumius ordered his horsemen to dismount and join the Roman battle line against the Latins at Lake Regillus. They quickly mounted up again for the pursuit when the Latins broke and fled. Some of this may represent what really happened, but it is easy to project imaginative scenarios into early battles, and Livy may be just as enthusiastically guilty as anyone else. Nothing significant is known of fighting methods. Weapons and equipment, and their use, are rarely mentioned in the literary sources, and are not specifically described. The consul Verginius is said to have ordered his men to ground their spears when facing an attack of the Volsci, to stand still to await the onslaught, and then to fight at close quarters using their swords. The Volsci were consequently winded by their energetic charge, while the Romans were still fresh, enabling them to win the battle.

The supreme commander in the fifth century would have been one or both of the consuls, or at times a Dictator and his *magister equitum*, or master of horse, each of them appointed for six months. Subordinate officers are not generally recorded in detail. At the battle of Lake Regillus, Livy records a few exploits where commanders of various sections of the armies of the Romans and the Latins suddenly espied their enemies in the battle line and went off to engage in individual combats, similar to modern epic films where the hero leader makes directly for the enemy leader, and depending on how long the film still has to run, he is gravely wounded to fight another day, or emerges victorious to bring peace to his people. Elsewhere Livy merely mentions that high-ranking officers, in addition to the cavalry, had to fight in the battle line at Lake Regillus.

The importance of the alliances with the Latins and the Hernici is that it enabled the Romans to furnish considerably greater manpower than they would have been able to muster from their own citizens. From the earliest years of the Republic, the Romans were able to field larger armies than their rivals, even when tribes or states united to oppose Rome. This was a significant factor in the ability of Rome to survive attacks, then to dominate Italy, then the Mediterranean, and to progress from there to the foundation of the Empire. When the fifth-century Romans faced a combined attack of the Sabines, Volsci and Aequi they raised an army of ten legions, according to Livy, four of them commanded by the Dictator and three by each of the two consuls. If 'legion' is not an anachronistic term when applied to the fifth century, it is estimated that there may have been 4,000–4,500 men in each one, which amounts to a minimum of 40,000 soldiers, probably accompanied by a similar number of allied and light armed troops. The story also illustrates that Rome could fight battles simultaneously on more than one front with different armies operating under different commanders.

Wars in the fifth century BC were not the long-term affairs that they later became, nor were they fought at considerable distances from Rome or Latium. The campaigns came to an end in the late summer or autumn, and often there was a peace agreement, or at least a truce was arranged, and everyone went home. Wars did not usually result in complete conquest or annexation of territory, so in the following campaigning season, hostilities would resume from where they left off last time. The fighting was probably still an amalgamation of raiding the neighbours, reclaiming stolen property, and defence of boundaries and farmlands, as it had probably been under the kings. From the end of the fifth century onwards, wars became more purposeful. It was discovered that they could be profitable too, so there were not only gains in personal prestige for the successful generals, but booty to bring back to Rome to be dedicated to the gods, and land could be appropriated, to be settled by the expanding Roman population. When this new kind of warfare came about, the problems of sustaining an army for a longer duration and covering more wide-ranging territory precipitated changes in the organisation of the army. The major change to a looser, more mobile formation probably came about in the fourth century, and is dealt with in the next chapter, but there may have been precedents where the Romans adapted to circumstances and terrain in previous years.

The army was probably not called out every year during the fifth century. Most of the recorded fighting was concentrated in the first half of the century, and again at the very end, leaving a gap of about forty years, from 454 to 411, when only fourteen wars were recorded. After the final defeat of the Sabines and the Latins, the Romans faced constant problems with the tribesmen of the Volsci and Aequi, who feature largely and constantly in the ancient accounts, until they were defeated during the first half of the fourth century and more or less disappeared. Another endemic problem for the Romans was the city of Veii. The tussle between the two cities was largely commercial as well as military. Everything depended on which of the two rivals was to control Fidenae on the left bank of the Tiber. If Veii controlled it, then Roman command of the riverbank and route to the north and south would be imperilled. If Rome controlled the right bank of the Tiber, Veii had no access to the sea and the salt pans of the coast.

After fighting against Veii from 483 to 474 and again from 438 to 425, the Romans did eventually manage to take control of Fidenae on the Tiber, but the hostilities did not end there. In 406, the Romans put Veii under siege. It was said to have lasted for ten years, which may have more to do with analogy with the siege of Troy than any approximation to the truth. It suffices to say that it went on for an unusually protracted length of time. The ancient authors were certain that this was the context for the introduction of pay (*stipendium*) for the soldiers. The siege could not simply be broken off and then resumed in the next campaigning season, so the men could not leave in order to go home for the harvest, and as a consequence they could not provide their own food for a sustained period of time. According to Livy the Senate decided to pay them. This raises the question of how they were paid and what they did with the proceeds. Probably the pay consisted of weighed bronze, but it is not clear whether this could be used to buy food and fodder from the surrounding countryside for the stationary army; maybe the soldiers could pay someone else to gather their crops at home, or perhaps the soldiers employed a combination of all kinds of schemes to enable the army to remain in the field, properly equipped and supplied. Pay would be for the duration of the campaign, and would cease when it ended.

The siege of Veii raises other questions. In previous wars between Rome and Veii, other Etruscan cities had sent help for Veii, but at the end of the fifth century, no other Etruscan city appeared to be willing to assist. Etruscan power was in decline by this time, and since there never was a unified Etruria, nothing was done to coerce other Etruscan cities to send troops to attack the Romans. The Etruscans may have realised that Rome was now too powerful to be vanquished, especially since she could call upon her allies to raise more armies if attacked either at Veii or closer to home. Veii was left to its own devices. It is not certain whether this was a siege in the conventional sense of troops scaling the ramparts with ladders, or hurling missiles at the walls from siege engines, or whether it was more properly classified as a blockade. City walls certainly became more common in the fifth and fourth centuries BC. Ardea had three earthen ramparts and ditches, and at Lavinium a stone wall was built. The cities of southern Etruria began to build walls in the fifth century, when they started to lose dominance and influence. Whatever it was, full siege or blockade, the city of Veii was eventually taken at the beginning of the fourth century. It was completely destroyed. This was a new departure. Cities were more usually taken and occupied, or left damaged but not beyond recovery, and bound to the victor by a treaty. The ultimate fate of Veii is considered to mark the beginning of Roman Imperialism. As Veii was obliterated most of its inhabitants were enslaved, while a smaller number were given Roman citizenship. The criteria that applied to the different treatment of these two groups probably concerned wealth. All the land that had belonged to Veii was taken over by the Romans and labelled *ager publicus*, public land, to be divided up into allotments and distributed among Roman settlers. It was the first significant expansion of Roman territory, and it would not be the last.

4

The Army of the Fourth Century BC

The Etruscan city of Veii and all its lands fell to the Romans in 396. Shortly after this victory and the consequent expansion of Roman territory, Roman achievement was obliterated by an ignominious defeat. The Gauls from northern Italy swept southwards and eventually approached Rome. The Gallic tribes on the south side of the Alps had made forays into Italy before, but Rome's neighbours, the Etruscans, had usually absorbed the impact and fought off the tribes. Now that Etruscan power was declining, the Gauls looked for other cities to plunder and marched further south. Livy explains that as the tribesmen approached the Etruscan city of Clusium, the citizens appealed to Rome for help, which was not given, but Roman envoys were sent to remonstrate with the Gauls. They acted in a very high-handed manner and offended the Gauls, who said they had never heard of Rome. They quickly became acquainted with the city.

The Gauls Attack Rome 390 BC

The attack of the Gauls occurred in 390 according to the chronology worked out by Varro, or 386 according to Greek sources, principally Polybius. The Gauls met the Romans at the battle of the River Allia, which joined the Tiber not far from Rome. There the Gauls inflicted such a heavy defeat on the Roman army that many of the soldiers ran away from these fierce northern fighters. The account of the battle in Livy's work may be mostly imaginative, but he blames the military tribunes for being too lax and not making adequate preparations to deal with the Gauls, whose advance seems to have been so rapid that it took the Romans by surprise. According to Livy, the Roman army drew up in a very long line so as not to be outflanked, and the commander placed his reserves on the heights to the right of the main army. The Gallic chief Brennus thought that these reserves would probably have been ordered to come down behind him or onto his flanks while he was occupied in attacking the main army, so he attacked the soldiers on the heights first, throwing the rest of the army into confusion and panic. There seem to have been little firm resolve and no coherent orders to stop the men and officers from running away. Some gathered in the area of Veii, others made it to Rome and fled straight to the Capitol Hill to await the arrival of the Gauls. All the men capable of bearing arms were summoned, and some of the people accompanied them, but the plebs gathered on the Janiculum and many people fled to nearby towns. Rome became a ghost town, and Roman legends were born. Some senators stayed in their houses to meet the Gauls, and were killed. The Gauls tried to take the Capitol by storm, climbing up the heights on the flanks of the hill by night, but the sacred geese set up such a commotion that the hero Marcus Manlius was alerted, and was able to save the day almost single-handed. These are the tales that have been repeated in storybooks from then until modern times. More realistically, the Gauls were not able to threaten the city with artillery and siege engines, and since they had burned parts of the city including the corn stores, they could not feed themselves without foraging further and further afield.

The sack of Rome by the Gauls was an infamous episode in Roman history, though their stay in the city has been played down; it probably only lasted a few days. The physical damage that they did was likely limited. Very few archaeological traces of destruction have been found dating to this period, so as yet it cannot be demonstrated that the Gauls wrecked the entire city. The Gauls were bought off, allegedly with one thousand pounds of gold, and left Rome. Although Livy says that the Gauls were searching for lands to settle, they probably had no ambitions to occupy Rome, or to find lands in Italy. In his lifetime, Livy would have known of this problem of mass migrations of tribesmen wanting lands to farm, since Augustus settled several tribes within the Empire, and started a trend that continued for centuries. In 390 it is more likely that the tribesmen were interested in portable wealth and plunder, not total conquest. It has been suggested that they were mercenaries on their way to join Dionysius, tyrant of Syracuse, but they may simply have been inquisitive and energetic warriors.

The capture of their city constituted a considerable shock to the Romans. The army had been defeated and discredited, the soldiers had run away, and the inhabitants of Rome had been forced to abandon the city for a short period. The fourth-century Romans probably felt that defence by the army alone was not sufficient, and a few years after the Gallic sack, the city was enclosed within walls, probably represented by the few remains of the so-called Servian wall that can still be seen today. There is a substantial section of this wall outside the railway station in Rome. The Gauls had made such an impression that it was decided to set up a fund for defence against them should they approach the city again. The money was still intact in the first century BC when Gaius Julius Caesar removed it from the temple where it was kept, in order to fund his army in the civil war against Pompey the Great. Caesar had just spent ten years in Gaul subduing the various tribes, and therefore claimed that as conqueror of the Gauls the money was his by right.

After the capture of Rome, although there was constant military activity in the first half of the fourth century, the fighting was still only on a small scale, and highly localised in comparison to the second half of the century, when the Romans started to fight wars in locations much further away from the city. From 350 BC until the end of the fourth century there were only three occasions, in 347, 344, and 328 BC, when Rome was not at war with another city state. On some occasions the Romans fought simultaneously on more than one front.

Changes in Army Organisation in the Fourth Century BC

The encounter with the Gauls may have prompted some changes in the organisation of the army. It is certain that important changes did take place during the fourth century BC, but it is not known exactly when new ideas were put into operation, so there is room for speculation that after the Gallic invasion the Romans looked at their army and its overall performance, and started to adapt it. The siege of Veii, the attack of the Gauls, and the prolonged and fierce Samnite wars of the fourth century have all been pinpointed as likely periods when Rome made changes to the organisation of the army. It cannot be proven whether the changes occurred all at the same time as a result of a corporately planned development, or in piecemeal fashion over a protracted period as and when problems were identified and solved.

The main developments for discussion concern a number of problems. One is the perennial debate about the method and the date of the establishment of the five Servian *classes*, and another problem concerns the rejection of the phalanx formation in favour of a looser organisation based on maniples, literally 'handfuls' of soldiers. Alongside these two main themes, there were changes in equipment and weapons. At some point the round *clipeus* was replaced by a different type of shield called the *scutum*, and the *pilum* was introduced, a throwing-spear mostly translated as javelin. It might be expected that new equipment and weapons went hand in hand with new methods of deployment, but this is not proven beyond doubt, and some authors favour a gradual introduction of the various new elements in the army of the fourth century BC.

In his book *The Making of the Roman Army* Lawrence Keppie assigns the introduction of the second and third of the Servian *classes* to the period of the siege of Veii which spanned the end of the fifth century and the beginning of the fourth. The men of the new second class were obliged to provide a shield, a helmet and greaves for protection, and a sword and spear for fighting. The third class had to provide a shield, a helmet and a spear. This would be a fitting occasion to introduce the *scutum* which is variously described as oval or oblong, but it seems that there were at least two variants, one a genuine oval and the other a cross between oval and oblong, or more precisely an oblong with rounded corners. Both these styles are shown in use together on a bronze bucket or *situla* from Certosa. The *scutum*, oval or oblong, protected more of the body than the round *clipeus*, and would be appropriate for soldiers of the second and third class who were not obliged to provide a cuirass or corselet for protection of the chest. The *scutum* was used widely in northern Italy and by the Gallic tribes. It was lighter than the *clipeus*, with a single grip instead of the arm and hand grip that the round shield required. The oval shield is usually shown in art and sculpture with a strengthening iron spine running along its length, and the oblong ones often have a central boss. Polybius says that the *scutum* had iron binding round the top and bottom edges, though this is not yet corroborated by archaeological or pictorial evidence.

Modern scholars suggest that there was a gradual replacement of the *clipeus* rather than an abrupt and total change, because that would involve expense and delay for the soldiers who were still armed in the old way and now had to have new equipment made. This means that for some time the army would contain soldiers with round shields fighting alongside soldiers with oval or oblong shields, and there is some support for this in art works. Tomb paintings and vase paintings show a combination of soldiers using hoplite arms and equipment together with others using the *scutum*.

It is not certain how an army equipped with different types of armour would have operated. It is possible that the phalanx was replaced by the new manipular organisation when the oval or oblong *scutum* began to be used, so there would be no requirement to lock shields and advance en masse. If they were not drawn up in the tight formation of the phalanx, it would not matter whether the men were protected by round or oval or oblong shields, because they would not be forced to maintain close contact with their neighbours. In effect, being able to move more freely in the looser formation of maniples, they would become individual fighters, operating in concert with the rest of the army but not locked into a solid line. Dionysius of Halicarnassus and Livy were certain that the introduction of the new type of shield and the division of the army into smaller maniples were associated, and occurred at the same time. There is a parallel in Greece in the fourth century, when the phalanx was falling out of favour and an oval shield was introduced.

It may have been in response to their failure against the highly mobile Gauls that the Romans abandoned the phalanx and created the smaller units of maniples that could move more rapidly and more freely in different combinations. According to Livy, a maniple contained 120 men, commanded by two centurions and two deputies called *optiones*. The maniples were drawn up in separate blocks, with spaces between each maniple, rather than in a solid mass or an extended line. Polybius, writing in the second century BC, says that the maniples could work together, or independently, depending on the needs of the moment. In book eighteen of his history, Polybius extols the virtues of the manipular system and contrasts it with the Macedonian phalanx, which was more highly evolved than the earlier versions, but the principles remain the same. As Polybius points out, the Roman army had met the phalanx several times and had always won the battles.

According to Polybius, who described the Macedonian phalanx, each soldier required a space three feet wide, as measured from the right shoulder of his neighbour to his own right shoulder. Likewise each soldier required another three feet from front to rear. The soldier would use both hands to grip his spear, which by the fourth century was over twenty feet long. The shaft and the head would extend fifteen feet in front of the soldier, and six feet to his rear, so that it was properly balanced. Some idea of the impenetrable wall of spear points can be formed when Polybius says that even the spears of the fifth rank would extend three feet in front of the men in the first rank, and then further forward there were the spearheads of the other four ranks, ranged progressively further out. No one would willingly hurl himself onto this formidable formation. The early phalanx was probably about twelve ranks deep, but the Macedonian phalanx had sixteen ranks, the last eleven of which could not take part in the initial fighting, but had to hold their spears above the shoulders of the men in front. Polybius says that these spears were so closely packed that they served to deflect missiles that were thrown over the heads of the first ranks.

The major drawback of the phalanx was that it required level ground, without ditches and streams, or large rocks and ridges. If a general could choose ground such as this on which to fight a battle, the phalanx had a tremendous advantage, and would often prevail. But the Roman manipular system was much more flexible. The soldiers moved as individuals, parrying blows with their shields, and cutting and thrusting with their swords. In order to perform effectively, the Roman soldiers in each maniple required the same space that a soldier of the phalanx required, three feet to front and rear, and the same on both sides. When a manipular army faced a phalanx, each soldier in the front rank of the maniple formation had to combat two men in the front rank of the phalanx, and also face the projecting spears of the ranks behind these two men, a total of ten spears. In theory, the Roman maniples ought not to have been able to defeat the phalanx if it maintained its formation and the impetus of the attack.

The disadvantage of the phalanx, apart from the need to find favourable ground on which to fight, was its uselessness as a formation in preventing the enemy from destroying crops, cutting supply lines, and sacking towns; flexible troops were needed for this. Another point that Polybius makes is that the Romans usually kept some part of their armies in reserve, which could be brought in if the phalanx forced its immediate opponents back, or if the phalanx was driven back on itself, because in either case its flanks would be exposed, and the reserves could easily attack them, or even come round the rear.

The command structure in the manipular system was greatly facilitated so that orders could be passed down from the commander to the subordinate officers. With two officers in command of the two centuries of a maniple the senior usually took charge of the whole, but there was also room for initiative during the battle, and if one officer was killed the surviving officer could take over. The looser formation also made it easier to replace the men in the battle line by bringing up the reserves to feed them into the line if the soldiers were in trouble.

Livy and the Army of 340 BC

In the eighth book of his history of Rome, Livy confidently describes the Roman army of the mid-fourth century, specifically 340 at the time of the rebellion of the Latins. It is possible that he combined elements of various different records, thereby indiscriminately amalgamating information that was either suspect or anachronistic, but he would have had no way of knowing whether his sources were reliable. It has been doubted whether the army that he described ever existed in reality.

According to Livy the army of 340 was drawn up in three main battle lines. The first line was made up of fifteen maniples of *hastati*, with spaces between each maniple. The *hastati* were composed of young men who were fit and mobile, fighting as heavy infantry armed with a spear. Attached to each maniple of *hastati* there were twenty light armed soldiers called *leves*, armed with a spear and light javelins. Their task was presumably to form a screen for the whole army, and to operate as skirmishers. Behind the *hastati* were another fifteen maniples of *principes* who were older and more experienced soldiers. These two lines were collectively known as the *antepilani*, which may be a throwback to an earlier formation dating to a time before 340, which comprised only two lines, the *pilani* in the rear and the *antepilani* in the front line. Another name that may be interchangeable with *antepilani* is *antesignani*, meaning in front of the standards.

The third battle line of Livy's army of 340 consisted of another fifteen maniples comprising three types of troops, first the older men, or veterans of several campaigns, called the *triarii*. Then there were the less experienced men of the *accensi* and the *rorarii*. Each of these fifteen maniples was divided into three parts, each part called a *vexillum*, a term that was later used to describe a particular kind of standard. In Livy's fourth-century army, each *vexillum* contained sixty men, plus two centurions and one man called a *vexillarius*, who carried the standard. The first *vexillum* of each maniple consisted of the *triarii*, the second contained the *rorarii*, and the third *vexillum* comprised the *accensi*, described by Livy as the least reliable of all the troops. Each group or maniple of three *vexilla*, according to Livy, contained 186 men, or three times sixty men plus six centurions. If each *vexillarius* was counted separately the total for each *vexilla* ought to have been 189, so the standard-bearer was presumably counted as one of the sixty soldiers.

The *triarii* were not expected to join in the fighting unless the circumstances were dire. They could sit or kneel while the first two lines did most of the work. If the battle was going badly they could dig their spear shafts into the ground to form a defensive line, but if it came to this, then the situation was very dire indeed. There was a saying in Rome for when everything was going wrong: 'So it has come to the *triarii*.'

The functions of the *rorarii* and *accensi* are not known. On a linguistic basis, the *accensi* were more likely to be attendants or orderlies, not soldiers, similar to the servants who carried the arms and armour of the hoplites. They may have acted as messengers as well. The *accensi* did occasionally take part in battles, notably in the war against the Latins under the general Decius Mus. The *rorarii* may have been light armed skirmishers, brought forward to open the battle. Rawlings draws attention to a fragment of the works of Varro, who refers to the *rorarii* as the shower before the rain, implying that their task was to soften up the enemy before the main heavy armed troops engaged. Writing in the early second century BC, Plautus produced a play with a reference to *rorarii* and *accensi*, implying that these were two separate types of soldiers, and also that the names were not too archaic to be understood by his audience.

There are some inconsistencies in Livy's fourth-century army. If the *rorarii* really were skirmishers in the front line, why does Livy assign them to the rear, and describe separately the numbers of *leves* attached to the *hastati*? The numbers of men in the army do not add up, either. At the end of the passage describing the organisation of the army, Livy says there were 5,000 infantrymen and 300 horsemen in each legion. In a different passage, not related to his description of the army of 340, Livy says that a maniple consisted of 120 men. It is not certain whether this number was also correct for the maniples of the mid-fourth-century army. Unfortunately, although Livy is quite specific about the numbers of men in the third-line maniples, he does not provide numbers in this particular context for the *hastati* and *principes*. If each of the thirty maniples of *hastati* and *principes* contained 120 men, the total number of soldiers, together with the *leves* and the fifteen maniples of the rear line, would have far exceeded the standard 5,000 men that Livy says comprised one legion. It is perfectly feasible that on occasion armies could be raised with many more men than usual. Writing in the second century BC Polybius says that a legion normally contained 4,200 men, but could contain 5,000 in emergencies, and in another passage he says that legions of 5,200 men were raised. Even so, the army of 340, as described by Livy, with fifteen maniples of *hastati* and *principes*, would have been very much larger than this, unless each maniple of the *hastati* and *principes* contained only sixty men, like the *vexilla* of the *triarii*, *rorarii* and *accensi*. In that case the totals would have been nearly 5,000, just as Livy says.

Polybius describes the army of the second century BC, but it is worthwhile to compare what he says with Livy's work on the fourth-century army. Polybius sometimes corroborates and sometimes contradicts what Livy says. The greater part of the sixth book of Polybius' history of Rome concerns the army. His information is generally considered reliable, because he had seen the army in action, in contrast to Livy, who wrote in the first century BC, and was forced to rely upon his sources to describe an army that had not been seen within living memory. This is not to say that Polybius was right and Livy was wrong, or that there are no problems at all in using the work of Polybius.

Polybius' account agrees with Livy's in that the three main battle lines were composed of *hastati*, *principes* and *triarii*, and that these consisted of three age groups, with the younger men in the ranks of the *hastati*, mature men in the *principes* and the more senior men in the *triarii*. Polybius says that the first two lines each comprised 1,200 men, divided up into ten companies or maniples, which would confirm Livy's figure of 120 men to each maniple, but Polybius' first two lines are only two-thirds of the size of Livy's version, with ten maniples instead of fifteen. Polybius says that the *triarii* were 600 strong. If a larger army was required, the extra numbers were placed in the first two lines, whereas the *triarii* always remained at 600 men. Though Polybius does not say so, it may have been more difficult to find a larger number of older men who were still fit enough to go to war. The army described by Polybius does not contain *rorarii* or *accensi*, but he does mention *velites*, which group comprised the youngest men and also the least wealthy. The mention of wealth implies that some sort of property qualification was still operative. The *velites* may have replaced the *leves* or the *rorarii* as skirmishers, but they did not operate as a permanent front line. According to Polybius they were split up into groups of 120 men, each attached to one of the maniples.

The arms and armour of each of the groups of fighting men are briefly described by Polybius. Since his work dates from the second century BC, caution should be exercised in applying his description to the fourth-century army when the manipular formation was first introduced. But Polybius cannot be ignored in this earlier context, because there is no better source. According to Polybius, the *hastati* were protected by the *scutum*, made of two layers of wood glued together and covered with canvas and then leather. It measured two and a half feet wide and four feet in length. Each *hastatus* wore a bronze helmet, with a plume made of three dark-coloured feathers, so he looked much taller than he really was. His legs were protected by greaves and his chest by a square metal heart-protector. His weapons included a two-edged pointed sword, and two spears or *pila*, one thick and the other much thinner, with a barbed point. Some men with a higher property qualification wore a chain-mail coat. The *principes* carried the same weapons, but the *triarii* wielded a thrusting-spear instead of the throwing-spears of the first two lines. The *velites* wore a helmet, often covered with the skin of a wolf or other animal, and carried a round shield about three feet in diameter. They were each armed with a sword, and javelins with pointed heads, hammered out so thin that they bent on impact, so they could not be picked up and thrown back by the enemy.

Polybius could confidently write of throwing-spears when he described the Roman army in the second century BC, but it is not certain if his account applies to the fourth century. This is bound up with the question of precisely when the manipular formation became the norm, at an unknown date in the years between the Gallic attack in 390 and perhaps the Samnite wars. Once the manipular formation had been adopted, the new-style army was better suited to missile combat than to close-quarter fighting. Whereas the *hasta* was designed for thrusting, the *pilum* (plural *pila*) was a throwing-spear, an ideal weapon for missile combat. It was perhaps introduced along with the new army formation. Archaeological evidence shows that there was a wide variety of spear types, most probably used in slightly different ways.

Bishop and Coulston point out that the type of *pilum* with a narrow shank and a pyramid-shaped head was designed to penetrate an enemy shield, and if possible carry on right through it to injure the bearer. Modern experiments show this was possible if the *pilum* was thrown from a distance of about five metres at a pinewood shield one inch thick. In addition, the *pilum* was designed to bend on impact, which was achieved either by leaving the iron untempered just below the head, or by using a wooden rivet instead of a metal one to attach the shank to the shaft, so that it would break. This was not the prime purpose of the *pilum* but it meant that if the enemy survived the missile attack he had to throw his shield away, and if he was killed, the *pilum* in his shield could not be hurled back. According to Polybius there were two kinds of *pila*, one heavy and thick, and one light and thin. He describes the thin variety as a medium-sized hunting spear with a barbed iron head, which was fitted into the shaft and riveted with iron clasps, so that it broke on impact.

Actual examples of the different kinds of *pila* are known from the end of the third century, but the only evidence that they may have been in use in the fourth century is from Etruscan tomb paintings from Tarquinii. The most numerous examples come from Spain, especially from Numantia, besieged by the Roman army in the second century BC, and from Renieblas nearby. Despite the lack of datable finds, some authors have strongly suggested that the Romans were already experimenting with the throwing-spear in the fourth century, and others have gone further still to suggest that the wars with the Samnites may have been the context when the *pilum* was introduced, because in the rugged hill country it was not possible to engage in close combat with the phalanx formation.

Argument continues about the origin of the *pilum*, as well as the date of its introduction into the Roman army. The Etruscans, the Spanish tribes, and the Samnites have all been credited with its invention, but as yet it has not been decisively shown that any of these were responsible for it. Once they adopted it, however, the Romans made full use of all the variant types, and it became one of the standard items of equipment of the Roman Imperial army.

The Five Servian Classes

Livy provides distinct names for five groups of soldiers in the army of 340, so it is easy but dangerous to equate them with the five Servian *classes*, on the assumption that the *hastati*, *principes* and *triarii* must belong to the first three classes, and the *rorarii* and *accensi* must represent the fourth and fifth *classes* of poorer men who could not afford the arms and armour stipulated for the other groups. The main problem with this theory is that the Servian *classes* were supposed to be drawn up on the basis of wealth, whereas the new formations of *hastati*, *principes* and *triarii* were drawn up based on age and fitness, therefore it is unlikely that there is a direct link between the manipular army and the five Servian classes. However there may be an indirect link. Cornell points out that when military pay was introduced at the end of the fifth century, a tax (*tributum*) was levied at the same time, presumably to provide the funds for the soldiers' pay while on campaign. In this context, the five Servian divisions based on wealth would serve to identify those citizens who could afford to pay the highest proportion of tax in return for greater political privileges and influence, given that the voting system was weighted in favour of the rich. Descending through the other classes there was a proportionate relationship between wealth, tax payments, and political privilege. Thus the five Servian classes could have been operative as a political and fiscal tool, while at the same time, the soldiers could have been recruited from all the classes, and then assigned to different sections of the army not according to their wealth but on the basis of age. Youth, agility, and fitness count for more than wealth in any army.

The Cavalry

In the days of the kings, the Roman cavalry allegedly numbered 300 horsemen, comprising 100 from each of the three tribes of Ramnes, Tities and Luceres. During the Republic, according to Livy and Polybius, each army had 300 cavalry assigned to it. Since horses and their maintenance do not come cheaply, the cavalry was necessarily formed from the very wealthiest men, originally those who could provide their own horses. As Rome expanded and wars became more frequent, this arrangement could not be sustained, so financial assistance from the state had to be provided if a larger cavalry arm was to be created. Livy associates this development with Servius Tullius and the institution of the five *classes*, indicating that there were six original centuries of cavalry, three of them raised by Romulus, and all six were known by their old names. In addition, twelve further centuries were enrolled, making a total of eighteen centuries. These men were the wealthiest of all in Rome, and their political influence far outweighed their actual numbers. Despite their wealth, Livy says that the treasury granted 10,000 bronze *asses* to each century for the purchase of horses, and taxed wealthy widows to provide 2,000 further *asses* to buy fodder. It is not known how long this arrangement would have survived, but it is known that during the Republic financial help was available to replace a horse if the cavalryman lost one on campaign. The cavalrymen were known as *equites*, from *equus*, horse, and those in receipt of state funds to buy or replace a horse were known as *equites equo publico*. Cavalrymen who provided their own horses were known as *equites equis suis*.

According to Polybius, the Republican cavalry attached to each army was divided up into ten groups called *turmae*, with thirty men in each *turma*, a figure that remained more or less the same throughout the Republic and Empire for cavalry units. Each *turma* was commanded by three decurions chosen from among its own members, and each decurion chose his *optio* or subordinate officer. The name decurion indicates that the man commanded ten men, though the first decurion to be chosen was regarded as the most senior, and commanded the whole *turma*. In his absence the other decurions would take charge.

Polybius is very scathing about the performance of the early Roman cavalry. The men wore no protective armour, he says, which gave them the advantage when mounting and dismounting but made them more vulnerable in combat. Their spears or lances were too flimsy to be of use because they shook and frequently broke with the action of the horse, and even if they survived the riding motion, they were susceptible to breakage on the first thrust. The shields carried by cavalrymen were also unfit for purpose. These were round with a central boss, and made of ox hide. This was useful enough in dry weather but peeled and rotted when the shields got wet. With some pride, Polybius tells how the Romans discovered the value of strongly made Greek shields, and the more rigid type of spear or lance, which was not susceptible to wavering around as the horsemen galloped, and had not only a strong head, but also a spike at the bottom end that could be used in combat. Since Polybius' Greek audience would know what these items looked like and how big they were, he does not go into details about dimensions or weight. Nor does he provide any indication of the date when the cavalry put into practice new ideas derived from the Greeks. The Romans did not come face-to-face with the Greeks in Greece until the first century BC, but there were Greek colonies in Italy whose cavalry may have provided the role models. Polybius merely adds a comment that the Romans were excellent at adopting and adapting new equipment and methods if they could see that other people performed rather better than themselves.

Very little is known about how the cavalry fought, and for the fourth century even the battles where the cavalry played a part are not fully documented. Livy describes how the Roman cavalry, 'drawn up in the best formation', attacked and scattered the Samnites who had stopped to loot the Roman baggage train. Unfortunately Livy does not describe what the best formation was. In 310, having broken the Etruscan phalanx at the battle of Sutrium, the Roman cavalry deflected the fleeing Etruscans from gaining the safety of their camp, and forced them to turn towards the mountains. A short time later, in a battle against the Samnites the cavalry attacked the enemy flanks, and precipitated a flight back to the Samnite camp. In an earlier confrontation with the Samnites, when the Romans were besieging Saticula, the enemy constantly harassed the Roman camp, and the master of horse Quintus Aelius Cerretanus gathered his horsemen, charged out of the gates and scattered the Samnites, only to be counterattacked by the Samnite general and his cavalry. Both the Roman commander and the Samnite commander were killed, and each fell into the enemy lines. The Roman cavalry dismounted, forcing the Samnite cavalry to do the same while each side fought to regain the body of their commander. In another battle against the Etruscans, when the Romans were not doing well, the cavalry fought on foot in the front line.

Conventionally, the cavalry could have been used for scouting and reconnaissance, but the Romans seem to have been especially lax about such procedures, and notoriously fell into carefully laid ambushes which might have been avoided if horsemen had been sent out to observe the surrounding terrain and enemy movements. Horsemen could obviously report back to the camp or the commander on the march more quickly than scouts on foot. In the Samnite wars, reconnaissance by the cavalry may have helped to avert the disaster of the Caudine Forks in 321, when the Romans marched into a trap, and ignominiously surrendered. Theoretically, cavalry was best equipped for pursuit of a fleeing enemy and killing or rounding up survivors, to ensure as complete a victory as possible. In battle, headlong pursuit could be disastrous, because it removed the cavalry from the field, and as everyone knows who has read about Prince Rupert and Oliver Cromwell, the hardest thing of all is getting them to come back.

Wars of the Fourth Century BC

Rome gradually emerged as the dominant state in Italy during the fourth century, after repeated battles against various tribes and states, which were sometimes enemies of the Romans and sometimes their allies in wars against other tribes. The shifting alliances among the Latins, Sabines, Etruscans, Volsci, Aequi and Samnites form a bewildering backdrop to the growth of Roman power in Italy. The inability of Rome's enemies to form lasting coalitions could only work to her advantage, since the Romans displayed a distinct talent for dividing their opponents and defeating them one by one.

Livy goes into great detail about the wars of the fourth century, but modern scholars suspect that his sources are not reliable. The hero cult is already apparent in Livy's history, because after all, history is made up of heroic or infamous personalities, and their exploits liven up any narrative. His readers could be forgiven for imagining that all Roman successes of the early fourth century must be due to Marcus Furius Camillus, just as Polybius' readers must have thought that if anyone was achieving anything in the Roman world in the second century BC, it was the past and present members of the Scipio family, who just happened to be his patrons.

In the fifth century, Rome and Latium had been potentially threatened on all sides, with the Sabines to the north-east, the Volsci to the south, and the Aequi to the east. The Sabines seem to have been absorbed by the mid-fifth century, but problems with the Aequi and Volsci continued into the early fourth century. It was the Latins who were most at risk, so the alliance with Rome guaranteed them protection, but reciprocally it was important to the Romans for the extra manpower that the Latins could contribute to the army. By 383 the Etruscans, Volsci and Aequi were subdued, and as far as possible they were kept under Roman control by the foundation of colonies. The institution of colonies had begun in the fifth century, or possibly even under the kings. Sometimes the new colony was founded in areas where there had been no urban settlement, and sometimes an existing town was converted into a colony. The original inhabitants were often included in the new arrangements. The colony was an independent self-governing community with its own elected magistrates. Settlers were not exclusively Roman, but it would be the Romans who supervised the allocation of land to the colonists, perhaps in consultation with the allies. The colonies could serve to safeguard territory and they provided manpower for the army.

In the first half of the fourth century the Gauls reappeared, and provided the catalyst for a renewal in 358 of the alliances between Rome and the Latins, and Rome and the Hernici, but this time on more favourable terms for Rome. The Latins were suffering from Gallic raids and were not inclined to argue, but some cities such as Tibur and Praeneste decided that they would be better off joining with the Gauls against Rome. These two cities were subdued and brought under Roman domination in 354. In the 350s and 340s Rome became more overtly aggressive and attacked and took over various towns and cities. From 358 to 351 the Romans fought the Etruscan city of Tarquinii, and then Falerii and Caere, though this struggle ended in a truce, not Roman domination. More serious struggles were to come, when Rome clashed with the Samnites.

The First Samnite War 343–341 BC

In the sixth century BC the Samnites were predominantly settled in rural villages, organised in administrative groups which the Romans called *pagi*. At the beginning of the fifth century BC the Samnite hill tribes of the Apennines spread out into the plains and coastal areas of Campania where they gradually took over the cities, though not by aggressive conquest. The

Samnites were not ethnically unified. There were four main tribes who all spoke the Oscan language and shared the same cultural heritage. In Campania they met the Etruscans and the Greeks, and eventually formed a Samnite-Campanian amalgam. Interstate wars were waged with monotonous regularity, though if threatened corporately the Samnite tribes could and did settle their differences and unite under one commander, which tended to make them a more formidable enemy than the squabbling tribes and city states of the Volsci, Aequi and Etruscans.

The Samnites had a warlike reputation, attested by the numerous hill forts in their Apennine homeland, and by archaeological finds of arms and armour. The weapons, cuirasses, shields and helmets that have been discovered show some Greek influence, and they differ widely from Livy's description of Samnite equipment. Livy says that the Samnites had two kinds of troops, one with gold shields and the other with silver shields, and the soldiers wore breastplates called *spongia*, and helmets with crests. Actual finds include triangular breastplates with three discs embossed on the metal and helmets with slots for feathers. The Samnites of the hill country may have used the *scutum*, but those settled near the coast commonly used the round shield of the Greeks.

The Samnites and the Romans initially had no quarrel with each other and were in fact allies, having agreed upon a treaty in 354. Virtually nothing is known of its terms, except that it is likely that the treaty arrangement recognised the River Liris (modern Garigliano) as the boundary between Latium and Samnite territory. If this is correct, the Romans were simply acknowledging the status quo. The war began when the Samnites attacked the Sidicini of Campania, and other Campanians went to aid them. The Samnites attacked Capua, the chief city of a Campanian federation, and the Campanians appealed to Rome.

According to Livy, the Campanian ambassadors pointed out that if the Romans helped to repel the Samnites, then Campania would belong to Rome, promising that 'no colony will surpass us in loyalty'. On the other hand, if no help was forthcoming, then they would inevitably belong to the Samnites, so it was now down to the Romans to decide whether they preferred to have the Campanians or the Samnites as neighbours. Livy points out that Capua, the chief city of Campania, was wealthy, and situated in fertile lands close to the sea, which represents the ethos of the Roman government, tending towards the principle of *cui bono*, who benefits? If there was a promise of tangible gains, then a war was always worth the effort.

The Romans at first very properly refused to be drawn into war without the necessary formalities, because they had an alliance with the Samnites. Accordingly they sent the fetial priests to ask for redress on behalf of the Campanians, which was refused. This meant that Rome could now embark on a just war because the Samnites had been given a chance to desist from their aggression and had not done so. War was declared probably in 343, though 341 is also suggested.

The first Samnite war has been dismissed by some modern scholars, or if it is accepted it is usually suggested that there was no fighting to speak of and no clear result. Livy fills in some details, which have also been dismissed as fiction. He describes how two armies were raised, one for each consul, Marcus Valerius Corvus, sometimes rendered as Corvinus, and Aulus Cornelius Cossus. Valerius led his troops into Campania, and fought a hard battle with the Samnites. Livy describes how Valerius tried to break the Samnite lines by ordering the cavalry to charge the enemy in a frontal attack, but when this failed he ordered the cavalry to move to the wings and brought in his infantry to take advantage of the confusion that the horsemen had caused. If this is true, it says something for Roman battle experience, in disengaging one element of the army, manoeuvring it in two different directions on to the wings, and committing another element to the attack. Due credit is given to the Samnites as determined fighters, without actually saying that since the Romans won they must have been even more determined.

The other consul Cornelius Cossus, operating in Samnite territory, led the army into a wood that concealed a ravine, where the Samnites were watching. This prefigures the similar story of the disaster of the Caudine Forks in 321, where a Roman commander committed the same error, but with consequences that were much greater. In this case disaster was avoided because the military tribune Publius Decius had noticed that a nearby hill dominated the enemy camp, and asked permission to scale the heights with the first two ranks of one legion. The implication in Livy's account is that Cornelius commanded two legions, and probably the other consul Valerius also commanded two legions. This is turn implies that the Romans were raising four legions each year. It is generally agreed that two legions were raised from 362 onwards, but there is no confirmation for four legions until 311.

When he had captured the hill, Decius was able to rain down missiles on the Samnites and hold them off until the main army had got out of its difficulties, then he extricated himself and his men by creeping through the Samnite camp after dark, with only a few losses. Before he marched into the consul's camp next day, Decius ordered his men to wait for the dawn so that they could tidy themselves up and present a proper military aspect. He was rewarded with the grass crown, for his exploits in rescuing the troops from what could easily have been disaster. According to Pliny, the grass for the crown was usually gathered from the area of the heroic action, so perhaps someone thoughtfully cropped some of it before leaving the hill.

This picturesque account of the events of the Samnite war may be true but it has a slight air of padding, and the events as described do not really account for the Samnite capitulation in 341, leaving a hint of unfinished business.

The Revolt of the Latins 341–338 BC

The Romans and Samnites renewed their alliance, and the Romans were assisted by their former enemies during their next struggles, primarily with the Latins, who had now allied with the Volsci and the Campanians. The Latins had honoured their treaty of the early fifth century for many years, but they now felt that they were considered as subjects of Rome, not allies. They had faithfully contributed soldiers to the Roman army, but they had not reaped many of the benefits, so they sought allies to help them shake off Roman control. The Volsci were knocked out of the combat in 341, but it took more battles with the Latins and their other allies to put an end to the revolt, as the Romans called it.

Two legendary events occurred during the Latin wars. In a battle fought at the foot of Mount Vesuvius, the consul Decius Mus saw that the battle was not going well, and decided to dedicate himself to the gods along with the enemy army. He asked the priests accompanying the army to preside over the religious ceremonial, and with his head veiled, standing on a spear, he invoked several gods to consign him and the enemy troops to the underworld, and let the Romans win. Then he rode into the thick of the fighting and was killed. The story is told that his son made the same sacrifice at the battle of Sentinum in 295. Even after the sacrifice of the general, it was still a desperate battle. Livy describes how the *rorarii* and *accensi* were ordered forwards to the front line, and finally the *triarii* were sent in to face the Latins. It was the decisive move, and the Latins fled to Minturnae.

Since disaffection with the Romans was strong among some of Rome's neighbours, the Latins were able to raise another army from different tribes and states, and rallied, to face the Romans again. The consul Manlius Torquatus defeated them, but it must have been a sour victory for him. He had given orders that the troops were not to engage in single combat with the enemy, and his son Manlius, leading the Roman cavalry, had done exactly that. Despite the fact that he had killed his adversary, Manlius the younger had disobeyed orders, and it was detrimental to discipline if the consul made exceptions in favour of his own family. He executed his own son.

Fighting between Romans and Latins continued into 339 and 338, but the cohesion of the Latins had been broken. The way in which Rome dealt with the defeated communities at the conclusion of the revolt in 338 introduced new ideas, with great consequence for the army. The communities closest to Rome remained as self-governing city states, or *municipia*, with full Roman citizenship for all the inhabitants. They had the right to vote at the assemblies in Rome, and it also made them eligible for Roman taxes and service in the Roman army, considerably increasing available manpower. The more distant Latin cities also remained as self-governing communities, with the right to intermarry with Romans (*ius conubium*) and to trade with Romans (*ius commercium*) but they did not possess the same rights of intermarriage and trading with any of the other Latin states. Each city state was bound to Rome and isolated from the other Latin cities. There was now no legal way of forming a Latin federation, or of allying with any other community outside Latium. The obligation to contribute men for the army was still in force, with the compensatory promise of Roman protection if the city or cities should come under attack. These obligations and privileges were classified as Latin rights, which was later regarded as a halfway house to the conferment of full Roman citizenship. Latin communities of the later Republic and the Empire were not necessarily inhabited by ethnic Latins, since the term denoted a political status.

For the city states further away from Rome, in Campania, the Romans made new arrangements, similar to those made with the Latin communities. The states became self-governing *municipia*, retaining their own forms of administration, and the inhabitants had the rights of intermarriage and conducting business with Roman citizens, while they themselves possessed a new form of Roman citizenship without voting rights at Rome. Each state became a *civitas sine suffragio*, a new institution that was more widely used during the later Republic and the Empire. The most important feature was that cities and communities with *civitas sine suffragio* were obliged to contribute soldiers to the Roman army.

The Second Samnite War 326–304 BC

Having entered the first clash with the Samnites by invitation of the Campanians, the Romans began to cast covetous eyes at the territory of Campania itself. There was fertile agricultural land, harbours and ports that would facilitate trade, especially with the Greeks, and there were mineral deposits, a feature which always loomed large in any decision to take over territory. The Romans can be accused of deliberately precipitating the second war by encroachment on Samnite lands. In 328 they founded a colony at Fregellae on the left bank of the River Liris, which the Samnites regarded as their own territory. The Samnites had seemingly not reacted when Rome took over parts of northern Campania, including Cumae, nor did they object when the Romans forged alliances with tribes surrounding Samnite lands, in Apulia and Lucania. But after 328 the Samnites did react, and attacked and took over Naples, the old city, which may or may not have been contiguous with the new city called Neapolis, the forerunner of modern Naples.

The war began in 327. The Romans found that it did not go quite as well as they had planned, and fighting rumbled on until 304. Before war was declared, the fetial priests set out to demand that the Samnites should evacuate Naples. After the expected refusal, the consul Quintus

Publilius Philo was sent out to wrest the city from the Samnites. The struggle continued until Philo's consulship was due to end, so rather than replace him and send out one of the new consuls, the Romans solved the problem with a novel idea which would allow Philo to continue as commander of the army, with the powers of a consul, but without actually being consul. This was the first time the proconsulship was instituted, and it would eventually become the norm as the Republic expanded its territory and acquired provinces which required a governor, ideally with experience of political administration at Rome and also of army command. In the end, someone betrayed Naples to the Romans.

There was some military activity against the tribes who had allied with the Samnites, such as the Lucanians and Vestini, but then, according to Livy, the Roman commanders operating in Samnite territory fell out with each other. The Dictator Lucius Papirius Cursor had to return to Rome, and left his master of horse Quintus Fabius Maximus Rullus (or Rullianus) in command with instructions not to engage the enemy. But Fabius saw a golden opportunity and attacked the Samnites, emerging the victor largely due to a cavalry attack that opened up a gap in the enemy front line, which the infantry exploited. Despite his success, Fabius was put on trial for disobeying orders, but the soldiers rioted and halted proceedings. According to Livy, the army was so disaffected that they decided upon a sort of work-to-rule when the Dictator Papirius next engaged the Samnites in 352, avoiding defeat, but not working hard enough to win a complete victory.

The Samnites assembled a large army to carry on the war in 323 and 322 and the Romans levied more troops. Livy accuses the Romans of neglecting to make a camp in the middle of hostile territory, though this is controversial, since it is not known when the Romans adopted the practice of building camps while on campaign. Livy also says that the Romans were forced into a battle on unfavourable ground, but the Samnites were distracted by the sight of the unprotected Roman baggage and began to plunder it, allowing the Roman cavalry to come up and disperse them. Disarmingly, Livy admits that for this period he had not been able to find any contemporary sources, and he suspects that his information consists of embroidered family legends making much of the achievements of various ancestors.

The following year, 321, was one that no Roman was likely to forget. In resuming the war, the Romans were duped by well-organised Samnite misinformation. Local farmers and shepherds were primed to drop hints that the main Samnite army was besieging Luceria in Apulia. The Romans set off to aid this supposedly beleaguered city, and marched straight into a defile near Caudium, better known as the Caudine Forks. No one had reconnoitred the area, so the Romans did not know that the Samnites had secretly assembled there, and had blocked the passage with uprooted trees and fallen rocks. Then they closed in behind the Romans. If the Romans had been soundly beaten in a pitched battle it would have been bad enough, but as it was they had to surrender without fighting. The Samnites did not massacre them, but forced the soldiers and commanders to divest themselves of most of their clothes and march under the yoke, so they had to bow their heads as if in submission. The Romans left behind 600 cavalry as hostages. The Capuans turned out to assist the defeated army as they marched through Campania. Livy blusters about Samnite recognition of Roman determination and courage, and he portrays wise elders declaring that in the long run the Samnites would rue the day.

The army raised for the resumption of the war in 320 was divided between the two consuls. Papirius headed for Luceria in Apulia, and Publilius remained in Samnite territory, where the Romans won a victory in an unnamed location, and Livy adds the interesting detail that in order to engage rapidly, the soldiers, on their own initiative, decided not to waste time throwing their javelins, but to lay them down and rush forwards with drawn swords. In Apulia, Papirius took Luceria and expelled the Samnite garrison, allegedly making them march under the yoke as the Romans had done at the Caudine Forks.

The long, drawn-out wars then became a series of sieges of various places, with towns and cities being taken and retaken, and both Romans and Samnites trying to detach the allies of the other. Even some of the leading men of Capua, hitherto loyal to the Romans, considered defection to the Samnites. The fighting escalated in 311 and 310 when the Romans faced the Etruscans as well as the Samnites and raised four legions for the two consuls to fight on two separate fronts. This is the first indication that there were four legions in the Roman army, but there are hints that there were already four legions in the first Samnite war in 343.

The Samnite wars dragged on, with campaigns fought every year. After a defeat in 310 the Samnites recovered sufficiently to embark on an offensive in 307 and captured two towns. In the following year they appeared in force in northern Campania. Two Roman armies were despatched into Samnite territory, one under the consul Postumius Megellus to Tifernum and the other under Titus Minucius to Bovianum. An indecisive battle was fought at Tifernum, and Postumius withdrew to a naturally defensible site in the mountains, where he built a camp, but it was all a ruse. He left a garrison behind and led the army to join Minucius at Bovianum. The combined armies soundly defeated the Samnites. Then they returned to Tifernum and surprised and defeated the other Samnite army. In 304 peace was finally made, on Samnite initiative but on Roman terms.

Soldiers of the Fourth Century BC

According to Livy, the Roman armies of the Samnite wars were manipular formations. There is some debate as to whether the Romans began their war in Samnite territory with the conventional hoplite phalanx formation, and then after discovering that it was not effective in hilly terrain divided by deep valleys, they reorganised and produced an army with a looser formation. It has been argued that there were several changes in army organisation during the Samnite wars. Some scholars argue that since wars were now fought on more than one front it would have been necessary to constitute the five Servian classes to facilitate the supply of recruits. It has also been suggested that the Romans first introduced military pay in the Samnite wars, because the soldiers were based much further away from Rome than they had been at Veii. The *scutum* and the *pilum* may have been introduced at this time, both being better suited to fighting in looser formations, launching javelins at some distance from the enemy. The theory fits the facts, but is not proven. Some authors have argued that the Romans would have been capable of evaluating in advance the difficulties posed by the Samnite territory, and would not have employed the phalanx in these wars. The jury is therefore still out on the demise of the phalanx and the introduction of the manipular army.

The commanders of the armies were consuls, or on occasion Dictators assisted by the master of horse, as documented by Livy. Serving under the consuls or Dictators were the military tribunes. In 362 Livy says that it was decided that the military tribunes, usually appointed by the commanders, should be elected by the people. Six were elected that year. Two tribunes commanded the whole legion for one month, perhaps with each one of the pair commanding on alternate days, then another pair would take over for the next month.

The strength of the legions is not known for certain. The figure of 6,000 has been advanced as the full complement of a legion from the time of the kings, and the Romans of the fourth century would have had access to such manpower. The six tribunes seemed to support the theory. If each tribune was in charge of 1,000 men, the legion must have numbered 6,000, but there is no evidence that the tribunes ever commanded a section of the army. Describing the army of 340 Livy gives the total number of men as 5,000, and Polybius' total for the legions of the second century BC is 4,200. Perhaps there is a flaw in expecting the legions to be always of a standard size. There is nearly always a difference between paper strength and actual strength, and in some wars units can be greatly increased in size according to the needs of the moment.

Several times in his narrative Livy refers to military camps, or the absence of camps, as though it was customary for armies of the fourth century BC to fortify a base or to construct marching camps, with earthen ramparts within a surrounding ditch. In one passage Livy describes how the Samnites attacked the camp of the consul Marcus Valerius, where soldiers were stationed behind the ramparts. On other occasions, the enemy is said to have come right up to the ramparts. The consul Postumius fortified a camp in the hills near Tifernum. When Livy was writing, the practice was usual, and Polybius describes the military camp of the second century BC, noting the precise locations of each section of the army within it, but there is some doubt that in the fourth century the army regularly dug marching camps. They may have built siege camps when there was an expectation that the process was to be prolonged.

As a historian devoted to the glory of Rome, it might be expected that Livy would have glossed over any dissension in the army, but he refers to such events more than once. The quarrel between the Dictator Papirius and his master of horse Quintus Fabius divided the loyalties of the army, and may have resulted in some reluctance on the part of the soldiers to fight to the best of their ability. In 362 Lucius Manlius was put on trial by the tribune Marcus Pomponius for his harshness in levying troops. There had been floggings and imprisonment when some men had not answered the call to arms. There were other incidents when the men refused to answer when their names were called out for the army, indicating an unwillingness to serve that contradicts the supposed reputation of the Romans for patriotism and martial vigour. In 342 the soldiers who were in winter quarters in Capua started to agitate against the Campanians who enjoyed a luxurious life in a rich land, while the Roman soldiers sent to help them had done all the hard work. The grumbling was likely to escalate, so the new consul Gaius Marcius Rutulus began the next season's campaign by quietly ridding the army of troublemakers, retiring some on account of their age or completion of the specified number of campaigns, and sending others home on periods of leave. Once they realised what was happening, the men who had been dismissed in this way banded together, chose a leader of their own, and set off for Rome where the newly appointed Dictator, Marcus Valerius Corvus (or Corvinus), had levied an army and was waiting for them. Civil war was narrowly avoided as the men came to their senses. Livy invents speeches for the leaders of the opposing troops, appealing to the better nature of the men and the glory and honour of Rome. Agreement was reached and a law was passed that reveals the genuine grievances of the soldiers. The law stated that no soldier on active service should have his name removed from the lists without his consent. If any man's name was not in the lists, this meant that his goods could be seized by creditors, and also the removal of his name meant that a serving soldier could not claim his share of the booty after a particularly profitable war. Another clause in the new law concerned military tribunes. It was enacted that a man who had served as tribune in a legion could not serve as chief centurion in the following year. This clause, according to Livy, referred to a notorious soldier and bully called Publius Salonius, who enlisted for successive campaigns, alternating as tribune and chief centurion. One of the clauses for which the soldiers lobbied was the reduction of the pay of the cavalry, because the horsemen earned three times as much as the infantry, but this was rejected. The cavalrymen had to feed themselves and look after their horses, so their pay reflected this.

The stories which Livy tells of the army and the wars of the fourth century BC may have no foundation, though on the whole he seems to have worked hard to compare his sources and evaluate them. What he does reveal is that the army was made up of people, subject to churlishness as well as heroism, generosity as well as meanness, and all those human attributes that it is easy to forget when working out how the armour fitted together, or how far a spear would travel and still penetrate a shield.

After the Samnites

Towards the end of the Samnite wars, it was almost certain that the Romans would win in the end, simply because of their dogged determination and their capacity to raise army after army until the enemy was worn down. The conclusion of the wars and the renewal of the treaty with the Samnites left the Romans free to concentrate on new theatres of war, especially in Umbria and Etruria, and then the gradual conquest of the rest of Italy. Wars of conquest always brought the Romans into contact with other city states and tribes, and then they needed to establish secure boundaries. They could not hope to avoid any relations, peaceful or otherwise, with the Greeks of southern Italy, nor ultimately with powers beyond Italy. In 348, according to Livy, the Carthaginians sent envoys to Rome to seek an alliance. In his account of the treaty of 348 Livy does not mention the previous arrangement with the Carthaginians in 509. In describing the treaty of 306, however, Livy says that the treaty was renewed for the third time, which lends some support that there had been a first treaty at some other time, most probably 509 when the Republic was established. The exact number of treaties with Carthage perhaps does not matter quite so much as the fact that a major maritime power had noticed how the Romans of the fourth century were progressing, and had decided that it was time to outline their respective spheres of influence.

By 348 the Romans had regained control of the Latins and had bound the various Latin city states to Rome by a series of treaties arranged on an individual basis and not corporately with the Latins as a whole. Internal politics had also quietened down, and although the struggle between patricians and plebeians had not yet ended, it had been resolved temporarily. By 306 Rome controlled the Pontine plain and the routes into and through Campania, and the port of Ostia had been founded. The Romans were not known as shipbuilders but their coastal allies, the *socii navales*, were experts, and could provide experienced crews. Towards the end of the fourth century the Romans appointed two new officials called *duumviri navales* to command a small fleet, most probably to defend the coasts from pirate attacks, and assist land forces operating near the coasts. Carthage was a long-established maritime power, and now it looked as though Rome was becoming more interested in control of the seas, not necessarily as a rival in commercial enterprises, but nonetheless perhaps a perceived threat to Carthaginian interests. According to the terms of the 348 treaty, Carthage won recognition for control of Utica in North Africa, and of southern Spain. In 306, in broad general terms, Carthage controlled Sicily, and Rome controlled Italy. It was control of Sicily that would cause all the trouble in the next century.

5

The Latins and Other Allies

The Latins or Latini were early inhabitants of an area called Latium, which survives today as modern Lazio, although the territorial boundaries of the modern region are not exactly the same as those of the ancient version. In Roman times, Latium was made up of two parts, Old Latium or Latium Vetus in the north, and an extension to the south-east to the borders of Campania, called Latium Adiectum. The Latini lived in Latium Vetus, between the Apennines and the coastal plain, extending as far north as the River Tiber. From early in their history it is probable that the Latins spoke the same language and shared the same cultural heritage and religious observances, but this did not mean that they lived in perpetual harmony with each other.

Rome's early alliance with the Latins, arranged by the consul Spurius Cassius in 493, applied to the Latins as a whole people rather than to individual city states. The Latin communities were allowed considerable freedom. Provided that they raised troops and joined with the Romans for specific campaigns for mutual defence, the Latin communities remained self-governing without undue interference, and they did not pay taxes to Rome. They were not prevented from waging war on their own account, so when they attacked the Samnites, the Romans did not interfere, explaining to the Samnites that there was nothing in the treaty that gave them authority to stop the Latins from going to war with whomever they pleased.

Latin Allies and Latin Colonies

Shortly after the treaty with the Latins, Spurius Cassius arranged a similar treaty with the Hernici, but with an important distinction between the two peoples, who were each allied to Rome individually and not brought into a tripartite alliance. Latins and Hernici were to be kept separate as far as possible. These arrangements endured until the Latins became disillusioned with the Romans and tried to shake off their domination. They joined together in a coalition that is termed by modern historians the Latin League, which term may not have been used by the Latins themselves, although modern historians can fall back on the authority of Dionysius, who used the word *koinos*, the Greek equivalent of league. The struggle ended in the defeat of the Latins in 338. Whatever the Latins called it, the League was broken up, and from this time onwards the Romans started to modify their system of alliances, starting with the Latins and then extending the concept to the Italian communities, though there was no standardised template to be applied to all communities in all circumstances. From the later fourth century onwards, on the pattern set after 338 with the Latins, treaties of alliance were more restrictive, with more closely defined terms. In the fifth century the Latins had been free to make war on other peoples without interference from Rome, but from the fourth century allied states were to have the same friends and enemies as Rome and could not go to war independently. With all alliances, there was always the stipulation that the allies should provide troops to fight alongside the Roman army.

There were two kinds of communities that came under the heading of Latins, the previously existing Latin city states allied to Rome, and the Latin colonies, which were founded from the fourth century onwards. Both types of Latin communities, the original settlements and the colonies alike, shared the same obligations, rights and privileges within the terms of their alliances, and both were obliged to furnish men for the allied contingents of the Roman army.

The allied Latin states shared some privileges with the Romans, such as the right to intermarry (*conubium*), and mutual trading and business rights were allowed (*commercium*). If a Roman male married a Latin woman, their sons were automatically counted as Roman citizens, and therefore eligible to serve in the Roman legions. The Latin colonies had the same status as the Latin cities, but without the ethnic connotations. The distinction was political, not racial, so a colonist's previous ethnic background or place of residence was of no account. A Latin colony did not have to be inhabited by Latins, or even be in Latium to qualify for Latin status. After 338 when the Latin League was dissolved, Latin colonies were quickly founded outside Latium, and some Romans as well as citizens of other communities either went there voluntarily, or were sent out to settle in them. It has been disputed whether the Latins and other people shared the responsibility for the foundation of a colony or whether they were all set up according to Roman initiative and under Rome's direction. It might be expected that Romans would far outnumber the inhabitants once the colony was established, but this does not seem to have been the case. As an inhabitant of the colony each individual acquired the citizenship of that colony and Latin status in the eyes of Rome, so the settlers from Rome became Latins, and the able-bodied men of military age served in the allied contingents, not the Roman army.

Citizenship in the Latin colonies was interchangeable with that of Rome. Any Roman who had settled in a Latin colony became a Latin citizen, but if he moved back to Rome he resumed his Roman citizenship. Migration to Rome was permitted, but by law any migrant had to leave a son in his home town, so that recruitment for the allied sections of the army was not jeopardised. Some people did not observe this precaution; Livy relates how a complaint was made about one of the inhabitants of a colony who had absconded, without leaving a potential recruit behind. The attractions of Rome proved too tempting, eventually creating a shortage of Latin recruits from the colonies and the Latin cities. In 187 and again in 173 the Romans agreed with the Latin communities to repatriate all those former inhabitants who had settled in Rome, which implies that proper records had been kept, with full names and details, and the dates of entry to the city. The repatriation of the Latins indicates that the allied troops were of great importance to the Republican Roman authorities when drawing up their armies. It also implies that the Romans had no trouble in filling the ranks of their own citizen legions, otherwise they might have been willing to turn a blind eye to the immigrant status of the Latins and enrolled them in the Roman legions to make up the numbers.

Since each Latin state was bound to Rome on an individual basis, and forbidden to make treaties with the other Latin cities, the Latin League was given no opportunity to rekindle itself. Rome controlled the military activity and foreign policy of each of her allies, who were obliged to have the same friends and enemies as the Romans and were forbidden to assist an enemy of Rome. The bonus for the Romans was a vast increase in military manpower, and for the allies the bonus was mutual protection. In theory any one of the allied states could call out the army and provide the commander for it, but in practice, it was the Romans who, in modern parlance, called the shots, assembled the army, and furnished commanding generals.

Allied Communities

The ancient historians, in their accounts of Roman warfare and descriptions of the appearance and organisation of the army, paid only scant attention to the thousands of allied troops that Rome was able to raise from the fifth century onwards. Although the allies contributed a great deal to the Roman army and to Roman military achievements, the emphasis in literature and in the Roman ethos was always firmly on the Roman citizen army, so the impression given by the literary evidence is that the army of the Roman Republic consisted of Romans from Rome and nowhere else. This is not the case, for without the allied troops the rise of Rome would have been much slower, if indeed it could have happened at all. The conquest of Italy and then most of the countries around the Mediterranean was greatly facilitated by the alliance system and the extra manpower that it afforded for Rome. As a consequence of the lack of literary references, the work of Polybius, who took more notice of the allies than most ancient authors, assumes a preponderant importance. He worked in the second century, but the information that he includes about the Roman army and the allied contingents is taken as valid for the third century, especially for the period of the Punic wars with Carthage. Other information concerning the allies has to be gathered from different periods of Roman history and welded into a whole that may not be entirely representative.

The alliances with the Latin states after 338 set the pattern for future alliances with other communities. From the fourth century onwards the Romans created and developed a method of binding defeated communities to them, without crushing them out of existence or taking them over and administering them as Roman territory. A hierarchy of different categories of citizens and allies was created. Some defeated peoples were absorbed into the Roman community and granted full citizenship, so that they could vote at elections and on political questions in Rome, and the men of military age were obliged to serve in the Roman citizen army. Other communities, further away from Rome, and not likely to make regular journeys there to exercise any vote, were given the status of *cives sine suffragio*, which meant that they were turned into Roman citizens, but without voting rights, and their states were called *civitates sine suffragio*. For military purposes no distinction was made between these two different categories of citizenship, so with or without the vote, all men of military age could be called up and enrolled in the army. Side by side with the two categories of citizens, there were two categories of allied communities, Latins and other allies, whose soldiers served in the allied contingents, not the Roman army.

Treaties were made with communities in Italy which had submitted to Rome after a military defeat, but it was not always a matter of coercion. Some free states entered into an alliance voluntarily, because there were tangible benefits to doing so. By agreeing to contribute troops to the allied contingents the individual states were guaranteed protection, but were otherwise left to govern themselves

Alliances were made for a variety of reasons, in addition to the need to control the activities of an erstwhile enemy. The treaty arrangements were not one-size-fits-all, but usually took into consideration the needs and capabilities of each ally, while at the same time the needs of the Roman army were paramount. Some alliances were made in order to secure routes, or river crossings, or staging posts, or because an area was particularly useful to the army, such as fertile land not yet under direct Roman control, where supplies could be obtained. Support for the military arm dictated some of the terms of the treaties. Some allies were noted for certain specialities, such as excellent cavalry or light armed troops, others could furnish materials and equipment. The *socii navales* on the coasts of Italy were obliged to furnish ships and crews, utilising their maritime expertise.

It has been suggested that some treaties were drawn up either on equal terms, or on unequal terms (*aequum* or *iniquum*). Livy refers to an unequal treaty (*foedus iniquum*), but this is the only literary reference so far known, and the whole concept has been disputed. Whether there were equal or unequal treaties, or only uniform kinds, it is certain that the Romans would make sure that they achieved all they wanted from the alliance. This does not necessarily mean that it was all good fortune for Rome, and doom, gloom and oppression for the allies. The Latin and Italian states were not taxed, except in the form of manpower, which may have been a preferable arrangement, since monetary taxes would presumably have been levied every year, but there may have been some intervals when no army was required. The main restriction on the allies was that relations with other states were precluded. Foreign policy was Rome's prerogative, with no opportunity for the allied states to formulate a policy of their own, individually or collectively. The inhabitants of many states, especially those which had willingly sought an alliance with Rome, realised that it was going to take an enormous force to defeat Rome and her allies, so it was more expedient to join the alliance rather than try to stand alone either against the Romans, or against the other potential enemies in Italy. The combined Roman and allied army was a more cohesive force than any temporary confederation of different states or tribes, and had a much greater chance of winning a war. Consequently there was a greater prospect of shared booty. There was a detectable reluctance to serve if a war was to be fought without the prospect of booty. One of the clauses of the fifth-century treaty with the Latins ensured an equal share of the spoils, and one of the several reasons why the allies rebelled at the beginning of the first century BC was a grievance over the unequal division of the spoils.

The allies were for the most part loyal to Rome and served her well. In the third century BC Hannibal failed to prise a large number of allies away from Rome. A few of the most recent of Rome's allies went over to him, and eventually so did Capua, which had remained loyal to the Romans all through the Samnite wars, but went over to Hannibal when food and manpower resources were running low, and it seemed that the fortunes of Rome were also in decline. The Romans recaptured the city, savagely, in 211. None of the Latins wavered during the struggle with Hannibal, even though their manpower resources were almost extinguished, and on one occasion several Latin states declared that they could not send any more troops. If they ever considered going over to Hannibal to ease their burdens, it would have been at that low point, but they did not waver.

There were occasions when loyalty to Rome was not quite so strong. Polybius relates how the people of Rhegium, sandwiched between Carthage and Pyrrhus of Epirus, asked the Romans for help. In total, 4,000 men were sent under the command of a native of Campania called Decius. He started out well, but then decided that Rhegium was a comfortable place to set up home, so he and his renegade soldiers ejected the citizens and settled in. It was a few years before the Romans could evict their erstwhile ally and bring home the original inhabitants.

By the beginning of the first century BC, relations between the allies and the Romans had deteriorated, culminating in war between Rome and the allies, an episode that was termed the Social War, after *socii*, allies. The war ground on for a few years, until the allies obtained Roman citizenship.

Assembling the Allied Troops

Every year the magistrates of the self-governing allied states drew up a list of their *iuniores*, or men aged seventeen to forty-five who were eligible for service in the allied contingents. Livy writes of names being called out when the Romans mustered the army, and Polybius refers to lists of names when he recounts the numbers of potential recruits that the allies could furnish for Rome, so it is likely that the lists of the allied soldiers were drawn up by individual names, with details of age and very likely with information as to previous service. The lists would need to be revised on an annual basis, because some of the men may have been killed, or simply died, and some younger men would have come of age since the last compilation was made.

The lists of available manpower were sent to Rome, where they may have been attached to the details of each treaty. Part of the text of an inscription concerning an agrarian law of 111 explains that the Romans demanded soldiers from the Latin allies *ex formula togatorum*, which suggests that there were documents which outlined the terms and perhaps stipulated the numbers of men that could be raised from each allied state. It has been suggested that the terms of each treaty stipulated a maximum number of men that could be summoned from each ally. The maximum would have to be tailored to the circumstances and manpower of each ally, rather than a standard figure applied indiscriminately, but the theory of maximum numbers has been disputed. There would be fluctuations in the birth rate and the death rate, so there would be times when manpower was short and other times when there was a surplus, which would render immutable maximum figures redundant. During the war with Hannibal, Livy records that there were two occasions in 219 and 217 when the Senate authorised commanders to raise as many men from the allies as they needed. It could be argued that the Senate could break the rules in emergencies, but such procedures weigh against agreed maximum quotas of allied troops.

At the beginning of the year the Roman consuls summoned the magistrates of the allied states from which they wished to raise troops. Consulting the *formula togatorum*, the Roman consuls and the allied magistrates agreed upon the date and place where the troops were to assemble. How quickly this could be done is revealed by Livy, who says that one muster was achieved in fifteen days. It is probable that unless there was a dire emergency, only a proportion of the allied states would be asked to contribute troops, and from these selected allies, it is probable that only a percentage of the available manpower would be actually mustered. The location of the projected theatre of war may have dictated which of the allies were to be asked for military contingents. The problem with this arrangement is that if wars were more frequent in a certain area than in other parts of Italy, then the same allies would be asked to contribute troops more often than some of the others. An alternative to this is that the system may have allowed for a levy of a uniform percentage of soldiers from each allied community.

As time went on and the alliance system expanded, the Romans were able to raise large armies and keep on raising new ones to a greater extent than any of the independent Italian or Greek states of the south could hope to do. The Romans did sometimes meet with defeats, and even catastrophic disasters, but they were usually able to field another army very quickly. Only if continuous warfare on several fronts had to be sustained for many years did Rome and her allies really begin to suffer. During the war with Hannibal, the Romans fought in Italy, Spain, Africa, and Sicily. They suffered massive casualties in 216 at Cannae, and yet fourteen years later they were still not completely overwhelmed, and found enough soldiers to protect Italy and Spain, and also allow Scipio to take the war into Africa, albeit that he had to raise the troops himself. Rome without her allies would probably have been extinguished in the first years of Hannibal's invasion of Italy. The alliance system engendered an unbreakable Roman and allied resilience, and it was this resilience in spite of defeats and reversals that greatly impressed the Greek Polybius when he began to write his account of Roman government and the army, choosing to start off with the disaster at Cannae to illustrate how Rome reached the nadir of her fortunes and yet still managed to re-emerge with fighting spirit intact. Roman warfare was on a different plane to what had gone before. Most wars were limited to the campaigning season, and at the end of the fighting, if there had been no outright victory to decide the issue, a truce might be arranged and the soldiers would go home, ready to fight another day. The Romans and their allies never gave in and simply raised more armies. It was a revolution, made possible by the fact that the Romans had extended their alliance system over most of Italy, and could call on more soldiers than any other state.

Organisation of the Allied Troops

One of the main benefits that the Romans derived from their alliances was not just the extra manpower, but also the fact that the allies had to supply and pay their troops for the duration of the campaign. This was not left to the allied units to administer themselves. The allies raised the necessary pay and supplies and turned everything over to the Romans for distribution. Roman supervision was probably undertaken to ensure a fair apportionment of cash and food, and it would serve to iron out glaring inconsistencies, so all allied troops received the same benefits. This method relieved Rome of what would otherwise have been a great burden. The allied states eventually had to adopt a coinage system to facilitate the payments.

The organisation of the allies is only sketchily understood, leaving many unanswered questions. Initially there may have been considerable variation in the numbers of men in the contingents of troops from each state, but it is possible that the size of contingents was eventually standardised, at about 500 men. Some of the larger allied states may have contributed more than one of these theoretically standard units. The allied contingents were led by their own magistrates, with the title of *praefectus* or prefect. Ten of the 500 strong units would be combined in in a larger formation, 5,000 strong, called an *ala sociorum*, indicating that the allies fought on the wings (*alae*). At this stage, the term *ala* does not signify a cavalry unit, as it invariably does in the Empire. By the fourth century the army was usually made up of two Roman legions, flanked by two *alae sociorum*, one on each wing.

The local magistrate acting as *praefectus* of his contingent would be subordinate to higher ranking Roman prefects, called *praefecti sociorum*. Polybius says that a total of twelve prefects of the allies were appointed by the consuls, so it is assumed that there were six of them to command each of the two *alae sociorum*, matching the six military tribunes who commanded a Roman legion. The *praefecti sociorum* were non-senators from the equestrian class, but despite their name the equestrians were no longer primarily horsemen. Since Polybius merely says that the consuls chose twelve *praefecti sociorum*, but does not specifically state that they were all Romans, it has been argued that there would be three Roman and three allied prefects in command of each *ala sociorum*. This remains theoretical, and on the whole it is perhaps unlikely, since the higher command was probably kept well under Roman control.

Polybius describes how the *praefecti sociorum* were responsible for the organisation and command of the allied armies, so it may be the case that there was some adjustment of the contingents once the allies had assembled alongside the Roman legions.

Polybius says that the allied cavalry contingents outnumbered the Roman cavalrymen three to one. The allied cavalry units were commanded by Roman prefects of senatorial rank, called *praefecti equitum*, and were divided into subgroups called *turmae*, a term which was still used of the divisions of the cavalry units during the Empire, when each *turma* contained about thirty men.

When the allied contingents were all assembled, the *praefecti sociorum* selected some men from the allied infantry and cavalry to serve in a special capacity as *extraordinarii*. The numbers were considerable, amounting to one-fifth of the infantry and one-third of the cavalry, so although the allied cavalry was three times as large as the Roman horsemen, with one-third of their strength syphoned off to become mounted *extraordinarii*, their operational numbers would have been only twice as large. These specially chosen men were allocated their own sections of the camp, separate from the rest of the allied infantry and cavalry, and were usually to be found close by the consul and his quaestor not only in the camp but also on the march.

There is a dearth of information about the internal organisation of the infantry of each *ala sociorum*. Livy was quite confident that the allied infantry of the fourth century was of the same strength as the Roman legions, and was also organised as the legions were, divided into *hastati*, *principes* and *triarii*. In his description of the fighting during the Latin revolt in 340 he recounts how Latin *hastati* and *principes* faced Roman *hastati* and *principes*, and the chief centurion or *primipilus* of each army took up a position with the *triarii*. It is not certain how reliable this is for the period. Livy does at least pay tribute to the fierce fighting qualities of the Latins, but then that merely serves to aggrandise the importance of the Roman victories.

Allied Manpower

Polybius remains the only detailed ancient source for the numbers of men that Rome was able to call upon from the allies as well as her own citizens, and his work is therefore invaluable. The reliability of Polybius' figures is not seriously called into question, and even if it were, there is nothing better which could quantify and back up the statements of modern historians that the alliance system afforded Rome unprecedented manpower for her armies.

Polybius enumerates the numbers of men that could potentially be raised from Rome and the allied states. The context is 225 when the Gauls were poised to strike at northern Italy. Polybius explains how each consul commanded a force of two Roman legions accompanied by allied troops. He gives legionary strength as 5,200, which contradicts his figure of 4,200 in another passage, but this may represent an extra number of men raised for a particularly dangerous circumstance. The total of four legions was matched by 30,000 allied infantry and 2,000 cavalry. In addition the Etruscans and Sabines, who would be in the front line when the Gauls arrived, mustered 50,000 infantry and 4,000 cavalry, and the Romans placed them all under a praetor, stationed on the frontier of Etruria, ready for the onslaught.

Also uncomfortably close to the frontier with the Gallic tribes were the Umbrians and Sarsinati, who raised 20,000 infantry, and the Veneti at the head of the Adriatic, always friendly to Rome, together with the Cenomani from the region of Lake Garda, raised another 20,000 men. Polybius then gives a list of available manpower from regions further to the south: from the Latins, 80,000 infantry and 5,000 cavalry; from the Samnites, 70,000 infantry and 7,000 cavalry; from the Iapygians and Messapians of Apulia, 50,000 infantry and 16,000 cavalry; from the Lucanians of the mountainous region of southern Italy, 30,000 infantry and 3,000 cavalry; and a combined total of 20,000 infantry and 4,000 cavalry from four tribes – the Marsi, living in the mountains of central Italy and friendly to Rome since the Samnite wars, the Marrucini of the Adriatic coast of central Italy, the Frentani on the borders of Apulia, and the Vestini of the mountains around the Gran Sasso. There were 20,000 infantry and 1,500 cavalry as a reserve in Rome, and two legions, each 4,200 strong plus 200 cavalry in Sicily and Tarentum.

The lists of Roman citizens contained the names of 250,000 infantry and 23,000 cavalry, the totals for all the available manpower being 700,000 Roman and allied infantry and 70,000 cavalry. These figures, more than any amount of words, bring home the importance of the allies to the Roman army.

After enumerating the staggering numbers of potential recruits, Polybius is at pains to point out that Hannibal invaded with only about 20,000 men, a puny amount compared to the resources of Rome, so it testifies to the quality of Hannibal's skill as a general, but at the same time the question has to be asked why Hannibal thought he could defeat the Romans in the end. If he had been able to detach Rome's allies and win them over to his own army, he must surely have defeated Rome in the end, from sheer exhaustion and attrition if not by his superiority as a general.

The Allies in War and Peace

Since the activities of the allies are never given as much attention in the literary sources as the Roman legions, there are only glimpses here and there of what they did and how they performed. One of the most common uses of allied forces seems to have been as garrisons for towns and cities where a military presence was deemed necessary, without using Roman soldiers. There are also some examples of allied armies being left in winter quarters while the Roman soldiers were allowed to go home, for instance in 197, according to Livy, each of the two praetors assigned to govern the two provinces of Nearer and Further Spain were granted 8,000 infantry and 400 cavalry, drawn from the Italian allies and those of Latin status. Opinion is divided on whether this means that each praetor took charge of half of this force, governing his province with 4,000 infantry and 200 cavalry, which seems a very small number of soldiers, or whether the total numbers raised from the allies were 16,000 infantry and 800 cavalry, divided between the two governors. Livy says that they were instructed to discharge the veteran troops, and settle the boundary between Nearer and Further Spain, so there were no Roman legions for a while in Spain and the allied troops did all the work. In Liguria in 170, the Roman legions were sent home only sixty days after the governor arrived, because there was little action and it was thought that it would be a peaceful year. The allies, of Latin status, according to Livy, remained behind and were put into winter quarters at Luna and Pisa.

Allied casualties are only rarely noted in the sources, but must have been considerable during the many wars in which they fought. At Cannae in 216, Livy says that there were 45,000 infantry and 2,700 cavalrymen killed, comprising roughly equal numbers of allies and Romans, which is corroborated by Polybius' information that the numbers of Romans and allies raised for this campaign were about the same. Elsewhere Livy rounds up his figure of 45,000 to 50,000, and Appian and Plutarch give the same statistics. Polybius sets the figure higher, at 70,000 allied and Roman dead at Cannae. In Spain in 206 under Scipio, figures specifically concerning the allies are given as 1,200 dead and 3,000 wounded. The ratio of casualties to the total numbers of allies assembled for each war cannot be estimated. At the beginning of the war with Hannibal the Romans fielded 24,000 Roman infantry and 40,000 allied soldiers, and the allied cavalry of 4,400 horsemen outnumbered the Romans, who provided 1,800 cavalry. Limited as these statistics are, they serve once again to illustrate the value of the allies to the Roman military forces.

In utilising allied manpower for garrison duty and keeping the peace in winter quarters, the Romans were relieved of the expense of maintaining the troops, since it was the allied communities which paid for the upkeep of their soldiers in their own military contingents. The system also ensured that if an emergency should arise, Roman citizen manpower was not otherwise engaged in garrison duty, and armies could therefore be raised fairly rapidly without jeopardising control of other areas. The use of the allied forces also meant that the Romans did not have to rely on mercenaries to form the backbone of their army, as Carthage did, with the potential problems that unhappy mercenaries could cause. This is not to say that the Romans never hired mercenaries, but they could pick and choose the best groups, with special skills, such as the Numidians who could do things with cavalry that most other horsemen could only aspire to, and Cretans who were the best archers that money could buy. Mercenaries had other qualities that home-grown Romans lacked, in that they were not generally tied to homes and families and did not have to go home for the harvest, but the Romans had solved the problem of maintaining control outside the campaigning season by using the allies to remain under arms in the field, or to garrison towns and cities.

Later Alliances

At the beginning of the first century BC, some of the Italian allies rebelled against Rome in the so-called Social War. The allies had begun to feel that Rome was exploiting them, and despite the fact that they had been promised that Roman citizenship would be granted to them, each time that a Roman politician attempted to frame the necessary legislation, it was always thwarted in the Senate. The rebels got tired of waiting, and tried to form a coalition in contravention of their treaty arrangements. They set up a new state at Corfinium and renamed it Italica. But not all the allies joined. The Latins and the Greek states of southern Italy remained aloof, and even within the rebel territory there were dissidents who did not want to fight against Rome. The main problem for the Romans was that the allies were experienced in the ways of Roman warfare. Hostilities began in 90 and rumbled on until 88 BC, by which time the Romans had grudgingly offered citizenship, first to the loyal Latins, Greeks, Etruscans and Umbrians, and then to the rest of the Italians provided that the hostilities ceased. In terms of military manpower, the army was not adversely affected, since the new citizens were still eligible for service, but in the Roman army, not in allied contingents. Allied troops now had to be assembled from further afield, but it was fortuitous that as the Social War ended and the Italians became Roman citizens, the constant wars between the tribes or states in Italy came to an end. There were occasional bouts of fighting that required armies to operate within Italy, such as the rebellion of Spartacus, which was put down with difficulty by Crassus. In general, wars of the later first century BC were fought beyond the Alps or overseas, and Roman commanders could usually raise units of natives to help them subdue more intransigent natives.

Even before the Social War and the enfranchisement of the Italians, it was usual practice to employ groups of native troops when the army was on campaign in other countries. These additional troops were commanded by their own leaders, but operating under the overall command of the Roman consuls or praetors. Gallic tribes had assisted the Romans in the fighting in northern Italy against other Gauls on more than one occasion. King Attalus of Pergamum commanded his own troops in the war against Philip of Macedon in 202, taking them away from his kingdom for the purpose, and suffering an invasion by the king of Bithynia during his absence. In the war against Antiochus the Great in 190 Lucius Cornelius Scipio, assisted by his brother Scipio Africanus, employed troops from Rhodes and Pergamum. At the battle of Magnesia in Lydia, the Pergamene horsemen forced the heavy cavalry of Antiochus' army back into their own ranks, and then turned to attack the exposed flank of the enemy phalanx, which greatly helped the Romans to win the battle. The native units would serve for the duration of the campaign and then return home.

From the third century BC Rome was brought into contact with states or tribes outside Italy, and extended the system of alliances to the rulers of such communities. Some alliances were made after a state or people had been defeated, for instance after the end of the war with Antiochus the Great, the Aetolians continued to resist the Romans, unwilling to accept unconditional surrender. The Roman general Fulvius Nobilior laid siege to their fortress of Ambracia, and when it fell the Aetolians were brought into an alliance with Rome, agreeing to support the Romans against their enemies, so they were on similar terms to the Italian allies. Other alliances were made on a friendly basis, without any previous hostilities. These new kinds of allies were usually on the edges of Roman territory, and alliances were made with a view to protecting Roman interests without having to resort to raising an armed force and despatching it to the territory concerned. The term 'client king' is used to describe the relationship between Rome and the allied rulers. The term is a modern one derived from the clientele system that operated in Rome around all important and wealthy men, whose 'clients' supported the great man in political and social life, and in return received assistance and benefits including money and food. The Romans used a formal description for these client-based alliances with states and kingdoms. The Senate formally recognised the king and his kingdom as *rex sociusque et amicus populi Romani*, meaning king and ally and friend of the Roman people. No strict standardised laws governed these arrangements.

The client king arrangement had several advantages for the Romans and their 'friends'. The client ruler, who could sometimes be a queen rather than a king, did not pay taxes to Rome, and was allowed to govern his or her territory according to custom, but each ruler was expected to contribute troops in the event of a war in his or her locality. The king or queen was also expected to keep the peace within his or her own kingdom, in return for Roman support on this score. Roman protection was assured in the event of an external attack. Thus the so-called client king system had many similarities with Rome's early alliances in Italy, the most important aspect being contribution of troops for the army when Rome requested assistance.

6

The Army of the Middle Republic from the Third to the Second Century BC

During almost the whole of the third century BC, Rome was involved in constant warfare. The last round of the Samnite wars spilled over into the beginning of the third century, but within three decades after the defeat of the Samnites, Rome finally brought all of central and southern Italy under her control. Scholars estimate that by 264 when the first Punic war began, Roman territory had increased from about 5,000 km² to an area more than five times as large. Polybius, writing in the second century BC, was amazed that it had taken such a short time to extend Roman control over the whole peninsula. The process is labelled the unification of Italy, but Romanisation was not enforced, and except in so far as Latin was universal for administrative purposes, the allied cities and tribes continued to speak their own languages, to worship their own gods and to carry on their own government within the wider Roman framework. Ethnic and cultural diversity was never totally stamped out in Italy, nor did the Romans express any desire for it to be eradicated.

In the third century BC, Rome fought wars in northern Italy against the Samnites and the Gauls, then in southern Italy against Pyrrhus of Epirus, followed by two major wars with the Carthaginians. The army was not always successful in battle, and manpower resources were greatly diminished during these almost continual struggles. Despite these problems, at the end of the third century the Romans emerged stronger than ever. Rome became a dominant power in the Mediterranean world.

The success of the Romans was due to several things, among them the effectiveness of their political and military institutions, their flexibility in adapting old established forms to new uses, their intransigent refusal to accept defeat even after losing battles, their pragmatic and unsentimental ruthlessness, and their alliance systems that gave them far greater manpower resources than they would have been able to muster if they had remained alone.

The Third Samnite War 298–290 BC

In 298 the third and final war with the Samnites broke out, escalating into a war on more than one front, involving not only the Samnites, but also Etruscans, Umbrians and Gauls. T. J. Cornell points out that from 298 until the Roman victory at the battle of Sentinum in 295, there was an unprecedented number of Roman commanders in the field all at the same time. Consuls continued as army commanders after their original office had expired, by means of *prorogatio imperii*, which allowed consuls or praetors to continue serving as proconsuls and propraetors, with *imperium* that enabled them to command troops. This arrangement had first been employed in 326 when the consul Quintus Publilius Philo had his command extended beyond the terminal date of his consulship. In 295 BC, in addition to the magistrates who had their powers extended when their office expired, four men were granted *imperium* and given command of troops even though they were private citizens, holding no office at all. The number of commanders indicates that the military situation at the opening of the third century was dire.

News arrived in Rome at the time of the elections in 296 that a combined force of Etruscans, Samnites, Umbrians and Gauls was assembling in northern Italy, and the armies were so large that two camps had been built to hold all the soldiers. Livy says that one of the consuls for 296, Lucius Volumnius, addressed the people to explain how serious the situation was, and that it would require more than one commander and one army to contain it. According to Livy, the Romans raised six legions for 295, with an even larger number of allied troops. Two legions fought in Samnite territory under the proconsul Lucius Volumnius, while the other four legions marched against the Gauls, Samnites, Etruscans and Umbrians. While these four legions were on the march, a Roman reserve force was ordered to attack Clusium (modern Chiusi) in Etruria, and to destroy the crops and farms, in the hope that this would force the Etruscans and Umbrians to leave the camp and come to the defence of Clusium. This they did, thereby reducing the forces ranged against the Romans at Sentinum in Umbria. There the Romans and their allies met the Gauls and Samnites and fought a hard battle. The consul Quintus Fabius commanded two legions on his right, opposite the Samnites, and the other consul Publius Decius commanded two legions on the left, facing the Gauls. The two consuls fared very differently. Fabius thought that the initial onslaught by the enemy was what counted, and if the troops could withstand this and hold firm, the Samnites facing his wing would tire, and then the Romans, who would not be as exhausted, could attack. On the other wing, Decius committed all his infantry at the beginning, and then tried to use the cavalry to drive off the Gallic horsemen. The Romans repulsed the Gauls with their first charge, but on the second charge they pressed on too far and were entangled in the Gallic infantry. Livy says that the Gauls also fought from chariots, and bore down on the Roman cavalry, causing them to panic. In their flight they mangled some of their own legions, who were then also attacked by the charioteers. At this point Decius decided to sacrifice himself and the enemy army to the gods, just as his father Publius Decius had done in the Latin war. He rode into battle and was killed, and the Romans rallied and won the battle, obviously with divine assistance. Sentinum has the distinction of being the largest battle ever fought in Italy until this time. Livy suggests that if the Etruscans and Umbrian forces had not been drawn off, the Romans would probably have been defeated.

The Samnites lost another battle in their own territory in 293. Three years later the Samnite wars were over. Fighting continued against the Etruscans and Umbrians until the 270s, but not on the scale of the battle of Sentinum. At the same time there was further trouble with the Gauls. The Gallic Senones, who had settled north of Picenum, attacked the city of Arretium (modern Arezzo). The Romans agreed to relieve the city, but were defeated. They assembled another army which defeated the Senones severely enough to force them to make peace, and also cede their territory to Rome. The land was added to the *ager Gallicus* in 283. Other Gallic tribes began to fear that the same fate might await them, and so they decided to pre-empt any encroachment. The Boii allied with the Etruscans, who also wanted to shake off Roman control and welcomed the extra manpower that the Gauls could provide. By 280 they had both been defeated by the Romans, in a battle near Volsinii. The Etruscans had their own internal problems, in the form of a dissident populace in several cities struggling against the rule of their aristocrats. The Romans agreed to help the Etruscans to reassert aristocratic control. When the disturbances were quelled, the Romans took over some Etruscan territory and planted a colony at Cosa, not precisely the result that the Etruscans had expected. They rebelled, but the only result was the destruction of the city of Volsinii in 265.

Pyrrhus of Epirus 281–272 BC

While the struggle between Etruscans and Romans was going on in the north, trouble had also been brewing in the south, and Rome was eventually drawn in to the fighting. In the second half of the fourth century, the Greek colonies were frequently hard-pressed by the Italian tribes, principally the fierce Lucanians and Bruttians. The colonies did not unite with each other to fight off the attacks, but turned to Greece itself for assistance. They persuaded King Archidamus of Sparta, to help them fight the Lucanians, but he was killed. King Alexander of Epirus was called in. He defeated the Lucanians and Bruttians, but then tried to take over the colonies, and was killed in 330. Next, Cleonymus of Sparta was brought in against the Lucanians, and Agathocles of Syracuse fought the Bruttians. Everything unravelled when Agathocles died, and Tarentum, one of the major Greek colonies of southern Italy, took the lead. Tarentum was one of the most successful cities, with control of the best harbour in southern Italy and rich grain-producing land in the hinterland. The Romans had arranged a treaty with Tarentum, probably in the mid-fourth century BC, whereby the Romans had agreed not to sail their warships within a certain distance of the harbour of Tarentum.

When the city of Thurii was attacked, the Tarentines said they could not help, so the Thurians asked the Romans for assistance, indicating how far the reputation of Rome had travelled. The Lucanians and Bruttians were duly defeated, and then as a precaution against further attacks, the Romans placed a garrison in Thurii, and made alliances with other Greek cities. They established a colony in Tarentine territory, and contrary to the terms of the treaty they sailed their warships into the Gulf of Tarentum. The Tarentines attacked the ships, and threw the garrison out of Thurii. War with the Romans was a daunting prospect, so the Tarentines asked for help from another king of Epirus, Pyrrhus, an accomplished soldier with a taste for adventure. He arrived in 281, equipped with the Macedonian-style phalanx, large numbers of cavalry and archers, and elephants trained for battle. When the two armies met at Heraclea, the elephants contributed heavily to the defeat of the Romans, who had never seen such animals before.

Pyrrhus followed up his victory by invading Latium, and sent his envoy Cineas to offer terms, but the Romans refused because they foresaw that there could be no peace while Pyrrhus was still in Italy. Aware that the Romans could call upon their many allies for troops, Cineas allegedly remarked to Pyrrhus that they were fighting a hydra. Another battle was fought at Asculum in Apulia, and the Romans were defeated again, but they had inflicted tremendous damage on Pyrrhus' army. The king said more victories like that would finish him, thus giving rise to the phrase 'a pyrrhic victory'.

The Romans were saved by the Carthaginians, who offered an alliance and cash. The Carthaginians were afraid that Pyrrhus, who had been asked to aid the Sicilian Greeks, would prove extremely detrimental to Carthaginian trading interests. Sicily was a fertile land producing quantities of grain, and the island possessed good harbours. Pyrrhus was called in to deal with the Mamertines, a group of Campanian mercenaries who had been hired by king Agathocles of Syracuse. When the king died, no one was interested in employing the mercenaries, much less paying them, so they seized Messana (modern Messina), which they used as a base for pillaging expeditions against any towns within their reach.

The Sicilians hoped that Pyrrhus would rid them of the Mamertines and the Carthaginians as well. Pyrrhus took on the dual task, campaigning from 278 to the beginning of 275, eventually ejecting the Carthaginians from the whole island, except for the town and harbour of Lilybaeum. The wily Sicilians had no intention of allowing Pyrrhus to become their next overlord, so they dismissed him, and made a separate peace with Carthage. Pyrrhus, now redundant in Sicily, returned to Italy in the spring of 275. The Romans had taken advantage of the respite to recoup their losses and raise more troops. The contribution of their allies enabled them to gather sufficient manpower to face Pyrrhus again, with more confidence, since they had learned a lot about his army and fighting methods. When the two armies clashed at Beneventum, the general Manius Curius Dentatus managed to turn the enemy's war elephants back into their own ranks, a significant factor in the defeat of Pyrrhus. The king decided to withdraw altogether, but before he left Italy he placed a garrison in Tarentum. He was killed in Greece in 272. The Greek cities were left without a leader, and even Tarentum could not take on the role of protector. The Pyrrhic garrison surrendered to Rome, and Tarentum became an ally like other Greek cities.

The First Punic War 264–241 BC

Rome was now free to concentrate on tidying up and consolidating southern Italy. Rebellious tribes were subdued, the Samnites gave up lands, colonies were founded, the Lucanians surrendered Paestum, and the Bruttians relinquished their forests. The Romans always recognised and exploited whatever was useful to them, but they also shared some of the benefits with their allies, at least at this stage. Rome was in an extremely strong position. Nearly all of Italy south of the Alps was now under Roman control, each city or community bound to Rome by the terms of a separate alliance, and most important, contributing manpower and war material for the protection of the whole. For the first time since the foundation of the Republic the Romans could imagine themselves on a par with Carthage, Macedonia, Syria, and Ptolemaic Egypt. In the course of the next two centuries Rome would absorb them all. The first contest was with Carthage.

Carthage was at least as old as Rome, having been founded probably in the eighth century BC by the Phoenicians, who had reached a more sophisticated and advanced culture than the early Romans. The Phoenicians were seafarers with trade networks extending beyond the Mediterranean, and their colony of Carthage likewise depended on commerce for its livelihood. The city of Carthage was governed and administered by its Senate. A small group of men prepared business for the meetings of the senators, and an assembly of the people elected the magistrates and the generals. The two chief magistrates presiding over the Senate were called *suffetes*, whose responsibilities included all religious, judicial and financial functions of the state. As in Rome, the status of the ruling class was based on wealth, and groups of aristocratic families had emerged, regularly squabbling with each other for political pre-eminence. In military affairs, the emphasis in Rome was on land-based armies levied from citizens and allies, while in Carthage the emphasis was on naval strength, with citizens serving as crews, and mercenaries provided the land forces, composed of Africans, Spaniards, Greeks, and some Italians from southern Italy. Provided that they received their pay and fair treatment, these mercenary armies fought very well for Carthage.

The first Punic war broke out in 264. The Romans responded to an appeal from the Mamertines of Messana, for help against King Hiero of Syracuse, who had attacked them in 265. The Mamertines had also asked the Carthaginians for help, and a Carthaginian garrison had been installed in Messana. The Romans were fully aware of this when they debated whether or not to get involved in the war, because it would mean that they would be fighting not just

Hiero, but Carthage too, a much stronger power. The Mamertines were irrelevant, because the conflict was about control of Messana and the straits between Sicily and Italy. The Romans construed the Carthaginian presence in Messana as a threat to the security of Italy, a concept commonly dismissed by modern scholars, but the Carthaginians possessed the strongest naval force in the Mediterranean, and if they wished to do so they could make life very difficult for the coastal cities by perpetual hit-and-run raids. The Carthaginians may have desired to establish a permanent foothold in Italy. This perceived threat precipitated Roman reaction.

The case for going to war was put to the vote before an assembly of the people, who were well primed and accordingly voted in the affirmative. Two legions were levied, commanded by one of the consuls, and the army set out for Messana. Part of the force sailed into the harbour there, which encouraged the Mamertines to eject the Carthaginian garrison. The Carthaginians asserted themselves and made an alliance with Hiero of Syracuse. Just as Rome was suspicious of the Carthaginian designs on Messana, Carthage was suspicious of Roman intentions in Sicily, especially since Rome had just gobbled up all of southern Italy, converting all the cities and communities into Roman allies.

The Romans were now committed to fighting Syracuse and Carthage. Typically they attended to one enemy at a time. In 263 they raised another army and concentrated their efforts on Hiero and Syracuse. After being mauled by the Romans during their first attacks, Hiero decided to ally with Rome against Carthage. The Romans were now strong enough to challenge Carthage for control of Sicily. They attacked Agrigentum, where the Carthaginians had placed a garrison. It fell in 262, and the Romans enslaved the survivors. There could be no clearer indication of Roman intentions to oust the Carthaginians from Sicily, but to achieve complete victory the Romans would have to face the Carthaginians at sea.

By 260, the Romans felt ready for naval warfare, with a new fleet of a hundred quinqueremes and some twenty triremes, commanded by the consul Gaius Duilius. In a trireme, each man operated one oar, and the oars were grouped in banks of three. The arrangement of the oars and rowers in the much more powerful quinquereme is not known, and so far no ancient source has been found to explain it. There was obviously some connection with the figure five, but it may not have been a simple increase in the number of banks of oars, three in a trireme, five in a quinquereme. There may have been only three banks, the lowest tier with one man per oar, and two men to each oar on the middle and top tier, making five rowers for the three banks. So far, the Romans had not yet felt the need for these larger ships, but when they met the Carthaginians at sea they changed their minds. The story goes that they modelled their ships on a captured Carthaginian quinquereme, but Rome's naval allies of the Italian coasts would be sufficiently well acquainted with warship design to be able to produce the vessels of Rome's first large fleet. The speed and scale of the achievement in shipbuilding was truly impressive. The Romans met the Carthaginians at the battle of Mylae in 260, and won their first naval victory.

The Romans decided to carry the war into Africa, and in 256 they assembled a very large fleet and thousands of men under the consuls Marcus Atilius Regulus and Manlius Vulso Longus. The Carthaginian fleet sailed to intercept them, and the two sides met at the battle of Ecnomus off the Sicilian coast. The Romans sank or captured nearly 100 Carthaginian ships for a loss of twenty-four of their own. Regulus landed in Africa, where he was so successful at first that the Carthaginians were ready to make peace, but the proposed terms were too harsh, so they decided that they had nothing to lose by continuing to fight. They called in the services of Xanthippus from Sparta, who thrashed the Romans and took Regulus prisoner. The Romans resorted to legend in recounting the fate of Regulus. The Carthaginians allegedly sent him back to Rome to deliver their terms, with the solemn promise that if he could not persuade the Romans to make peace, he would return to Carthage for judgement. When he arrived in Rome, Regulus argued against making peace, and dutifully returned to Carthage and execution.

Large-scale hostilities ceased for a while. The remnants of the Roman army set sail from the African coast, but many ships and men were lost in a storm. The Romans resumed the offensive against the Carthaginians in Sicily. They besieged Drepana (modern Trapani) and Lilybaeum, near the modern town of Marsala. The Roman blockade of Lilybaeum dragged on for years, because the Carthaginians could expertly navigate through the shoals outside the harbour and bring in supplies for the defenders of Lilybaeum. At the blockade of Drepana the commander, Publius Claudius Pulcher, failed to watch all the exits from the harbour, so the Carthaginians came out and attacked his fleet from the rear. The situation was made even worse when what remained of the Roman fleet was destroyed in yet another storm.

In 247, when the war had been going on for several years, the Carthaginian general Hamilcar Barca took over in Sicily and began to turn the tables on the Romans. He occupied the fortress of Eryx, seizing every opportunity to harass the Roman armies in Sicily, and he also raided the Italian coast. By 242, the Romans were almost exhausted. They were bankrupt, short of manpower, and needed yet another fleet. There were no resources to build one, so the senators decided to use their own funds to pay the bills. When the new ships were ready, the consul Gaius Lutatius Catulus took command.

Catulus attempted to cut the supply lines of the Carthaginian citadels of Drepana, Lilybaeum, and Eryx, but he was wounded and had to relax his attention while he recuperated. He used his recovery period to good effect. He set about training his sailors in naval warfare, and found out as much as he could about Carthaginian military and naval dispositions and procedures. Consequently, when the Carthaginians put to sea in spring 241 with supplies for their Sicilian garrisons, Catulus was ready for them. Realising that he would never meet with such an opportunity again, Catulus risked a battle off Aegates (modern Aegusa), despite the strong March winds which threatened to wreck the Roman fleet. The Romans sank about fifty Carthaginian ships, captured seventy, and took over 1,000 prisoners. The victory finally put an end to the war. It had lasted for more than two decades.

Wars in Italy and Illyricum 241–218 BC

As part of the peace terms, Rome gained control of Sicily, and a large indemnity was imposed on Carthage that would help the Romans recoup some of the costs of the wars. The Carthaginians were in no condition to carry on fighting, because their mercenary troops rebelled and it took the commander Hamilcar Barca three years to subdue them. The Romans lent assistance to the Carthaginians to combat the mercenaries.

Meanwhile the Carthaginian garrison troops in Sardinia were finding it difficult to keep the natives under control, and were not receiving any help from home. They appealed to Rome for assistance. The Romans politely refused at first, but when the revolt of the mercenaries in Carthage was over, they changed their minds and sent troops. The Carthaginians attempted to recover control of Sardinia, but the Romans converted these efforts into an act of aggression against themselves, and declared war. The Carthaginians were too weak to go to war, and backed down, surrendering Sardinia, and Corsica as well, along with an instalment of cash as an indemnity.

Both the Romans and the Carthaginians were occupied with their own affairs for most of the next twenty years. The Romans were increasingly drawn into foreign wars in order to protect the interests of weaker states which appealed to them for help against their oppressors, and then against other neighbouring states which felt threatened by Roman interference, even though Rome was not in the habit of automatically annexing territory at this stage. A war outside Italy began in 229, shortly after the death of King Agron of the Illyrians in 231. Agron had formed an alliance with the king of Macedon, and had welded the tribesmen of the Adriatic coast into a nascent state, for which the Roman name, when the area became a province, was Illyricum. The widow of Agron, Queen Teuta, pursued his aggressive policy of piratical raids against the cities of the western coast of Greece and the Greek colonies of Italy. In the guise of protector of the Greeks, Rome went to war in 229, combining a strong fleet and army for operations on land and sea. Queen Teuta was compelled to give up the territories that she had taken over, and the Romans awarded some of them to the rulers who had helped them in the war, such as Demetrius of Pharos, who was confirmed as ruler of an enlarged territory.

In 225 a serious war broke out with the Gallic tribes of Cisalpine Gaul on the south side of the Alps. A coalition of four tribes, including the Boii and the Insubres, threatened to invade Italy. Two Gallic tribes joined with Rome. The two consuls for 225 each raised an army, one stationed at Ariminum to watch for the Gauls as they came south, and the other sent to Sardinia in case the Carthaginians used the opportunity to regain the island while Rome was preoccupied in the north. The consul at Ariminum heard that the Gauls had bypassed him, heading for Etruria, so he followed as fast as possible, and while the tribesmen were making their way back northwards, laden with booty, the other Roman army from Sardinia disembarked. A great battle was fought at Telamon, with the Gauls disastrously trapped between two Roman armies. They gave a good account of themselves, and one of the Roman consuls was killed, but in the end the tribesmen were almost wiped out. The Romans spent the next few years campaigning against the Boii and Insubres, and then subduing the inhabitants of the southern side of the Alps. By 219, only the Ligurians remained outside Roman control in northern Italy.

The so-called second Illyrian war broke out just as the wars with the Gauls were ending. Demetrius of Pharos, who had helped the Romans and been rewarded, joined forces with Antigonus Doson, the new king of Macedon. From 222 onwards, Antigonus had pursued an aggressive policy and had taken over nearly the whole of Greece in an incredibly short time. Sheltering under his alliance with Antigonus, Demetrius attacked some of the communities of Illyricum, and in order to protect them the Romans mobilised for a war, even though there had been no formal alliances, and therefore no obligation on Rome's part to do so. By 219 the threatened cities were liberated, and the Romans left the country, having achieved their aims. Demetrius was forced to flee to Macedon, where Antigonus had been succeeded by the new king, Philip V, of whom the Romans were to hear more in the future.

The Second Punic War 218–201 BC

While the Romans were engaged in these various wars, the Carthaginians were quiescent in Africa, but after quelling the revolt of the mercenaries, in 237 Hamilcar Barca had turned his attention to Spain, in the hope of reviving the fortunes of Carthage to compensate for the loss of Sicily and Sardinia. The Carthaginians had once controlled large areas of Spain, but opposition from the inhabitants of Marseilles, who were not tolerant of competition in trading ventures, combined with incursions by the native Iberians, had whittled Carthaginian acquisitions down to a handful of the old Phoenician cities, principally Gades (modern Cadiz), the centre of trade with the west.

After the Roman victory in 241, Hamilcar may not have harboured any intention of opening further hostilities, though Roman legend insists that he tutored his son Hannibal in extreme hatred for Rome almost from birth. Hamilcar required an army to control the native Iberians while he exploited the wealth of the country, not least the lucrative silver mines. In 229, before he had gained control of the whole country, Hamilcar was drowned. He had three young sons, Hannibal being the eldest, but at eighteen years old he was not experienced enough to succeed his father. Instead, Hamilcar's son-in-law Hasdrubal took charge, founding another city, New Carthage, or Cartagena, which functioned as a supply base for his troops.

The inhabitants of Massilia were increasingly alarmed at the growing powers of Hamilcar and his successor Hasdrubal, and appealed to Rome. The Romans sent an embassy and came to an arrangement with Hasdrubal in 226. They proposed that Spain should be divided by the River Ebro, and the Carthaginians should not interfere in the lands to the north of it, but were free to act in the area to the south, despite the fact that the Massilians dwelt there, and depended on their trading connections for their livelihood. It is worth noting that Carcopino, followed by G. and C. Picard, have suggested that the river name Iberus in the text of the treaty between the Romans and Hasdrubal actually refers to the River Jucar, not the Ebro, and this river marked the limits of the territory that Hasdrubal had managed to bring under control. If this is correct, it would cast a different light on the story, but the Ebro as the agreed boundary is now so entrenched in history books that it would be difficult to prevail against it.

When Hasdrubal was assassinated in 221 his power passed to his brother-in-law, Hamilcar Barca's eldest son, Hannibal, now in his twenties. The war was precipitated when a Spanish tribe allied to Carthage attacked Saguntum. Though this city lay south of the Ebro and was allegedly in the Carthaginian zone (but north of the River Jucar which just might have been the agreed boundary) the Saguntines were allied to Rome, so the scene was set for another conflict between the two great powers. The alliance is what counts, rather than the question of whether Saguntum lay inside or outside the Carthaginian zone. The Romans sent an embassy in 219 to protest at the attack on Saguntum. Hannibal referred the matter to Carthage, and during the consequent delay, he mobilised to blockade Saguntum. The city surrendered after eight months. Hannibal was encouraged by the lack of any Roman reaction when Saguntum fell, and he marched across the agreed boundary line. This time the Romans did react. The second Punic war had begun.

Rome prepared by raising two armies for the consuls of 218, hoping to wage war outside Italy. The consul Publius Cornelius Scipio set off overland for Spain to deal with Hannibal, and the other consul, Tiberius Sempronius Longus, embarked for Sicily, a staging post on the way to Africa where he would deal with Carthage. In the event the Romans were thwarted before they were able to put their plans into practice. When Scipio arrived at the River Rhone, Hannibal had already crossed it and was heading for the Alpine passes. Scipio failed to stop his progress into Italy, and had to make new plans. He decided to entrust the conduct of the war in Spain to his younger brother Gnaeus Cornelius Scipio. As consul he had the legal right to bestow praetorian powers on Gnaeus Scipio, so that he could command the armies. The intention was to keep the Carthaginians in check in Spain, and especially to prevent Hannibal's brothers, Hasdrubal and Mago, from bringing more troops to join Hannibal. The consul then took part of the army intended for Spain, and marched into Italy along the coastal route, chasing after Hannibal and hoping to get ahead of him, but when he arrived he learned that the Carthaginians were through the Alps and had defeated the tribe of the Taurini, around modern Turin. The Gallic tribes of northern Italy who had been recently defeated by the Romans were willing to join Hannibal, so the new recruits for his army made up for his losses in crossing the Alps. Scipio finally engaged him in battle at the Ticinus (now called Ticinio) near modern Pavia. This was the first of several defeats that Hannibal inflicted on the Romans during his long sojourn in Italy. The consul Scipio was wounded in the battle, allegedly rescued by his young son, also called Publius Cornelius Scipio, who was destined for greater fame in the near future. The Scipios and their followers had to take refuge at Placentia (modern Piacenza), one of the colonies founded after the recent battles against the Gauls.

The consul Tiberius Sempronius Longus hurriedly returned from Sicily, and joined Publius Scipio. They engaged Hannibal again at the Trebia, but lost the battle and a great number of soldiers. As soon as he had recovered from his wounds, Publius Scipio left for Spain to join his brother Gnaeus, where they scored some successes against the Carthaginians over the next few years. In Italy, the new consul for 217, Gaius Flaminius, fared no better against Hannibal. He had been consul in 223, and had commanded an army in the battles against the Gauls, but at most stages of his career he had incurred senatorial hostility. Fearing that he might be forcibly ejected from his command, he left Rome in a great hurry, without observing the proper rituals. His actions offended the gods, so it was not surprising that he was defeated and killed, with the loss of 15,000 men, at the battle of Lake Trasimene.

A new strategy was required, since three successive defeats indicated that pitched battles were not the way to deal with Hannibal. After the disaster of Lake Trasimene, the middle-aged Quintus Fabius Maximus was made Dictator. He was elected by the people, instead of being more properly appointed by one of the consuls, but Flaminius was dead and the other consul nowhere near Rome, so the Romans found other legal methods to make him Dictator. Two more legions were raised, but Fabius did not commit them to battle. He used his troops to harass the Carthaginians, keeping them on the move and denying them supplies. The Romans nicknamed him the Delayer, Cunctator in Latin. His method was correct, but it was a long-term plan with no rapid results, and meanwhile lands around Rome, especially in Campania, were being devastated, farms destroyed, and the population killed. Impatience won the day. Fabius' second in command, Publius Minucius Rufus, was appointed a general in his own right. He immediately engaged in battle without proper reconnaissance of the area and Hannibal's dispositions. Fabius had to rescue him.

Ignoring this near defeat, the consuls for 216, Gaius Terentius Varro and Lucius Aemilius Paullus, were urged by the Senate to take on Hannibal in battle. A massive recruitment campaign was undertaken to raise enormous new armies, with which the consuls faced Hannibal at Cannae (modern Canne) in August 216. Since they were under pressure from the impatient Senate, they probably felt that there was little time to wait for a more propitious occasion to fight the Carthaginians. The battle was fought on ground that they had not chosen, but perhaps they felt confident that their sixteen legions of Romans and allies would give them the advantage, since they outnumbered Hannibal by nearly two to one.

The consuls seem to have had no previously agreed corporate strategy. When both consuls were present, each one commanded on alternate days, a procedure that allowed each individual to put into operation his own particular plan, whether or not his colleague approved. Aemilius Paullus was the more cautious of the two consuls, and would perhaps not have risked battle, but on the fateful day, Varro was in command, and chose to fight. Varro placed the legions in the centre, the Roman cavalry on his right wing and the allied cavalry on the left. Hannibal put his lighter-armed Spanish troops in the centre, and his more heavily armed African infantry troops on the wings. The Celtic and Spanish cavalry on the Carthaginian left wing faced the Roman cavalry, and the Numidian horsemen on the Carthaginian right faced the allied cavalry. Hannibal gave instructions that the men in the centre should gradually withdraw after the battle had started, as though they were being steadily beaten back, and then the African troops on the wings should start to close in. This drew the Romans forward out of their lines and into the trap. They had shortened their front by closing or narrowing the gaps between the maniples, and were therefore formed up in a compact mass like the old-style phalanx, presumably hoping to batter their way through Hannibal's Spanish infantry. They pushed too far into the line and were enveloped by the African soldiers. It is possible that Hannibal's screen of light armed troops had obscured these infantry wings from the Roman commanders. The final blow fell when the Celtic and Spanish cavalry of Hannibal's army routed the Roman cavalry contingents, and then rode round the rear of the Romans to help the Numidians fight off the allied cavalry. Both the Roman and allied cavalry wings were driven from the field, so the Carthaginian horsemen rode back around the rear of the Roman infantry. The ring was closed. The greater part of the Roman army was annihilated, but some men escaped, and Hannibal took a few thousand prisoners. He tried to persuade the Romans to ransom them, but Roman pride could not countenance this disgrace, so they refused. They even sent the survivors of Cannae to Sicily to live in leather tents until further notice, which came when Scipio took them to Africa and the final battle of Zama in 202.

The battle of Cannae was the greatest disaster that had ever befallen the Romans. Some junior officers such as Publius Cornelius Scipio, the son of the consul, and Fabius Maximus, the son of the Dictator, had escaped the slaughter of Cannae and tried to rally the remnants of the troops at Canusium, where they learned that Terentius Varro had survived. The defeated consul sent word to the Senate that his consular colleague Lucius Aemilius Paullus was dead, and that most of the soldiers were killed or captured. Varro had with him about 10,000 men, or the strength of about two legions out of the enormous numbers that had been raised, 80,000 according to some sources, but the figure is disputed. Exact truth as to the numbers that were originally raised could hardly clarify or obscure the fact that Cannae was a disaster of epic proportions. The Romans had lost so many men that it stretched resources to breaking point, and for a short time, Rome was at the mercy of Hannibal's army. But he did not try to take the city. He had no siege engines. He could have tried to blockade the city and starve the Romans out, but if he managed to take Rome, he would then have to obliterate it or hold it, and with the small number of troops at his disposal he could not afford to tie any of them down in garrisoning the city. His way of war depended on mobility and flexibility. Besides, Rome was by now a cohesive federation, so even if the city fell, he would still not be master of the Romans. He had been in Italy for two years but had not succeeded in detaching many of Rome's allies. The Gauls of the north, and the Bruttians and Apulians of the south, only recently absorbed into the Roman world, were disaffected and therefore sympathetic to him, and he had conquered some of the other allies. The most important gain was Capua, which went over to him voluntarily in 216, after the Roman defeat at Cannae. The Capuans were short of food, and it now looked as though Rome was almost finished, and would never be able to help them, whereas Hannibal might do so. Capua was a prestigious gain, but unless Hannibal could win over the core of the Roman federation he would have to take each city one at a time.

The Romans held their breath for a while, but then began to repair the damage as far as possible. They enlisted the *capite censi*, the poorest men who were not eligible for army service, emptied the prisons, and recruited and armed 8,000 slaves with the promise of freedom if they fought for Rome. The Romans did not attempt to meet Hannibal in a pitched battle. Instead they concentrated on reconquering their allies who had gone over to the Carthaginians. For these campaigns the Romans employed smaller forces, with Fabius Maximus in command of one of them, and in command of the others they placed generals who would not rush headlong into battle.

Hannibal's victory at Cannae still failed to shake the loyalty of the Latins, but it did encourage other interested parties to make overtures to him. In 215 Philip V of Macedon proposed an alliance, which the Romans discovered when their fleet patrolling the Ionian Sea captured a ship with a Carthaginian passenger carrying the treaty. It was vital to stop Philip from arriving in Italy to join Hannibal, so the Roman fleet played its part in patrolling the seas, while the Aetolians, the Spartans, and the Pergamenes were persuaded to keep Philip occupied on land while the Romans attended to other spheres of the war.

As well as fighting in Italy, the Romans had to maintain a military presence in Sardinia, Corsica and Sicily to ward off Carthaginian attempts to regain the islands. There was a severe setback in 215-214 when Hiero of Syracuse died and was succeeded by his son Hieronymus, who allowed the Carthaginians take over the city. The Roman fleet patrolled the seas around Syracuse but the Romans had to wait until they were in a position to attack in strength on land. The general who finally did take Syracuse, Claudius Marcellus, had been on his way to Sicily as praetor in 216, but was recalled after the disaster at Cannae and spent the next couple of years clearing up, restoring order and retaking Casilinum, one of the cities of Campania which was under Hannibal's control. In 214 he set off once again for Sicily, this time as consul, and in 213 began the siege of Syracuse in earnest. It took him two years to take the city, where Archimedes contributed to the defence by his invention of the 'claw', a war engine imperfectly understood in modern times, but which was said to have lifted the Roman ships out of the water and dunked them back in again, probably stern first. In 211, Syracuse fell to the Romans. Marcellus tried to prevent a massacre of the inhabitants. During the proceedings, Archimedes was killed, allegedly while studying designs for some unknown engine or mathematical problem, which he asked the soldiers not to disturb.

The war in Sicily was not entirely over when Syracuse fell in 211, but it was a step forward. In the same year, the rebellious city of Capua was retaken by the Romans. During the siege of Capua, Hannibal had not attempted to relieve the city by attacking the besieging force, but he tried to frighten the Romans into withdrawing their troops by marching to Rome itself. He camped a few miles from the city and then rode up to inspect the Porta Collina. There were skirmishes outside the city walls, but nothing serious occurred, and Hannibal went away. According to Livy, he was discouraged because it was clear that the Romans did not intend to raise the siege of Capua, nor would they divert the latest levies which were destined for Spain. But the most discouraging news, from Hannibal's point of view, was that the lands around Rome were being sold to raise much needed funds, and somebody had bought the whole area where his soldiers were camped, for the normal price.

The recapture of the two major cities of Syracuse and Capua enabled the Romans to release seasoned troops for the war in Spain where, after an auspicious start, things were not going well. When Gnaeus Cornelius Scipio took command in 218, he had managed to stabilise the situation in the north. His brother Publius joined him in 217. The Carthaginians were weakened by the diversion of some of their troops to Africa, to counter the attacks of Syphax, prince of the Numidian tribesmen. The Scipio brothers defeated the Carthaginians in Spain in 216 or possibly 215, temporarily averting the threat that troops might be sent to aid Hannibal in Italy.

When the revolt of Syphax was quelled in Africa, fresh Carthaginian troops arrived in Spain, assisted by a Numidian cavalry contingent under their chief Masinissa. From 214 the Carthaginian commander was Hasdrubal son of Gisco, who brought the Romans to battle in 211.

The Scipio brothers had split their forces. They were both defeated and killed. The remains of the Roman army were collected by one of the surviving officers. The Senate appointed the praetor Gaius Claudius Nero to command the northern part of Spain in 211-210. He did not attempt to gain control of the rest of Spain, probably because he was preoccupied in restoring order, but he was accused of being too cautious and was replaced by Publius Cornelius Scipio, the son of the late consul Publius Scipio. He was only twenty-five years old, and though he had served in the army with distinction, he had no political experience. He was too young for the consulship, and except for the office of aedile, he had held none of the other requisite magistracies that would have qualified him for election. At the time of his appointment to Spain he held no office at all. It was all very irregular. In order to command the armies in Spain, he needed the rank of consul or proconsul, and would require the bestowal of *imperium*, all of which was arranged legally by the *comitia centuriata*, which passed a special law to grant him proconsular powers.

Scipio arrived in Spain in 210. His first task was to restore discipline and boost morale. Then he spent some time training the troops and gathering information about the country, the geography, the people, and the dispositions and habits of the enemy. He learned that Cartagena, an important supply base with a large harbour, was protected on the south side by the harbour and on the north side by a lagoon, but at low tide the water level of the lagoon dropped, and it was possible to wade across it. In 209 Scipio decided to try to capture the city. He set up a three pronged attack. The main force approached the main gate, and the fleet under an officer called Laelius attacked from the harbour. Another smaller force was instructed to cross the lagoon as soon as the water level dropped, and attack the north wall, where there were fewer defenders. The Romans were able to surmount this wall, drive off the opposition and use the wall walk to approach the main gate, which they then attacked from inside. The city was captured, and shortly afterwards the citadel was surrendered.

The war in Spain was approaching its end. Scipio defeated Hannibal's brother, Hasdrubal Barca, who then set off in 208 with his remaining forces to join Hannibal in Italy. Modern scholars have criticised Scipio for failing to stop Hasdrubal, but by this time, Hannibal's army had dwindled in size, and although he had persuaded or forced some of Rome's allies to contribute soldiers, he had not managed to keep his army up to strength. Scipio ignored Hasdrubal and concentrated his energies on the Carthaginian forces that were left in Spain, under Hannibal's youngest brother Mago, who was defeated at the battle of Ilipa in 206. Carthaginian power in Spain was broken for ever, and Scipio returned to Rome.

As Hasdrubal was making his way to Italy, Hannibal inflicted another blow on the Romans at Venusia (modern Venosa), where his Numidian cavalry discovered both the consuls for 208, Claudius Marcellus and Crispinus, on an ill-advised reconnaissance, and killed them both. The consuls for 207 raised more men and took command of two armies, Marcus Livius Salinator proceeding northwards to await the arrival of Hasdrubal from Gaul, and Gaius Claudius Nero to Bruttium to face Hannibal. As soon as he heard that his brother was in Italy, Hannibal marched north to meet him. Claudius Nero shadowed Hannibal but did not attack. Then his troops captured messengers with a letter from Hasdrubal, informing Hannibal where their armies should meet in Umbria. Claudius Nero had been censured for inactivity in Spain in 210, but he more than made up for it now, by leaving some troops to watch Hannibal and then hastily setting off with most of his army to reach Hasdrubal's rendezvous point. His army marched fifty miles a day for five days to join Livius Salinator at his headquarters at Sena Gallica (modern Senigallia). The two consuls caught up with Hasdrubal at the Metaurus River, and wiped out the army, killing Hasdrubal in the process. The energetic Claudius Nero wasted no time in marching back south, setting off that same night with Hasdrubal's head in his baggage. The Romans reached Hannibal's camp and threw his brother's head over the defences. Hannibal probably realised now that he could not defeat the Romans, but he remained at large in Italy for another three years. The wonder is that he had been able to sustain his army for so long, keeping them enthusiastic enough to continue to follow him, and not letting them starve. As a commander he far outshone most of the Romans who faced him, but while he fought them he also tutored them in generalship.

Now that Spain, Sardinia, Corsica and Sicily were denied to Carthage, the time was ripe for the Romans to strike at Carthage itself. The young Scipio urged this course of action when he stood for election to the consulship for 205. Fabius Maximus opposed the plan, and the Senate refused to grant Scipio any troops or resources, but agreed that he could undertake the expedition, provided that he raised his own army. This he did very quickly, enlisting volunteers and recruiting the disgraced survivors of Cannae. Scipio set sail for Africa from Lilybaeum in 204.

The likely success of the expedition had been underlined, probably in 205 when the Romans consulted the Sibylline Books, a collection of oracles which had been part of Roman religious culture since at least the fifth century BC. Prophecies could usually be found in these books to solve any problem. In this case the prophecy stated that if a foreign enemy invaded Italy, he would be defeated if the Romans imported the religious cult of the mother goddess Cybele into the city. This was corroborated by another prophecy from the Delphic oracle, so arrangements were set in motion to bring Cybele to Rome. The statue of Cybele was brought from Pessinus in Phrygia in 204. The goddess was installed in the temple of Victory on the Palatine Hill. It was a good investment. In the following year Hannibal was recalled to Carthage.

When Scipio landed in Africa he was opposed by the Carthaginian army reinforced by their Numidian allies. The Romans promptly put the city of Utica under siege, and the Carthaginians marched to its relief. Scipio placed the army in winter quarters, and waited until spring when he won another victory. A fresh Carthaginian army was raised with Hasdrubal Gisco in command, but at the battle of the Great Plains the Carthaginians were defeated again. Scipio now called in a new ally. While he was in Spain he had fought against the Numidian chieftain, Masinissa, who was allied to the Carthaginians at the time, but was won over by Scipio after the victory at Ilipa in 206. This chieftain was recognised as an ally of Rome, and he brought reinforcements for Scipio's army, mostly the famed Numidian horsemen.

The Carthaginians made overtures for peace, and during the truce that followed Scipio dictated terms, but both sides knew that if Hannibal was ordered to come home the peace terms would be meaningless. Since this was precisely what Scipio wanted to bring about, he waited and did nothing, certain that Hannibal would be recalled and the war would begin again. Hannibal left Italy in 203, and as soon as he arrived the Carthaginians broke the truce and attacked. The two armies met at Zama in 202, where victory was not a foregone conclusion for Scipio. He ordered the Romans to leave gaps between their ranks and allow the Carthaginian elephants to charge through them, and he placed Masinissa and Laelius in command of the cavalry on each wing. Hannibal stationed his Numidian cavalry opposite Masinissa and the Carthaginian horse opposite Laelius. During the battle the Romans drove all the enemy cavalry off the field, but they did not pursue the Carthaginians. Had they done so, Scipio would have been at a disadvantage without them. Fortunately the Roman and Numidian horsemen turned around, and charged the rear of Hannibal's army. It was all over for the Carthaginians. Hannibal escaped and turned up later at the court of King Antiochus the Great in Syria.

The Romans were able to dictate peace terms, by which Carthage was disarmed completely. All the war elephants and all the warships except ten triremes were to be given up, and more importantly, the Carthaginians were not to make war on anyone without the approval of Rome. Carthage had to pay another large indemnity and send hostages to Rome. Their territory was reduced to the area of the city itself and the lands immediately surrounding it. All other territorial possessions were to be surrendered. As a sort of insurance policy, Masinissa was confirmed as ruler of his own territory on the borders of Carthage. Scipio was at the zenith of his career, and justifiably took the victory title Africanus.

Development of the Army in the Third Century BC

The prolonged and drawn out Punic wars moulded Roman society and its military ethos, and launched Rome into the Mediterranean world as a power that could rival most other states. The Roman army and its commanders had learned a great deal from all the battles of the third century BC, from Sentinum in 295, through the invasion of Pyrrhus, to the battle of Zama at the end of the century. The alliance system had proved its worth, and most of the allies had remained loyal, especially the Latins, whose communities had been exhausted by the protracted wars. The Romans had proved that they could fight in several different theatres of war at the same time, and still raise more armies after defeats. Polybius' manpower statistics for the time when the Gauls were poised to attack in 225, show that the Romans and their allies were able to raise 700,000 infantry and 70,000 cavalry. These would not be static figures, but would fluctuate depending on birth rates and death rates, but it still gives an impression of inexhaustibility.

Although there was no standing army in Rome until the time of Augustus, there were several armies in the field for many years at a time in the course of the third century wars. The obligatory term of service was set at six years, which usually meant enlisting on six separate occasions in different armies until the term was fulfilled, but in the third century, with armies in Italy, Spain, and Sicily for prolonged periods, it was possible to serve continuously for six years in succession. After serving for the obligatory six year term, the soldiers were eligible for discharge, but had to remain on the books as *evocati*, literally meaning 'those called out', until they had served in a maximum of sixteen campaigns. This is the most likely explanation of a passage in the sixth book of Polybius' history, where he says that an infantryman was required to complete sixteen years' service before he reached the age of forty-six. Cavalrymen had to serve for ten years. In normal circumstances infantry soldiers would have about thirty years from the age of seventeen to the age of forty-six in which to fulfil their obligations to the state, so they would not have to serve in the army every year to reach their target of sixteen years or campaigns. During the third century there were only a few gaps between wars, so the *evocati* were probably called out more frequently as the wars progressed and losses mounted. Polybius adds that in times of emergency, the term of service was raised to twenty years.

Some men could make a professional career in the army at this time, re-enlisting on a voluntary basis for successive campaigns and even serving for longer than the stated term. Despite the willingness of some soldiers to continue serving, there was no career structure to follow in Republican armies. If a soldier had reached a higher rank in one campaign, he could not guarantee that he would be reappointed to the same rank in the next campaign, so one of the main attractions would be the prospect of booty, and if that failed, it seems that patriotic duty only applied if the homelands were threatened. Wars in distant places with no prospect of enrichment did not attract so many eager candidates.

By means of many men re-enlisting for successive campaigns, a corporate military expertise would be built up. When magistrates were recruiting new armies, they would be glad to enlist men who were known to have fought in, and obviously survived, previous campaigns. Fortified by experience, they would be better fighters and they would serve to steady inexperienced recruits. It is taken as read that there must have been some formal training when armies were assembled, and indeed it is common sense to try to ensure that all the soldiers can at least handle their weapons before committing them to battle. The information from the ancient sources does not lay great emphasis on when and how any training may have been organised, and there is an unavoidable impression that when episodes of training are reported, they were somehow exceptional. Lutatius Catulus trained his naval crews, and he won the battle against the Carthaginian fleet in an opportunistic attack in adverse weather conditions. Scipio began his command in Spain by formally training his troops. When training is mentioned in the sources, it can usually be seen to have paid off, but in literary terms, it would be nothing short of disgraceful if training was undertaken, but the Romans still lost the battles. The importance of training is underlined in a negative way by the Senate's reaction to the disaster at the Trebia in 218. As Nathan Rosenstein points out, Hannibal defeated the Romans because he was a better general, but there was no question of putting the blame on the Roman commander. The lack of training for the soldiers was held to be the cause of the disaster. Perhaps the ancient historians did not mention training because it was obvious that it was done. For officer training there was nothing approaching a staff college, unless the gap was partially filled by talk around the dinner table. The first hints of military manuals belong to the second century, when it is thought that Polybius may have derived some of his information from manuals intended for military tribunes. In the same century Hellenistic military manuals became popular, and at the very end of the second century, the author Sallust in his work on the Jugurthine war in Africa says that Marius sneered at consuls who took command of armies with only book learning to back them up. Commanding generals of the third century and later would have gained some experience of how armies worked if they served as tribunes or quaestors with the legions, but beyond this they were simply expected to know how to wage war, move troops from one place to another, maintain discipline, organise supplies, and deal with sick and wounded. In the long run, they managed very well.

Another defect in the army was the lack of reconnaissance and intelligence gathering, and once again Catulus and Scipio stand out in the sources as the successful proponents of the art of knowing where the enemy was and what he was doing, and the equally important art of investigating the lie of the land, or of the coasts and harbours. When the two consuls Claudius Marcellus and Crispinus did make an attempt at reconnaissance, they were so ill-prepared that they ran into Hannibal's troops and were killed. Information could have been gathered by soldiers specially trained for the purpose, and then it would have been the task of the consuls to assess the information and act upon it, not to go riding out themselves, at least until they knew where Hannibal was. The same lack of information had already led the Romans into the Caudine Forks in 321, and straight into the path of Hannibal in the fog at Lake Trasimene. Livy reports that the consul Lucius Cornelius Merula, fighting against the Gallic Boii of northern Italy in 193, sent out horsemen to scout the route, even though he was moving off in daylight, as though reconnoitring in these circumstances was something unusual.

The command structure of the army also left something to be desired. In the early days, with two consuls to command armies, most wars and skirmishes could be dealt with successfully without the need to appoint other commanders, but the coalition of the Etruscans, Umbrians, Gauls and Samnites at the beginning of the third century had stretched the capacity of the political structure to cope with fighting on several fronts with different armies. During the build-up to the battle of Sentinum, some magistrates had to have their powers extended and some private individuals had to be invested with *imperium* to provide enough army commanders to take the field during this dangerous period. It speaks volumes for the political and military flexibility of the Romans that they were able to provide more than the usual quota of commanders and still remain within the confines of their legal framework.

The deep-felt detestation of one-man rule necessitated annually elected magistrates, short-term six-month Dictatorships, and consular collegiality, but this precluded any long-term overall planning from being undertaken, much less put into effect. The Senate was the supreme authority, but for the Carthaginian wars what was required was a man or a small committee like a war cabinet, that could decide on a policy and stick to it, rather than allowing annual consuls to reverse the previous strategy. No one can say whether the delaying tactics of Fabius Maximus would have forced Hannibal out of Italy in the end, because succeeding consuls overturned his ideas. Attrition and denying food supplies to the enemy wears down the defenders as well, so it probably would not have worked. Even though it was the Senate which was urging the army commanders to engage Hannibal in 216, it is just possible that if the cautious consul Aemilius Paullus had been in sole command of the army with no contradictory colleague, there would have been no battle of Cannae, but his caution was overruled by Varro, who was no match for Hannibal; probably only Scipio Africanus could have reached that high goal. The point is that an army commanded by two equal-ranking generals, who do not agree with each other about the best way to defeat the enemy, is not very effective. Napoleon said that one bad general in command of an army is better than two good ones.

The Punic wars also witnessed a phenomenon that was to repeat itself during the later Republic, in which the law had to be circumvented to allow young men who were not politically qualified to command armies. Scipio was the first who showed extraordinary ability to command troops without having gone through the political career path as aedile, quaestor, praetor and consul, which would have brought him to the accepted age and rank for army command. The Romans were adept at getting round their own legislation to deal with such circumstances, but extraordinary commands in the later Republic led directly to civil wars and ultimately to the demise of the Republic. Augustus established the standing army and a controlled career path to senior promotions, which were mostly in his gift, and put a stop to the precocious commands for which Scipio set the example. In Scipio's case, it was not such a bad thing. Without him, Hannibal might have remained in Italy until Rome really was exhausted.

The consuls, or sometimes a praetor, directed campaigns, and each legion was commanded by six military tribunes, working in pairs for one month at a time. There was no single legionary commander or legate until Augustan times. Livy mentions centurions and chief centurions, called *primipili* or first spears, who would have exercised authority in the legions, subject to the tribunes. It is not known how large the legions would have been during the third century. In fact it is never very clear how many men there were in a legion, despite Livy's and Polybius' figures of around 4,200 to 5,200 men. J. Roth has suggested that there was never any standard size for a legion, and Polybius gives different numbers for different campaigns, so this may reflect what actually happened, with armies varying in size depending on the urgency of the situation and different circumstances, always subject to manpower availability at the time.

By the time of the Punic wars, it is most probable that the Roman army was manipular in formation and the phalanx was a thing of the past, except that at Cannae the Romans formed up in a compact mass which proved too inflexible. The characteristic weapons of the Roman army were in place, the *pilum* for throwing, and the *gladius* for cutting and thrusting. Polybius explains how the Romans had the advantage in fighting the Gauls in 225 at the battle of Telamon, first with their showers of throwing-spears which greatly harassed the Gauls and prevented them from engaging at close quarters, and then when the Romans advanced, their swords could be used for stabbing and cutting, whereas the Gauls were limited to cutting with theirs.

According to Polybius, by the end of the third century if not earlier, the Romans had begun to organise their troops by cohorts in place of maniples. In 206 at the battle of Ilipa, Scipio grouped together three maniples, one of *hastati*, one of *principes* and one of *triarii*, to form one cohort, which ought to have contained 300 men, 240 in total from the *hastati* and the *principes*, and sixty from the *triarii*. Livy uses the term cohort to describe the allied contingents as far back as 294, and again for allied military units in 217 and 212. It is possible that Livy's use of the term is anachronistic in these instances, but between 210 and 195, as Cagniart points out, Livy mentions cohorts in the Roman army in Spain seventeen times, so it may be the case that Roman commanders were employing the three-maniple cohort more frequently. By the 160s when Polybius was writing his history, he knew what a cohort was, but it may have been used temporarily for specific tasks rather than a basis for forming the legions. The credit for introducing the new legionary organisation based on cohorts instead of maniples goes to Gaius Marius at the end of the second century BC. The cohort had definitely replaced the manipular system by the time of Julius Caesar. As yet, no direct link can be established between the possibly temporary cohorts used in Spain from 210 onwards, and the more permanent cohorts of the legions of Marius and Caesar.

There are two conflicting theories about the Roman practice of building entrenched camps when they ended the day's march or needed to bivouac for a while. One source states that it was Pyrrhus who taught them this useful habit, but another source is convinced that Pyrrhus admired the disciplined way in which the Romans made camps when they were fighting him. Livy refers to camps several times in his account of Roman wars, and although all his many references could be anachronistic, on the whole there are too many accounts of the enemy approaching right up to the ramparts, and Romans fending off attacks, for them all to be complete fiction. At some point the Romans began to protect themselves on the march and during campaigns by digging in. Polybius took great pains to describe the orderly layout of a Roman camp. He says that the *extraordinarii* were encamped parallel to the ramparts at the sides of the camp, and refers to ramparts at the rear, so by the middle of the second century it was standard practice to enclose the whole camp within earthen fortifications. If the Romans were not already making camps by the time of the Samnite wars, the area of hills and valleys where they were operating would have been a good place to adopt the habit.

7

The Army of the Second Century BC

In the second century BC the Roman army emerges in a clearer light than at any previous era. Information is more abundant and more reliable. It is the century of Polybius, whose close observation of the Roman army has been projected backwards to the Punic wars and forwards to the wars with Philip of Macedon and Antiochus III the Great. For the second century, archaeology and literature converge to a greater extent than before. Polybius writes in the 160s of camps and weapons, and especially at Numantia and Renieblas in Spain, camps and weapons of the 130s have been discovered, and can be compared with Polybius' descriptions.

During the first half of the century a number of colonies were established in Italy and the Po valley, and in the second half more provinces were created, including Macedonia and Africa in 146, and Transalpine Gaul in 121. The new territories all required armies to keep the peace and protect the boundaries, and governors to administer them. At Rome there were internal problems, typified by the turmoil engendered by Tiberius and Gaius Gracchus, who tried to put into effect reforms by means of their tribunician powers and were both killed for their pains.

Foreign Wars

The Romans did not actively seek to annexe territory during the first half of the second century. With a reputation for military success, the Romans were occasionally asked to intervene in the affairs of countries outside Italy, to repel an invader or stop the ruler of one state from oppressing another. The initial response was usually to send someone to investigate the circumstances, and then, if it was considered appropriate, the Romans assembled an army, fought the battles until they won, and then returned to Rome. The wars of the third century BC had concerned Italy and the west, but now Rome was drawn into conflicts to protect states and communities in the east which they had officially recognised as friends and allies.

By the second century BC Hellenistic culture, from Hellenes, the collective name of the Greeks, had spread over much of the eastern Mediterranean. After the death of Alexander the Great in 323, his generals, known as the Successors, seized much of the territory that he had conquered and created kingdoms for themselves. Ptolemy Soter fled to Egypt with the body of Alexander, and placed it in a splendid tomb in Alexandria. Egypt became a Hellenistic kingdom under a succession of rulers all called Ptolemy. Another of Alexander's generals, Seleucus, took over the kingdom of Babylonia, and eventually northern Syria, where he founded the city of Antioch in 300. These large and powerful kingdoms of Egypt, Syria, and Macedon dominated the eastern Mediterranean. Freedom and independence were jealously guarded among the surrounding smaller states. To become a friend of one state almost automatically meant becoming an enemy of some other state. This lack of unity made it easy for Rome to divide and rule in Greece.

Freedom and independence continued unopposed by the Romans, provided that Rome's friends were not threatened in any way, and Roman military and trading interests were not compromised. The city states which had been recognised as friends and allies of the Roman people were not bound to Rome by treaties outlining mutual rights and obligations, as the Italian allies were. Formal treaties would have involved an obligation for Rome to intervene if the protected state were attacked. The Romans preferred to maintain informal relations with friends in the eastern half of the Mediterranean, so they could monitor events and decide whether or not to intervene. Roman expansionist policies began only after many years of diplomatic and military activity designed to preserve the harmonious relations that Rome desired. After 146, when the Romans destroyed Carthage and Corinth, some states lost their independence, passing from semi-free status under Rome's wing, to absorption under Rome's thumb.

The Second Macedonian War 200–196 BC

During the war with Hannibal, Philip V of Macedon had proposed an alliance with the Carthaginians, but the Romans were too preoccupied with the war in Italy to send troops. They were assisted by the Aetolians and other Greek states, and ended the struggle in 205, without a crushing victory, and with lenient terms for Macedon. At the end of the third century envoys from Rhodes and from King Attalus of Pergamum arrived in Rome, bringing news of an impending alliance between Philip of Macedon and Antiochus the Great, the ruler of Syria. They were preparing a joint attack on Egypt.

Though there was no direct threat to Italy, the Romans sent ambassadors to Philip, but they failed to deter him, so the Senate decided on war. There was an unforeseen problem. When the proposal was put before the *comitia centuriata* the people of Rome voted against a war with Philip of Macedon. The Romans were exhausted. They had fought on more than one front for several years during the war with Carthage, sending armies to Spain to prevent the Carthaginians from sending assistance to Hannibal. They had condoned the first war against Philip of Macedon to prevent him from allying with Hannibal. This time the trouble did not seem to concern Italy, and the Roman people did not want to fight. The senators could not overrule the assembly, so they spread propaganda to convert Philip and his ambitions into a direct threat to Rome, repackaged the proposal for war, and the *comitia centuriata* voted 'yes'.

In 200 the consul Sulpicius Galba set out to make war on Philip, assisted by troops furnished by the Aetolian confederacy, and contingents from Pergamum, Rhodes and Athens. The consul Titus Flamininus took over in 198. Within a short time he had driven Philip out of Epirus. He proposed terms, but Philip would not give up control of Thessaly, or the fortresses of Corinth, Chalcis and Demetrias, so the fighting continued. In 197 Flamininus' consulship was due to end, but in Rome two tribunes called for a *prorogatio imperii* to extend his command. Flamininus and Philip V joined battle in 197 in Thessaly, at Cynoscephalae, which means Dog's Head, named after the shape of the rocks in the hills near the battlefield. Antiochus the Great was marching to join Philip but had not yet reached him. On the day when the battle was fought there was a rainstorm with thick cloud that obscured the sun. Philip's troops were dispersed in the gloom, but managed to pitch camp near the hill, where they placed an outpost. Flamininus sent some cavalry and 1,000 infantry to reconnoitre, and they came upon the Macedonian outpost, where after an initial hesitation both sides started to fight, each sending messengers to their respective commanders to ask for assistance. Neither Flamininus nor Philip would have chosen to fight at this time or in this place, but they were now committed to battle. The Romans had the worst of it, until two military tribunes arrived with 500 cavalry and 2,000 infantry. Then Philip's reinforcements came up, and forced the Romans down into the plain below. Livy says that the Aetolian cavalry, the best horsemen in Greece, shielded the Romans. Both commanders now threw in all their troops. Flamininus led the left wing composed of light armed troops, while on his right wing he placed his elephants and support troops. When the Romans reached their comrades at the bottom of the hill, they charged the enemy. Philip formed the phalanx, which was driven back. At this point, Livy says that Philip ordered the phalanx to put down their spears and fight with their swords, but modern commentators have recognised that Livy misunderstood the phrase that Polybius used, which simply meant that the Macedonians were ordered to lower their spears for action, pointing forwards, not lay them down on the ground. At the same time the phalanx started to close up to present a solid front. Flamininus launched an attack before the Macedonians completed the manoeuvre. The elephants on the Roman right wing dispersed the enemy, but the Roman left was in trouble, until one of the military tribunes gathered some men and led them round to the rear of the Macedonian right wing. The phalanx was now in serious trouble because the ground was unfavourable, and the formation was too tightly packed to allow the men to turn round. From then on it was more slaughter than battle. The Macedonians raised their spears, which was the customary signal for surrender. Flamininus was informed of this and tried to stop the battle, but the soldiers either could not hear or chose to ignore the order to cease fighting, and cut the Macedonians down. Philip saw that all was lost and fled the battlefield.

The battle was a complete Roman victory, proving the superiority of the looser formation of the Roman army over the compact phalanx of the enemy, which lost cohesion in the broken ground. The victory put an end to Philip's ambitions for the time being, and stopped Antiochus in his tracks. Peace was declared, and Flamininus ignored the pleas of the Greeks for revenge on Philip. The terms were crippling enough, entailing surrender of all Philip's territories in Greece and Illyricum, surrender of his warships, and the payment of an indemnity. In 196 Philip became an ally of Rome. In the same year, Flamininus famously explained to the Greeks at the Isthmian games that henceforth they were free of the domination of Philip of Macedon, and under Roman patronage they were free to govern themselves. Flamininus was nearly killed in the enthusiastic reception of his speech. The Roman troops were withdrawn. The Greeks did not yet realise that their ideas of freedom did not match the concepts of the Romans.

While the Romans fought the war with Macedon, other Roman armies were fighting the Gauls in northern Italy, principally the Boii, Insubres and Ligurians. From 198 to 191 this war dragged on, and at its conclusion 40,000 Ligurians were transplanted to the south of Italy, where Hannibal had based his army for much of his stay in Italy.

The War with Antiochus the Great 192–189 BC

The Aetolians who had assisted the Romans in the war against Philip had hoped for extra territory and financial gains, but they were disappointed. They asked Antiochus the Great to help the Greeks to liberate themselves. Antiochus mobilised, and the Romans declared war. The consul Acilius Glabrio won the battle at Thermopylae in 191, but Antiochus refused to accept the peace terms. The next Roman commander was the consul Lucius Cornelius Scipio, but the real commander was his more famous brother, Publius Cornelius Scipio Africanus, officially acting in an advisory capacity. Africanus was the logical choice of commander to combat Antiochus, but he had been consul in 194, and by law there had to be a gap of several years before he could become consul again. The Roman senators were not willing to bend the laws by bestowing *imperium* on him, despite the precedents.

Antiochus had built a fortified camp at Magnesia, surrounded by a ditch with a palisade on its outer lip, and a wall with towers on the inner edge. The Romans camped nearby. For a while Antiochus refused battle, but eventually had to engage because his army was becoming restless, which was fortunate for the Romans, because unless they could win a victory within a very short time, the army would have to go into winter quarters.

One day the Romans saw that Antiochus had paraded his men some distance from his camp, ready to fight. Livy describes the composition of the Roman army, with two legions in the centre, arranged in the three-line formation of *hastati, principes* and *triarii* and two *alae sociorum* on the wings, each 5,400 strong, comprising Latins and Italian allies. There were also extra troops on the right flank, consisting of 3,000 infantry made up of Achaeans, and Pergamenes contributed by King Eumenes II. In addition there were about 2,000 Roman cavalry assisted by 800 Pergamene horsemen, and 1,000 Cretans and Trallians. The left flank was protected by the river, but Scipio placed some cavalry there. At the rear of the *triarii* there were sixteen elephants. Macedonian and Thracian volunteers guarded the camp.

Antiochus' army was a cosmopolitan force, with troops from many different countries. The centre was made up of 10,000 soldiers organised and equipped like the Macedonian phalanx, but divided up into ten sections with spaces between them, where two elephants were stationed. The battle was fought in damp conditions, which hindered vision and ruined the bowstrings and slings of Antiochus' troops. In the front line the king had stationed his chariots which according to Livy bristled with scythes on the axles and the yokes, some of them pointing downwards to make short work of anyone who fell underneath them. Eumenes of Pergamum knew what damage these could do, but he also knew that it was possible to panic the horses and turn the chariots into the ranks of their own army, so before the battle was properly started he ordered the archers and slingers to attack the chariots from different directions and make a lot of noise, and the result was as he expected. The Romans took advantage of the disorder, and repulsed the centre of Antiochus' army. Meanwhile Antiochus himself ordered an attack on the Roman left flank, which was supported by the river but protected only by the small numbers of cavalry, who were quickly dispersed, leaving the infantry exposed. The situation was saved by a military tribune commanding the Roman camp, who rallied the soldiers somewhat brutally by ordering his own men to cut down anyone who was running away. The rest turned back to the fighting. Attalus, brother of King Eumenes II of Pergamum, brought 200 horsemen from the Roman right flank to the assistance of the left. Antiochus left the battlefield while his men were fleeing, pursued by the Roman cavalry and the horsemen of Eumenes.

The Roman victory at Magnesia at the end of 190 or the beginning of 189, ended the war. The Romans took the states of Asia Minor into their protection, and rewarded the kingdoms of Rhodes and Pergamum with territories from Antiochus' domains. Ironically, Hannibal, the adversary of Scipio Africanus, was with Antiochus. The Romans demanded that the king should surrender him, but instead the king helped his famous guest to escape.

The Aetolians refused to accept the terms of unconditional surrender, and carried on fighting alone. A Roman army under Fulvius Nobilior besieged and took their fortress of Ambracia, and the Aetolians accepted peace terms. They became allies of the Roman people, with the obligation to support the Romans against their enemies.

Another war had been dragging on for some years between Attalus, king of Pergamum and King Prusias of Bithynia, who had taken over part of Attalus' kingdom. After the battle of Magnesia, the Romans instructed Prusias to return the territory to Eumenes, the new king of Pergamum. This merely provoked further attacks, with Hannibal aiding Prusias. Hannibal won a sea battle, but the Romans won the war in 182. Eumenes recovered his territory, and the Romans once again demanded the surrender of Hannibal. This time there was no opportunity for escape. The great Carthaginian general took poison.

The Third Macedonian War 176–168 BC

The next few years after the defeat of Antiochus the Great were relatively peaceful except for a revolt in Sardinia, which occupied the Romans from 181 to 176. The Romans clung to the island because it provided grain and minerals, but had to deal with the determined banditry of the Sardinian people for the next seventy-five years.

Having been forced to give up territory, Philip V was not content with his lot as an ally of Rome. He had been rearming and assembling a war chest, but he died before he was ready to make war. His son Perseus cultivated other disaffected Greek states, and this made the states that were friends of Rome feel very insecure. The Romans sent an embassy, with impossible demands, and declared war in 171. Livy says that the army destined for this war was assembled with care and attention. Experienced veterans volunteered, and there was a surplus of ex-centurions, for whom there were not enough posts. One of the compelling motives for volunteering would have been the anticipation of acquiring booty. There were few spectacular results in the first years of the war, and then in 168 the consul Aemilius Paullus took over. The army was demoralised, so Paullus concentrated on restoring vigour and enthusiasm, then brought Perseus to battle at Pydna in Macedonia. The Macedonian phalanx at first repulsed the Romans, but the soldiers could not keep close together, and with the sun shining in their eyes they began to break up. The Romans saw their opportunity and destroyed the phalanx by closing in and using their short swords.

The Macedonian state was now divided into four self-governing Republics. Many prisoners were taken to Rome including Perseus, who was shamefully maltreated and died. About one thousand Achaeans were transported to Rome as hostages to ensure the good behaviour of other Greeks. Fortunately for historians and archaeologists, one of these Achaean captives was the historian Polybius. He was taken into the circle of Scipio Aemilianus, the natural son of Aemilius Paullus, adopted as a child by Publius Cornelius Scipio. When Polybius wrote his history of Rome, he made all due reference to the Scipio family, especially Africanus, the adoptive grandfather of Aemilianus.

The Greeks soon realised that they had exchanged domination by Macedon for domination by Rome. The Romans became suspicious and peevish. They objected when the Rhodians tried to mediate between Perseus and Rome, and forced them to give up territories in Asia Minor, and then they ruined Rhodian trade, which was the main support of the economy, by converting the island of Delos into a free port. The Romans had obviously forgotten that Rhodes had furnished troops for their wars. They also turned against Eumenes of Pergamum, who had also helped them in the wars. They attacked the towns of Epirus and enslaved large numbers of the inhabitants. The freedom of the Greeks, declared with pomp and ceremony by Flamininus less than thirty years earlier, was now revealed as an illusion.

The subjugation of Macedon taught the Romans that war could be profitable. The wealth that poured into the city made it possible to remit the property tax on Roman citizens in Italy (*tributum civium Romanorum*) from 167 onwards.

Wars in Spain 198–133 BC

In the two new Spanish provinces, Hispania Citerior, or Nearer Spain, and Hispania Superior, Further Spain, each governed by a praetor, rebellions went on for years, with escalating cruelty on both sides. The provinces were worth keeping because they yielded valuable resources, especially silver. In 155 separate revolts were raised by Celtiberian tribes in Nearer Spain, and the Lusitanians in Further Spain. The Lusitanians were defeated by the praetor Servius Sulpicius Galba in 151, but with great losses. In 150 BC Galba resorted to treachery, promising a treaty with the tribes and then turning on them. Many tribesmen were killed, and the rest were enslaved. Among those who escaped was a shepherd called Viriathus, or more correctly Viriatus, who successfully waged a guerrilla war for eight years. He would perhaps have been surprised to learn that a tribune in Rome, supported by Marcus Porcius Cato, had proposed that Galba should be brought to trial for his betrayal of the Lusitanians, but the senators closed ranks and Galba escaped condemnation. Such a blatant miscarriage of justice only served to underline the callous attitude of the Romans to the Lusitanian tribesmen. By 147 Viriatus had welded the Lusitanians and the Celtiberians together, operating in guerrilla actions in both the Spanish provinces. In 140 BC he defeated a Roman army under Quintus Fabius Maximus Servilianus, and made peace, but even though the arrangements were ratified by the Roman people, in the following year the Senate reneged on the peace settlement, allowing the new commander Gnaeus Servilius Caepio to resume hostilities. Viriatus was betrayed by one of his own men in the pay of the Romans, and after his death resistance collapsed. The Lusitanians surrendered in 138.

The wars in Spain were not yet over. The Celtiberians rebelled again in 143. Most of the tribesmen surrendered to the consul Quintus Caecilius Metellus, but the diehards held out, using the town of Numantia as their stronghold. The Romans sent another commander, Quintus Pompeius Aulus, who blockaded Numantia through the winter, and made peace in 140, but the Senate refused to ratify the terms. The next commander, Gaius Hostilius Mancinus, managed to get himself surrounded in 137, and surrendered with his army of 20,000 men. One of the officers in his army was Tiberius Sempronius Gracchus, whose father had treated the Spanish tribes well, and was remembered with gratitude. The Numantines would negotiate only with Tiberius, and in the end they let the Roman army go free, provided that they left their equipment behind.

It was clear that special efforts were required to defeat the Celtiberians, so the Romans called in the top man, Scipio Aemilianus, who had won his laurels in the third war with Carthage in 146. He was elected to the consulship for 134, despite the legislation intended to prevent men from holding the office for a second time. He spent some time instilling discipline into the disillusioned soldiers. He cleared the camps of all unnecessary personnel, including the slaves of the officers and men, and the camp followers that inevitably clustered around any army. He also recruited local tribesmen to swell the ranks of his army. Then he put Numantia under siege. He built a stone wall and ditch all around the site, with towers at regular intervals, and a series of camps for the soldiers, for which modern archaeologists are very grateful. In a predominantly dry country the internal arrangements of the camps have not been eradicated, and the layouts suggest that the army was still organised in manipular formation, but it is thought that Scipio may have formed prototype cohorts made up of three maniples, like those that Cornelius Scipio and other commanders had used in Spain. This does not mean that Scipio reorganised the legions into cohorts, like the legions of the first century BC. The temporary cohort made up of three maniples, or possibly more than three, was neither too large nor too small, an ideal size and formation for use in the Spanish terrain against mobile guerrillas, and given the example of

Mancinus who surrendered with 20,000 men, there would be a need for mobility and vigilance in the areas around Numantia. There were some skirmishes from which the Romans did not always emerge unscathed, but Scipio accomplished his main aims of cutting off the supplies to the Numantines, and preventing other Spanish tribes from rendering assistance to them. In the end the Numantines were starved out, and sold as slaves, in 133. Peace of a sort came to Spain, on Roman terms.

The Third Punic War 149–146 BC

After their defeat in 102 the Carthaginians were forbidden to make war on anyone by the terms of their agreement with Rome, so they concentrated on revitalising their commerce. A constant source of discontent had been engendered in Carthage, because Rome was allied with the Numidian chief Masinissa, who raided Carthaginian territory with impunity, because the Carthaginians were not allowed to fight back. They appealed to Rome several times, and each time a commission was sent to Africa, but ended by condoning Masinissa's actions. In 153 the elderly Marcus Porcius Cato was included in the group of Roman senators who were sent to investigate the latest dispute with Masinissa. Cato saw how wealthy and potentially powerful Carthage had become, and on his return to Rome, whenever he spoke in the Senate, no matter what the subject was, he always ended with the words 'Carthago delenda est', meaning Carthage must be destroyed.

Around 150 the Carthaginians attacked Masinissa, but they were defeated. Rome declared war. An army was sent out to remove all Carthaginian war material and siege engines. At first the Carthaginians complied, but they realised that they faced annihilation. The Romans decided that the old city of Carthage was to be abandoned, and a new city was to be built, ten miles from the coast. Trade, the lifeblood of Carthage, could not survive under those circumstances. The Carthaginians now had nothing to lose, and went to war in 149. They had to manufacture weapons, since the Romans had seized their war equipment. The story goes that the Carthaginian women donated their long hair to make the torsion springs for the catapults, with which the Carthaginians defended their walls.

One of the officers in the Roman army was Scipio Aemilianus, who was not yet politically important, some years before he achieved fame at Numantia. He was not eligible for any of the higher magistracies, but when he returned to Rome the Scipio family mustered a large following of clients and friends who could influence the Roman populace, who were soon agitating for the election of Aemilianus to the consulship. There was the precedent of Aemilianus' adoptive grandfather, Scipio Africanus, and the added pressure of a war against Carthage that was not going very well. The Carthaginians were fighting for their lives, more effectively than the Romans had anticipated.

As consul, Scipio Aemilianus took command of the army, defeated a Carthaginian force, and besieged the city of Carthage. The Carthaginians were outnumbered and ran out of food, so the fall of the city was a foregone conclusion, but they made the Romans fight for every building and every inch of ground. Anyone who survived after the Roman victory was enslaved, the city was utterly destroyed and the agricultural land was sown with salt. In times past the Romans would have arranged a peace settlement and withdrawn the troops. Those days were over. The territory formerly ruled by Carthage was annexed and named the province of Africa.

Wars in Greece 149–146 BC

Two wars in Greece had started at the same time as the Carthaginian war. The Achaeans who had been taken to Rome in 168 after the battle of Pydna were finally allowed to return home in 151. With the exception of Polybius, their opinion of Rome had deteriorated, and their homecoming inflamed the rest of the Achaeans. About this time, a pretender to the Macedonian throne called Andriscus turned up claiming that he was the son of Perseus. He took over the old kingdom, and managed to defeat a Roman army sent to remove him, but in 148 Andriscus was defeated by the praetor Metellus, and Macedonia became a Roman province.

The Achaean confederacy decided that the Romans would be too preoccupied with other battles to notice if they made war on Sparta. They defeated the Spartans, and took over the whole state. The Romans protested, but the Achaeans ignored them. Finally the consul Lucius Mummius was sent out with two legions. Critolaus, leader of the Achaeans, risked battle and was defeated and killed. Mummius defeated the Aetolians again at Leucopetra in 146. Metellus, the general who had put down the Macedonian revolt, squashed any remaining embers of rebellion in Greece. In order to underline the power of Rome and make an example that would be crystal clear to other cities, Corinth was treated in the same way as Carthage. It was completely destroyed, looted for its art treasures, and the inhabitants enslaved.

Roman Expansion 135–121 BC

From 135 to 132 Roman armies fought in Sicily, where a serious and well organised slave revolt had started, led by Eunous, a Syrian slave who called himself King Antiochus. He set up his capital in the area of Henna. It was estimated that about 70,000 slaves joined the revolt. Some of Eunous' associates took over Agrigentum, and others captured Tauromenium (modern Taormina), Messana and Catania. The Romans under Calpurnius Piso had to recapture the towns one by one, and it took the best part of three years to do it.

The kingdom of Pergamum was bequeathed to Rome by King Attalus III on his death in 133. Taking over the new province was not a simple matter of imposing a Roman administrative system and collecting the taxes. Battles had to be fought against Aristonicus, the illegitimate son of King Eumenes, the predecessor of Attalus. Rallying the people and promising freedom and equality for everyone, Aristonicus defeated the Romans army led by Licinius Crassus, who was killed in the battle, but then Aristonicus was defeated and killed by the consul for 130, Marcus Perperna. During the next four years the kingdom was pacified and organised as the new Roman province of Asia. Some of the original territory ruled by Attalus near the eastern borders was given away to local rulers. These lands were not fertile and would not have yielded a sufficient return to offset the cost of administration. The new province on the shores of the Aegean Sea provided a stepping stone for Rome to monitor events in the east and to expand further if necessary, but above all it was very wealthy, and therefore unfortunately fell victim to greed, as a province where governors and tax collectors could line their pockets, pay all their debts, and still come home as rich men, with the noble exception of Lucius Licinius Lucullus, to whom the provincials erected a statue.

In the 120s the people of Massilia were harassed by the Gallic tribes, principally the Saluvii, and appealed to Rome for military assistance. The campaign was begun by the consul Fulvius Flaccus in 125, and continued under the consul for 124, Gaius Sextius Calvinus, who defeated the Ligurians and took the main Saluvian settlement at Aquae Sextiae (modern Aix-en-Provence), which the Romans fortified and occupied. The route from Italy to the Rhone was now under Roman control, but as usual, when the Romans took over territory, the nearest neighbours felt threatened. The tribes of the Arverni and Allobroges, settled on each side of the Rhone, formed an alliance. The Romans asked them to hand over any Saluvians who had taken refuge with them. The result was war, ending in 121 in defeat of the Allobroges by the proconsul Gnaeus

Domitius Ahenobarbus, and of the Arverni by the consul Fabius Maximus. Throughout the hostilities, the Aedui, settled north of the Arverni, remained pro-Roman. Massilia remained free, but the rest of the territory of southern Gaul from the Alps to the Pyrenees was now under Roman control, converted into the province of Gallia Transalpina. Travel from Italy into Spain was facilitated by the Via Domitiana, named after its builder Domitius Ahenobarbus. A colony of Roman citizens was founded at Narbo Martius, which became the capital of the province under Augustus when its name was changed to Gallia Narbonensis.

Recruitment Problems

The wars of the second century BC stretched manpower resources and revealed some problems. In the previous century during the war with Hannibal, twelve of the Latin cities had reached the point of exhaustion and had been unable to provide any more recruits, but even after the departure of the Carthaginian army, some of the allies found it difficult to reach their quotas of manpower because many of their menfolk had migrated to Rome. The allied cities themselves agitated for the return of their citizens, and on two occasions some of the Latins who had settled in Rome were sent back to their places of origin. Some other men were expelled from Rome because they had fraudulently claimed Roman citizenship, which indicates that citizenship was worth having. Also in 177 the Samnites complained that at least 4,000 families had gone to live in the colony of Fregellae, reducing the number of recruits that the Samnites could furnish.

Although there was no standing army at this period, there was an army in the field somewhere in the Roman world for most of the time, so a sort of professionalism grew out of continued service. Some men made a career out of the army, voluntarily re-enlisting for different campaigns, and thereby accumulating experience that could be handed on. Despite this growth of experience and the numbers of men who were willing to re-enlist, there was a growing reluctance to serve in the wars, especially if there was nothing to be gained except hard work, potential injuries or death, and no booty to bring home. The location of the wars and the reasons for fighting them had a preponderant influence on recruitment. Service in Spain was very unpopular, but recruitment for the third war with Carthage in 149 was easier, indicating that half a century after the second Punic war, ordinary Romans were still inflamed with hatred and the desire for revenge, and not just attracted by portable wealth.

Military service in the foreign wars from 200 onwards was unpopular. On two occasions, in 151 and 138, the call to arms had been resisted, and the tribunes had lent political support to the resistance. The property qualification for army service had already been lowered during the war with Hannibal, and it was probably reduced again in the 120s, though this is not universally accepted. The property qualification had been set in the first place to produce men who were wealthy enough to provide their own military equipment. If poorer men were recruited they had to be equipped at state expense, or occasionally by the general who was raising an army. For the Numantine war Scipio Aemilianus did not raise a new consular army, but instead he enlisted his clients and many volunteers. Polybius hints that some of the soldiers in the legions received their equipment from the state, but their daily pay of three *asses* was docked to recoup the costs. The ancient authors were certain that the army was manned by increasing numbers of poorer men in the second century BC.

At first sight there seems to be some evidence that the Roman population declined in the second half of the second century BC. The census figures progressively dropped from 337,022 citizens in 163 to 318,828 in 130. Then within five years in 125, the number of citizens had increased dramatically from 318,828 to 394,736. As with all statistics, there are problems. Who exactly was registered in the census? Brunt argued that all males from seventeen years old were registered, up to and beyond those aged forty-five. There could have been several reasons why the population declined, such as a falling birth rate, combined with the numbers of casualties in the wars. If soldiers were absent from home it is possible that they did not marry, or if they were already married then they did not produce children because they were serving in the army. This is perfectly feasible, but on the other hand Nathan Rosenstein and Luuk de Ligt have argued that the decline in the census figures was artificial, caused not by a fall in population, but by the fact that some men avoided registration because of a widespread reluctance to serve in the armies, most especially in Spain. It is also possible that rural impoverishment removed many small farmers from the ranks of men who were eligible to serve because they fell below the property qualification. A few questions arise under this heading: were the censors not assiduous enough to find men who might be avoiding registration, and did they leave out the poorest men who were below the property qualification? Did the sudden increase in the census figures in 125 come about because the property qualification was lowered once again, and therefore many more potential recruits registered and were included in the census? These ideas are not impossible but at the same time they are not capable of proof.

The land question was closely bound up with service in the army and the lack of recruits. The majority of the soldiers were drawn from the farms, so if the numbers of farmers declined, so did the availability of recruits. The system worked well enough in the early days when the Romans were fighting their neighbours, raising an army on an annual basis, conducting the campaign and then disbanding the troops so that the soldiers could go home for the harvest. But this system was soon outmoded, even during the wars in Italy. Campaigns continued through the winters and soldiers were retained on active service or in winter quarters. Then the expansion of Rome necessitated foreign wars and even longer continuous periods of service, and also a greater number of men would be levied at one time, especially when the Romans were hard-pressed. The theory goes that for several years, for several reasons, more men were taken from the farms, but the alleged decline of the small farms for these reasons has been disputed. Nathan Rosenstein suggests that it is likely that the levy never included all the eligible manpower, so that there would be some of the younger men as well as older farmers who remained at home and looked after the farms, and there is the contributory factor that women are just as capable as men of carrying out most work on the farm.

The spread of the *latifundia*, the enormous landed estates of the wealthy, has been blamed for rural depopulation. The public land (*ager publicus*) had been won by conquest and was theoretically open to all Roman citizens, and after 338 when the Latin League was dissolved, it was available to the Latins as well. There had been disputes from the earliest times about how the land should be used, whether it should be distributed to the poorer classes, or leased to the wealthier citizens who would pay rent, providing an income for the state. Attempts were made to limit the size of individual holdings to 500 *iugera*, the equivalent of about 14 hectares or 350 acres. The first attempt was in 367 when the Licinio-Sextian laws were passed, and the second attempt occurred at some time between 201 and 167, indicating that landowners had continued to expand their holdings.

The growth of these large estates, combined with other factors such as the enforced absence of the soldiers, the death rate during the various wars, and the devastation caused by Hannibal's long sojourn in Italy, probably did entail the abandonment of *some* farms, whose occupants would migrate to the towns, and most especially to Rome, where the urban mob swelled in proportion to the decline of the rural population. It has been suggested that competition from slave labour and the imports of cheap food reduced the profits of the small farmers, with the result that even those farmers whose lands were still under the plough were forced to give up, and also migrated to Rome and the smaller Italian towns and cities. In the 130s the Senate started to worry about the decline of the small farmers, the numbers of landless men thronging the city of Rome, and the lack of recruits. The senators thought that these factors were causally related, but modern scholars have pointed out that the decline of the small farmers may not have been as serious as once thought, the landless men in Rome were not necessarily displaced farmers but men who could not find lands because there were none to be found, and the lack of recruits may have been due to reluctance to serve in the armies and avoidance of registration for the census.

The Romans were aware that something had to be done. In 133 the tribune Tiberius Sempronius Gracchus tried to find a solution to the redistribution of land. Tiberius was well connected, a member of the plebeian nobility. His father, also called Tiberius Sempronius Gracchus, had been consul twice, and had reached the pinnacle of his career when he was made censor in 169. The younger Tiberius' proposals for reform had allegedly been instigated by his observation of the sorry state of the Italian countryside and the farmers who tried to scratch a living from it, all of which he witnessed while he was on his way to the wars in Spain. There was much in Rome that was in need of reform by the latter half of the second century BC, and some of the problems concerned the Roman army and the allies.

Tiberius' proposals for reform included a law that would redistribute parcels of the public land to the urban poor, reverting to the limit of 500 *iugera* for each landowner. Farmers who were already in occupation of the public land could keep this much land rent-free, and were allowed an extra 250 *iugera* for each child, up to a maximum of four children, which would provide an estate of 1,500 *iugera*, approximately 900 acres. The rest of the public land was to be allocated to landless farmers in small parcels of thirty *iugera* each, which they were not allowed to sell. Modern scholars have questioned whether the thirty *iugera* allocation would provide small farmers with enough profit to reach the relevant property qualification for service in the army, so the only result would have been to reduce the size of the Roman mob without benefiting the army at all. There were other considerations about reallocating the land. Families who possessed nothing to start with would need gifts or loans to be able to set up. Another problem was that not all the urban poor or time-served veterans would make good farmers, so the drift back to Rome would begin again.

Despite these potential shortcomings, the proposed law was supported by the public. Opposition came from men who might lose lands, principally the senators who owned large estates. The tribune Marcus Octavius was persuaded to veto Tiberius' bill. The result was an undignified scuffle when Tiberius had Octavius deposed by force and arranged for a replacement tribune to be elected. The commission of three men to put the land law into effect consisted of Tiberius, his brother Gaius Gracchus, and his father-in-law Appius Claudius. Tiberius then announced that he was going to stand for election as tribune for a second term in 132. In anticipation of Tiberius' future proposals, and aware of his habit of bypassing the Senate by laying everything directly before the people's assemblies, the senators decided to block him. At the elections, while people were still voting, Tiberius was removed as a candidate. None of this adequately conveys the build-up of violent feelings towards him in the Senate. Urged on by Scipio Nasica, the *pontifex maximus*, or chief priest, Tiberius was killed and his supporters were rounded up and executed.

Ten years would elapse before Tiberius' younger brother Gaius followed in his footsteps as tribune for 123, and again in 122. The brothers had listened to the problems of the serving soldiers as well as the small farmers, and the legislation that Gaius enacted illustrates some of the grievances of the army. It was made illegal to recruit soldiers under seventeen, and Gaius put an end to the docking of military pay to cover the cost of clothing and equipment issued by the state. He may also have passed a law to reduce the length of military service, though this is not proven. The legislation reveals the main grievances of the soldiers.

Very little had been done for Rome's allies, save for the laws that gave them some redress against extortion. During his consulship in 125, Gaius' supporter and fellow tribune Fulvius Flaccus had proposed that citizenship should be given to Latins and the Italian allies, or if the allies did not wish to be incorporated into the Roman state, then they should be given the right of appeal against the actions of Roman magistrates, which to some communities was more important than the right to vote in the Roman elections. The Senate circumvented these suggestions by sending Flaccus off to fight against the Saluvii who threatened Massilia, so the scheme had to be abandoned. It seems that Gaius entertained plans for conferring Roman citizenship on all the Latins, and a limited franchise on the Italian allies, perhaps in the form of Latin rights. Such suggestions always provoked opposition. There were more Latins and allies than there were Romans, so senators feared that their own influence would be diluted, and likewise the Roman people did not want the allies to share in their privileges. The Senate persuaded another tribune, Marcus Livius Drusus to propose an alternative to citizenship, namely that Latins serving in the army under Roman officers should be immune from flogging, which highlights what had been going on among the allied troops. None of this came to anything, nor did Gaius Gracchus' proposals for enfranchisement of the allies. He stood for re-election for a third term as tribune, and was murdered. The Italians would not forget that they might have come close to a greater equality with the Romans, and thirty years later they prepared to fight for it.

The Army of Polybius

Anyone who studies the Roman army has to take into account the work of Polybius, most especially his sixth book on the organisation of the army. His work belonged to the middle of the second century BC, and he probably used some written sources to supplement his personal observations. It is suggested that he consulted a manual for military tribunes, and although no such material has survived there are hints that such manuals existed.

Polybius goes into great detail about the method of assembling the army. After the consuls had been elected, 24 military tribunes were appointed, fourteen of them with five years' service and ten of them with ten years' experience. At the time when Polybius was writing, four legions were usually raised, and on the day of assembly, six tribunes were assigned to each legion, with responsibility for choosing the soldiers, four at a time, in a strict rotation system to ensure a fair distribution of men in each legion. Polybius says that there were 4,200 men in a legion, or 5,000 in emergencies, so this process must have taken a very long time. He also says that the place where the men of military age mustered was the Capitol Hill, which modern authors have questioned, on the grounds that the area was too small to accommodate the numbers of men. The assembly of the army was carried out at other times on the Campus Martius.

An important feature of the Roman army was the oath that the soldiers took to obey their officers. This too must have taken a long time to achieve, even though it was abbreviated by selecting one man to repeat the full oath, with the rest of the men coming forward to say that they would do the same, the phrase in Latin being *idem in me*. This procedure survived into the Empire.

After the legions had been assembled it remained to muster the cavalry and the allies. Each legion was accompanied by 300 horsemen, who used to be chosen on the day of assembly, but by Polybius' time they were appointed by the censors on the basis of their property qualification. These would be wealthy young aristocrats. The allied contingents were raised by the magistrates of the cities where they were raised, the numbers having been prearranged by the Roman consuls. The magistrates administered the military oath and appointed a commanding officer and a paymaster, then the allied soldiers were sent to Rome. It is permissible to question whether they all marched to Rome, especially if the war was to be fought near their own areas, which would entail two marches, one there and one back, instead of mustering at a place selected by the consuls that would have been more convenient.

The selection process for the legions was only the first stage. The military tribunes announced the date and location where each legion was to muster without arms, so that the division into 1,200 *hastati*, 1,200 *principes*, 600 *triarii* and a varying number of *velites* could be effected. If the legion was to be enlarged, the first two lines were increased, but the *triarii* remained at 600 men. The *velites* were chosen from the youngest men and also men with the lowest property qualification, so they would not be entirely composed of younger men. They were armed with javelins, a sword and a shield, and wore helmets covered with wolfskin. The *hastati* carried two throwing-spears or *pila*, and wore a short sword (*gladius*) on their right side, called a Spanish sword. Modern historians debate when this first appeared in the Roman army. It may have been adopted during the first Punic war when the Carthaginians employed Spanish troops, and the Romans on the receiving end of their weapons started to adopt the swords. A bronze helmet with plumes, a breastplate, greaves, and the *scutum* completed the panoply of each soldier of the *hastati*. Polybius says that the other two ranks, the *principes* and *triarii*, were armed with the same weapons, except that the *triarii* carried thrusting-spears instead of the *pila*.

The centurions, elected by the soldiers of each legion, appointed their own *optiones*, and then divided up the soldiers into maniples, with two centurions and two *optiones* in command of each one. This was the second stage of assembling the army. Once each man knew which maniple he belonged to and who were his officers, he was told where and when to assemble with his arms and armour, and dismissed. The soldiers' names were listed, so there was no excuse for not turning up on the appointed day. Polybius adds that each of the two consuls were allocated two legions and accompanying allied troops, and the consuls sometimes named two different locations for the assembly of their respective armies.

The 300 cavalry for each legion were divided into ten *turmae*, each commanded by three decurions and three *optiones*. The earlier cavalry, according to Polybius, was equipped with unsuitable weapons and armour, including shields covered in leather which suffered badly in the rain, and lances which were so slender that they shook with the motion of the horse and sometimes broke. But when the Romans adopted Greek-style lances which were much more firm, and Greek-style shields, they overcame these problems. Polybius was proud of the superiority of Greek equipment, but also he admired the adaptability of the Romans.

The allied infantry usually equalled, or sometimes exceeded, the numbers of the Romans, but the allied cavalry were three times the size of the Roman units. The consuls appointed the *praefecti sociorum* to command the infantry, twelve in total, six to each *ala sociorum*. The *praefecti* picked out about a third of the allied cavalry and one-fifth of the infantry to act as *extraordinarii*, who were given special duties and were allocated specific places in the military camp.

The camps were laid out according to a standard plan, so that the legions, the allies and the cavalry would always know where to go when they arrived. Polybius says that he will describe the layout 'as far as this can be done in words', which highlights the need for a plan, but despite his attention to detail, there is still room for some discrepancies in the plans that modern authors have produced, based on his information. The description given here is an abbreviated version; there is no substitute for reading the original.

Polybius describes a camp to accommodate two legions and two allied contingents, each legion comprising possibly 4,000 or 5,000 men, though there are problems with Polybius' figures that are still debated. Two legions commanded by one consul comprised half the army of four legions, the normal number that was raised when Polybius wrote his history. He explains that it was only on rare occasions that the whole army of four legions operated together, but if they did, then the camp that he describes was doubled in area.

The tribunes and some of the centurions surveyed the ground where the camp was to be laid out. They measured the area where the general's tent, or *praetorium*, was to be sited, usually in the best location for viewing the whole camp. The general's tent was flanked by the *quaestorium* on one side and the Forum on the other side, the spaces were measured by the tribunes and marked by means of flags. Polybius says that the *quaestorium* and the Forum could be reduced in area if a large number of allied troops needed accommodation, indicating that the allied contingents were not of a standard size. Facing the *quaestorium*, *praetorium* and Forum were the tribunes' tents, lining the Via Principalis that ran across the camp. This arrangement ensured that the commanding officers were all grouped together. There was also space near the tribunes' tents for their horses, and their baggage and mules.

A road was laid out running at right angles to the Via Principalis, and parallel to it on either side, each of the two legions placed their tents. Each of the legions contained some cavalry, who were accommodated with their horses on either side of the street, flanked by the *triarii*, *principes* and *hastati*. On either side of the legions were the allied troops, with their cavalry and infantry. The tents of the legions and allied troops occupied about two-thirds of the camp. Behind the *praetorium* there were the *extraordinarii* comprising the cavalry and infantry picked out from the allied troops.

Polybius describes earthen ramparts surrounded by an outer ditch. Two lines of the ramparts were dug by the Roman legionaries, and two by the allied troops. The ramparts were laid out 200 feet away from the tents, all round the camp. The space was necessary to allow the soldiers to march in and out of the camp in an orderly fashion. At night the cattle were placed in the wide road, and any plunder that had been captured was stacked there. The width of the road served as additional protection if the camp was attacked, since missiles generally did not have the range to clear the ditch, the ramparts, and the road.

When the camp was finished, the tribunes assembled all the men, soldiers and slaves alike, and made them all take an oath individually that they would not steal anything from the camp. Then the *hastati* and *principes* were assigned to various duties for the tribunes, such as guarding their tents and keeping the area in front clean and free of obstacles, because this was where most daily business was carried out. The *triarii* and *velites* were excused this work, but the *triarii* provided the guards for the cavalry whose tents adjoined theirs, paying special attention to the welfare of the horses.

When the time came to break camp, the tents of the consul and the tribunes were taken down first, then those of the soldiers. A signal was given for the striking of the soldiers' tents, and another to load the baggage on the pack animals. The *extraordinarii* led the column from the camp, followed by one of the wings of the *alae sociorum* and their pack animals, then the Roman legions each with their pack animals, the rear brought up by the other wing of the allies. On alternate days the order was reversed, so the rearguard became the advance guard. This ensured that the same wing and the same legion did not always arrive at the fresh water and foraging ground before the others.

Security of the camp, especially at night, was an important issue. The watchword was set and written down on a wax tablet by the tribune on duty for the night, and collected by one man from the tenth maniple of each of the classes of infantry at sunset. The tablets were passed along all the maniples, finally received by the first maniple, and then delivered to the tribune, who could see from the marks on the tablets if maniples had been missed out, which would mean that the watchword had not been delivered to all the men. There was a maniple on duty every night to guard the consul's tent, other men were chosen by the tribune to guard their tents and those of the cavalry, and the consul chose all the remaining guards. The *velites* guarded the perimeter of the camp, and ten of them formed the gate guards. The Roman cavalrymen attached to the legions were responsible for doing the rounds, with each *turma* taking its turn on successive days to provide four men for the four watches of the night, assigned to each man by the tribune on duty. The cavalryman on each watch usually did his rounds accompanied by a few friends, who could bear witness that the duty had been fulfilled. The beginning of each watch was signalled by a trumpet or horn blown by a soldier from the first maniple of the *triarii*, and it was the duty of the centurion of this maniple to see that it was done. Lapses in doing the rounds were investigated, and the culprits were court-martialled by the tribunes. If the men were found guilty, they were beaten to death by the soldiers, whose lives had been endangered because of the potential lack of security. As Polybius comments, this harsh punishment ensured that the night watches were scrupulously observed.

Polybius lists other offences considered to be crimes which incurred the severe penalties, including stealing from the camp, homosexual activities, or having incurred three successive punishments for lighter offences. There were other transgressions not listed as crimes, such as leaving a post through fear, or throwing away weapons and armour. Soldiers who lost these items in battle made strenuous efforts to recover them, risking death to do so. If an entire unit ran away in battle, the tribunes decimated the unit, by selecting one man in every ten, who were then beaten to death, while the remaining men were put on barley rations and expelled from the camp to remain outside without protection.

The information provided by Polybius is invaluable because no other source includes such attention to detail. However, various commentators have questioned some of this, and warned against projecting it backwards to the third or even the fourth century BC, because the organisation of the army was not immutable over a long time span. Polybius outlines what he saw for himself, or possibly read about in military manuals, or learned from conversation with other people, but his static portrait of the army applies to a single point in time. Nevertheless, it is the most informative source about the Roman army, and used with caution it illustrates better than anything else how the army operated during the middle and later Republic.

A detail from a sculpture depicting Republican legionaries and a cavalryman attending the sacrifice of a bull, a sheep and a pig (*suovetaurilia*), from the so-called Altar of Domitius Ahenobarbus, now known as the Temple of Neptune, and housed in the Louvre, Paris. The soldiers all have helmets with crests, which may be made of horsehair, since they do not look like the feathers that Polybius says the *hastati* wore. The helmets of the two soldiers on the left each have cheek pieces and small neck guards, and the middle soldier appears to have a brow guard. Over their cloth tunics the infantrymen and the cavalryman wear mail armour reaching to their thighs, and with square neck-holes and short sleeves. The oval shields were usually made of two or three layers of wood, and the spine running down the length of the shield was also made of wood nailed to the shield, with a boss in the centre to allow for the handgrip. Redrawn by Susan Veitch after M. C. Bishop.

Two Republican soldiers from the Temple of Neptune, previously known as the Altar of Domitius Ahenobarbus. On the sculpture they accompany a scene showing the taking of a census. The mail armour of the left-hand soldier is shown in more detail, with shoulder guards. Redrawn by Susan Veitch after M. C. Bishop.

A Republican officer, perhaps a tribune, from the Temple of Neptune/Altar of Domitius Ahenobarbus. He is shown on the sculpture between the census officials and the sacrifice of a bull, a sheep and a pig. Tribunes of the Republic were the legionary commanders directly responsible to the consuls, since there was no legionary legate until Imperial times. This officer is distinguishable from the legionaries by his fine armour and equipment, including his cloak (*paludamentum*) the end of which is draped over his left arm. The style of dress and the draping of the cloak survived into the Empire, as shown by the tombstones of some legionary centurions, notably that of Marcus Favonius Facilis at Colchester. Redrawn by Susan Veitch after M. C. Bishop.

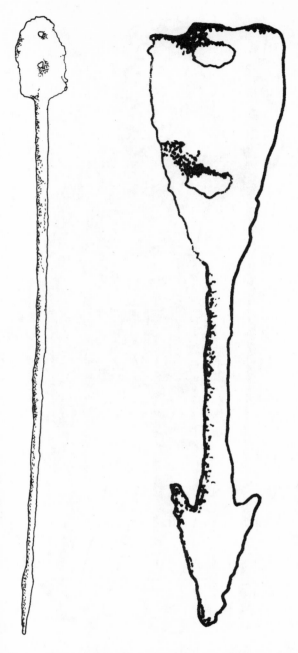

During the Republic the spear known as the *pilum*, embracing various types, was adopted by the army. The long example with elongated spearhead is from Numantia in Spain, and the short barbed version comes from Entremont in France, each showing how they were fitted on to the wooden shaft. Not to scale. Redrawn by Susan Veitch after M. C. Bishop.

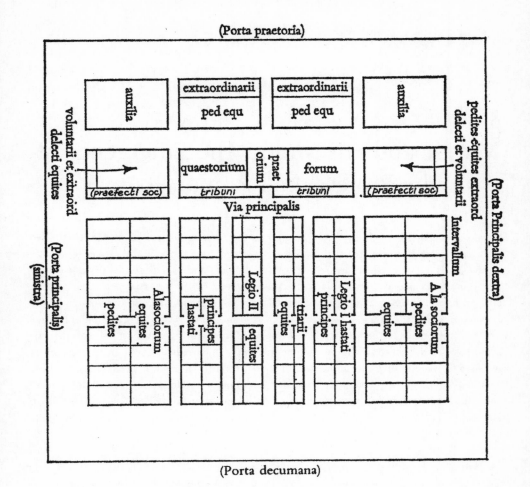

The historian Polybius goes into great detail about how the Romans laid out their camps for a consular army, usually consisting of two legions and the allied contingents. This plan shows a possible reconstruction based on Polybius' description, but there are alternatives. In this plan, the Porta Praetoria is at the top, and the first row of accommodation, in mirror image, contained the *auxilia*, usually hired for the duration of the campaign, and the *extraordinarii* chosen from the infantry and cavalry of the allies (*socii*) for special duties. The central section of the second row contained the officers, facing the main road through the camp, the *via principalis*. The *praetorium* for the consul was placed in the in the middle, flanked by the *quaestorium* and the forum with the tribunes' tents in front. To the left and right the prefects of the allied contingents were accommodated, with more *extraordinarii*. The barracks were for the allied contingents nearest the walls, and the two legions between them. Redrawn by Susan Veitch from Ian Scott-Kilvert *Polybius: The Rise of the Roman Empire*. Penguin, 1979.

8

Marius and His Mules: The Emergence of the Professional Roman Army

Marius' career owed much to the patronage of the Caecilii Metelli, a very distinguished aristocratic family. It was quite usual for aspiring younger men to attach themselves to wealthy patrons at the outset of their careers, for political support and sometimes for finance, just as Julius Caesar was associated with Marcus Licinius Crassus. Marius was a late starter in politics, being primarily a military man. He had served with Scipio Aemilianus at Numantia in Spain, alongside an ally of the Romans, Jugurtha, adoptive grandson of Masinissa of Numidia. The two were to be opponents in the war in Africa some years later. Having served in the army, Marius turned to politics, backed by the Metelli. He was thirty-four years old, well above the normal age, when he was elected to the junior post of quaestor in 123. Marius was elected tribune in 119. In 115 he was one of the praetors in Rome, and then propraetorian governor of Further Spain. When he returned from his province, he married Julia, sister of the elder Gaius Julius Caesar. Marius and Julia became the uncle and aunt of the younger and much more famous Gaius Julius Caesar, born in 100.

The War with Jugurtha 112–105 BC

When the war with Jugurtha broke out in Africa in 112, an opportunity opened up for Marius to display his military talents. Jugurtha was not in the direct bloodline for the succession as king of Numidia, but had been adopted by King Micipsa, the son and successor of Masinissa. Micipsa already had two sons of his own, Hiempsal and Adherbal. When Micipsa died in 118, Jugurtha quickly removed Hiempsal by assassination, but Adherbal escaped from an attack made on him and fled to Rome for help. The Senate decided to split the kingdom into two parts, Jugurtha ruling the western half and Adherbal being given the more fertile eastern half. Despite the warnings of the Romans, Jugurtha captured Adherbal at Cirta (modern Constantine) and had him murdered, in 112. The Romans became more deeply involved because Jugurtha also massacred the Italian businessmen and traders who had settled in Cirta. Two consuls fought against Jugurtha, without result. Eventually Quintus Caecilius Metellus Numidicus was given the command in 109. Marius was made one of his legates, as was Publius Rutilius Rufus, who like Marius had served at Numantia. During the African campaign, if not earlier, Rufus and Marius became mortal enemies.

During the war with Jugurtha, Marius asked permission to return to Rome to stand for the consulship of 107. Metellus let him go, probably convinced that Marius had no hope of election. The consulship of 107 was Marius' first out of a total of seven, an unprecedented number. None of Marius' plebeian ancestors, from Arpinum (modern Arpino), was distinguished in any way, so as the first man in his family to reach the consulship, Marius was a *novus homo*, or a new man, in Rome, looked down on by the aristocracy, whose illustrious forebears had been elected to the consulship for many generations.

Metellus had been successful in two battles against Jugurtha, and he captured some cities, but these actions did little to bring the war to an end. As consul Marius set about persuading the Senate to install him as commander in Africa in place of Metellus.

Marius' New Recruits

When he was confirmed in his command, he began to recruit more soldiers to fill the gaps in the army in Africa. This was not the usual levy to raise new legions, but to augment the troops already in action, and the numbers of men were not prohibitively large. Marius found the men he wanted by asking for volunteers, and departed from tradition by accepting men below the property qualification, the *capite censi*, who did not normally serve in the army, but this was not a complete innovation, since these men below the property qualification had been used before when there were emergencies and a shortage of manpower. In any case the property qualification had been successively lowered, in 212 or 211 during the war with Hannibal, and again in the 120s, though opinion is divided on the exact dates. The property qualification had dropped to the point where the state had to provide the necessary clothing, weapons and equipment, and by Cicero's time there were state-owned factories producing these items. The soldiers had money docked from their salaries to pay for their equipment, so there was hardly any cash left for the men themselves, a situation that Gaius Gracchus had attempted to relieve.

The most dangerous precedent, one for which Marius is eternally blamed, is the likelihood that the poorer classes would be more loyal to their commander than they were to the Senate, and when they were discharged they would be dependent on the commander for rewards and veteran settlement. Such a commander, with troops at his beck and call, would then be in a very powerful position, able to dominate the Senate and the people by sheer force. Within a very few years after Marius' recruitment campaign, this is exactly what happened, but the blame cannot be laid entirely at his door. The lengthening campaigns in foreign countries and the need for continuity of command surely contributed to the growth of loyalty of the soldiers to the commanders whom they served for many years. If the unresponsive Senate had attended to the needs of their returning armies by regularly settling them on the land, the soldiers may have displayed more loyalty to the government, but they were thrown into the arms of their commander, because he was the one person who could arrange for land settlements, reimbursement of some kind, or alternative employment for veterans. If they could not be granted plots of land, the next best thing for discharged soldiers was another war, preferably one which offered some profit other than the meagre soldiers' pay.

Marius took his new recruits to supplement the army in Africa, and resumed the war against Jugurtha. His quaestor in Africa was Lucius Cornelius Sulla, an impoverished aristocrat of few scruples, decisive, clever, ambitious, and ruthless. Though Marius possessed undoubted military talents it was through Sulla's intrigues that the war was finally ended, when he persuaded Jugurtha's father-in-law Bocchus, who was fighting alongside Jugurtha, to hand over the self-made king to the Romans. Bocchus was king of Mauretania, and after his co-operation with the Romans, he was also confirmed as ruler of the part of Numidia which Jugurtha had originally ceded to him in return for his help. There was to be no Roman annexation of Numidia, as long as the borders with the province of Africa were secure.

The Cimbri and Teutones 113–101 BC

While the war with Jugurtha was going on, a much greater danger to Rome was playing out in the north of Italy. Two Germanic tribes which the Romans called the Cimbri and Teutones had started to migrate, and their wanderings disturbed other tribes who fought each other and the Romans as well. Great battles were fought by the Roman armies to try to stop the tribesmen from entering Italy, and in each case the Romans were defeated, losing vast numbers of men. In 105, at Arausio (modern Orange), the two Roman commanders allowed their personal animosity to interfere with the campaign. Quintus Servilius Caepio, a blue-blooded aristocrat who had been consul for the previous year, would not co-operate with Gnaeus Mallius Maximus, a *novus homo* like Marius. It was said that this lack of co-operation and co-ordination led to the defeat of the Roman army. The tribesmen killed probably 80,000 men, the worst disaster since the battle of Cannae. This calamity occurred as Marius was winding up his campaign in Africa, and even though he was not in Rome to stand for the elections, the people chose him as one of the consuls for 104. This was not strictly legal, because it was not the custom to stand for election *in absentia*, and there were laws designed to prevent ex-consuls from taking up office again. In 342 a ten-year gap had been set between consulships, and in 151 a law was passed in an attempt to stop men from holding a second consulship at all. But since there was a dire emergency, the illegality was overlooked or reconciled by some means.

As soon as he could, Marius marched north, to find that the Cimbri and Teutones had passed through southern France and were heading for Spain. This fortuitous event gave him the time he needed to toughen up the army, which was encumbered with civilians and camp followers. Marius chased them all away except for the necessary personnel, as Scipio Aemilianus had done in Spain. Then Marius turned his attention to training. Some of the credit for training is due to Marius' enemy Publius Rutilius Rufus, who deserves more recognition than he has received. Rufus was consul for 105, and after the terrible Roman defeat by the tribesmen at Arausio he had managed to collect the army together and build up morale. He had started to train the soldiers by means of arms drill and a physical fitness regime based on the training programmes of the gladiator schools. According to Sextus Julius Frontinus, the author of *Stratagems*, Marius liked what he saw and adopted the same methods. He continued with the weapons training, and instituted route marches with full equipment.

Marius' Army Reforms

There was no sign of the tribesmen for some considerable time, but since the danger was not yet over, the people elected Marius as consul for 103 and again for 102, so he was allowed time to reform the organisation of the army and develop it into a cohesive and effective fighting force, ready for the return of the Cimbri and Teutones. The need for continuity had been demonstrated before, but the problem had sometimes been solved by extending a consul's command when his office ran out. This was not the method by which Marius' command was prolonged. He was continually elected consul without being present in Rome for the elections, and he held successive consulships without regard to the laws that had been designed to prevent this monopolisation of power.

Marius is credited with reforms of the Roman army that laid the foundations for the legions of the Empire. The most important change in the Roman army occurred at some point between the wars in Spain at the end of the second century BC, and Caesar's wars in Gaul in the 50s. This was the abandonment of the manipular formation in favour of a different one based on the cohort. In the Imperial era, there were ten cohorts in a legion, each containing six centuries of eighty men. The reorganisation is generally attributed to Marius. As mentioned in previous chapters, there were antecedents for the cohort in the Roman armies in Spain. Cornelius Scipio had grouped three maniples together to form a cohort in 206 BC. Cagniart points out that Livy makes a total of seventeen references to the employment of cohorts in Spain between 210 and 195. In the late third and early second centuries, the cohort was ideally suited to combatting guerrillas in the Spanish terrain, but it was not a permanent arrangement and was not yet the basis of army organisation. Just as the term *ala* originally denoted the allied infantry contingents of the Republic, and was eventually applied to the cavalry units of the Imperial period, the term cohort had a long history from the late third century BC to the early first century, so over that long time span it would not necessarily denote exactly the same kind of unit, employed in the same way, with standard numbers of men, until it became the normal subdivision of the legions. The army of Scipio Aemilianus at Numantia in the 130s was still organised in maniples, but he may have grouped some of the maniples into temporary cohorts, as Cornelius Scipio had done. If so, Marius would have seen the cohorts in action, so he was probably not so much a brilliant innovator as a shrewd adaptor. He retained the three-line battle formation of the old-style army, with four cohorts in the first line and three cohorts in each of the second and third lines. Traces of the manipular formations still remained in the Imperial armies, since every two centuries shared a standard or *signum* with a hand (*manus*), palm facing outwards, redolent of the Republican maniple or 'handful' of men, made up of two centuries.

One problem, still unsolved, is that there is as yet no evidence of a cohort commander in any of the legions, from Marius' time to the end of the Roman army, though Cagniart is certain that there must have been an officer in charge of the cohort. The six military tribunes were retained, but there was as yet no single legionary commander like the legates of the Imperial period. In the absence of firm evidence for a cohort commander, modern scholars have to assume that the most important officers in the field, subordinate to the commanding general of the entire army, and the six tribunes of each legion, were the centurions.

It is worth pointing out that no ancient source contains evidence that Marius reformed the tactical organisation of the army, though there is literary evidence for some of the other changes, such as the introduction of the eagle standard, and the change in design of the *pilum*. The change from manipular formation to organisation by cohorts is attributed to Marius largely because it was not the norm before his battles with the Cimbri and Teutones, but it had become the norm by Caesar's day, half a century later. It is not absolutely certain that all the changes that had been accomplished in the army by the mid-first century BC were put into effect by Marius. Even if the reforms were definitely his own ideas, they may not have been put into practice all at the same time, and they may not all belong to the period while the Romans waited for the Cimbri and Teutones to reappear, though clearly the two years of respite would have offered Marius a great opportunity to rethink the organisation and operation of the army, while the soldiers were kept busy with their training and fitness programmes.

Marius is credited with modifications to the *pilum*. Two metal rivets held the head firmly to the shaft, so that when it plunged into an enemy shield, it remained intact and could be reused by the enemy. Marius replaced one of the metal rivets with a wooden one, so that it would break on impact with a shield, then the *pilum* would bend and the shaft would drop down, rendering the shield too unwieldy to use. But Marius was not the first commander to equip his men with *pila* that bent on impact. The long metal shank of the *pila* used in earlier armies often ensured that the shaft would drop down, and the army of Scipio Aemilianus left some examples of bent *pila* behind at Numantia. Marius was an innovator in that he devised a new method of achieving the desired result. G. R. Watson says that it was not entirely successful, and it was Caesar who perfected the *pilum*. In a passage in the first book of his account of the Gallic wars, Caesar describes how the Gauls were greatly encumbered by the Roman *pila* embedded in their shields, because the iron bent and the shaft dropped down. This was achieved by leaving the metal behind the head untempered and soft, so it bent under the weight of the shaft when it embedded itself in a shield.

Since Marius knew he would be fighting a highly mobile army of Cimbric and Teutonic tribesmen, he aimed at a comparable mobility, stripping down his army to bare essentials. It was not a new idea, since Scipio had done the same in Spain and so had Metellus in Africa, and Marius would have observed the effects. He limited the number of wagons, which encumbered the army on the march. Deprived of transport, the soldiers had to carry everything themselves, using a forked stick with a sack dangling from it, containing equipment, entrenching tools, rations for at least three days, and pots and pans for cooking. They called themselves Marius' mules, but mostly in good humour and with a sense of pride, not grievance. Perhaps Marius was more rigorous in eliminating baggage trains than other commanders, since the phrase Scipio's mules, or Metellus' mules has not entered history.

The soldiers shared a strong sense of corporate identity and purpose. The army was gradually becoming a society in its own right, separate from civilians. In the old days Romans from the four tribes would assemble in the city, march out and fight the war, then return home again to resume civilian life with the neighbours. The army was now fighting a long way from Rome for longer periods, and was becoming more professional by dint of prolonged service and experience. Distinctions of wealth and age had ceased to apply in Marius' army, which contained many more of the poorer men who were equipped by the state.

The sense of professionalism and community was enhanced by Marius' new legionary standard, the eagle, carried by the *aquilifer* in the front rank when the legion marched into battle. The eagle was a unifying influence on the semi-professional army. When not in use it rested in a shrine, a religious icon of tremendous importance. If it was lost in battle the legion was disgraced. Before Marius adopted this one potent symbol the legions had carried five animal standards. The eagle had always been one of them, but in addition there were the wolf, the boar, the horse, and the man with a bull's head. These five symbols are reminiscent of the five classes of the early Roman army, but they possibly indicate even earlier origins deriving from a more primitive tribal era.

Marius' Victory 102–101 BC

The Cimbri and Teutones reappeared in Transalpine Gaul in 102, and Marius marched to intercept them before they could attack Italy. He was elected consul for 101 in his absence. Encamped on the River Rhone, Marius dug a canal to the sea to facilitate the delivery of supplies. He made alliances with the Gallic tribes who did not welcome the presence of the Cimbri and Teutones in their lands, and placed Quintus Lutatius Catulus in charge of guarding the passes into Italy through the Alps. When the tribesmen returned intent on an assault on Italy, Marius and his troops were ready, but Marius did not immediately engage in battle. Instead he followed the tribesmen, wishing to choose the right moment to fight, and in the meantime he wanted to accustom his men to the sight and sound of the enemy.

At Aquae Sextiae (modern Aix-en-Provence) he judged the time ripe for battle. Marius camped near the tribesmen but the Romans did not have ready access to water, so a battle would have to be commenced quite soon, or they would have to move. It began accidentally, or at least not in planned fashion, before the camp was completely finished. Some of the army slaves were bringing water from the river when they clashed with a group of tribesmen. The allied troops went to help them, and repulsed the tribesmen, but this skirmish did not decide the issue. Another battle was required. On the next night, Marius sent Marcus Claudius Marcellus with 3,000 men to work their way behind the tribesmen, with instructions to remain hidden until they heard that battle was joined. Marcellus was to use his discretion as to when his troops should emerge. When the main battle began, Marius fought in the front rank, which as Goldsworthy points out was very rare, and reduced the general's chances of directing the battle to virtually nil. In the end the Romans won, and the tribes fled, but some of them got through the passes into Italy, because Catulus' men panicked and could not hold them. The Romans suffered many casualties in this episode. Marius marched to the assistance of Catulus, and with their combined troops he finally stopped the tribesmen at Vercellae in the high summer of 101.

Marius in Rome 100–99 BC

As the hero and saviour of the Roman people Marius was elected consul for a sixth term for 100, but his reputation was tarnished during his term of office. He was not a successful politician, and because he associated with the wrong sort of people he was almost dragged down with them. Initially his associates appeared to be useful and above board, but it all degenerated into chaos and yet more civil strife. The association stretched back to the African campaign, when the volunteers from Rome fought for Marius against Jugurtha. After their service in the army, they required a reward which would prevent them from drifting back to Rome, penniless and potentially troublesome. In 103, the tribune of the plebs, Lucius Appuleius Saturninus, had ushered through the necessary legislation to grant land allotments of 100 *iugera* to the time-served soldiers, though not without a certain amount of fisticuffs to add persuasion. After the successful conclusion of the wars with the Cimbri and Teutones, Marius and his veterans required the same magic formula that Saturninus had put into effect for the veterans of the African campaigns. Since Saturninus was tribune for an additional term in 100 when Marius was consul, and Saturninus' friend Gaius Servilius Glaucia was praetor, it seemed like the perfect partnership that would enable Marius to settle his time-served soldiers on plots of land.

Saturninus' proposals for settlement of the veterans carried much wider implications. The well-worn question of citizenship for the allies was also bound up in his schemes, though not quite as overtly as it had been in the programme suggested by Gaius Gracchus. There had been several armies in the field besides those of Marius in the north of Italy, notably in Greece and Sicily, so Saturninus included them in his scheme, proposing that lands in the countries where they had served should be awarded to the time-served soldiers. Several colonies were to be founded, and land allotments were to be given to Roman citizens in Cisalpine Gaul. The colonies were presumably not limited to Romans, because there was a clause allowing Marius to bestow citizenship on a limited number of settlers, indicating that some of the intended settlers were allies. The people of Rome reacted badly to the extension of citizenship to the allies because it threatened their own superior position, and the senators were in agreement with them. The meetings of the assembly did not go well. Saturninus decided to underline his point by bringing in some of Marius' veterans who had a vested interest in seeing the necessary laws passed. They lined the assembly area to keep out hostile voters, and there were some violent episodes in which the soldiers were naturally the winners. This was bad enough, but apart from the use of physical force to push through his legislation, Saturninus used moral pressure on the senators by forcing them to swear an oath to uphold the laws that he had passed. They were given five days to do this, and they all did so, grudgingly, except for Quintus Metellus, who packed up and left Rome when Saturninus moved to have him exiled.

Marius was in a difficult position. He could no longer control his assistants. The use of his soldiers to enforce the passage of laws was something he had probably not foreseen, and it made him doubtful whether the laws passed in this way could be valid. Eventually Saturninus went too far and Marius was thrown into the arms of the Senate. When Saturninus stood for re-election as tribune for 99, he also tried to obtain the consulship for Glaucia. Marius had to make a decision, either to support his erstwhile colleague, or to try to block him. As consul Marius presided over the elections. He rejected Glaucia as a candidate, so Saturninus proposed a law to overturn this judgement, and meanwhile his followers, not necessarily all soldiers, turned into gangsters, and killed one of the other candidates. In the face of complete disorder the Senate passed the last decree to allow the consuls to look to state security. Marius managed to persuade both Saturninus and Glaucia to surrender to him along with several of their entourage. He promised them that there would be no executions, herded them into the Senate house and locked them up. Unfortunately emotions were running as high as they had been in the days of Tiberius and Gaius Gracchus. Someone had the bright idea of entering the Senate through the roof. The mob that had gathered removed the tiles and climbed in. Saturninus, Glaucia and their friends were beaten to death.

The power of the tribunes was escalating out of control, prompting violent reactions in the city. Tiberius and Gaius Gracchus had used the assemblies to pass their laws, deliberately bypassing and undermining the Senate, but they had not forced the senators to swear oaths to uphold their laws, nor had they brought in armed force to persuade the voters to do as they were told. It was very embarrassing for Marius, who left Rome in the year after his consulship, insisting that he was on a religious quest in the east. His finest hour had passed, and he was never to regain the prestige that he had won as the saviour of Italy and Rome when he defeated the Cimbri and Teutones. Though it was Saturninus and not Marius himself who lined the streets with soldiers on the day of the elections, Marius had unwittingly set the precedent for others to use the army to obtain what they wanted. A couple of decades later, Lucius Cornelius Sulla was to do it on a somewhat grander scale than Marius.

9

The Rise of the Great Generals 100–60 BC

By the second century BC a regular career path had been established for Republican Romans, ideally embracing political offices and military posts in more or less alternating succession. There were junior posts on the political ladder that sons of senators could take up, the most useful being that of quaestor, with mostly financial duties. Sulla made this post the automatic entry qualification for the Senate. The post was usually followed by a stint as aedile with responsibility for keeping the city clean, and putting on lavish shows and games that could ensure votes in the elections for the next rung on the ladder. Young men ambitious for advancement would serve in the army as military tribunes, probably in different armies for a number of years, and thereby gain experience of military affairs. The ultimate aim would be to become praetor, then consul, both of which offices could entail command of armies. Praetors and consuls would then hope to go on to govern a province when their terms of office came to an end.

Not all politicians wished to command armies, which was fortunate because, except in times of severe danger, there would not always have been enough military opportunities for all the men who held office in one year. Some men like Cicero were content with their civilian careers, in Cicero's case as a lawyer, though he was forced out to govern a province when Pompey's new laws stipulated that there should be a gap between magistracies, which for a few years created a shortage of eligible provincial governors. A successful and ambitious politician who sought fame as a general would expect to move on to ever more prestigious military appointments at each stage of his career, and successful generals, popular in Rome because of the prestige and profit that they brought, would be almost guaranteed the highest office in the electoral stakes, give or take the rampant bribery and corruption that had become a feature of Roman life by the first century BC. Governors of provinces where there was an opportunity for military renown engaged in combat with various tribes if the province was not completely subdued, and there were enough foreign wars in the first century BC to satisfy some of the more ardent commanders.

Successful generals were able to attract soldiers eager to join their armies, all the more so if there was a hint of personal enrichment during the course of the wars. Gradually a mutual dependence grew up between commander and soldiers, since no general could achieve anything without his troops, and when it came to the (hopefully) victorious return to Rome, the soldiers often had no chance of any rewards unless their general helped them to wring land settlements out of the Senate. Various attempts to solve the problem of land settlements, for the urban poor and for veteran soldiers, dominated Roman politics and the army in the first century BC. There was no satisfactory solution until Augustus established a pension scheme for veterans in AD 6.

The proper way to assemble an army was by summons from the chief magistrates, with the backing of the Senate, but at the beginning of the first century, private individuals raised armies without asking permission of anyone. Marcus Licinius Crassus said that no one could count himself rich unless he could raise an army, which presumably entailed equipping and supplying it as well, which he did on behalf of Sulla when the latter returned from the war against Mithradates. In the third century BC Publius Cornelius Scipio had shown that a single individual could raise armies of willing soldiers, when he collected troops to carry the war against Hannibal into Africa. Admittedly he had the authority of the Senate behind him, but he was not granted official funds or the means to assemble an army, which he had to undertake on his own initiative. Perhaps more significantly Scipio had also shown that there was a way around the established stages of the political career, and also the careful legislation to exclude unqualified or underage men from military command. These rules were to be broken several times in the first century BC.

Scipio Africanus could be said to be the first of the great generals in terms of leadership and tactical and strategic brilliance. He was also the first to gain commands before he was qualified for them in age or political experience, and for whom the rules had to be bent to accommodate him. Other men such as Aemilius Paullus and Scipio Aemilianus also qualify for the distinction as great generals, but their careers, though brilliant, were relatively short-lived. They were the servants of the Roman people and the Senate, stepping down after their achievements and allowing others to command armies and defend Rome's growing empire. Marius was the first to overstep the mark in his old age, in pursuit of personal power and also bloody revenge, and his career ended disastrously. The first century BC saw another kind of great general, who dominated politics and military affairs for a long time and wielded more personal power and influence than any of the previous generals had achieved. Lucius Cornelius Sulla and Pompey the Great, both quite different in character and in the effect they had on Rome, are the two most significant great generals before the advent of Gaius Julius Caesar.

Sulla was not a great general in the sense that he won splendid victories, or saved the Roman people from destruction as Marius had done, but he persuaded men to follow him and he used the army to obtain what he wanted. Then he used it less overtly to maintain himself in a position of supremacy as Dictator, until he thought his work was done, and then he abdicated. Pompey was a great general in all respects. His soldiers were loyal to him, he did win splendid victories, he was a talented organiser and administrator, and he did not march on Rome as Sulla did.

As Sulla and Pompey pursued their careers, the darker side to the mutual dependency of generals and soldiers emerged. There was an escalating tendency of ambitious generals, from Sulla onwards, to utilise the soldiers to force their wishes on the Senate and people of Rome. After his conquest of Mithradates and the east, Pompey could have kept his soldiers together and forced through his desired legislation, but he chose not to, and almost failed because of the opposition he encountered in the Senate. This intransigence and the political system that supported it gave returning generals little choice except to use armed force, and in the end the Senate was relegated to the background while powerful leaders and their henchmen controlled Roman politics and military affairs, and finally fought two cataclysmic civil wars to decide who was to be the ruler of the Roman world.

The Social War 91–87 BC

The first military conflict of the first century BC was the rebellion of Rome's allies, known as the Social War. The Italian allies tired of waiting for the continually postponed grant of Roman citizenship that had been dangled before them by politicians in Rome. In 91 BC the tribune Marcus Livius Drusus proposed solutions to several problems at once. His programme included distribution of public land to poorer citizens, the foundation of colonies to relieve population pressure, and perhaps the most radical of all, Roman citizenship for the Latins and the Italian allies.

The allies monitored the proceedings in Rome, but since they were accustomed by now to disappointment, they had joined forces, prepared to thrash out their demands by force. The results were as they expected. The consul Lucius Marcius Philippus invalidated Drusus' proposals, and then Drusus himself was assassinated. Thwarted once again, the allies not only mobilised, but set up a separate state of their own, based at Corfinium. One of the prime instigators of the revolt was Quintus Poppaedius Silo, a man of the Marsi, a tribe which was one of Rome's early opponents at the beginning of the Republic. Hence the Social War is sometimes known as the Marsic war.

The rebels renamed the city of Corfinium, calling it Italica, signifying a shared purpose if not total agreement. The new state had a Senate and appointed its own magistrates. Coinage was issued, with their legends in Oscan, the most common language among the Italian allies. More important, the rebels mustered an army of about 100,000 soldiers willing to fight for their rights, and they were all perfectly acquainted with the latest Roman fighting techniques. This federation of several allied cities was a development that the Romans had probably never anticipated, since each ally was individually bound to Rome and was forbidden to join with any other state. Fortunately for the Romans, Poppaedius Silo was unable to achieve complete unity among the Italians. The Latins could not be persuaded to join, nor could the Greek states of southern Italy. There were many other Italian states which kept out of the war. Even within the areas where communities joined the Marsi and the new state, some of the populace remained loyal to Rome.

The war began in 90, and the rebel allies scored some successes. They gained control of Campania, Apulia and Lucania. Some of the Etruscan cities had not yet joined the revolt, so some of the rebels aimed for their territory north of Rome, in the hope that the rest of the Etruscans might join them. Hastily the Romans made political moves to stem the rebellion. A law was passed by Lucius Julius Caesar in 90, offering Roman citizenship to the Latins, and to allied cities such as the Greek states of the south which had not taken part in the fighting. This meant that the Romans could now rely upon the faithful Latins, the Etruscans, the Umbrians and the Greek states of the south. In 89 citizenship was offered to the Italians provided that they applied for it within sixty days, and some communities of Cisalpine Gaul were enfranchised by the consul Gnaeus Pompeius Strabo, the father of Gnaeus Pompeius, later to be called Magnus. Pompeius Strabo also arranged for the Transpadane Gauls, settled on the north side of the River Po, to receive Latin rights. He was able to bring the war to an end in the north by a combination of diplomacy and fighting, and in southern Italy Lucius Cornelius Sulla mopped up the rebels. The war petered out, except for a few troublesome cities which aimed at the higher goal of total autonomy, for instance the city of Nola, which Sulla besieged. Although some hostilities rumbled on for a few years, the fighting was much reduced by 88 because the offer of citizenship proved more tempting than continuing to fight, and the cohesion of the rebels was undermined.

The Roman Army after the Social War

The consequences of the Social War affected the army in that all or most Italians were now Roman citizens and were eligible for service in the legions, which broadened the recruiting base extensively. The allied contingents disappeared, but at the same time so did the wars in Italy against other tribes, since nearly the whole peninsula south of the Alps was under Roman control. With the exception of the struggle with Spartacus and his slave army, wars were now fought outside Italy. The units once provided by the Italian and Latin allies were replaced with contingents raised from foreign allies in the vicinity of the war zone, who served for the duration of the campaign. It was not a sudden innovation, since commanders of the second century had raised considerable numbers of extra troops drawn from the kingdoms or states allied to Rome.

The alliances with kings and leaders of foreign states were not made on the same basis as those with the Italian allies, where contribution of troops, with Roman *praefecti sociorum* in command, was a stipulated term of the treaty. The allied contingents in Roman campaigns outside Italy were usually led by non-Romans, usually high-ranking men, and quite frequently the king of the state concerned. These would be subject to the consul commanding the whole Roman force, but there seems to have been no co-ordinating officer in command of all the allied units, as there had been for the *alae sociorum*. The practice of employing foreign allied contingents under their own commanders continued into the Empire, until the procedure was eclipsed but not eradicated by the gradual establishment of the properly organised permanent auxiliary units.

Sulla, Marius and the Mithradatic War 88–83 BC

The conflict with Mithradates VI Eupator Dionysus that broke out in the 80s had its roots in the previous decade. Mithradates had succeeded as king of Pontus while he was very young, with his mother as de facto ruler, until about 115, when he seized power for himself. His constant ambition, like his ancestors before him, was to create an Empire by extending his territorial boundaries at the expense of his neighbours. Previous kings of Pontus had taken over some of the Greek colonies founded on the Black Sea coast; others had absorbed the few cities of the interior. Immediate neighbours of Pontus were Galatia, Paphlagonia, Bithynia and Cappadocia. Mithradates VI co-operated with his neighbour Nicomedes II of Bithynia in a joint expansion programme, taking over and dividing most of Paphlagonia, but when they took Cappadocia, the strongest of all the neighbours of Pontus, the two kings quarrelled, so Mithradates abandoned his alliance with Nicomedes and arranged a new one with Ariarathus of Cappadocia. This was possibly a scheme developed and encouraged by Gaius Marius, who was present in Asia Minor at the time, and would have liked nothing better than an excuse to go to war against Mithradates. Complications arose when Tigranes of Armenia invaded Cappadocia, and Parthia began to take an interest in her own western borders that faced Rome's eastern ones. The end result of the scheming was that the Romans forced Mithradates to give up most of his empire; it was Lucius Cornelius Sulla who sorted it all out in 92 BC, acting in concert with a representative from Parthia. It would have been impossible to withstand pressure from both Rome and Parthia.

Within a few years, Mithradates was active once again. He chose his moment to strike into Bithynia and Cappadocia when the Romans were fully occupied with the problems of the Social War in Italy. He knew that the Romans would not countenance any threat to these eastern territories, which were wealthy and exploitable and well worth fighting for, so eventually the Romans were bound to challenge him. For the time being, Mithradates was able to exploit the hatred of Rome that united most of the eastern states; he encouraged the massacre of Roman and Italian officials and tax gatherers. Cappadocia and Bithynia were lost, and the murder of Romans and Italians demanded retribution.

Both Sulla and Marius were intent on leading the Roman armies against Mithradates. The command had already been granted to Sulla, but that did not deter Marius. Laws could be passed by the people's assemblies, so he recruited the tribune Sulpicius to put forward a proposal that the command should be wrested from Sulla and bestowed on himself. It was passed by the assembly, but only with the assistance of violent street riots organised by Sulpicius. Marius was still popular because his reputation as a general who had saved Rome was still intact after nearly twenty years, so although he was over seventy years old, he was appointed commander in the war against Mithradates.

The ensuing scenario bordered on comedy. The consul Sulla withdrew to observe the heavens for portents. Technically this meant that all public business should cease, but it merely increased the violence. Sulla was personally caught up in the riots, and hounded through the streets, until he dashed into a nearby house for safety. It was Marius' residence. Marius offered his unexpected guest two choices: Sulla could leave his house and take his chance with the mob, or he could cease to observe the heavens and withdraw his obstruction to the passage of the bill through the assembly.

Sulla agreed with the safest proposal, then left the city and rounded up his old soldiers, pointing out to them that if Marius, the new commander in the east, began to recruit different troops, the opportunities for glory and booty would be given to other soldiers, thus once again highlighting the main motivational force behind volunteering for army service. Theoretically the soldiers ought to have accepted the new commander whose appointment had been made by the Senate, but senatorial authority now counted for less than loyalty to any general who offered the best deal. When Marius' officers arrived to take charge of Sulla's army, they were stoned to death. With six legions, Sulla set out on his infamous march on Rome. This was a momentous step, not only outrageous but sacrilegious, because there were religious taboos attached to crossing the *pomerium* or city boundary at the head of troops. It is to the credit of most of Sulla's officers that they refused to accompany him. Sulla moved so fast that the Marians were unable to defend themselves. Marius sailed to Africa, and the tribune Sulpicius was killed. This was not the use for which Rome's armies were originally designed.

Sulla was concerned to protect himself at home during his absence in the campaign against Mithradates. There was a potential rival in Pompeius Strabo, who still commanded an army. Sulla tried to counter the military threat by recalling Strabo to Rome, but Strabo intrigued with the tribune Caius Herennius, who vetoed the proposal. Sulla despatched his consular colleague Quintus Pompeius Rufus to take over Strabo's army, probably by decree of the Senate, which may have been achieved via coercion. Strabo did not protest or even react strongly when Rufus arrived to take charge of his army, but he had probably already made plans. Rufus must be removed, but Strabo's hands should remain clean. As Rufus left his tent next morning to conduct the sacrifices, he was killed by the soldiers. Strabo went through the motions of extreme shock, horror, and anger, but immediately assumed command of the troops, seemingly unchallenged by either Sulla or the Senate.

The assassination of a consul ought to have been an enormity, but it was overshadowed by even more ghastly events in Rome itself. As soon as Sulla left for the war zone, Marius returned from exile. The consuls for 87 were Caius Cornelius Cinna and Gnaeus Octavius. Trouble was inevitable. Octavius was prepared to uphold Sulla's principles and Cinna was determined to undermine them. Octavius expelled Cinna, but shortly afterwards Cinna returned with Marius himself, and an army. It was said that Pompeius Strabo negotiated with both sides, motivated by self-interest. He waited until he was officially asked to intervene, so that he could act with the sanction of the Senate. This waiting game was something that Pompey developed to a fine art in his later career. But by standing aloof, it was said that Strabo and Pompey had granted Marius, and his colleague Quintus Sertorius, enough time to recruit armies.

By this time there were several armies in the field, and civil war had begun in earnest. Marius attacked Ostia, the port of Rome at the Tiber mouth. His ally Sertorius had also gathered an army, and Cinna marched on Rome. Strabo was eventually summoned, and mobilised first against Sertorius, then came to Rome to help Octavius beat off Cinna, in a dreadful battle outside the Colline Gate. But Rome was still not safe. Marius persuaded a guard on the Janiculum hill to open the gates, and his troops and then Cinna's entered the city. Marius' illustrious career was about to end in disgrace. He had recruited a number of Samnites, still hostile to Rome, and a body of slaves who had been promised freedom, but he allowed these to go on the rampage in the city to eliminate his rivals. The consul Octavius was killed. Marius could not control the slaves and had to have them executed. He entered on his seventh consulship in January 86 with Cinna as colleague, but before he could engage in further bloodbaths, he mercifully died. Lucius Valerius Flaccus replaced Marius as consul and set out to replace Sulla in the eastern command.

A plague broke out after the battles, and Pompeius Strabo died. It was rumoured that he had been struck by lightning. His body was dragged through the streets by the mob, until order was restored by the tribunes. The young Pompey disappeared. Cinna rapidly took over Strabo's army, which was battle hardened and experienced, and a valuable asset as well as potentially dangerous; on both counts it must be brought under the control of Cinna's party before the soldiers could be attracted to someone else's banner with the promise of money and rich rewards. The Roman armies had become a commodity for sale to the highest bidder.

While the struggles began in Rome, Sulla was on his way to the east. He chose to besiege Athens, which had gone over to Mithradates. The city and the port of Piraeus fell in the spring of 86, for the loss of many of Sulla's men. With Athens secured, Sulla marched to central Greece to meet Mithradates, and defeated him in two battles, at Chaeronea and then Orchomenus, but there was a stalemate because Mithradates controlled the Aegean Sea, and Sulla could not challenge him because of lack of ships. His quaestor Lucius Licinius Lucullus set about collecting some vessels. Around this time, the consul Lucius Valerius Flaccus arrived, ostensibly to take the command from Sulla, but he did not succeed and instead chased Mithradates into the Roman province of Asia, using the overland route via Macedonia and Thrace. He won back all these territories from Mithradates. Flaccus was poised to enter the kingdom of Bithynia, but was killed in a mutiny, and command of the army was assumed by Gaius Fulvius Fimbria, who possibly had a covert hand in the murder of his predecessor. Fimbria won a victory over Mithradates in 85 BC but did not press on into Pontus to finish the war. Sulla called a halt because he could not waste too much time in getting back to Rome. He placed his troops in Asia to keep order, and levied huge sums from the cities as redemption for having sided with Mithradates. The cities had been impoverished first by the Roman tax collectors, then by Mithradates, and now had to borrow money, ironically from Roman moneylenders, to pay Sulla.

The Return of Sulla 83–82 BC

The city and the wider Roman world were dominated by Cinna, who held the consulship every year from 86 to 84, with Papirius Carbo as his colleague for the last two years. Cinna had tried and failed to wipe out Sulla by sending armies to fight against him in Greece, but the last troops that were sent out never completed their journey, being battered by storms at sea in which many lost their lives. The survivors returned to Italy in no mood to hear a speech by Cinna about discipline and the interests of the state, so they killed him, and went home. Carbo remained in office as sole consul after the death of his colleague, but his star was waning, while Sulla's star was growing ever brighter. Carbo did not attempt to raise another army to fight Sulla in Greece, but concentrated upon preparing to meet him in Italy. In 83 BC news arrived that Sulla had left Athens and was on his way home.

Pompey had been unsuccessfully prosecuted after his father's death, and after the trial he had disappeared from the historical record for nearly three years. Since he was indelibly dyed with the colours of his father Strabo, he was not a natural ally of the party of Marius and Cinna, so he presumably chose to lie low and wait for better times. Now he quietly made a decision that was to shape the rest of his life. He gathered his friends and started to recruit troops from his estates in Picenum. When he started out he had no idea whether he would be annihilated before Sulla arrived in Italy, or whether Sulla himself might be defeated. Having declared for Sulla so firmly it was doubtful that Pompey would survive whatever regime arose after Sulla was gone. It was a gamble, but Pompey was not alone in taking it. Quintus Caecilius Metellus Pius had escaped the slaughter organised by Marius and Cinna by fleeing to Africa, and Marcus Licinius Crassus had gone to Spain. These two men were both recruiting from among their clients on behalf of Sulla. Pompey was certainly the youngest and the least well connected of the three. He began recruiting at Auximum, with nothing but his own resources with which to pay and equip his troops. There was at first fierce competition from Carbo's recruiting agents, but Pompey was more popular, and within a short time he was also the stronger, with about 6,000 men, or roughly one legion. This modest beginning is perhaps more credible than Plutarch's account, in which it is suggested that Pompey raised three legions all at once. Certainly by the time he finished the campaign his army had grown to three legions, but this might have been a gradual process as his successes were reported and his reputation spread far and wide.

It may have been during his first recruiting drive that Titus Labienus, Aulus Gabinius, Lucius Afranius and Marcus Petreius joined Pompey. These men, all from his home area of Picenum, were probably the first to be offered posts in his army. Labienus became a trusted and capable officer of Caesar's army in Gaul, but returned to Pompey when the civil war broke out in 49. Aulus Gabinius was to be instrumental in gaining for Pompey the eastern command that sealed his reputation as the foremost general of the day. Lucius Afranius was with Pompey until the end. He was defeated by Caesar in Spain during the civil war, but was allowed to join Pompey in Greece, and survived the battle of Pharsalus, but was captured and executed after the battle of Thapsus. Marcus Petreius was already a soldier before the Social War, and may have been one of the officers in Strabo's army.

Before he could join up with Sulla, who was marching north from Brundisium, Pompey had to fight three armies sent by Carbo under three different generals. They had not yet united, so Pompey attacked the nearest one, taking an energetic part in the fighting against the Celtic cavalry that Carbo had hired. The three generals could not agree on what to do next, thus losing the opportunity to converge on Pompey.

Sulla was finally blocked on his march towards Rome by two armies, one at the River Volturnus and the other near the town of Teanum. It was the first time that the Marian troops had encountered Sulla and his experienced soldiers, and they failed to unite to meet him. Having carved his way relatively easily through the army attempting to hold the river line, Sulla moved on to Teanum, where he won by a calculated ruse rather than by bloody fighting. The Marians had seen how easily Sulla defeated the army on the Volturnus, and were not eager to fight. After a short armistice, while his men infiltrated the enemy ranks and spread fear and discontent, Sulla drew up his army in battle order, but the enemy troops came over to him en masse.

Much of Italy was still loyal to the Marian cause, except around Picenum where Pompey was operating. At the earliest opportunity Sulla marched to meet him. Pompey brought up his victorious troops and hailed Sulla very properly as Imperator, an honorary title bestowed on victorious generals by their soldiers, a name that would be absorbed into the titulature of the emperors as part of the infrastructure of their power. It was not a word to be idly used, and it carried wide-ranging connotations, so it meant a great deal when Sulla dismounted, approached Pompey on foot, and returned the compliment by also hailing the young man as Imperator. He would have been fully aware of what he was doing, and once he had uttered the title he could hardly retract it. With Sulla's approval, the faith that his troops already had in the young Pompey could only be enhanced when the soldiers saw how the great general favoured his young protégé. Rome and the Senate had faded away in the glowing fame of Sulla and Pompey

The war in Italy had still to be won. Rome was not prepared to welcome Sulla, and most people acquiesced when Papirius Carbo and the young Marius, son of the dead general, were elected consuls for 82. They declared all those senators who had joined Sulla *hostes*, enemies of the people of Rome, and therefore outlaws, to be denied fire, water, or shelter, and their property was confiscated. It would make people think twice before declaring for Sulla.

The two hostile forces moved in scattered groups around Italy. One of the Marian armies under Carbo faced Sulla's general Metellus Pius in the north of Italy, while another under the young Marius faced Sulla in Latium, in an effort to prevent him from reaching Rome. Pompey had joined Metellus Pius as a subordinate officer, alongside Marcus Licinius Crassus, also serving under Pius. Pompey conducted military operations independently, chasing Carbo's army into Ariminum (modern Rimini), and winning a battle at Sena Gallica. Sometime later, Pompey and Crassus won another victory near the town of Spoletium, and a short time after that, Pompey trapped some of Carbo's troops in a defile and then encircled them on the hill to which they had retreated. It ought to have been an easy victory, but Pompey was perhaps overconfident and did not prime his guards properly. The enemy commander and his men left their camp fires burning while they evaded Pompey's lookouts and escaped. It was the oldest trick in the book.

The civil war between the Marians and Sulla began to spread into the rest of the Roman world. One of the Marian generals, Quintus Sertorius, had decamped to Spain, where he was eventually joined by others of like persuasion. He was an able administrator and a brilliant general, and was able to survive for many years without completely alienating the natives or being defeated by any of the armies sent against him, thus prolonging the war for at least another decade. Nearer to Rome, the civil war began to affect the tribes of Italy. The Samnites, still fierce and intransigent, had refused to disarm after the Social War, and as a consequence their leaders had been executed by Sulla. They marched to the aid of young Marius when Sulla ran him into Praeneste and besieged him there. It ought to have signalled defeat for Sulla, but the approach to Praeneste was through a narrow pass, of which he immediately gained control by placing men on the heights on either side of it. In several battles he prevented the Samnites from approaching the city, and also beat off attempts by Marius to break out.

Carbo decided to attack Metellus in the north, but he abandoned the project when he discovered that the Gauls of northern Italy had joined Metellus. Carbo gave up and fled to Africa, abandoning his soldiers, who carried on fighting until Pompey defeated them near Clusium. The soldiers and civilians of Praeneste now had no hope of any relief from an outside source, so they surrendered. The young Marius committed suicide, and his head was sent to Rome.

There were now two potential wars to be fought outside Italy, one with Sertorius in Spain and another with Carbo in Africa, where many veterans of the Jugurthine war had been settled. Since they had fought under Marius, they would probably join Carbo. But the Samnites were aiming for Rome, and Sulla was forced to race after them. He left Pompey in the north, and took Crassus and his men with him in a desperate march, engaging battle as soon as he arrived outside the city. He placed Crassus in command of the right wing, taking the left for himself, fighting immediately outside the Colline gate. His troops were tired and were steadily overrun. They were forced to take refuge in the city, and the gates were closed in the faces of the Samnites. Sulla had no idea what had happened to Crassus. During the battle it had been impossible to keep in touch with the right wing. Then news arrived that Crassus had driven the enemy off and routed them. He had saved the day, and perhaps Sulla rewarded him with the same praise that he bestowed on Pompey; but he did not give him independent commands or promote him as he promoted Pompey, and there, perhaps, the seeds were sown of the famous rivalry between the two men.

Sulla's Constitution

Sulla was made Dictator and set about strengthening the Senate, giving the senators complete control of the jury courts, which had been detached from them by previous legislation and had been a bone of contention ever since. He passed strict laws about the magistracies, the number of years that should elapse between them, and the age at which they could be held. The number of quaestors was raised to twenty each year, and holders of this post were guaranteed entry to the Senate. There were to be no meteoric rises to the consulship. Candidates must become praetors first, and by dint of the age restrictions and the stipulated number of years between each post, no-one could conceivably become consul until he was in his forties. These laws would ensure that office holders gained relevant experience before taking up their posts. In Sulla's world there were to be no more young generals like Scipio Africanus, or indeed any more like Pompey, who had also been appointed as commander of armies at an age well below the norm.

One of Sulla's most resented measures was his treatment of the tribunes of the plebs. He intended to muzzle them and prevent them from becoming the tools of ambitious politicians. Tribunes were banned from holding any further magistracy, so only the most dedicated men would choose to become tribunes. They were also forbidden to present bills direct to the people's assembly, and had to have them vetted by the Senate. The rules and regulations illustrate what had been going on in politics, but the tribunate was far too useful to politicians to lose it, and after Sulla's death it was restored bit by bit, the final touches being made in 70 by the consuls, Pompey and Marcus Licinius Crassus.

In 81 Sulla relinquished his Dictatorship, but was consul in 80 with Metellus Pius. He died in 78, and Pompey organised a state funeral for him.

The Rise of Pompey the Great

Pompey's career started with his voluntary support of Sulla, and would have foundered if Sulla had not actively promoted him, even offering him his step-daughter Aemilia as his wife. Pompey the Great was an anomaly all his life. He was a wealthy plebeian who never followed the prescribed career of Roman equites or senators, and yet he was appointed to extraordinary commands and achieved some spectacular successes. He never lost a war until he fought against Julius Caesar in 48.

As a protégé of Sulla, Pompey was given the command against the fugitive Marians, who had spread out to Spain, Africa and Sicily. The Sicilian command was Pompey's first task. The provincial governor of Sicily, Perperna, was a known Marian sympathiser, but Pompey had very little to do. His reputation as a successful commander ensured that Perperna fled, turning up later in Spain with the rebel Quintus Sertorius. Pompey's troops discovered the consular Papirius Carbo, and brought him to their young commander in chains. To put an end to the war in Sicily, Pompey executed Carbo, earning for himself, much later, the title of *adulescentulus carnifex*, or the 'boy butcher' from one of his enemies. He settled affairs in Sicily and was appointed to command in Africa against other Marian sympathisers. Here too he brought his campaigns to a swift end, displaying the talents that he would use in later life to great effect against the pirates of the Mediterranean, and against Mithradates. His administrative and organisational skills matched his capacity to lead soldiers, and he gained his first experience of diplomatic procedures in his dealings with the natives of Sicily and Africa.

He also experienced the potential problems faced by other highly successful generals, in that once his usefulness was outlived in one campaign, he needed to obtain another command, but without being too precocious about it. A display of extraordinary talent could lead to jealousies and even prosecution, so when his troops hailed him spontaneously as Imperator, he tactfully refused the title, and let it be known that he had done so. Later, when the troops protested at Sulla's order that he should return to Rome with only one legion, he had to work very hard to convince the men and the outside world that he had no intention of seizing power.

Outward display, not too politically orientated, satisfied him. He added the title Magnus, 'the Great' to his name, and demanded a triumph in Rome, to which Sulla reluctantly agreed, because the triumph was meant to be reserved for senators, and Pompey was still of the equestrian class, not having held any political office and therefore not yet a member of the Senate. When he was refused permission to hold a triumph, Pompey told Sulla that more people worshipped the rising than the setting sun; perhaps not believing his ears, Sulla asked his associates what Pompey had said. When it was explained to him, instead of subjecting everyone to the expected tirade, he simply said 'Let him triumph!' Pompey became the only equestrian to hold a triumph. He was a little disappointed because the elephants that he wished to use to draw his triumphal chariot would not fit through the arches on the route to the Capitol Hill, so he had to make do with horses like other Roman commanders.

When the triumph was all over he needed employment, and certainly did not consider humbly taking up one of the junior magistracies in Rome, working his way up to military commands and provincial governorships like other men. He found his opportunity just after Sulla's death, when Marcus Aemilius Lepidus attempted to take over the state, and the Senate needed an army to put an end to the disturbance. When asked to take action Pompey did so with his customary speed and skill, and then innocently kept his troops together, knowing that in Spain the war against the rebel Sertorius was not going very well, and soon a new commander and more troops would be needed to help Metellus Pius.

In 76 Pompey went to Spain to eradicate the rebel Sertorius. One of the major problems of fighting in Spain concerned supplies, so Pompey aimed to capture the coastal towns to supply his armies by sea. His next concern was to win over the Spanish tribes and towns in order to deprive Sertorius of assistance, thus drawing the Spanish peoples into a war that was nothing to do with them and was hardly likely to benefit them. One of the towns which turned to Pompey and Metellus was Lauron, so Sertorius besieged it. When Pompey came to the rescue, Sertorius positioned himself behind Pompey's troops and neatly trapped him, splitting his forces and holding one part of his army at bay while he massacred the other group. Lauron fell, and Pompey was seen as a commander who could not protect his allies.

In the following year he captured the city of Valencia and defeated the Marian commander Perperna, who had fled from Sicily to join Sertorius. The success was more or less negated by another defeat, because Pompey attacked Sertorius at what he considered to be an opportune moment, without waiting for Metellus to join him with more troops. He got into difficulties, but was saved the next day when Metellus marched up and the Sertorians withdrew. The war descended into one of small scale attacks, and the constant search for supplies while the opposing armies chased each other. In the winter Pompey remained close to Sertorius' camp in the mountains, and Metellus took his troops to Gaul, since dividing the forces reduced the problem of feeding them. Pompey wrote an impassioned letter to the Senate, pointing out that he had used up all his own money in supplying his army, and if he did not receive help soon he might have to withdraw. The consuls for 74 BC were Lucius Licinius Lucullus and Marcus Aurelius Cotta, and another war was about to start in the east against Mithradates, whose predatory designs on Roman territory had begun once again. Lucullus had been appointed to the command and realised that disaster in Spain would threaten the success of his own enterprise, so Pompey got his supplies. The trouble was that the Mediterranean pirates had now allied with Sertorius and this made deliveries to the Spanish ports much more difficult.

The war was dragging on because throughout 74 and 73 Pompey and Metellus did not risk pitched battles, concentrating instead on securing ports, cities and towns and wresting them from the control of Sertorius. War weariness on both sides began to tell on the troops. Sertorius had been fighting specifically against the government of Sulla, who was now dead and much of his draconian politics overturned. Since his troops and the Spanish allies were exhausted, treachery soon raised its head in Sertorius' army. Perperna arranged to have his leader assassinated, and took over the army, which he unwisely committed to a pitched battle against Pompey, who had set a trap. Perperna walked straight into it. Only two Spanish cities still held out and came to an ignominious end, besieged until they starved. Pacification of Spain could begin, though it was to take a long time; Roman generals could still cut their teeth and win or lose reputations against the Spanish tribes. Julius Caesar achieved success in his first independent military command as governor of Further Spain in 61.

On his way home Pompey set up a monument in the Pyrenees, proclaiming that he had conquered 876 cities between the Alps and the borders of Further Spain. No-one got anywhere in the Roman world by being modest. He hastened back to Italy because the slave army of Spartacus was wreaking havoc and unexpectedly defeating Roman generals. By the time Pompey reached Italy, Marcus Licinius Crassus had defeated Spartacus, but Pompey met up with about 5,000 of the survivors and routed them, thus robbing Crassus of the complete victory. Pompey said that Crassus had won battles, but he himself had ended the slave war, cutting it out by the roots.

Though Crassus and Pompey persisted in rivalry all through their lives, they had to work closely with each other for the following year, since they were both elected consuls for 70. At the end of December 71, still only an equestrian, Pompey held his second triumph, and on the next day formally entered the Senate as consul. Not having been in the Senate before, and therefore not knowing much about senatorial procedure, he had asked his literary friend Terentius Varro to write a handbook for him to explain the protocol. As consuls, Pompey and Crassus finally unravelled the Sullan constitution that had placed power firmly in the hands of the aristocrats. They made the final arrangements to restore power to the tribunes of the plebs, but they were not innovators; they merely finished off what other politicians had started since Sulla's death.

From the end of his consulship in 70 until his command against the Mediterranean pirates in

67, little is known of Pompey. He had a family by this time, so perhaps he attended to them and to his estates. He had been married briefly to two women, first as a youth to Antistia, whom he divorced so that he could marry Aemilia, on the recommendation of Sulla. This lady was already pregnant to her first husband and she died in childbirth. Sometime later Pompey married Mucia, who belonged to the clan of the Metelli. Together they produced two sons, Gnaeus and Sextus, and a daughter, Pompeia. It was normal for the Romans to marry into powerful families in order to gain patronage and advancement, and even though his military reputation was established, in the political field he needed support if further commands were to be obtained.

Pompey and the Mediterranean Pirates 66 BC

The pirate menace had enlarged to such proportions that in 67 there was agitation for the appointment of a commander to eradicate them all. Politically, Pompey stayed in the background while his supporters did his work for him, not wishing to seem too eager for the post. When the command was finally arranged through the good offices of the tribune Aulus Gabinius, Pompey was granted wider powers than anyone before him, admittedly only for a specified duration. He was granted 500 ships and twenty-four legates, or twenty-five according to some sources. Some of these are named by two ancient authors, the most reliable being Appian, and other names are provided by Florus, but the two lists do not agree with each other on all counts.

Pompey had obviously devoted some thought to dealing with the pirates. He divided the Mediterranean and the surrounding coastal areas into thirteen regions, and appointed a legate to each region. The remaining eleven or twelve legates are not known by name, and presumably they controlled land forces in the coastal areas, though 'coastal' is not really adequate to describe the extent of Pompey's powers, which included all territory around the Mediterranean up to fifty miles inland. It is speculated that there would be land-based Roman troops, and also perhaps local levies, who would know the terrain and the likely bays and inlets where pirate fleets could hide, and strongholds that the pirates held along the coasts.

Pompey's extraordinary command was not the only one of its type but it was certainly the largest extent of territory controlled by one man until Augustus took over the Roman world. The command was important for another aspect, in that Pompey's legates reported to him and took orders from him, without recourse to the Senate. Some of his legates were not simply junior officers who were eager for promotion, but ex-consuls and praetors who were willing to work to Pompey's instructions. No one else had ever been given such wide-ranging powers over such a vast extent of territory, but the pirate menace had been going on for so long, and previous attempts to round them up had failed, bringing shame and opprobrium on the men who had been defeated, one of whom was Marcus Antonius the elder, father of a son of the same name, better known as Mark Antony. The efforts to eradicate the pirates had hitherto been piecemeal and inadequate, not properly supported by naval resources and manpower. Pompey made sure that he was given enough of everything, including ships and crews and land forces, and authorisation for him to give orders to and overrule the governors of provinces which bordered the Mediterranean. Augustus learned some of his statecraft from Caesar, but there were also valuable precedents in Pompey's career and his extraordinary commands.

The detailed planning paid handsome dividends. When news broke that Pompey had accepted the command, before he had even assembled his forces the price of grain dropped in Rome. Pompey cleared the seas via his legates in a very short time, forty-nine days according to the sources. He had thought about what to do with the defeated pirates, and arranged for land settlements for them so that they could earn a living without resorting to raids on shipping and the coastal areas. The pirate problem was to re-emerge later, and ironically it was his younger son Sextus Pompey who controlled the seas, driven to do so because he had nowhere else to go after Caesar had defeated the Pompeians at Pharsalus, and then rounded up the survivors at Thapsus and Munda.

Pompey and Mithradates 66–62 BC

At the end of the pirate campaign, Pompey's assistants started proceedings to obtain the command against Mithradates, currently in the hands of Licinius Lucullus. More political wrangling began in Rome, culminating in the success of the tribune Gaius Manilius in bestowing the command on Pompey in 66.

The eastern command, another with wide-ranging powers, lasted from 66 to 62, and ultimately encompassed most of the eastern provinces and allies. Pompey was at his peak both as a general and an administrator. The details of the eastern campaigns are not as clear as historians would wish, not least because the chronology is not understood. Pompey took with him writers and philosophers, just as General Bonaparte took scientists and artists with him to Egypt, but the works of Pompey's literary friends only survive in fragments relayed by later authors such as Plutarch, Appian and Cassius Dio, leading to some confusion. There seem to be two reports of events in many cases, for instance Pompey pursued Mithradates twice, received two embassies from him, and laid two ambushes for him, all of which is perfectly possible, but may indicate that some events have been duplicated.

The salient points of the four-year eastern war revolve around the delicate balance of power between the various smaller kingdoms and Rome's relationship with Parthia. Though the war against Mithradates theoretically concerned only the kingdom of Pontus and the territories invaded by the king, in fact the fighting and the diplomatic activity extended much beyond these areas. The political and military control of Armenia was always disputed between Parthia and Rome, but Armenia was more directly involved in this war because its ruler, Tigranes, had married the daughter of Mithradates, who now chose to take refuge with his son-in-law. Lucullus had achieved early successes against them both, but failed to contain the two kings, who soon won back the territories and the influence that they had lost. At this point Pompey took over. Lucullus, greatly embittered, lingered for a while trying to win over his troops, and finally went home.

Pompey immediately came to an arrangement with the Parthians under King Phraates, encouraging them at best to attack Armenia, or at worst to refrain from attacking the Romans while the campaign went ahead against Mithradates. Just as he had done in Spain when fighting Sertorius, Pompey needed to isolate Mithradates and persuade his existing and potential allies that co-operation with Rome was more advantageous. He chased Mithradates back to his own kingdom, avoiding pitched battles. Having failed to capture Mithradates, Pompey turned away from the pursuit into Lesser Armenia, to find supplies for his army, hoping at the same time to lure Mithradates into battle on more favourable ground, but the king was too well-versed in military tactics to engage. At one point Mithradates used the old trick of slipping away at night while leaving the camp fires burning, but Pompey's scouts reported that he had gone, and Pompey managed to get ahead of the enemy troops and ambush them by gaining control of the high ground flanking a narrow pass. Many of Mithradates' soldiers were killed, but the king escaped. This time, though, Armenia was closed to him, and Tigranes even put a price on his head to underline his refusal to take him in and risk war with the Romans. Tigranes was already at war with his own son who had tried to usurp him with Parthian help. Pompey temporarily gave up chasing Mithradates, persuaded the Parthians to withdraw, and turned the squabbles of the Armenian royal house to Roman advantage and profit. He restored the old kingdom within its former limits to the elder Tigranes for an indemnity of 6,000 talents, gave small territories to the younger Tigranes, and dated Roman domination of Syria from this moment when he detached it from Armenian control. As added security, Pompey placed one of his legates, Lucius Afranius, in Armenia, with a watching brief. The next potential war broke out when Phraates extended Parthian control over Armenia's neighbouring territories, attacking Gordyene, but Pompey soon expelled the Parthians and sent Afranius to take over Gordyene.

The states that had been allied to Mithradates attacked Pompey in winter quarters, just before the campaigning season of 65, so he spent some time in restoring peace, principally with King Oroeses of Albania (not to be confused with the modern state of Albania) and Artoces of Iberia. By this time, Pompey's troops were spread over most of the east, operating under his legates. Lucius Afranius was still watching Armenia, Aulus Gabinius was in Mesopotamia, some of the troops were guarding communication and supply routes, and some units were patrolling the coasts in case of renewed pirate activity. Pompey took the troops that were not engaged in these activities on an expedition to the Caspian Sea, but achieved little military success. According to the Greek author and geographer Strabo (who was born around the time when this campaign took place) the region was infested with poisonous snakes, and huge spiders whose bite was eventually fatal, but first made people hysterical, so that they literally died laughing. The Romans, victorious against most of their two-legged opponents, withdrew in the face of adversaries with eight legs.

In 64 Pompey abandoned the pursuit of Mithradates, turning southwards to Syria, Judaea, and Nabataea, where everyone seemed to be fighting everyone else. His legates had already overrun Syria and captured Damascus, and Pompey wasted no time on diplomacy, but annexed Syria, in order to put an end to the attacks of the Arabs and the Jews. From there, he went to Jerusalem, to disentangle the quarrel between Hyrcanus and Aristobulus for the throne of Judaea. He had already met the two contenders in Syria and listened to their claims, but made no judgement, with the result that Aristobulus determined to fight the Romans, and installed himself in Jerusalem where Pompey put him under siege. Though Aristobulus came to Pompey to negotiate, his supporters would not give up, so when the Romans finally won there was a great loss of life. Pompey notoriously entered the inner sanctuary of the temple, probably an act of curiosity rather than deliberate sacrilege, since he respected most other Jewish religious customs. He made Hyrcanus High Priest, not king, in order to lessen the stability of the Judaean state in favour of a strong Roman-controlled Syria.

In the meantime, Mithradates died, and his sons made peace. Pompey was able to concentrate on settling the whole of the east, mostly with reference to the needs of Rome, but also with consideration to the natives. His arrangements were fair and feasible, and some of them lasted throughout the Empire until the late third century. He created the Roman provinces of Pontus, Bithynia, Asia, Cilicia, and Syria, all around the coast of Asia Minor and the southern shore of the Euxine Sea, altering the boundaries of Cilicia and Bithynia to take in related areas and to rationalise their populations. He installed garrisons as appropriate, one in Bithynia and two each in Syria and Cilicia. Pompey's extended eastern command prefigured the government of the Roman Empire in Imperial times. He commanded a large army and a number of subordinate commanders of high rank who were answerable to him and not the Senate, and he controlled a very large area covering several kingdoms which he either allied to Rome as clients, or made into provinces with readjusted boundaries. He installed garrisons at strategic points to watch routes and guard cities. All this could have evolved without Pompey's administrative talents, but in many respects he showed the way it could be done.

Pompey and Caesar 62–59 BC

The greatest general of his day, Pompey returned home in 62 and celebrated a magnificent triumph. He gave games and shows and made arrangements to provide Rome with its first stone theatre, based on the one he had seen at Mytilene. His popularity and prestige were assured, and he was the most eligible bachelor in Rome. While on his way home, he had divorced his wife Mucia by letter. His standing in the Senate, however, was not so high and he had made enemies other than Lucullus. When the time came to ratify all his eastern arrangements and to settle his veterans, he was blocked at every turn. Pompey had supporters who had reached the consulship, Marcus Pupius Piso, consul in 61, and Lucius Afranius, consul the following year, but although they tried to secure the legislation that would have solved the problems of veteran settlement and the administration of the eastern provinces, they had proved ineffective against the intransigent attitude of some of the senators. The tribune Flavius had introduced a land bill aimed at settling the veterans, but that too met with defeat. As the months and then years went by, bringing no results, he realised that he needed an ally who could forge a path through the political maze.

The partnership of Pompey and Caesar began probably in 60 when Caesar returned to Rome from his command in Spain, to stand for the consular elections for 59. Pompey was the senior of the two, six years older, and undeniably a great general who had enriched Rome, and himself, beyond measure. Caesar was not yet a great general, but he intended to become one. His ambition would lead to civil war and assassination. Pompey gets a mention in Shakespeare's *Henry V* but many more people know the name of Caesar, and he lent it to the rulers of Germany and Russia, as Kaiser and Czar.

It is not known whether Pompey approached Caesar, or whether Caesar came up with an offer of assistance, but news of Pompey's difficulties must surely have reached Caesar even in Further Spain, and there is a hint of some collusion before the elections, since Caesar as consul had already worked out in fine detail what his programme was to be, not least for the land bill that he intended to introduce, designed not only to help Pompey settle his veterans, but also to solve several other problems at the same time.

It may have seemed to contemporaries that an alliance between Caesar and Pompey was impossible, because Caesar was unofficially allied to Marcus Licinius Crassus and had allegedly borrowed large sums from him, and Pompey and Crassus had never been on friendly terms. This time, however, they joined forces. Modern historians have labelled the partnership of Caesar, Pompey and Crassus the First Triumvirate, because it is reminiscent of the Second Triumvirate between Octavian, Marcus Aemilius Lepidus and Mark Antony, formed after the assassination of Caesar. This second alliance was official and sanctioned by law, albeit under coercion, but the so-called First Triumvirate was a private coalition limited to the achievement of certain goals. The partnership may not have had an official title, but the people recognised its potential power, and called it the Three-Headed Monster.

Caesar's colleague in the consulship of 59 was Marcus Calpurnius Bibulus, the son-in-law of Marcus Porcius Cato. Bibulus had been elected by dint of large-scale bribery, condoned by the usually upright Cato, who distrusted both Caesar and Pompey. Caesar came to the consulship with a ready-made agenda. The land bill was the most urgent, chiefly for the settlement of Pompey's veterans. He had framed his bill very carefully, to iron out all the problems that had caused other bills to fail. There were to be no compulsory purchases of land, so only the men who wished to sell would be approached. The earlier settlements of Sulla's veterans would not be disrupted, and no one should feel under threat of eviction. Priority was to be given to Pompey's veterans, but there would still be enough allotments to accommodate numbers of landless men, even though the Campanian lands were not to be touched. The price to be paid for lands was to be related to the last census ratings, and the cash for the purchase was already lying in the coffers, thanks to Pompey's eastern conquests. War could be seen to have paid for war, still with tangible profits to the state. Caesar had pre-empted all the potential criticism of his bill, but his enemies spoke against it anyway, especially Cato, who did so at great length. Caesar lost patience and had Cato imprisoned, but many senators said that they preferred to be in prison with Cato than in the Senate with Caesar. So Caesar had Cato released and adjourned the session.

It cannot have taken Caesar and Pompey by surprise that the land bill did not have a smooth passage through the Senate, so presumably when they went on to the next stage it was already planned in advance. There were plenty of Pompey's veterans who could be called upon to demonstrate solidarity in Rome. Caesar took his land bill to the people's assembly, where Pompey made a speech outlining the benefits of the land settlements. When asked by Caesar what he would do if there was violence from the opponents of the bill, Pompey declared that if anyone opposed it with the sword then he would use both sword and shield. On the day when voting on the bill was conducted, Bibulus and his retinue of three tribunes were prevented from approaching the scene by Pompey's soldiers. Bibulus was dowsed in mire, but his friends saved him from becoming a martyr to the cause by dragging him into a temple.

Caesar's land bill became law, and a committee of twenty men was appointed, including Pompey and Crassus, to oversee its operation. All senators had to take an oath to support the law; Cato and some of his die-hard friends held out for a while, but were persuaded by Cicero that there was little to be gained by refusing to take the oath. Bibulus retired to his house, watching the skies for omens. This religious ploy meant that no public business could be conducted while he was engaged in observing the heavens, and it ought to have nullified all Caesar's acts. But Caesar had his destiny in mind as well as his *dignitas*, so he ignored Bibulus' omens. He still had a lot to do, and the year was passing by.

Pompey's eastern settlements were ratified, this time without the tiresome senatorial debates. Caesar turned his attention to the problems of the *publicani*, the private tax gatherers, who had put in a bid for the taxes of the province of Asia, but they had overestimated the profits to be milked, and were now in financial trouble. Caesar pushed through the necessary legislation and told the *publicani* not to do it again. Next, Caesar took up the cause of King Ptolemy Auletes, ruler of Egypt, who was in debt to Roman moneylenders, and was seeking recognition as a friend and ally of the Roman people. Caesar and Pompey pulled the necessary strings, at a price. They both made fortunes out of the arrangement. Egypt was to feature largely in Roman history some years later.

In the spring of 59, the association of the two men was strengthened by marriage ties. Pompey had divorced his wife when he returned from the east, and now he married Julia, Caesar's daughter. The consensus of contemporary and modern opinion is that this marriage was much more than a political expedient, and that Pompey genuinely loved his new wife. The marriage made it clear that the First Man in Rome had thrown in his lot with Caesar.

After his consulship, Caesar required a province, ideally a long-term military command, and since Pompey had sorted out the eastern question for the time being, Caesar had to look to the west or towards the Danube for a suitable location to show that he could be a great general as well as an effective politician. There had already been warning signs of potential trouble in Gaul. The Aedui, one of the more sophisticated tribes, were allied to Rome. Their chief Diviciacus appealed to Rome for help against the raids of another tribe, the Sequani. The war threatened to escalate because the Sequani had called upon the German chief of the Suebi, Ariovistus, and he had gladly given assistance but then he demanded lands from the Sequani to settle some of his tribesmen. The turmoil affected the Helvetii, who had previously migrated to Switzerland from the Rhine and Main region and now wanted to move again. They would probably move through Roman territory. Rome prepared for war. Quintus Caecilius Metellus Celer was to be governor of Transalpine Gaul but he died before he took up his command, so there was a convenient vacancy for Caesar, who obtained his proconsulship of Gaul in two stages. The tribune Vatinius went direct to the people's assembly to propose that Caesar should become governor of Cisalpine Gaul and Illyricum, with three legions, for a fixed term of five years, terminating on 1 March 54 BC. At this stage it was not certain whether he would concentrate on Gaul, or whether he would perhaps be called upon to fight beyond Roman territory in Dacia (modern Romania) where the tribal leader Burebista was growing uncomfortably powerful. The command in Illyricum was conveniently close to Dacia, but was also close enough to Italy to enable him to monitor events in Rome. Unusually, Caesar was to receive the provinces with immediate effect, in the early summer of 59, which meant that he held a military command while still consul, a practice that had been normal in the earlier days of the Republic when the consul commanded two or more legions, but this had changed when Rome began to acquire provinces. The consuls held office for the year and then were assigned to various tasks, not all of which concerned the government of territories, but could concern mundane things like repairing the roads. For a short time in 59, Caesar was consul with all the customary powers, while at the same time he had access to troops, which would give him a slight edge in anything he proposed during the remainder of his office. Caesar's command in Cisalpine Gaul and Illyricum would not allow him to achieve very much in the military sphere, unless he chose to intervene in Dacia. The conquest of the tribal territories of Gaul on the other side of the Alps would offer far more military prestige. It was Pompey who proposed in the Senate that Caesar should be given the province of Transalpine Gaul with one legion. This command was granted, to commence on 1 January 58 for one year, so it would have to be renewed annually.

Transalpine Gaul in its wider sense indicated the whole of Gaul beyond the Alps, but in reality it comprised the old province formed in 121 to protect the Greek colony and port of Massilia (modern Marseilles), and also the land route from Italy to Spain. The capital was at Narbo (modern Narbonne), which gave the province its later name of Gallia Narbonensis. In Caesar's day, the area under Roman control was referred to as the Province, *Provincia*, a name that still survives today as Provence. Beyond the Province, the Romans labelled the rest of the country Gallia Comata, or Long-Haired Gaul. It was to be this area where Caesar would fight his battles.

When Caesar's consulship came to an end, the situation in Rome would change unless he could find some means of protecting his legislation and also some means of influencing political events. Pompey and Caesar presided over a ceremony whereby the patrician Publius Clodius Pulcher was adopted as the son of a plebeian, to enable him to stand for election as tribune. Clodius' task was to prevent Caesar's political enemies from undoing his legislation. Through Clodius' manoeuvres, Cicero was exiled because he had executed without trial the men who had been involved in the so-called conspiracy of Catilina, a move that the rising politician Caesar had warned against. Another potential troublemaker, from Caesar's point of view, was Cato, who was sent to govern the new province of Cyprus.

10

Caesar 58–49 BC

Caesar's Gallic wars are known almost wholly from his own descriptions in his *Commentaries*, which are better known under the title *Gallic War*. The account is admittedly biased, because Caesar's purpose was to impress his Roman audience, but despite this strong personal bias, without Caesar's work there would be very little else to reconstruct the decade-long wars in Gaul. Only a small amount of archaeological evidence has been discovered which can corroborate Caesar's account, and the epigraphic habit was not yet widely established, so there is little supporting evidence to be gleaned from inscriptions. The *Commentaries* may have been written from notes that Caesar kept during his decade in Gaul. He would have collected reports from subordinate officers, who documented briefly what had happened and which soldiers had distinguished themselves in battle and in military operations. Other historians such as Livy tell the stories of heroic individuals in previous wars, but there is an immediacy in Caesar's accounts because even if he had not seen for himself who did what and where, he was present at the battles, and he slots into his accounts several names of officers, centurions and, less frequently, ordinary soldiers, which enlivens the narrative.

Gaul in the First Century BC

Gaul was not a unified country with a central government and a capital city. The several tribal groups who inhabited what is now modern France would identify themselves first as Allobroges, or Aedui, or Senones, and only secondarily as Gauls. Intertribal rivalries engendered restlessness, as native chiefs allied with each other against other tribes, and then, like the tribes of Italy had done, they allied with their former enemies against different neighbours. The shifting alliances meant that territorial boundaries were mobile, and sometimes tribes could be absorbed by larger groups. Nascent states were emerging as Rome extended her influence into the Celtic west, but the concept of a city state like Rome, with a fixed territory and a corporate government that could make treaties, wage war and direct operations, had not yet universally taken root. The state was embodied in the king or chief; alliances were made with another chief, and were considered null and void when either of the chiefs died. The tribesmen viewed their relationship with eminent Romans in the same impermanent way. After the death of the Roman representative that they knew and honoured, they no longer considered themselves bound by the terms that they had arranged with him. There was much for Caesar to exploit in tribal divisions in Gaul.

The Roman Army in the First Century BC

Caesar's legions and additional auxiliary troops represent a transitional stage between the armies of the Roman Republic and the Empire. The legions of the late first century were in existence for longer than usual. Some of them had acquired numbers. Towards the end of his account of the Gallic wars, Caesar noted that the Eleventh legion had served for eight campaigns, but it had not gained the same reputation as the other legions for length of service and courage. The days were long gone when legions were raised for a specific campaign and disbanded when the campaigns ended. As far back as the fourth and third centuries BC, wars could not be broken off at the end of the campaigning season, so some if not all the troops were occasionally assigned to winter quarters until the new campaigning season began. The legions of Caesar's day, especially those he commanded in Gaul, served continuously for many years. From the third century onwards, soldiers had been able to make a career out of army service by enlisting for successive campaigns in different legions, but now some soldiers could serve for most of their careers in one legion. Some legions were kept in existence for so long that instead of discharging the veterans all at once and disbanding the whole legion, time-served men could be discharged on a periodic basis, and new recruits brought in to replace them, or to make up the losses incurred in battle, or as a result of accidents and disease. There was as yet no standing army, but the legions of the Gallic wars and the ensuing civil wars came very close to the permanent force that was finally established by Augustus and developed by his successors. Perhaps this long service was one of the reasons why Caesar doubled army pay to 225 *denarii* per annum. Although a pay rise would bind the troops to him personally, it was not simply applied to those who had served him in Gaul on the civil wars, since there were armies in other provinces as well. No one thought of raising army pay again until the late first century AD, when Domitian increased military pay to 300 *denarii* per year.

In the late Republic there were no legionary legates in command of one legion. This was the pattern adopted during the early years of the Empire, but command of a legion in Caesar's day was the responsibility of the six tribunes assigned to it, acting in pairs for a specified term, usually one month, and then replaced by a succeeding pair. The tribunes served for a number of years and therefore gained valuable military experience.

Legates did exist in Caesar's army, but they were not in command of a legion, or any permanent body of troops. They were usually given special tasks for short terms, which could include temporary command of more than one legion, or groups of mixed troops. Caesar employed his most senior officer Titus Labienus as one of his legates, to hold bases or mount special expeditions. Publius Crassus and Mark Antony were also designated as legates for similar purposes. These commands did not result in a permanent command over the same body of troops that they had led while performing their appointed tasks.

The manipular formation, along with the light armed *velites* and the 300 cavalry assigned to the legions, had disappeared by Caesar's time. The legions were now divided into ten cohorts each numbering about 480 men, comprising six centuries with a complement of eighty men, each commanded by a centurion and his second, the *optio*. The six centurions in each cohort were ranked in seniority with titles that reflected the organisation of the manipular legions. In descending order they were *pilus prior, pilus posterior, princeps prior, princeps posterior, hastatus prior, hastatus posterior*. As mentioned in the chapter on Marius, at no time in the history of the legions is there any evidence of a cohort commander, but it has been suggested that the *pilus prior*, the most senior centurion in each cohort, may have commanded not only his own century of eighty men, but also the cohort. The chief centurion of a legion was the *primus pilus*, literally meaning first spear. He and senior centurions, called the *primi ordines*, attended Caesar's councils and planning meetings, along with the tribunes and the various special legates.

Legionaries were now equipped by the state, and were paid salaries minus the cost of the equipment, weapons, armour, and food. In the early Republic soldiers had to feed themselves, but now there was a supply system organised by the commanding officer. Body armour could vary, but for the most part legionaries wore a mail coat, like those depicted on the Altar of Domitius Ahenobarbus, now renamed the Temple of Neptune, dating to the first century BC. The sculpture is now in the Louvre in Paris. The soldiers were protected by the *scutum*, and wore helmets made of bronze or iron, probably with cheek pieces, and plumes fixed in a slot at the top. The weapons were the *pilum*, and the short sword or *gladius*.

Enfranchised Italians now served in the Roman legions, so the Romans recruited allied troops from the city states or tribesmen near the theatres of war. These additional non-Roman troops were commanded by their own officers, often their chiefs or kings. They were armed in their national styles and fought according to their own customs. Roman commanders would have to be aware of their methods in order to employ them in the most useful way. Their numbers were not standardised. Non-citizen troops such as these were classified under the heading of *auxilia*, and Caesar uses this description in his *Commentaries* for the native troops in his army. These were not yet the auxiliary cohorts and *alae* of the standing armies of the Empire. These later auxiliary troops were commanded by Roman officers and not native leaders, served for twenty-five years and not just a specific campaign, and were of a standard size with approximately 500 or 1,000 men.

There was an increased need for cavalry after the Italian allies were converted into citizens, and after the 300 cavalry assigned to each legion had disappeared. The Romans had always recognised talent when they saw it and had made use of specialists such as the Numidian horsemen. Caesar employed Numidians and also Spanish, Gallic and German cavalry, commanded by their own leaders. Some of the German horsemen were accompanied by footsoldiers who ran alongside the horses, holding on to their manes. These units were flexible and could be used for different purposes.

There was one other element that made Caesar's army effective, namely Caesar himself. He was a natural psychologist who knew how to get the best out of his men. Loyalty to a commander had blossomed in late Republican armies, but Caesar took it to new heights. He recognised courage and merit and rewarded his men, and he punished transgressions to encourage discipline. Soldiers enlisted for a variety of reasons, for personal profit or to escape from problems at home, but now there was also a growing element of pride in belonging to the army, which was becoming more and more divorced from civilian society. The men belonged to a tent group or *contubernium* of eight men, who would usually form a very strong bond. They were part of a century of eighty men, belonging to a cohort of six centuries, and above all they belonged to a legion with its eagle standard and its traditions and battle honours. This sort of esprit de corps could not grow and flourish in the less permanent Republican armies. A charismatic leader like Caesar could foster this unifying force and use it to great advantage.

In Caesar's account of the Gallic war, the Roman army emerges as a living entity. The practical operations of the army are described in detail. Caesar pays great attention to securing the food supply, storing the supplies and guarding them. There are constant references to baggage trains, realistically called *impedimenta*, without which no army can function. Caesar's narrative makes it clear that his legions were sometimes under strength, for instance in his fifth book he says that two legions and their accompanying cavalry numbered 7,000 men.

For the first time in the history of the army, several names and personalities are known from Caesar's narrative. Livy always notes the names of the consuls and some notable officers, but Caesar's account brings the army to life. Caesar knew the names of many if not all of his officers, including the centurions. In at least one instance, when Caesar had to rush to the front ranks and rally the troops, he called to the centurions by name. Individual exploits are recorded, including in one case the number of missiles that had struck a man's shield. These are very important features, valued by the men, who would perform all the better for being noticed as people and not just faceless individuals. Promotions could be earned on the battlefield, public honours could be achieved, and more important cash rewards could be earned. On one occasion Caesar gave 200 *sestertii* to the soldiers, and 2,000 to the centurions, which on his own admission served as compensation for the lack of booty. Caesar knew the priorities of his men, and came up with the goods to keep them loyal. The legions were now the tools of their commanders, not the Roman Senate.

The Migration of the Helvetii 58 BC

The Helvetii had comparatively recently settled in what is now modern Switzerland to escape from the Germanic tribes across the Rhine, but now felt threatened when the Suebian Ariovistus arrived with his tribesmen to help the Sequani. Since they would be surrounded by the Germanic tribes, the Helvetii planned to move westwards to the territory of the Santones (modern Saintonge). Caesar interpreted the movement of the Helvetii as a potentially hostile act, in order to create a war for himself. The Helvetii had once defeated Roman armies, and had a reputation as a fierce and warlike enemy.

Caesar dashed northwards in March 58 to organise defence from Geneva. The Helvetii had built a bridge across the Rhône. Caesar destroyed it and then erected a fortified barrier for sixteen miles along the river valley to prevent the passage of the tribes. The effect was to turn the Helvetii to a different and more difficult route, this time through the territory of the Sequani. Caesar declared that this was just as much a threat to Roman territory, but with only three legions he could not hope to stop the migration, so he hurried back to Cisalpine Gaul to recruit two more legions, leaving Titus Labienus in command on the Rhône. Strictly, the recruits ought to have been Roman citizens, but Caesar was never one for rules and regulations when speed and expediency were required. The army was becoming less Roman, in the sense that many of its soldiers had never seen the city of Rome and probably never would.

The Helvetii passed through the lands of the Aedui and Allobroges, causing damage, foraging for food, perhaps even pillaging. The afflicted tribes appealed to Caesar for protection, which justified his actions. In his *Commentaries*, Caesar carefully set out the reasons for this war. His allies among the Gauls were not united in their support. The Aedui were split into two opposing groups, one led by Diviciacus, who appealed to Caesar, and the other led by Dumnorix, the brother of Diviciacus, who had set his hopes on an agreement with the Helvetii. Caesar followed the Helvetii to the River Saone, where he held a meeting with their leaders, but with no result. The whole tribe pressed on. Difficulties beset the Roman pursuit. The Aeduan horsemen attached to the Roman army were attacked, and fled. The food supplies were deliberately disrupted; the culprit was Dumnorix. Caesar placed him under guard. In order to secure supplies, Caesar diverted his march and aimed for Bibracte (Mount Beuvray), the capital of the Aedui, but the Helvetii construed the manoeuvre as a retreat, so they followed and attacked. In the ensuing battle, the whole tribe was present, with the women and children and the baggage drawn up behind the warriors, potentially blocking their route if they needed to withdraw. Caesar was probably outnumbered, and as the battle progressed he also had to deal with a flank attack by the Celtic Boii and Tulingi, which nearly stopped the Roman advance, especially when the Helvetii took advantage of the panic and surged forwards again. The fighting lasted until nightfall. In the end the Helvetii were broken and repulsed, and survivors fled towards the territory of the Lingones. Caesar let it be known that he would make war on any tribes who offered assistance to the scattered tribesmen. Ultimately the remnants of the Helvetii were sent back home, where they rebuilt their houses, and agreed to keep the Germanic tribes beyond them at bay.

Caesar had won his first battle in Gaul. Within months of assembling an army he had welded his troops together, inspired them with confidence and led them to victory over an enemy. The report that Caesar sent to Rome would not be a modest little note.

Ariovistus and the Suebi 58 BC

The next stage of Caesar's Gallic war centred on Ariovistus and the Suebi, brought into Gaul by the Sequani in their feud with the Aedui. The Romans intervened to protect their Aeduan allies, threatened by a further influx of Suebi. Neither the Sequani who had started it all, nor the Aedui, could stop them. For the Romans there was a slight problem. Caesar himself had been instrumental in proclaiming Ariovistus a friend and ally of the Roman people only the year before. Diplomatic wrangling preceded the fighting, so that Caesar could be seen to have pursued all possible channels to find a peaceful solution to the problem. He asked politely if Ariovistus could restrict his followers to the agreed boundaries, which met with refusal, but Caesar would probably have been quite irritated if Ariovistus had meekly withdrawn, because then another excuse would have to be found for fighting him.

Preparing for confrontation, Caesar moved to the capital of the Sequani at Vesontio (modern Besançon) to prevent Ariovistus from occupying it. At this point the Roman troops began to lose heart, because the reputation of the Suebi was fearsome. It was time to make a stirring speech and a grand gesture, something for which Caesar was particularly talented. He reminded the soldiers that the Cimbri and Teutones had once been defeated by the Romans, perhaps implying that he had absorbed some special prowess from his uncle Marius. He said that if the troops were afraid then he would face the enemy alone with the Tenth legion which he trusted with his life. The Tenth legion would now follow him into Hades, and the others would follow him to prove that they were not afraid. Six days later the Roman army was drawn up within a day's march of Ariovistus' camp. Caesar and Ariovistus arranged a meeting, and the speeches as reported in Caesar's account serve as a useful exposition of the plot, each opposing viewpoint neatly condensed for Roman audiences. Caesar's main point was that although most of Gaul was technically free, Rome's interests in the whole country were paramount, therefore infiltration or conquest by another power could not be condoned. In a nutshell what Caesar really meant was that if anyone was going to conquer Gaul it would be him, not a Germanic chief from across the Rhine.

Ariovistus declared his intentions by imprisoning Caesar's envoys, then he took up a position to the rear of Caesar's camp, threatening the Roman supply lines and communications. To protect these lines Caesar built a smaller camp a short distance from the first. He offered battle fruitlessly for five days. There was a skirmish outside the smaller Roman camp on the sixth day, and on the following day the real battle commenced, progressing so rapidly that the two sides closed before the Romans could throw their spears. They drew their swords and went straight in. Caesar stationed himself opposite Ariovistus' left wing, which he thought was the weakest point. On his own left wing he owed his eventual success to the prompt action of Publius Licinius Crassus, who brought troops up when the wing began to falter. Caesar made special mention of it in his *Commentaries*. Ariovistus' forces were scattered, and the Suebi decided against crossing the Rhine into Gaul.

It had been a highly satisfactory first campaign. Caesar called a halt, placing the troops in winter quarters under the command of Titus Labienus, while he himself went to Cisalpine Gaul to attend to the civil government of the province. From his headquarters he communicated with his agents in Rome, never entirely out of touch with political developments there. Clodius was ruling the roost in Rome, and had become a liability. Before cannons had been invented, Clodius was the first loose one. He had turned against Pompey, and had tried to have all the acts of Caesar's consulship declared illegal because they had all been put into effect when Bibulus was watching the heavens. Clodius was a law unto himself, and his actions ultimately benefited neither him nor anyone else. Without becoming too personally involved, Pompey organised a rival street gang to curb Clodius and his friends.

The Confederation of the Belgae 57 BC

The presence of the Romans in Gaul unnerved the tribes of the interior. Titus Labienus had agents with receptive antennae, who gathered information that the various groups of the Belgae of north-western Gaul had joined forces. Caesar began to move in spring with two new legions, the Thirteenth and Fourteenth, raised in Cisalpine Gaul. Diviciacus and his Aeduan cavalry and infantry were also at Caesar's disposal, so he sent them to harass the Bellovaci to prevent them from joining the main group of the Belgae. Caesar made for the territory of the Remi, around modern Rheims and Châlons. The Remi submitted instantly, throwing in their lot with the Romans and handing over the hostages that Caesar demanded. In return the Romans beat off a Belgic attack on one of the settlements of the Remi. Operations shifted to the River Aisne. Somewhere along its course Caesar fortified a bridge and crossed to the northern bank where he built a camp. The Belgae soon followed, selecting a site to the north of the Roman troops, where they made their own camp. They tried to circle round and come up behind Caesar by crossing the river some distance away and doubling back, but Caesar defeated them with a cavalry attack. The Romans had attended to logistics and had secured their supply lines, so it was now a question of waiting until the tribesmen ran out of food and moved to better foraging grounds. When they moved away, Caesar waited until he was certain that it was not just a ruse, then he followed, sending the cavalry to harass the tribesmen while he occupied the native towns of the Suessiones and Bellovaci.

At the River Sambre he faced some of the tribes of the Belgic federation, the Nervii, the Viromandui and the Atrebates. Caesar was badly prepared. The tribesmen chose their moment well and attacked while the legionaries of the vanguard were setting up camp near the river, and the rest of the army was still on the march. There was only a cavalry screen protecting the builders of the camp instead of the larger forces that Caesar normally posted to serve this function, and the horsemen were quickly dispersed. Fortunately the legionaries were disciplined enough not to waste time trying to form up with their proper units, and simply downed their digging tools, armed themselves and gathered round the nearest standard. They held firm against the onslaught. The Viromandui and the Atrebates were forced back across the river where there was a separate battle, but on Caesar's right, the Nervii began to push the Romans back and threatened to come round behind them. Caesar was now fighting not only for his reputation but also his life. He rose to the challenge with panache, borrowing a shield and pushing his way to the front, calling to the centurions by name, then sounding the charge. His career might have ended on this glorious note had it not been for the simultaneous arrival of three legions, the Tenth under Labienus who had disengaged from the battle on the other side of the river, and the two recently recruited legions who were last in the line of march. Labienus managed to trap the Nervii between the Tenth and the two less experienced legions. Only a few of the Nervii survived the battle. The tribesmen came to terms, which were lenient enough. They were allowed to keep their lands, and other tribes were warned not to attack them. Caesar was merciful, but it cost him very little, because the Nervii were reduced to a few warriors with the women, children and old men. These remnants, however, were to give a good account of themselves in the winter of 54.

Caesar's report to the Senate was well received, and even his enemies had to admit that it was a momentous achievement to extend Roman arms into uncharted territory. Trading interests would soon follow where the army led. The Romans did not think in humanitarian terms about the annihilation of their enemies.

The political climate in Rome had changed subtly. The wilder activities of Clodius had been subdued, and Pompey had brought about the recall of Cicero from exile in 57. Both Cicero and Pompey spoke in favour of Caesar in the Senate, voting him an extraordinary fifteen days of thanksgiving for his victories. Pompey had merited only ten days for his eastern campaigns.

The Extension of Caesar's Command 55 BC

Caesar spent the autumn in Illyricum, which he had hitherto neglected. He required an extension to his command because his campaigns were nowhere near a satisfactory conclusion, and Pompey was building up another power base by means of an extraordinary command to regulate the corn supply, which Clodius had put under strain by instituting a free corn dole to the urban poor. Who but Pompey could be entrusted with such a momentous task? He was given powers for five years and a staff of fifteen legates to assist him. There was a possibility that he might soon eclipse Caesar, because he was dealing with matters of immediate interest, while Caesar was far away and dealing with problems that did not affect the populace at first hand. He had considerable influence through his agents, one of whom was the wealthy, loyal and influential Cornelius Balbus, originally from Spain, but given Roman citizenship when he was part of Pompey's circle. Caesar could ensure that some of his adherents were elected to appropriate magistracies, but if his influence weakened his enemies could destroy his political achievements. Already at the end of 57 the tribune Publius Rutilius Rufus had begun to dismantle Caesar's agrarian law, and worse still Lucius Domitius Ahenobarbus was intent on removing him from his Gallic command.

On a tour of inspection of his provinces he came to Ravenna in the spring of 56, and met up with Crassus and Pompey at Luca. Though the meeting is known as 'the conference at Luca', it is not certain if all three men met at the same table at the same time, but however it was arranged the three men confidently carved up the Roman world between them. Pompey and Crassus were to be consuls for 55; bribery, corruption and the presence of many of Caesar's soldiers in Rome at the time of the elections made this proposal a certainty. Caesar's command was to be confirmed and extended, and Pompey and Crassus were to obtain similar proconsular commands. All the commands were to be for five years, with definite terminal dates, before which all discussion was forbidden. For Pompey and Crassus the crucial date was 1 March 50, but the lack of certainty about the exact terminal date of Caesar's command makes it impossible to unravel the political position that he occupied in 50 and 49, as the Romans approached civil war. For the moment, Caesar's command in Illyricum, Cisalpine and Transalpine Gaul was assured for the next five years. His plans were ambitious, including an invasion of Britain.

The Veneti 55 BC

The coastal tribes of north-west Gaul anticipated that any invasion of Britain would involve Roman control of their territory. Initially the Veneti became friends of the Romans, but their resistance stiffened during the winter, and when Crassus sent envoys to negotiate for supplies of grain for the army, the Veneti detained them. Caesar declared war. Since this war would be fought at sea as well as on land, he ordered the building of warships on the Loire, and gave the naval command to Decimus Brutus, while he himself attended to the land battles.

The fleet could make little progress against experienced seamen like the Veneti, who were familiar with the ports and inlets and understood the vagaries of the tides and the weather. They possessed ships strong enough to withstand the frequent rough seas, and they were in less danger of going aground at low tide. Decimus Brutus achieved nothing until he adopted grappling hooks on long poles, with which he brought down the yardarms and sails of the enemy ships. After being disabled in this way, the Veneti tried to sail further out to sea, but they were suddenly becalmed, and their ships were taken one by one. Caesar was able to secure the whole coastal area. He executed the leading men of the Veneti because they had imprisoned his envoys, and he enslaved everyone else. It remained to mop up resistance from smaller coastal tribes nearer to the Rhine, but the tribesmen went into hiding in the forests. Caesar did not waste any more time because a winter campaign in forested country would be foolhardy and profitless. He could begin again next spring.

The Rhine Bridge 55 BC

The movements of the Suebi displaced other tribes on the Rhine, among them the Usipetes and Tencteri, who crossed the river in the winter in search of new lands. They sent representatives to Caesar to explain that circumstances had forced them to leave their homes, and that they wanted to settle in Gaul. The tribesmen stalled for time, while Caesar pressed on closer and closer, professing to agree to their proposals. He camped a short distance from the tribesmen, promising to receive their envoys next day. Until this meeting was over there was supposed to be a truce, but some German cavalry attacked Caesar's Gallic cavalry. Caesar's next action was treacherous, but coldly expedient. The tribal leaders came to his camp as arranged. He took them all prisoner and then mounted a surprise attack on the Germans in their camp. It was a massacre, continuing all the way to the Rhine as the Romans chased the tribesmen and their women and children. Anyone not killed by the army was drowned.

The point had been made that Caesar would not tolerate the infiltration of German tribes into Gaul, but he followed it up with a celebrated demonstration of strength and Roman ingenuity by building a bridge to carry his army across the Rhine. The plentiful forests provided the timber and the army completed the task in ten days. His description of the bridge and how it was built does not clarify all the details, with the result that more than one reconstruction is possible. The Romans crossed into German territory and the tribes prepared for war, but Caesar was interested only in making a display of Roman prowess. He returned to Gaul after only a few days, and destroyed the bridge to prevent the Germans from using it. But they now knew that Caesar could invade across the Rhine whenever he wished.

The Expeditions to Britain 55 and 54 BC

Winter was approaching, so the projected invasion of Britain would have to be reduced to a quick reconnaissance of the southern parts of the country. There had been considerable contact between Britain and Gaul, and there was a flourishing cross-Channel trade which enabled the

British tribes to import Roman goods. Caesar alleged that the Britons had sent help to the Gauls and provided refuge for them when they fled. This was the official reason for the landing in Britain. Another reason was the quest for military glory.

Caesar sent Gaius Volusenus to reconnoitre the British coast to find suitable landing places. Commius, chief of the Atrebates of Gaul, was despatched to Britain (where there was a branch of the Atrebates) to encourage the tribes to submit to Caesar. The Roman invasion fleet was small, comprising the ships that were built for the war against the Veneti, and vessels commandeered from other coastal tribes of Gaul. The ships set sail from Portus Itius (modern Boulogne), and perhaps also from Ambleteuse. Caesar took the Seventh and Tenth legions and some cavalry, but the horse transports were unable to land in the stormy weather, so it was with infantry alone that Caesar faced the British opposition. The cliffs were lined with tribesmen, who marched overland, following the Roman ships as they sailed round the coast, probably to Deal, where the battle began. The troops were reluctant to disembark, but the eagle bearer of the Tenth legion leapt into the shallow water and headed for the shore with the standard held high, so everyone could see that it would be captured unless the soldiers followed.

According to Caesar's account, the Britons still used chariots in battle, a fighting method that had gone out of fashion on the continent. Caesar admired the nimble handling of the chariots, manned by a charioteer and a warrior. Once the battle was fully engaged, the charioteer deposited the warrior who fought on foot while the chariots withdrew to await the outcome. In the event of a defeat, the tribesmen could escape via the chariots.

Despite their skills and their bravery the Britons were defeated, and submitted to Caesar, delivering the hostages that were demanded, but they quickly rallied when the unpredictable weather damaged the Roman ships, which had not been beached. Caesar lost twelve ships, but the rest were not irretrievably damaged. He did not conceal the disaster in his account of the British expedition.

The Britons seized the moment to attack the Seventh legion while the soldiers were out foraging. Caesar rallied the troops and led them to victory, but it had been a close call. When the ships were repaired and the weather calmed down, he demanded hostages from the defeated tribes, and sailed back to Gaul. Two of the British tribes sent hostages, but none of the rest did so.

For the second expedition to Britain, Caesar ordered his officers to build more ships and to repair the old ones. Before he could embark he had to suppress a hostile coalition of several of the Gallic chieftains, instigated and led by Dumnorix. The Treveri had made overtures to the Germans, but fortunately for Caesar the Treveri were disunited, with two rival leaders. All Caesar had to do was to promote one at the expense of the other. Once this was settled, Caesar journeyed to Portus Itius (Boulogne) to embark his legions, summoning the Gallic chiefs to meet him there. They arrived, not suspecting that Caesar intended to take them all hostage and carry them to Britain with him. Dumnorix fled, but was overtaken and killed.

The second British invasion started in July, with a huge fleet of 800 ships, according to Caesar's account. The Britons did not attempt to oppose the landing, but took up a position on high ground and waited. Caesar left his ships at anchor in order to disembark the troops and get them marching more quickly. For a second time a storm wrecked the ships because while they were riding at anchor they collided with each other. Caesar was forced to return to the coast, where he placed Labienus in charge of repairing the ships.

The Britons settled their differences under the leadership of Cassivellaunus, chief of the Catuvellauni, who knew that guerrilla tactics would be more effective than open battle.

Nonetheless, he did make a stand. Caesar marched cautiously inland, coming upon the Britons at the Thames, where they had fortified the riverbank with stakes. The Romans in Caesar's army had some years' battle experience by now, and did not let the river itself or the fortifications stop their advance. It was a victory, offset by the fact that Cassivellaunus roused the Kentish tribes to attack the troops who were repairing the ships at the naval base.

As he progressed further inland, Caesar needed to cultivate allies among the tribes who could lend him support. He made great play of generous treatment of the Trinobantes, whose crops he spared, and they submitted to him. Shortly afterwards Cassivellaunus asked for terms. The Britons were not uneducated savages. They were aware of what was happening in Gaul and in Rome, and Cassivellaunus had probably concluded that Caesar was not intent on complete conquest of Britain, being too preoccupied with Gaul. For Cassivellaunus, surrender was more likely a means of bringing the war to a conclusion. Caesar exacted immediate tribute, which the Britons perhaps readily assembled and paid in order to rid themselves of Caesar and his army. The Britons were not to see another invading Roman army for the best part of a century.

Rebellion in Gaul 54–52 BC

The two expeditions to Britain brought no profit to Rome and nothing but a reputation for daring to Caesar and his army. In 54 BC, Caesar's daughter Julia died trying to give birth to Pompey's son. The child died shortly after. Opinion is divided about the influence that Julia may have had over Pompey and Caesar if she had lived. Her death need not signify the beginning of the rift between Caesar and Pompey at this stage, nor did the death of Crassus in Parthia in the following year loosen the ties between the two men. The irretrievable breakdown still lay a few years in the future.

During the winter of 54/3 Caesar remained in Transalpine Gaul. The harvests had failed, so each legion had to set up camp some distance from the others so that their foraging areas would not overlap. Before all the arrangements were finalised, the occupants of one of the camps were annihilated. The Treveran chief Indutiomarus bore a grudge against Caesar, and he had spread disaffection among other tribes. He encouraged Ambiorix, chief of the Eburones, to attack the Romans encamped at Aduatuca, which he did, but then Ambiorix resorted to subterfuge. He sent a message to the commanders Sabinus and Cotta that he had attacked only because he was obliged to do so, as part of a plot that had spread among the Gauls to launch an assault on all the Roman camps at once. He convinced the Romans that German tribesmen were en route for their camp at that very moment, and suggested that it would be better to leave their fortified camp and join Quintus Cicero, whose camp was about two days' journey from theirs, in the vicinity of Namur. Cotta and the officers were against making any move, but Sabinus and the soldiers overruled them. The troops marched out and were slaughtered. Only a few escaped to Labienus' camp, where they passed on the gory details. Sabinus and Cotta would have benefited from regular reconnaissance.

Other tribes started to arm themselves. The Nervii besieged the camp of Quintus Cicero, brother of Cicero the orator. The tribesmen adapted their techniques to Roman methods; being soundly defeated is an educative process. Cicero erected more fortifications and towers, defending his camp ably, but he was aware that his soldiers would be worn down by repeated attacks. He tried to send messages to Caesar at Amiens. One messenger got through, and Caesar acted with characteristic speed. He summoned troops from other camps but by this time Labienus was pinned down by Indutiomarus, so it was with fewer troops than he would have preferred that Caesar approached Cicero's camp. The Nervii broke off the siege to meet him.

According to Caesar's account he was outnumbered by about ten to one, so a pitched battle was out of the question. He built a camp on an extremely small scale as though he had only a very small number of troops, and he ordered the legionaries to simulate disorder and panic. The Nervii read all the signals and launched an attack, but Caesar's men rushed out from all the gates and attacked from all directions. The cavalry dispersed the rest of the tribesmen.

The forests soon swallowed up the Nervii, so Caesar wasted no time on pursuing them, marching instead straight to Cicero's camp. When Indutiomarus heard of the failure of the Nervii he raised the siege of Labienus' camp. A short time later he was killed. The Treveri and the Eburones allied and other tribes started to arm, and there was the perennial threat posed by the Germans across the Rhine. Caesar gave orders to raise two more legions in Cisalpine Gaul, and sent to Rome to ask Pompey to lend him one of his. By the end of the winter all three legions were at his headquarters.

He summoned the Gallic chiefs to a conference, but the Senones, Treveri and Carnutes did not attend. They removed the chiefs imposed on them by Caesar. The Senones banished theirs, while only assassination suited the Carnutes. These anti-Roman demonstrations could not be ignored; other tribes might rebel, and even the tribes which had submitted to Caesar might choose to bid for independence. Caesar transferred his base to Lutetia (modern Paris) and marched towards the Senones. Without a battle both they and the Carnutes submitted.

The Aedui and the Remi remained firmly with Caesar, which gave him leeway to turn his attention to Ambiorix and the Eburones, and their allies the Menapii and Treveri. Labienus attacked the Treveri and restored Cingetorix to power, while Caesar first attacked the Menapii at the mouth of the Rhine, and then the Eburones. This was not a war of pitched battles but a very thorough wasting of the entire land. Caesar invited the surrounding tribes to join him in pillaging the homesteads of the Eburones. Exploiting intertribal rivalries, setting tribe against tribe, was effective. The Eburones were never heard of again, and the fate of Ambiorix is unknown; he was never found, alive or dead.

One of the undesirable results of the invitation to other tribes to help in the destruction of the Eburones was that some of the Sugambri crossed the Rhine to join in, but they diverted and instead attacked the camp at Aduatuca, where Caesar had left Quintus Cicero with the baggage and the Fourteenth legion. A forage party was caught unawares and wiped out. Caesar summoned the Gallic chiefs to Rheims, and executed Acco, the leader of the Senones. With winter approaching, he quartered six of his ten legions in the lands of the Senones, to watch them and to punish them by the heavy burden of supplying the troops.

Caesar was about to face the most difficult years of the conquest of Gaul. His harshness did not quell the tribes, but inflamed them, not en masse, but some tribes who would not otherwise have worked together now began to think of co-operative action. The moment for the Gallic revolt was propitious. Circumstances in Rome were worsening. Pompey and Caesar were no longer in mutual agreement about their candidates for the consulship of 53, and the elections were delayed. There were riots, and rumours spread that Pompey was to be made Dictator to pacify the city and restore order. He said that he did not desire the office, which was just as well, because Cato made sure that he did not get it.

In 52 the situation degenerated further. Clodius intended to stand for the praetorship, but before the elections were held he was killed. Deprived of their whimsical benefactor, the people overreacted and gave Clodius a splendid funeral in the Forum, during which they managed to burn down the Senate House as well. Pompey was entrusted with the safety of the state, but not as Dictator, despite appeals that he should be appointed as such. Eventually he was made sole consul, an anomalous and unprecedented situation, since consuls had always come in pairs since the ancient kings had been expelled from Rome.

Pompey was not yet ready to sever all ties with his former colleague, and arranged for Caesar to stand for the consulship of 48 *in absentia*. This would mean that he could remain in his province until 49 and step from proconsulship to consulship unhindered by irritating prosecutions. It is unlikely that he would have been convicted if anyone prosecuted him, but a court action would debar him from standing for the consulship.

Caesar would now need all his resources to fight on two fronts, one in the political arena against his enemies who were determined to remove him from his command, and the other in the purely military sense, against a Gallic chief called Vercingetorix.

Vercingetorix 52 BC

When Caesar returned to Gaul at the beginning of 52 the position was probably worse than it had been in 58. The Gauls who had been co-operative had begun to turn against Rome. While it was not a complete pan-Gallic rising, it was both widespread and intense.

The opening round was won by the Carnutes, with their massacre of the Roman traders at Cenabum (modern Orléans). Two rebel leaders had emerged, Commius of the Gallic Atrebates, and Vercingetorix of the Arverni. Both had been cultivated as friends of the Roman people by Caesar, but they had now rebelled and also persuaded neighbouring tribes to join them in revolt. Caesar's problem was to discern which areas were disaffected, and how to reach his army. He had only new recruits and a provincial militia at his disposal, and with these he marched towards Narbo (modern Narbonne) immediately after hearing that some tribesmen were closing in on the town.

Vercingetorix was with the Bituriges, trying to detach them from their connection with the pro-Roman Aedui. Caesar decided to attack the Arverni in the expectation that Vercingetorix would come to their defence. Once he knew that the Gallic leader was on his way home, Caesar dashed non-stop for the two legions based near Langres, and from there he set about assembling his whole army. He then besieged and took a settlement of the Senones, and went on to attack Cenabum, where the revolt had started. Then he turned his attention to the Bituriges. Vercingetorix tried to prevent Caesar from crossing the Loire into the lands of the Bituriges. Caesar was besieging Noviodunum, which was just about to capitulate, but as Vercingetorix approached, the occupants were emboldened, and closed their gates. Caesar's German cavalry, a legacy from his defeat of Ariovistus, drove off the warriors of Vercingetorix, and Caesar was then free to march on Avaricum (modern Bourges), the wealthiest and most important settlement of the Bituriges.

Knowing that it would be folly to risk a pitched battle, Vercingetorix focused on cutting off Caesar's supplies. To this end he ordered his allies to fortify their towns, or if the settlements could not be defended, then they were to burn them along with all food stores and any other supplies that might help the Romans. The Bituriges were unwilling to sacrifice Avaricum, but otherwise they co-operated with Vercingetorix, and burnt twenty settlements in one day.

The leadership of Vercingetorix was a new phenomenon. He inspired such confidence in the Gauls that he was able to unite several tribes and was then able to persuade them to take this drastic step of destroying their homes. The Gauls had seen the Romans in action, and that gave them the incentive to sink their differences and fight together for their survival and freedom. It is significant that though the Aedui and the Remi remained loyal to Caesar, the tribes in revolt did not even consider the option of submitting to him before they joined Vercingetorix.

The new policy of Vercingetorix put Caesar's army under stress. Food supplies ran low while the Romans were besieging Avaricum, but the soldiers would not hear of abandoning the siege. Vercingetorix camped nearby. The Romans attacked his camp by night, but the defences proved too strong. Meanwhile Caesar was building a ramp to reach the defences of Avaricum. It was presumably framed in timber, since the Gauls were able to set it alight from a mineshaft that they had sunk underneath it. The Roman troops on guard duty were able to cut a fire break, and they also beat off the Gauls who rushed out of the gates. The fighting was prolonged. Next day Caesar noted the determination and bravery of the Gauls on the ramparts. One man was killed by Roman missiles, and another stepped into his place, until he too was killed, and so on, one man after another, until the fighting ceased. Caesar was impressed with the pertinacity and self-sacrifice of the Gauls, but perhaps he appreciated for the first time the depth of the extreme hatred of Roman rule.

Avaricum fell in the end, on a day of heavy rain, when the ramparts were not strongly defended and the Roman siege towers could be pushed close to the walls. The Romans massacred the inhabitants, including the women and children. A lesser man than Vercingetorix would have crumbled, but by force of personality he was able to retain and even increase the faith that the Gauls invested in him. It was disquieting for Caesar that the loyal Aedui were now beginning to waver, and there was a danger that the anti-Roman party would persuade the rest to throw in their lot with Vercingetorix. Caesar spent valuable time on public relations, bringing the Aedui back to their alliance. It was of vital importance to him since he wished to use their territory as a base, and to be able to rely upon the tribe to supply his army.

Besides the host gathered by Vercingetorix, there were additional threats to the north from the Senones and Parisi. Caesar divided his forces, sending Titus Labienus northwards with four legions while he himself took the rest of the army and aimed for Gergovia, the chief settlement of the Arverni. To reach it he had to cross the River Allier from the east. Vercingetorix destroyed all the bridges, but the Romans succeeded in getting across. Vercingetorix dashed straight for Gergovia to reach it before Caesar. It was a naturally strong settlement on a high plateau. On the southern edge of the town Vercingetorix built a camp protected by a dry stone wall, and garrisoned a nearby hill, nowadays called La Roche Blanche, to secure the water supply and the pasture. It was this area that Caesar decided to attack, since one look at the place was enough to convince him that he could not take Gergovia by force. He encamped and then set about taking La Roche Blanche. He built a smaller camp to the south-east of the town, took the hill by night, placed two legions on it and joined the small camp to the large one by two parallel ditches.

At this point, trouble erupted among the Aedui. A rumour had spread that all the Aeduans in Caesar's army had been executed, and in response the tribesmen, led by Litaviccus, had killed all the Romans in charge of one of the supply convoys. Caesar mobilised, leaving a garrison to hold the camps at Gergovia. About twenty-five miles from the town he met Litaviccus and the rebel Aeduans. There was no battle because the Aeduan leaders in Caesar's army were patently not dead, so the tribesmen surrendered. Caesar did not exact revenge. He allowed the soldiers a short rest, then marched them back to Gergovia, where the Gauls had attacked his camp while he was absent.

The blockade of Gergovia was fruitless, and Caesar knew that he would have to abandon it, but he made one last assault. The hill to the south-west of Gergovia was the key. Caesar pretended that he was going to attack there. He put his baggage men on their mules as fake cavalry, and sent a legion towards the hill, then when the Gauls took the bait and began to move to this point, he attacked the camp that Vercingetorix had built to the south of the town.

According to Caesar, the original plan was to pull back once the damage had been done and the score was settled, but the troops did not hear the signals to retreat. They forced their way through the camp until they came up against the town defences, where the Gauls put up a fierce fight and stopped them. The cost was high: 700 soldiers and forty-six centurions dead, and many wounded. The story about the planned retreat being ignored sounds like a cover-up for an assault that went wrong.

The rebels among the Aedui had not given up. Caesar's headquarters and administrative centre were at Noviodunum in their territory. Without warning, the Aeduan leaders of the troops in Caesar's army joined the rebels, and attacked Noviodunum, where they killed the soldiers and Roman traders, and destroyed the food stores. The whole area was roused against the Romans. Caesar was now almost surrounded by hostile Gauls, and his army was not united. He marched to join Labienus, who had fallen back with his four legions to the Roman Province in the south when he learned that the blockade of Gergovia had failed. He started to march to join Caesar. The two armies met up, but the situation of the united Roman army was far from safe. The defection of the Aedui was a bitter blow, but fortunately the Remi, the Lingones, and the Allobroges of southern Gaul held to their allegiance. Meanwhile the Aedui challenged Vercingetorix over leadership of the revolt, but the tribesmen voted for him, and he persuaded them that the best policy was to avoid pitched battles, to attack on a small scale whenever there was an opportunity, to deny the Romans any supplies, and to wait.

Vercingetorix moved his headquarters to Alesia (modern Alise Sainte-Reine) in the territory of the Mandubii. He encouraged the Aedui and other tribes to attack the Province, and in response Caesar appointed a relative of his, Lucius Caesar, to attend to its defence. Twenty-two cohorts were recruited and strung out along the borders of the Province, and the pro-Roman Allobroges prevented the Gauls from crossing the Rhone. Caesar knew that the defence of southern Gaul was inadequate, but his troops needed rest, and he needed reinforcements. He sent for contingents of German horsemen from the tribes across the Rhine, but when they arrived he found their horses unsuitable, and to remedy the defects he made his officers give up their riding horses for use as cavalry mounts. Then he set out for the Province, through the lands of the Sequani.

Hoping to surprise Caesar on the march, Vercingetorix advanced from Alesia. His plan was to place his infantry in battle order in front of his encampment and send the cavalry to attack the head and flanks of the marching column. It seems that Caesar was not aware of the presence of the Gauls, and the plan had every chance of success, but the Gallic cavalry attack did not have sufficient initial impetus to roll the column back. That short delay allowed Caesar time to assess the situation, bring up his own cavalry to hold off the Gauls, and order his legions to form squares with the baggage in the centre. Details are lacking in Caesar's account of this battle, but the manoeuvres he briefly describes attest to the experience and training of the Roman legions in changing from column to square while under attack. There may have been more confusion and panic than Caesar was prepared to admit, and he had clearly neglected to send out scouts to reconnoitre the road ahead of his troops.

Vercingetorix withdrew into Alesia, and began to fortify the weakest parts of the stronghold. The settlement lies on a plateau surrounded on three sides by rivers, the Ose and Oserain to the north and south, both flowing into the River Brenne on the western side. When Caesar arrived, he reconnoitred and concluded, as at Gergovia, that a siege was not a viable option, so a long blockade was the only choice available. He started to encircle the whole area with banks and ditches, distributing the troops in camps at intervals along the fortifications. Before he had fully completed the works, Vercingetorix attacked Caesar's cavalry on the west side of the town. The battle was going badly for the Romans until Caesar sent in the German horsemen. The Gauls turned and made for their camp, but they could not ride in through the gates quickly enough, and had to stand and fight. For the German cavalry, it was not a battle but a slaughter. The Gauls then tried to escape up the hill towards the town but Vercingetorix ordered all the gates to be shut.

There were no further Gallic cavalry attacks on the Roman works. Vercingetorix sent all his horsemen away by night, with orders to recruit more tribesmen to come to the aid of Alesia. He no longer needed to feed the horses, but was forced to ration food for his warriors. Caesar heard about this from deserters, and tightened the cordon around the town. At the same time he started to build an outer circuit of defences, fourteen miles long, to protect his army from external attack by the Gauls who were probably already on their way to Alesia.

Caesar's army has been estimated as 70,000 strong, requiring vast daily supplies of food and fodder, but Caesar also needed to build up reserve stores, in case he was cut off from the countryside by the Gallic relief force. Foraging was an increasingly time-consuming operation, taking the horsemen further and further away on each expedition, but fortunately Vercingetorix evidently had no intention of attacking the foraging parties. Meanwhile a huge army of Gauls was assembling to relieve Alesia. The Aeduans contributed about 250,000 infantry. This enormous army occupied the high ground to the west of the beleaguered town. Next day they brought the cavalry down into the plain to attack Caesar's outer defence works, while at the same time the Gauls in Alesia attacked the inner lines, implying that there was effective communication between the two Gallic armies. Caesar manned both lines and sent out his cavalry to engage the enemy. The battle lasted until evening, when the German horsemen scattered the Gauls of the relieving force, and Vercingetorix recalled his men from the attack on the inner lines.

The next attack on both the inner and outer lines occurred at night, but the Roman defences held. The Gauls had observed that to the north of the town, where the River Rabutin joined the Ose, the outer Roman lines were not joined up. Two legions guarded this spot, chosen as the focal point for the next attack. The relieving army marched round to the north, while from inside Vercingetorix mounted a number of assaults at different points to keep the Romans occupied and prevent them gathering together. At one point the Gauls started to breach the inner defences, and Caesar had to take command himself to drive them off. The Gallic relief force were making headway against the two legions guarding the gap in the outer defences, so Caesar sent Labienus and six cohorts to help the legions, but it was not enough. Caesar gathered some cavalry and infantry and set off to join Labienus. As a safeguard he sent another force round the outside to come up behind the Gauls, who were taken by surprise. The tide turned in favour of the Romans. According to Caesar, their attack slowed down when they recognised his red cloak, the badge of Roman commanders. The Gauls were heavily defeated, and so many were killed that the survivors decided to abandon the camp. The Romans pursued, killing all the way. It signified the end of any attempt to relieve Alesia.

The Gauls of Alesia could not hope to hold out any longer. Food stocks were already dangerously low, and there was no time to raise another relief army before it ran out. Vercingetorix offered to surrender himself to the Romans. Caesar was informed, and prepared to receive the Gallic leaders next day. He demanded the surrender of all weapons. Vercingetorix rode in, dismounted, and knelt before Caesar. It is one of the most moving moments of history. Vercingetorix had almost united the Gauls and forged them into a nation. His policy of guerrilla warfare, patience and waiting could have won the war in the end, but the promised rewards of freedom from Roman domination were too far off, uncertain and nebulous. Caesar had the edge because his legions could look forward to pay, rewards and booty. Vercingetorix could offer nothing like this, only hardship for the present, and years of slow recovery even if he won. Death for a cause is a noble sentiment, but it lacks the pulling power of cartloads of portable wealth.

Vercingetorix could have died gloriously in battle, or he could have disappeared from Alesia, to continue the fight somewhere else. As it was, he waited for six years in a Roman prison, then walked behind Caesar's chariot in one of his triumphs, and was finally strangled. When his country became a nation, he became a national hero, as the gigantic statue at Alise Sainte-Reine attests.

After Vercingetorix 52-49 BC

The fall of Alesia did not signify the end of the revolt. Caesar went some way to diffuse opposition by a display of clemency. The Aeduan and Arvernian prisoners were sent home. The Aedui resumed their former status as friends of the Roman people, allowed to govern themselves. Caesar put his troops into winter quarters, and remained at Bibracte in Aeduan territory, anticipating further trouble from the Bituriges, who mobilised at the beginning of 51. Caesar marched against them, leaving Mark Antony in charge of the winter camp. Antony had been with Caesar for some time, but was mentioned in Caesar's account of the Gallic war only in its later stages.

The Bituriges were defeated, but this time Caesar did not take bloody revenge, perhaps counting upon leniency to persuade the Gauls that there was more to be gained by co-operation with Rome than by fighting. As resistance fell away the tribes started to fight each other. The Carnutes raided the Bituriges, and Commius of the Atrebates encouraged the Bellovaci to attack the Suessiones. Caesar waged an energetic campaign to subdue the Bellovaci, who were led by Correus and Commius, who brought in some 500 German horsemen. Caesar started to enclose the camp of the Bellovaci, who saw clearly the parallel with Alesia, and escaped at night behind a massive smokescreen. Correus made another camp and raided the Roman foraging parties. Caesar sent out a foraging party accompanied by concealed infantry and cavalry, who counter-attacked when the Gauls appeared. The victory shattered resistance. Once more Caesar treated the tribesmen leniently, instead of exacting terrible revenge. Other tribes submitted to him voluntarily.

Commius was still at large. He may have been the prime force behind the other chiefs who determined to resist the Romans. They were all savagely defeated. Caesar eradicated what was left of the Eburones, Labienus was sent against the Treveri, and other officers were sent on operations in north-west Gaul. Caesar's policy of clemency did not apply in this part of the world. There was little time left now to consolidate his gains and pacify the country before his term as governor expired. Consequently he had little patience with the tribesmen who still refused to submit. Two leaders called Drappes and Lucterius occupied Uxellodunum (modern Puy d'Issolu), where they had amassed quantities of food and stores to last them and their army through a siege. They probably reasoned that Caesar would be recalled to Rome and that his replacement would perhaps prove less durable. When Caesar arrived at Uxellodunum he ordered his engineers to cut off the water supply, which brought about the inevitable surrender. On this occasion, Caesar acted more ruthlessly than ever before. He lined up all the captives, and cut off their hands. Killing them was not memorable enough, because he had seen how readily the Gauls died in battle or for a cause. He wanted the survivors to remain as visible reminders of the power of Rome, *pour encourager les autres* as the modern descendants of the Gauls would say.

The last of the Gauls to surrender was Commius. He gave himself up to Mark Antony. Organisation of the country could begin. Most of Gaul was exhausted, some of the land completely wasted or pillaged out of existence, some of it resettled by tribes who hailed from other parts of Gaul. It was time to establish tribal boundaries, recognising each tribe as a different state, organising its relations with Rome, and assessing the tribute to be paid. Common sense ruled, instead of Imperialist greed. The Gauls could not pay fantastic sums from their devastated lands, so Caesar settled for a total of 10 million *denarii*, a sum that any Roman aristocrat would probably have considered loose change. The organisation of Gaul involved Caesar in a great deal of personal negotiation, promoting chiefs who were well disposed to Rome, sending lavish gifts to keep them loyal. All this came with the tacit understanding that Roman armed support would be forthcoming at the least sign of trouble, the corollary being that armed Roman persuasion would also be forthcoming at the least sign of disloyalty. It was of the utmost importance to Caesar to avoid any further outbreaks of fighting so near to the end of his governorship.

In Rome, the consuls of 51, 50 and 49 were hostile to Caesar, and manoeuvred to have him recalled from Gaul. The major problem for historians is the uncertainty over the terminal date of Caesar's command, and the major problem for Caesar's contemporaries was the fact that he wished to stand for the consular elections in 49 without coming to Rome or laying down command of his army. Complications arose because Pompey had remained in Rome as sole consul in 52 while commanding armies via his legates in Spain, and he still commanded armies from Rome in 49, which gave Caesar some leverage to seek equality with Pompey: either they both held on to their commands, or they both laid them down at the same time. This was proposed several times in the Senate by the tribune Curio, who was a friend of Mark Antony and had come over to Caesar. On 1 December 50, the senators voted by an overwhelming majority in favour of the proposal that both commanders should lay down their commands, but despite its obvious popularity it was not adopted. Caesar sent a message to the Senate via Curio to insist that he would not relinquish his command unless Pompey did so at the same time. This put the onus on Pompey to act, either by giving up his armies and retiring into private life, or coming to some agreement with Caesar in which he would be very much the junior partner, or allying with the Senate. The consul Gaius Marcellus had already entrusted Pompey with defence of the state, and Pompey had accepted.

The Senate proposed that a date should be set for the termination of Caesar's command, and if he refused to comply he should be declared an enemy of the state. The tribunes Curio and Mark Antony vetoed the proposal, but the Senate passed the ultimate decree, empowering the consuls to protect the state. Antony and Curio were physically ejected from the Senate House, and set off for Caesar's camp. By the time they reached him, Caesar had crossed the Rubicon, an insignificant stream in geographical terms, but deeply significant in political terms because it was the boundary between Caesar's province and Italy, and to cross it with troops was an act of war.

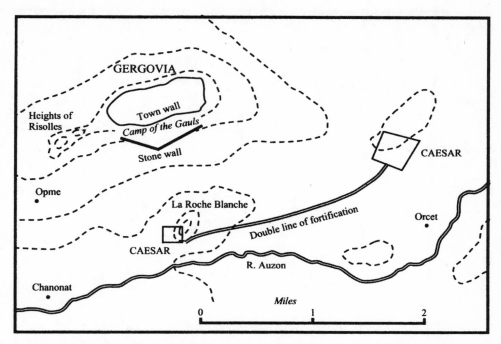

Sieges were a common feature of Republican wars. During Caesar's conquest of Gaul, his most competent enemy Vercingetorix made camp at the town of Gergovia, situated on a plateau with steep slopes to the north and east. There was a defensive wall on the southern side where the slopes were less steep and Vercingetorix built a second wall in front of it. Caesar made his first camp to the south-east, captured the high ground south of the town, made a second camp and linked the camps via two communication trenches. Despite the preparations, Caesar's attack failed, and Caesar had to move into the territory of the Aedui. Drawn by Jan Shearsmith.

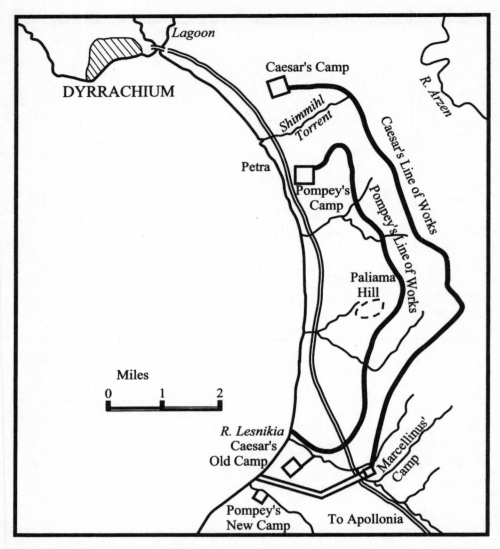

Plan of the Dyrrachium campaign. When Mark Antony ferried the second half of Caesar's army
from Italy to Greece, both Caesar and Pompey raced for Dyrrachium, where Pompey arrived first
and secured his base which could be supplied by sea. As Caesar began to invest the camp Pompey
extended his lines so that Caesar had to do the same. Although this gave Pompey more foraging
ground, he eventually had to send his cavalry horses away to find fodder. The plan shows the
double lines of entrenchments at the southern end of Caesar's lines, where he had not closed them
off at the seashore. Pompey tried to break out by launching an assault here from land and sea,
attacking from the north and south, with more of his troops between the lines. His men fought
well, and he was only driven off by the arrival of Mark Antony with fresh troops, and Caesar with
thirteen cohorts. In the end, it was Caesar who had to move to find food, and the two armies finally
arrived at Pharsalus and the final battle. Drawn by Jan Shearsmith.

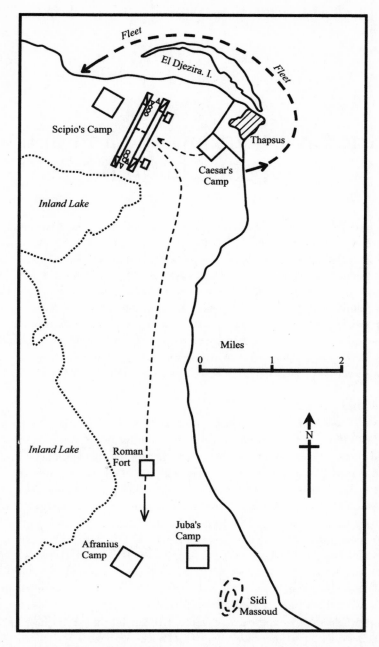

The Thapsus campaign. Thapsus was held by the Pompeians, so Caesar blockaded the town from the sea and besieged it from the landward side, but it seemed as though he was in an awkward position, in a narrow corridor between the sea and an inland lake. The Pompeians under Metellus Scipio thought that they could trap him by making camps at both ends of this corridor, but when Scipio offered battle west of Thapsus, Caesar trapped him instead by sending ships round the promontory to come up behind Scipio's forces. This Pompeian defeat ended the civil war in Africa, but started another war in Spain where the survivors gathered under Pompey's elder son Gnaeus. Drawn by Jan Shearsmith.

11

The Civil Wars and the End of the Republic 49–30 BC

The army and politics had always been inextricably linked in Rome, but after Marius and Sulla the army had begun to dominate Roman life to a greater extent than ever before. Armies were no longer the sole preserve of the Senate but the instruments of the generals, who exercised larger commands for longer periods of time than the early Republican consuls had done. During the first four centuries of the Republic, the army was predominantly made up of local men from Rome, and from Italian allies, whose generals were subordinate to the Senate, but by the time of the civil wars of the later first century BC, the army was a mixed bag, composed of different peoples from distant lands, a Roman army in name but not devoted to Rome, probably not even familiar with it. During the civil wars this diversification enabled each successive group of rivals to raise armies who would willingly fight other Roman armies for their favoured commander.

Caesarians and Pompeians

Caesar's invasion of Italy took the Senate by surprise. Pompey had boasted that he only had to stamp his foot in Italy and armies would rise up, but recruits did not flock to him, and he was not granted enough time to train those who did join him. He had lent one of his legions to Caesar, and though Caesar had returned it along with one of his own, Pompey could not trust either of them. On 17 January, Pompey arrived at Capua, his main recruiting ground, declaring that those who did not join him would be classed as enemies. On 22 January, Titus Labienus joined Pompey, after ten years as Caesar's deputy.

Caesar proposed that both he and Pompey should disband their troops, that elections should be held, and that Pompey should go to Spain. Pompey would comply if Caesar would return to Gaul and disband his armies, which was a non-starter. Pompey prepared to occupy Picenum in the hope of cutting Caesar off from Rome, but Caesar occupied it first. Domitius Ahenobarbus, at Corfinium with thirty-one cohorts, decided to make a stand against Caesar, before he had assembled his whole army. Pompey advised Domitius to join him at Luceria, because they could never resist Caesar with split forces. Domitius would not budge but was soon writing to Pompey seeking help, because Caesar was encamped outside Corfinium.

Pompey replied that he would not gamble the fate of the Republic on one pitched battle with untrained troops. Two days later he marched to Brundisium, to evacuate the army to Greece. Domitius surrendered. He was allowed to go free, but his troops were absorbed into Caesar's army. It is debated whether Pompey decided at the start of the war to withdraw from Italy. Given that Pompey's campaigns in the east had brought him clients, wealthy investments, and a knowledge of the terrain and its potential for maintaining an army, it is feasible that he had decided to fight Caesar in the east. He had troops in Spain under loyal subordinates, and with headquarters in Macedonia and Greece he could perhaps converge on Rome from east and west.

Caesar arrived at Brundisium and besieged the town, but most of Pompey's army and the consuls had sailed for Greece. The transports were to be sent back for Pompey himself and his remaining cohorts. Caesar invested the city on the landward side and attempted to block the harbour by anchoring rafts covered with earth to create piers on both sides, but Pompey's returning transports got through on 17 March. The evacuation of Brundisium is considered masterly by many authors. Pompey had installed light armed troops on the defences, and embarked the heavy armed troops in strict silence. At a given signal, the defenders left the ramparts and hurried to the ships. Caesar's men stormed the defences, only to find that trenches had been dug across the main streets, and pits had been excavated, covered with hurdles to disguise the sharp stakes set inside them. There were barricades across other streets, and huge palisades guarded the route to the harbour. By the time Caesar reached the harbour, Pompey was at sea.

For lack of ships Caesar could not follow Pompey. He had to organise a shipbuilding programme. Caesar concentrated on securing his food supply, which entailed control of the grain-producing provinces. He took Sardinia, and Curio won Sicily without a fight, because Pompey's governor Marcus Porcius Cato had refused to go there when ordered, and when he did arrive, he had to start recruiting and training troops. He abandoned the island on 23 April and joined Pompey in Greece with his new troops. In Africa, Curio was killed when his army was defeated by King Juba and his Numidians.

Meanwhile Caesar had returned to Rome. He installed guards on all the ports, but gave special permission for Cicero to leave for Greece. He enfranchised the Cisalpine Gauls and appointed Marcus Crassus as governor, in order to secure northern Italy. Marcus Aemilius Lepidus was made prefect of the city to secure Rome. Mark Antony was put in charge of all troops in Italy, while his brother Gaius Antonius occupied Illyricum. Caesar decided to deal first with the Pompeians in Spain, saying that he would fight the army without a leader, then he would go to Greece to fight the leader without an army.

Spain 49 BC

Pompey's legates in Spain were Lucius Afranius, Marcus Petreius and Terentius Varro, with seven legions. Caesar brought six legions and a complement of auxiliary troops, 6,000 of which were cavalry, highly experienced after ten years in Gaul. Varro held Further Spain with two legions. Afranius joined Petreius in Nearer Spain where they commanded the other five legions. They were encamped on a hill near Ilerda (modern Lerida), on the River Sicoris (modern Serge) when Caesar's troops arrived. Afranius repelled an attack by the Fourteenth legion, and attacked one of Caesar's convoys, but he was driven off when Caesar began to create a man-made ford across the river, which his troops could cross to prevent the Pompeians from foraging. Afranius and Petreius moved off towards the River Ebro; Caesar overtook them, forcing them to turn back. They made for Ilerda, but on the march they were trapped on a hill without access to water, and surrendered. With two legions, Varro could not hope to stand against Caesar.

While Caesar was in Spain, Decimus Brutus defeated a Pompeian fleet, but in turn the Pompeians defeated Caesar's naval commander Dolabella. In Illyricum, Gaius Antonius surrendered. In northern Italy Caesar's legions, tired of fighting civil wars with little profit, had mutinied, the Ninth legion being the most discontented. Caesar prepared to decimate it, but after protests he rounded up 120 of the ringleaders and decimated them instead, so for a loss of twelve lives the mutiny was quelled.

In Greece, Pompey trained and augmented his army. He had five legions from Italy, and filled gaps in their ranks with the troops of Gaius Antonius. He raised two legions from veterans who had settled in Cilicia, Greece and Macedonia, and the consul Lentulus raised two more from veterans in Asia. Pompey requested more troops from the allied kings of Commagene, Cappadocia, and Galatia, whom he had installed after the Mithradatic war. He raised auxiliary troops from Thessaly, Boeotia, Achaea and Epirus. Pompey also recruited specialist troops, such as Cretan archers, and two cohorts of slingers. His son Gnaeus brought ships and 500 men from Egypt, and Pompey requisitioned ships and crews from Phoenicia, Cilicia, Syria, Bithynia, Pontus, Athens, Corcyra, and Asia. The struggle between two rival Romans was becoming a world war.

Pompey employed his usual impressive organisational skills in troop raising, fund gathering and shipbuilding. Similarly his training programme was energetic and thorough, and he did not shirk the exercises that he put his men through. Plutarch describes how, at fifty-seven years old, he rode at full gallop in his armour, performed all the sword exercises and hurled a javelin faster and further than the young men in the army. Perhaps because of his display of organisational ability and military skills, he was belatedly made supreme commander by the senators who had accompanied him.

Caesar returned to Rome at the end of 49 and was made Dictator, which enabled him to hold the elections. The new consuls were Caesar himself and Publius Servilius Isauricus. The other magistrates were appointed, and the vacant priesthoods were filled. Laws were passed to relieve debts, and food was distributed to the people; both of these problems were potential flashpoints, which Caesar wished to avoid while he was finding and fighting Pompey.

The Dyrrachium Campaign 48 BC

As soon as possible Caesar embarked 15,000 legionaries and 500 cavalry at Brundisium, leaving Antony to embark the rest when the transports returned. Pompey's army was in winter quarters in Dyrrachium and Apollonia, and other Adriatic coastal towns. Leaving two legions in Macedonia under his father-in-law Metellus Scipio, Pompey set off for Dyrrachium in January 48. Caesar evaded the Pompeian fleet commanded by Bibulus, and landed some eighty miles to the south. Bibulus captured about thirty of Caesar's transports on their way back to Brundisium, and burnt them with the crews on board.

Caesar discovered Pompey's stores at Oricum, where the inhabitants opened their gates rather than stand a siege. Then Caesar took Apollonia. Having lost control of two cities and his supplies, Pompey made every effort to reach Dyrrachium ahead of Caesar. Pompey won the race. He made camp on the northern bank of the River Apsus, and Caesar faced him on the southern bank. Pompey's army outnumbered Caesar's, and he controlled the sea lanes so he was not short of supplies. The sources tell of cavalry encounters, and hint that Pompey tried to cross the river, perhaps to cut Caesar's supply lines. Pompey summoned his father-in-law Scipio from Macedonia with two legions, but Caesar detached two legions under Domitius Calvinus, who successfully prevented Scipio from moving.

Caesar occupied the coastline opposite the Pompeian fleet-base on the island of Corcyra, to prevent the ships from coming ashore for fresh water. Blockaded in Brundisium, Antony did the same, preventing the Pompeian commander Libo from obtaining water. Caesar tried once more to open negotiations, but Pompey said that he did not wish to live to old age courtesy of Caesar. He knew that Caesar would soon be short of food.

Pompeians and Caesarians on either side of the river were beginning to mingle. Labienus ended the fraternisation, brutally. News arrived that Antony had landed at the harbour of Nymphaeum, north of Dyrrachium. To prevent the Caesarian armies from uniting, Pompey marched to tackle Antony, planning to trap him at a narrow pass at the Genusus River, but the local Greeks warned Antony, so he made camp, and waited for Caesar. Pompey had to withdraw, or be trapped between two armies. Caesar followed and camped opposite him. Next day he drew up in battle order, but Pompey did not respond. On the following morning, Caesar moved off. Pompey thought that he was going in search of supplies, but when his scouts returned with the news that Caesar was heading for Dyrrachium, Pompey had to follow. He allowed his men to rest, and nearly lost the race this time. When he reached Dyrrachium he camped on a hill called Petra, sending orders for part of his navy and the supply ships to assemble in the bay.

Caesar camped to the north of Pompey's army. Without ships, he could not cut Pompey's supply lines, but he could prevent him from gathering fodder for the horses. He enclosed Pompey within siege lines by occupying the hills running in an arc to the east of Pompey's camp, building camps on them and joining the hills with a series of trenches. Pompey began to build an inner ring of lines, in order to enclose as much land as possible for foraging, occupying all the territory from Petra to the River Lesnikia (modern Gesnike) to the south. Caesar was forced to extend his own lines, stretching his troops to the limit to guard them.

Pompey knew that inactivity was the best policy while Caesar starved, but his main problem was the cavalry, which he was unable to use, and the animals were suffering. Major-General Fuller says that Pompey ought to have removed the cavalry from the camp, and used it to attack Caesar's foraging parties and supply convoys, then Caesar would have been forced to march, and Pompey could have decided whether to follow, or to turn his attention to Italy.

For his water supply, Pompey was dependent on the streams running from the mountains towards the sea, so Caesar cut them. Pompey's men dug wells in the strip of land near the shore, but it was high summer and they dried up, so the shortage of water combined with the lack of forage decided Pompey to remove the cavalry to Dyrrachium, where the horses could be properly fed and watered.

In order to draw Caesar away from the blockading lines Pompey sent a false message saying that the city of Dyrrachium was ready to open its gates to him. Caesar took the bait and attacked Dyrrachium, but was ambushed by Pompey's waiting troops. Simultaneously, Pompey's men attacked Caesar's lines in three separate places, but were repulsed. Caesar managed to cut off Pompey's cavalry from their foraging grounds, and the horses had to be ferried back to the ground enclosed by Pompey's lines.

It was imperative for Pompey to break out. Two Gauls, deserters from Caesar's camp, informed Pompey that there was a weak point at the southern end of Caesar's lines. There was a double line of trenches, one facing Pompey's camp to the north, and another 200 paces distant, facing south. The trenches were protected by a camp some distance from the sea, manned by Lentulus Marcellinus with the Ninth legion, but the two parallel lines were not joined together where they met the coast, so troops could get between them. Pompey ferried his troops down the coast, one group landing in the gap between the lines, and the other to the south. The Caesarians between the two lines were rolled back, and clashed with reinforcements under Marcellinus. Then Antony arrived with twelve cohorts, followed by Caesar with thirteen cohorts. Even though Pompey had to abandon the attack, he had successfully broken through the blockade and had established a camp south of Caesar's lines near the coast, which enabled him to bring his cavalry to forage in safety. Caesar attempted to storm Pompey's new camp before it was fully garrisoned. His troops broke through the ramparts and herded the Pompeians into a corner, but then Pompey arrived with five legions. The Caesarian soldiers fled, but their route was blocked by the rampart they had just broken through. Many were trampled to death, and Caesar lost thirty-two standards, thirty-two tribunes and centurions, and 960 men. Pompey did not follow up this victory, but it signalled the end of the blockade, and Caesar moved off in search of supplies.

Pompey followed as soon as he knew what was happening, and apart from a skirmish where Pompey's cavalry caught up with Caesar's rearguard at the River Genusus, the two armies peacefully occupied their old camps at Asparagium, facing each other as before. Pompey lost the advantage when his officers decided to return to their base at Dyrrachium to collect their baggage, and Caesar escaped while Pompey's camp was in turmoil. Pompey pursued for four days, then returned to Asparagium, where he held a council of war, still advocating his policy of attrition. Afranius recommended that the Pompeians should prolong the war in the hope of wearing Caesar down. Another alternative was to decamp without delay and invade Italy. Pompey sent part of his fleet to blockade Brundisium and to attack Sicily, perhaps preparing to invade Italy. But instead he marched to join Scipio, Caesar followed, and the two armies moved around Thessaly without joining battle.

The Battle of Pharsalus 48 BC

This phase of the war came to an end when Caesar entered the fertile territory near Pharsalus, and made camp. The exact location is not established, because there are two separate sites about seven miles apart, Pharsalus and Old Pharsalus, on the River Enipeus (Kutchuk Tcharnali). Pompey camped on a hill in a strong defensive position, and there he remained, steadfastly ignoring Caesar's attempts to entice him into a pitched battle. The opposing armies drew up each day facing each other, but Pompey's troops remained near their camp high up the slope. Pompey's insubordinate subordinates continually urged him to fight. On the morning of the battle, Caesar had decided to strike camp, but while the soldiers were packing up, Pompey's army formed up much further down the hill than usual. Caesar hastily countermanded his orders and brought his army out in battle order.

Pompey rested his right wing on the River Enipeus and strengthened his left wing by placing his huge cavalry force there, much enlarged by the addition of many horsemen from his native allies. He may have siphoned off about 600 cavalry and stationed them near the river on his left, but no source except Frontinus says this. Announcing his plans the previous night, Pompey explained that he intended to demolish Caesar's right wing with a cavalry attack under Titus Labienus, who was to force a way around the flank and rear to close the trap. The plan was sound, especially as the Pompeians knew that Caesar was outnumbered in both infantry and cavalry, with only eight under-strength legions to Pompey's eleven legions, and a mere 1,000 cavalry to Pompey's 7,000.

Caesar entrusted the left to Mark Antony, facing Lucius Afranius, and the centre to Gnaeus Domitius Calvinus, opposite Metellus Scipio. On the right, opposite Pompey's large numbers of horsemen, Publius Sulla, son of the Dictator, was in command, and Caesar remained there himself. His famous Tenth legion was positioned on the right of the infantry. Caesar also formed up a fourth line by withdrawing one cohort from the third line of each legion. He placed these cohorts out of sight as a reserve, in case the right wing should crumble. One other factor was perhaps instrumental in Caesar's victory: he ordered his troops to strike at the faces of the Pompeian soldiers, judging that the psychological impact would spread fear and panic.

The battle opened with a Caesarian charge, which the Pompeians received without moving, since Pompey did not want his men to be winded. Once battle was joined, Pompey's right and centre held firm and fought hard. Labienus began the envelopment of the Caesarian right, but the horsemen did not move round rapidly enough, and a flank attack by the troops that Caesar had concealed scattered them. The Pompeian left was now in danger. When Caesar sent in the third line to help the first and second, Pompey saw that the battle was lost and rode back to the camp, escaping just as Caesar's men approached. He and a few attendants went to Larissa, where he advised the citizens not to resist Caesar. Then he made for the coast, and ultimately Egypt, where he was killed by the advisers of the young Ptolemy XIII.

Pharsalus was a decisive battle, but Pompey's sons and many of his legates were still at large, and it would take four more years and two major battles to end the civil war.

The Alexandrian War 48–47 BC

When Caesar arrived in Alexandria, there was a private war going on between the young Ptolemy XIII and his half-sister Cleopatra VII, joint heirs of the deceased Ptolemy XII Auletes. Ptolemy XIII was only a boy, so his ministers dealt with most matters, and Cleopatra had been driven out of Alexandria, encamped with her army near the city. When Pompey came to Egypt, Ptolemy's ministers decided that he must be eliminated to avoid a war with Caesar, so when Caesar arrived, he was presented with Pompey's head and signet ring. Caesar could have returned to Rome, but instead became embroiled in the war between Ptolemy and Cleopatra. There was potential profit in doing so. Ptolemy XIII and Cleopatra had a young brother also called Ptolemy, and a sister, Arsinoe. If Caesar could install one of these royal offspring as ruler, he or she would be grateful to Rome, but specifically to Julius Caesar.

Cleopatra came to Alexandria secretly to avoid capture by the ministers of Ptolemy XIII. Her arrival at Caesar's feet in a rolled-up carpet may be true. Caesar probably reviewed the available royal candidates, and judged Cleopatra to be the most sensible, knowledgeable, conscientious, independent, and resourceful of the four, and the most fit to rule. Before he could make Cleopatra queen, Caesar had to endure a siege from an unaccustomed angle, from the inside. Ptolemy XIII's general Achillas invested the royal palace with all four heirs to the throne inside it. Caesar had already sent for reinforcements to be brought in by sea, and had contacted his ally Mithradates of Pergamum, sending him to recruit in Syria and Cilicia, but it would be some time before these reinforcements arrived. His first concern was to clear the way into the harbour, so he burnt the Egyptian fleet. It is a good story, but disputed, that he accidentally burnt the library as well. He seized the lighthouse, which takes its name from the Pharos island on which it stood, and then took possession of the causeway on the western side of the harbour linking Pharos island with the mainland. While he was fortifying it Caesar's men were attacked, and many were drowned, and Caesar had to swim for his life. Fortunately the reinforcements arrived. Mithradates took Elysium, east of Alexandria, and Caesar was able to trap the Egyptians between his two forces. Ptolemy drowned in the Nile. By Egyptian lore, this conferred divinity upon him; Caesar had him fished out and put on display, patently mortal and dead.

Cleopatra was made Queen of Egypt with her young brother Ptolemy XIV as consort. Her true consort for the time being was Caesar himself. After Caesar had departed, she gave birth to a son, Ptolemy Caesar, but the Alexandrians nicknamed him Caesarion. The boy united Rome and Egypt, representing Cleopatra's hopes of avoiding annexation by Rome.

Caesar remained in Egypt until the summer of 47, for the war against Pharnaces, son of Mithradates whom Pompey had defeated. The Roman territories of Bithynia and Pontus were threatened by the empire-building tendencies of Pharnaces, who defeated a Roman army under Domitius Calvinus, and occupied Pontus. Caesar defeated Pharnaces at Zela in Pontus, but failed to capture him. This war is the context for his famous phrase *veni, vidi, vici*, I came, I saw, I conquered.

The Thapsus Campaign 47–46 BC

In the autumn of 48, Caesar had been made Dictator for one year, and Mark Antony was *magister equitum*, master of horse, Caesar's deputy in Rome. There had been riots in Rome related to debt problems, and the Senate had authorised Antony to restore order, which he did, but with bloodshed. When Caesar at last returned to Rome in the autumn of 47, Antony was coolly dropped.

Caesar was made Dictator for the second time. The Pompeians were gathering strength at sea, in Africa and in Spain. Since there was soon to be a campaign, Caesar's soldiers came to Rome, thinking that because he would need them he would accede to their demands, mostly concerning pay. Caesar met them without a guard, but Antony was close by with troops. The soldiers bluffed that they wanted to be discharged, not mentioning pay. Caesar simply addressed them as *Quirites*, citizens. He added that he would give them everything that he had promised when he returned from the wars in Africa, for which he would now employ other troops. The soldiers capitulated.

Part of the army sailed from Lilybaeum in Sicily just as the winter season was beginning. A storm blew up and scattered the ships. There was no prearranged rendezvous, because Caesar did not know which harbours and coastal towns were in Pompeian hands. Caesar landed with only 3,000 men and 150 cavalry near Hadrumetum (modern Susa), which was held by the Pompeian Considius Longus. Caesar marched south-east down the coast towards Leptis Minor (modern Lemta). The towns on the route welcomed him, including Leptis, where some of the transports arrived, but Caesar still did not have an adequate campaign army. He sent the transports back to Sicily to bring over the rest of the troops, and sent out warships to look for the lost fleet.

The Pompeians had congregated at Utica where the governor Atius Varus was replaced by Cato. King Juba of the Numidians joined them with his experienced horsemen, infantry and archers. The citizens of Utica favoured Caesar, and Metellus Scipio advocated their massacre, but Cato successfully protested. He emerged as the true political leader, advocating a policy of wearing Caesar down by preventing him from foraging and keeping him away from the harbours and ports. But Metellus Scipio was chosen as overall commander.

After a few days, more transports delivered troops to Caesar, who made camp at Ruspina, a plateau north of Leptis Minor. He led out a foraging party of thirty cohorts and some cavalry, flanked by 150 archers, but ran into Labienus with 1,600 Gallic and German horsemen. Caesar summoned the rest of the cavalry from the camp, about three miles away. Labienus tried to encircle Caesar's men without engaging, riding round them and assailing them with showers of missiles to wear them down. Caesar formed a line with cavalry on the wings and archers in front, but the wings were gradually forced back until the line almost became a circle. Somehow Caesar reformed the line and then made an unusual manoeuvre, by ordering every alternate cohort to face about, so that the line faced in two directions. Precisely how he did this is not explained. Turning alternate cohorts around in the middle of a battle demands some form of elaborate signalling or command relays, and the fact that the soldiers performed the manoeuvre under extreme pressure testifies to their experience and discipline.

Caesar broke through the encircling enemy, and escaped to the hills to the east. There are two versions of what happened next. According to the account of the African war, which was written by an unknown author probably using Caesar's notes, the Caesarians were attacked by Marcus Petreius. Eventually Caesar and the surviving soldiers broke through to higher ground, and he led them back to camp in the dark. The historian Appian says that the Pompeians withdrew because Metellus Scipio was coming up with more troops and they wished to give him the opportunity of delivering the final blow. The episode is suspicious, because Scipio did not deliver the final blow.

After this battle Caesar's main concern was food. Scipio camped near Ruspina, endangering Caesar's foraging parties. Caesar built two lines of entrenchments from Ruspina to the sea so that he could bring in supplies and reinforcements from his ships. Caesar and his ally, King Bocchus of eastern Mauretania, had fostered a rebellion in Numidia, which drew King Juba away, so the Pompeians lost some men while Caesar gained some with the arrival of the Thirteenth and Fourteenth legions, plus cavalry and archers. With his enlarged army Caesar moved south to Uzita and made two camps, one on the high ridge to the east of the town and another nearer to Uzita itself. Caesar carefully protected his foraging parties. His troops clashed with Scipio and Labienus, but Caesar tipped the balance by summoning the cavalry that he had hidden behind some farm buildings. There were no serious actions after this battle. Caesar put the town of Uzita under siege, hoping to take it and use the supplies stored there, but lack of food forced him to move away.

Caesar ordered ships from the fleet at Leptis to guard the approaches to Hadrumetum, and also Thapsus on an eastward-facing promontory further along the coast, in order to allow his transport ships to approach with reinforcements from Sicily. The Pompeian admiral Varus set out from Utica with a large squadron to intercept the transports, but Caesar was informed. He rode straight for Leptis, put out to sea in a small boat, located one of his squadrons, leapt on board one of the ships, took command, and drove away Varus and the Pompeian fleet. He saved most of his ships from destruction and cleared the way for the Sicilian transports, which arrived shortly afterwards carrying the Ninth and Tenth legions. He moved off and camped fifteen miles from the town of Thapsus, with the Pompeians close behind him. Scipio camped to the west of Caesar's camp, and started to forage around the town of Zeta (modern Beni Hassan). By risking a march past the enemy camp, Caesar occupied Zeta and installed a garrison, then on the return journey he was attacked by Labienus and Afranius, with the Numidian cavalry attacking from all sides. They could draw off very quickly and regroup for the next onslaught, without suffering many casualties. Caesar kept on moving slowly, beating off attacks, and resisting the temptation to make camp, because there were no supplies and more importantly no water. Discipline held and the soldiers finally reached their camp at night. The experience decided Caesar to meet like with like; he began to train some of his soldiers, 300 men from each legion, to fight in loose formation, instead of in the usual battle lines. This involved teaching them to fight as individuals, more like gladiators, as Rutilius Rufus had done before Marius took over against the Cimbri and Teutones. Caesar used the new formations against Labienus when the latter attacked him on the way to seize Scipio's stores-base at Sarsura.

Caesar's problem was how to make the Pompeians risk a pitched battle. He required a battlefield where it would seem that he was at a grave disadvantage, preferably where the legions could engage each other, but the Numidian cavalry could not operate. He found it to the south of Thapsus, where a strip of land was enclosed between the sea and an inland lake. Any army camped near to Thapsus could be boxed in by closing both ends of this corridor. Caesar's fleet was already guarding the approaches to Thapsus from the sea, and now he made a camp west of the town and besieged it, as though he had not noticed that he had walked into a potential trap. He placed a small camp at the south end of the corridor.

Scipio also made a camp at the southern end of the corridor, placing Juba and Afranius there. With the rest of the army he made a larger camp at the northern end. Caesar was ready. He attacked Scipio, sending orders to the fleet blockading Thapsus to sail round the promontory to the rear of Scipio's army, watch for a signal from Caesar, and make a great noise as if troops were disembarking. Scipio drew up in battle formation with elephants on both wings. Caesar formed up extra troops out of sight on both wings to deal with the elephants. Scipio's troops started to mill about in confusion, and the soldiers, noticing the turmoil, urged Caesar to give the order to engage, but he refused. Suddenly, without orders, one of the trumpeters sounded the charge, and the centurions could not restrain the men. On Scipio's right the elephants panicked and ran through the Pompeian troops. The Numidian horsemen left the field, and the whole Pompeian army collapsed.

Scipio's surviving soldiers fled to Utica, where they forced their way in, killing many of the inhabitants. Cato stopped the massacre, but he had to resort to bribery to persuade the soldiers to leave. It was the end of the war in Africa, but the fleet was still free, and there were groups of Pompeians in Spain. Cato did not wish to join them. He made arrangements for the welfare of his family, and committed suicide, as the preferred option to being forgiven by Caesar.

One by one the other Pompeians were hunted down. Shortly after the battle of Thapsus, the town surrendered. Caesar occupied Utica, Hadrumetum and Uzita, and took over the kingdom of Juba, some of which he handed over to Bocchus of Mauretania for his part in distracting Juba from the Pompeians. The majority of the kingdom was converted into the new province Africa Nova, with the proconsul Gaius Sallustius Crispus as the first governor. Fines were imposed on communities which had supported the Pompeians, and Caesar settled some of his veterans in colonies along the coast, where they could keep the Pompeian fleet at bay.

Rome 46 BC

For Caesar's victories in Africa, an unprecedented forty days' thanksgiving had been decreed by the Senate, and Caesar emphasised his achievements by holding four triumphs, over Gaul, Egypt, Pharnaces and Juba. There was no mention of Pompey, or of victories over Romans. He was made Dictator for ten years, and numerous honours were voted to him.

Cleopatra was invited to Rome, and stayed in one of his villas. Cleopatra needed official status as friend and ally of the Roman people, and recognition of her son Caesarion as her successor, to secure the freedom of Egypt beyond her own lifetime. Caesar acknowledged the boy as his son, and after Caesar's death Antony presented Caesarion's claims to the Senate.

For the settlement programme for his veterans, Caesar appointed legates to purchase land, attending personally to those cases which were not straightforward. In a very short time, he produced a staggering amount of legislation. He reformed the calendar to synchronise the months with the seasons, instituting a year of 365 and one-quarter days. He enacted laws to control the mob, and reduced the number of people entitled to receive the free corn dole. Without unduly upsetting creditors, he passed laws to alleviate the problems of debtors. Provincial government was reformed. Praetors were to govern for one year and consuls for two years, something of an irony after Caesar's ten-year command in Gaul. All this was pushed through at great speed. Caesar short-circuited senatorial debate, simply telling senators what he had decided. It was not his ideas that met with opposition, but his methods.

The Munda Campaign 46–45 BC

A war in Spain against the surviving Pompeians could not be postponed. Caesar planned to take his great-nephew Gaius Octavius with him on campaign, but the boy was ill. Pompey's sons, Gnaeus and Sextus, were in Spain, raising a considerable army. Caesar's nephew Quintus Pedius and Quintus Fabius Maximus were sent to contain the Pompeians, until Caesar arrived, with the Tenth legion, and the Fifth, nicknamed *Alaudae*, 'Larks', raised in Transalpine Gaul. Gnaeus Pompeius was besieging Ulia, and Sextus held Corduba with two legions. In order to draw Gnaeus off from Ulia, Caesar laid siege to Corduba. Gnaeus moved, but refused to risk a battle, and Corduba held out until lack of supplies forced Caesar to raise the siege, but twenty miles to the south-east there were stores of grain at Ategua, guarded by Pompeians. Caesar besieged it. The garrison commander Munatius Plancus massacred all the Caesarian sympathisers in the town, and had the bodies thrown over the walls. Brutality was a feature of the second Spanish war.

The garrison of Ategua tried twice to break out, but finally surrendered. Gnaeus Pompeius and Caesar chased each other from place to place until they arrived at Munda. The site has not been identified, but was probably west of Urso, which Caesar later chose as a site for one of his many colonies. Here Gnaeus offered battle. Caesar had not expected this, so it was a repeat of the battle of Pharsalus. The soldiers were breaking camp when Caesar noticed the enemy formations, so he gave the orders for attack. Gnaeus Pompeius had chosen his site well, and had every chance of winning. There was a stream and a surrounding marshy area between the two armies, which delayed the Caesarians trying to cross it. Caesar had to dash to the front to rally his troops, then the Tenth legion became the main driving force of the attack, pushing the Pompeians back on their left wing. Gnaeus ordered Labienus to move from the right wing to assist the left, but before he got into position Caesar ordered up the Mauretanian horsemen who drove Labienus away. The Pompeian line collapsed. Caesar said afterwards that he had often struggled to achieve victory, but this was the first time that he had fought for his life. Gnaeus Pompeius escaped, but was captured and decapitated. Sextus Pompeius fled from Corduba, leaving his two legions behind. Caesar took the town amid tremendous slaughter.

Caesar crushed any remaining resistance by harsh methods, but there were rewards for those communities which had been loyal to him. Their taxes were reduced and their territories were enlarged at the expense of the communities which had declared for the Pompeians. Some towns received Latin rights, and Caesar founded several colonies of Roman citizens with the obligation of defending their own territories. During the last phase of the Munda campaign, while he settled communities and made his administrative arrangements, Caesar was accompanied by his great-nephew Gaius Octavius, who had arrived on his own initiative, too late for the battle, accompanied by a few companions, including his lifelong friend Marcus Vipsanius Agrippa. Octavius acquitted himself well, and travelled back to Rome in Caesar's own litter. On the journey from Transalpine Gaul, the party was joined by Mark Antony, who was now back in favour, destined for higher things. He was to be consul with Caesar for 44.

The Ides of March 44 BC

The Roman Empire in nascent form can be discerned in Caesar's domination after Pharsalus. Pompey had shown how to govern provinces and command several armies via legates, who were answerable to him and not the Senate. Caesar took this one step further. As Dictator he did not feel the need to seek ratification for his arrangements in Spain. He had established colonies named after himself whose inhabitants would direct their allegiance to him rather than the Senate and People of Rome. He appointed governors and deployed legions, so both the governors and the armies were Caesar's rather than Rome's. The veterans settled in the colonies owed their livelihoods to him.

The civil wars had ended but foreign wars were beginning. After the victory over Pharnaces, Caesar had installed a relative, Sextus Caesar, as governor of Syria, but the Pompeian Quintus Caecilius Bassus had emerged from hiding and taken over the province. Sextus Caesar was murdered. The Caesarians Quintus Cornificius and then Gaius Antistius Vetus were sent with two legions to remove Bassus. It remained a purely Roman matter until Pacorus, son of the Parthian king, entered the scene, expressing a strong interest in the eastern Roman provinces. A war with Parthia loomed, and Caesar intended to conduct it himself, as soon as he had organised the Roman world.

On his return to Rome towards the end of 45, Caesar did not immediately enter the city, because he wanted to preserve the proper forms, not entering Rome as a general in command of an army until he held his triumph. At his estates at Labici, not far from the city, he wrote his will. In a codicil, he made Gaius Octavius his heir, adopting him as his son. Then he held his triumph, officially over Spain, but the victory was over Romans.

Caesar received the command against the Parthians via a law of the people. He estimated that the campaign would take three years, since he intended first of all to make war on the troublesome Dacians across the Danube, then to go to the east. He filled the public offices of Rome with his adherents, in order to direct policy while he was absent, lining up his consular candidates for the next few years. In December 45 the new tribune, Mark Antony's brother Lucius, passed a law granting Caesar the right to recommend half of the candidates for all other offices.

Most of the state was now in Caesar's hands. He controlled the armies and the finances, he appointed provincial governors, and he recommended most of the candidates for office in Rome. He created new patricians and elevated men to the Senate, including recently enfranchised citizens from outlying parts of the Empire. He had founded colonies in Gaul, Spain, and Africa, and he revived Corinth and Carthage, destroyed by the Romans half a century before he was born. Honours flowed in his direction, voted by the Senate. Anniversaries of his victories were to be marked by festivals and games, and fifty days of thanksgiving were voted after the victory at Munda. He was granted Imperator as a hereditary name, and he was entitled to wear triumphal clothes on public occasions, as well as a laurel wreath, which happily disguised his baldness. A temple was to be built in his honour to Libertas, Freedom, ironic in the circumstances. A statue of him was to be set up in the temple of Quirinus, with an inscription 'to the unconquerable god'. These honours were greater than any hitherto accorded to one man, elevating Caesar far above his peers.

Caesar was in a hurry, and autocracy saved so much time. He was made Dictator for life, so there was now no possibility that he would ever lay down his powers, no possibility that the government of Rome would ever be restored to the Senate, no paths to promotion except through Caesar. There was no debate, no discussion, not even any real share in government, no place for individuality or initiative, and certainly nothing to be gained from holding opinions that differed from Caesar's.

There had already been murmurs of dissatisfaction while Caesar was in Spain. Mark Antony had been sounded out about removing Caesar. He is censured for not warning Caesar, but it is possible that Antony went to meet Caesar on his return from Spain with the express purpose of warning him, and they both decided to do nothing. Absolutism runs the risk of assassination, and Caesar knew it.

It was known by early February 44 that Caesar had accepted the Dictatorship for life. Suspicion that Caesar intended to be king was made worse at a festival celebrated on 15 February, the Lupercalia, a fertility rite of extreme antiquity. The consul Antony took part, running round the streets of Rome with other young men, wearing only a loincloth, striking young women with goatskin thongs, which made them fertile, to bear sons for Rome. Antony carried a diadem with him, which he offered to Caesar, in effect handing him the kingship. Caesar refused it. The audience roared approval. Antony offered it again, with the same result. Motives in this little scenario are obscure. Caesar may have wanted to test popular opinion. If the crowd roared for him to take the diadem, then he could become king with relative immunity. Alternatively it may have been a public demonstration that he did not wish to be king.

As a preliminary for the Dacian and Parthian wars Caesar had sent his great-nephew Gaius Octavius to gain military experience among the legions already stationed in Macedonia. While he was occupied with preparations to go to war, a conspiracy evolved. Marcus Junius Brutus was the son of Caesar's mistress Servilia. He had been brought up by Cato with lofty ideals about the Republic. Gaius Cassius Longinus had fought for Pompey and been pardoned by Caesar, but never settled down in the shadow of Caesar's clemency. Then there were Caesarians like Decimus Brutus and Gaius Trebonius who had held commands under Caesar, but thought that they should have advanced their careers a little faster. The plotters, who called themselves Liberators, would have to act quickly. There was a meeting of the Senate planned for 15 March, and Caesar was to leave for the war three days later. The conspirators decided upon 15 March, the Ides; they swore oaths of loyalty to themselves and Rome, and braced themselves for the event.

The meeting was to be held in Pompey's theatre, because the Senate House had been burnt down at Clodius' funeral and was still being rebuilt. On the appointed morning, Caesar felt ill, but Decimus Brutus was sent to fetch him. Spurinna the augur had warned Caesar about the Ides of March, and on entering Pompey's theatre, Caesar said, 'The Ides of March have come,' and Spurinna, according to legend, replied, 'But not yet gone, Caesar.' Gaius Trebonius drew Antony aside before he entered. Inside Pompey's theatre, the conspirators were waiting. Caesar died from twenty-three stab wounds, pulling his cloak over his head as he fell at the foot of Pompey's statue.

After the Ides

Incredibly, the Liberators had made no plans to take over the state after Caesar's death. They had failed to grasp that without the armies behind them they could not hope to govern Rome. They had spared Antony, mainly at the behest of Brutus, though Cicero lamented the lost opportunity. As consul, Antony took charge, first securing armed assistance from Lepidus, who brought troops to the Tiber island. Then Antony summoned the Senate for 17 March. It is to Antony's eternal credit that he prevented another civil war from breaking out. In the two days since Caesar's murder, Antony had cultivated Caesar's *clientelae* as well as his secretaries and assistants, who gave him all Caesar's papers. He did not call out the troops to line the streets, but his soldiers were close by, and there was a prearranged signal should he find himself in difficulties. At the Senate meeting, Antony let everyone have their say. Cicero proposed a general amnesty, which was accepted.

Antony came to a precarious understanding with the conspirators, who had fled to the

Capitol Hill. Antony attended to government, using Caesar's notes to put forward measures which had been planned but not implemented. He allegedly mixed up his finances with Caesar's, and managed to pay off all his debts, fostering suspicions that he had defrauded the state. Having established order, Antony and the Senate ratified the terms of Caesar's will on 18 March. There was a sum of money for every Roman citizen in the city, and legacies to most of the conspirators. Antony was not in the first rank of the legatees. Caesar had left a quarter of his fortune to his kinsmen Pedius and Pinarius, but the main beneficiary was Gaius Octavius, Caesar's great-nephew, who was to be adopted as his son. Since he was only nineteen, and frequently ill, Antony and the Senate devoted little thought to Octavius, currently in Macedonia with the legions destined for Parthia.

Brutus and Cassius were sent out of Rome to administer the corn supply in Asia and Sicily. Antony passed a law to exchange his province of Macedonia for Cisalpine Gaul, where Caesar's governor, the conspirator Decimus Brutus, was already in command. Antony installed his brother Gaius as governor of Macedonia, with one of the five legions stationed there, taking command of the other four for his province of Cisalpine Gaul. In the midst of all these arrangements, Gaius Octavius returned to Rome. He changed his name to Gaius Julius Caesar, never using the name Octavian, by which historians identify him. Caesar had been destined for deification after his death, so Octavian called himself son of the god, *divi Juli filius*, or simply *divi filius*, eventually issuing coins bearing this proud legend.

The Second Triumvirate 43 BC

Octavian required support in the Senate and found it in Cicero, who required support against Antony and found it in Octavian. Antony marched his troops to Cisalpine Gaul, instead of marching on Rome, proving Cicero wrong in his prediction that Antony would attack Rome. Decimus Brutus would have to be ejected from Cisalpine Gaul, and Antony knew that since his consulship was almost at an end, the Senate would empower the new consuls to make war on him, so he would be fighting on two fronts. He blockaded Decimus Brutus in Mutina (modern Modena).

Cicero persuaded the Senate to confer a military command on Octavian, convinced that the young man would fight against Antony, who was declared an enemy of the state. In the spring of 43, the consuls Aulus Hirtius and Vibius Pansa, accompanied by Octavian and his troops, marched north. Antony decided to attack Pansa before the armies could unite. Pansa was defeated and received a fatal wound, but then Hirtius arrived with the other army, and Antony withdrew. After a second battle at Mutina, Antony had to acknowledge defeat. He set off with his soldiers over the Alps into Transalpine Gaul. It attests to his leadership that they followed him through the wintry passes, without food.

Decimus Brutus was ordered to pursue Antony, and Octavian was ordered to help, but seemed reluctant to march. Decimus was one of the assassins of Caesar, and Octavian was Caesar's heir. While Cicero thought he could use Octavian to eliminate Antony, Octavian had been using Cicero to obtain a legitimate military command. He used it to march to Rome and demand the consulship. The Senate was in no position to argue, and so Octavian became consul, aged nineteen, with Caesar's nephew Quintus Pedius as colleague. One of Octavian's first acts was to have his adoption by Caesar ratified by law. Then he had all Caesar's assassins tried in court in their absence, and secured their condemnation. This meant that they were outside the law, as Antony was. While Octavian marched north against Decimus Brutus, Pedius revoked the law declaring Antony an enemy of the state.

In Gaul, Antony had made spectacular progress. Marcus Aemilius Lepidus joined him, followed by Munatius Plancus, governor of Transalpine Gaul, and Asinius Pollio, governor of Further Spain. This gave Antony control of fifteen legions. When Octavian arrived in northern Italy, he met Antony and Lepidus at Bononia (modern Bologna) and the three of them decided the future of Rome. On 27 November 43, the tribune Publius Titius passed the legislation designating them 'three men appointed to reconstitute the Republic' (*tresviri rei publicae constituendae*). This is usually termed the Second Triumvirate, but officially there had never been a first triumvirate, merely an informal agreement between Pompey, Caesar and Crassus. Antony, Lepidus and Octavian were formally appointed with equal powers to the consuls for five years. They were empowered to make laws, and to nominate magistrates and the governors of provinces. Antony was to govern Cisalpine and Transalpine Gaul, Lepidus was to take control of Gallia Narbonensis and all Spain, Octavian was to control Sardinia, Sicily and Africa. Since they intended to declare war on the Liberators, they would govern their provinces via legates. The eastern provinces were out of their reach, since Brutus and Cassius had seized them and started to raise armies.

Before they could embark on a major war, the three men required the removal of real and potential enemies, and lots of money. They proscribed seventeen men and posted up the lists, but many more names were quickly added. Cicero was one of the first victims. Antony takes most of the blame for the proscriptions, but Octavian had just as much reason to eliminate rivals. As for money, the revenues of the eastern provinces were not reaching Rome, because Brutus and Cassius were diverting them, and since the western provinces were not so wealthy, the heaviest financial burden fell on Italy. The Triumvirs seized all the personal savings entrusted to the Vestal Virgins, and they revived old taxes and invented new ones, including a tax on wealthy women.

The Liberators controlled most of the eastern provinces. Brutus commanded Macedonia, where Antony's brother Gaius had been captured and killed, and Cassius gained Syria by marching there before the Caesarian governor Dolabella could take command. Cleopatra sent four legions to help Dolabella, but Cassius seized these too. In the Mediterranean, Sextus Pompeius had built up a fleet after escaping from Spain, and had gained control of Sicily posing a threat to the corn supply. Fortunately he did not unite with the Liberators.

When the war began, Lepidus was left in Rome with some troops. Antony did not have enough ships to take his whole army across the sea. Cleopatra sent a fleet from Egypt to aid the Triumvirs, but the ships were wrecked in a storm. However, they served their purpose because the Liberators sent out their fleet to search for them, which gave Antony and Octavian the opportunity they needed to send eight legions under Decidius Saxa and Norbanus Flaccus across the Adriatic to Macedonia, where the landed and set off eastwards towards Thessalonika. Brutus and Cassius moved into Thrace and then along the Via Egnatia to meet them. Taking advantage of a brief moment when the enemy fleet drew off, Antony and Octavian landed at Dyrrachium with the rest of their army. Norbanus and Saxa had established a base at Amphipolis, and Brutus and Cassius had camped to the west of Philippi. Antony marched to Amphipolis, left a garrison there, and took the army to reconnoitre the situation at Philippi. Octavian had to be left behind at Dyrrachium, because he was too ill to travel.

The Battle of Philippi 42 BC

At Philippi, Brutus and Cassius had chosen their ground well, utilising all the defensive aspects of the terrain to form two separate camps, Brutus in the northern camp, straddling the road with mountains protecting his flank, and Cassius in the southern camp, protected by a marsh. They had also erected defensive earthworks to prevent the approach of attackers.

Antony made camp to the west of the conspirators, joined by Octavian who had not really recovered but could not afford to be absent at the forthcoming battle. But no battle was likely to occur unless Antony could force the conspirators out of their defences, so he decided to cut their supply line by building a causeway across the marsh, around the southern defences of Cassius' camp, towards the Via Egnatia to the east. His troops built quite a long section of this causeway in secret, while each day Antony drew up the rest of his army to offer battle and to distract attention from the building works, but when Cassius discovered what was happening he started to build a line of defences north of Antony's causeway.

The first battle of Philippi began with a skirmish over these defences, when Antony sent out some of his men across the causeway and Cassius attacked them. The fighting escalated as Antony poured more men into the struggle, and Brutus' army joined in, thinking that they could take Antony in the flank and crush him. The outcome was not decisive. Although Antony took Cassius' camp, Brutus took Octavian's, so that the two armies swivelled round through ninety degrees, still facing each other and neither side victorious. What tipped the balance and prepared the way for final victory for Antony was that Cassius misunderstood what he saw. He had been driven out from his camp, and he assumed that Brutus had likewise been defeated, so he committed suicide.

Alone now, Brutus repaired the damage, entrenching himself even more firmly behind defences, prepared to wait until lack of supplies forced Antony to move. Perhaps like Pompey at Pharsalus, he succumbed to the firebrands among his officers who considered Antony weakened and therefore easily defeated. Brutus offered battle, and Antony hastily accepted. His first move was to try to outflank Brutus, but Brutus sent in his reserve to stop him. Antony switched to an all-out attack on the centre. It may be that he deliberately feigned an attack on the flanks to make Brutus commit his reserve, and once that was out of the way, he then launched his assault on the centre, or he may simply have seen an opportunity and attacked the centre at the right moment. Whichever it was, Antony's manoeuvres won the day. Brutus fled, with four legions, leaving Antony master of the battlefield. During the pursuit, an officer pretending to be Brutus gave himself up. Antony may have been glad that it was not Brutus, because then he would have been forced to execute him. In the end Brutus committed suicide, so Antony could be generous and grant him an honourable funeral, but he allowed Octavian to cut off the Liberator's head and take it to Rome to throw it down at the foot of Caesar's statue. Since Antony had nailed Cicero's head and hands to the Rostrum in the Forum, he was not in a position to refuse on ethical grounds.

The Triumvirs Divide the Roman World 42–37 BC

The victory at Philippi was Antony's. The troops hailed him as Imperator, and when the provinces were carved up once again between him and Octavian, Antony won control of Cisalpine and Transalpine Gaul via his legates, with about seventeen legions, plus the whole of the east. It was the lion's share, and for about a decade Antony was the most important man in the Roman world.

Octavian's part in the two battles had not been impressive, but he was far from negligible in the political sphere. He was to govern Spain, Sardinia, Corsica and Sicily, and Lepidus would control Africa. Octavian would have to fight for Sicily since Sextus Pompey still controlled the island, and there had been rumours that Lepidus was seeking an alliance with him, so Octavian would have to tread carefully. His first major task would be to find lands for his discharged veterans, in fulfilment of the promise made to the troops when the Triumvirs had held their meeting at Bononia.

Antony remained in the east, repairing the damage that the Liberators had caused by extracting supplies and money. Some cities had been impoverished, others had tried to resist, but in the end they had all suffered. It was not only the cities of the Roman provinces that had been affected. The fragile relationships with rulers whose kingdoms bordered on the provinces also required attention. Unfortunately the sources do not elucidate Antony's arrangements in the east. Greater emphasis is laid on the fact that he went to Athens for the winter of 42/1. In the spring of 41 he travelled to Ephesus, where he was hailed as the new Dionysus, the god of wine and beneficence. The Romans did not approve of treating living persons as if they were divine, but in the east it was quite normal and Pompey had been treated in the same way when he campaigned against Mithradates. Antony's newfound divinity would counterbalance Octavian's claims to be the son of the god Caesar.

At Pergamum, Antony met with delegates from the eastern states, and demanded ten years' taxes, from communities which had already paid vast sums to the Liberators to support their armies. One of the delegates asked if Antony could arrange a second summer and a second harvest. Antony settled for nine years' tax payable over two years. He needed to pay his troops, and to supply them, no light task given the number of legions he had at his disposal, but he could not disband them because the ultimate aim was to fight the war against the Parthians that Caesar had planned. For the time being he concentrated on making friendly overtures to the states which bordered the Parthian Empire.

One state in particular, which could scarcely be said to border on Parthia, was vital to his plans. Egypt was wealthy, possessing all the resources to supply food for the soldiers and to build a fleet of ships. Queen Cleopatra had been placed securely on her throne by Caesar and she had tried to help the Triumvirs by sending soldiers and ships to fight against the Liberators. Antony asked her to meet him at Tarsus, in Cilicia (modern Turkey). She agreed. Antony wanted financial assistance for his Parthian campaign. Cleopatra wanted recognition for herself and her son Caesarion as independent rulers of Egypt, and at the moment Antony was the most important man in the Roman world, as Caesar had been in 48. This famous meeting started out as a political expedient for both Antony and Cleopatra, but their relationship transcended any formal alliance. It played into Octavian's hands, when the time came to use it against Antony.

After their meeting, Antony attended to problems in Syria, and left Decidius Saxa in command when everything was settled. The sources are hostile to Antony, even accusing him of creating more problems than he solved, but it is significant that all was calm for some time thereafter, although the peace was disturbed by the Parthians. Antony spent the winter of 41/40 BC in Egypt. His relationship with Cleopatra was confirmed when Antony acknowledged the twins that she had borne him, Alexander Helios (named for the sun) and Cleopatra Selene (named for the moon).

In Italy, Octavian was having trouble in finding lands for the veteran soldiers. There was active opposition from Lucius Antonius, Antony's brother, and Fulvia, Antony's wife. They said that Antony's veterans were being treated unfairly, but Octavian defused the situation by allowing Antony's men to supervise the settlement of veterans. Lucius then took up the cause of the displaced farmers. The problems escalated into war, in which Lucius was blockaded in Perusia (modern Perugia). In February 40, the town was burned – no one seems to know who was responsible – and Lucius was captured. He was sent to govern Spain, but was supervised by several of Octavian's supporters. Antony did nothing at all, so that nobody could decide whether he had instigated the whole event, or whether Lucius and Fulvia had acted with misguided zeal on his behalf. Seeds of distrust were being sown. After the fall of Perusia and the capture of Lucius, many of the Antonians fled, including Antony's wife Fulvia, and his mother, Julia. Fulvia, accompanied by the ex-Pompeian Munatius Plancus, arrived in Athens to meet Antony, with the news that Plancus' legions had gone over to Octavian. Another blow to Antony was the unexpected death of Fufius Calenus, Antony's legate in Gaul. Octavian quietly assumed command of the legions in Gaul and sent out Salvidienus Rufus as governor.

Antony could not immediately regain control of Gaul because the Parthians invaded Syria in the spring of 40, killing the governor Decidius Saxa. Antony delegated his general Ventidius Bassus to restore order in Syria, and then in the autumn he sailed to Italy. Sextus Pompeius had given refuge to Antony's mother as she fled from Octavian, and now proposed an alliance with Antony, who guardedly said it depended on the agreement he made with Octavian, but he would put Sextus' case before the Senate.

Antony arrived at Brundisium with his new ally Domitius Ahenobarbus, originally the commander of the fleet raised by Brutus and Cassius. Brundisium had closed its gates. Antony started to besiege the town, but Octavian arrived and a treaty was made. Antony would hold the east, relinquishing his command in Gaul, and Octavian would control the west. The two men travelled to Rome, where they were met by a relieved population. In order to cement their new alliance, Antony married Octavia, the sister of Octavian.

There remained the problem of Sextus Pompeius, who had reapplied his stranglehold on Rome's corn supply. There were riots in the city. Neither Octavian nor Antony had enough ships to combat Sextus, whose crews were by this time far more experienced than any that the Triumvirs could assemble. Negotiation was the only alternative, so the three men met at Misenum in 39 and another treaty was made. The terms were that Sextus was to control Sardinia, Corsica, and Sicily, which merely ratified the status quo. In return, Sextus was to guarantee the corn supply for Rome. He was promised the consulship, and control of the Peloponnese. Neither promise was fulfilled.

The Triumvirs had already filled all the main magistracies up to 31. They declared an amnesty for anyone who had taken refuge with Sextus, and some of the magistracies went to them, in multiples in some cases, to give them administrative experience as well as rank. In 39 there were more than two consuls, and sixty-seven praetors in the following year. The Triumvirs had all their acts ratified by the Senate, by a law applied retrospectively to the beginning of the Triumvirate, which would soon be coming to the end of the five-year term.

Later in the year the prospect of peace was shattered. Sextus Pompeius had not received the Peloponnese, so he raided the ships carrying food to Rome. Octavian invaded Sicily, but was badly beaten. He lost many ships in a battle off Cumae, and most of the surviving vessels in a storm the next day. He was forced to ask Antony for help. Antony had spent the winter of 39 in Athens, preparing for the Parthian campaign. His general Ventidius had restored order in Syria, and it remained to ensure the loyalty of the kingdoms and tribes of the east before the army set off to make war on King Pacorus of Parthia. When Octavian's request for assistance arrived, Antony put everything on hold and sailed once again to Brundisium. There was no one to meet him, so he sailed back, having wasted a lot of time. He arrived in Syria in the middle of the summer. Ventidius had fought a battle with the Parthians at Gindarus in northern Syria, in which the Parthian king had been killed. The remnants of the Parthian army had taken refuge with King Antiochus of Commagene, at Samosata on the River Euphrates. Ventidius marched there and laid siege to the place. Antony took over in autumn 38, and Ventidius returned to Rome to celebrate a well-deserved triumph.

Antony made peace at Samosata and returned to Athens for the winter, intending to resume his preparations for the Parthian campaign in the spring of 37, but was interrupted for the third time. Octavian had lost another battle against Sextus. Antony assembled 300 ships and sailed to Brundisium, then on to Tarentum, where Octavian met him. Antony gave up 120 ships to help Octavian in the struggle against Sextus, and was promised 20,000 soldiers for the Parthian campaign.

The Renewal of the Triumvirate 37–33 BC

Technically the Triumvirate had expired in 38, but Antony and Octavian had retained the command of their armies, and their adherents had been appointed to the most important magistracies. For the sake of appearances, they renewed their powers for another five years, and the necessary law was passed by the people's assembly in Rome.

It was too late to begin the campaign against the Parthians, so Antony deferred it until the spring of 36. The delay was frustrating because the Parthian royal house was in turmoil after Pacorus had been killed in battle against Ventidius. The new king Phraates was busily eliminating all his relatives. In coming to the aid of Octavian, Antony had lost the chance to exploit the distracting mayhem among the Parthians. He spent the winter in Antioch, and in spring he drew up his army at Zeugma in north-eastern Syria, as if he intended to invade at that point, significantly opposite Carrhae where Crassus had been killed in 53, but instead he made a dash northwards to march through Armenia and Media, hoping that the Parthians would assemble in the wrong place and he could attack them from the north. The plan failed because he was stalled in Media trying to besiege the capital at Phraaspa. His siege train was destroyed and he had to retreat, through the horrendous terrain and bitter wintry weather of Armenia. He lost many of his men, and finally put his generals Domitius Ahenobarbus and Canidius in command of the army, while he travelled ahead to the Syrian coast, sending messengers to Cleopatra, asking her to meet him with clothing, food and money. She gathered the supplies and set off in person, probably in January, risking her life in an inadvisable winter sea voyage.

There was no question of mounting another campaign against Parthia in 35. The army would have to be rebuilt and Antony needed money. When his wife Octavia arrived in Athens with supplies, soldiers, and cash, Antony did not go to meet her, but simply sent her a message. He went to Alexandria with Cleopatra. It was not a sound policy. By maltreating his wife and linking himself with Cleopatra, he had broken with Octavian.

In contrast to Antony, Octavian's campaign in 36 against Sextus Pompeius was a resounding success. Marcus Vipsanius Agrippa had built a new fleet, constructed an artificial harbour and used it to train the crews. He adapted the grappling iron called the *harpax* that could be catapulted on to enemy ships to draw them close enough to board. He had added protective covering on the ropes that were attached to them so that the enemy could not cut them and break free. There was an indecisive sea battle off Mylae, then in September 36 Agrippa won the naval battle of Naulochus. The victory elevated Octavian to new heights in Rome, except for an unpleasant episode when the forgotten Triumvir Lepidus tried to gain control of Sicily, but Octavian simply purchased Lepidus' soldiers. Lepidus was allowed to retain his office as Pontifex Maximus, but was closely watched for the rest of his life.

Octavian was the man of the hour in Rome, showered with tremendous honours voted to him by the Senate and people, and yet more power, this time that of the tribunes. It is debatable whether he was granted full tribunician power at this time or whether he achieved it by gradual stages, but it was to become the mainstay of Imperial power. As Octavian went from strength to strength, Antony's reputation had begun to tarnish. If there had been a splendid victory over the Parthians, Antony may have been able to redeem himself, and he may have been forgiven for associating with the Queen of Egypt.

Civil War 32–30 BC

It was perhaps not inevitable at this stage that another civil war would break out. Antony ought to have gone to Rome, to exercise the same level of self-advertisement as Octavian, but he remained in the east and his agents in Rome were ineffective, allowing Octavian to eclipse him. In 34 Antony mounted a campaign against Armenia, hoping to consolidate his power in that kingdom so that he could attack Parthia. His conquest of Armenia has been belittled, but it was sound enough, even if not permanent, and Antony issued coinage with the legend *Armenia Devicta*, Armenia conquered. This was wholly in keeping with the Roman ethos, and it would have greatly assisted Antony's cause if he had celebrated his victory in Rome, dedicating the spoils of war to Jupiter in the Capitoline temple. Instead Antony chose to celebrate it in Alexandria. He held a parade through the streets of the city, perhaps not intending to make a mockery of the Roman triumph, but it was easy to interpret it as such. Next day Antony sealed his fate with Octavian and Rome. He held another celebration, known as the Donations of Alexandria. Seated on a dais with Cleopatra at his side and their children before them, Antony bestowed on them kingdoms and territories of the east, including kingdoms that were not yet within his gift. What was more threatening, from Octavian's point of view, was Antony's proclamation of Caesarion as the true heir of Caesar.

Octavian was engaged in campaigns in Illyricum, which gave him legitimate grounds to command armies, and hopefully military prestige to match Antony's. There was the possibility that Antony would defeat the Parthians and become a hero, so there would be no reason to make war on him. Octavian began a political campaign against Antony. As consul in 33 Octavian tested public feelings with a speech against Antony, but he shifted most of the opprobrium onto Cleopatra, who was a foreign and therefore legitimate enemy.

In 33 Antony abandoned any idea of a Parthian campaign and turned away from the east, focussing on Rome, but too late. He started to prepare for war against Octavian, but tried to soothe public feeling in Rome by offering to lay down his Triumviral powers if Octavian did the same. The Triumvirate had probably ended in December 33, which meant that in 32 neither Octavian nor Antony was entitled to command armies. The consuls of 32, Sosius and Domitius Ahenobarbus, were both Antony's men, but they were overwhelmed by Octavian, who convened a meeting of the Senate where he arrived with his bodyguard, and forcibly seated himself between the two consuls. The illegality of his actions was ignored. He said he had obtained documentary evidence to condemn Antony and would produce it at the next meeting. It precipitated a mass exodus. The consuls and about 300 senators fled to Antony. The Roman world was once again dividing itself into two opposing camps. About 700 senators remained with Octavian, and some of Antony's men came to Rome, sensing that they might be on the losing side if they stayed in the east. It was said that two of them revealed to Octavian that Antony had lodged his last will and testament with the Vestal Virgins in Rome, so Octavian seized it and read it out at a meeting of the Senate. Antony reaffirmed Caesarion's status as the heir of Caesar, and expressed a wish to be buried in Alexandria with Cleopatra.

The indignation of the Senate and people fuelled their support for war. Octavian took the precaution of having all the inhabitants of Italy swear an oath of allegiance to him, save for the towns such as Bononia where Antony had many clients. It was an unprecedented gesture which gave Octavian the moral support to make war on Cleopatra, and by default on Antony. The war was fought in Greece. Antony strung his army out to watch the inlets and harbours on the western coast, concentrating on the Gulf of Ambracia, where two projecting peninsulas almost encircled the waters of the gulf. In the spring of 31 Octavian arrived and made camp on the northern peninsula, facing Antony on the southern arm. Antony crossed the mouth of the gulf with his allied cavalry and tried to cut off Octavian's water supply, but his native troops deserted to Octavian. The second attempt may have been more successful. Coin evidence shows that at some time in this campaign the soldiers hailed Antony as Imperator for the fourth time, and this is the most likely context.

Most of Antony's fleet was now bottled up in the gulf. Agrippa steadily annihilated Antony's troops on the islands and coasts. The morale of Antony's army deteriorated as malaria and dysentery decimated them. Desertions began, and Antony's punishments for indiscipline grew more and more severe. Finally, he decided to risk a naval encounter. The battle of Actium is significant as the turning point in the civil war, but it was less of a battle than a break-out. Antony had already lost. He burnt some ships, assembled the rest and told the crews to ready their sails. A light offshore wind usually began in the afternoons, which would help the ships to escape if they got through Agrippa's lines.

Cleopatra escaped carrying the treasury and after desultory fighting Antony followed. Most of his ships were captured or sunk. Canidius was ordered to march the army overland to Alexandria. Cleopatra entered Alexandria with flags flying as though they had won a great victory, while Antony hid himself away in a hut on the shore. It was certain that Octavian would follow. He had already purchased the Antonian troops in Greece, except for their commander Canidius, who refused to be bought and went to join Antony in Egypt. Octavian allegedly offered lenient terms for Cleopatra if she would surrender Antony, but she refused. She probably distrusted Octavian, knowing that what he really needed was access to her treasure and the wealth of Egypt. The people were prepared to go to war on her behalf, but she refused to embroil them in death and destruction, knowing that Octavian would have no interest in them beyond gathering their tax payments.

When Octavian appeared in Egypt in 30, Antony took some of his troops to combat him, hopelessly outnumbered. His cavalry routed Octavian's advance guard, and he came back to Alexandria to celebrate, but it was only a matter of time. The soldiers and the fleet went over to Octavian. Antony watched the mass desertion and rode into Alexandria to find that Cleopatra had locked herself into her mausoleum, and was probably already dead. He fell on his sword, but did not die immediately. The story goes that he was hauled up into the mausoleum to die in Cleopatra's arms. It may be true. It may also be true that after a few days, Cleopatra was bitten by an asp hidden in a basket of figs, and died rather than be led as a captive in Octavian's triumph.

Caesarion, the son of Cleopatra and Caesar, was killed, as was Antony's son Antyllus. There the vendetta ended. Antony's younger son Iullus Antonius, and the three children of Antony and Cleopatra, were all spared. Octavian was undisputed sole ruler of the Roman world. Arriving at this point had been difficult and protracted; now he needed a legitimate means of staying there, which ultimately depended on the army.

Part II
The Imperial Roman Army

1

Historical Overview 30 BC–AD 260

Ancient and modern historians have dated the beginning of the Empire to the battle of Actium in 31 or the fall of Alexandria in the following year, but the transformation of the Republic into the Empire was a gradual process. The Republic as a form of government was dead on its feet by Caesar's day, and long before 30 BC Rome already controlled an Empire which embraced most of the territories around the Mediterranean, including Sicily, Sardinia, Corsica, Spain, Gaul, Illyricum, Macedonia, Achaea, Asia, Bithynia, Syria, Cyrenaica, Crete, Cyprus, Africa, and latterly Egypt.

The Supremacy of Augustus

Octavian's victory over Antony and Cleopatra ended two decades of political and military turmoil. Octavian took over Egypt as his personal preserve, which provided most of his wealth. He made Cornelius Gallus, an equestrian, the first governor, with the title of prefect. From then onwards, senators were forbidden to enter Egypt, and the governor was always an equestrian prefect, appointed by and answerable to the emperor. In 30 there were probably sixty legions in existence. Octavian disbanded many of them, establishing colonies in Italy, Gaul and Spain for the veterans, leaving twenty-eight legions under arms. Little is known about auxiliary units, which at this period would have been engaged on a temporary basis. Many were probably sent back to their homes. The military reforms were undertaken stage by stage, and resulted in the establishment of the first standing army.

In 29, when Octavian was consul for the fifth time, the Senate confirmed all his acts, which exonerated the past, but he needed to ensure his future as head of state. For that he required money, political supremacy, and control of the armies, but without making it too obvious that his supremacy ultimately depended on armed force. The unprecedented honours that were voted to him were significant, but did not provide him with the long-term legal basis that he required. That would have to be arranged by degrees, slowly and tactfully.

In his sixth consulship in 28 Octavian was made the leader of the Senate, *princeps senatus*, which gave him a preponderant influence in discussions. Aware that his prolonged hold on power would not continue unchallenged, at the beginning of his seventh consulship in 27 he proclaimed that he would restore the Republic and hand over the government to the Senate. This was a calculated risk. Octavian probably had alternatives in mind if the senators readily assumed control of the Empire, but fortunately many of them owed their positions to him and had a vested interest in maintaining him in power. It was agreed that Octavian would govern the provinces of Gaul, Spain, Syria, Cilicia, Cyprus, and Egypt, all of which bordered foreign powers, or were subject to internal unrest. All of them required armies, which would be commanded by Octavian, via his legates, who would owe their promotion to him. Men of consular rank would govern provinces with two or more legions, and less important armed provinces would be governed by men of praetorian rank. Whether they were ex-consuls or ex-praetors, all the legates were titled *legati Augusti propraetore*, or propraetorian legates of the emperor. In the fully evolved system, smaller Imperial provinces with only auxiliary troops would be governed by equestrian prefects, like Egypt. Senators of praetorian or consular rank would govern all the other non-Imperial provinces, with the title of proconsul. A few of them would command armies, but this did not last for a long time. It seems that Octavian could intervene in the government of the proconsular provinces, but there is much debate about the technicalities of how this was done. After this political settlement, the Senate bestowed on Octavian the name Augustus, a tremendous honour. It gave him enormous influence but no legal powers. He represented himself as first among equals, adopting the title *Princeps*, from which the term Principate is applied to the early Empire, as opposed to Dominate describing the changed circumstances of the later Empire.

In 23 Augustus was seriously ill. His son-in-law Marcellus, husband of Augustus' daughter Julia, was his intended heir, but was too young and inexperienced, so Augustus chose his friend and colleague Marcus Vipsanius Agrippa as his deputy and successor if he should die. Fortunately he recovered, and the crisis was averted. He relinquished the consulship from then onwards, and in return he received *imperium proconsulare*, the powers of a proconsul. There is considerable debate concerning his status with regard to the provincial governors, and whether his proconsular power was equal or superior to theirs, but it was perhaps never formally expressed as *aequum* or *maior*, allowing him leeway to act as appropriate if circumstances demanded his intervention. It has been argued that there was never any such concept as *aequum* or *maior*, but the debate has not yet been concluded.

Proconsular power was important, but even more significant was tribunician power, *tribunicia potestas*, renewed each year. Octavian-Augustus may have acquired these powers in stages from 36 onwards, receiving the full powers in 23. This gave him the right to summon the Senate and put motions to the senators, to initiate legislation, to summon the people's assembly, and to veto any proposals from whatever source. Contrary to custom, other tribunes did not have the right to veto any of Augustus' proposals. Only Agrippa, and later Tiberius, shared in Augustus' tribunician power, but it was adopted by future emperors.

Confirmed in his supreme position for the time being, Augustus could now make long-term plans, though he was careful to put a temporal limit on his powers, usually five or ten years. There was never any trouble in renewing his powers, but the need for renewal avoided any hint of limitless or permanent power. Gradually, Augustus laid the foundations of a more structured career path for senators, so that they could exercise some influence, and could look forward to promotion, otherwise they would either sink into apathy, or erupt in revolt. Augustus increased the senatorial property qualification from 400,000 *sestertii* to one million *sestertii*, but gave financial assistance to some of those who fell short of the required total. The sons of senators were ranked as equestrians until they began their careers, the quaestorship being the first important post, which automatically made them senators. The next politically important post was that of aedile, then praetor, followed by a gap of some years, so that no one could reach the consulship until his mid-thirties. Praetors and consuls could look forward to promotion as provincial governors, but each man would have to be known to, and trusted by, Augustus.

For the equestrians, too, there were opportunities for promotion. The Prefects of Egypt were always equestrians, and Augustus created more prefectures. The Praetorian Guard was formed in 2 BC, with two Praetorian Prefects in command, and the *Vigiles*, the police force and fire service of Rome, with one prefect, was created in AD 6. Two years later Augustus created the post of *Praefectus Annonae* to administer the food supply, to ensure that the people did not go hungry, thereby pre-empting riots.

Self-advertisement was an integral part of Augustus' scheme, utilising his literary circle co-ordinated by his friend Gaius Maecenas. His image was promoted all over the Empire via the coinage, statues, and sculptured reliefs. He was always presented as a youthful figure whatever his real age. He allowed himself to be worshipped via the Imperial cult, which varied in practice in different parts of the Empire. Soon after the battle of Actium, Octavian-Augustus allowed the Greeks to worship him together with the goddess Roma, but Roman citizens worshipped instead the deified Caesar and Rome. In the west, the Imperial cult started in Spain where worship of the spirit, or *genius*, of Augustus, as distinct from the living person, began around 25 BC. The cult spread to Gaul, Germany, and Italy. The development of the cult relied on local initiatives, and was never imposed. Sacred altars were established at Lyon for the Three Gauls, and another for the tribe of the Ubii on the Rhine, at a place which was called literally the altar of the Ubii, *Ara Ubiorum*, the early name for modern Cologne.

There was a continuous problem about the succession. In 13 Augustus' powers were renewed for another five years. He could not be certain how much longer he would live, so he needed to ensure the succession. The hereditary principle had not yet been applied to the government, so he needed to ensure that the Senate and people of Rome, and above all the army, accepted the designated heir. Augustus' dilemma was that all his heirs predeceased him. His first choice, his nephew Marcellus, died late in 23, leaving Augustus' daughter Julia a widow. She was then married to Marcus Vipsanius Agrippa, and together they produced three daughters, and two sons, Gaius and Lucius, who were adopted by Augustus and groomed for succession. They were introduced at an early age into public life, under his supervision. Unfortunately Lucius, the younger of the two boys, died in AD 2, and Gaius died two years later. In AD 4, Augustus' stepson Tiberius was granted tribunician power for ten years, and Augustus adopted him, and also Agrippa Postumus, the son of Agrippa and Julia. As further insurance for the succession, Tiberius adopted his nephew Germanicus, the son of his brother Drusus, who had died in Germany in 9 BC. Tiberius was the most experienced of Augustus' heirs, and Germanicus was the most popular. Agrippa Postumus was allegedly involved in a plot and banished in AD 7.

On his way to Capri in AD 14, Augustus fell ill. He reached Nola, where he owned property. He gathered his friends around him to ask if they had enjoyed the performance. On 19 August the greatest showman and most astute psychologist of the Roman world died. He was deified, and his adopted son Tiberius reluctantly inherited the government of the Empire.

The Julio Claudians AD 14–68

The four successors of Augustus were Tiberius (AD 14–37), Gaius Caligula (AD 37–41), Claudius (AD 41–54), and Nero (AD 54–68). They combined the bloodlines of Julius Caesar and the Claudian house, as represented by Tiberius, whose full name was Tiberius Claudius Nero. The name Augustus became an official title, and all four emperors assumed or were granted tribunician power, which was the political mainstay of Imperial rule. All emperors were commanders in chief and paymasters of the armies, and the higher promotions were in their gift.

The problems of the succession that Augustus had experienced were avoided by the next four emperors, but transmission of power by inheritance was not necessarily a peaceful process. Tiberius ruled for twenty-one years, latterly by remote control from Capri, before he felt the need to name his heirs in AD 35. His son Drusus had died in AD 23, leaving only two candidates, his grandson Tiberius Gemellus, and Gaius Caligula, the son of Germanicus and Agrippina. In AD 37 Tiberius died. He was seventy-eight years old and had led an arduous life, so there was probably no need for Caligula to smother him, as legend has it. Supported by the Praetorian Prefect Macro, Gaius Caligula became Emperor. He adopted Gemellus, and bestowed the consulship on his uncle Claudius, who had played little part in public life, ignored by the Imperial household because of his stammer, his lameness, and his tendency to drool. Caligula did not name an heir, so after he was assassinated his successor Claudius was chosen by the soldiers. Claudius had a young son, Britannicus, by his third wife Messalina, who was executed after a sex scandal. He then married his niece, the younger Agrippina, daughter of Germanicus and Agrippina the elder. He adopted her son Lucius, who took the name Nero Claudius Caesar, and began to eclipse Britannicus, especially since Claudius promoted Nero, designating him consul for the year AD 58. In 54, when Nero was sixteen, Claudius died, probably poisoned by Agrippina. Without protest from the Praetorians, the Senate, the people or the army, Nero became Emperor on 13 October 54. In 68, Nero was not given the chance to designate his heirs. He committed suicide as provincial armies converged on him and he was followed by four successive emperors all fighting for supremacy.

The provinces were static under Tiberius, who left his governors in command for many years. The continuity benefited the provincials, but blocked promotion for senators and equestrians. Caligula did little for the provinces, except to annexe Mauretania, and he nearly wrecked Augustus' careful administrative arrangements for the east, especially where provinces and client kings bordered on the Parthian Empire. He installed Herod as king of Judaea, but Claudius converted Judaea to a province again, and he annexed Lycia together with Pamphylia, and also Thrace. He conquered Britain, and after a rebellion in Mauretania, pacified by Suetonius Paullinus and Hosidius Geta, he created two provinces, Mauretania Tingitana and Mauretania Caesariensis. The Mauri, or Moors, provided excellent cavalry for the Roman army.

Claudius has been credited with the organisation of the administrative machinery of the Empire, but his role is now played down by modern historians. Nonetheless separate departments with a secretary over each eventually evolved. The staff were mostly freedmen, though some equestrians were given posts. Finances were looked after by Pallas, the freedman secretary *a rationibus*, and Narcissus dealt with correspondence in the office *ab epistulis*. The library and archives were supervised by *a studiis*, legal matters and petitions by *a cognitionibus* and *a libellis*. The system was retained by succeeding emperors. Claudius improved the water supply for the city of Rome, extended the boundary (*pomerium*) and built roads in Italy to the coasts and to the Alps. He built a new harbour at Ostia, the port of Rome, and tried to increase trade and to improve agriculture.

In his dealings with the Senate, Tiberius had tried to foster discussions and independent thought, but the relationship between the senators and the Emperor gradually soured. Caligula scared the senators to death because of his unpredictability and his appetite for treason trials, but fortunately the Praetorians assassinated him in 41. Claudius encouraged the senators to contribute to debates, but his benevolent attitude was not wholly trusted, and eventually there were executions. About thirty-five senators were killed, along with many more equestrians as their clients. Nero largely ignored the Senate, but did not ignore the activities of individuals. Senators began to fear him, and in the end their alienation was complete.

From Augustus onwards, all emperors were dependent on the support of the armies. Tiberius was the only successor of Augustus who had any military experience. Between 12 and 9 BC he subdued Pannonia and annexed it. In 9 BC he took over the campaigns in Germany after his brother Drusus died, remaining there until 7 BC, and returning from AD 4 to 6. Immediately after that he suppressed revolts in Pannonia and Illyricum, and cleared up in Germany after the loss of three legions under the governor Varus in AD 9. After this disaster Augustus instructed Tiberius not to expand the Empire, and, as Emperor, Tiberius complied; he had seen enough fighting. Immediately after the death of Augustus, Tiberius made sure of the Praetorians by paying them a donative, and secured the loyalty of the armies in the provinces by administering the military oath that had been established by Augustus. Early in his reign the armies of Germany and Pannonia nearly mutinied over pay and long terms of service. Tiberius kept his distance from the Praetorians, allowing the infamous Praetorian Prefect Lucius Aelius Sejanus far too much leeway. The Praetorian cohorts were distributed through Italy, but Sejanus brought them to Rome and installed them in a camp on the outskirts of the city. Significantly, no emperor reversed this decision. Sejanus eliminated rivals and became sole Praetorian Prefect, and began to eliminate anyone else who might stand in the way of his ambition. Sejanus demonstrated how far a determined officer with the backing of soldiers could rise while the emperor was not paying attention. When Tiberius was informed of what had been happening by Antonia, daughter of Mark Antony and mother of Claudius, he appointed Naevius Sutorius Macro as Praetorian Prefect with orders to eliminate Sejanus.

Gaius Caligula had grown up in the military circles of his father Germanicus, but he had not taken part in any wars. As Emperor, Gaius led an expedition to the Rhine, in response to a suspected plot, which was suppressed by two competent military men, the future emperors Sulpicius Galba, and Titus Flavius Vespasianus. It was said that Gaius also planned an invasion of Britain. Allegedly he reached the coast of Gaul and made his soldiers collect seashells. The word *musculi* denotes shells, but it is also the term used for military siege equipment, which explains part of the puzzle, but not why the expedition was aborted. The conquest of Britain was undertaken by Claudius, via his legates. Claudius had no military experience, but he was the only one of the Julio-Claudian successors of Augustus who expanded the Empire by conquest, and he earned twenty-seven acclamations as Imperator. Not even Tiberius could rival that. Nero very nearly abandoned Britain after the revolt of Boudicca in AD 60–61, and was content to combat the Parthian threat via his legate Gaius Domitius Corbulo, who campaigned in Armenia to keep the Parthians out, and was made governor of Syria in AD 60. Corbulo commanded a large territory and large armies, keeping the eastern part of the Roman world secure until Nero realised that such a powerful general represented a threat, and drove him to suicide in AD 67. Nero appointed Gaius Licinius Mucianus as governor of Syria, and gave the command in Judaea, where a revolt was in process, to Titus Flavius Vespasianus.

At the beginning of his reign, Nero recognised his dependence on the armies. His first task was to ensure the loyalty of the Praetorians by distributing cash to each man, which became an Imperial habit. By the end of his reign, Nero had upset so many people that four provincial governors marched to Rome with four different armies, intent on replacing him. Tacitus called the armed intervention the secret of Empire, in that emperors could be made elsewhere than in Rome, but it had not really been a secret, just a veiled possibility.

The Flavian Emperors AD 69–96

Titus Flavius Vespasianus was governor of Judaea when the revolt against Nero began in 68, instigated by Gaius Julius Vindex, governor of Gallia Lugdunensis, and then led by Servius Sulpicius Galba, governor of Hispania Tarraconensis. Vindex had no troops. Galba commanded one legion, and raised a new one, then marched on Rome with Marcus Salvius Otho, governor of Lusitania. Galba arranged the assassination of the governor of Africa, and of Fonteius Capito, governor of Lower Germany, installing Aulus Vitellius in Capito's place. The Praetorians initially supported Galba, but observing how he eliminated Nero's soldiers and installed his own adherents in various posts, the Praetorians cooled, especially since Galba did not pay them the promised donative. Ignoring his supporter Otho, Galba named Lucius Calpurnius Piso as his heir, so Otho joined with the Praetorians, who murdered Galba and made Otho Emperor.

There was a rival candidate, Aulus Vitellius, appointed governor of Lower Germany by Galba. The soldiers declared him Emperor, and he marched towards Rome. Otho was outnumbered, and left it too long before he tried to stop Vitellius in northern Italy. Vitellius' generals Fabius Valens and Aulus Caecina Alienus marched through the Alps, and Otho's commander Suetonius Paullinus failed to halt them. Otho committed suicide, advising his supporters to declare for Vitellius and avoid unnecessary bloodshed. The Senate acknowledged Vitellius before he reached Rome. The new Emperor arrived in the city with 60,000 troops, which he could not control. The mayhem in the city provided the excuse for Gaius Licinius Mucianus and Titus Flavius Vespasianus to rescue the city from Vitellius. This was not a sudden decision. After news arrived of Nero's suicide in 68, both Mucianus and Vespasianus had been in communication with each other, waiting for an opportunity to intervene. At the beginning of July 69, the troops in Egypt, Judaea and Syria all declared for Vespasian, as he must now be called. A considerable amount of preparation had gone into this spontaneous acclamation.

When the Flavian party began to move, they had an ally in Antonius Primus and the legions of Pannonia. He set off before Mucianus marched from Syria. Primus won the battle near Cremona against Vitellius' commander Caecina, but he could not prevent his troops from sacking Cremona, a stain on the Flavian regime that led to Primus' downfall later on. Vitellius abdicated, but his troops ran amok, endangering Vespasian's brother Sabinus, and his son Domitian, who gathered their supporters and fled to the Capitol Hill. They were rescued by Antonius Primus, but then the soldiers of Primus' army ran riot in the city. Order was restored when Mucianus arrived in Rome.

The war in Judaea could not be abandoned. Vespasian put his son Titus in command, and journeyed to Rome at the end of 70. He was made consul with his son Titus as colleague, and his younger son Domitian was urban praetor with consular powers. The Senate conferred Vespasian's powers upon him, as they did for all emperors, but in Vespasian's case there was a special law, *lex de imperio Vespasiani*, which may have differed from the usual procedure, especially as Vespasian was not related to the Julio-Claudians. He was also the first Italian to become Emperor. His title was Imperator Caesar Vespasianus Augustus, using Imperator as a name, distinct from the title derived from acclamations by the troops, setting the format for the nomenclature of future emperors.

Vespasian reconstituted the Praetorian Guard, which had been disbanded by Vitellius in favour of his German soldiers. Titus was made Praetorian Prefect. Vespasian cultivated the provincial armies, and the soldiers were kept busy in some provinces during the first part of his reign. The Jewish revolt was suppressed by Titus in 70, with the destruction of the Great Temple in Jerusalem, and the dispersal of the Jews, termed the Diaspora. The Jews of Masada held out until 74. There was a revolt in 69 in Gaul and Germany led by Julius Civilis, a Batavian who had served in the Roman army. Mucianus sent Petillius Cerialis to squash the revolt.

Vespasian strengthened the Rhine army, and authorised an advance into the north of Britain and Wales under three successive governors, Petillius Cerialis, Sextus Julius Frontinus and

Gnaeus Julius Agricola. During the remainder of his reign there were no further wars, allowing Vespasian to concentrate on repairing the damage during the mayhem of 69. He and Titus took the office of censor and overhauled the Senate, replacing the casualties of the civil wars, and opening up the Senate to enfranchised provincials. In the provinces, colonies were founded, and some cities were upgraded to municipal status. In the east, special attention was devoted to the territories on the borders of the Parthian Empire and Armenia, and the troops in Syria were increased.

The greatest achievement during Vespasian's reign was the overhaul of the finances. Largely due to Nero, the state was bankrupt, despite Claudius' careful administration. As censors Vespasian and Titus were able to assess the wealth of the Empire and its potential tax revenues, which they began to collect assiduously. Vespasian also limited public spending. He spent money in the provinces on necessary projects like road building, and in Rome on part of the site of Nero's Golden House he built the Colosseum, but this project was funded by the spoils of the Jewish war.

The Emperor Titus took over without opposition when Vespasian died in 79, not long before the destruction of Pompeii and Herculaneum. Titus was generous with relief funds for the victims, and he came to the rescue in the following year when a serious fire destroyed much of Rome. Titus' reign was too short to discern what his policies may have been. He died in September 81, succeeded by his younger brother Domitian, who was hailed by the troops as Imperator on the day of Titus' death. The Senate confirmed Domitian's accession. He held tribunician power, commanded all the armies like his predecessors, and was Pontifex Maximus or chief priest. He held the consulship for ten years, putting his administrative measures into effect during the first few months of each year and then stepping down to allow a suffect consul to take his place, so he did not block promotions. He treated the senators fairly, and promoted the equestrian class by appointing many of them to administrative posts. He took over control of the mint in Rome and issued coinage with the finest silver content that was ever achieved; any graph showing the standard of Roman coinage displays a sharp peak under Domitian.

The army came in for special attention when Domitian gave the soldiers a pay rise of thirty-three per cent, the first pay rise since Julius Caesar's time. The Romans generally wanted defence at little cost, but Domitian's attention to the troops was timely, since he was involved in serious wars for most of his reign. The conquest of Britain was completed in 83 or 84 by Julius Agricola, and about the same time Domitian personally conducted a war in Germany against the Chatti, across the Rhine. In 83, another conflict broke out on the Danube. The Dacians from what is now Romania crossed the Danube into the province of Moesia, defeated the army and killed the governor. Domitian gathered another army, with the Praetorian Prefect Cornelius Fuscus in command. Domitian took troops from the Rhine, possibly filling their places with troops from Britain, which entailed abandoning Agricola's conquests in Scotland. The progress of the Dacian war is not clear, except that Domitian received three acclamations as Imperator in 86, but in 87 the Romans were defeated by the Dacian leader Decebalus, and the Praetorian Prefect was killed. Domitian assembled yet another army in 88, and won a victory at a place called Tapae. There is no record of a treaty or a proper conclusion to the Dacian war, which may have been cut short by a rebellion in Upper Germany at the beginning of 89, led by Lucius Antonius Saturninus, who commanded four legions, two at Mainz, one at Strasbourg and one at Windisch. Domitian set off from Rome for Mainz, summoning Marcus Ulpius Traianus from Spain with his legion, *VII Gemina*. There was no battle, because the governor of Lower Germany had already defeated Saturninus, whose followers were hunted down and killed.

The rebellion seems to have shaken Domitian. In *The Twelve Caesars*, Suetonius says that Domitian only became the oppressive tyrant of legend after the revolt. Having fostered good relations with the army and given them more pay, it was shattering to find that soldiers would march against him under a persuasive leader. Saturninus had financed his rebellion by seizing the cash at the fortresses containing two legions, so Domitian limited the amount of money that could be held in military strongrooms, and two-legion fortresses were never to be used again.

Shortly after the revolt of Saturninus, the tribes of Marcomanni and Quadi threatened Pannonia. Domitian travelled to the scene of action, but it is not known what he achieved, except that he stationed four legions in Pannonia, whereas no other province held more than three. Dacia was made a client kingdom of Rome, receiving subsidies, perhaps to buy off further trouble and to encourage the Dacians to keep other tribes at bay. Roman advisers helped the Dacians to build forts.

From AD 92, the Empire was more or less peaceful, but in Rome there was suspicion, distrust and ultimately executions. Domitian did not feel secure, and consequently nor did anyone else. Suspected plots and executions escalated, until Domitian was assassinated by his household staff in September 96. No senators were implicated in the murder, but without delay they proclaimed as Emperor the aged Marcus Cocceius Nerva, suggesting that they were merely waiting for a message from the Imperial Palace that the deed was done.

The Adoptive Emperors AD 96–161

Given that the hereditary succession had bequeathed Domitian to the Roman world it is perhaps not surprising that the next four emperors, Nerva (AD 96–98), Trajan (AD 98–117), Hadrian (AD 117–138) and Antoninus Pius (AD 138–161), designated their heirs by adoption, but they had little choice, since none of them had sons. Nerva was not a military man, and was the first emperor to be chosen by the Senate. Nerva distributed cash to ensure the loyalty of the troops and the Praetorians. A welfare scheme was introduced in Italy called the *alimenta*, whereby the state lent money at low interest rates to small farmers to assist them to work the land, and the farmers paid back the loans not to Rome but to their local municipalities, which used the money to feed young children. Nerva adopted Marcus Ulpius Traianus, who came from an Italian family whose ancestors had settled in Spain. Trajan was granted Imperial powers immediately, and appointed as governor of Upper Germany. He became Emperor in his own right when Nerva died in 98.

Trajan inherited the Dacian war, so instead of coming straight to Rome he marched to the Danube, where he may have strengthened the frontiers of Pannonia and Moesia. He arrived in Rome in 99. He paid a cash donative to the Praetorians, and gave 300 *sestertii* to each citizen. He also increased the number of recipients of the free corn dole.

He fought two Dacian wars from 101 to 102 and 105 to 106, finally converting Dacia into a Roman province. The Dacian leader Decebalus had not invaded Roman territory, but perceived threat on the part of the Romans, and the subsidies paid by Domitian, may have played their part in instigating further hostilities. Trajan prepared by reconstructing the road originally built by Tiberius along the Roman side of the Danube. He assembled nine legions and a large number of auxiliary troops, crossed the river, and fought a battle, but without conclusion. In the following year Trajan defeated Decebalus. He put garrisons in Dacian territory, took possession of all weapons, and recruited numbers of tribesmen for the Roman army, a customary measure after a victory, because it reduced the enemy manpower while augmenting the auxiliary troops of other provinces, probably causing headaches for the military trainers and commanders.

By 105, Decebalus had rearmed. He attacked the Iazyges, allies of Rome, and invaded Moesia. Trajan's arrival with his legions was delayed until 106, because tribes which had once been friendly or neutral were leaning towards Decebalus rather than Rome. When their loyalties had been established, Trajan invaded Dacia, building a stone bridge across the Danube to bring the troops across. Eventually, after strenuous fighting, the Romans took the Dacian capital of Sarmizegethusa. Decebalus committed suicide. Dacia was made a province, with a consular governor and two legions, and extraction of the iron, gold and silver of the Carpathians began. The Dacian wars are commemorated on Trajan's Column in Rome, in idealised fashion but with fascinating detail, and by three monuments at Adamklissi in southern Romania.

From 106 to 113, there were no serious wars. Trajan devoted the intervening years to building works, including his market complex in Rome, complete with two libraries for Greek and Latin books. He repaired roads and built bridges in Italy, and improved ports and harbours, especially at Ostia, where most of Rome's food supply was brought in. He appointed officials known as *curatores* to some towns and cities to oversee financial affairs, which had deteriorated for various reasons. Trajan's military and administrative achievements earned him the honorary title of *Optimus Princeps*, the best of emperors.

The eastern provinces were threatened by renewed Parthian activity in 113. The Roman provinces on the borders of Parthia had been strengthened, and the new province of Arabia was created when the client king of Arabia Petraea died in 105. One of the legions of Syria was sent to Bostra, the capital of Arabia, and Trajan raised a new legion, *II Traiana*, to take its place in Syria. The main source of trouble between Rome and Parthia was the control of Armenia, where the Parthian king had just installed his nephew on the throne. Trajan declared war, and assembled an army with the intention of annexing Armenia rather than trying to control it via a friendly king. Having occupied Armenia, Trajan decided to protect it by gaining control of Mesopotamia as well. In 115 he reached the northern half of Mesopotamia, but had to go into winter quarters at Antioch, resuming the campaign in 116. He reached the Parthian capital of Ctesiphon, and annexed vast territories as the province of Parthia, but he did not have enough troops to consolidate and hold the new provinces. There was further trouble in Mesopotamia, Egypt, and Africa, and in 117 there was unrest in Dacia. At this point Trajan died at Selinus in Sicily. It was proclaimed by Trajan's wife Plotina and the Praetorian Prefect Acilius Attianus that on his deathbed Trajan adopted as his heir and successor his relative Publius Aelius Hadrianus, who was currently governor of Syria.

Hadrian's family was from Italica in Spain, like Trajan's, and his father was a cousin of Trajan's. After his father died Hadrian had been Trajan's ward, and had been given important appointments when Trajan became Emperor. He had accompanied Trajan in the two Dacian wars. In the eastern campaigns he was a staff officer and he was made governor of Syria. It was clear that he was the intended successor, but had never been officially designated as such. Fortunately the soldiers accepted him, and the Senate followed suit, but there was an obscure plot which resulted in the execution of four senators.

Hadrian was the first Emperor to pay attention to the provinces and the provincials, and to the armies. He visited Germany and Britain in 121–122, then Gaul, Spain, Greece, Asia and Sicily. He was back in Rome in 128 and then went to Africa, where he reviewed the troops. The speech that he made after the review is preserved on a long inscription, called the *Adlocutio* or address. The African climate is kind to inscriptions, so if similar ones were set up elsewhere in wet climates it is likely that they did not survive.

Hadrian was never popular. One reason was his abandonment of part of Dacia, and most of

Trajan's territorial gains in the east, and another was that he put an end to Roman expansion. Roman traders approved of expansion because there were profits to be made. Hadrian probably considered that the costs of administration and defence would outstrip the resources of the Empire. There had always been boundaries, some of which were guarded by towers and patrolled by the armies, but Hadrian called a halt and began to consolidate by building solid running barriers manned by forts and watchtowers. These are described in the chapter on frontiers.

The succession was provided for by Hadrian's adoption of Lucius Ceionius Commodus, who became Lucius Aelius Caesar. But Hadrian outlived Lucius, whose son Lucius Verus was only a child. New arrangements were made. Titus Aurelius Fulvius Boionius Arrius Antoninus, more familiar as Antoninus Pius, was adopted by Hadrian on condition that Antoninus adopted Lucius Verus and Marcus Annius Verus, the future Emperor Marcus Aurelius. In 138 Hadrian died, still largely detested. His mausoleum survives in Rome, because it was converted into the fortified residence of the Popes.

Antoninus Pius inherited a peaceful Empire, with little recorded internal unrest and no serious threat on the frontiers, save for some minor skirmishes in Numidia and Mauretania, and in Dacia. Hadrian was deified, after some opposition from the senators, who advocated the repeal of all Hadrian's acts. As Antoninus explained, he would not then be the adopted son and designated successor, so it was best to leave things as they were. He reigned for twenty-three years without recorded plots against him. Antoninus was not a military man and the army was not called upon to fight wars for defence or for campaigns across the frontiers. The soldiers of most provinces would assist the peace-keeping process, but in Germany and in Britain the armies were put to work in building new frontiers in advance of the Hadrianic lines. The new German line was retained, but the British one was occupied for only a short time. The reign of Antoninus Pius was considered a golden age, but after he died in 161, Cassius Dio described the succeeding years as an era of iron and rust.

The Antonines AD 161–193

Lucius Verus and Marcus Annius Verus, who became Marcus Aurelius, both succeeded Antoninus Pius with equal powers and the title Augustus. Their joint reign had precedents. Trajan held Imperial powers while Nerva was Emperor, and Vespasian shared power with his son Titus, both father and son holding the title Augustus. The peace of Pius' reign was shattered when serious wars broke out soon after the accession of the two Emperors. In 162 the Parthians began to show an interest in Armenia. The Romans would not tolerate Parthian control of Armenia, so they mobilised for war in the east. Lucius Verus was the nominal commander, but his generals directed the campaigns, which were successfully concluded in 166. Probably in the same year, the tribes beyond the Danube invaded Dacia and Pannonia, and both Emperors took command of the armies to repel the tribes. It was to be a prolonged process, lasting until Marcus' death and the accession of Commodus in 180.

Lucius Verus died in 169, probably of the plague that broke out in the 160s, killing many people. Marcus ruled alone for some years. In 175 he gave his young sons Commodus and Annius Verus the title of Caesar, which from then on denoted junior partners to the Augusti. Annius Verus died young. In 177, aged sixteen, Commodus was made co-Emperor. The Empire was too large to be administered by one man, especially when there were wars on extended fronts, or on more than one front, which became more common from the late second century AD, and usually the emperor commanded the armies in person rather than relying on his senior officers. Probably because he was absent from Rome for long periods, Marcus gave the Praetorian Prefect responsibility for keeping order in Italy, and the city prefect took on more juridical powers.

Greater social mobility characterised Marcus' reign, which became a limited meritocracy. If a man displayed obvious talent, Marcus gave him appointments most suited to his abilities, promoting him in the army and in the government, but he elevated his chosen magistrates and officers to the appropriate social status by making them senators, in some cases also providing the qualifying wealth. The equestrians were employed in administrative posts, some of them newly created to augment the departments of the civil service. There were graded ranks for equestrians, staring with *egregius*, distinguished, then *perfectissimus* or most perfect, rising to *eminentissimus* or most eminent, the superlatives prefiguring the more rigidly hierarchical structure of the late Empire.

The wars on the Danube consumed vast manpower resources. In order to fill gaps, and to operate over large areas, Marcus required trained soldiers and particularly officers who could act independently. The increased social mobility and Marcus' policy of promoting men of proven talent enabled officers like Publius Helvius Pertinax, son of a freedman, to rise from the ranks of the army to the consulship. Marcus personally promoted his friend Avidius Cassius, appointing him as governor of Asia. It was a bitter blow when Avidius raised revolt in 175, taking over most of the eastern provinces. He did so probably because he had heard that Marcus was dead, and therefore he tried to consolidate the east to protect it, but Marcus had no choice except to retaliate, and after only three months the rebellion was crushed. Avidius was killed.

Another eminent officer was Marcus Valerius Maximianus, whose career is documented by more than one inscription. He was an equestrian who was made a senator and given the rank of praetor, then appointed to legionary commands in Pannonia, Moesia and Dacia. He was also given special commands, sometimes in charge of large forces made up of detachments of various legions, and he was responsible for bringing supplies to the Pannonian troops via a fleet on the Danube.

The tribes who threatened the Danube provinces, and penetrated into Italy, were the Marcomanni, Quadi, Sarmatians, and Iazyges. They were not necessarily always in collusion, and some of them were more interested in finding lands in which to settle than in making war. Marcus accommodated many of them in parts of the Danube provinces, and in return the tribes contributed recruits. The more warlike tribesmen made raids across the frontiers, damaging lands and property. Marcus' response was to penetrate their own territory and keep them perpetually on the move, harassing them wherever they settled down, breaking them up into smaller groups. It was a new kind of warfare without pitched battles and the takeover of a capital or central place. With only a few years' respite this policy continued until Marcus' death in 180. It was said that the long-term plan was to create two provinces called Marcomannia and Sarmatia, but if so, it never materialised. Commodus succeeded his father and made peace, which lasted for several years.

Commodus achieved a notorious reputation in his own lifetime, documented by the historian Cassius Dio, who lived through his reign. The diplomatic peace settlement on the Danube in 180 was criticised by Romans who thought that the tribes should have been completely extinguished. The treaty with the Marcomanni and Quadi demanded a large number of recruits to be delivered immediately, which augmented the Roman army at the expense of tribal manpower. The frontier wars diminished in scale to raiding, and the role of the army likewise scaled down to policing and patrolling. Commodus built watchtowers or *burgi* along the frontiers to assist supervision. Inscriptions record the building work, listing the purpose of the towers as control of *latrones*, or robbers.

The reign of Commodus began well, but ended in a reign of terror. Like Tiberius who allowed the Praetorian Prefect Sejanus far too much power, Commodus promoted a freedman of his father's, Marcus Aurelius Cleander, who quickly became powerful enough to control the Praetorian Prefects and to make or break men who sought promotion for themselves. Cleander was put in charge of the Imperial household so no one could approach Commodus directly. All emperors required a security system, but Cleander took it to extremes, and Commodus acquiesced, until there was a food shortage, causing riots in Rome. Cleander took the blame and Commodus executed him, but without the protection of Cleander, Commodus became frightened and suspicious, much like Domitian in his later years. Executions began. It was inevitable that Commodus would eventually be assassinated. The Praetorian Prefect Laetus and the palace chamberlain Eclectus chose their moment on the last day of 192, and Commodus was killed.

The Severans AD 193–217

While Commodus alienated more and more people, events in Rome were being monitored by the provincial governors, among them Septimius Severus in Pannonia, Clodius Albinus in Britain, and Pescennius Niger in Syria. Before any of them could make a move when Commodus was assassinated, Helvius Pertinax was declared Emperor at the beginning of 193. He had been governor of Lower Moesia, Upper Moesia, Dacia, Syria and Britain, where he gained a reputation as a strict disciplinarian. Pertinax failed to win over the Praetorian Guard, despite paying them 12,000 *sestertii* per man, and he made the mistake of persuading the Senate not to execute Laetus for the murder of Commodus. After only eighty-seven days as Emperor, he was murdered by the man he had spared. There was no designated successor, but two candidates came forward offering cash to the Praetorians, who sold out to the highest bidder, Didius Julianus.

The soldiers in Syria, Britain and Pannonia declared for their respective governors. Septimius Severus was the nearest to Rome, and had secured the support of sixteen legions on the Rhine and Danube, which may explain why the Senate executed Didius Julianus and confirmed Severus as Emperor before he set foot in Rome. Severus cast himself in the role of avenger of Pertinax as the excuse for his march on Rome.

The Praetorians tried to negotiate with Severus while he was en route. He summoned them to a meeting, surrounded them with his soldiers and disbanded them. Later, he reconstituted the Praetorian Guard, recruiting legionaries and reducing the predominance of Italians who had formed the majority of the Praetorians. On entering Rome, he changed into civilian dress before he crossed the *pomerium*. He needed to cultivate the senators and the populace of Rome, especially since he faced two rival Emperors, Clodius Albinus and Pescennius Niger at opposite ends of the Empire. He promised to rule like Marcus Aurelius, and made strenuous efforts to connect his family with that of Marcus, but this involved the reinstatement and deification of Commodus, whose memory had been damned by the Senate. Severus renamed his elder son Septimius Bassianus as Marcus Aurelius Antoninus, better known as Caracalla, from the Gallic hooded cloak that he usually wore. Severus gave Caracalla the title of Caesar, and also *Imperator destinatus*, leaving no one in any doubt about the succession. Severus' younger son Geta was promoted when he reached the appropriate age.

In the east Pescennius Niger had gained control of Egypt, and his ally Asellius Aemilianus, governor of Asia, occupied Byzantium. Towards the end of 193, Severus set off for the east via the Danube provinces, ordering the troops in Moesia to move against Niger. The first target was Aemilianus, who was defeated by Severus' general Candidus, but Byzantium was still in the hands of Aemilianus' troops. Severus besieged the city, which held out for nearly two years. Niger had set up headquarters in Antioch, but some of the eastern cities went over to Severus. Niger was killed early in 194. When Byzantium surrendered in 195, Severus destroyed it, but the site was too strategically important to let it remain unoccupied, so he rebuilt the city.

Learning that some of Niger's supporters had gone to Parthia, Severus concentrated on strengthening the frontier provinces, putting down an insurrection in Mesopotamia and Osroene, which was controlled by Rome but not yet annexed. Severus converted it into a province. He may have divided Syria at this time, creating a larger northern province called Syria Coele with two legions, and a smaller southern province called Syria Phoenice with one legion. The eastern frontier had to be strengthened to allow Severus to turn his attention to Clodius Albinus in the west. Severus had bestowed on Albinus the title of Caesar, implying that he would be the successor if Severus died, but he also gave the same title to Caracalla in 196. Albinus took the title Augustus, gathered some troops in Britain and crossed into Gaul, setting up headquarters at Lyon, ancient Lugdunensis. The Rhine legions remained loyal to Severus, and the governor of Lower Germany, Virius Lupus, made a stand against Albinus. The final battle came in 197 near Lyon. Albinus was defeated and committed suicide.

There were no further challenges to Severus from provincial governors or army commanders. Aware that service in the army must be made more attractive if willing recruits were to be found, Severus rewarded the soldiers with the first pay rise since Domitian's reign, a century earlier. He also allowed soldiers to marry, which had hitherto been illegal, but he merely acknowledged the status quo, because as the army became more of a static force, liaisons with local women became the norm, and when soldiers were discharged these relationships, and any offspring, were officially recognised.

The reconstituted Praetorian Guard was a larger force than the previous version. In 197 Severus' fellow African, Caius Fulvius Plautianus, was made Praetorian Prefect, a mistake, because Plautianus was as ambitious as Sejanus had been, and ended badly. Severus also installed a legion a short distance from Rome at Alba (modern Albano). This was II *Parthica*, one of three new legions, all with the same name, and all commanded by equestrian prefects, not senatorial legionary legates. Social mobility, first glimpsed under Augustus and increased under Hadrian and Marcus Aurelius, reached new levels. Soldiers could rise from the ranks to military commands, and new administrative posts were created for the equestrians.

The reign of Severus was notable for wars in Parthia and Britain, and the expansion of territory in Mesopotamia and Africa, earning him the epithet of *propagator imperii*. The Parthian war began in 197, in response to the occupation of Mesopotamia by King Vologaeses. It was more of a demonstration than a war. Mesopotamia was made a province with two legions, *I* and *III Parthica*, with their equestrian commander, and an equestrian prefect as governor. The city of Hatra stood in the way of communications, but though he besieged it in 198 and again in 199, he was not strong enough to take it. The eastern desert between Parthia and the province of Syria Phoenice and Arabia was guarded by Palmyrene soldiers, not part of the Roman army, but there was an understanding with Severus because the city of Palmyra had a vested interest in avoiding Parthian interference.

Since his appointment as Praetorian Prefect, Plautianus had been busy working his way closer to the Imperial family and eliminating rivals. He arranged the betrothal of his daughter to Caracalla, and was sole Praetorian Prefect for a while before Severus was informed by his dying brother of Plautianus' ambition. He was executed in 205, and two Praetorian Prefects were appointed, one of them an ex-Prefect of Egypt and the other a jurist.

In 208, Severus mounted an expedition to Britain, for reasons which remain obscure. Cassius Dio says that the governor Virus Lupus bought peace from the Maeatae, who lived close to the Roman wall that divided the country into two. The Antonine Wall had probably been abandoned by this time, but it is still not certain whether the trouble began in northern England beyond Hadrian's Wall, or in Scotland. Severus decided to subdue the whole island, and arrived in Britain accompanied by extra troops from the Rhine and Danube, together with *II Parthica* and detachments of the Praetorian Guard. He set up headquarters at York. The most certain evidence for the campaign derives from the Severan supply bases at South Shields and Corbridge, and sites at Cramond on the Forth, and Carpow on the river Tay. Severus died at York in 211, and Caracalla made peace, and like Commodus' arrangements after the Danube wars, the peace endured, in this case for nearly a century. If Severus had not already done so, Caracalla divided Britain into two provinces.

After his arrival in Rome, Caracalla murdered his brother Geta, along with many of his supporters. All portraits of Geta and all mentions of his name on inscriptions and official records were destroyed. Inscriptions survive with chiselled spaces where his name once existed.

The most famous administrative measure of Caracalla's reign, giving rise to endless discussion, is the *Constitutio Antoniniana*, traditionally dated to 212. By this edict, Roman citizenship was granted to all freeborn inhabitants of the Empire, and since it was usual to take the name of the man who enfranchised new citizens, after 212 there was a great preponderance of men and women all over the Empire with the family name Aurelius, from Caracalla's official name Marcus Aurelius Antoninus. Roman citizenship had already declined in status and after 212 a new elite evolved. Instead of Romans and provincials, or citizens and non-citizens, the yardstick shifted to a distinction between upper and lower classes. The new groups were labelled *honestiores* and *humiliores*, beginning as a social distinction but soon crystallised in law. *Honestiores* were possessed of greater legal privileges than *humiliores*, for whom punishments were much more severe.

Caracalla's reign lasted for only six years, punctuated by wars on the Rhine and Danube, and in the east, which are not well documented. He campaigned in Raetia in 212–213, where inscriptions attest road building and repair, and it is known that he brought extra troops from Egypt and Pannonia, but how he achieved a peace lasting for about twenty years is not known. The Parthian campaign appears to have been an act of aggression on the part of the Romans when the king of Parthia was at odds with his brother. Caracalla failed to take over Armenia, and had to go to Alexandria in 215–216 to quell a rebellion, which he stopped via tremendous slaughter. By the time he returned to the east, the Parthians were much stronger under the new King Artabanus V. There was no war, and the Roman troops began to feel restless. A rumour started that Caracalla intended to kill the Praetorian Prefect Marcus Opellius Macrinus, because a prophecy stated that he would become Emperor, which came true when Macrinus decided to pre-empt any action by Caracalla and killed him.

The Soldier Emperors AD 217–260

Macrinus was not a military man, but an experienced jurist, and an administrator with a wide knowledge of how the Empire functioned. He was the first non-senator to become Emperor, but his elevation did not upset the senators because they were too relieved about being rid of

Caracalla to be overly concerned about Macrinus' lower social rank. Macrinus wrote to the Senate to announce his adoption of the Severan name and gave himself the additional titles of Pius Felix Augustus. Caracalla's memory was not damned, but nor was he immediately deified, a compromise on Macrinus' part to satisfy both the soldiers and civilians. Macrinus was consul in 218, with Oclatinius Adventus as his colleague. Adventus was of even lower class than Macrinus, an ex-mercenary who had been a member of the *frumentarii* or secret police. Macrinus made him city prefect, but replaced him soon afterwards by Marius Maximus. Men of low status were appointed to various offices which were usually the preserve of senators, for instance the new governors of Pannonia and Dacia were Macrinus' own men, Marcius Agrippa, a slave who had been convicted and banished, and Deccius Triccianus, once a doorkeeper to the governor of Pannonia, rising to commander of *II Parthica* and then to provincial governor. This was social mobility gone mad.

In Parthia, King Artabanus launched an offensive against Mesopotamia. Macrinus prepared for war, but negotiated and bought peace. He awarded himself the title *Parthicus Maximus* in his report to the Senate. In attempting to provide for the future succession, Macrinus bestowed on his young son Diadumenianus the name Antoninus and the title Caesar, confirmed by the Senate. In deference to the army, he finally deified Caracalla. The army was essential as the main prop for his regime, but he needed to strike a balance. Macrinus tried to curb the expenses of the army, without unduly offending the troops. While he did not attempt to withdraw any privileges, he did not celebrate the Parthian victory by gifts to the soldiers, and worse still, he reverted to the Severan rates of pay, ignoring the rise that Caracalla had awarded the army. Cost-cutting would appeal to tax-paying civilians, but the soldiers were disgruntled, and began to think of a new Imperial ruler. It would have been less easy for them to foment rebellion if Macrinus had dispersed the troops in different winter quarters, but they were all together in one place, so they were well prepared when the members of the Severan family produced their own Imperial candidate. The Empress Julia Domna did not long survive her son Caracalla, but she had a sister, Julia Maesa, whose two daughters Julia Soaemias and Julia Mammaea each had a young son. Julia Maesa persuaded the soldiers that Caracalla was the true father of Soaemias' son Varius Avitus Bassianus, and on 16 May 218 the army declared the boy Emperor, with the name Marcus Aurelius Antoninus, nicknamed Elagabalus, after his devotion to the eastern god of the same name.

The soldiers killed Macrinus and his son Diadumenianus, and Elagabalus entered Antioch early in June, paying the soldiers 2,000 *sestertii* each to persuade them not to sack the city. He wrote to the Senate as Emperor, styling himself Imperator Caesar Antoninus, grandson of Severus. At the end of September 219, Elagabalus arrived in Rome. The character of the new Emperor and the overpowering influence of the Syrian princesses would soon be revealed. Elagabalus embarked on the usual round of reshuffling military and government officials, installing his own supporters. Publius Valerius Comazon, an equestrian who had once been condemned to the galleys, was made Praetorian Prefect, though he had absolutely no experience. He was soon made consul, and he held the post of city prefect three times. Opponents to the new regime were quickly despatched and the Senate obligingly condemned them posthumously.

The historical sources give no attention to what was happening in the provinces, being wholly absorbed in the enormities of Elagabalus' reign and his outrageous sexual behaviour. Politically the main problem was that Elagabalus was strongly influenced by his unsuitable courtiers, and the controlling authority of his mother Julia Soaemias. His grandmother Julia Maesa began to favour her other grandson, the son of Julia Mammaea, Gessius Bassianus Alexianus. She arranged his formal adoption by Elagabalus, which was ratified by the Senate. Alexianus was renamed Severus Alexander, and was made consul in 221. Before long Elagabalus was intriguing against his cousin, but found that Alexander was too well protected by his grandmother and the Praetorians. On 6 March 222 the soldiers declared Severus Alexander as Emperor, and killed Elagabalus, his mother, and many of his adherents, including Fulvius the city prefect. Once again Comazon, the only one of Elagabalus' court to survive, filled this sudden vacancy, for the third time.

One of the first Imperial appointments was the elevation of the *Praefectus Annonae* Domitius Ulpianus, or Ulpian, to sole Praetorian Prefect in December 222. He was a jurist, not a soldier, but at this moment administrators and legal experts were required to a greater extent than soldiers. His achievements were worthy, but unfortunately he was murdered, perhaps in the spring of 223, but some sources give the date 228.

The guiding forces in the government were the women of the Severan dynasty. Julia Mammaea was honoured with several titles which gave her no actual political powers but extended her influence. In particular she took on the role that Julia Domna had held with regard to the army, with the title *mater castrorum*, or mother of the camp. Not content with that, eventually she was known as *mater Augusti et castrorum et senatus atque patriae*, indicating that her influence if not her authority extended over most aspects of Roman life, including the Senate. She chose sixteen of the noblest senators to guide the young Emperor as part of his council, or *consilium*. It was fortunate that there was a peaceful interlude from 222 until 230, which allowed for the restructuring of the government. Some the notables of the Severan regime re-emerged during the 220s, infiltrating government posts and the Imperial court.

Meanwhile the Parthian royal house had its own internal troubles. A vassal of Artabanus V was rising to power. This was Ardashir, or Artaxerxes, son of Sasan, of Iranian lineage. In 224 the Sassanid Persian dynasty with Ardashir at its head supplanted that of the Parthian Artabanus, after the latter was killed on the battlefield of Hormizdagan. Within a few years, Ardashir had begun to expand his empire to incorporate the states around the old Parthian kingdom. This naturally brought him into contact with Roman frontier territories. He attacked Hatra in 229, and by 230 Severus Alexander was gathering an army, recruiting soldiers in Italy and the provinces. He left for the east in 231. Using Antioch as a base, Alexander attacked in three columns, leading the central one himself, while the others marched to the north and south, one to Armenia and then into Media, and the other towards the Persian capital city of Ctesiphon. Alexander's achievements were perhaps not as abysmal as they have been painted. The Persians remained quiet after the campaigns, not causing any serious trouble until the 240s under Ardashir's successor Shapur I.

While he was still in Antioch, Alexander received news of disturbances on the Rhine and Danube. Without concluding an official peace with Ardashir, Alexander returned to Rome at the end of 232. He held a triumph, and then began preparations for the war on the northern frontiers. He took with him troops which had fought in Mesopotamia, such as the archers from Osroene and the units of Moors. As part of the preparations he placed an experienced officer in command of the recruits, Caius Julius Verus Maximinus, a soldier of Thracian origin who had risen from the ranks, who would be responsible for training the troops for the coming campaign.

The destruction of several forts along the Taunus-Wetterau frontier in Germany has been dated to 233 or thereabouts, suggesting that this area was where the German tribes concentrated their attacks, an assumption corroborated by the fact that Severus Alexander chose Mainz as his base. The offensive was launched in 234 against a new federation of Germanic tribes, the Alamanni. Alexander won a victory, but instead of pursuing the enemy and eradicating them, he began to negotiate, offering money and perhaps food and supplies. It was an accepted Roman policy to give subsidies to tribesmen and since the tribes had attacked the fertile areas of the Taunus-Wetterau region it is possible that their prime need was for food. The Emperor's policy caused much resentment. In spring 235, Severus Alexander and his mother were murdered, and the Pannonian soldiers proclaimed as Emperor the trainer of the troops, Caius Julius Verus Maximinus, nicknamed Thrax, the Thracian.

Maximinus Thrax had a proven military record. He was the first soldier-Emperor to rise from the ranks, only a few decades after Septimius Severus had broadened the base of recruitment and facilitated promotions for outstanding soldiers and junior officers. Maximinus was perceived by the Senate as a barbarian, but nevertheless the senators passed the necessary decrees investing him with Imperial powers. His young son was declared Caesar, marking him out for the succession. Without wholesale slaughter the immediate entourage of Severus Alexander was removed. Some men were relegated to lower-grade posts, such as the equestrian Timesitheus, one of the close associates of Alexander, who was sent out of the way to a provincial command.

The war against the Germans was resumed. By the end of 235, Maximinus was calling himself *Germanicus Maximus*, and in 236 he had transferred the army to Pannonia, basing himself at Sirmium to fight against the Sarmatians and Dacians. Maximinus ignored the Senate and concentrated wholly on the frontiers, consuming vast amounts of money to pay the soldiers. The usual taxes did not prove sufficient for his needs, but to be fair to him, income had not matched expenditure for some considerable time. He complicated matters by giving the soldiers a pay rise, never a popular move because the inhabitants of Rome, secure now for many years, did not experience at first hand the threats to their frontiers. To the Romans of Italy and the more peaceful provinces, the army was far away, full of semi-barbarous men who were troublesome and greedy. The army was literally a foreign body, and its services were not appreciated, particularly when money was wrested from unwilling hands to pay the soldiers. Taxation began to weigh heavily on the provincials. Some of the wealthy nobles in Africa rebelled, killed the Roman procurator in Thysdrus (modern El Djem), and then raised the proconsul Marcus Antonius Gordianus Sempronianus as the Emperor Gordian I with his son as Gordian II.

In April 238 the Senate confirmed the two Gordians in power, but in Africa, the new emperors were quickly routed and killed by the governor of Numidia, Capellianus, who was loyal to Maximinus, but not interested in seizing power for himself. Maximinus, outlawed by the Senate, gathered his troops and marched towards Italy. The Senate elected two Emperors, Marcus Clodius Pupienus Maximus and Decimus Caelius Calvinus Balbinus, but the people and the soldiers of the Praetorian Guard agitated in favour of the thirteen-year-old Marcus Antonius Gordianus, the grandson of Gordian I. The Senate recognised the boy as Caesar and designated successor of the two senatorial Emperors. As Maximinus approached Italy, Balbinus remained in Rome, while Pupienus marched north to meet the outlawed Emperor, and won a victory of sorts. Maximinus' army, besieging Aquileia, was disaffected, because food supplies were low and morale was even lower. Eventually the soldiers of *II Parthica*, thinking of the safety of their families at their base at Alba, not far from Rome, decided to kill Maximinus and his son. Pupienus sent the troops back to their bases and returned to Rome, keeping the German contingents as his bodyguard, but this made the Praetorians uneasy. They murdered both Pupienus and Balbinus, and declared Gordian III Emperor.

The main sources for the history of Rome now expire altogether or lose themselves in fantasy, so only an outline can be given of the events of the next few years. With the accession of Gordian there was a temporary peace, and measures were taken to reorganise the state. Attempts were made to reduce taxation without compromising the state treasury, and control of the army was tightened up. *Legio III Augusta* in Africa was disbanded for its part in the defeat and deaths of the first two Gordians, but without the legion to keep order and to take charge of defence, trouble broke out afresh in Africa. The governor of Mauretania Caesariensis had to restore order. By 241, the most important man in the Roman world was Timesitheus, who was appointed Praetorian Prefect and directed policy and military matters on behalf of the teenage Gordian III. The Imperial peace did not last long. There was trouble on the Rhine, and the Carpi and the Goths had erupted into Roman territory through Dacia and Moesia. The Emperors Pupienus and Balbinus had arranged a treaty with these tribes, favourable to the Goths, who received subsidies, but the Carpi received very little. It may have been a deliberate ploy to set one tribe against another.

In 239 the Persian King Ardashir attacked Dura Europos (modern Salihiye) on the Euphrates, and possibly captured Hatra. He overran the greater part of Mesopotamia, threatening Syria. The Praetorian Prefect Timesitheus prepared for war, but first he had to deal with the Goths and Germans in Illyricum. After a short war against them in 242, Timesitheus concluded peace, and he and Gordian III turned their attention to the east. By this time Ardashir had raised his son Shapur as his colleague, and the latter may have taken over Edessa. Timesitheus wrested Osroene from Persian control, and after a battle at Rhesaena the Persians left Nisibis and Singara, but at this high point of the war Timesitheus died. The Romans did not recover from the blow, though Gordian III and the Praetorian Prefect Marcus Julius Verus Philippus (Philip the Arab) followed the original plan and marched to Ctesiphon. From unknown causes, Gordian III died and Philip was blamed for his death, but there are four different literary versions of Gordian's demise, so even the ancient historians were not sure of the facts.

Philip was declared Emperor by the troops, and began to extricate the army from the clutches of the Persians. He negotiated peace, by means of an indemnity to the Persians of 500,000 *denarii*, and giving up control of Armenia, but retaining Osroene and Mesopotamia. Philip was accused of hastening back to Rome without settling the east, but he had placed his brother Priscus in command as equestrian prefect of Mesopotamia. Documents show that Priscus was also governor of Syria, and an inscription reveals that he held the title *rector Orientis*. This does not signify an actual office, but it does indicate that he held wide-ranging powers over the eastern provinces. Philip gave his wife, Otacilia Severa, the title Augusta, and made his son Caesar, elevating him to Augustus in 247. The new Emperor enjoyed good relations with the Senate, and from the outset of his reign he reaffirmed the old Roman virtues and traditions. From 246 to 247 he fought the Carpi and Quadi on the Danube, taking the titles *Germanicus* and *Carpicus Maximus*. In 248, back in Rome, he celebrated the Secular Games, always a significant festival for the Romans, marking their development and power over the centuries, but this time the celebrations were even more meaningful, since it was the first millennium of Rome.

Philip stopped paying subsidies to the Goths in 248, with the result that by 249 the tribes had formed a coalition, united in opposition to Rome. They invaded Moesia and Thrace, and about the same time two revolts also broke out among the Roman army commanders in the north and the east. One of the usurpers, Pacatianus, had been given an extended command over Pannonia and Moesia, though it is not specified exactly where his authority lay. His command is symptomatic of the need to combine the armies of more than one province in order to defend large areas, because the enemies of Rome now ranged far and wide, moved rapidly and could not be dealt with by one provincial governor acting alone and keeping within his own defined territory. The corollary to this requirement was that usurpation was rendered more feasible when such commands over large areas and large numbers of soldiers were instituted. Philip lost his nerve, but the Senate made a show of solidarity, shored up by a senator called Caius Messius Quintus Decius, who was entrusted with the defence of Moesia and the Balkans, and the command against Pacatianus. He put down the revolt but was declared Emperor by his troops. Civil war followed, despite Decius' attempts to come to terms with Philip. Two Roman armies, one from Rome and the other from the Danube, converged on northern Italy. The location of the final battle is disputed, but wherever it was fought, Decius was the victor and Philip was killed, and the Praetorians killed Philip's young son.

As Emperor, Decius started off by reaffirming the old Roman religion, reinvigorating the cult practices and rituals, and repairing the temples. He outlawed the cults that he saw as most threatening to unity, chiefly Christianity. Philip had been tolerant towards the Christians, so the new persecution surprised the Christian community. An order to sacrifice to the gods of the Empire was rigorously enforced throughout the Roman world. Compliant participants were issued with a certificate to prove that they had obeyed the order. The non-conformists were singled out, to be tried and executed. The trials embraced not just the lowly adherents, but were aimed at the chief officials of the Church, so Decius became the arch-tyrant in the works of the later Christian authors.

For the persecuted Christians it was seen as divine retribution when the Carpi attacked Dacia and the Goths invaded Moesia in 250. Decius was granted the name of Trajan by the Senate when he became Emperor, and like the earlier conqueror of Dacia he won the battles and brought peace to the province, earning himself the title *restitutor Daciarum*. He faced a more resolute enemy in the Gothic leader Cniva in Moesia and Thrace. The Goths had become more closely united and had learned a lot about how to wage war against the Romans. They succeeded in taking Philippopolis. Decius could not dislodge them, so he waited for them to move off in search of food. Meanwhile he made his son Herennius Etruscus, who was already Caesar, his colleague in his regime; his younger son Hostilianus was in Rome with a respected senator, Publius Licinius Valerianus (the future Emperor Valerian) in charge of the civil administration while Decius led the army. The presence of a respected senator delegated by the Emperor did not prevent the Roman mob from raising a candidate of their own, Julius Valens Licinianus, to replace Decius, whose name they removed from inscriptions in the city.

Decius was probably too embroiled in the struggle in the Danube provinces to notice that he had been usurped. In 251 the Goths began to move northwards, so Decius followed, fighting battles but unable to bring them to final confrontation until he reached the Dobrudja. He risked battle at Abrittus (modern Razgrad in Bulgaria) and was killed. His son Herennius Etruscus may have been killed in one of the earlier skirmishes. There was now a power vacuum. The legions declared for the governor of Moesia, Caius Vibius Afinius Trebonianus Gallus. The new Emperor did not feel strong enough to defeat the Goths decisively, so he made peace with them, reinstating their subsidy payments. They were allowed to go free, taking their booty and prisoners with them.

In Rome, Gallus adopted Decius' younger son Hostilianus and raised him alongside his own son Volusianus, making them Caesars and then Augusti. Hostilianus succumbed to the plagues of 252–253, leaving Volusianus and his father as Emperors. It seemed that Gallus was powerless to stop invasions from across the Danube, or to deal with the threat to the eastern provinces, where the Persian King Shapur I captured Nisibis. Shapur went on to take Antioch, probably in 263. Given that no help came from Rome, the usurper Uranius Antoninus, Priest-king of Emesa, seized power to organise defence against the Persians.

On the Danube frontier the soldiers chose the governor of Lower Moesia, Aemilius Aemilianus, as Emperor. He put an end to the subsidies to the Goths and defeated them in battle. Aemilianus realised that his claims would be received in a much better light if he adopted a respectful attitude towards the Senate. Regardless of the fact that Trebonianus Gallus was the legitimate Emperor, he sent a letter to Rome suggesting that the Senate should exercise supreme power, and he would be the general in chief commanding the Danube and the east. Gallus sent his general Valerian with the Rhine legions against Aemilianus who was marching on Rome, but the legions proclaimed Valerian as Emperor. Valerian perhaps reasoned that he might as well fight on his own behalf, instead of trying to support an emperor who seemed to be rapidly losing control. Within a short time, Gallus and Volusianus, and soon afterwards Aemilianus, were all killed, leaving Valerian as sole Emperor. He set about confirming his power immediately. The Senate bestowed the title Caesar on his adult son Publius Licinius Gallienus, who was shortly afterwards made Augustus, as colleague of his father. Now at last there were two emperors who would be able to deal with the problems in the two halves of the Empire at the same time, Gallienus taking the west and Valerian going to the east as soon as he could, to combat the Persian menace.

In 253 Shapur I turned his full attention to Armenia, killing King Chosroes, whose son Tiridates fled, leaving Armenia wide open to Persian domination. Valerian set up headquarters at Antioch and started to rebuild the city. From 253 to 255 the situation slowly improved. Gallienus celebrated victories over the Germans in Illyricum, but in 256 the Franks threatened Gaul and Germany. Gallienus left the Danube provinces, leaving his son Valerian the younger at Viminacium as Caesar, while he set up headquarters at Cologne. He opened a mint, which issued coins naming him as *restitutor Galliarum*, the restorer of the Gallic provinces. In 258 Gallienus was threatened by a usurper called Ingenuus, proclaimed Emperor by the troops in Illyricum. It is probable the younger Valerian may have been killed in this revolt. While Gallienus was re-establishing his authority over Illyricum, there were more invasions by the Goths threatening the Black Sea coastal cities, and the Alamanni were restless on the frontiers of Germany and Raetia. The simultaneous defence of all the western provinces was impossible. Gallienus placed his younger son Saloninus at Cologne as the new Caesar, while he returned to northern Italy and set up headquarters at Milan.

The disasters piled up. In the summer of 260, Shapur captured the Emperor Valerian and his army. The Persians were now free to dominate the entire east, because there was no one to stop them except the ruler of Palmyra, Odenathus, with some Roman troops and his own Palmyrenes. Usurpers appeared in several places, because in the absence of Imperial troops, self-help on the frontiers had become the only alternative. At Carnuntum the soldiers chose Regalianus to lead them against the Iazyges and Roxolani. In the east Callistus (also called Ballista in some sources) and Macrianus took charge of the remnants of Valerian's defeated army. Neither Macrianus nor Callistus declared themselves emperors, but Macrianus proclaimed his two sons, Titus Fulvius Junius Macrianus and Titus Fulvius Junius Quietus, as Augusti. In Gaul the governor Postumus was declared Emperor. An inscription found at Augsburg shows that the domain of Postumus extended over Raetia as well as the Rhine frontier and the Gallic provinces; Britain was with him and Spain came over to him later. The Emperor Gallienus was backed into a corner in Milan, with only a fraction of the armies and resources of the Empire at his disposal. AD 260 was the darkest year of the Empire.

2

Augustus and the Establishment of the Standing Army

After the fall of Alexandria in 30 BC Augustus created the first standing army; a simple phrase, and even a simple concept, but it conceals a vast amount of organisation and administration. It is estimated that in 30 BC there were about sixty legions under arms. There had been several legions in the field on a more or less permanent basis before and during the period of the civil wars, and some of these legions survived into the Empire, though it is not always possible to discern which of them did so.

The major task facing Octavian-Augustus was what to do with the numerous armies, some of them with him in Egypt and others distributed over the provinces. He had a few options, some of them impractical. He could have chosen to keep them all in existence, but the problems of where to house them and how to pay them would have been immense. Alternatively he could have disbanded them all and returned to the Republican system of raising armies whenever there was a need for them, but that would have created other problems, the first and most immediate being how to retain his power, and the second problem being what to do with thousands of discharged soldiers. It would not have been wise to allow so many men trained in the art of fighting to roam loose around Italy and the provinces with no means of financial support or making a living. All discharged soldiers would have to be settled on land allotments, or given cash payments, both of which were difficult if not impossible to achieve within a short time period. Another problem was that if there were no readily available troops, in the event of an external war or an internal rebellion, it would have taken far too long to raise armies, train the men who had not seen action before, and get them to the war zone. The annual or periodic levy worked reasonably well during the early Republic when wars were fought in Italy, but when Rome acquired provinces, which had to be defended, there was clearly a need for troops to be stationed in them. This did not necessarily mean that that the troops would always be the same soldiers in the same units in the same locations. Even when the standing army had been established there was constant movement of legions and accompanying auxiliary troops from one province to another during the early Empire, indeed movement never ceased entirely, but it dwindled from the end of the first century AD. Augustus created the standing army but he did not make it a static one, housed in forts and fortresses on a permanent basis. That was a development of the second century with the advent of fixed frontiers.

The happy medium between retaining all the armies and disbanding them all was to keep some of them. A fortunate by-product of retaining a number of troops, ultimately twenty-eight legions, was to provide support for Octavian's regime, and for all succeeding emperors, though this facet of armed force was not overtly stated. When Octavian made the gesture to return the government of Rome and the Empire to the Senate in 27 BC he emerged as governor of most of the provinces which contained armies, with only a few areas where senatorial governors could command troops. The loyalty of all troops was directed to Augustus via the oath of allegiance that all soldiers swore when they enlisted. The oath was transferred to succeeding emperors and was renewed annually. When the standing army was created, Augustus was its paymaster, and all the higher appointments and promotions were in his gift. He directed operations via his legates, and deployment of the legions and auxiliaries would be supervised by him.

At the end of the war with Antony and Cleopatra, armies would have been stationed in Spain, in Gaul, near or on the Rhine and Danube, in the east in Syria and Asia Minor, and in Egypt and northern Africa. Some of the legions were originally raised by Caesar for the Gallic war, and more were raised for the civil war by Pompey and by Caesar, and by Pompey's sons. Other legions dated from the Triumvirate, when Antony and Octavian raised troops to fight against Brutus and Cassius, who had also raised legions in the eastern provinces. Later, Antony raised troops from the east for the Parthian campaign, and latterly he and Octavian brought large armies to Greece to fight each other. Not all of these legions would have survived until 30 BC, but it suffices to say that there would be a collection of troops from different periods and different places all gathered under Octavian's control when Antony was removed from the scene.

Once Augustus was secure as supreme commander, he could begin to rationalise the organisation of the army. This process was extended over a number of years and did not spring fully fledged from a couple of all-embracing decrees passed in any particular year. Afterwards the army continued to evolve from the foundation created by Augustus.

Each legion was given a number and often a name, but although there were twenty-eight Augustan legions, they were not renumbered from I through to XXVIII. The highest number assigned to the legions at this time was XXII. Some of the legions already possessed their own identity when Augustus reformed the army, for instance *V Macedonica* had been formed during the latter days of the Republic, and *V Alaudae*, 'the Larks', was one of Caesar's legions, and neither of them wished to give up their numbers and names. There was therefore some duplication or even triplication of numbers, with the result that besides *V Macedonica* and *V Alaudae*, there were *III Augusta*, *III Cyrenaica*, and *III Gallica*, *IV Macedonica* and *IV Scythica*, *VI Ferrata* and *VI Victrix*, and *X Fretensis* and *X Gemina*. The name *Gemina* usually indicates that the remains of two legions had been formed into one. Some legions were lost in wars, spectacularly so in AD 9 when three legions, probably *XVII*, *XVIII*, and *XIX*, were annihilated by the German tribes. These numbers were never used again.

Veteran Settlement

Before any reorganisation of the existing armies could proceed, more than half of the sixty legions of 30 BC would have to be disbanded. Provision for the settlement of veterans, and the eventual institution of cash pensions, is one of Augustus' most important reforms of the army.

Some of the soldiers under arms in 30 BC may have wanted to remain in the army, and if their legions were to be disbanded, they would probably have been sent to fill gaps in the legions which were to be retained, since there had presumably been some casualties during the Actium and Alexandrian campaigns, and the other legions in the provinces would still need to recruit to keep numbers as near to full strength as possible. On the other hand, many men would have no wish to be kept on in any army. Several legions had been levied from unwilling recruits during the civil wars, and even willing recruits were probably getting tired of fighting. Some of these men may have had homes to go to, and could be sent off with a cash payment, especially the troops who were in Egypt with Antony, and latterly Octavian, which had been raised in the eastern provinces. Perhaps it is fanciful to imagine hundreds of ex-soldiers queuing up at the harbour in Alexandria, clutching their discharge payments and possibly some form of certificate attesting that they had been honourably discharged from the army, all seeking ships to take them home. In the third chapter of Augustus' account of his reign, the *Res Gestae Divi Augusti*, he specifically states that he sent men back to their towns (*remisi in municipia sua*), though the passage concerns the sum total of men discharged and settled during the whole of Augustus' reign, and is not necessarily connected with the troops in the east in 30 BC.

Octavian-Augustus had been settling discharged soldiers from different armies since the beginning of the civil war after Caesar's assassination. When the Triumvirs were recruiting soldiers for the war against Brutus and Cassius, they had to make military service more attractive because a civil war did not yield much in the way of booty, so among other measures they promised at the outset that veterans would be settled in eighteen designated cities in the most fertile areas of northern Italy. The historian Appian names some of them as Capua, Rhegium, Venusia, Beneventum, Nuceria, Ariminum and Vibo. After the Philippi campaign, it was Octavian's task to oversee the veteran settlements, with all the disruption that it entailed in redistributing the land. After the naval victory at Naulochus in 36 BC there would be more veterans to cater for, who may have been settled in Sicily.

The numbers of veterans to be discharged after the fall of Alexandria have been estimated at 40,000 to 50,000. Those who were not given cash would be settled in colonies, and Augustus mentions in chapter fifteen of the *Res Gestae* that he gave 250 *denarii* to each of the 120,000 men who had served in his armies and were now settled in colonies. This total probably includes the veterans of Philippi and Naulochus, as well as those discharged after 30 BC. Apart from direct cash payments, there were other privileges for veterans. Octavian issued an edict in 31 BC to the effect that veterans should be exempt from taxation and requisitioning of supplies.

Colonies for veterans had been established in Italy until the Triumviral period, and then were increasingly established in the provinces. Octavian's veterans were given lands in towns which had supported Antony, while veterans who had fought for Antony were either given cash, or were settled in various places, including Macedonia, perhaps in Africa around Carthage, and some in northern Italy. Some unfortunate Italians from Augusta Baggienorum in Liguria who had served in Antony's army were not allowed to go home, because their lands were given to Octavian's soldiers.

In chapter twenty-eight of the *Res Gestae* Augustus lists the provinces where he established veteran colonies, in Libya, Sicily, Macedonia, Nearer and Further Spain, Achaea, Asia, Syria, Pisidia, and in Gaul around Narbo, and Pisidia. He says that he founded twenty-eight colonies in Italy, which has been queried because Augustus was probably responsible for more than this number of colonies in Italy. The number twenty-eight is significant since it corresponds to the number of legions that were retained from the sixty that were extant after the fall of Alexandria. The problem in identifying which colonies were founded by Augustus is that both he and Julius Caesar gave them the same name, Julia, so unless there is other corroborative evidence as to the date of foundation, it is impossible to discern which belong to Caesar and which to Augustus, though it is known that some colonies were reserved for the veterans of specific legions. Boris Rankov provides a list for Caesar's legions: veterans from the Seventh and Eighth legions were settled in Campania at Calatia and Casilinum, the Ninth in Picenum, the Eleventh at Bovianum in Samnite territory, the Twelfth at Parma, and the Thirteenth at Spello in Umbria. In Gaul, veterans of the Sixth legion settled at Arles, and those of the Tenth at Narbonne. Alison Cooley adds three more colonies in Narbonensis, Arausio (modern Orange) for *legio II*, Baeterrae (modern Béziers) for *legio VII*, and Forum Julii (modern Fréjus) for *legio VIII*.

Augustus enumerates how much he paid for all the lands for veteran settlement in Italy and the provinces in chapter sixteen of the *Res Gestae*. The figures appertain to the whole of his reign: 600 million *sestertii* for Italian lands and 260 million *sestertii* for provincial lands. He says that he was the first and only individual to pay for lands, by which he means out of his own funds, whereas land for veterans had previously been paid for by the state, for instance as consul in 59 BC, Caesar had included in his land bill for the settlement of Pompey's veterans provision for land purchase out of the state treasury, which had been filled by the spoils that Pompey had brought to Rome from the east. Lawrence Keppie has estimated that 600 trillion *sestertii* for land in Italy would have purchased allotments of about fifty *iugera* for 24,000 veterans, though the size of the allotments is not known for certain. The aftermath of the civil war would have involved one of the largest mass settlements of veterans ever undertaken, and there would have been many more men than the estimated 24,000, but many of the veterans after the fall of Alexandria were settled in the provinces, where land may have been less costly.

Sixteen years after the reorganisation of 30 BC there was another large settlement of veterans in 14 BC, sixteen years being the standard term of service at the time. When it was being decided which legions to retain and which to disband, it may not have been possible to bring the twenty-eight legions up to full strength by filling the gaps with volunteers from other legions, so there may have been large-scale recruitment to provide the full complement of soldiers, who would have signed up for the full term of sixteen years' service, and those who survived would have been ready for discharge in 14 BC.

The settlement of so many discharged soldiers on the land could not continue indefinitely, particularly if civilians had to be relocated in order to provide farms for the veterans. Even if new colonies were to be founded, lands would eventually become too scarce to continue with the programme. In 13 BC two changes were made. Land allotments were largely but not entirely commuted into cash payments, and service in the legions was extended to twenty years. Soldiers would be on active service for the usual sixteen years but would be retained for another four years as reserves, excused from ordinary fatigues. This would defer their discharge for a short time and allow the accumulation of funds to ensure their cash payments, which for the first twenty years or so derived from Augustus' own private resources, including the further settlements listed in the *Res Gestae* in 7, 6, 4, 3, and 2 BC.

In AD 5 the length of service in the legions was extended to twenty years with five in reserve, though this is an assumption because no source states this unequivocally. Service for twenty-five years seems to have become the norm for legionaries and auxiliaries alike, perhaps from this time onwards. Also in AD 5 the cash payment for discharged veterans was fixed at 12,000 *sestertii* for each soldier, equivalent to thirteen or fourteen years' pay. These cash payments were still funded by Augustus himself, but he regularised the procedure in AD 6, by establishing a military treasury (*aerarium militare*), financed initially by 170 million *sestertii* from his own funds, and thereafter from taxation, in this case a 1 per cent tax on sales at auctions in Italy, usually of property, and a 5 per cent tax on inheritances where the legates were not the immediate family members.

The foundation of colonies did not abruptly cease altogether in AD 6. In Pannonia the colony of Julia Emona was founded as late as AD 14, and settlement of veterans would probably have gone well if the land had been fertile, but it was mostly marshland, and there was a mutiny in protest because the soldiers wanted cash.

From AD 14 when Augustus died, there was finally an end to the undignified scramble to redistribute lands on which to settle discharged veterans, which had plagued the Republic every time a victorious general returned home, to be confronted by the Senate's reluctance to provide lands. Provided with their pensions, some of the veterans of the standing army set up businesses, or bought farms on their own initiative. As the army became more static in subsequent years, located in permanent fortresses, some soldiers were already running businesses while still serving in the army, and continued to develop them when they retired.

Organisation of the Standing Army

There were clear advantages in the establishment of the standing army. For the first time, the soldiers were guaranteed pay and a reasonably prosperous future, which would facilitate recruitment. Cash payments on discharge were probably more acceptable to soldiers than land, because it allowed them to be more flexible about their futures, instead of tying them to farms. Not all veterans would have adapted to a life on the land. They came from widely different backgrounds, unlike the soldiers of the early Republic who were mostly engaged in agriculture for a living and served when called up.

The interdependent link between the generals and the army that had increasingly featured in Republican politics was now severed. All the soldiers swore an oath of loyalty to Augustus and to all future emperors, and the generals and the provincial governors were likewise dependent on Augustus for appointments and promotions. The men who governed the Imperial provinces were legates of Augustus with praetorian rank, even though they were ex-consuls. They were senior members of the Senate, but their career paths would have given them experience in the army as young men, so they would understand, or ought to have understood, the mindset of the officers and soldiers in the troops under their overall command. Until the disastrous reign of Nero none of the provincial governors with access to troops, nor the army commanders, made a determined bid for Imperial rule, although some of them may have entertained the idea and finally decided against it. This does not mean that everyone was contented with the new system of army command and provincial government, but it was better than civil war.

Augustus made few alterations to the organisation of the legions of Caesar's day. Caesar had raised pay to 225 *denarii* per annum, and Augustus did not see fit to increase it again. The historians Suetonius and Cassius Dio seemed to think that the *aerarium militare* funded not only the pensions for the retired soldiers but also military pay, but this is not the case. Army pay was derived from provincial taxes. There was no alteration to legionary command until late in Augustus' reign, when the first legionary legates began to appear. Until then the six military tribunes had been in command, in pairs, for one month at a time. Legates had been employed by various generals of the later Republic, but these men would command one or more legions, or detachments of various legions, for a specific purpose. When the tasks assigned to them had been fulfilled, the legates would retain their status, but they were never appointed as long-term commanders of a single legion. This was an innovation introduced by Augustus, by adapting procedures that had been in existence for a long time, though his legionary legates were of lower status than the legates of Caesar or Pompey. Legionary legates were senators, usually ex-praetors, appointed by Augustus himself and his successors. They would usually be about thirty years old, having gained some military experience as young men, usually as legionary tribunes. After three or four years in command of a legion, the legates would go on to higher appointments. The six military tribunes of Republican times were retained as assistants to the legate. The most senior was the *tribunus laticlavius*, literally the broad stripe tribune, of senatorial rank, but younger and less experienced than the legate. The post was held for a short time, perhaps a year, and then the young man could embark on a career that combined administrative posts and military appointments. Some young men might serve as broad stripe tribune in more than one legion, which would provide wider experience of the army and its organisation, before going on to other appointments.

Ranking below this officer were the five equestrian officers serving as tribunes, distinct from the senatorial tribune, and designated *tribuni angusticlavii*, or narrow stripe tribunes. These would serve for a year or two, and then perhaps move on to appointments as tribunes in other legions or to the command of auxiliary units. Continuity of command was provided by the next most senior officer, the *praefectus castrorum*, or the prefect of the camp, who would be a professional soldier and would have served in the legions for a long time. The men who held this post had usually served as centurions, possibly in different legions, and then been promoted to senior centurion, the *primus pilus*, literally 'the first spear'. Commonly described as the backbone of the army were the sixty centurions commanding the sixty centuries, containing eighty men. These were grouped together into ten cohorts, six centuries in each, but there is no evidence that there was ever a cohort commander in the legions, so the centurions were the men upon whom the senior officers depended. This organisation had been in existence since before Caesar's day and Augustus did not alter it

The disposition of the armies in the provinces was authorised by Augustus, but it was constantly changing as circumstances changed over the Empire. The legions and the auxiliary troops were stationed in the provinces where internal policing was necessary, or where the borders required vigilance and sometimes armed combat. In the Augustan period, the camps and forts where the armies were housed were not of a permanent nature and had not yet attained the regular layouts of the later Imperial era, though some of the bases would be in use for long periods, or subject to repeated occupations as winter quarters. When wars broke out troops could be moved from other provinces to the war zone, and extra troops could be recruited, for instance in AD 6 when the Pannonian revolt began on the Danube, conscription was applied in Italy, and the future Emperor Tiberius gathered a large army, including legions brought in from the east, to put the rebellion down. Most of the troops were stationed on the borders of the provinces, on the Rhine and Danube in the north, and on the borders with Parthia in the east. It is only in the reign of Tiberius that it is possible to discern where the legions were placed, thanks to the historian Tacitus. In the fourth book of the *Annals* he provides a survey of the provinces and the number of legions in them in AD 23, but he does not actually name the legions. His list indicates where the main perceived threats to security were located. There were eight legions on the Rhine to deal with problems in Gaul and Germany, three legions in Spain, two in Africa and two in Egypt, four in Syria and the lands bordering the Parthian Empire, and two each in Dalmatia, Pannonia and Moesia. Mauretania was held by King Juba II, who had been taken to Rome as a young boy when his father Juba I was killed after the battle of Thapsus. Juba II married Cleopatra Selene, daughter of Antony and Cleopatra, and was sent to govern his kingdom as an ally of Rome. Allied kings kept order in Iberia and Albania, small kingdoms between Armenia and the Caucasus. The coasts and the Mediterranean were patrolled by fleets based at Misenum and Ravenna, and a squadron of ships was based at Forum Julii (modern Fréjus) which was then on the coast, but is nowadays situated over a mile inland. The total number of legions in Tacitus' list is twenty-five, which falls short of the twenty-eight that

Augustus originally retained because three legions had been wiped out in the Varian disaster in Germany in AD 9.

There is little information about the auxiliary cavalry and infantry troops of Augustus' reign, so it is not possible to say if he reorganised them and laid the foundation for the formalised auxiliary units of the early Empire. Tacitus says that the auxiliary forces were about equal in numbers to the legions, but their numbers fluctuated and they were frequently moved around as circumstances demanded, so Tacitus felt unable to say where they were located. Reading between the lines, it is possible that some units labelled as auxiliaries were still being recruited from tribesmen who fought under their own leaders for the duration of a campaign, and then returned home. At Augustus' death in AD 14 the *auxilia* was probably not a permanent force in all the provinces. Unit size may not yet have been universally standardised, and terms of service may not have been set at twenty-five years, so it may have been left to his successors to complete what he had begun. In the evolved system, the auxiliary troops consisted of cavalry units called *alae*, and infantry units called cohorts, each 500 or 1,000 strong, and mixed units combining some mounted men and some footsoldiers, called *cohortes equitatae*. The equestrian commanders of these units would follow a prescribed career path, beginning with about three years as an infantry cohort commander and working up to the command of a cavalry unit of 500 men. There were only a few 1,000-strong infantry units, and even fewer 1,000-strong cavalry units, of which no province had more than one. The commanders of the large cavalry units were important officers who could expect to go on to further military commands and prestigious civil posts. It was Augustus who laid the foundations of the equestrian career path, gradually establishing the four great equestrian prefectures of the Praetorians, of the food supply or *annona*, of the fire brigade or *Vigiles* in Rome, and the most prestigious appointment, the Prefect of Egypt. It would therefore not be out of character if he also instituted the auxiliary commands as the first steps towards the equestrian career, gradually substituting equestrians for the native leaders, a process that continued under Tiberius and Claudius.

Troops in Rome

One of Augustus' important innovations was to station different kinds of troops in the city of Rome. Troops had appeared in Rome before, but there had never been a permanent body of soldiers in the city. Antony had assembled a bodyguard in 44 BC, much as the Republican generals had assembled a *cohors praetoria* originally consisting of their friends and advisers, but latterly of soldiers to guard the commanders in camp and on campaign. Antony may not have retained his guards through the Triumviral period, but after the battle of Philippi he and Octavian formed a prototype Praetorian Guard from soldiers who did not wish to be discharged with the other veterans of the civil wars. They were divided into cohorts, and were still in evidence at Actium.

After 30 BC Octavian organised nine cohorts as the first Praetorian Guard. Six of the cohorts were stationed in various locations in Italy, and three were placed in Rome, where each cohort guarded Octavian and his residence for one month at a time. The Praetorians were of higher status than the legionaries. They were paid more, and served for shorter periods, though their length of service was increased at the same time as that of the legionaries. In 13 BC legionary service was increased to twenty years, while the Praetorians served for twelve years, then in AD 5 when legionary service was set at twenty-five years, service in the Praetorian Guard was set at sixteen years.

The functions of the Praetorians were largely ceremonial, accompanying the emperor on campaign and in Rome, though many of the guards had military experience in the legions, and on occasions the Praetorians fought in campaigns, notably under Domitian. Centurions were often drawn from the legions, and unlike the legions where no cohort commander is attested, the commanders of Praetorian cohorts were tribunes, who were usually men with long experience, who had served as *primi pili* in the legions. The commanders of the Praetorian Guard were equestrians, with the title of prefect, and there were usually two of them acting together, though notoriously Lucius Aelius Sejanus managed to eliminate colleagues and serve for some time as sole Praetorian Prefect. His example was followed on occasion by other ambitious men as time went on.

Throughout the long history of the Republic, there had never been a police force or a fire brigade in Rome, though there were many occasions when one or the other would have been supremely useful. Since the Praetorian Guard were too high-status to be comfortably assigned to police work, Augustus created two groups of military forces to undertake police work and fire watching. Alongside the Praetorians were the Urban Cohorts, *cohortes urbanae*, which Augustus established in 13 BC. There were three cohorts, all under the supervision of the *praefectus urbi* or city prefect, an office which had originally been of minor importance but had evolved into a high status appointment, held by ex-consulars. The Urban Cohorts were each divided into centuries commanded by a centurion, and as in the Praetorian Guard, tribunes commanded the cohorts. The soldiers served for twenty years, without the five years as reserves that pertained to the legionaries. The Urban Cohorts were closely associated with the Praetorians, and their cohort numbers followed on from the original nine Praetorian cohorts, adjusted as more Praetorian cohorts were added, for instance Domitian added an extra Praetorian cohort, making a total of ten, so the Urban Cohorts would have to be renumbered, starting at eleven.

Little is known of the way in which the Urban Cohorts operated until after the reign of Augustus, but it is reasonable to suppose that succeeding emperors employed them as Augustus had done. The men of the Urban Cohorts were called out in force to keep the peace when the news of the Varian disaster reached Rome in AD 9, and some of the Urban Cohorts were sent to arrest conspirators in AD 65 in Nero's reign. There are some recorded instances of soldiers from Rome being sent to put down trouble in other Italian cites, but the sources do not usually distinguish between Praetorians and the Urban Cohorts. Probably both forces would be called out in the case of food riots and other demonstrations in Rome.

The history of the fire brigade in Rome could be said to have begun with the bands of slaves trained to fight fires by Marcus Licinius Crassus in the first century BC. Crassus did not work purely for the benefit of the Roman populace. His fire brigade would turn up at various conflagrations with their equipment, and Crassus would first negotiate a price for the building or buildings before he put his slaves to work. Most owners of property would probably prefer to accept a knock-down price for their burning building, than to see it crumble into a pile of ash. As it was the building would disappear anyway, because the best method of combatting fires was to demolish buildings. The neighbours of the unfortunate owner would no doubt encourage him to sell as quickly as possible in the hope that the fire could be stopped from spreading.

The next recorded private initiative was that of Egnatius Rufus. He funded the project when he was serving as aedile, gathering and training slaves as Crassus had done, but he simply put fires out and rescued people rather than venturing into real estate. Instead of snapping up property he gained votes from a grateful populace when he stood as a candidate for the praetorship. Unfortunately Rufus overreached himself, becoming a little too overtly ambitious for comfort, and he was condemned and executed by the Senate while Augustus was absent in the east.

Sporadic attempts to combat fires were made by some of the other aediles, and by the board of *tresviri nocturni* responsible for the night watch, in charge of groups of public slaves. Augustus assembled 600 of these public slaves in 22 BC and placed the aediles in charge of them to watch for fires. After a serious fire in 7 BC, Augustus divided the city into fourteen regions, divided into *vici*, each one with a *vicomagister* in charge. The public slaves trained for firefighting were placed under their supervision, but with a total of 265 *vici* the system was perhaps too unwieldy to be effective. What was required was a permanent military force with commanding officers who could direct operations over the whole city.

When the finishing touches were being put into effect for the standing army and its pay and pensions, Augustus created the *Vigiles* in AD 6. This force translates as watchmen, and they probably combined police work and the fire service. The *Vigiles* consisted of seven cohorts, each divided into seven centuries, and not the usual six centuries of the legionary cohorts or the Praetorians. The numbers reflect the fourteen administrative regions, or districts, of Rome that Augustus had established. One cohort of *Vigiles* was placed in charge of two of the regions, with a permanent station in each one where equipment could be stored and the firemen accommodated. Whereas Crassus and Egnatius Rufus had used slaves for their fire brigades, Augustus recruited freedmen. The centurions of the *Vigiles* were commonly drawn from the legions, and the tribunes in command of each of the seven cohorts were usually men who had served as *primus pilus* in the legions, as were those of the Urban Cohorts and the Praetorians. The overall commander of the *Vigiles* was an equestrian, with the title of *Praefectus Vigilum*.

As firefighters without the sophisticated modern equipment of fire brigades today, the *Vigiles* could only prevent fires from getting a hold, so their patrols, especially at night, were their main feature. If fires got out of control, their only option was to demolish buildings in the path of the fire to prevent it from spreading. As for police work, the *Vigiles* would probably arrest anyone they found doing something suspicious, despatching the offender to the office of the *praefectus vigilum* who was expected to be on duty, or at least on call, during the night.

The number of military police and guardsmen in Rome has been estimated by Christopher Fuhrmann as 23,840 men, subject to some guesswork like all other statistics in the Roman world, but revealing nonetheless when it is remembered that each member of these military-style units in Rome swore an oath of allegiance to the emperor, and their combined numbers were the equivalent of more than four full-strength legions in the immediate environs of the Imperial residence. Somehow Augustus managed to establish these forces in Rome for the benefit of the populace without reminding people that they also benefited him.

3

The Legions from the First to the Third Century AD

The Latin term *legio* was used during the early Republic for the levy, or the procedure of raising an army, and as time went on it was applied to the body of heavy armed infantry known as the legion. The early Republican legions were organised as a hoplite phalanx, which had originated in Greece, in which the soldiers fought in very close formation, armed with long spears and protected by large, heavy round shields. Service in the army was based on wealth because the soldiers had to provide their own armour and weapons. This organisation was superceded around the middle of the fourth century BC by a looser arrangement based on small number of men in maniples, or 'handfuls', each containing 120 soldiers, the whole army being usually drawn up in three battle lines, each based on age and fitness instead of wealth. Two legions of Roman citizens, one for each consul, were usually raised until the end of the fourth century BC, when the usual number was upgraded to four legions, two for each consul. Experiments began in the third century BC in combining three maniples into a cohort, but only on a temporary basis for specific tasks, but the cohort was found to be a useful body of troops, not too large like the whole legion, and not too small like the individual maniple, and by the end of the first century BC the legions were organised in cohorts containing six centuries, each century commanded by a centurion. The legions of Caesar's day were in most respects the same as those of the Empire. Although the cohort and its centuries superceded the maniples, soldiers of the Imperial period were still sometimes called *manipulares*.

The late Republican legions were raised to fight in specific campaigns and disbanded when the wars ended, though some campaigns lasted for so long that legions were kept under arms for extended periods, and the soldiers gained in experience by continuous service. A sense of corporate identity gradually developed, especially as some legions acquired names as well as a number, but they were technically only temporary organisations, and the soldiers were still subject to discharge as campaigns ended. Augustus established the standing army after the defeat of Antony and Cleopatra in 30 BC.

Even when the standing army had been formed, the legions were not stationed permanently in the provinces. With the passage of time some provinces were demilitarised, while others required greater protection; for instance under Augustus, Tiberius and their successors there were three legions in Spain and eight on the Rhine, but the Spanish garrison was afterwards reduced to one legion and the number of Rhine legions were halved to four, while Pannonia and Moesia on the Danube had four each. Later still these provinces were divided so that the concentration of legions in a single province was reduced, but the actual number of legions of the Danube area remained the same for many years. All through the Imperial era, the legions could be sent to other provinces when necessary, either for the duration of a campaign, or as a permanent move to replace another legion, or to increase the size of the garrison.

While the Empire was still expanding, campaign armies had to be assembled on occasion, but not necessarily by raising new legions for each campaign as in the Republic. When Britain was annexed in AD 43, the four legions that took part in the conquest were drawn from other provinces, and there was a consequent reshuffling of legions after they left their bases. The original four main legions in the invasion of Britain were *II Augusta*, which had served in Spain and then on the Rhine; *IX Hispana* which also served in Spain as its name suggests, and then in Numidia; *XIV Gemina*, which had a long history, having served in the civil wars between Caesar and Pompey, then the Actium campaign and latterly on the Rhine; *XX Valeria*, which served in Spain, Pannonia, the Rhine and then in Britain. *XIV Gemina* was removed from Britain at the time of the civil war of AD 69, sent back for a while, and then it was removed permanently, leaving a garrison of three legions in Britain. *X Hispana* disappeared from its base at York in the second century AD, probably not by vanishing into a Scottish mist, but by moving first to the Rhine, then perhaps to Judaea where it may have been annihilated during the Jewish revolt. The Emperor Hadrian replaced it at York with *VI Victrix*, which had served on the Rhine and then perhaps in the Dacian wars of Trajan. This enumeration of the movement of legions in just one province is matched by similar movements in other provinces, and serves to demonstrate that neither the Roman Empire nor its troops remained in stasis throughout their history.

In the early Empire, although there are archaeological traces of camps, especially in Gaul and Germany where much of the archaeological work has been done, there were no permanent forts or fortresses, though some sites were used many times on a temporary basis, for instance at Neuss (ancient Noviomagus), traces have been found of several camps in the area where the later legionary fortress was built. As time went on the legions gravitated towards the borders of the Empire, and their bases became more static, especially in the mid-second century AD when the frontiers were established by Hadrian. The frontiers were adjusted but not abolished by subsequent emperors. Legionary bases were usually situated some distance from the frontiers, while the smaller forts closer to, or actually on, the border line were manned by auxiliary units. Several of the legionary bases were occupied for many years, not necessarily by the same legions, but once they had been established the sites were usually maintained until the troublesome times of the late Empire, because they were usually strategically placed at nodes of communication. It can be an interesting exercise to compare maps of legionary bases and large auxiliary forts with modern maps of main railway stations.

The number of legions did not remain constant throughout the centuries. There were spectacular losses, the most serious being the annihilation of three legions in Germany under the governor Quinctilius Varus in AD 9. These were *legiones XVII, XVIII*, and *XIX*. They were never reconstituted, and the numbers were never reused when new legions were raised. For some years after this disaster the total number of legions did not exceed twenty-five. The distribution of the twenty-five legions under Tiberius is described in a famous passage of Tacitus, already mentioned in the previous chapter on Augustus' reforms. New legions were created when necessary, *XV Primigenia* and *XXII Primigenia* in 39, and *I Italica* under Nero in 67. In the civil wars that brought Vespasian to power in 69, two more legions, *I Adiutrix* and *II Adiutrix*, were created from marines from the fleet, but at the same time no less than five legions were disbanded for their rebellious actions, even though one of these had only just been created. There is another list of legions, dating from the reign of Antoninus Pius, on an inscription found in Rome and now in the Vatican museum. It extends over two columns and lists the legions by their numbers and titles, arranged in their provincial groupings. At some unknown date the names of the legions that were created after the reign of Antoninus Pius were added to the list at the end, out of geographical sequence; these are *II Italica* and *III Italica* raised by Marcus Aurelius, and *I*, *II*, and *III Parthica* raised by Severus. Significantly most of the emperors who created new legions, such as Vespasian, Domitian, Trajan, Marcus Aurelius and Severus, were involved in protracted civil or foreign wars.

Some legions were awarded extra titles after they had performed well in battles or proved loyal to the emperors in civil wars, for instance *XX Valeria* may have been awarded its title *Victrix* after the suppression of the Boudiccan revolt in Britain, and *I Flavia Minervia*, raised by Domitian in 83, declared for him in the revolt of Saturninus six years later, and was henceforth known as *I Flavia Minervia pia fidelis*. As well as their distinguishing names the legions adopted symbols, usually real or mythical animals, for instance a Capricorn was adopted by *IV Scythica* in Moesia, and *XXI Rapax* in Germany, and a running boar was the symbol of *IX Hispana* and *XX Valeria Victrix*. These symbols are sometimes found on antefix tiles made in legionary depots.

Command of the Legions

Legions of the Republic were commanded by six military tribunes, under the overall command of the consuls. During the late Republic the generals in command of armies appointed legates or *legati* to take charge of one or more legions, or a collection of detachments of various troops, called vexillations, because they operated and fought together under a special standard or *vexillum*. These were only temporary commands which remained in force until an allocated task had been completed. The legions themselves were not permanent units, and there were no single commanders until the reign of Augustus. When the standing army was created after the civil wars with Antony, Augustus retained the six military tribunes, but inserted an extra layer of command between the tribunes and the provincial governors, using the title legate that had been employed by Pompey and Caesar for temporary commands. The full title was *legatus Augusti legionis*, emphasising that the appointment was made by the emperor, by Augustus himself at first and then succeeding emperors who each adopted the name Augustus, which became an Imperial title.

One of the six military tribunes was always a young man of the senatorial class, the *tribunus laticlavius* or broad stripe tribune, and the other five were equestrians, called *tribuni angusticlavii* or narrow stripe tribunes. The senatorial tribune ranked as second in command of the legion after the legate, despite the fact that he had no previous military experience. The equestrian tribunes undertook staff work, but could also command vexillations composed of groups of different troops.

Third in command after the legate and the senatorial tribune, and in authority over the equestrian tribunes, was the camp prefect, *praefectus castrorum*, a post that was usually held after that of *primus pilus* or chief centurion. The camp prefect would usually be a career soldier with long experience of the army. He was responsible for all aspects of administration of the camp, as his title suggests, but also the smooth running of the legion, including maintenance of arms and armour and artillery engines, and discipline of the soldiers. A camp prefect called Aufidienus Rufus rather overdid things in this respect. In the first book of the *Annals*, Tacitus records how Rufus served for a long time as an ordinary legionary, rose to centurion, then camp prefect, in which post he determined to restore the old hard discipline (*antiquam duram militiam revocabat*). Naturally he was not popular.

At the end of the second century the Emperor Septimius Severus raised three new legions, *I*, *II*, and *III Parthica*, and appointed equestrian prefects to command them in place of the more usual senatorial legates. This is often seen as the beginning of a revolution in legionary command, and the first signs of the demise but not total obliteration of senatorial influence in the army. This is eventually what happened, but it may not have started out as a deliberate Imperial policy. Brian Campbell points out in *The Emperor and the Roman Army* that the three new legions and their equestrian commanders were located where they would be subject to another equestrian, so it would not have been politically correct to appoint senators who would be answerable to an officer of lower social rank. One of the new legions, *II Parthica*, was stationed in Italy at Albano, and would probably have been subject to the Praetorian Prefect, who was always an equestrian, and *I* and *III Parthica* were stationed in the new province of Mesopotamia, created after Severus' eastern campaigns. Mesopotamia was governed by an equestrian, perhaps because there was a lack of senators who satisfied the two criteria of having sufficient experience and being trusted by Severus. In the later Empire there were considerably fewer senators in command of armies. The Emperor Gallienus, who ruled when the Empire was in danger of falling apart after the crises of 260, takes the blame for finally divorcing senators from military commands, but if this really was his policy he did not remove every single senator in favour of equestrians, and he did not achieve the changes overnight. Senators are found in command of armies in the years after his reign.

Organisation of the Legions

One of the most fundamental questions about the organisation of the Roman legions cannot be answered. No extant source states how many men there were in any of the Imperial legions. Livy and Polybius give figures for the Republican legions at various times, but the two authors differ in their estimates, and it cannot be said that legions organised on Republican lines contained the same number of men as the Imperial legions. It is possible that in different provinces and at different times legionary strengths varied; there may have been less rigid uniformity than modern authors expect. Most scholars opt for a legionary strength somewhere between 5,000 and 6,000, because there simply is not enough evidence to be more specific. Archaeological excavations have revealed plans of barracks from which the numbers of men in a century can be deduced, but only if the entire plan of a fortress is recovered, at a single point in its life, can it be shown how many men were accommodated in it, and even then one fortress does not necessarily provide a standard template for all fortresses.

The term of service for legionaries was originally six years during the Republic, with an obligation to serve for a further ten years, but these years need not be consecutive. Augustus increased the obligatory term to twenty years for legionaries of the standing army, but after serving for sixteen years they were designated as veterans or reservists, whose duties were much lighter, for the remaining four years. This term of service was increased at a later date to twenty years with probably five more as a veteran, and though this is not unequivocally stated, most modern scholars opt for twenty-five years as the standard term of service in the legions. Before the systems for discharge had been properly organised at the beginning of the Empire, there is some evidence that soldiers were retained into old age, and this, among other things, caused resentment. In the mutiny on the Rhine at the beginning of Tiberius' reign, the Emperor sent his adopted son Germanicus to suppress it, and allegedly one of the men seized Germanicus' hand and thrust it into his mouth to demonstrate that he had no teeth left and should have been discharged some time ago.

The smallest group of men within the legion was the *contubernium*, denoting eight men sharing a tent, or quarters in the barracks. These eight men would share the restricted space of the barrack room, cook their food and eat together, and more importantly they would fight together in the battle line. Though there would be separation by deaths, transfers or retirements, this would be the closest-knit community in the legion. The *contubernium* had no tactical significance, but each soldier would form close bonds with his seven colleagues (*contubernales*) and such associations would help foster a strong esprit de corps in the legions.

Ten *contubernia* constituted one century, which totalled eighty men rather than the hundred implied by the title 'century'. Each century was commanded by a centurion, whose subordinate officers, called *principales*, included those familiar from the old Republican army, the *optio*, who commanded in the absence of the centurion, the *signifer* who carried the standard (*signum*) of the century, and the *tesserarius*, whose main responsibilities concerned guard duties and giving out the watchword. The *tesserarius* earned one and a half times standard pay, termed *sequiplicarius*, and the standard-bearers and *optiones* were on double pay, termed *duplicarius*. Some men held all these posts in succession, while others were rapidly promoted to the rank of centurion after holding only one of the posts. It is possible that all the *optiones* were qualified to become centurions eventually, but some of them felt obliged to point out that they were destined for promotion by expanding their titles to *optio ad spem ordinis*, or *optio spei*, or other variations on the theme, the word *spes* meaning hope or expectation.

Some men bypassed service in the ranks and the post of *optio*, and entered the legions directly as a centurion. On occasion an officer from an auxiliary unit could become a legionary centurion, and some centurions came from the Praetorian Guard. These men had some military experience, but it was also possible to obtain a direct posting as centurion without having served in any army. Influential men could obtain the post of centurion for their friends via a letter of recommendation, regardless of the fact that their chosen candidate had no military experience. It was not always a successful process. Some men tried and failed to obtain an appointment as legionary centurion. Suetonius quotes the case of Marcus Valerius Probus who gave up after waiting for some time for a vacancy, and in the third century the future Emperor Pertinax failed to become a centurion in a legion and instead obtained a post in an auxiliary unit.

Six centuries, each commanded by a centurion and *optio*, constituted one cohort, and ten cohorts made up one legion. From the late Republic onwards the cohort was the tactical unit of the legion, and although the cohorts of the Praetorians and the Urban Cohorts were commanded by tribunes, there is no record of a cohort commander in any of the legions. The cohort was the equivalent of three of the old-style maniples, though with an adjustment to make up the numbers to 480 men per cohort. Although the early Imperial army dispensed with the two-century manipular formation, the centuries were still paired off in camp, and traces of the maniples remained in the military standard showing a hand (*manus*) with the palm facing outwards. The titles still used in the Imperial army for the six centurions of each cohort reflected the manipular organisation of the three Republican battle lines of *hastati*, *principes* and *triarii*, except that *pilus* replaced *triarius*, and the old order of the battle lines was reversed. The youngest men in the Republican legions formed the front rank of *hastati*, so there is a certain logic in labelling the most junior centurions as *hastatus posterior* and *hastatus prior*, followed by *princeps posterior* and *prior*, whose names derived from the Republican middle line of *principes*. The most senior centurions were *pilus posterior* and *pilus prior*, just as the Republican *triarii* were made up of the older men. It is possible that the most senior centurion of the six centuries, the *pilus prior*, commanded his own century and also the cohort, but this is not attested.

Significantly, the term *manipularis* was still used to describe a soldier, but maniples did not feature in tactical formations or on inscriptions, where soldiers generally described themselves as belonging to a particular century, distinguished by their centurion's name. Official military records of the soldiers were also arranged by centuries under the names of the centurions, as shown in several surviving papyri.

The First Cohort

From the late first century AD the first cohort in some legions contained almost twice as many soldiers as the ordinary centuries, comprising only five centuries instead of the usual six, but each of the five centuries contained 160 men instead of eighty. The centurions of the first cohort were senior to all the others in the legion, and their titles were slightly different, staring with the most junior as *hastatus posterior*, then *princeps posterior*, rising to *hastatus,* then *princeps*, and finally the most coveted of posts, *primus pilus*, which translates literally as 'first spear'.

The legionary fortress at Inchtuthill in Scotland, a single-period fortress dating to the late first century AD, not built over in ancient or modern times (an archaeologist's dream), provides unequivocal evidence that the first cohort of the legion stationed there was divided into five double-strength centuries. Next to the headquarters building, five houses with courtyards stood at the ends of five pairs of barracks. One of the houses was more refined than the other four, with a larger courtyard and underfloor heating in some of the rooms, and it is postulated that this was the residence of the *primus pilus*. No archaeological or epigraphic evidence attests the name of the occupants of the fortress, but Inchtuthill is now ineradicably associated with *legio XX Valeria Victrix*, ever since the 1950s when A. R. Burn deduced its presence there by extrapolating from its absence everywhere else. For much of its residence in Britain *legio XX* was housed at Chester (*Deva*). Archaeological excavations at Chester are restricted because the modern city overlies the fortress, so it cannot yet be shown whether the layout compares or contrasts with Inchtuthill, which in turn leaves the possibility that *legio XX* contained a double-strength first cohort while on campaign in Scotland, but not necessarily when it was brought south to the fortress at Chester. The likelihood that Chester does in fact conceal accommodation for a double-strength first cohort is supported by the fact that it is situated on the River Dee in a good position to supervise North Wales, in a similar situation to the legionary fortress at Caerleon (the Welsh version of *castra legionis*, the camp of the legion) which is in a corresponding position on the River Usk to watch South Wales, and excavations there have shown that its garrison, *II Augusta*, contained a double first cohort. The legionary fortress of Neuss in Germany and of Lambaesis in Numidia also contained accommodation for double-strength first cohorts.

Vegetius, the late Roman author of a military handbook now called *Epitoma Rei Militaris*, provides additional evidence that at least in the third century, if not at all times, the first cohort in a legion was double the size of the others. Writing of the legionary cavalry (*equites legionis*) of the third century, Vegetius indicates that the cavalry of the first cohort was twice the strength of the horsemen of each of the ordinary cohorts. Thus there is some evidence that the first cohort in some of the legions was double strength, but it is still not possible to state categorically that all legions in all provinces and at all times had a double first cohort. It has been suggested that the first cohort was largely composed of veterans, but this does not answer the question whether all legions adopted the same policy. There may have been special circumstances in which the first cohort was strengthened, for instance for a campaign and the pacification of the country afterwards, as may have been the case with the legion at Inchtuthill in Scotland. Some modern armies recruit extra soldiers in wartime, so it is possible that only a few of the legions had an enlarged first cohort, and it is also possible that this was not intended to be a permanent situation.

The Legionary Cavalry

Each legion contained 120 mounted men (*equites legionis*). Only one source, Flavius Josephus, attests to this number, and strictly interpreted this simply means that when Josephus wrote his description of the army in Judaea under Vespasian and Titus, the legionary cavalry numbered 120 men. Lacking any other evidence, it is usually assumed from Josephus' statement that the same number applied to all legions of the first two centuries AD.

For administrative purposes the *equites legionis* were allocated to different legionary centuries, which may signify that they all trained as infantrymen on enlistment, and after being appointed as cavalrymen they remained on the registers of their original centuries. Epigraphic evidence attests that the horsemen were commanded by centurions like the rest of the soldiers, and not by decurions who were the commanders of all other cavalry. One inscription records an *optio equitum* serving in the fifth century of the seventh cohort of *legio III Augusta* in Numidia, and a tombstone from Lincoln in Britain shows that the horseman Quintus Cornelius served under the centurion Cassius Martialis. It cannot be proved whether the *equites* lived in the barracks of the centuries where they were first enrolled or whether they remained on the century records for administrative purposes, but were in fact housed all together somewhere in the legionary fortresses. There is no information as to where they kept their horses.

Apart from the literary evidence of Josephus there is no further documentation about the numbers of legionary cavalry until the middle of the third century. During the reign of Gallienus when the Empire was under threat of disintegration, the numbers of the *equites legionis* were vastly increased to 726 horsemen. This figure derives from the work of Vegetius, who says that there were sixty-six cavalry attached to each cohort, and 132 in the first cohort. The functions of the legionary cavalry are not firmly established at any time in its existence. It has been suggested that the horsemen were mounted messengers, but it seems that they trained together as a unit and performed the same exercises as the ordinary cavalry, using the same weapons. When Hadrian addressed the troops after their military exercises at Lambaesis in Numidia, he praised the *equites legionis* for their javelin throwing, specifically mentioning that they performed while they were wearing the legionary cuirass.

Though it is known that the legionary cavalry trained as a unit and the men were grouped together on the march, it is not known if there was an officer in command of the *equites legionis*. Some authors have suggested that if there were such an officer, he would be the *optio*, mainly because an *optio equitum* is attested on an inscription, but if there was an *optio* then there is at least a chance that there was also a centurion. In the third century, when the Emperor Gallienus required an armed force of great mobility and speed to deal with threats on several different fronts, he amalgamated all types of cavalry from the auxiliary units and from the legions and used them to assemble a mounted army, commanded by an officer called Aureolus. Vegetius says that the legionary cavalry of the later Empire was divided into *turmae* and commanded by decurions.

The immunes: Engineers, Artillerymen, and Other Specialists

The Roman legions were as self-sufficient as possible, and therefore employed soldiers with special skills in manufacturing, engineering, building, clerical work, and medical and veterinary capacities. The men who performed specialist duties were *immunes*, who were exempt from fatigues, such as guard duties, labouring jobs and other tasks like latrine cleaning, but not exempt from fighting, and they trained and marched together with the other legionaries, so they ought to be regarded as soldiers with specialist skills and functions. *Immunes* are first attested in the mid-second century, but the concept probably dates from a much earlier period. There was no extra pay for specialists, and *immunis* was not a rank, but the men were allowed to devote their time to their specific tasks without having to do fatigues like the ordinary soldiers. It would have been somewhat wasteful to employ a man on latrine cleaning if he could have been more usefully employed on mending weapons and armour.

The jurist Tarrutienus Paternus, sometimes named as Tarruntius, compiled a list of the *immunes* of the legions, perhaps when he was appointed Praetorian Prefect in the reign of Marcus Aurelius. The list is preserved in a late Roman corpus of law known as the *Digest* compiled on the orders of the Emperor Justinian in the sixth century AD. The list of *immunes* appears to be in no particular order, but broadly categorised it includes the personnel who performed engineering duties, those who manufactured and repaired weapons and armour, the clerical staff who kept the records of the unit, the staff of the hospitals and assistants to the surgeons, and the staff who dealt with the animals belonging to a legion.

In the Imperial Roman army there was no separate engineer corps. The engineers and artillerymen, as well as all other specialist workers, were registered as members of individual centuries. Of those who can be included under the modern heading of engineers, Tarrutienus includes surveyors and ditchers, who would be necessary when marking out new camps or fort sites, and those who were most likely involved with building works and the transport of materials, such as roof makers, stone cutters, carpenters and woodworkers, metal cutters, glass workers, plumbers and water-pipe makers, cartwrights, blacksmiths, coppersmiths, lime burners and charcoal burners. Specifically associated with the manufacture and repair of weapons and equipment were the men who made arrows, bows, and swords, and those who made trumpets and horns. The clerical staff included a range of assistants, with responsibility for keeping records of the grain store, and for various financial accounts such as the cash on deposit and the monies left by soldiers who had no designated heirs. Inscriptions attest clerical *immunes librarii*. One was set up by Septimius Licinius, *immunis librarius* of *legio II Parthica* at Albano in Italy, commemorating the death of his daughter, who lived three years, four months, and twenty-four days. The other *librarius* inscription was set up by Marcus Ulpius Firminus at Potaissa in Dacia (modern Torda in Romania).

Building work played an enormous part in a legionary's working life. It was the legionaries who built the roads and bridges, and the forts and fortresses in any province, and they are also attested working on canals and river-widening projects, and even sinking mines. Tacitus reports in the *Annals* that a commander called Curtius Rufus employed soldiers to excavate a silver mine in the territory of the Mattiaci, around Mainz and Wiesbaden in Germany. Curtius received triumphal honours (*ornamenta triumphalia*) for his exploits in Germany, and the soldiers wrote to the Emperor, suggesting that he should award an honorary triumph *before* a commander set out, so that if he had already received an award, he might not be so keen to earn glory by working them so hard.

Roads were of particular importance to communications and troop movements, and the legions built thousands of miles of roads all over the Empire. Much of the information about who built the roads comes from milestones and other inscriptions. One milestone from the province of Arabia mentions paving for the road that was built by troops of the provincial governor Gaius Claudius Severus in the reign of Trajan. Paving for roads was a comparatively late development and was not universally adopted in all provinces, and in this instance the fact that it is specifically pointed out indicates that it was a worthy and unusual achievement. Legionaries from *III Flavia* and *VII Claudia* built Trajan's road along the River Danube by cutting back the cliff face, and an inscription found near the River Orontes in Syria attests to road building by four legions, *III Gallica*, *IV Scythica*, *VI Ferrata*, and *XVI Flavia*. The inscription also attests to the presence of soldiers from twenty auxiliary units, which are not mentioned in building inscriptions as often as legions, but probably regularly contributed to the work.

Each legionary fortress contained a workshop (*fabrica*), where the production and repair of arms and armour were carried out. Some of the workmen attached to the *fabricae* also made bricks and tiles, which was an important section of any legion, but the place of manufacture was sometimes at a depot situated a short distance from the legionary headquarters, as at Holt near the legionary fortress of Chester in England.

The Romans employed various types of artillery to throw stones and shoot bolts. The heavier engines were employed only in sieges, but some Roman artillery was light enough for use in the field. Artillerymen (*ballistarii*) are specifically mentioned in Tarrutienus' list of *immunes*, but there is little evidence of their numbers or how they were organised. Vegetius indicates that eleven men from each century were allocated to the operation of the *carroballista*, which fired large arrows. Marsden points out that on Trajan's Column, only two men are shown working with an arrow-firing machine, but there would be other soldiers who were designated to look after the animals and the carriage used for transport. By the middle of the first century AD it is probable that each century had one artillery engine, firing arrows or stones, and Adrian Goldsworthy estimates that seventy wagons and 160 animals would be needed to carry the artillery of one legion.

The men who manufactured and maintained the artillery pieces would probably be *architecti*, who are mentioned as *immunes* in Tarrutienus' list. The legionary workshops could easily produce and repair artillery pieces, with the help of the *ballistarii*, under the supervision of the camp prefect (*praefectus castrorum*). A tombstone found in Rome records the career of a legionary *architectus* called Gaius Vedennius Moderatus in the first century AD. Vedennius started his service in *legio XVI Gallica* in Lower Germany, but was transferred to the Praetorian Guard, and after discharge was asked to remain in service in the Imperial arsenal, because of his skills as '*arcitect[us]*' (sic). In 2014, an inscription recording an *architectus* was found at Binchester in northern England

Headquarters Staff

Soldiers who possessed a high standard of literacy could be appointed to the administrative and clerical staffs of the legionary officers. The equestrian tribunes, the camp prefect, the *tribunus laticlavius*, and the legionary legate all employed a staff of clerical and other assistants in their *officia*, or offices. These men, like the small group of lesser officers attached to each centurion, were called *principales*. The standard-bearers, the *aquilifer*, who carried the legionary eagle, and the several *signiferi* and *imaginiferi*, who carried the lesser standards, all ranked as *principales* of the headquarters, which was served by a collection of clerical staff, commonly called *librarii*, who attended to the financial and administrative functions of the legions under the watchful eyes of the *cornicularii*. These are described more fully in the chapter on officers and men, below. Records were kept of all the men for various purposes, for example there were daily rosters to show where the men of each century were located and what they were doing, and annual strength reports. Financial records would detail the pay and deductions for each man at the three pay parades per year, and show how much money the soldiers had in their savings accounts. According to Vegetius, the standard-bearer was responsible for the money contributed by all the soldiers for the burial club, which was used to pay for the funeral services of men who had died. Other financial records would document the expenses of the whole legion for various purchases. Copies of all financial records would be sent to the office of the provincial procurator, who was responsible for army supplies and pay. There would be letters incoming and outgoing, reports to be sent to provincial headquarters, records of punishments and disciplinary hearings, and a variety of clerical work and bureaucracy that would keep many soldiers doing the pen-pushing that most armies require.

Recruitment

During the Republic the Romans were able to recruit enough citizens to raise several armies in times of war, provided that the crisis did not last for many years. The second Punic War stretched resources almost to breaking point, and recruitment reached unprecedented levels as the Senate committed more and more troops to foreign campaigns even while Italy was threatened. There were about twelve or fourteen legions on active service in 215 BC, rising to eighteen in 214, and about twenty-five in 212–211 BC, each accompanied by an equally high number of allied troops. Roman and allied manpower was not inexhaustible, as demonstrated by the refusal of some of the Latin colonies to provide any recruits for the *alae sociorum* in 209 BC, and there were no levies at all in the following year. The Romans were forced to enrol younger and older men than normal, and more of the poorer men as needs pressed. Manpower remained problematical, and Gaius Gracchus introduced a bill in 123 BC making it illegal to recruit men younger than seventeen.

After the Punic Wars the Romans fought wars outside Italy. In the first half of the second century there were Roman armies in Syria fighting against Antiochus III, and also in Macedonia, Greece and Spain. Though there was no standing army there was an almost perpetual military presence, enabling some men to follow what amounted to a military career, with the growth of experience and professionalism that automatically built up as men re-enlisted over and over again in different armies. The career of Spurius Ligustinus demonstrates how it was possible to remain as a soldier almost all the time. Livy relates how Ligustinus volunteered for many campaigns, and fought in Macedonia, Greece and Spain, sometimes reaching the rank of centurion, then staring afresh as an ordinary solider in the next campaign, but usually being promoted for exemplary service and serving as centurion once more.

With the growth of Empire, recruitment patterns inevitably changed. The enfranchisement of the allies after the Social War made more men available for service as legionaries, but reduced the number of allied troops, which were from then onwards recruited from the non-citizen provincials or peoples outside the Empire, such as the Batavians of the Rhineland. The anarchy of the civil wars at the end of the Republic interrupted the pattern, when more or less anyone who could use a weapon was recruited into the legions regardless of status. Augustus re-established Roman citizenship as a requirement for legionary service. Recruits had to state on oath that they were freeborn Roman citizens, but it seems that there was no readily available documentary proof that cancelled all doubt as to whether a man was freeborn, and a Roman citizen, or not as the case may be. Adrian Goldsworthy quotes the case of an *optio* who was denounced as a non-citizen and had to produce witnesses to vouch for him. Slaves and criminals were excluded from the armies, and suspicions about the legal standing of recruits were closely examined. Pliny wrote to Trajan asking what to do about two recruits who were thought to be slaves, and received the answer that it was important to find out whether they were conscripts or volunteers. Trajan explained that if the recruiting officer had not noticed that the men were slaves, then he was at fault. If the slaves had volunteered and lied about their status then they should be executed, but if they were substitutes (*vicarii*) then the men who sent them to the recruiting officer in their place were to blame.

In the legions, Italians predominated until the second century when citizens from the western provinces such as Gallia Narbonensis, Baetica (southern Spain), Africa and Macedonia began to serve as legionaries. Citizenship gradually spread over much of the Empire during the first two centuries AD, producing more eligible candidates for the legions, with the result that provincial recruitment broadened and Italian recruitment declined. New legions were normally raised in Italy, but replacements for the existing legions were increasingly found in the provinces, especially after expansion slowed and legionary fortresses became more permanent establishments.

In Britain, the origins of some of the legionaries who died at the fortresses of Caerleon, Chester and York show that they came from various different provinces. Quintus Julius Severus, veteran of *II Augusta* at Caerleon, came from Digne in the Basses-Alpes. Gaius Valerius Victor, standard-bearer of *II Augusta*, came from Lugdunum (Lyon). At Lincoln, the legionary base that preceded York, one soldier of *IX Hispana* came appropriately from Spain, and another from Heraclea, in Macedonia. At York Lucius Duccius Rufinus, *signifer* of *IX Hispana*, who died aged only twenty-eight, came from Vienne in France, and a soldier of the same legion, whose name is lost, hailed from Navaria, modern Novara, west of Milan. Far more tombstones survive at Chester, giving the origins of soldiers of *II Adiutrix* and *XX Valeria Victrix*, which two legions occupied the fortress in succession. Four soldiers of *II Adiutrix* came from Aprus in Thrace, one from Celeia in Noricum, one from Savaria in Pannonia, one from Aequum in Dalmatia, and one from Aosta in northern Italy. The legion was raised in 69 according to Tacitus, and may have accompanied the governor Petillius Cerialis to Britain in 71. The fortress at Chester was built in the 70s; the water pipes were being laid down when Gnaeus Julius Agricola was governor, from 77 or 78 to 83 or 84. The soldiers recruited in 69 would still be serving in *II Adiutrix* until about 84, when *XX Valeria Victrix* may have arrived at Chester, though the exact date is uncertain. Though the tombstones of the soldiers of *II Adiutrix* cannot be precisely dated, it is likely that the men died before the end of the 80s, and must therefore represent the original recruits, drawn from a wide area, or replacements brought in to fill gaps from a variety of other provinces. The soldiers of *XX Valeria Victrix* at Chester came from a similarly wide area. The camp prefect Marcus Aurelius Alexander came from Osroene in northern Mesopotamia, but on his tombstone he is described as a Syrian tribesman. It would be usual for senior officers to serve in different legions in different parts of the Empire, but this was presumably Alexander's last posting. He died at Chester aged seventy-two, probably still in service. Of the legionaries and lower-ranking officers, four men came from Gaul, from Lugdunum (Lyon), Arelate (Arles), Vienna (Vienne), and Forum Julii (Fréjus). Four others originated from Noricum, one from the *municipium* of Virunum (Mariasaal, Austria) and three from the *municipium* of Celeia. From northern Italy, one man came from the district around Turin, another from the *colonia* of Cremona, and another from Brescia (Brixia). One man came from Emerita (Merida) in Spain; one from Oea (Tripoli, North Africa); one from Ulpia Traiana (Xanten, Germany). These tombstones represent only a small proportion of the legionaries who were based at Chester. There are many more tombstones where no origin is stated. The picture can never be complete because it cannot be said that every single tombstone set up at Chester has been discovered, and there were probably many soldiers who died without benefit of a stone memorial.

Yann le Bohec envisages a progressive recruitment pattern, firstly from a wide area covering more than one province, which is supported by the British examples for four different legions, then from the regions surrounding the individual legionary fortresses, then eventually in the immediate locality of the fortress, when men from the *canabae*, or civil settlements near the fortresses, were brought into the legions. These may have been sons of soldiers, who were listed in the records *origo castris*, indicating that they came 'from the camp'. It has been suggested that this phrase may indicate occasions when the rules about eligibility to serve in the legions were relaxed, especially for men drawn from the vicinity of the fortress, and the fictional description of their origins and citizenship satisfied the regulations.

There is some debate as to whether there were always enough volunteers to pre-empt the need to fill up the ranks by conscription (*dilectus*). Some authors suggest that conscription was only used in emergencies, when preparations were being made for wars, but others consider that sometimes volunteers were in short supply, and that compulsory service, or at least Rome's right to enforce it, remained the norm all through the Empire. High-ranking officers were put in charge of conscription, called *dilectatores* in the Imperial provinces and *legati ad dilectum* in senatorial provinces. As demonstrated by Trajan's response to Pliny about the slaves, conscription and voluntary entry were both feasible, and the fact that men who did not want to serve in the armies were entitled to produce willing replacements presupposes that conscription was in force in some provinces at certain times, since eager volunteers were not likely to send substitutes. An inscription from Africa, dated to the first century AD, refers to a soldier of *legio III Augusta*, Lucius Flaminius, who was 'chosen in a levy by Marcus Silanus'.

It is estimated that about 18,000 replacements were needed over the whole Empire in peacetime during the first two centuries, but this is not an impossibly high number for such a vast expanse of territory. The Romans were usually scrupulous about the physical and mental qualities of their legionary recruits, and therefore many men would probably have been rejected, unless wars were being fought and there were many casualties who would have to be replaced. Vegetius outlines the qualities that were normally sought in recruits. Candidates for the legions had to be of regulation height, between five feet ten inches and six feet tall in Roman measure, which approximates respectively to five feet eight inches and five feet ten inches in modern measure. The recruits were expected to be in good health, with good eyesight, ideally able to understand Latin, and in some cases recruiting officers looked for men who could read and write so that they could fulfil the several clerical roles. The Roman army was a bureaucratic organisation, and some men may have spent much of their military careers in offices keeping records up to date, the ancient equivalent of pen-pushing or more recently keyboard bashing and number crunching. But as stated above, these men were soldiers first and foremost and would march and fight if necessary. For the majority of recruits, physical strength was the most important criterion. Vegetius dismisses certain occupations as not worthy of consideration for recruitment purposes, such as weavers, but young farm labourers were prized because they were used to working hard in the open air for long hours. They would also be accustomed to digging, and soldiers of the Empire spent a lot of their time digging trenches, and digging up turf blocks to build ramparts. The ideal age for joining the legions was about eighteen to twenty-one, but from gravestones and other inscriptions it is known that men joined up anywhere between the ages of seventeen and their late twenties. In emergencies men up the age of about thirty or thirty-five could be recruited.

Weapons and Armour

The Roman soldiers of the Republic were responsible for providing their own arms, armour and equipment. In the mid-second century BC, soldiers were paid salaries by the state, but as the legislation of the tribune Gaius Gracchus shows, money was deducted for the clothing and armour, the deductions being a source of grievance among the soldiery. In the Imperial army, the system was the same, as surviving records show. Pay was allocated with deductions for food, clothing and equipment, and if a soldier lost any items he had to pay for replacements, so in a sense the men still provided their own arms and armour but in a roundabout way. Since they owned the equipment, it is possible that some men embellished it while others were contented with the basic material. There may have been some uniformity in the soldiers' appearance but the modern concept of military uniform is probably wide of the mark for Roman armies.

The weaponry of the Roman legions consisted of different types of spears for throwing, and swords for thrusting or slashing. The *pilum*, a deadly missile weapon, was adopted by the legions at an unknown date and remained in use for centuries. Describing the armaments of the Republican army, Polybius says that the *hastati* carried two *pila*, one heavier than the other, one with a thick shaft, either rounded or squared, and the other with a thinner shaft. Polybius compares both types to medium-sized hunting spears, and the evidence from archaeological finds supports his description, especially those from the Republican siege works at Numantia in Spain, specifically the camp at Renieblas nearby. From the archaeological record there are several different designs of *pila*, varying not only in size, but in the shape of the head and the method by which the metal shank was attached to the wooden shaft. In some earlier examples the shank was quite short, and the business end was shaped like a large arrowhead, whereas the later versions had a longer shank and the tip was shaped like a small pyramid.

Some *pila* were attached to the shaft by means of a flat tang riveted to the wood, held by two rivets in the late Republican and early Imperial examples, but this style seems to have died out since *pila* of this type are not represented among the finds from the Rhine and Danube frontiers. The most common type of *pila* are like those from Oberaden in Germany, where the metal shank is set inside a wooden block shaped like a flat-topped pyramid and held by three rivets. Other examples of *pila* were equipped with a socket at the base of the iron shank, and the wood was seated inside the socket and held with an iron collar. Since there are very rarely any complete finds of the metal parts and hardly anything at all of the wooden shaft, it is difficult to discern exactly how long the *pila* may have been, but it is commonly suggested that the iron shank measured about two feet and the wooden shaft was about four feet long, so on average the whole weapon measured approximately six feet.

The *pilum* was designed for throwing, and had great penetrative power. Effectively used, it could pass through a shield and injure the man holding it, and since it was difficult to remove it quickly, at the very least it would render the shield unwieldy and therefore useless. A battle would start with the discharge of *pila* before the legions closed in using their swords. An additional feature of the *pilum* appears on some sculptural reliefs, in that a spherical object is shown, sometimes more than one, at the top of the shaft. This has not yet been attested in the archaeological record, so it is not possible to say what the ball-shaped object was made of, but it is probable that its purpose was to add extra weight to the weapon.

The legionary sword or *gladius* was commonly termed the *gladius Hispaniensis*, which was adopted by the Romans either when they met mercenaries from Spain employed by the Carthaginians, or when they first campaigned in Spain themselves. The Republican *gladii* tend to be longer than the Imperial examples, but there are so few known examples that it is impossible to be dogmatic on this score. The early Imperial *gladii* were shaped like an elongated leaf with a long tapered point, like the examples found at Mainz in Germany, from which they take their name in modern terminology. These Mainz-type swords are common on Augustan sites and probably survived until the Claudian period, when they were eventually replaced by the so-called Pompeian types, straight sided with a shorter point. The handgrips of wood, bone, or ivory usually had four grooves for the fingers and ensured a good hold; pommels were of wood, possibly covered with sheet metal, or ivory, and the scabbards were usually made of wood with sheet metal covers, often very highly decorated.

The *gladius* was effective either for cutting or for thrusting, and was used by legionaries and also by auxiliaries. The sword was worn on a belt, suspended from the four rings on the two circlips around the top of the scabbard, but no one knows precisely how the attachment to the belt was achieved, or whether all four rings were used. Tombstones from the Rhine frontier show auxiliaries wearing the *gladius*, like the legionaries, on the right side, which enabled the soldiers to withdraw it easily without hindering their shield arm. Sculptural evidence shows that centurions and officers wore their *gladii* on the left.

The long slashing sword known as the *spatha* is traditionally associated with the Roman cavalry, but it was used by infantry as well from the late second century, so the presence of a *spatha* in an archaeological dig does not always signify a cavalry unit. This type of sword could vary in length from twenty to thirty-six inches, and in width from one and a half to three inches. The ends were usually rounded, or only slightly tapered, and the handgrips were of wood, sometimes reinforced with metal. Two cavalrymen of the second century AD were buried at Canterbury in England, each with a *spatha*, with some traces of wood still adhering to the top of the blade. The *spatha* was suspended from a baldric over the shoulder, usually on the right side during the first century AD. Modern experiments have shown that it is possible to withdraw the sword quite easily from the right side while on horseback, but there was a change in the second century when according to sculptural evidence the *spatha* began to be worn on the left side, which would facilitate extracting it with the right hand across the body. A funeral monument from Augsburg shows a soldier called Tertiolus, and his servant handing to him a baldric and *spatha*.

Legionaries and auxiliaries are shown on sculptures wearing a dagger, called the *pugio*, on the opposite side to their swords. These may not have been used for combat, and they are not mentioned at all by Polybius, even though examples have been found in Spain dating from the second century BC, so they were used by the soldiers whom Polybius described. The daggers and particularly their scabbards were very often more highly decorated than the *gladii* and were clearly of importance to the soldiers. They had a leaf-shaped blade, and were shorter than the swords, generally about thirty-five centimetres long.

The legionaries were protected by their oblong, curved shields, known as the *scutum* since Republican times, but the earlier examples were more oval and not so sharply curved. The shield was made from layers of plywood and covered with leather. There was a central boss, and the edges were covered with iron. The *scutum* protected most of the body from the neck to the shins, and could be used in the famous tortoise formation at front, sides and top of an advancing group of legionaries that would have been the closest thing in the ancient world to a tank. It presumably took considerable practice to achieve this formation in a hurry.

Armour consisted of the helmet and various types of body armour. The several designs of Roman military helmets have been well documented, but an attempt to produce a strict chronology to illustrate their evolution is always problematic because the links between types have not necessarily been found, and it may be mistaken to assume that there was a chronological linear development covering the whole Empire. A whole range of modern terminology has been invented to distinguish between types of helmets, but none of the labels would be meaningful to the men who wore them. In simplistic terms, helmets were developed to provide protection from blows, downwards via the forehead, across the back of the neck, to the cheeks, and primarily to the top of the head. The latter function was served by the early helmets, which were little more than an inverted bowl made of one piece of metal, with a rudimentary neck guard at ninety degrees to the body of the helmet. Hinged cheek pieces could be attached to the sides. The hinges made it easier to put the helmet on and take it off. This is typified by the so-called Montefortino type in its fully developed stages, a type which had been used in its simplified form since the third century BC. In the first century AD, the Coolus type superseded this helmet, with a similar neck guard and an additional brow guard. The Imperial Gallic and Imperial Italic helmets improved on these designs in that the neck guard was provided with ribs, and angled down to reduce the space between the old-type neck guard and the shoulders. At the front of the bowl, close to the bottom, there was usually a metal strip running from ear to ear that would act as a brow guard, and also as some protection for the nose, since Roman helmets of the Imperial era did not have nose guards like the helmets of the eleventh-century Normans. Cut-outs were made to accommodate the ears, and protective ear pieces were added to some helmets. The cheek pieces became more elaborate with the rear section angled outwards, to deflect blows from connecting with the side of the neck. Some helmets were very elaborate, made of iron with decorative bronze fittings and studs. On Trajan's Column, some legionaries are depicted with reinforcing cross pieces on the tops of their helmets, but no actual examples were known until comparatively recently. A significant feature of Roman helmets is the so-called 'drawer handle' that was attached to the neck guard for ease of carrying it; these pieces survive in greater numbers than the helmets themselves.

Most of the helmets had a knob or some other attachments at the top for fitting a crest, and the Coolus type was equipped with a slot at the side for plumes. Polybius says that the Republican soldiers sported black or purple feathers in their helmets, to make themselves seem taller and more imposing, and according to Vegetius centurions were distinguished by a wide crest running transversely over the helmet, rather than running from front to back as they invariably do in modern films, but no fittings have yet been discovered to verify Vegetius' statement. It is not certain whether the Romans went into battle wearing their crests and plumes. On Trajan's Column it seems that these were fitted only for parades and ceremonies, but Caesar describes an occasion when fighting broke out unexpectedly, giving the soldiers no time to take off their shield covers, or to fit their plumes to their helmets. It may have been a case of fashionable practice at certain times, or perhaps it was left to the discretion of the general in command.

The body armour of legionaries of the first century AD consisted of a mail or scale cuirass reaching down to the thighs, but hitched up by a belt in order to take some of the weight off the shoulders. Mail armour or *lorica hamata* was manufactured from small metal rings fastened together, so it was heavy but flexible and could be folded up, as demonstrated by an archaeological find of such armour inside a helmet. Scale armour, or *lorica squamata*, was made of pieces of metal shaped like scales, all held together with wire, and sewn on to a cloth backing, which would not be as flexible as mail. The traditional portrayal of Roman legionary armour, fostered by films and TV programmes, is *lorica segmentata* which is a modern term derived from appropriate Latin terminology for the bands of metal round the body and over the shoulders, with copper alloy fastenings. Armour of this type was found at Corbridge in

Northumberland, south of Hadrian's Wall. In a box which had been deliberately buried, various pieces were discovered belonging to six incomplete sets of *lorica segmentata* dated to the second century AD. The box may have belonged to an armourer who intended to repair the various tools and weapons that were found with the armour. The find enabled archaeologists and historians to fathom out how the metal plates were joined together by leather strips, and to recreate one complete suit of armour. Bishop and Coulston suggest that this type of armour originated with the gladiatorial schools in the first century. An important point about the Corbridge find is that the box was buried in what would then have been an auxiliary fort, not a legionary base, which suggests either that legionaries were present, or much more likely that the distinction between legionary and auxiliary armour is a modern fabrication. The current thinking is that soldiers in all types of military units would wear what was available, especially as they had to pay for their armour and it is known that some items were handed down to one or more soldiers who put their names on them. It is highly likely that there were no strict rules about uniforms and standard appearance. The hackneyed theme in modern war films of soldiers being roundly chastised for not having their top buttons fastened would probably not have applied to the Roman army.

Senior officers wore a more elaborate type of cuirass, usually moulded to enhance the muscled appearance of the wearer, with fringed leather strips (*pteryiges* or *pteruges*) at the waist and the shoulders. The relief sculptures of the Temple of Neptune, previously known as the Ahenobarbus altar, together with the sculptures of Trajan's Column, show officers in this type of armour, which was also worn by the emperors. Apart from the sculptures, there is little other evidence for the muscled cuirass, which may have been made of metal, or perhaps of leather, or possibly both.

Discharge and Legionary Veterans

After completing the stipulated term of service, which is generally agreed to be twenty years plus an extra five as reservists, soldiers would be discharged from the legions. There seems to have been no hard and fast rule that soldiers should retire at a certain age, so if a man was fit and healthy he could serve for a longer period. It was not unknown for centurions to serve for longer, perhaps because it took a long time for ordinary legionaries to reach the centurionate so some of those who achieved this goal remained in service to enjoy the rank, the pay and the privileges. Men who had reached the exalted ranks of *primus pilus* or camp prefect were sometimes still in post over the age of fifty. On the tombstone of the camp prefect of *XX Valeria Victrix*, Marcus Aurelius Alexander, who died at Chester aged seventy-two, there is no indication that he had completed his service, and he is not described as a veteran, so it is possible that he remained in service until he died. Lucius Maximus Gaetulicus, *primus pilus* of *II Traiana*, had served for fifty-seven years by AD 184. If he enlisted between the ages of seventeen and twenty, he would be between seventy-four and seventy-seven years old in AD 184.

The soldiers who had been reasonably well-behaved, and had served well, received *honesta missio* or honourable discharge. When the legionaries were discharged they do not seem to have received documentation to prove that they had completed their service and had been released from the military oath that they had sworn when they enlisted. It is generally agreed that they did not receive the bronze diplomas such as the time-served auxiliary soldiers did when they were honourably discharged and granted Roman citizenship. This is a much debated question, but a papyrus document from Caesarea in Syria Palaestina, concerning twenty-two Egyptian soldiers from *X Fretensis*, provides unequivocal proof that at least in the second century legionaries did not receive any written confirmation of their discharge. The soldiers of *X Fretensis* had joined the fleet at Misenum as non-citizens in 124 and 125, but under the Emperor Hadrian they were made Roman citizens and transferred to *X Fretensis*. This legion was based in Jerusalem and had probably lost many casualties in the Jewish revolt in the 130s, so the marines would have been recruited to fill gaps in the ranks and would have been made Roman citizens when they joined the legion. If they had remained in the fleet, the Egyptian soldiers would have received diplomas like the auxiliaries, and the grant of citizenship would have been given to them at that time, but as citizen legionaries they had received no documentation on discharge, so they petitioned Vilius Cadus, the governor of Syria Palaestina, which embraced Judaea, to furnish them with documents proving that they had been discharged from the legion and released from their military oath, so that they could all produce written evidence if they were asked to do so when they went back to Alexandria. The crucial evidence is in the reply to the petition, which states that veterans of the legions do not normally receive written documents, but the governor of Syria understands that the Prefect of Egypt needs to be informed of the circumstances, and Cadus therefore agrees to provide written documents. It is known that any veteran who wanted to settle in Egypt had to undergo an examination called an *epikrisis* to ascertain that he had completed his service and had been honourably discharged. It is possible that the regulations concerning veterans in Egypt were stricter than in other provinces, since Egypt itself differed from most other provinces in many respects. The governors of Egypt and the legionary commanders were equestrians, and senators and probably other equestrians as well were forbidden to enter the province without Imperial permission. The twenty-two ex-sailors probably knew that the authorities would be more rigorous in demanding their ID and evidence as to their status when they went home to Alexandria. On present evidence it cannot be shown that all provincial authorities were equally rigorous about the documentary proof of honourable discharge of veterans, but it is generally assumed that this would be the case all over the Empire.

The status of any children born to legionaries while they were serving is debated. Since the right to marry (*conubium*) was denied to them while they were in the army, it is possible that the children born to legionaries before they had been discharged and received permission to marry would be considered illegitimate. This seems to have been the case for the children of auxiliary soldiers, and these were usually legitimised and included in the citizenship grant after discharge, but it is not known if this also applied to children of legionaries. Any children born after the soldiers had been discharged would be considered legitimate Roman citizens, deriving their status from their citizen fathers. The situation was much simplified at the end of the second century when the Emperor Severus legalised soldiers' marriages, which ought to mean that any children born to legionaries during or after military service would be legitimate, and Roman citizens.

The importance of having been granted *honesta missio* is demonstrated by the fact that soldiers mentioned it so often on inscriptions. Veterans recording their achievements and careers usually included the phrase, or the formula *missus honesta missione* sometimes in full, and sometimes abbreviated to M.H.M. In their wills, which soldiers were allowed to make only when they had been entered on the records of their units, the men who died after retirement usually instructed their heirs to include the fact that they had been honourably discharged in the text of their tombstones, and the heirs dutifully record that they have done so according to the terms of the will. The tombstone of Attonus Constans, veteran of *XXII Primigenia*, was set up by his wife Attia Florentina at Lyon, noting that her husband was *missus honesta missione*.

Gaius Julius Valens set up a tombstone near Lambaesis in Numidia for his wife Vibia Maxima, mentioning that he was *missus ex III Augusta*. The tombstone of Marcus Aurelius Primus describes him as *veteranus* of *I Minervia missus honesta missione*.

There were two other kinds of discharge from the army, on medical grounds (*causaria missio*), and dismissal for bad behaviour (*ignominiosa missio*). In the case of medical discharge, both physical and mental problems were recognised as reasons for discharge. The Romans seemed to recognise battle fatigue and the equivalent of shellshock. If the soldier was discharged for medical reasons before he had completed his full term of service, the grant of *honesta missio* was usually given. An inscription recording a legionary from *II Parthica* states that the soldier was *ex causa missus* but also makes it clear that he had been honourably discharged. The full pension was probably given to soldiers who had completed twenty years of service before they were discharged on medical grounds, but if they had not served for this length of time pensions were calculated on a sliding scale according to how many years they had completed. If a soldier who had been dismissed in this way subsequently recovered and wanted to join the army again an examination by two doctors was required to show that he was fit. Dishonourable discharge, usually involving reprehensible behaviour or disobedience, involved penalties. Pensions were automatically lost, and the tax exemptions and privileges of veterans were not granted.

Up to the reign of Hadrian some soldiers were given plots of land as they had always been during the Republic, but this usually involved the settlement of groups of soldiers in colonies rather than individual allotments, which were called *viritim* grants. Colonies were still established in areas that had been newly conquered so that veterans could provide security and defence if necessary. After Hadrian's reign land was usually granted in allotments to individuals. Veterans did not always make good farmers after twenty-five years of serving in the armies with comrades around them all the time and hardly any knowledge of agriculture. They could have run their farms via slaves, but this would still require some knowledge and the life may not have appealed to them. Some men left their farms and went back to the settlements outside their fortresses where they were familiar with the life and would feel part of a community that they understood and which understood them.

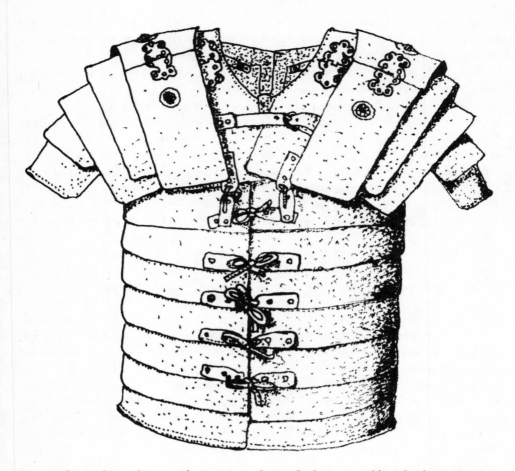

For a modern audience this type of cuirass instantly signifies legionary soldiers, but legionaries also wore scale or mail armour during the Republic and into the Empire. The description *lorica segmentata* is modern, so no one knows what the soldiers called their armour. This drawing is based on H. R. Robinson's reconstruction of the armour found in a box at Corbridge, dating to the second century AD, though some pieces found on archaeological sites date from the first century under Claudius. The strips and shoulder plates were usually made of iron, the fittings were of copper alloy, and fastenings and straps were of leather. One of the problems in reconstructing this type of armour was to work out how the iron strips were held together by their leather straps inside, which the Corbridge find helped to elucidate. It is worth noting that the Corbridge cuirass is small, much too tight to fit most modern well-fed males. Redrawn by Susan Veitch after M. C. Bishop.

These legionaries are depicted on a column base from Mainz, dating to the second half of the first century. The soldier on the left carries a clearly sculpted *pilum* with his helmet apparently slung over it, and a typical curved shield. On his right shoulder and arm, sculpted lines may indicate that he wears *lorica segmentata* under his cloak. His companion is a standard-bearer wearing a fine cloak knotted at his neck. There are six very similar column bases at Mainz, showing other equally grim and determined rather squat legionaries, one depicted frontally, wearing his helmet, with his curved shield at his side just revealing his sword suspended on a baldric, and two others shown in close formation with drawn swords, wearing helmets and carrying curved shields, going into battle. Legions most closely associated with Mainz in the second half of the first century are *XXI Rapax* and *XXII Primigenia*, though they moved around after the civil war of AD 69 and the revolt of Saturninus in AD 89. Redrawn by Susan Veitch from a photograph.

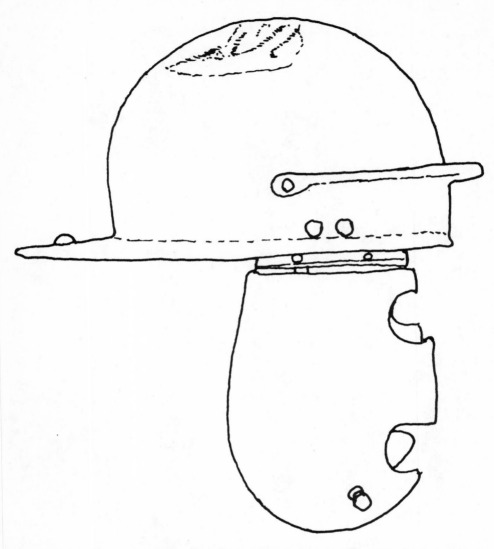

Many examples of Roman helmets have been found in various parts of the Empire and scholars have attempted to classify them into categories, labelled for the sites where they were found or by period. Without the entire corpus from all sites and all periods it is not possible to say that there was a steady evolution of helmet design. This helmet is known as the Coolus Type, which is divided into subcategories, beginning with Republican bowl helmets with rudimentary neck guards. This helmet has a brow guard and hinged cheek pieces. The original has a soldier's name inscribed over the front under the brow guard, and some helmets are known with more than one name, indicating that armour was handed on after the retirement or demise of the owners. Redrawn by Susan Veitch after M. C. Bishop.

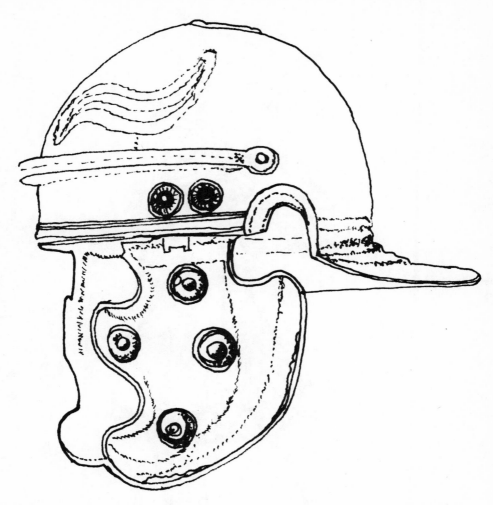

This helmet from Mainz is classified as Imperial-Gallic, which types have been pronounced the finest helmets produced by the Romans. It has a more pronounced neck guard and elaborate protection for the ears. It is made of iron with brass piping, especially around the hinged cheek guards. Redrawn by Susan Veitch after M. C. Bishop.

This legionary in battle is from the Tropaeum Traiani monument at Adamklissi in Romania, set up *c.* AD 108, to commemorate Trajan's Dacian wars. The soldier is wearing scale armour, a greave on his left leg if not his right, and a helmet braced by cross pieces. He has enhanced protection for his arms, which some scholars have associated with the enemy's use of the *falx* (plural *falces*), variously described as a scimitar, curved sword, or large billhook. Weapons of this description are shown on the Adamklissi monument, but they may have been used by other tribes allied with the Dacians, and not the Dacians themselves. Whoever used it, the wounds to shoulders and arms were fearsome, so the Romans adapted segmented arm guards that they were already using in other areas, rather than inventing them anew to meet the Dacian threat. Redrawn by Susan Veitch after M. C. Bishop.

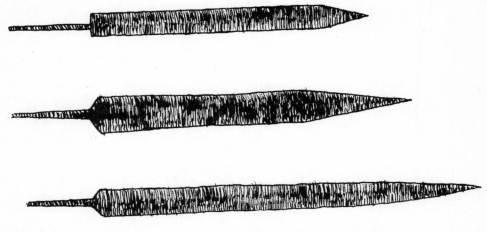

Examples of *gladius* types showing the evolution of shapes and sizes, as suggested by research based on dated examples. The longer example represents the swords of the late Republic, the middle one with a slight waist and much longer point represents the so-called Mainz type used in the early first century. It is not certain whether the waist is part of the design, or is the result of continued sharpening, because some swords with long points have straight sides. The slightly shorter sword at the top with the less severe point is the Pompeian type, which must have come into use at some time before AD 79 when Pompeii was destroyed, burying the swords for archaeologists to find. The modern typology and dating does not imply that the Romans suddenly stopped using one type and re-equipped the entire army with new types. Redrawn by Susan Veitch after M. Feugère *Weapons of the Romans*. Tempus, 2002.

Sword or *gladius* of Mainz type from Rheingönheim, with a fine handle made of wood with silver plating. The four grooves in the handle gave the user a better grip. Scabbards for these swords rarely survive intact. They were usually made of wood, with metal fittings, or sometimes they were encased in bronze metal sheeting. There were normally two metal bands near the top of the scabbard, each with two metal rings, showing how the sword was suspended. Drawn by Susan Veitch after M. Feugère *Weapons of the Romans*. Tempus, 2002.

Long sword or *spatha* from Cologne, dating to the late third or early fourth century. Cavalrymen used the longer sword to give them the further reach that was necessary for fighting on horseback, but infantry troops also used it from the later second century. The *spatha* was usually suspended from a baldric on the left side. Susan Veitch after M. Feugère *Weapons of the Romans*. Tempus, 2002.

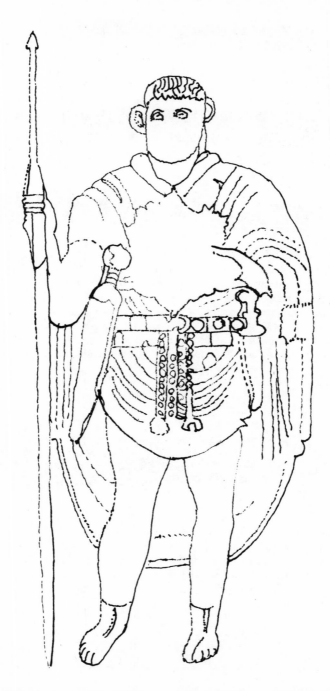

Damaged tombstone of the legionary Petilius Secundus from Bonn, who died aged twenty-five after serving for five years in *XV Primigenia*. This legion was created *c*. AD 39/40 and was destroyed in the Batavian revolt of AD 69. Petilius' pyramid-head *pilum* is clearly shown. He wears two belts with a short sword on his right and a dagger on his left. Redrawn by Susan Veitch after M. C. Bishop.

4

Auxiliary Infantry Cohorts

The auxiliary units of the Imperial Roman army were the successors of a long line of support troops which accompanied the Roman legions from the beginning of the Republic. The very early history of such troops is not properly documented, but the hoplite phalanx formation used by the Romans until the fourth century BC would not have been effective without light troops to protect its flanks, or skirmishers to soften up the enemy army before the main body of the army engaged in combat. It is possible that the poorer Roman citizens, who could not afford the armour of the hoplites, fulfilled these functions.

The Republican Roman army consisted of citizen troops serving in the legions and in the Roman cavalry, and non-Roman troops which were contributed by the Latin and Italian allies. At the end of the fourth century BC the Romans began to extend their control over the Italian peninsula, and by the middle of the third century they had absorbed all the states and tribes south of the Alps. As the conquest of Italy progressed, the Romans established a network of alliances, with each city state or tribal community bound by the terms of their treaty only with Rome. Not all the city states were converted into allies after a defeat in war; some of them joined Rome voluntarily for the benefits that an alliance brought, chiefly protection against other tribes and city states. The allied cities were allowed to govern themselves, and did not pay taxes to Rome, but were not allowed to ally with any other state or to direct their own foreign policy. The most important clause in the treaties of alliance concerned the obligation of each ally to furnish troops for the combined Roman and allied army whenever there was a war to be fought. The number of men to be raised was agreed by the Roman consuls and the magistrates of the allied states at each levy. Contributions of men would be tailored to the circumstances of each ally, and the needs of the war, but probably only a percentage of available manpower was raised, unless there was a dire emergency.

The individual allied contingents from each city state may have been allowed to fight wearing their own armour and using their own weapons, but eventually their equipment was brought into line with that of the Roman legions. The soldiers of each contingent were commanded by one of their own local magistrates with the title of *praefectus*. The allied contingents were amalgamated into units called *alae sociorum*, literally meaning 'the wings [*alae*] of the allies [*sociorum*]', reflecting the usual position of the allies on the wings of the Roman legions. During the Empire, an *ala* was invariably a cavalry unit, the title indicating that the cavalry also fought on the wings of the army, but the *alae sociorum* were not their direct ancestors. The allies did contribute cavalry, but the horsemen all fought together in battle, separate from the allied infantry.

The overall command of the *alae sociorum* was entrusted to Roman citizens appointed by the consuls. These commanders were of equestrian rank and called *praefecti sociorum*, usually six to each *ala*, matching the six tribunes of the Roman legions. The *alae* equalled or sometimes exceeded a Roman legion in size, though the exact number of men in a legion at any one time is not known and much disputed. Legion size seems to have varied in different circumstances, and similarly there was no standardisation of numbers of men in the *alae sociorum*. Polybius says that certain areas of the Roman camp could be reduced in size if an exceptionally large number of allied troops required accommodation.

For a long time Rome resisted granting Roman citizenship to the Latins and Italians, but after the Social War of 91 to 87 BC, all the inhabitants of Italy became Roman citizens, and therefore eligible for service in the legions. This meant that while there was a much broader base for legionary recruitment, the *alae sociorum* disappeared and it was necessary to find replacements to fulfil the functions of the allied troops. The gradual evolution of the permanent auxiliary units of the Empire can be traced in part to the temporary use of native troops in various campaigns of the late Republic and early Empire. When campaigns were fought outside Italy, the commanders usually recruited local tribesmen from the environs of the theatre of war. It was not unusual for different tribes to fight on Rome's behalf against other tribes, for instance many Gauls and Germans were recruited by various generals for wars in Gaul, and Spanish tribes fought for the Romans in Spain. During his eastern campaigns Pompey called upon local rulers and petty kings to furnish his additional troops. These contingents were often allowed to fight in their own way and with their own equipment, under their own native commanders. They were not a permanent feature in the Roman armies, but were engaged for the duration of a specific campaign. When peace was concluded, the troops went home. It is not known who paid these troops, but on analogy with the Italian allies, if the soldiers were paid at all, it would be their own communities who provided the cash and probably their food supplies.

Organisation of Auxiliary Cohorts

As the Roman Empire expanded, the need for permanent, more regularly organised units increased. The early history of the *auxilia* of the Imperial army is not clear. Tacitus informs us that the provincials outside Italy contributed recruits for naval crews, cavalry *alae* and infantry cohorts, but in his enumeration of the troops in AD 23 he excuses himself from listing the auxiliary units because they were constantly moved around, and the numbers of units under arms varied from time to time, reflecting the fluid situation before permanent forts were established. The stages in the transformation of the temporary auxiliary troops into the regular units have been examined by Saddington, and though Cheesman's book on the *auxilia* is now a century old, it is still useful.

The development of the standing army was the work of Augustus after the civil wars ended with his victory at the naval battle of Actium in 31 BC, and the fall of Alexandria in the following year. There were about sixty legions under arms, probably accompanied by troops contributed by allies of both sides in the civil wars. This huge army was reduced to twenty-eight legions, and the veterans from the other legions were settled on the land, mostly in the provinces. Any additional auxiliary troops that had been raised from the eastern states would most likely have been engaged on a temporary basis for the duration of the war, and would now be disbanded and sent home. Some auxiliary units were presumably retained, but at this point there are few collections of troops that can be identified as prototype auxiliary infantry and cavalry units.

The practice of raising native troops on a temporary basis was never entirely abandoned during the early Imperial period, especially when important campaigns were mounted, but these forces fought under their own commanders and were not integrated into the Roman army, usually being discharged when the campaign ended. From Augustus' reign onwards permanent auxiliary units were created, commanded by Roman officers, fully integrated with the Roman army, with stipulated terms of service, regular pay and supplies, and eventually a plan for discharge and retirement. There was probably no single date when temporary native units all over the Empire were replaced by, or converted into, standing auxiliary cohorts and *alae*. It is more likely that older units commanded by their own chiefs operated alongside new regular units for some time until they were phased out.

The development of the auxiliary units was not completed all at once when Augustus created the standing army, which was in any case a prolonged process. The terms of service of the legions were adapted gradually in stages. At first, the sixteen years' service of Republican times was retained, then increased to twenty years, by adding four years as reserves, then to twenty years with probably five years as reserves. The formation of auxiliary units also went through successive stages, but they are not so well documented as the legions. In developing the auxiliary units, Augustus or his successors could have reverted to Republican practice, creating units of the same size as the *alae sociorum*, on a par with the legions. Instead, the permanent auxiliary infantry cohorts and cavalry *alae* were smaller, organised on the same lines as the cohorts of the legions. The term cohort as used to describe auxiliary infantry troops is first attested at the end of the first century BC. The campaign armies of Augustus contained infantry cohorts and cavalry *alae* so the two terms had presumably acquired their distinct meanings by this time, though they were probably not used in the sense of regular units like those of the Empire.

The auxiliary forces of the early Imperial era were gradually standardised. In their developed form, auxiliary infantry cohorts contained six centuries of eighty men commanded by centurions, making a total of 480, like the legionary cohorts. For descriptive purposes the numbers were rounded up to 500, as reflected in the unit title *cohors quingenaria*. Augustus may have been responsible for the early standardisation of unit size, but even under the Emperor Claudius who reigned from AD 41 to 54, the auxiliary forces were still evolving. Later in the first century, perhaps under Nero, or more probably Vespasian or his sons Titus and Domitian, larger auxiliary units of 1,000 men were established, called *cohortes milliariae*, comprising ten centuries of eighty men. The auxiliary cavalry units were likewise nominally 500 or 1,000 strong.

Cohortes equitatae or mixed units containing both infantry and cavalry began to appear during the early Empire. These were organised like the infantry cohorts as quingenary or milliary units. Their ancestry is obscure, but these units may be related to the native German units raised by Caesar, predominantly cavalry, but accompanied by infantry running alongside the horsemen. Such native contingents may have provided the concept for mixed units, or perhaps the Romans emulated Caesar and continued to recruit some of the German cavalry and infantry, converting them into cohorts. An inscription from the reign of Tiberius records a cohort of Ubii, tribesmen from the Rhine area, who are described as *peditum et equitum*, footsoldiers and horsemen.

It is usually considered that the horses and riders of the *cohortes equitatae* were somehow inferior to those of the cavalry *alae*. The inference is found in the *Adlocutio* or address delivered by Hadrian at a military review at Lambaesis. The speech conveys the impression that the cavalry of the cohorts were not usually expected to perform as well as the cavalry of the *alae*. This should not be interpreted to mean that the horsemen of the *cohortes equitatae* were nothing more than mounted infantry who rode to battle, but then dismounted to fight on foot, as some scholars have suggested in the past. It now seems certain that the cavalry of the mixed units fought alongside the cavalry of the *alae* and not with the infantry centuries of their own cohorts.

An unresolved problem concerns the exact number of horsemen in the *cohortes equitatae*.

It is assumed that quingenary mixed units contained six centuries of infantry with the usual total of 480 men, accompanied by four *turmae* of cavalry totalling 128 horsemen, while milliary units contained ten infantry centuries and perhaps eight *turmae*, totalling 256 horsemen. Some scholars prefer to round down these totals for the horsemen to 120 for quingenary units, and 240 for the military units. This is one of the unresolved problems in the study of auxiliary troops. In the end, despite much use of scholarly ink and keyboard skills, no one knows the full complement of horsemen in the *cohortes equitatae*. In any case, unit sizes may have varied in different provinces, and the paper strength of any Roman unit was probably never precisely matched in reality. A strength report dated to 31 August AD 156 for *cohors I Augusta Praetoria Lusitanorum equitata* in Egypt shows that the rounded figure of 120 horsemen for a quingenary part-mounted unit did not apply to this particular cohort at this particular time. On 1 January AD 156 there were 505 men in the unit, comprising six centurions, three decurions, 363 infantry, 145 cavalry, and eighteen camel riders. The report then lists all the additions to the unit between 1 January and 31 August 156. One centurion, Sextus Sempronius Candidus, had been directly appointed from civilian life, so he must have had someone to recommend him. One decurion had been promoted and transferred from the *ala I Thracum Mauretana*, and nine recruits had been received, comprising seven infantrymen, one cavalryman and one camel rider. The 145 cavalrymen in this cohort do not support the theory that the standard numbers for a quingenary part-mounted unit would have been 120 horsemen. The papyrus records found at Dura Europos in Syria reveal that the part-mounted *cohors XX Palmyrenorum equitata* was sometimes under strength, and sometimes over strength, and in wartime units of all kinds may have deliberately recruited extra men, over and above their paper strength.

In the eastern provinces, Roman army units often contained a few camel riders (*dromedarii*), who were usually but not always attached to a *cohors equitata*. The camel riders of the *cohors Lusitanorum* mentioned above had been augmented by the addition of one new recruit in AD 156. Between thirty-two and thirty-six *dromedarii* are listed at different times in the rosters of *cohors XX Palmyrenorum equitata* at Dura Europos in Syria during the early third century. Small numbers of *dromedarii* were sent on missions with the infantry and mounted troops of the unit. There was no consistency in the organisation of the *dromedarii* as either infantry or cavalry, which perhaps has implications for their pay. The camel riders in *cohors XX Palmyrenorum equitata* were attached to the infantry centuries rather than the cavalry *turmae*, and their names were listed in the records as infantry, after those of all the other infantry soldiers. On the other hand an entire 1,000-strong camel unit, the *ala I Ulpia dromedariorum milliaria*, was raised by Trajan and stationed in Syria. If this unit was classified as cavalry, the soldiers were presumably paid as cavalry. It is generally considered that a *dromedarius* would usually enlist as an infantryman and serve for a few years in that capacity before becoming a camel rider, just as cavalrymen often served as infantry for a few years before being promoted to the cavalry. However, this assumption does not apply in the case of *cohors I Augusta Praetoria Lusitanorum equitata* in Egypt. The *dromedarius* called Cronius Barbasatis, one of the nine new recruits added to the unit in AD 156, was assigned to the cavalry *turma* of the decurion Salvianus. He was a volunteer, and had not been transferred from another unit, so his skills in handling and riding camels were presumably recognised immediately on enlistment.

Commanders and Officers

There may have been initial experiments in organising the command of auxiliary units. It is known that Augustus appointed young men, the sons of senators, as commanders of the cavalry, working in pairs, and he may have organised auxiliary infantry in the same way. The system reflects the pairs of military tribunes who commanded the early legions for one month, though an auxiliary cohort commander would not be of the same rank. The fully developed auxiliary infantry and cavalry units were commanded by men of equestrian rank, who possessed the property qualification of 400,000 *sestertii*, placing them just below the senators. A standard career path for equestrians developed during the early Empire, and an equestrian could become a senator if he gained sufficient wealth and experience in civil government and military posts. It was usual in the early Empire to intersperse civilian administrative posts with military postings, and equestrians could rise high in the Imperial civil service, with the ultimate goals for a select few being the four great prefectures, of the *annona*, the *Vigiles*, the Praetorian Guard, or as the Prefect of Egypt.

A *cohors quingenaria* was commanded by a *praefectus cohortis*, the most junior of the equestrian officers, who would remain in command of his 480 auxiliary infantrymen for two or three years, before going on to serve as one of the five *tribuni angusticlavii* or 'narrow stripe' tribunes in a legion. The next most senior military command for men who had served as cohort commander and military tribune was a cavalry command as *praefectus alae*, prefect of a quingenary *ala*. This was the third rung of the equestrian career path, as commander of a nominal 500 cavalry, serving for another three to four years.

In all provinces the milliary cohorts were fewer in number than the quingenary cohorts, so there was a corresponding reduction in opportunities for promotion to the command of the 1,000-strong units. The commanders were called tribunes, not prefects, and the post was the fourth on the career path, termed *militia quarta*, which terminology sometimes appears on career inscriptions of successful soldiers who survived their service, and went on to endow their towns with public buildings or other benefits. It also appears on tombstones, presumably on the instructions of the deceased to their executors. The *militia quarta* was a considerable achievement. The tribune of a milliary cohort was outranked in the auxiliary forces only by the tribune of a milliary *ala*, but because there was only ever one of these units in any province, and consequently only a few of them over the Empire, only a very small number of men would reach this elevated position.

The auxiliary cohort commanders were housed in the central range of the fort in a Mediterranean-style house with rooms arranged around a courtyard, usually sited next to the unit headquarters building. The house was called the *praetorium*, which was the name for the general's tent in the Republican camp described by Polybius. These houses could be quite well appointed, with their own private bath suites, and some of the other rooms heated by hypocausts and probably wall-flues. There is evidence that the walls would be plastered and painted, and some floors would have been adorned with mosaics. The commander often brought his family with him for his three- or four-year command, and there would be several slaves to run the household. It is possible to imagine the new commander and his wife entering the rooms for the first time, disapproving of the décor, and deciding to have the whole place redecorated straight away. Commanders' wives do not feature in the historical record, except in the letters from the fort of *cohors IX Batavorum*, or Batavians, at Vindolanda, pre-dating Hadrian's Wall, which was laid out to the north of the fort. The commander of the Batavians in the late first century AD was the prefect Flavius Cerialis, and his wife, Sulpicia Lepidina, was famously invited to the birthday party of Claudia Severa, who is revealed in another letter as the wife of Aelius Brocchus. Lepidina is mentioned in other letters from Vindolanda.

The prefects of the quingenary and milliary infantry cohorts, like all auxiliary commanders, were well-travelled, cosmopolitan men, with experience of military service in several different provinces. Some men became patrons of cities, or builders of civic amenities, leaving career inscriptions proudly listing the appointments that the individual had held, and occasionally including details of where they had held them, revealing that they moved about from province to province in a variety of posts.

The junior officers of auxiliary infantry units are less well known than the commanders. The cohorts were divided into centuries of eighty men, like the legions, commanded by a centurion. The second in command to each centurion would be the optio. Very little is known about the rank structure below the auxiliary centurionate, except that *duplicarii* and *sesquiplicarii* are attested, respectively men on double pay and one and a half times pay, so it assumed that the junior officers were modelled on those of the legions. There would be a clerical staff working in the headquarters, keeping financial records and duty rosters. The unit would have a standard-bearer of officer status, and each century would probably have had its own standard, called a *signum*, with its own standard-bearer or *signifer*. A junior officer called the *tesserarius* is known, responsible for giving the watchword, and probably for other clerical duties. Auxiliary forts usually contained a hospital, and each unit would have employed a medical team, with the chief *medicus* probably of equal rank to the centurions.

Recruitment

Non-citizens in the provinces were termed *peregrini*, which means 'foreigners', or more specifically people who were not Romans. The *peregrini* were less privileged than citizens, but Roman citizenship was not impossible to attain. The men who served as leaders of their town or city councils were rewarded with Roman citizenship, and for the less wealthy another method of obtaining citizenship was through the army. Since the legions were theoretically composed of Roman citizens, the provincial *peregrini* and various tribesmen could not enlist as legionaries, so they were recruited into the auxiliary units, and after serving for twenty-five years they received Roman citizenship for themselves and their descendants. The recorded instances where men had fraudulently claimed Roman citizenship show that the award was valuable to the non-Romans who joined the army.

Most of the auxiliary units were originally raised from the various tribes inside and sometimes outside the Empire. Gauls were recruited in large numbers, and there were several units of Thracians. Although all provinces contributed soldiers, and there were several units originally of eastern origin all over the Empire, it was the western provinces which supplied the majority of the auxiliaries. Unit titles in the *auxilia* reflect the nationality of the original recruits, and included a distinguishing number, especially if more than one such unit had been drawn from the same tribe or area, for instance *cohors V Lingonum* was the fifth auxiliary infantry unit raised from the Lingones of Gaul, and *cohors I Tungrorum* was the first cohort raised from the Tungri, from the region of modern Tongres. Some units were given additional titles from the family name of the emperor, for instance under the three Emperors, Vespasian, Titus and Domitian, whose family name was Flavius, several cohorts were given the title *Flavia*, often in conjunction with a national name, such as *cohors I Flavia Damascenorum*. The Imperial names are not necessarily clues to the date when the units were raised, since the name could be awarded for distinguished conduct to units which had been in existence for some time.

When expansion of the Empire slowed down and the provinces became more settled, permanent forts began to appear mainly on the borders of the provinces, and on important routes, and the auxiliary units which occupied the forts became more static. When the Empire was at its height, stretching from Syria in the east to Spain and Britain in the north-west, and from the Rhine and Danube to northern Africa, the numbers of replacement troops to fill the gaps in all the legionary and auxiliary units would have been staggering. Vacancies would be created when some of the men had completed their twenty-five years of service, and there would have been deaths from accidents and diseases. Desertion was not unknown, and would have to be counted as part of the natural wastage rate, which would be vastly increased if there were casualties of war. During the Empire, most of the auxiliary units remained in the same locations for many years, and recruitment from the homelands of the original soldiers ceased in favour of recruitment from the areas where the units were stationed. After a few years there would be none of the original tribesmen left in the unit, but the names were retained even though they no longer reflected the ethnicity of the soldiers.

There were long-term exceptions to this practice of drawing replacements from the local area. The specialist units such as the Hamian and Palmyrene infantry archers and horse archers from Syria, titled *cohortes* or *alae Hamiorum sagittariorum*, or *cohortes* or *alae Palmyrenorum sagittariorum*, continued to recruit from their original homelands, where young men were trained in their specialist skills and arrived as effective archers in their units stationed in other provinces, which spared the time and expense of training local recruits in the art of using and maintaining their bows and arrows. This would probably be undertaken only in times of emergency and shortage of men.

Throughout the Imperial era, entire auxiliary units were sometimes raised, often by coercion, especially after a war when the terms of a peace treaty usually included a demand for a contribution of fixed numbers of men, often on an annual basis, but sometimes en masse as a one-off arrangement. When Marcus died, his son Commodus made peace and ended the Danube wars, and demanded a number of recruits immediately, waiving the need for an annual levy that was more usual in peace treaties. A compulsory levy could be carried out among any of the subject people of the Empire, whenever there was a need for soldiers. The procedure was called a *dilectus*, the same term which was applied to recruiting the legionaries in the Republic. It derives from the verb *diligo*, meaning I choose or pick out. The *dilectus* was resented if it was carried out among the same people too often, for instance it was one of the main reasons behind the Thracian rebellion in AD 26. Even existing auxiliary troops could be disaffected, as shown by the Batavian revolt in 69, led by Julius Civilis, a native Batavian leader who had been granted Roman citizenship. This was a nationalist revolt affecting not only the Batavian units in the army but tribes of Gaul and Germany who joined Civilis. They chose their time well. The legions at the bases of Vetera (modern Xanten) and Novaesium (modern Neuss) were much depleted because Vitellius took troops to Rome to support his bid for rule of the Empire. The legionaries were forced to surrender to the Batavians.

After this unexpected rebellion, newly raised units of tribesmen were usually sent away from their homes to another province. In the late first or early second century, Britons from northern England or Scotland were formed into small units called *numeri* and sent to man part of the frontier of Germany. The scheme did not always work as planned. In his biography of his father-in-law Gnaeus Julius Agricola, the historian Tacitus tells the tale of the Usipi, tribesmen from Germany, who had been sent to serve in Britain during the 80s when Agricola was engaged in conquering what is now northern England and Scotland. The Usipi tried to return home, and stole three warships in which they set off, probably from the River Clyde. They had to come ashore on occasion for water and food, for which they fought the native Britons. They travelled all the way around northern Scotland and down part of the east coast, eventually finding their way to the coast of Germany where the Suebi and Frisii killed some of them and sold the rest as slaves. Tacitus says that some of these slaves eventually turned up in Rome, where their story was made known.

As time went on, the military authorities did not always rigidly adhere to the distinctions between citizens and non-citizens when they were recruiting replacements for existing units, or raising new units. The legions relaxed their rules and regulations, and took on non-citizens, converting them by a legal fiction into Romans, and Romanising their original native names for the records. Similarly the non-citizen auxiliary units took on more Roman citizens, so that the distinctions between the legions and the auxiliary units became somewhat blurred.

Some auxiliary units had already been formed from Roman citizens from the earliest years of the Imperial Roman army. Augustus created such citizen auxiliaries from freed slaves when there was an urgent need for troops during the Pannonian revolt in AD 6, and after the disaster of Quinctilius Varus in Germany in AD 9, when three legions were lost. Slaves legitimately received citizenship when they were freed, but Augustus insisted that only freeborn Roman citizens should serve in the legions, so he bent the rules a little by forming the units of ex-slaves as citizen *cohortes* and *alae*. Besides these original formations, if an auxiliary unit had performed exceptionally well, all the soldiers could be enfranchised, and their unit became a citizen cohort or *ala*. The original citizen units formed from groups of slaves, and also those which had been enfranchised on merit, can be distinguished by their names, usually expressed on inscriptions by the initials *c.R.*, standing for *civium Romanorum*, in the genitive case to match the ethnic name of the unit, for instance the Thracian *cohors I Thracum c.R.* Only the original enfranchised soldiers would be Roman citizens, and as these were discharged they would be replaced by non-citizens from the region where the unit was stationed or operating. These non-citizens would not automatically become citizens on enlistment, even though the units retained their distinguished titles of *civium Romanorum*, which after some years simply denoted a historical honorary award, not status. In 212 or 213, the Emperor Caracalla extended Roman citizenship to all freeborn inhabitants of the Empire in 212, thus changing the face of military recruitment, and also broadening the base of taxpayers liable to contribute to the Imperial coffers.

New recruits were not immediately sent to their units as replacements, or formed up as complete units and placed in a fort. They had to be inspected and trained. In his book *Epitoma Rei Militaris* the late Roman author Vegetius was concerned to bring the army of his day back to the supposed golden age of the earlier Empire, so his work is more an instruction manual on how things ought to be done, rather than a true depiction of reality. Nonetheless, most of what he says is perfectly plausible and makes good sense. He describes the training of recruits before they were enrolled in their units. This initial training lasted for four months. Dummy weapons and shields were used in basic infantry training, made of wood, but twice the weight of ordinary weapons, so that the men would develop the muscle power to wield their real weapons to greater effect. The recruits were also trained in digging ditches and erecting palisades, which would occupy a lot of soldiers' time and energy. They were taught to keep ranks, which implies that there was a programme of marching drill, and they were exercised in swimming, which entailed teaching non-swimmers how to do it. During this four-month period the men who lacked stamina or showed themselves to be reluctant or even timid could be weeded out, so that precious time would not be wasted in enrolling them, kitting them out, testing them in their routine tasks, or in battle, and then finding out that they were not suitable. In the case of volunteers or men conscripted from the provinces they could safely be sent home again, but tribesmen levied en masse after a war may have been forcibly moulded into shape and retained under strict discipline, rather than letting them loose in the province where they were to be stationed.

Terms of Service

The auxiliary soldiers signed up for twenty-five years' service, during which they would be subject to the sometimes harsh discipline of the centurions, and to a whole series of military laws covering their behaviour in peacetime and during battle. Any soldiers who endangered the lives of others were subject to capital punishment. During the Republic, soldiers who failed to guard the camp properly were tried by the tribunes in a military court and if found guilty were clubbed to death by their fellow soldiers. Desertion to the enemy, running away from the battle line, disobeying commands during battle, violence or insubordination to an officer were all subject to the death penalty. Soldiers found guilty could be beheaded, hanged, burned alive or made to fight in the arena against wild animals. Other punishments for lesser offences which did not endanger the lives of other soldiers included flogging, or monetary fines.

Rewards for soldiers of auxiliary units were not given on an individual basis, but if the unit had performed exceptionally well, an award was made to all the soldiers, and added to the unit title. Honorary titles were awarded after particularly loyal service, usually expressed as *pia fidelis*, abbreviated in documents and on inscriptions to *p.f.* As mentioned above, sometimes the entire cohort could be granted Roman citizenship, denoted by the initials *c.R.* added to the title.

The rate of pay of the auxiliary troops is a perennial problem for modern historians. It has long been considered by some scholars that auxiliaries must have been paid less than the legionaries, perhaps only five-sixths of legionary pay. Since it is known from Polybius' work and from Hadrian's address to the troops of Numidia that cavalrymen were paid more than the infantry, pay scales have been reconstructed that show three basic rates, with the auxiliary infantry as the lowest paid, then the next highest the legionaries and the cavalrymen of a *cohors equitata*, and finally at the top of the scale, the cavalry of the *alae*. There are some different permutations of these rates, none of which can be backed up by firm evidence. More recently R. Alston argued for parity between legionary and auxiliary pay, on the premise that when regular pay was instituted for auxiliary troops, only the standard rates for infantry and cavalry would have been applied. Like the junior officers in the legions, some of the auxiliary junior officers were paid at double and one and a half times the normal rate, indicated by their respective labels *duplicarii* and *sesquiplicarii*. The lack of precision as to what exactly *was* the normal rate hampers any calculation of the likely figures represented by one and a half times ordinary pay and double pay.

Augustus created the *aerarium militare* or military treasury in AD 6 to provide cash pensions (*praemia*) for discharged legionary veterans, but it is not known whether the auxiliaries received cash pensions when they were discharged. Some modern authors state categorically that they did not, while others have wondered whether the auxiliaries, who constituted half of the army of the Empire, could have been excluded from cash pensions at the end of their service. This has enormous implications for anyone trying to calculate the total cost of the army at any one time. Auxiliaries were usually rewarded with Roman citizenship after serving for twenty-five years, so the Romans may have considered that citizenship for non-Roman soldiers, with the privileges and tax concessions that this would confer on them, was sufficient reward in itself without the addition of pensions, which would have been costly to the state. In the fully developed auxiliary units, the soldiers were encouraged to save part of their salaries, and their accounts were studiously kept by the unit clerks. Their savings were perhaps the only financial support that auxiliaries received. It would be difficult to prove that auxiliaries were not given pensions, because documentation is usually restricted to things that did happen, and there is little to prove that things did not happen, but there is always the possibility that in the future some document will be discovered that shows that auxiliaries received pension payouts on discharge, like the legionaries.

When the auxiliary soldiers had served for twenty-five years, they were discharged and were usually granted Roman citizenship, which extended to their children, but not to the soldiers' wives. The origins of this arrangement can be traced to the reign of Claudius, who initially set the length of service at thirty years, and gave citizenship grants to certain individuals and some whole units, but the fully operational system of granting citizenship when auxiliaries were discharged probably did not come into force until the turn of the first and second centuries, when the system was regularised and citizenship became part of the package after twenty-five years' service.

Peace and War

During the Empire, when expansion more or less ceased after the reign of Trajan, except for some military expeditions in one or two provinces, the auxiliary units were stationed in forts ranged along the borders of Roman territory, or on routes which required protection. There were serious wars from the first to the third centuries AD, but for much of the time the auxiliaries would not be engaged in fighting, but in performing many of the duties that in modern times are carried out by non-military uniformed officials, such as police and customs guards. The men did not remain in their forts all day, but were kept busy on various tasks. Duty rosters that have survived among papyrus records show that soldiers were sent out for several different purposes, such as guarding markets, where gatherings of people would need supervision, and road patrol, called *vianico* in the records. The soldiers stationed in forts close to the mining areas in frontier provinces such as Dacia and Britain would probably have provided convoy guards when the produce of the mines was transported.

At the boundaries between provinces, and particularly on the frontiers when running barriers had been created by the Emperor Hadrian, the designated crossing points would be guarded by auxiliary soldiers, who would examine people and goods travelling into and out of the province, and possibly collect the customs dues and tolls that were applied on specific items. A list of tolls survives from Africa, enumerating the charges for two-wheeled and four-wheeled vehicles, and all kinds of animals charged for *per capita*. Frontier crossings would be particularly sensitive, not only because of potentially undesirable people and goods entering the province, but in some areas there were items which it was forbidden to take into the non-Roman zones beyond the frontiers. There are two well-known gateways across frontiers, one at the fort at Dalkingen on the frontier of the province of Raetia, now in Germany, and the other at the Knag Burn on Hadrian's Wall, east of the fort at Housesteads. Since both these gateways are close to auxiliary forts, it is fairly certain that the auxiliaries would be responsible for guarding them.

When the Empire was enclosed within frontiers in the second century AD, most military activity in many provinces would concern police work behind the frontiers and patrolling beyond them, and engaging in skirmishing rather than full-scale war. Only when large expeditions were mounted would whole or part units be involved, on occasion removed far away from their forts, as when Domitian and Trajan conducted the long-drawn-out Dacian wars, or when Marcus Aurelius fought the tribes of the Danube area, or when Severus arrived in Britain intent on conquering Scotland, bringing extra troops with him.

Auxiliary troops would accompany the legions and take part in any fighting, but like the *alae sociorum* of the Republic their contribution is not always documented. Some of the duties of auxiliary units on campaign may have included guarding semi-permanent camps, and convoying supplies. On the march, the auxiliary infantry cohorts were usually positioned between the scouts and cavalry *alae* which formed the head of the column, and the legions. At the rear they would often march in a mirror image arrangement, with the infantry cohorts following the legions and preceding the cavalry. In battle, the auxiliaries commonly fought on the wings, but there were instances where the auxiliary troops bore the brunt of the fighting, leaving the legions fresh for battle if the auxiliaries were overwhelmed. By the late first century AD, it was not unusual to keep the legions in the rear and employ the auxiliaries in the battle line, until the commander decided that the legions could be sent in to decide the issue. One of the best known examples is the battle of Mons Graupius, fought in 83 or 84 at an unknown location in Scotland, where the governor Gnaeus Julius Agricola faced the Britons under their leader Calgacus, which means 'the swordsman'. Instead of placing his legions in the centre flanked by auxiliaries, Agricola drew them up just in front of the camp, and put the auxiliary infantry cohorts in the centre, with the cavalry *alae* on the wings. He kept four cavalry units in reserve, so that he could quickly reinforce any part of the battle line that wavered. This battle was won solely by the auxiliaries, who withstood the initial charge of the Britons, no mean feat against an estimated 30,000 warriors, and held firm while the reserve cavalry rode round to the rear and trapped the Britons between the two Roman lines. This battle illustrates the value of the auxiliary forces, and testifies to their discipline, training and experience, which cannot have been far short of the performance of the legions.

Weapons and Armour

The auxiliary cohorts were armed and equipped for war in similar fashion to the legions, but there were important differences, because the auxiliary infantry units and part-mounted units fought in a less uniform manner than the legionaries, and some of them were armed in different ways. There were some units composed of archers, whose main attributes were obviously bows and arrows, but the majority of auxiliary infantry were probably armed with spears and a sword.

Since there are very few archaeological finds of equipment which indisputably belonged to auxiliaries rather than legionaries, information about their arms and armour is derived mostly from depictions on tombstones, which usually show considerable detail even if they are eroded, and would have shown even more detail when pristine because they were usually painted, so the finer lines that cannot be sculpted would have been much clearer. Sculptured representations on the great monuments such as Trajan's Column and the column of Marcus Aurelius in Rome show different kinds of troops, but these portrayals must be used with caution. The auxiliaries and other types of soldier on Trajan's and Marcus' columns are often stylised in order to convey to viewers which kinds of troops are depicted, so the details of dress, armour and weapons may not be absolutely accurate. With these provisos in mind the sculptures are well worth studying, and it is possible to make some broad generalisations.

For protection, auxiliary infantry carried an oval or sometimes rectangular shield or *scutum*, with a central boss, usually flat or only slightly curved, compared to the more sharply curved rectangular shields of the legionaries. There are variations in auxiliary shields, but the oval version is the most common representation. On tombstones auxiliaries are not normally depicted wearing a helmet, but on Trajan's and Marcus' columns auxiliaries are shown with helmets resembling legionary examples, although the neck guards tend to be shorter, at least in the artistic representations. Their armour is most commonly shown as mail, made up of metal rings all joined together. The mail coat is usually shown with short sleeves, extending at least to the hips. Some auxiliaries wore scale armour, consisting of small metal scales wired together and stitched on to a cloth backing. Both mail and scale armour is shown on the Marcus column, the mail depicted by drilled holes and the scale by overlapping scalloped-edged scales.

There is some debate about whether or not the auxiliaries wore *lorica segmentata* like the legionaries. This arises because several examples of such armour have been found inside auxiliary forts, not known to have been occupied by legionaries, and too frequent to be explained away by the possibility that some legionaries visited auxiliary forts often enough to leave armour behind. The theory developed that there was no difference between legionaries and auxiliaries, who would both wear *lorica segmentata* indiscriminately, but Bishop and Coulston pointed out that there are no representations of auxiliaries on monuments or tombstones, or any other art form, showing auxiliaries in this type of armour.

The main weapon of auxiliary infantry appears to have been the spear, in a variety of styles. According to artistic representations the soldiers usually carried more than one spear, clutched in the left hand with the shield, so the portraits show the spears protruding at the top and bottom of the shield. The number of spears carried by each man indicates that they were for throwing. An auxiliary is shown on a column base from Mainz, with two spears in his left hand protruding beyond his oval shield, and a much thicker spear in his right hand, pointing downwards as though he is thrusting it. The *lancea* was a spear with a leaf-shaped head, sometimes with very elongated points, which presumably enhanced penetration. The translation as lance is tempting but not strictly accurate, since the *lancea* was not necessarily used in cavalry actions for thrusting. The auxiliaries among Arrian's troops in Cappadocia were ordered to throw their *lanceae* over the head of the ranks in front of them. Whereas the legionaries armed with the *pilum* would throw their javelins from a distance and then engage in close combat with the sword, the auxiliaries probably used a variety of different types of spear in a variety of ways, though they did have swords, as shown on several tombstones, where the men are sometimes depicted with their shields in their left hands, partially hidden behind them, two spears held upright in their right hands, and a sword on their right sides. Auxiliaries used the short sword usually termed the *gladius* and also the long sword called the *spatha* which was usually worn on the left.

The Romans employed several auxiliary units of archers (*sagittarii*), both infantry and mounted, usually recruited from easterners whose expertise was highly valued, and unlike other units where new recruits were found from the local population, the ranks of the archer units were refilled from the east. Usually the only surviving evidence in the archaeological record for bows consists of the antler tips, since the wooden parts have disappeared. A distribution map of the find spots of antler tips virtually marks the Rhine and Danube frontiers in Europe, and several have been found in Britain.

Bows were quite elaborate in construction, known as composite bows because they were made of different types of materials glued together and held with bindings. When not in use the bow was unstrung, and to restring it the archer used his leg to bend it until the string could be attached. Bows and bowstrings were particularly susceptible to damp weather, and archers could be put out of action in rainstorms. Arrowheads were usually made of iron, often triangular in cross section, though some are squared. Bone arrowheads have been found near Porolissum in Dacia, and were used by the Germans, Scythians, Sarmatians and Huns. Arrowheads were either socketed or tanged and the shafts were most commonly of reeds, pine or hazel. Shafts and fletchings have been preserved only in the eastern provinces where the climate is dry, but some examples of arrowheads with wood still attached have been found at Housesteads and Corbridge in northern England, and at Caerleon. In the west, barbed arrows were often used, which would have been very effective against tribesmen who wore no armour. The arrows were kept in a cylindrical quiver, examples of which are shown on Roman sculptures, and there would have been a reserve of arrows for archers to use when their quivers were empty. Horse archers probably used lighter and shorter bows than the infantry, and lighter arrows, so the infantry archers would have had a longer range than the mounted *sagittarii*.

Depictions on tombstones often show soldiers with elaborate belts and straps, and tunics worn underneath the armour. Some soldiers are shown wearing a cloak called the *sagum* fastened over the right shoulder which would leave the right arm free, or on occasion a different kind of cloak called a *paenula* which was put on over the head, rather like a poncho.

This brief overview merely scratches the surface of a complex subject, for which whole volumes are necessary to encompass the range of different auxiliary units in different provinces. There is an abundance of finds and artistic representations of auxiliary soldiers, but they derive from the whole Empire and from a very long time span, so it is not possible to be too dogmatic about what the soldiers looked like and how they fought at any single point in time.

Veterans

The soldiers of auxiliary units all over the Empire have left numerous inscriptions. Living soldiers are commemorated on altars that some of them set up to various gods, most commonly in fulfilment of a vow, which means that the soldiers had asked the gods for a favour and it had been granted. The most common inscriptions concerning auxiliary soldiers are tombstones, often showing the soldiers in military dress, some of them with their weapons or a military standard, with an inscribed text below the portrait giving details of their names and which unit or units they served in. A considerable number of soldiers commemorated on tombstones never completed their twenty-five years' service, dying before they reached honourable discharge, but even those who died after being discharged felt it necessary to mention their military service.

If the soldiers survived long enough to complete their twenty-five years' service, they were granted Roman citizenship on discharge, and the citizenship grants extended to their children, but not to the soldiers' wives. The soldiers who achieved honourable discharge were entitled to receive confirmation of their new status as veterans and Roman citizens, in the form of a bronze two-leaved diploma, but according to current opinion not all the discharged men would necessarily obtain one, because it is probable that soldiers had to put in a request for a diploma and pay for it. The name diploma is a modern term describing the two leaves of bronze, wired together, with engraved text on both sides. No one knows what the Romans called them. There are as yet no dated examples of diplomas before the later first century. Each diploma bears the individual soldier's name, and a list of all the units in the particular province that were discharging men at the same time, usually in January, and it is thought that this happened every two years, not annually. If a unit had no men to discharge it would not be listed, so a diploma does not provide a complete enumeration of auxiliary units in a province at any one time, and conversely the diplomas cannot be used to list the full garrison of a province because the units would move about, some being moved out and some being brought in at different times.

In some provinces soldiers may also have obtained a certificate in less durable form than the bronze tablets to prove that they had completed their term of service and were now legitimate Roman citizens. Since there were penalties for claiming Roman citizenship falsely, there were probably occasions when the men had to show their ID, just as in modern times when a variety of documents are necessary attributes of travelling about. Diplomas for auxiliaries disappear in the third century, the latest one so far discovered dating to 203. When Caracalla converted all free born citizens of the Empire into Roman citizens in 212 or 213, auxiliary soldiers would not need the individual grant of citizenship. Another factor is that sons of auxiliaries who had survived their twenty-five years' service would be made Roman citizens along with their father, and even after Antoninus Pius ruled that citizenship would be given only to children born after the auxiliary soldiers were discharged, there would still be a proportion of Roman citizen sons who might aspire to a military life. Not all of them opted to join the legions, but chose their local cohort or *ala*, so auxiliary units would contain an increasing number of citizens as time went on. Diplomas continued to be issued to Praetorians and the sailors of the fleets during the third century.

Copies of the diplomas were put on public display in Rome, and the text of each diploma stated where the copies were to be found, for example 'on the Capitoline in front of the military treasury on the base of the monument of the Claudii Marcelli' or 'on the wall behind the temple of the Divine Augustus by the statue of Minerva'. This indicates that there was contact with officials in Rome when batches of auxiliaries were to be discharged in any province, and requests had been made to purchase a diploma, so that arrangements could be made to display the bronze equivalents in the city.

Like the legionaries, auxiliary soldiers were forbidden to marry while serving in the army, but often formed associations with local women. The association was tacitly condoned all through the soldiers' serving lives, and then officially recognised as a legal marriage by the grant of *conubium* or the right to marry a non-Roman woman when the soldier was honourably discharged. This arrangement had to be properly sanctioned because a union between a man and a woman was only considered to be a full Roman marriage if both were Roman citizens, unless a grant of *conubium* had been made to an individual or a group of people, such as the grant to all Latins during the early Republic. Since many of the soldiers died before they had completed their terms of service, there were presumably many women whose partners died before their marriages had been legalised, thus depriving them of financial support and legal status, and the children would remain technically illegitimate non-Romans.

Many soldiers settled down after retirement in the *vici* or civil settlements outside their forts, where their families lived. As forts became more permanent, so did the *vici*, some of which could be quite extensive, so some soldiers preferred to settle there. They would have connections with local people and could probably set up small businesses in the *vicus*. Some soldiers ran businesses while they were still serving, though most of the evidence concerns legionaries. Not all the discharged auxiliaries chose to remain near their forts. It used to be thought that it was very unusual for soldiers to return to their original homes, and the case of an auxiliary who went home to Pannonia was usually recorded as an exception, but discoveries of more and more bronze diplomas, particularly in the Danube area, show that some veterans did return to their homes after service. These men may have opted for purchase of a bronze diploma, which would not wear out, in order to travel across several provincial boundaries, where they may have been examined by military guards. In some provinces, if not all of them, there were tolls for crossing internal boundaries as well as frontiers that faced the non-Roman world. Veterans from the time of Augustus were exempted from tolls, along with members of their families including their parents, wives and children. Durable documents which proved their veteran status would therefore be vital for travelling any distance.

Tombstone of an auxiliary infantry soldier of the first century AD. This is Annaius Daverzus from Bingen. He carries two spears and wears two belts with a sword and dagger, and in appearance he is very similar to the legionary Petilius Secundus. According to M. C. Bishop and J. C. N. Coulston the distinguishing factors that mark him out as an auxiliary and not a legionary are his spears and his flat shield, since legionaries carried *pila* and had curved shields. Redrawn by Susan Veitch after M. C. Bishop.

5

Auxiliary Cavalry *Alae*

Much of the information recounted in the previous chapter on auxiliary infantry units concerning recruitment, terms of service, discharge and veterans, applies to the cavalry soldiers of the *alae*, with the obvious important difference that the cavalry also had horses to procure, train and look after. Some if not all cavalrymen probably started out as infantrymen and underwent the same induction and training as the men of the cohorts, served for a while in an infantry unit, and were then transferred to the cavalry.

The army of the late Republic was usually assisted by native cavalry contingents operating under their own commanders, and presumably supplying their own horses and remounts as and when necessary. They were not permanent adjuncts to the legions, just as the legions themselves were not permanent, even though some legions were continuously employed in several successive campaigns. When the standing army was created at the end of the first century BC, there were probably several of these native units in existence, some of which may have been disbanded while others may have been employed on the same temporary terms as previously. Some native infantry and cavalry were still being employed under their own leaders in the middle of the first century. The establishment of permanent Roman cohorts and *alae* with Roman commanders would involve the organisation of regular units, a hierarchy of junior officers, institution of pay for the soldiers, and in cavalry units there would need to be a system of provision of horses and a constant supply of remounts, and for accommodation and care for the horses in each unit.

Organisation and Command of the Alae

The commanding officers of the auxiliary *alae* were equestrians, like those of the auxiliary infantry. A quingenary *ala* would be commanded by a prefect, still a relatively young man who would normally have served in two preliminary posts, first as prefect of a quingenary infantry cohort, and then as a military *tribunus angusticlavius*, perhaps in more than one legion. As prefect of a 500-strong cavalry unit, he would be on the third stage of his military career. After three or four years in this post, his choices would be more limited. The next promotion would be to gain a posting as tribune of a milliary infantry cohort, the fourth stage in the military career, called *militia quarta* and sometimes proudly displayed in the text of career inscriptions. Since there were fewer milliary cohorts than there were 500-strong infantry and cavalry units, the chances of gaining one of these commands would be limited, and the next and most senior stage, as tribune of a milliary *ala*, would be even more limited, since there was usually only one in any province, and not all provinces contained armies.

Equestrians with experience of military command who did not receive further promotion to command of a milliary *ala* could then turn to civilian administrative posts, probably starting out as procurator. There were several posts with this title, with different functions, held by equestrians. The less important provinces were governed by procurators who would be in command of troops and were responsible for all legal and financial matters. Other procurators served as financial officials in Imperial provinces, collecting taxes and supervising the pay of the troops, and in provinces where there were estates belonging to the emperor a procurator was placed in charge of them.

The cavalry units were divided into *turmae*, not centuries, each *turma* being commanded by a decurion, who was often promoted from the ranks, having served as an ordinary soldier for some time. Occasionally a decurion could be appointed from a legion. There were reasonable prospects for promotion of decurions who had started out as legionaries, and were therefore Roman citizens. Some of them attained the much more influential and more lucrative post of centurion in a legion. One of the most famous decurions, self-advertised on his career inscription set up while he was still alive, is Tiberius Claudius Maximus, who claimed to have captured the Dacian leader Decebalus. Maximus began his service as a legionary cavalryman in *VII Claudia*, was promoted to standard-bearer after holding junior posts, transferred to *duplicarius* or soldier on double pay in *ala II Pannoniorum*, and was then promoted to decurion of the same *ala* by Trajan, as a reward for bringing the head of Decebalus to the Emperor. Promotions could be earned in less grisly ways. Maximus did not obtain a post as centurion.

It has been suggested that an inscription recording a *decurio princeps* must mean that the decurions were graded according to seniority, or at least there may have been a senior decurion in an *ala*. Without further corroborative evidence this must remain a possibility. The duties of the decurions concerned everything to do with their *turma*, including discipline, welfare and training, and supervision of the clerical work necessitated by military administration such as strength reports and daily rosters. Below the decurions, the officers were differentiated, as in the infantry units, by their pay scales, *duplicarii* on double pay, or *sesquiplicarii* on one and a half times pay. The most senior officer after the decurion was the *vexillarius*, who carried the standard called the *vexillum*, a square of purple or red cloth, usually with a fringe, suspended from a cross bar attached to the top of a lance. There were also *signiferi*, carrying other standards. These men and the *vexillarii* were on double pay. It is thought that the *cornicularius* at the head of the prefect's staff would also have been a *duplicarius*. There was a *curator* or accountant attached to each *turma* who probably kept records of the soldiers' pay and savings and perhaps the expenses of the decurions. All this information would be collated and filed by the headquarters clerks.

The number of men in each *turma* is not known for certain. To simplify matters it is usually stated that there were thirty men plus the decurion and his second in command. This figure of thirty-two men is supported by statements of two ancient authors, and an inscription from Egypt. Lucius Flavius Arrianus, better known as Arrian, wrote his book called *Ars Tactica* in the second century AD during the reign of Hadrian, and in chapter eighteen of this work he gives a total of 512 men for a *quingenary ala*. The author Hyginus, whose work is not dated, wrote a manual called *De Munitionibus Castrorum*, or alternatively *De Metatione Castrorum*, on the layout of a military camp while the army was on the march. Hyginus says in chapter sixteen of this work that a *quingenary ala* was divided into sixteen *turmae*. In order to accommodate the various units in the camp that he described, Hyginus would have to know their relative sizes, so he can probably be taken at his word, but since it is not known when he wrote his book, it cannot be said that his figures apply to all armies of all provinces at all times. There is corroboration for the sixteen *turmae* in an inscription from Alexandria dated to AD 199, which mentions two different cavalry units, and lists sixteen decurions for each of them. The total of 512 men, as stated by Arrian, divided into sixteen *turmae*, produces the figure thirty-two, which probably includes thirty men and two officers.

This neat reckoning is thrown into complete disarray by two other pieces of evidence, one from papyrus records, and another from archaeological excavations.

The papyrus evidence concerns a part-mounted cohort, not an *ala*, but it throws out any notion of a standard number of men in a *turma*. At the beginning of the third century, lists of men in the *turmae* of *cohors XX Palmyrenorum milliaria equitata* were drawn up, and the names of cavalrymen under each decurion number sixty or more. Five decurions are listed. Decurion Zebidas had sixty men, Tiberinus had sixty-six, Demetrius sixty-eight, Octavius seventy-one, and Antoninus sixty-one. Even more puzzling are the totals given at the ends of the lists for each *turma*, because all of these totals are greater than the number of named individuals listed under each decurion. There is no supporting evidence to explain the discrepancies, nor is it known if the Palmyrene cohort constituted an anomaly, or standard practice.

The archaeological evidence comes from Wallsend fort on Hadrian's Wall, where complete cavalry barracks were excavated, each with the house for the officers at one end, and nine double cubicles. It was always postulated that there would be ten cubicles in cavalry barracks each housing three men, amounting to thirty troopers with two officers, and thereby arriving at the seemingly well-established thirty-two men as found in the combined statements of Arrian and Hyginus. Even if the entire cavalry block had not been excavated in a fort it was usually shown in reconstructions with the attested number of rooms plus however many more were required to arrive at ten cubicles. At Wallsend this was certainly not the case. New thinking about stabling was applied at Wallsend, derived from the excavations at Dormagen, where barrack blocks or stable blocks were discovered, consisting of rows of double cubicles with soakaway pits in the rooms on one side and hearths in the rooms on the other side. This was taken as evidence that the men and their horses were housed together. It is now suggested that each of the nine double cubicles at Wallsend was probably occupied by three men and three horses, which means that there were twenty-seven men in the block, plus officers, and therefore about thirty men in the *turma*. The literary evidence and the archaeological and papyrus evidence are at odds with each other, and the problem will not be solved until every single barrack block in every single cavalry fort over the whole Empire has been excavated, which is about as feasible as porcine aviation.

Milliary cavalry *alae* with a nominal strength of 1,000 men first appeared under the Flavian Emperors between AD 69 and 96. These were much fewer in number than quingenary units and on present evidence milliary units were limited to one in each province. In some cases a quingenary unit was increased in size to form a larger *ala*, which would reduce the numbers of new recruits to be trained in horsemanship and cavalry operations, and the existing men in the unit would be able to help with this. If new milliary units were raised there was normally a small core of experienced men who could help with training the new soldiers. The numbers of men in these milliary units present the same problems as those for the quingenary units, but it is likely that an *ala milliaria* was never intended to be twice the size of an *ala quingenaria*, but only one and a half times larger. Hyginus says that there were twenty-four *turmae* in a milliary cavalry unit, which at thirty men and two officers per *turma* would give a total of 768 men, with the fictitious title of *milliaria*, much as a legionary century contained eighty men and not 100.

The Supply of Horses

The supply of good-quality horses for the cavalry units was probably a constant headache. It is known that there were times when some cavalrymen lacked a horse, as attested by a papyrus document from Dura Europos in Syria, where the garrison was the part-mounted unit *cohors XX Palmyrenorum equitata*. The papyrus lists the men and their horses, including the men who had no horses when the record was compiled. The top of the document is missing, so it cannot be said that all the men belonged to the same *turma*, but this is the usual way of listing men in military documents, under the name of their officer, and then by the date of enlistment of each soldier. In this particular document, some men are listed with their horses, but against the names of other soldiers the words *amisit equum* appear, 'lost his horse'. Most of these entries have a date attached, which presumably records the day when the horse was lost. The reason for the loss of each horse is not given, but it has been suggested that the horsemen of the unit at Dura Europos would be involved in constant border raids and skirmishes with the natives, so there would be some horse casualties as a result. There would be many other reasons for horse losses at Dura, and indeed in all provinces, such as deaths from accidents or diseases, or there could have been thefts of horses. In the late first century in Judaea when Vespasian's son Titus was in command, the Jewish author Josephus records that horses were always being stolen, so the cavalrymen learned that leaving a horse unattended was not an option, and went about clinging to their mounts as though their lives depended on it.

The provision of horses seems to have been the responsibility of the provincial governor, who was legally responsible for retaining military horses in his province. A law dating from the second century AD, reproduced in the late Roman compilation known as the *Digest*, states that the governor had a duty to prevent any military horse from being removed from the province: *equum militare extra provinciam duci non permittere*. The documentation from Dura indicates that the governor was also responsible for approving new horses, just as he was responsible for new recruits. In Egypt, six recruits were sent to a unit approved by the governor, *tirones sex probatos a me*, and at Dura a four-year-old horse, reddish in colour, was approved by the governor, using the same formula, *ecum* [sic] *quadratum russeum probatum a me*. The inspections were presumably carried out by officials from the governor's staff, not by the governor himself even though the records state that he approved recruits and horses. On occasion a horse could be approved by the procurator of the province. The governor probably cast an eye over the reports, or perhaps held briefings with the men who had inspected the horses. There may have been a permanent group of men with responsibility for finding and inspecting horses intended for the army.

It is likely that copies of the Dura list of men and horses would be sent to provincial headquarters. This may have been done on an ad hoc basis when horse losses had become severe, or on a regular cycle as a matter of routine, as part of the strength reports that were compiled each year. For the purpose of obtaining remounts, perhaps only a copy of the *amisit equum* records were sent to headquarters, where the need for remounts for each unit could be assessed and measures taken to supply horses. This is supported by the fact that the horses which arrived at Dura were usually listed in a letter from the governor and were assigned to named cavalrymen, implying that the batches of horses were sent in response to a report listing the men who needed them.

The system for obtaining remounts was probably organised at provincial level, in preference to leaving everything to individual unit commanders. In emergencies, it is possible that any equine that was reasonably fit would serve the purpose, on the tacit understanding that a cavalryman without a horse in any army in any era was duty bound to provide himself with a mount by fair means or foul. But in normal circumstances, central control of provision of horses would make more sense, and it is possible that the provision of baggage animals for all units, not just mounted ones, was also under central control. Two kinds of officials are known who may have been responsible for remounts. One is the *equisio*, which admittedly could denote a groom attached to an officer, but the governor's *equisio* attested at Vindolanda south of Hadrian's Wall may have been connected with obtaining horses. A group of *equisiones* of *II Adiutrix* is mentioned on an inscription at Aquincum on the Danube. These may simply be grooms, but at best this is an imprecise job description, and there is nothing on the inscription describing the functions of the *equisiones*. They were most likely connected to the legionary cavalry and may have been responsible for providing remounts. The other official who may be connected with the remount service is the *strator*. Provincial governors and legionary legates had a number of *stratores* on their staffs, and in the late Empire these men were supervised by an *architrator*. They all belonged to the staff of the *comes stabuli*, literally count of the stables, which is the origin of the English word constable. With these late Imperial *stratores*, the connection with the remount service is based on firm evidence, since the *comites stabuli* were responsible for the levy of horses for the army and for members of the Imperial court. In Britain the brief text on the tombstone of Anicius Saturninus, which was found at Irchester, describes him as *strator consularis*, which places him on the staff of the provincial governor. It is thought that there was a horse-breeding centre at Irchester, so Saturninus may have been stationed there to inspect and collect horses. At Dover an inscription probably attests another *strator*, though only the first two letters are extant in the text.

Horses could be obtained in various ways, by capturing large numbers of mounts from an enemy, by a mass levy according to the terms imposed on a defeated enemy, by requisitioning from the provinces, and by breeding, which may have been left to private enterprise with certain breeders under contract to the army. The existence of horse-breeding centres in most provinces is taken as read with hardly any evidence, because across the Empire it would have been common sense to establish a method of replacing horses on a regular basis. The possible importation of horses to improve the breeding stock is also postulated. At the fort at Newstead in southern Scotland, the remains of horses found there were said to represent unimproved native British horses and also slender-limbed animals like the smaller breeds of Arab ponies of modern times. Sometimes military authorities would perhaps purchase horses on the open market, as officers and some cavalrymen probably did on an individual basis. During the Danube wars of Marcus Aurelius, 5,500 Sarmatian horsemen were sent to Britain, presumably with their own horses, and when the Quadi made peace in 170 they surrendered large numbers of cattle and horses to the Romans. The receipt of such huge numbers of horses would necessitate the creation of a depot where they could be inspected and entered into the records, but rather than driving all the horses to a permanent depot, if such establishments existed, such an installation could have been temporary, requiring only fencing and some huts or tents for the staff, and would not leave much trace for archaeologists. When all the horses were allocated to units the depot would probably cease to exist.

More regular supply of horses from breeding centres, or from occasional requisitioning expeditions, would probably have been catered for by a more regular system at established bases. New horses may have been collected and sent to permanent depots for inspection and distribution, though there is not much evidence for this, except that the *strator consularis* Anicius Saturninus, mentioned above, may have been inspecting horses at a depot at Irchester. In times of war, horses may have been collected and brought straight into the units which needed them. A military record on papyrus dating to the period of the Dacian wars under Trajan shows that some cavalrymen of the *cohors I Hispanorum Veteranorum equitata* were absent from their base at Stobi in Macedonia, having gone 'across the Erar' which may be a river, for the express purpose of collecting horses. The existence of central depots for collection of horses, if not for breeding them, is implied by the papyrus records from Dura Europos, which show that horses arrived at all times of the year at Dura. This is clear from the useful Roman habit of putting dates on most of their documentation, and filing records. If horses could be delivered as and when necessary, they probably came from a holding depot rather than from a special round-up each time requests for remounts were sent in.

Horses in the Army

Advice on what to look for in a military horse derives from several sources. In the *Georgics*, Virgil describes an ideal horse as high-necked with a clean-cut head, short belly, plump back, and well-muscled chest, and he says that preferably the mane should be thick and fall to the right. The Roman agricultural author Columella adds that a horse should have wide nostrils and straight legs. Modern horse trainer Ann Hyland says that in a military context all this makes perfect sense. Wide nostrils and a broad chest indicate better respiration and therefore stamina, and straight legs mean that the joints will not be under too much strain. A mane falling to the right leaves the left side of the neck free, so that a cavalryman holding his weapons in his right hand, and his shield in his left hand together with the reins would be better able to convey instructions to the horse via its neck unencumbered by the mane. The Greek author Xenophon, who wrote *The Art of Horsemanship* long before the Romans created their auxiliary cavalry units, provides the most comprehensive advice on inspecting military horses. He recommends starting with the feet and legs, listing the common problems with hooves and the most frequent causes of lameness. As the saying goes, no foot, no horse.

As a means of estimating the size of Roman cavalry mounts, the various artistic representations are not especially reliable. On tombstones of cavalrymen a horse is usually depicted with its right side facing the observer, so the rider can be seen wielding his weapons in his right hand. These sculptural depictions cannot help to determine how large the horse really was. More refined sculptures such as those on Trajan's Column in Rome show fine, idealised horses that perhaps do not represent the reality of war, when on occasions anything answering the loose description 'horse' may have sufficed. Nevertheless it has been estimated from these Trajanic sculptures that the average Roman cavalry horse was about 14 hands high, which is supported by the horse skeletons found in excavations at Krefeld-Gellep, the ancient Gelduba in the province of Lower Germany. It is suggested that this was the site of the final battle of the Batavian revolt under Civilis in 69, and that most of the horses belonged to the Batavian auxiliary units. The evidence from these excavations shows that the average size of the horses was between 13 and 15 hands. Only two of the horses were below 13 hands.

Three of the horses at Krefeld-Gellep were under four years old, which may indicate that horses were in short supply during the Batavian revolt, so younger horses were brought in to fill gaps. The Roman writers Columella and Varro, who both produced works on farming, recommend that no horse be put under strain by severe exercise until it is four years old, since at three years old a horse is still growing and putting on muscle. The Dura papyrus records show that the reddish-coloured horse mentioned above was four years old, but on the other hand four horses that were assigned to the *cohors XX Palmyrenorum*, one in 208 and three more at some time before 251, were only two years old. They may not have been expected to perform strenuously at that age, but on the other hand the soldiers were perhaps not too sentimental about their animals. At Krefeld-Gellep, one horse was over twenty years old, and several others ranged between eight and thirteen years, but it is not known how old they would have been when they were first brought into the unit, so no estimate can be made of the average working life of cavalry horses.

When the horses were allocated to soldiers they were entered into the records, as instructed by the governor, *in acta ut mos referre*, 'enter in the records according to custom'. This formula did not change over the years. The horse was described by its colour and any distinguishing marks. Some horses may have been branded when they arrived, and these marks were duly noted in the records, with their locations in abbreviated form. The initials n.f.a.d. probably stand for *nota femore armo dextro*, or brand marks on the right shoulder or thigh, or n.f.a.s for *sinistro* if the brands were on the left. Some horses had no marks at all so it is suggested that the Roman army did not brand their horses as a rule, which raises the question of proof of ownership if horses were stolen. Perhaps all military horses were marked in some way, and this need not be noted down because it was standard practice. In the records, horses were not given names, but racehorses and chariot horses had names, as shown on mosaics, so the soldiers perhaps unofficially named their mounts too.

The care, feeding and general welfare of the horses would be largely the responsibility of the individual cavalryman, who received an allowance for fodder. The horse was almost regarded as part of the trooper's equipment, and just as money was deducted from military pay for weapons and armour when they were first issued, or when items had been lost and replaced, it seems that a standard figure of 125 *denarii* was deducted for a horse, no matter what it had cost the army to obtain it. This derives once again from the papyrus records at Dura, so there may have been variations in provincial practice all over the Empire and at different times, but the principle that horses were paid for by the cavalry soldiers was probably universal. It would at least make the soldiers take more care of their mounts so as to avoid the expense of paying for a replacement. 125 *denarii* constituted a large slice of the soldiers' annual salaries.

For the care of sick and injured horses, there were veterinarians in the unit, usually with the title *medicus* like the doctors and surgeons who looked after the men. Occasionally the titles were more specific, such as *medicus veterinarius*, which appears on the tombstone of Quartianus, *medicus veterinarius* of the first Praetorian cohort in Rome. All units, whether they were cavalry or infantry, would have riding horses for the officers and baggage animals that would need care and attention. Another designation is *mulomedicus*, which appears most commonly in a work called *Ars Mulomedicinae*, a manual on the care of equines in general written by Publius Vegetius. Some scholars argue that he was not the same man as Flavius Vegetius Renatus who wrote *Epitoma Rei Militaris*, while others have stated that Flavius and Publius were two names for one man. A tombstone from Gaul shows a *mulomedicus*, carrying a *hipposandal*, examples of which can be seen in museums, made of metal with a flat base and curved sides with rounded hooks, most probably to take the cords or tapes which held it to the horse's foot. Hipposandals would have impeded a horse's movements, especially if equipped with protruding curved hooks as most of them were, and they may have been used on a temporary basis to hold medicines in place, like modern poultice boots. These items are usually listed as 'horseshoes', but the shoeing of horses in the modern sense was probably not a feature of the Roman army. No certainly attested Roman horseshoes have been found. Some examples once thought to be Roman may be medieval horseshoes which had worked their way down into lower levels, thus appearing out of their proper archaeological context. More telling is the fact that Publius Vegetius' manual does not include details of injuries to hooves caused by misplaced nails, which ought to have featured if shoeing horses was a regular process.

The Romans probably did not geld their stallions as a routine procedure. Depictions of horses on cavalry tombstones and sculptures on monuments such as Trajan's Column clearly show that the horses are entires. Military records do not mention gelded horses, but simply denote gender, though it is possible that some horses had already been gelded when they arrived at the unit. Stallions and mares together could cause trouble in a unit, but so could groups of mares if they took a dislike to each other. It is likely that each horse was considered on its own merits, and gelding was only undertaken as a last resort if behavioural problems could not be solved by altering a horse's position on the march or in picket lines.

The Search for Stabling

The question of stables inside forts was studied by archaeologists for some time, but new discoveries and new thinking have overturned the theories that somewhere inside a fort there ought to be stable blocks, separate from the barracks. There were only a few forts where stables were tentatively identified, usually without knowing the entire layout of the fort. Excavators would make educated guesses about the number of horses to be accommodated and the amount of space available inside the fort, then put the two figures together, which is obviously not as satisfactory as uncovering undoubted stable blocks with some evidence that horses had been kept inside them. In Britain, traces of what were thought to be stable blocks were identified at Halton and Benwell on Hadrian's Wall and at Brough-on-Noe and Ilkely in the Pennines. The presence of drains underneath or close to the buildings, and of water tanks nearby, was usually taken as supporting evidence that horses were accommodated, which may still be true, but horses were not necessarily housed in free-standing, separate stables. The small fort of Hod Hill in southern England, fully excavated in the 1950s, was built inside an Iron Age hill fort to take advantage of two of its ramparts. It dates to the very early period of the conquest when the most serious fighting was over and there was time to build forts and fortlets to pin down the country. The occupants of the fort were mixed, perhaps two units, or parts of two units, probably comprising both infantry and cavalry. At this site, the presence of horses inside the fort was unequivocal. Six rectangular blocks were identified as stables and two of the buildings had traces of partitions dividing them into large and small cubicles. Judging from the worn and stained patches on the floors, it seems that the animals were tethered to the cross walls, three horses in the smaller cubicles and in the larger cubicles a total of six horses, three against each opposing cross wall with their backs to each other. It was a surprising discovery, since it would have been more economical of space to arrange the horses in two rows down the length of the buildings with a passage in the middle, facilitating access for feeding and for mucking out. Hod Hill may not represent standard practice inside Roman forts, but in Germany the fort at Dormagen, between Neuss and Cologne on the Rhine, was excavated much later than Hod Hill, and the same arrangements for tethering horses to cross walls were revealed. This pattern has been adopted in reconstruction drawings of possible stables at other forts in Germany.

The evidence from Dormagen has been described above in connection with the number of men in a *turma*, but it is worth going over the main points again in connection with stabling. The Dormagen excavations seem to negate the need to search for separate stable bocks inside forts, since at least at this fort the men and their horses were housed together. In at least three of the Dormagen stable blocks, there were double cubicles, with soakaway pits in those along one side, and hearths in those on the other, indicating that men and mounts probably shared the blocks. Similar evidence was found at Wallsend in the excavations of the late 1990s. Strictly speaking the evidence from two forts is not sufficient to prove that the arrangement was universal in all forts where an *ala* or a *cohors equitata* was stationed, but the results from these two sites will direct further research.

Horses demand much more labour on a daily basis if they are stabled. The horses require grooming, and the floors of the stables must be kept dry and clean, otherwise in ill-kept stables the animals may suffer from respiratory problems. In a fort containing nearly 500 troopers, each with at least one horse to be accommodated, the problems of what to do with the end product, so to speak, invite the scenario of constant traffic along the streets to the fort gates with piles of dung, which was perhaps eventually put on to the fields belonging to the unit, where crops were grown. This would not have been totally impossible to organise, since large numbers of cab horses were kept in stables in British town centres, some of them on two storeys.

In some Roman forts, it is possible that a few horses were kept in a separate stable block. The officers would probably have had more than one horse, and it is not clear whether the men were accommodated with their animals. Perhaps sick or injured animals would be housed separately, to facilitate the tasks of the *mulomedici* in caring for them. It is not known if the Roman veterinary staff understood infection, or the isolation that would have been necessary to prevent infections from spreading.

The main problem for the cavalrymen would be to keep the horses fit and ready for action. It is not likely that all of the horses would be stabled with their riders all of the time, nor is it likely that all of the horses would be in peak condition all of the time. Some horses were perhaps put to grass in the meadows outside the fort. If horses were kept outside forts in the meadows, fences would be necessary and guards would have been called for, but fences would leave little trace, and guards none at all, unless they were particularly careless with their belongings. At Stanwix near Carlisle, where a milliary *ala* was stationed, a line of post holes was found outside the fort, which may represent such a fence. Corrals and temporary paddocks may have been used outside forts, and groups of horses may have been kept outside or put to grazing on rotation. Horses at grass are not ready for action since they would not have been fully exercised, and in a meadow it would take some time for each trooper to find his own horse and prepare it. A rotational system would seem the best solution, with some horses out grazing, and others fully exercised and in peak condition, located for easy access, perhaps in their quarters with their riders, who would be on call, in case of emergencies.

Training the Men and the Horses

Before each new cavalryman and his horse were paired up, it is likely that both would undergo separate preparatory training. Some if not all cavalrymen would probably undergo the same training routine as the infantry, because they would probably be called upon to dismount and fight on foot on occasion, and if they were unhorsed at any point it would be useful to know how to fight like infantry. Cavalrymen probably trained on foot with the infantry recruits before they ever mounted a horse, then after their basic training was completed they would have to learn how to use their weapons while mounted and moving. Before they reached this point they would have to learn how to ride. Even if the men had been good riders as civilians, they would probably be told by their instructors to forget everything they had ever learned and to start all over again. What is not known is whether this part of the training took place at the same location as the basic training, or at a central depot specially concerned with cavalry training, or if the recruits who had survived their four months' basic training and had been accepted as potential soldiers were assigned to their units, where instructors would take over from where basic training left off. A central depot would be the most economical in terms of provision of instructors, and could be manned all the time to train both horses and men, whereas the training of new cavalrymen at their forts would require personnel at each one. The titles *campidoctor* and *magistri campi* or *kampi* are attested, and are usually taken to be instructors of some kind, but it is not known if there was such an instructor at each fort where cavalry or part-mounted units were housed. According to the historian Herodian, when the future Emperor Maximinus Thrax was serving under Severus Alexander, he was made an instructor on account of his expertise. He had started out as a cavalryman, gained Roman citizenship, joined the legions and risen to high rank as a member of the equestrian class. Herodian says that he was put in charge of training all the recruits, which could be taken as an indication that the recruits were initially all in one place, and could have been intended for both infantry and cavalry units.

The units of horse archers may have been treated differently. Using a bow and arrow on horseback requires special skills because the rider needs both hands to fire his weapon, and needs to twist and turn and exert pressure with his knees in order to stay on the horse, and his horse must be trained to ignore this pressure, in contrast to other cavalry horses which would normally take instruction to do something specific from leg and knee movements. It is thought that most of these soldiers, who comprised foot archers as well as mounted archers, came from the east, such as the Hamians from Syria and the Palmyrenes from the eastern frontier of the Roman Empire, facing the Parthians. These units were kept up to strength by recruiting from their original homelands, so that the new men would be well versed in horse management and archery when they were enrolled in the unit records, and conversely if they brought their own horses with them, which is likely but not attested, the animals would be accustomed to their riders' movements.

The recruits may initially have been given horses that had been specially schooled for the purpose of introducing new soldiers to riding. The recruit would have to learn how to mount and dismount, and how to relax while seated. Xenophon recommends that the riders' lower legs and feet must be loose and flexible, because if the leg is stiff and rigid and the rider hits something the leg could break. The upper body should also be loose so as not to tire the rider. The tendency would be to tense up at first, a modern equivalent perhaps being a novice pillion rider on a motorbike failing to relax and sway with the machine, and arriving at the destination completely exhausted, terror as well as tension having played a part. After mounting and dismounting in a civilised manner, recruits would have to learn how to do it by vaulting onto the horse, and getting on and off while the horse was moving. This would have to be accomplished wearing armour and holding weapons and a shield. These procedures would be essential to prepare for the possibility of being unhorsed in a skirmish or a battle and remounting if the horse was still standing or any horse was available.

The Romans did not use stirrups, so there would be no question of hauling oneself up with one foot supported. Soldiers would perhaps grab the manes of their horses and vault into the saddle. For a long time it was declared in most books on the Roman army that the cavalrymen did not use saddles, but sat on nothing more elaborate than a blanket with a fringe, which is of course what can be seen on several military tombstones. But the blanket is placed underneath the saddle, the horns of which, on closer inspection of relief sculptures, can also be seen behind the rider's seat. Thanks to the research of Peter Connolly who reconstructed Roman saddles, leather expert Carole van Driel-Murray, and Marcus Junkelmann who rode horses using the reconstructed Roman saddles, it is now fairly certain what a military saddle looked like. The component parts and the effectiveness of the saddle are discussed below in the section on arms, armour and equipment.

Having become proficient at mounting and dismounting, the recruit would ideally learn to ride in all kinds of terrain, to jump over ditches and raised obstacles, to throw javelins at targets and to wield a sword without damaging the horse. Even when all the necessary skills had been learned, regular practice would be necessary when the new cavalryman joined his unit. Practice sessions may have taken place on the parade ground outside, which most forts possessed, though many horses constantly moving around would have churned up the surface, which the Romans usually took pains to level off.

The training of the horses was probably begun at the postulated remount depots, though it has to be admitted that the existence of such establishments has not been proven, except possibly at the fort at the Lunt at Baginton, in Warwickshire, where there is a circular enclosure just inside the eastern ramparts, which were built to curve around the structure. The circle, with a single entrance facing west, has been interpreted as a *gyrus* for training horses. No other similar structure has yet been discovered in other Roman forts. The animals may have been put on a long lunge-rein and made to walk round in clockwise and anti-clockwise circles inside the *gyrus* before having a saddle placed on their backs, and then sometime later a rider would sit on the horse, or sometimes lie across its back to accustom the animal to carrying the weight. The British army training programme for horses in 1937 was divided into three sections, each lasting for seventeen weeks. In the first stages the horse was led around, and not saddled until after about six weeks. Much would depend on the temperament of the horse. Some are quick learners, others are lazy, and some of them are stubborn or vicious. It may have been in these early stages that a trainer could assess whether the horse was to be of use or not, and would reject unsuitable candidates, just as recruits with insufficient stamina or courage would be weeded out during basic training. It is not known if a recruit would be trained to ride any horse, or whether he was matched up with his own horse at this stage and the trainers would then school both man and horse together. In the British army, the rider merely sat on the horse at first, while the trainer directed operations, then the rider would learn how to control the horse with the reins and leg movements. Weapons training would begin when the rider and the horse gained confidence in each other and the horse responded to the rider's commands.

When the riders were fully trained and could perform all the manoeuvres that were required, the training would have to be kept up by exercise. Horses suffer if they are worked too hard, but they also lose condition if they are not exercised. As mentioned above, there may have been a rotational system to keep some horses in peak condition and fit for work, since it is unlikely that all the unit's horses could be ready for action all at the same time. Fitness in horses cannot be achieved without exercise, and expertise and constant practice can only benefit the riders, so the two can be combined. Both Xenophon and Vegetius recommend that horses should go on route marches, and be ridden over all kinds of terrain, learn to leap over ditches, and gallop up and down hills. This is common sense, but it may not have been possible for all cavalrymen to take their horses out every day. Some of the men would be appointed to the tasks necessary in the day-to-day running of the fort, such as guard duty at the headquarters or the gates. When several horses were to be exercised it is possible that one rider would lead another horse, or more than one horse, and exercise them all together. In the duty rosters of *cohors XX Palmyrenorum equitata* at Dura Europos, against the names of cavalrymen there are some entries in abbreviated form that do not appear for any of the infantry. Between two and four horsemen from different *turmae* were given the task described as *ad m. ambul.*, or *ad man. ambul*, or just *m. ambul*. This was not fully understood when the papyrus records came to light. *Ambul.* is clearly short for *ambulare* but it was suggested that *man.* may be an abbreviation for a place name. Professor Jo-Ann Shelton of the University of California suggested in a letter to the present author and Karen Dixon, authors of *The Roman Cavalry*, that the phrase *ad man. ambul.* probably means *ad manum ambulare*, referring to leading by hand, which sounds perfectly obvious once it is pointed out, one of those kick-yourself moments after the publication of a book. The Latin phrase could entail exactly what it says, walking a single horse on a march or around in a paddock, but it could also mean that the cavalrymen in the duty rosters were assigned to taking several horses out, riding one and leading the others.

In bad weather it is possible that some horses could be exercised indoors in special halls. Excavations at several forts over the past two or three decades have revealed the existence of forehalls attached to the headquarters building. Some of these were timber extensions to a stone *principia*, so it was easy to miss the post holes unless the excavation could be extended beyond the outer walls of the buildings. Later, it was discovered that there were stone forehalls at some forts, one of the best examples being at Aalen in Germany, which clearly takes its name from the *ala II Flavia milliaria* that was stationed there in Roman times. The Aalen forehall extended across the entire street in front of the *principia* and projected beyond the front of the building at both sides. There were entrances on each of the short sides, and the building had two aisles flanking the central area. Other forehalls were constructed on this general pattern. The existence of forehalls attached to the headquarters buildings is not in doubt, and most of them have been found in forts where an *ala* or a *cohors equitata* was stationed, but there is no absolute proof that they were used to exercise cavalry horses and riders. On the other hand the existence of exercise halls for cavalry is attested by an inscription dated to 222, found at the fort at Netherby, north of Hadrian's Wall. The text mentions the *cohors I Aelia Hispanorum milliaria equitata* and refers to the erection of a *basilica equestris exercitatoria*, leaving no doubt as to its purpose. The stone had been reused as a drain cover, so the point where it was found need not be related to the building it commemorates. The only question is whether the archaeologically attested forehalls and the epigraphically attested exercise halls are one and the same thing.

Another method of developing the skills of the riders and their horses is performances in tournaments and displays. Special events were organised, called *hippika gymnasia*, much like the precision riding performed by the cavalry at modern festivals, where riders perform elaborate manoeuvres weaving in and out and threading through rapidly moving lines of horsemen. These manoeuvres are described by Arrian in *Ars Tactica*, especially the Cantabrian gallop in which groups of riders circled round in two lines, throwing spears at the shields of their opposite numbers in the other line. The spears did not have iron tips and the shields were lighter than normal versions, but the potential for injury was always present. The skills learned in these displays would benefit the horsemen in battle.

Arms, Armour and Equipment

Cavalrymen used longer swords than those of the infantry, and carried a variety of spears with different names. The sword was called a *spatha*, ranging in length from twenty-six inches to thirty-six inches. It was used for slashing, and was worn on the right side in the early Empire. From the second century onwards, the sword was worn on the left, and from the second and third centuries onwards infantry units also started to use the *spatha*, so discoveries of long swords without any other cavalry gear do not automatically mean the presence of horsemen at a particular site.

Spears for throwing or thrusting were about six feet long, held overarm for throwing or for stabbing downwards, or underarm for use as a shock weapon. An even longer weapon was the *contus*, probably adopted from the Sarmatian tribesmen of the Danube area. This was a much heavier spear about twelve feet long, which had to be held with both hands and was used as a shock weapon. It would be held parallel to the horse's right side, or if striking to the left it could be held diagonally over the horse's neck. The use of both hands with this weapon meant that the *contarii* could not use a shield. The *ala I Ulpia Contariorum milliaria*, distinguished by Trajan's family name, was probably created by him during the Dacian wars.

Mounted archers probably used bows that were shorter than those of the infantry, who had the advantage of standing still and could therefore use longer bows with heavier arrows. The bows were made of several different components, wood for the central sections, with bone, horn and sinew attached, called in modern parlance a composite bow. When fully drawn back the shape of the bow resembles a rounded letter W. In archaeological contexts, very little survives of the bow except the bone or antler tips. Horse archers had to learn how to fire arrows to the left or the right of the horse, and sometimes to the rear, the famous Parthian shot, so they had to be supple and rapid in their movements. Since they had to use both hands to fire arrows they did not usually carry a shield, but probably had a sword. They may have attached the ends of the reins to a strap worn on the ring finger of their right hands, so that after using the bow and arrow they could pick up the reins quickly. There is not much evidence for bow cases, because they would not leave much archaeological trace, but quivers are sometimes depicted on tombstones, hanging from the archer's right side, and usually cylindrical in shape. Many arrowheads have been discovered, made of iron and usually barbed, which caused horrendous wounds and were difficult to extract except by careful surgery.

Mail or scale body armour was worn by cavalrymen, usually in the form of a short-sleeved shirt extending to the hips or just slightly lower, sometimes with slits to allow the man to sit astride his horse. The mail coat covered the upper parts of the cavalryman's trousers, which reached just below the knee, as shown on several sculptures. Mail armour, or *lorica hamata*, was made from iron or bronze rings, each passed through two rings above and two rings below. There were variations in ring size, and some mail was made of alternate rows of solid rings and wire with the flattened ends riveted together. Scale armour or *lorica squamata* was made of small plates of iron or bronze, with two holes at the top where it would be stitched to the leather or linen backing, and two holes at each side where the scales were attached to each other. Both these types of armour were clearly depicted on tombstones and sculptured reliefs.

Helmets are not always shown on cavalry tombstones, but examples have been found, and a gradual evolution giving greater protection to the face has been detected. The earlier helmets had a bowl-shaped head piece, with hinged cheek pieces but only a short neck flange and initially no reinforcement across the forehead, which seems to have been adopted by the second century. By the later second century the cheek pieces were larger, extending further round the face, leaving only the eyes, nose and mouth visible.

A variety of different shield types are depicted in sculptures, including rectangular, hexagonal, round and oval shapes. It is thought that round shields had become more common by the third century, even though an oval shield would afford greater protection for the rider from his lower legs to his shoulder. The shields were generally made of wooden strips or planks held together by glue, with binding of metal or hide round the edge. There was a hole in the centre of the shield, with the *umbo* made of metal on the outside to accommodate the soldier's left hand, and the grip on the inside made of wood or metal, sometimes extending a long way across the hole for extra strength. Some shields were covered on both sides with leather or linen, and some were elaborately painted like the examples from Dura Europos, one of which shows Greeks fighting

Amazons. Remains of leather shield covers with drawstrings have been found at the fort of Valkenberg in the Netherlands, indicating that shields were protected when not in use.

The Romans employed heavy armoured cavalry units called *cataphractarii* and *clibanarii*. There is some dispute as to whether these were synonymous terms for the same kind of horseman. *Clibanarius* literally means 'oven', graphically describing how it felt to wear the heavy armour in a hot climate. Some authors suggest that the *clibanarii* were purely eastern troops from Parthia and Palmyra, still qualifying as cataphracts. Other scholars have suggested that the distinction in terminology reflects the respective armament styles, the *cataphractarii* being armed with the lance and shield in the western tradition, while the *clibanarii* adopted the eastern tradition of bow and lance.

The Parthians used armoured cavalry or *cataphractarii* to good effect against the invading Roman army of Marcus Licinius Crassus in 53 BC. The defeat was decisive and the balance was not redressed until Augustus negotiated a peace over three decades years later and arranged for the return of the captured standards. The Romans themselves adopted *cataphractarii* perhaps in the late first or early second century AD, but there is no firm evidence of cataphract units until the reign of Hadrian, when the *ala Cataphractariorum* is attested. The armour extended to both the rider and the horse. Plutarch in his biography of Crassus describes the horses clad in plates of bronze and steel, and the late Roman historian Ammianus Marcellinus says that the men wore armour of iron plates that fitted the curves of their bodies, completely covering their limbs, so that they looked less like men than polished statues. A graffito from Dura Europos in Syria shows an armoured cavalryman enveloped in heavy armour, and what appear to be thigh guards or cuisses, perhaps of the type found at Dura, which were made of rawhide. The graffito also depicts the barding or scale armour of the cavalryman's mount, like a blanket covering the horse's body and reaching halfway down its legs.

Heavy armoured cavalry were not as mobile as the lighter armed mounted units, and were soon exhausted by too much exertion, but they served their purpose as shock troops, when armed with the *contus* or long lance. Some of the *cataphractarii* used bows and arrows as well as the lance.

The most important pieces of equipment for the horses were the bridle and bit, and the saddle, to enable the rider to control the horse, and to stay on its back. The leather sections of the bridle have not survived in the archaeological record, but there are many depictions of horses on tombstones and sculptures which show the details. Where the strapwork joined together on the bridles and other parts of the harness there were usually metal discs called *phalerae*. These are also shown on sculptures, and several examples have survived along with the different styles of bits. The mouthpiece of the bit could be a solid bar or a two-section jointed bar, with rings on either end to attach the reins. The Romans used more severe curb bits, allowing for greater control of the horse. These had a U-shaped bar in the horse's mouth, with another bar or chain running under the animal's chin. An example of this kind of bit was found at Newstead in lowland Scotland.

The shape of Roman cavalry saddles has been determined from finds of leather at Vindolanda, south of Hadrian's Wall in Northumberland, and at Valkenberg in the Netherlands. The saddle had two upright horns at the rear to clasp the rider's buttocks, and two angled horns at the front which curved inwards over the rider's thighs. On sculptural representations the horns at the rear are often visible, but at the front the horns are usually obscured by other details. Saddles have been reconstructed using two different methods, one with a wooden frame or tree, and another with the same shape but simply tightly stuffed, with no frame. This kind of saddle would hold the rider in place, as demonstrated when an experimental archaeologist using one of these saddles accidentally collided with a tree branch, and was knocked backwards but remained on the horse. However, it is considered more likely that saddles were supported by a wooden frame, and though no conclusive proof of the existence of such a frame has been found, analysis of the leather covers shows that stretch marks exist, indicating where the leather was pulled over the horns rather than being stuffed. Bronze plates in the shape of the horns were discovered at Newstead, and were initially thought to have been used as templates for the shaping of the horns, but since names were inscribed by lines of punch marks on the insides of the plates, it is now thought that the metal pieces were placed over the wooden tree and covered by the leather. The identification of the owner of the saddle would help the saddlers who might have to undertake repairs. The saddle was fitted to the rider as far as possible, but not necessarily to the horse, as modern saddles are. The horse's back was protected by a thick blanket, or possibly by a fur or sheepskin, with a saddle cloth over it. Some of these cloths as shown on tombstones and sculptures are decorated with fringes, and seem impossibly long for practical use. They may represent the horse and its rider in their best turn out for ceremonial occasions. Some sculptures show a shorter cloth over the long one, and others simply show the short one, which would be more practical for action. The harness of Roman horses is also shown in some detail on sculptures. There were straps from the saddle to the rear, passing under the horse's tail, and straps extending forwards around the horse's breast. The method by which these were attached to the saddle was reconstructed by Peter Connolly.

Protection for the horse comprised the chamfron, the peytral, and armoured barding. The chamfrons covered the horse's face, with ear guards and holes for the eyes. They were usually made of leather, often decorated with studs. Some were made of metal, and it is thought that these items may have been reserved for the tournaments or *hippika gymnasia*, not that there was anything to stop a cavalryman from using these in combat. The peytral made of leather was suspended from the harness around the horse's chest and may have afforded some protection, though its purpose may have been to prevent the metal pendants of the harness from constantly banging against the horse as it moved. Barding was obviously intended to protect the body of the horse, shaped much like modern coats for horses in winter weather, draped over the horse's back to hang down at the sides. An extant example from Dura Europos, where three bardings were found, was made of two layers of linen backing, with scales of bronze stitched on to them, the whole coat edged with red leather. There was a hole in the centre to fit over the saddle, and in the other surviving example, made with iron scales instead of bronze, there were curved sections at the front which fastened together over the horse's chest. No such protective coverings have been found in the western provinces.

Highly elaborate helmets and armour have been discovered, usually described as parade armour, used for ceremonials and tournaments. The use of this term has been revised in recent years on the basis that some of the items so described could have been worn in battle as well as in parades, where it could be spruced up to look splendid, whereas the really ornate items would be better described as sports equipment, definitely not used in combat but reserved for tournaments. Whatever the terminology, it boils down to the fact that the cavalry used two types of equipment, one for display and another for battle. In his *Ars Tactica*, Arrian describes the special clothing that the soldiers wore for the *hippika gymnasia*, leather tunics and tight trousers, but from about the third century, bronze breastplates with embossed decoration were probably worn. Helmets with partial or full face masks were also used for these tournaments. According to Arrian they were made of bronze or iron, and gilded. The most commonly cited example of such a helmet from Britain is the one in the British Museum, originally from Ribchester, with a full face mask and slits for the eyes. Another helmet was found at Newstead in Scotland, but more recently a splendid helmet made of bronze was found at Crosby Garrett in Cumbria. It is undamaged with a complete face mask and a Phrygian cap over a stylised representation of curled hair, and a griffin on the peak of the cap.

In order to put one of these helmets on, the face mask was usually hinged at the brow, or the whole mask could be furnished with a slot at the top which was fitted on to a hook on the inside of the helmet, and held in place with straps at the sides extending round the back of the helmet and fastening at the side. Some members of re-enactment societies have made their own versions of the elaborate armour and helmets, and they are very impressive, if not slightly unnerving, when the wearers are seen close up, mounted on a horse, with an almost disembodied voice issuing from behind the face mask.

The spears or javelins that were used in the *hippika gymnasia*, according to Arrian, were made without iron heads, and the shields were oblong, weighing less than normal ones. Everything in these displays was highly decorated and colourful, and the main object was to display highly developed skill and elaborate turnout, not violence and bloodshed, though the manoeuvres would help the riders and horses to achieve exactly those objectives in battle.

Veterinary services for the animals of the Roman army were probably as well developed as medical services for the men. This drawing of a sculpture from Gaul shows a civilian *mulomedicus* or horse doctor, carrying a metal hipposandal, of which several examples have been found. They were probably not used as regular horseshoes, but as medical aids like modern poultice boots, to keep ointments and dressings in place and allow hooves to heal. There were Roman manuals on veterinary medicine and practice, and a *medicus veterinarius* is known in the Praetorian units in Rome. Drawn by Graeme Stobbs.

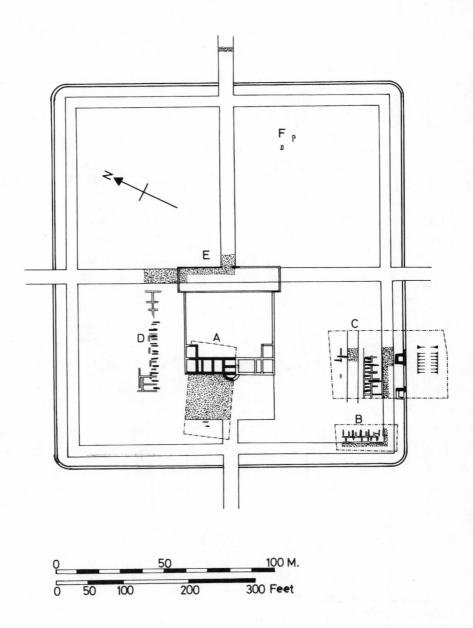

While accommodation for the soldiers in a fort or fortress is easily recognised, accommodation for horses has long been sought. Stables have been tentatively identified in several forts, but the definitive version was discovered in the excavations at the fort at Dormagen in Germany. At sites labelled B, C and D on the plan there are rows of double cubicles, one of each pair containing a soakaway pit, which was taken as evidence that horses had been kept there, and the companion room in each pair containing a hearth for the use of the soldiers. This arrangement with men and horses living together was also discovered at Wallsend on Hadrian's Wall. Redrawn by Graeme Stobbs from G. Müller *Durnomagus: Das Römische Dormagen*. Cologne: Rheinlandverlag GMBH, 1979.

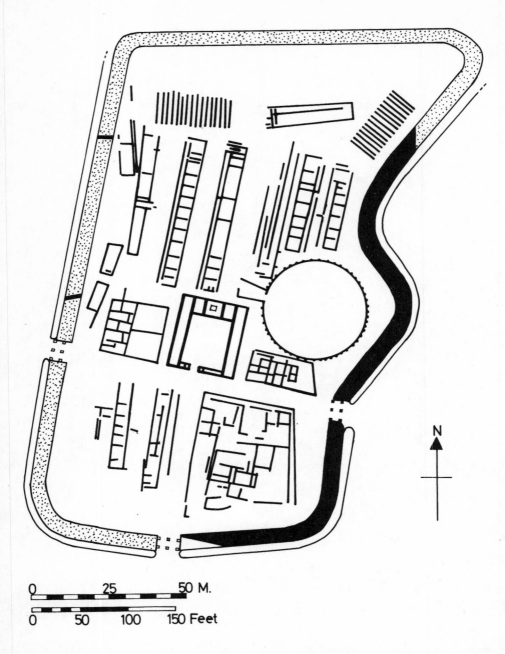

The circular structure in the middle of the Lunt fort at Baginton has been interpreted as a gyrus for exercising and training horses. The internal buildings of forts and fortresses of the first to the third centuries usually conformed to a broadly similar pattern, though more recent excavations such as this one have shown that the layout was not always standardised. The fort wall on the western side made a detour to accommodate the gyrus. Redrawn by Graeme Stobbs from B. Hobley 'A Neronian-Vespasianic Military Site at the Lunt, Baginton, Warwickshire'. *Transactions of the Birmingham Archaeological Society* 83, 1969, 65–129.

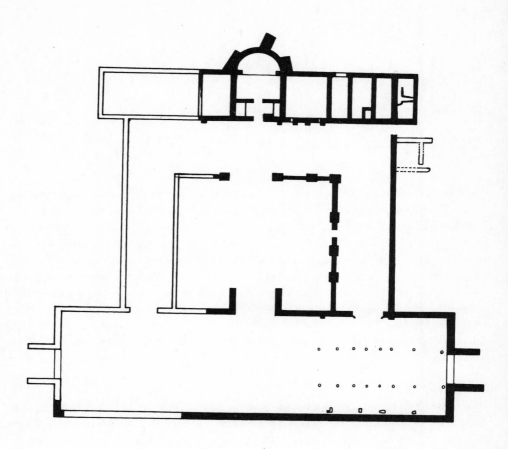

0   10   20m

The headquarters building or *principia* in most forts was usually situated in the centre range of the fort, flanked by the commander's house and the granaries. This plan shows the headquarters of the auxiliary cavalry fort at Aalen in Germany, which held a milliary *ala* from which the modern town presumably took its name. The building had a chapel of the standards with a projecting apse and a central courtyard. The long aisled building at the front is interpreted as an indoor exercise hall for the cavalrymen and their horses. The existence of such exercise halls is attested on an inscription from Netherby in northern England, recording the building of a drill hall (*basilica equestris exercitatoria*) in AD 222. Redrawn by Graeme Stobbs from *Der Obergermanisch-Raetische Limes der Römerreiches*.

6

Special and Elite Military Units

The Roman army was not simply made up of legions and the three kinds of auxiliary units, consisting of infantry cohorts, mixed infantry and cavalry cohorts, and cavalry *alae*. Augustus established new units of soldiers in the city of Rome, the Praetorians, the Urban Cohorts, and the *Vigiles*, and from a later period there were the mounted bodyguards of the emperors, the *equites singulares Augusti*. In the provinces, there were groups of soldiers specially picked from infantry and cavalry units to form the *singulares* guards of the provincial governors. Probably from the reign of Trajan, there were various units called *numeri*, units of varying sizes which were stationed mostly on the frontiers. These did not readily slot into the legionary or auxiliary categories. Only the Praetorians and the *equites singulares Augusti* among these different units can be described as elite in the sense that they were privileged and benefited from being close to the emperor.

The Praetorians

During the Republic a general at the head of troops was forbidden to cross the city boundaries, and there were no official bodyguards for any of the magistrates when they were in Rome. On campaign, military commanders assembled a *cohors praetoria* to guard them, taking the name from the *praetorium* or camp headquarters. Both Mark Antony and Octavian assembled praetorian cohorts. In 44 BC, when the consuls Hirtius and Pansa were fighting against Antony in the north of Italy, they each brought their own praetorian cohorts. These soldiers did not simply guard their commanding officers but fought in the battles.

At the end of the civil wars against Brutus and Cassius many of the legionaries did not want to be discharged after the battle of Philippi, and 8,000 men were formed into two praetorian units, one for Antony and one for Octavian. When Antony was defeated in 30 BC Octavian did not disband his praetorians. In 28 or 27 BC he established nine cohorts of praetorians, which can now be called the Praetorian Guard, though this is not the official Roman designation. Augustus, as he became after 27 BC, tried to establish his rule on a legal basis, but in reality he was backed by armed force, so it may have been in an attempt to play down this fact that he did not bring the whole Praetorian Guard into Rome. Only three of the cohorts were based in the city under Augustus, with each cohort mounting guard at his residence for one month in rotation. They did not wear armour for this duty but even though they were in civilian dress they carried weapons. The Praetorians had no barracks in Rome until the reign of Tiberius, and were at first placed in various lodging houses in the city, with the other six cohorts billeted in towns in Italy, but there is no information to elucidate exactly where they were based.

The Praetorians were trained as legionaries, and from the end of the first century they accompanied the emperors on campaign and fought in some battles. Career inscriptions show that Praetorians received military decorations from the emperors, though it is not usually stated what they had done to earn them. Like the legionaries, they carried military standards. On a long march, they were allowed to use pack animals to transport the standards, a ruling of the Emperor Gaius Caligula which subsequent emperors seem not to have revoked. There is some evidence that they carried an eagle standard. On the famous relief sculpture of Praetorians now in the Louvre Museum in Paris, an eagle standard can be seen behind the first soldier on the left. On one of Antony's coins issued to his troops before the battle of Actium, two standards with discs are shown, flanking an eagle with its wings raised, accompanied by the legend COHORTIUM PRAETORIARIUM. On Trajan's Column, Praetorians can be seen in more than one section of the column, with an eagle standard usually surrounded by a wreath, which may be an artistic symbol, not necessarily representative of the appearance of their standards.

When they were on campaign the Praetorians probably wore legionary armour, although their ceremonial dress, armour and equipment were much more elaborate than that of ordinary legionaries, and they carried an oval shield instead of the rectangular version of the legionaries. On the Louvre relief, all the Praetorians carry oval shields. The status of the Praetorians was much higher than that of ordinary legionaries, and their terms of service were shorter, at only twelve years from 13 BC onwards, raised to sixteen years in AD 5. During the early Empire they were paid one and a half times more than the legionaries and auxiliaries. They also received a higher proportion of Imperial donatives when emperors paid cash to the soldiers, sometimes on their accession, or for military victories, and on other occasions to celebrate the promotion of family members, or the marriages of their sons or daughters. The Guardsmen and officers could soon accumulate a small fortune, and since they served for only sixteen years they could progress to further military posts while still only in their mid-thirties.

The commanding officers of the Praetorians were all equestrians. Augustus appointed two equestrian prefects in 2 BC to work together as colleagues, though there were several periods when only one prefect was in command, the first being the infamous Lucius Aelius Sejanus who was sole prefect from AD 14 and spent much of his time trying to build up his personal power under Tiberius. Each Praetorian cohort probably contained about 480 men like those of the legions and the auxiliary infantry units. Unlike the legions, where no cohort commander has yet been attested, each Praetorian cohort was commanded by a tribune, often a man of long military experience, who would probably have reached the rank of *primus pilus* in a legion, and then gone on to hold commands in the *Vigiles* and Urban Cohorts. Each Praetorian cohort was divided into ten centuries, commanded, as in the legions, by centurions. The most senior centurion of the Guard was the *trecenarius*, and his second in command was the *princeps castrorum*. The title of the *trecenarius* is indicative of his command of 300 mounted Imperial guardsmen or *speculatores*, an elite force of horsemen created in the early first century. They were called *speculatores Augusti*, but lost this designation as 'the emperor's own' when they were incorporated into the Guard after Sejanus founded the Praetorian camp in Rome. The horsemen formed a special bodyguard for the emperor, clearing the way through crowds as he progressed through the city. They were distinct from the German bodyguard of the emperors and also from the mounted guards or *equites singulares Augusti*.

The recruits for the Praetorian cohorts were usually Italians in the first century, who joined somewhere between the ages of seventeen and twenty, so they would be relatively young when they retired. Whereas the legionaries did not receive discharge diplomas, on completion of their service the Praetorians did receive them, unless they had been discharged with dishonour for some misdemeanour. Since they were already citizens they did not require the citizenship grant like the auxiliaries, but they received the right of *conubium* with a woman of non-Roman status, and could bring up their children as though they were born of two Roman citizens. This right extended to one woman only, the first one that the soldier married. Diplomas for auxiliaries disappear from the archaeological record from the early third century, but they continued to be issued to the Praetorians, although there seems to have been an unexplained gap from the mid-third century to the establishment of the Tetrarchy. Then the issue of diplomas resumed during the reigns of Diocletian and his successors, until Constantine dissolved the Praetorians.

There were good career prospects for Praetorians. A Praetorian Guardsman could be directly promoted to centurion in one of the provincial legions. It used to be thought that most of the legionary centurions were ex-Praetorians, but as more and more evidence has accumulated, principally career inscriptions and tombstones, it is now seen that centurions in the legions were drawn from a wider variety of sources. The earlier theory of the predominance of Praetorians as legionary centurions derives from the fact that there are more inscriptions from Italy than from other provinces, and consequently there is also a greater number of tombstones and documented Praetorian careers among these inscriptions. This skewed the picture somewhat, but in the absence of other evidence from other provinces, it was statistically correct some years ago that the majority of legionary centurions had served as Praetorians. Nowadays the promotion of a soldier of the Praetorian Guard to centurion in a legion is seen as only one of several methods of becoming a centurion.

An ex-centurion of the Guard had even greater advantages than the ordinary Praetorian soldiers, and could reach the rank of *primus pilus* in a legion and then perhaps return to Rome and go on to a succession of commands in the various military forces in the city. Some of them could progress to an administrative career, becoming Imperial procurators in the provinces.

Under Tiberius, when the influence of the Praetorian Prefect Sejanus was at its zenith, the Praetorians were housed all together in their newly built camp (*castra praetoria*) on the north-eastern outskirts of Rome. It may have been built of timber, since the first stone camp is said to have been built by Claudius. There were several rebuilds after the first-century versions of the camp. In the later third century the Praetorian camp was incorporated into the walls built round Rome by Aurelian. Its location is immediately recognisable on the north-eastern section of the ancient city, where the line of the wall running towards the north-west makes a diversion to the east to enclose three sides of a rectangle, and then resumes its course round the northern edge of the city. The Metro station just outside is called Castro Pretorio and the site is still occupied by military forces.

The Praetorians had no executive political power, but the Prefects could aspire to considerable personal power and influence as Sejanus had done, and the support of the Praetorian Guard was crucial for new emperors at their accession, or to put it another way, if the Praetorians objected to a new emperor they could make his life miserable, and by the end of the second century the prefects could and did remove an emperor and create another. Claudius had been proclaimed and supported by the Praetorians, and he gave each of them a hefty donative to keep them loyal. At an unknown date before AD 47 three more cohorts were added to the original nine to make a total of twelve. Nero managed to offend almost everyone in Rome and the Empire but he clung on to power while he was supported by the Praetorians, until they too turned against him. During the civil war of 69 which followed Nero's suicide, Vitellius dismissed the Praetorian Guard and created a new one with sixteen cohorts, each 1,000 strong. It has been argued that the Praetorian Cohorts were 1,000 strong from the very beginning, but Yann Le Bohec has suggested that the *castra praetoria* at 16.7 hectares was too small to accommodate so many milliary cohorts. Lawrence Keppie points out that although Suetonius says that Vitellius disbanded the Praetorians and replaced them from his legionaries, this cannot be entirely true, because in order to establish sixteen cohorts of 1,000 men, almost the entire legionary force that Vitellius had at his immediate disposal would have been needed. As a complete outsider from the Julio-Claudian family Vitellius had no dynastic claims to rule the Empire and would need to ensure his own security and that of his regime, so cultivation of the Praetorians was vital. He issued coins with the legend CONCORDIA PRAETORIANUM, and if he had survived he would probably have increased Praetorian pay. The new arrangements for the Guard would scarcely have been put into effect before Vespasian was declared Emperor. A special law was passed by the Senate to define the Imperial powers of Vespasian, and since he was secure in his position even though he was not a member of the Julio-Claudian dynasty, he could afford to reduce the Praetorians from Vitellius' sixteen cohorts to the original nine, as had been the case under Augustus, but if he retained the milliary strength that Vitellius had established for each cohort, he still had at his disposal an armed force that was probably twice the size of the original Praetorian Guard. He made his elder son Titus Praetorian Prefect, which kept it in the family, so to speak, and underlined Vespasian's grip on Rome and the Empire. The treasury had been annihilated by Nero's extravagances and the civil wars, and there was no possibility of a permanent pay rise for the Praetorians, but Vespasian allowed them some privileges. He was prepared to reduce Imperial income by allowing the Praetorians tax immunity on the lands that the men were given after discharge, and any lands that they had owned before their military service.

Vespasian's younger son Domitian, who became Emperor in 81, created a tenth Praetorian cohort. Opinion differs as to whether or not he also increased the size of the cohorts. Perhaps he did, if Vespasian had reduced the nine cohorts that he retained to normal quingenary size of 480 men. The addition of the new tenth cohort to the Praetorians entailed the renumbering of the three Urban Cohorts, which had been numbered consecutively after the Praetorians from X to XII, and were now numbered from XI to XIII.

A pay rise for the Praetorians and the whole army was awarded by Domitian, who gave the soldiers of the whole Empire an extra 33 per cent, so that legionary pay went up from 225 to 300 *denarii* per annum. The differential which had always existed between legionary pay and that of the Praetorians was also increased. There is little evidence to show the actual amounts that Praetorians were paid, so modern historians have to rely on estimates which differ quite widely. Under Augustus the Praetorians earned probably 375 *denarii* per annum, but by AD 14 it had been doubled to 750 *denarii*. G. R. Watson speculates that this pay rise may have occurred in AD 13, the probable date when Augustus appointed the first permanent city prefect, who was put in command of the three Urban Cohorts, providing additional troops in the city. Domitian raised Praetorian pay to three times that of the legionaries. His generosity was rewarded by the loyalty of the Praetorians, a reciprocal arrangement since both parties knew that the power of the emperors ultimately rested on armed force, and the soldiers would perform all the better for proper remuneration.

The Praetorians under their prefect Cornelius Fuscus accompanied Domitian on campaign in the Dacian wars at the end of the first century AD. The wars broke out probably in 85 when the Dacians overran the Danube to invade Moesia where they defeated the Romans and killed the governor Oppius Sabinus. The army that Domitian assembled to fight the Dacians would normally have been commanded by a senator, but Domitian chose the Praetorian Prefect Cornelius Fuscus as overall commander, regardless of his social rank as an equestrian and the ruffled feathers of the senators. The first campaigns went well. The Dacians were pushed back, and Domitian celebrated a triumph in 86, though the chronology and even the triumph are disputed. In Dacia, Fuscus prepared for a new punitive campaign, and crossed the Danube into Dacian territory, perhaps from Oescus. Unfortunately Fuscus was killed and his army annihilated. The Dacians captured an eagle standard, which may have belonged to the Praetorians. It was once suggested that it belonged to *V Alaudae*, but this legion was lost long before the disaster of Cornelius Fuscus. Domitian assembled yet another army and won a victory in 88.

When Domitian was assassinated in 96 one of the Praetorian Prefects knew about the plot, but the soldiers had no quarrel with Domitian and did not have anything to do with the murder. They forced the new senatorial Emperor Nerva to execute the assassins. If Nerva had enjoyed a long reign his relationship with the Praetorians may have deteriorated still further, but he was elderly when he became Emperor and was careful to choose as his adoptive successor the military man Trajan. When Trajan became Emperor, his relationship with the Praetorians started badly. He executed the prefect and some of the officers who had browbeaten Nerva. After this, he restored confidence in the Guard, and he took the Praetorians with him on his Danube campaigns against the Dacians. Some of the Praetorians are depicted on the column that he erected in Rome to record the Dacian wars. They are not distinguishable from the legionaries by their arms and armour, but as mentioned above, their eagle standard usually has a wreath. In the second century the Praetorians began to be recruited from men from Pannonia and Dalmatia. It is suggested that this is when the Praetorians acquired their reputation as bullies who went around terrorising the inhabitants of Italy, as though Italian Praetorians were not equally capable of bullying civilians. One of the duties of the Praetorian Guard was arresting suspects on the emperor's orders, so the population would see them not as agents obeying orders but oppressors. Some soldiers in all armies at all times abuse their powers, and the Praetorians were in a special position owing to their high rate of pay and not least the support of the emperors, who could not take a stand against them without risking their own security. Gibbon thought that the 'licentious fury' of the Praetorians was one of the causes of the demise of the Empire.

Under Commodus the Praetorian Prefect Tigidius Perennis exercised considerable power. He was said to have replaced the legionary legates in Britain with equestrian prefects, and when a delegation of British soldiers arrived in Rome to protest, they were allowed to lynch Perennis while Commodus turned a blind eye. For some time thereafter Commodus was strongly influenced by Cleander who had started out as a slave but attained the position of Imperial freedman under Marcus Aurelius. He became chamberlain to Commodus, and he engineered the removal of the Praetorian Prefects Regillus and Julius Julianus. With the appointment of Quintus (or Marcus) Aemilius Laetus as Praetorian Prefect, things began to change. Laetus arranged the assassination of Commodus on New Year's Eve 192, and installed Pertinax as Emperor. It was said to be quite spontaneous, but none of it could have been left to chance. However, Pertinax proved too strict for the Praetorians, so Laetus removed him after only a few months. After the assassination of Pertinax there was no clear successor. The city prefect Sulpicianus, father-in-law of Pertinax, set himself up as the next candidate and offered money to the Praetorians, but they sold out to the highest bidder, Didius Julianus, who was Emperor for just over two months after paying the Praetorians a large donative.

When Severus became Emperor in June 193, he disbanded the original Praetorian Guard. He summoned the Praetorians to meet him, and the soldiers did so on the understanding that they would perhaps be awarded some cash or a pay rise, but they found themselves surrounded by Severus' troops. In order to provide himself with a legitimate reason for his bid for Imperial power, Severus had presented himself as the avenger of Pertinax, and now he accused the Praetorians of betraying Pertinax, and neglecting to pursue and execute the assassins. The Guardsmen were formally dismissed, made to give up their weapons, armour and belts, and most important, they were to leave Rome and remain beyond the hundredth milestone from the city. The historian Cassius Dio complains that Severus was to blame for creating hordes of unemployed ex-Praetorians roaming the countryside and endangering the inhabitants. The old Praetorian Guard was abolished, and then reconstituted by recruiting loyal soldiers from Severus' own armies, mostly from the Danube provinces. The cohort strength was a nominal 1,000 men. The ancient sources relate that Severus increased the pay of the Praetorians without giving precise figures, so once again modern estimates differ. The Praetorians probably earned 1,500 *denarii* per annum under Severus, but no source confirms this.

The new Praetorians were eventually commanded by Caius Fulvius Plautianus, from Africa, like Severus himself. Plautianus quickly eliminated his colleague and enjoyed sole power as Praetorian Prefect. Like another Sejanus, he tried to insinuate himself into the Imperial family. His daughter Plautilla was married in 201 to Severus' elder son, Caracalla. By the beginning of 205 Plautianus had gone too far and he lost favour. Severus executed him and replaced him with two Prefects, Quintus Maecius Laetus (not to be confused with the Laetus who eliminated Commodus and Pertinax) and Aemilius Papinianus. Maecius Laetus had been Prefect of Egypt, and Papinianus was a reputable jurist who may also have been *Praefectus Annonae*, in charge of the food supply. This prefigured the later role of the Praetorian Prefects, whose duties included administrative tasks, not least the military food supply.

When Severus was dying at York in February 211, his advice to his sons Caracalla and Geta was to pay the soldiers and ignore everyone else. Caracalla lost no time in killing his brother Geta, probably in 212, and thereafter he ruled alone, fostering the army by awarding another pay rise, so that the Praetorians may have been in receipt of 2,250 *denarii* per year, as well as the frequent donatives that emperors gave to their troops. This was the zenith of the Praetorian Guard, which soon lost influence under the emperors of the third century. The frontier wars necessitated the presence of the emperors in the war zones with their armies, and it was these armies who raised emperors and eliminated them in quick succession for most of the third century. The focus was already turning away from Rome. Diocletian reduced the number of Praetorians in his entourage, and since the emperors were hardly ever in Rome from the middle of the third century, the Praetorians became simply a garrison of the city with no political influence. The Praetorian Guard finally met its end at the hands of Constantine, who abolished it in 312, because the soldiers had fought for his rival Maxentius at the battle of the Milvian Bridge. By this time the emperors were guarded by different units, and the Praetorian Guard was unnecessary and obsolete. The Praetorian Prefects fared much better than the soldiers. They were retained, eventually multiplied in number, and accrued considerable power. Several Prefects were jurists and took on legal responsibilities, and they were also in charge of supply and recruitment for the armies, but they were deprived of the command of troops. Although they were very high-ranking important officials they were basically civilians with administrative, legal and financial responsibilities.

The Urban Cohorts

The need for a city police force in Rome was glaringly apparent at the end of the Republic, but the establishment of such an organisation was not really possible under the old system, when there was no tradition of standing army units and the scramble for personal power escalated to the point of civil war. Access to troops in the city would have been frowned upon because of the potential power base that they would provide for anyone unscrupulous enough to use them. Significantly Augustus waited for some time before creating the three Urban Cohorts (*Cohortes Urbanae*), commanded by the senatorial city prefect (*praefectus urbi*). During the Republic a city prefect was appointed only when both consuls were absent. Augustus launched a failed attempt to create a permanent city prefect in 26 BC by appointing Marcus Valerius Messalla Corvinus, but after only six days in office, Corvinus resigned, allegedly because he felt that he did not have enough experience fulfil his new role. Augustus bided his time, something at which he excelled, and reintroduced the post at a later date. The first permanent city prefect was the senator Lucius Calpurnius Piso, who may have been appointed in AD13, and the three Urban Cohorts were placed under his command. They may already have existed by 13, but were perhaps not known by this title. It has been suggested that when the nine Praetorian cohorts were increased to twelve at some time in the early first century AD, and then reduced to the original nine, the extra three cohorts may have been converted into the Urban Cohorts, which could explain why they were numbered consecutively after the Praetorians.

The three Urban Cohorts were quingenary, probably containing 480 men, divided into six centuries like the legionary cohorts. Each cohort was commanded by a tribune assisted by six centurions. There were three cohorts in Italy, and at a later date other Urban Cohorts were established, perhaps by drawing men from the original units in Rome. Probably under Vespasian, one Urban Cohort was stationed at Lugdunum (Lyon), where there was an important mint. Others were located at the ports of Puteoli and Ostia in Italy, and at Carthage. It is thought that at these three ports the main duties of the extra Urban Cohorts concerned the security of the corn supply. Just as Augustus did not bring the whole Praetorian force into Rome, he placed some of the Urban Cohorts in other Italian cities so that not all of them were brigaded together, but when the Praetorian camp was built in the reign of Tiberius, the Urban Cohorts were housed there, even though they were answerable to the senatorial prefect of the city and not to the equestrian Praetorian Prefects. Some of the soldiers of the Urban Cohorts may have occupied smaller watch-houses within the city. The men of the Urban Cohorts served for twenty years, four years longer than the Praetorians, but a shorter term than the legionaries or auxiliaries. They were probably recruited from Italians, though there is not as much information for their origins as there is for the Praetorians. The Urban Cohorts were not taken on campaigns as the Praetorians were, though on one occasion it is recorded that the soldiers did fight, especially during the civil war of 69, when their commander was the city prefect Flavius Sabinus, brother of Vespasian and uncle of Domitian. Sabinus and Domitian had to take refuge on the Capitol Hill when Vitellius' troops went on the rampage against any Flavian supporters.

The principal duties of the Urban Cohorts are usually listed as police work and keeping order in the city, but in reality there is not much information to elucidate what their tasks were. There would be several occasions in Rome when crowd control would be needed, especially during games and shows, similar to football matches in the modern world. It would be an interesting exercise to find out how a force of three Urban Cohorts and perhaps some of the Praetorians would police events in the Colosseum, with entrances and exits all around it and thousands of spectators converging on them. The potential for food riots was always present in Rome, so the Urban Cohorts would perhaps be called out to deal with them. The policing function is assumed because the Urban Cohorts did not guard the emperor or take part in expeditions and campaigns, so it is thought that they must have been concerned with the city and its environs.

As city prefect, the commander of the Urban Cohorts was a senator, and therefore ranked higher than the Praetorian Prefect. Aufidius Victorinus, city prefect under Marcus Aurelius and a personal friend of the Emperor, was entrusted with the virtual rule of Rome while Marcus was absent fighting the wars on the Danube. By the time of Severus if not earlier, the duties of the city prefect reflected his role as the main agent for policing in Rome. The jurist Ulpian says that the city prefect was responsible for all criminal cases, not limited to the city of Rome, but also including crimes committed in Italy. It is likely therefore the soldiers of the Urban Cohorts were responsible for arresting criminals and bringing them to the headquarters of the prefect, or possibly anyone deemed to be acting suspiciously. Ulpian goes on to describe how the prefect should keep order at the games by using the Urban Cohorts, and having men posted to watch the areas where the people sat at the games, so as to be able to report what was going on.

One of the reasons why not much is known about the Urban Cohorts is that their treatment in ancient historical sources ranges from cursory to non-existent. The troops were stationed alongside the Praetorians, and their cohorts were numbered consecutively after the Praetorians, so to all intents and purposes they were part of the same organisation. When ancient writers described various disturbances, they often described the men who were sent to restore order simply as 'soldiers', or they described the units that were involved as 'cohorts' without distinguishing between Praetorians and the *Cohortes Urbanae*.

Later emperors after Augustus increased the number of Urban Cohorts. There were six at some time before AD 47, the extra ones probably being added at the same time as the number of Praetorian cohorts was increased from nine to twelve. The maximum of seven Urban Cohorts was reached under Claudius. When Vitellius seized power in 69 he reduced the number to four cohorts, but is said to have increased the number of men in each one to 1,000, presumably by adding extra centuries to each cohort. In some sources it is said that the Flavian Emperors were responsible for this increase, which may be correct, but it is more likely to have been Domitian, rather than his father or his brother. Vespasian had returned to the Augustan number of Praetorian cohorts, and he had an empty treasury to fill, so he would probably not have indulged in a large increase in the numbers of men in the Urban Cohorts, who would all have to be paid from funds that were not immediately available. It is more likely that Vespasian reduced the numbers of men in each Urban Cohort to 500 as a cost-cutting exercise, though there is no evidence for this. He would perhaps have found alternative employment for the soldiers as replacements in the legions.

When Domitian added a tenth Praetorian cohort, he may also have increased the size of the Urban Cohorts at the same time, but this is disputed. When he awarded a 33 per cent pay rise to the armies and the Praetorians, it is likely that he included the Urban Cohorts, whose pay was probably one and a half times that of legionaries, but less than the Praetorians.

Antoninus Pius returned to the old Augustan number of three Urban Cohorts, and when Severus became Emperor he retained the three, but increased the numbers of men in each one, though actual totals are not firmly attested, especially as the cohorts were supposedly already milliary by the middle of the first century. Aurelian moved the Urban Cohorts in AD 270 to a new purpose-built camp, called the *castra Urbana*, which was situated on the Campus Martius. Constantine spared them the fate of the Praetorians, but they became less and less of a military force.

The Vigiles

The *Vigiles*, or city fire brigades, were created by Augustus in AD 6. Republican Rome was a closely packed city with many timber or half-timbered buildings and was therefore always at risk from fires. During the late Republic, Marcus Licinius Crassus had notoriously kept a force of trained slaves to fight fires, not for the good of the city, but so that he could buy up burning properties at ridiculously cheap prices, put the fire out, and develop the site. If the owner would not sell, then the property burned and Crassus remained as rich as he was before. Under Augustus, the aedile Egnatius Rufus gathered another slave fire brigade with which he successfully controlled several fires, but political ambition led to his downfall. He was accused of conspiracy by the Senate, and executed. Other aediles took on the task of combatting fires, and there was a board of *tresviri nocturni* in charge of the night watch, using groups of public slaves. In 21 BC Augustus took over the remnants of Rufus' gangs, and placed a force of 600 slaves at the disposal of the aediles to put out fires. These men formed the basis of the units of *Vigiles*, but were not yet properly organised or at full strength. After a serious fire in 7 BC, Augustus divided the city into fourteen regions, subdivided into *vici*, with a *vicomagister* in control of each one, responsible for the area and also the public slaves trained for firefighting. The system lacked co-ordination between the 265 *vicomagistri*, one major problem being that there was no single person in charge of all fire-watching and firefighting duties.

In AD 6 Augustus created the *Vigiles*, divided into seven cohorts each 1,000 strong. One cohort was responsible for two regions of the city. There was a camp for the *Vigiles* in the city and there was a station (*excubitorium*) in each region where equipment could be stored, and some members of the cohort would be based there, perhaps on rotation. They were to go on patrols, especially at night. Remains of the *excubitorium* of *cohors VII* of the *Vigiles* can be seen in the Fourteenth Region of Rome, in modern Trastevere, not far from the bridge leading from the Tiber Island. Another site is known, the *excubitorium* of *cohors V*, on the Caelian Hill, but it is underneath the ninth-century church of Santa Maria in Domnica. Each cohort was commanded by an equestrian tribune, many of whom had been *primus pilus* in a legion, and unusually each cohort contained seven centuries, not six as in the legions, commanded by centurions. The overall commander of the *Vigiles* was an equestrian prefect (*Praefectus Vigilum*), ranking below the other equestrian prefectures, and those of the food supply (*annona*), Egypt, and the Praetorian Guard. After commanding the *Vigiles*, the prefect was sometimes promoted to Praetorian Prefect. From the reign of Trajan onwards the prefect of the *Vigiles* was assisted by a sub-prefect. The two commanders may have worked alternate shifts, since the prefect was supposed to be available at all times, especially at night when the patrols were out watching for fires and arresting anyone who was on the streets with nefarious intent, or probably even if they only looked as if they were about to commit a crime. Suspects were escorted to the office of the city prefect, who commanded the Urban Cohorts and acquired juridical responsibilities as time went on. Career inscriptions and tombstones show that a centurion of the *Vigiles* could often progress to the post of centurion in the Urban Cohorts, then in the Praetorian Guard, and thereafter to varied careers in the legions, sometimes reaching the post of *primus pilus*.

Tacitus did not include the *Vigiles* in his list of armed forces in AD 23, indicating that they were not regarded as soldiers, even though they did take part in the fighting in the civil wars in 69 and 193. Although the original prototype units were formed from slaves, the status of the *Vigiles* steadily rose. The ranks were filled by freedmen under Augustus, and in Tiberius' reign the term of service was set at six years, after which the men received Roman citizenship. Later this was reduced to three years, and citizens began to enrol in the *Vigiles*. Severus increased the numbers of the Urban Cohorts and the *Vigiles* and recruited from the local population, perhaps in part as compensation for having removed Italians from the Praetorian Guard. At the beginning of the third century, the *Vigiles* were regarded as soldiers, but they did not fulfil military functions.

The Equites Singulares

The forerunners of the *equites singulares Augusti* can be discerned in the group of German horsemen that Julius Caesar gathered together as a bodyguard while campaigning in Gaul. The *Germani corporis custodi* were taken over by Augustus, but were disbanded after the Varian disaster of AD 9, when the German tribes wiped out three legions. Under Tiberius the German guard units reappeared. The name *Germani* is attested by Josephus and Suetonius, but on gravestones the more usual title is *Caesaris Augusti corporis custodes*. In the first century AD, these bodyguards were quite separate from the Praetorian Guard, and were not even regular army units. They could be commanded by anyone whom the ruling emperor thought fit. Caligula appointed a gladiator called Sabinus, but then Caligula was always somewhat eccentric.

The emperors of the first century were also accompanied by a small group of horsemen called *speculatores*, who may originally have been scouts in the armies of the Republic. These men were eventually housed in the Praetorian camp, fully integrated into the Guard and listed in the centuries, even though they were horsemen, just as the cavalry of the legions were incorporated into the centuries.

There were two kinds of mounted *singulares* units. In the provinces there were units of *equites singulares* who were chosen from the *alae* for the guard contingents of the provincial governors and for legionary legates. The more prestigious units were the *equites singulares Augusti* who guarded the emperors. The *equites singulares Augusti* were probably established under Domitian or Trajan. Trajan's 1,000-strong *singulares* unit, largely recruited from the Batavians of Lower Germany, was housed in a camp in Rome on the Caelian Hill near the modern Lateran palace, until Severus doubled the size of the *singulares* and built a second camp (*Castra Nova*) next to the old one (*Castra Priora*) for another 1,000 men. Both camps remained in occupation throughout the history of the guards.

The *equites singulares Augusti* were commanded by a tribune, and divided into *turmae* under decurions, like other cavalry units. They accompanied the emperors on campaigns and provided cavalry support for the Praetorians, so during active service in wars it is possible that the Praetorian Prefects were ultimately responsible for them, as they were for the separate units of mounted *speculatores*, which were fully integrated into the Praetorian cohorts. Recruitment for the *equites singulares Augusti* was predominantly from auxiliary cavalry units of Germany, Raetia, Noricum and Pannonia. A cavalryman called Ulpius Titus was selected from an *ala* in Pannonia in the late second century. Thracians enlisted from around AD 114, and in the early third century more Batavians were recruited, earning the units the nickname of Batavi, just as the German guards had been called under Caesar. The soldiers of the *equites singulares Augusti* became Roman citizens when they were selected for service, and completed whatever remained of their twenty-five years as the emperor's horse guards.

The *equites singulares Augusti* did not spend all their time on horseback, since there are records of some of them acting as footguards in the Imperial palace. Occasionally they may have been outposted to the provinces, as shown by an inscription in Greek naming a horseman called Zotikos as a *stationarius* in Bithynia. The Praetorians were sometimes sent on such missions as *stationarii*, so one interpretation of this inscription is that the *eques* was of a similarly important rank, probably a member of the *singulares Augusti*. The usual translation of *stationarius* is road guard, but the term had different shades of meaning and did not always refer to lowly posts such as this. Zotikos may have been personally chosen by the emperor for special duties in an extraordinary situation.

In the provinces, the governors assembled bodyguards called *equites singulares*, together with an infantry equivalent, *pedites singulares*, but these were not permanent units. It is not known if an incoming governor would retain the guards of his predecessor, or whether he would form his own units. The full title of the guard would be *equites singulares consularis*, since the governors of provinces containing armies would be ex-consuls, and the term would distinguish the horsemen from those of the emperor's bodyguard. The men were seconded from the cavalry and infantry units of the provincial garrison, on temporary postings. They remained on the registers of their original units, and received the same pay as before; the honour of serving in the provincial guard units did not extend to a pay rise. Arrangements for their pay to be brought to the points where they were serving were probably made when the men were seconded, though the records would still be kept at their original bases.

The numbers of *singulares* attached to a governor's entourage may have varied. In a large province there may have been units of 1,000 men, made up of 500 infantry and 500 cavalry, but this is only speculative. The commander of the *singulares* was usually listed as a *praepositus*, which often signifies an officer in a temporary or extraordinary command, in keeping with the temporary nature of the governors' bodyguard. The units were probably divided into *turmae*, since the presence of decurions is attested. The *singulares* were sometimes used in battle and since a *signifer* is known from a *singularis* unit, the *turmae* appear to have possessed standards just as those of the *alae* did. The terms of service remained the same as for the troopers of the *alae* who would be eligible for *honesta missio* at the end of twenty-five years, but it appears that some of the officers of the *singulares* could remain in service for longer.

The frumentarii

A new unit of soldiers called *frumentarii* is first attested in the second century, but some scholars think that the *frumentarii* were instituted under Domitian. At the latest it is considered that they were fully operational by Hadrian's reign. Soldiers with this title had originally been in charge of the supply of grain (*frumentum*) to the army, and some of them retained this function throughout the Empire, being sent to procure supplies and perhaps to organise transport, especially when armies were on campaign and supplementary sources of supply were necessary. The sinister reputation of the *frumentarii* as spies, leading modern scholars to label them as secret police, is blamed on Hadrian, but this has been dismissed as anachronistic for the Roman period, conjuring up as it does the image of the Roman equivalent of seedy-looking men lurking in taverns, listening to conversations and reporting any potential disaffection. If they did fulfil this function they performed many other tasks as well, but it is thought that on occasion they may have quietly despatched people whom the emperors wished to have removed rapidly and without fuss, and without resorting to legal means such as a prosecution leading to a messy trial.

The *frumentarii* did not constitute a large unit, their numbers perhaps never exceeding about 100 men, though there is no documentation to show the size of the unit, or how they were organised. They were housed in a camp on the Caelian Hill as their headquarters in Rome, but they travelled through the whole Empire on widely different missions for the emperors. They could act as Imperial messengers, or as procurers of grain, or as overseers of military requisitioning, or as tax collectors, either working independently or attached to a provincial governor's headquarters staff. The use of the title *frumentarius* perhaps does not always mean that the soldier so named was part of the unit of *frumentarii* in Rome. Some of them could perhaps act in this role for a short period for special tasks, sometimes still connected to the grain supply. In their capacity as tax collectors and supervisors of requisitioning, the *frumentarii* are known to modern historians via lurid accounts of their notorious behaviour in literary sources, and in official complaints from provincials, which are documented in papyrus records or on inscriptions. These complaints can be partially offset by two statue bases from Aphrodisias, which document the grateful thanks of the inhabitants to two centurions acting as *frumentarii* who had served honourably and bravely in the province of Asia. The existence of these two inscriptions implies that the grateful inhabitants had expected something far worse, but had been pleasantly surprised.

The National Numeri

In contrast to the more prestigious city troops and the *equites singulares*, the Roman army contained smaller units which do not readily slot into the category of auxiliary infantry cohorts and cavalry *alae*, such as the *numeri* and *exploratores* usually found on frontiers of the Empire, principally in Germany, Dacia, Africa and Britain. Some units combine the two terms, being described as *numeri exploratorum*.

The term *numerus* is a catch-all for different bodies of troops, simply meaning 'unit' and not necessarily a permanent body of troops in all cases. Authors such as Caesar and Livy use the term to describe 'a number of soldiers' and Tacitus uses it to describe the military units of all types in Britain. Unlike *ala* or *cohors* the title *numerus* does not denote a troop of a standard size or organisation. The so-called ethnic units, or national *numeri*, recruited from tribesmen on the fringes of the Empire, may have been created by Trajan or possibly by Hadrian, who perhaps adapted the temporary troops which were often used on campaigns, and converted them into permanent units. The *numeri Palmyrenorum* attested in Africa and Dacia may have had their origins in the Palmyrene archers who were employed as extra troops on campaigns. Some of these were attached to the Roman army in Judaea under Vespasian and Titus in 70–71. Similarly groups of Moorish tribesmen (*Mauri*) were attached to the troops of the governor of Mauretania Caesariensis in 68, and may have been the forerunners of the *numeri Maurorum*.

The *numeri* probably took part in campaigns, and attempts have been made to identify some of them on Trajan's Column, where some soldiers are shown wearing loose trousers and no body armour, but there is not proof that these are *numeri*. On the frontiers the functions of the *numeri* could have been to patrol the less populated regions, and to protect convoys, particularly in Dacia where the *numeri*, principally Palmyrene archers, may have patrolled the routes to and from the mining areas. They perhaps acted as scouts beyond the frontiers, if the titles of the *numeri exploratorum* from the British and German frontiers are indicative of their purpose.

There is archaeological and epigraphic evidence that from the second century onwards ethnic units of varying sizes were established in frontier forts, in particular in the Odenwald region of Germany, where several small forts of 0.6 hectares were garrisoned by a number of *numeri Brittonum*, British tribesmen perhaps withdrawn from northern England and southern Scotland by Trajan. A likely context for this would be the preparations for the Dacian wars of the first years of the second century. In the later 80s Domitian had abandoned Scotland, only recently conquered by Gnaeus Julius Agricola, and Trajan seems to have pulled back even further to northern England, to the road now called the Stanegate which runs from Corbridge in the east to Carlisle in the west, just south of the future Hadrian's Wall. For the Dacian campaigns, troops would be drawn away from the German provinces, and the raising of smaller units from Britain would serve two purposes, to remove potentially troublesome tribesmen from the British frontier region, and to provide protection for the borders of Germany.

The British units are described on inscriptions either as *numeri Brittonum*, or simply as *Brittones*. It seems that the title *numerus* was not as important as the ethnic name, and often this was followed by another distinguishing name derived from the place where the unit was stationed, for example *Brittones Triputienses*, or *Brittones Elantienses*, meaning the Britons of the River Elz. Similarly *numeri* composed of soldiers from the eastern provinces were designated by an ethnic name and a place name, such as a unit of Syrians in Africa called the *numerus Syrorum Malvensium*, and the *numerus Palmyrenorum Porolissensium*, Palmyrenes stationed at Porolissum in Dacia.

There was no uniformity of unit size in the *numeri*, which were perhaps organised on a tailor-made basis for different purposes, with footsoldiers in some places and mounted men in others where wider-ranging patrols were required. The *Brittones* of the Odenwald appear to have been infantry units, but there is evidence that other *numeri* were horsemen. The *numerus exploratorum Germanicianorum Divitiensium* occupied the large fort of Niederbieber in Germany from the early third century AD, and may have been at least 1,000 strong. A *numerus Brittonum* of unknown size was stationed with this unit, and some buildings in the fort have been identified as stables, which may indicate that one or both of these units was mounted or part-mounted, but the existence of separate stable blocks in forts is disputed. More certain evidence for mounted units derives from the fact that decurions are attested for a *numerus Maurorum* serving in Dacia, and for a *numerus Palmyrenorum* in Africa, implying that these *numeri* were organised like the *alae*, divided into *turmae*.

The *numeri* were frequently commanded by legionary centurions, who were sometimes given the title *praepositus*. This did not denote a specific rank like prefect or tribune, but was a title often given to an officer in a temporary command, who would keep his original rank, so the term *praepositus* conceals a wide variety of officers. Occasionally the centurion in command of a *numerus* was also called *curator*, or the unit was described as 'in charge of' (*sub cura*) a centurion. Some *praepositi* commanded a *numerus* and also a unit of *exploratores*, or even an auxiliary unit and a *numerus*. In the third century, commanders of *numeri* were more often prefects and tribunes.

There was some debate in the past as to the status of the *numeri*, which were described as irregulars, not properly integrated into the Roman army. The excavation of the *numerus* fort of Hesselbach in the Odenwald in Germany overturned this view, because the small fort of 0.6 hectares possessed a recognisable headquarters building, suggesting that the *numerus* stationed there was organised like other units, with military standards, pay, and regular terms of service. The *numeri* attested at the other very similar 0.6-hectare forts of the Odenwald were presumably organised in the same way, but the problem is that the terms of service are not known for any of the *numeri*. The soldiers of the *numeri* did not receive diplomas at the end of their service, which may have been twenty-five years, as for the auxiliaries. There may have been special cases where the men of a *numerus* would receive a diploma, but it does not seem to have been standard practice. Citizenship grants for time-served *numeri* may have been made when they were discharged but this is not attested. It seems certain that the *numeri* were paid, since coin finds at *numerus* forts in Germany are comparable with those of auxiliary forts, and the *numerus* fort at Neckarburken Ost where the *Brittones Elantiensium* were stationed possessed a strongroom. There is no information about the rates of pay, which are generally considered to have been less than the auxiliaries because many of the *numeri* are regarded as low-grade troops. This cannot have been the case for all units, since the *numerus exploratorum Germanicianorum Divitiensium*, probably 1,000 strong, was commanded by an equestrian prefect, who was serving in his *militia quarta*, or fourth term as commander, comparable to the commander of a milliary cohort. This begs the question why the *numerus* was not constituted as an auxiliary cohort, which on present evidence no one can answer.

There are other groups of soldiers in ancient literature which may or may not have some relevance to the *numeri*. In Hyginus' *De Metatione Castrorum* describing the laying out of a camp, specifically in wars in the Danube area, there is mention of the *nationes* and *symmachiarii*. The *nationes* are conceivably units of tribesmen who may have been hired for the duration of a campaign. The *symmachiarii* are more problematic, and the word has been variously rendered as *summactares* or even *supernumerarii* in some versions of the ancient text. In Greek *symmachia* means fellowship in fighting, reminiscent of the Roman practice of employing troops from allied rulers during their wars. Arrian refers to *symmachikon* in the *Ars Tactica*, and Dio describes the Moors in Trajan's army as *Mauron symmachias*. Herodian describes Caracalla's German troops as *symmachoi*. On balance it is likely that these troops were temporary and not comparable to the established units of *numeri* on the frontiers, but with future discoveries of inscriptions and papyri some links between the different kinds of troops could be revealed. In the third century, units with the title *cuneus* began to appear, which are sometimes said to be the mounted equivalents of the *numeri* but since it is clear that some of the *numeri* were mounted units without this title, this cannot be entirely true. The name *cuneus* literally means 'wedge', probably referring to the battle formation of such units, but whether they were all horsemen is not known for certain. In the later Empire, units called *cunei* were stationed on the Danube frontier, but these were larger and not recruited from ethnic people around the Empire. They may have developed from the mounted vexillations brought together from different cavalry units when the Empire was in crisis in the AD 260s.

7

Officers and Men

The commander-in-chief of the armed forces of the Roman Empire was the emperor, who directed the deployment of the legions and auxiliary troops, and decided where the boundaries of the Empire should be, and whether there should be peace or war. In war, some emperors with little military experience directed operations through their legates. Augustus was fortunate in that his lifelong friend Marcus Vipsanius Agrippa and his stepson Tiberius were content to win victories on his behalf and never seemed to desire supreme power for themselves. Claudius was the conqueror of Britain, wholly responsible for the concept but not its execution, which was initially undertaken by his legate Aulus Plautius. Other emperors took command of armies in the field, for example Domitian in the war against the Chatti across the Rhine, and against the Dacians; Trajan commanded armies in person in the continued Dacian wars and then in the east. In the second half of the second century, Marcus Aurelius spent much of his reign in the Danube area fighting against the tribes of Marcomanni, Quadi and Sarmatians. Emperor Severus led armies against his two rivals for Imperial rule, then to the east, and finally to Britain where he died in 208. In the third century the situation changed, with mounting pressure on the frontiers. The German frontier and the Danube regions were under almost continual threat, and the borders with Parthia became unstable with the rise of the Sassanid rulers, who were more aggressive towards Rome than their predecessors had been. The presence of the emperor in the war zones was imperative and in the second half of the third century, the armies made and unmade emperors from among their own military commanders.

The emperor was accompanied by his circle of friends and advisers in peace and in war, just as any senator was surrounded by his friends and assistants at home or abroad. The *amici* of the emperors were members of the *consilium principis*, which usually included one or both of the Praetorian Prefects and some men of military experience as well as personal friends of the emperor. Other men might be invited to join because of their particular expertise in a variety of fields. In war, the commanders of the armies would be part of the circle, presided over by the emperor. The *consilium* was not a formally constituted body with permanent membership or officially graded ranks. Marcus Aurelius began to employ legal experts with salaries, but there was no official coterie of military advisers and nothing that approached a high command with a hierarchical rank structure.

All senior appointments which involved command of troops were in the emperor's gift. The Imperial provinces containing the armies were under the direct control of the emperor via his legates, while the senatorial provinces with no troops were governed by the Senate. The senatorial governors of these provinces were chosen by lot and were given the title of proconsul, governing for one year. In the early Empire the senatorial provinces were mostly unarmed, though there were originally three with armies, Macedonia, Illyricum and Africa. By

1. This sculpture marks the site of the Lacus Curtius in the Forum Romanum in Rome. According to legend a chasm opened up in the Forum and Marcus Curtius rode his horse into it to save the city. It sounds like a distant memory of an earthquake, but there are at least two other legends, involving Mettius Curtius who sank into a marsh, and Gaius Curtius who consecrated an area that had been struck by lightning. The sculpture shows an early Roman cavalryman with flying cloak, plumed helmet and distinctive round shield. He also carries a spear, much eroded on the sculpture, aiming downwards behind the horse's head.

2 (left). Modern copy of the Prima Porta statue of Augustus, placed beside the Forum of Augustus in Rome. Over a number of years from the fall of Alexandria in 30 BC Augustus established the first standing army with regulated pay, standard terms of service, and pensions, though the auxiliary troops were not fully developed until the end of the first century AD.
3 (right). The Arch of Titus in Rome celebrates the conquest of Judaea in AD 70. Titus died in AD 81 before the arch was completed and dedicated by his brother the Emperor Domitian.

4. This scene from one of the inner faces of the Arch of Titus shows the trophies brought back from Jerusalem and displayed in the triumphal procession of Vespasian and Titus in AD 71. Triumphal displays were still appreciated by the Romans but were limited to the Imperial family, while other successful generals were denied the actual procession but could be awarded *ornamenta triumphalia*.

5. Replica of a statue of the Emperor Trajan near the Markets of Trajan in Rome. Trajan extended the Empire after defeating the Dacians in two major wars, and campaigning in the east. The Dacian wars are commemorated on Trajan's Column, which is located just off this photo to the left of and behind the statue. Relief sculptures spiral round the column, reading from bottom to top like an elongated strip cartoon. The Emperor and his artists were hardly likely to depict bedraggled soldiers and horses, so the portraiture is idealised and ennobled to represent the victorious Roman army, but if used with caution there is no better source for the legions and auxiliaries of the second century AD.

6. Statue of the Emperor Hadrian in the gardens behind Castel Sant'Angelo, the refuge of the Popes created from the remains of the Mausoleum of Hadrian in Rome. The Emperor is conventionally depicted in military dress, but he was not warlike. He put an end to expansion of the Empire and created solid frontiers, but he took an interest in the army, reviewing troops and issuing congratulatory speeches to them on his tours of the Empire.

7. The Arch of Severus next to the Senate House in Rome commemorates the Parthian campaigns of the late second century AD. Four large panels, two on each side over the smaller arches, depict significant events in the Parthian wars. The Arch was half buried in the earth until the nineteenth century, and has been dug out to its foundations. The modern road level is marked by the wall supported by the mound of earth.

8. The left-hand panel of the Arch of Severus on the side facing the Capitol Hill. It reads from bottom to top, showing the Roman attack on Seleucia on the River Tigris, and the final submission of the city. The Emperor and some of his officers and military standards are depicted at the top right of the panel, while on the left side some of the soldiers are shown wearing mail armour, which is depicted in stylised fashion by means of drill holes, similar to the soldiers on the Column of Marcus Aurelius.

9. Much of a Roman soldier's life would be spent digging ditches and extracting turves to build camps and forts. Scenes XI–XII from Trajan's Column show legionaries wearing *lorica segmentata* of the early second century AD, while they build a fort. Auxiliaries wearing their helmets and carrying oval shields stand guard. Photograph by Dr J. C. N. Coulston.

10. Scene XX from Trajan's Column shows legionaries cutting and transporting timber to build a fort. The four blocks in the foreground may not be stone, but turf. Until the later second century, Roman forts were commonly built in turf and timber, only being replaced in stone as conditions in the provinces became more settled. Photograph by Dr J. C. N. Coulston.

11. The Romans were not always on the offensive. In scene XXXII from Trajan's Column the Dacians attack a Roman fort defended by auxiliary troops, conventionally shown with stylised oval shields and using spears. Photo by Dr J. C. N. Coulston.

12. Roman military medical services were quite advanced for their time, and manuals were written on the treatment of wounds and diseases. In this scene from Trajan's Column wounded men are being helped and one man is having his thigh bandaged, while on the left Dacian prisoners are being roughly handled.

13. Different kinds of ships were utilised by the Roman army for war and for transport. In scenes XXXIII–XXXIV from Trajan's Column an oared ship is rowed along the River Danube, and two other ships transport horses and men. Photograph by Dr J. C. N. Coulston.

14. Legionaries carrying their shields and helmets cross the river on a bridge of boats in scenes IV–V on Trajan's Column. In the background soldiers carry their equipment on poles, just as they did in Marius' day in the late Republic. On the right of the photograph the standard-bearers wearing animal skins carry a variety of different standards. Photograph by Dr J. C. N. Coulston.

15. This sculptured panel from the side of the Arch of Constantine is Trajanic in date. It shows Roman cavalrymen in the Dacian wars of the early second century. The soldier on the left of the panel wears scale armour and trousers extending below the knee, and carries his sword on his right side, and behind him a soldier holds up the head of a Dacian warrior. On the right the horsemen armed with spears and protected by oval shields ride over defeated Dacians in the conventional style of many cavalry tombstones. The soldiers in the background with elaborate plumes on their helmets may be Praetorians, who are known to have taken part in the Dacian Wars.

16. Cavalrymen riding their horses are shown in scene XXI on Trajan's Column. The horses are always depicted as noble steeds of approximately fourteen hands, which most likely did not represent reality. Cavalrymen lost their horses to disease, wounds and theft, and especially in wartime they probably rode anything remotely equine, or remained as footsoldiers until remounts could be supplied. Photograph by Dr J. C. N. Coulston.

17. The lower panel of the tomb of Longinus Biarta in the Römisch-Germanisches Landesmuseum at Cologne shows his horse being exercised on a long rein. The details of the harness and trappings can be clearly seen and the saddle horns are most prominent. The Romans did not use stirrups, and for some time it was thought that they did not use saddles either, but it is now accepted that they did. There is some controversy as to whether there was a wooden saddle tree supporting the horns, or whether tight stuffing was used. Both methods have been shown to keep the rider in place, but Carol van Driel Murray has shown that stretch marks on surviving pieces of leather are consistent with having been drawn over a frame.

18. There are many cavalry tombstones from all over the Empire that have survived intact or in part, bearing the soldiers' names, the units they served in, and their ages at death. This is a copy in the EUR Museum in Rome of a stone found in Germany near Xanten, revealing that Caius Julius Primus died aged twenty-seven after serving for seven years in the *ala Noricorum*. He is described as *stator*, an official who may have been connected with providing horses for the remount service. The saddle horns and long saddle cloth are shown on his horse in the lower panel.

19. This photograph shows the reconstructed *gyrus* at the Lunt Fort, Baginton, two miles south of Coventry. Between AD 60 and AD 80 the Romans built a fort of indeterminate size, then rebuilt the internal structures on a different alignment, and included this circular structure inside the fort, which was reduced in size. The circular area, with a diameter of 107 feet, was enclosed by timber walls, and the floor was two feet lower than the ground level of the fort. There is as yet no comparable structure in the entire Roman Empire. The new and very unusual layout of the fort suggests a specific purpose, and it is thought that the *gyrus* may have been used for training cavalry horses and perhaps their riders, if these were new recruits. In the nineteenth century the US cavalry trained its new horses and recruits in a similar but smaller circular enclosure at Jefferson Barracks. Photograph courtesy of the Lunt Fort, Baginton.

20. These scenes from the Column of Marcus Aurelius show stylised legionaries wearing long skirts and segmented armour, while the auxiliaries wear mail armour depicted by drill holes. The horse in the foreground has a short saddle cloth, and the rear and front horns of the saddle can be seen.

21. The transport and delivery of supplies to the army, especially while on campaign, required detailed organisation. River transports were utilised where possible, in this case on the Danube. Well-packaged sacks (?) are being unloaded from a transport ship near a fort in scene XXXIII from Trajan's Column. Notably, the auxiliaries carry their helmets and shields while working. Photograph by Dr J. C. N. Coulston.

22. Military transport in Severus' campaigns as depicted in a narrow frieze on the Arch of Severus in Rome. Two- and four-wheeled carts are shown laden with goods and driven by legionaries.

23. This scene from Trajan's Column shows portable artillery engines or *carroballistae* mounted on two-wheeled carts drawn by mules. The machines were operated by legionaries, who were trained as specialists but remained with their centuries rather than being formed into an artillery unit.

24. A detail from scene XVI on Trajan's Column shows artillery in action, operated by legionaries, during the Dacian wars of the early second century. The torsion springs can be clearly seen, but because it is difficult to portray a *carroballista* face-on, the slider seems to be pointing to left of the artillery engine. Photograph by Dr J. C. N. Coulston.

25. Military horn blowers at the top of a Trajanic panel on the Arch of Constantine. The soldiers (*cornicines*) are using the *cornu*, which wrapped around the arm and shoulder, with the mouth of the instrument above the user's head. The soldiers are shown in the action of blowing with puffed-out cheeks.

26. Legionary fortresses were designed to impress and overawe as well as to protect the soldiers inside them. At the fortress at York in the early fourth century AD Constantius I built a series of multi-angled towers facing the River Ouse. This photograph shows one of the surviving towers with medieval additions. Fortresses in other parts of the Empire, especially on the Rhine and Danube, made similar statements of dominance.

27. Most forts had four gates, one in each side of the usually rectangular defences, and they were well defended, with towers flanking the entrance or joined by a platform over the whole gate. This is the reconstructed timber gateway, viewed from the inside of the fort at the Lunt, Baginton, near Coventry, which is anything but the usual rectangular shape. First-century forts almost always had earthen or turf ramparts with timber superstructures, and timber gates. In the second century, when fort sites became more permanent, forts were often rebuilt in stone. The gate, based on the sculptures on Trajan's Column in Rome, has two carriageways and an elevated platform across both, and timber steps lead up to the rampart walk. This gate and earth rampart are now over forty years old, and are still standing, though the earth has settled, just as the experimental rampart has done at Vindolanda near Hadrian's Wall. The Romans would have constantly repaired their forts, or rebuilt them, or moved to another site. Photograph courtesy of the Lunt Fort, Baginton.

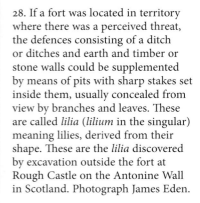

28. If a fort was located in territory where there was a perceived threat, the defences consisting of a ditch or ditches and earth and timber or stone walls could be supplemented by means of pits with sharp stakes set inside them, usually concealed from view by branches and leaves. These are called *lilia* (*lilium* in the singular) meaning lilies, derived from their shape. These are the *lilia* discovered by excavation outside the fort at Rough Castle on the Antonine Wall in Scotland. Photograph James Eden.

29. The foundations of these legionary barrack blocks at Prysg Fields, Caerleon (the Welsh version of the Latin *Castra Legionis*), have been reconstructed after excavation, and laid out on top of the original remains. To the right of the photograph on lower ground can be seen the only original Roman foundations that have been exposed. Traditionally each barrack would have ten cubicles to house one century of eighty men, with a larger house at the end for the centurion.

30. The headquarters building or *principia* of a fort was normally placed in the centre range, flanked by the commander's house and the granaries, though on occasion the terrain precluded this arrangement. Inside the *principia* there was usually an underground strong room, except where the fort was built on solid rock. This photograph shows the remains of the strongroom at Chesters fort on Hadrian's Wall in England. A narrow stairway descends into the vaulted room, where the original wooden door was still in place when excavators found it in the nineteenth century, but on contact with the air it crumbled. All the fort's cash would be kept here, though the Emperor Domitian put a limit on how much money could be stored in forts and fortresses after the rebel Saturninus seized all the resources of several legions in Germany to finance his failed coup in AD 89.

31. Each Roman fort contained a granary for the storage of food, with the floors usually raised on posts or pillars to allow for air to circulate in order to prevent the food from being affected by damp, and to guard against the entry of rodents. In early forts, granaries were timber built on these principles, and the ground plans of some of the timber versions have been revealed in excavations. It is not certain what kinds of food would be stored, though it would be principally grain, and it is not known how it was stored, in bins or sacks. This timber granary is a reconstruction at the Lunt Fort at Baginton. It is raised on posts and timber-clad, though as with nearly all Roman buildings the design of the roof is based on guesswork. Photograph courtesy of the Lunt Fort, Baginton.

32. This photograph shows one of the two rectangular stone-built granaries lying very close together, and probably under a single roof, at Housesteads, on Hadrian's Wall. These granaries show the characteristic ground plan with heavy buttresses all around the outer walls. The stone flags of the floor have disappeared, but the uprights that supported them are still visible. This is sometimes confused with a hypocaust for the underfloor heating, as in houses and bath buildings, but fires were definitely not lit under this building.

33. At all forts the soldiers had to draw their grain rations from the granaries, grind it to produce flour and bake their own bread. It is probable that one man from each tent group or *contubernium* of eight men would take charge of the procedure. Stone ovens were usually set into the earthen rampart back, which would reduce the risk of setting the fort buildings alight. The circular stone structures in this photograph are the remains of some of the ovens in the rampart back at the legionary fortress of Caerleon, and others are known at the fort of Vindolanda south of Hadrian's Wall.

34. Most legionary fortresses, and some auxiliary forts, possessed an amphitheatre which would be used for training purposes as well as gladiatorial combats and sports events. This is the amphitheatre at Caerleon, the most complete example in Britain. The superstructure and upper seating were probably built in wood on the stone foundation.

35. This photograph shows a reconstruction of a stone tower on the Roman frontier in Germany, which started out as a road guarded by timber towers under the Flavian Emperors, but in its final form under Hadrian consisted of a timber palisade with the timber towers replaced in stone. The style and shape of the roof cannot be detected archaeologically, but the roof and external gallery of this tower are based on the representations of towers in the first scenes of Trajan's Column, where they are usually shown with a very large torch projecting from the upper storeys.

36. From the middle Rhine to the province of Raetia, a timber palisade constituted the frontier of Roman Germany, reconstructed here by modern archaeologists. The auxiliary forts were usually sited some distance behind the line of the palisade, which is larger than it seems on this photograph, but it still does not look substantial. The palisade was not continuous but had gaps, usually guarded by towers, some of which were rebuilt several times, and there were small forts, not large enough to hold a full auxiliary unit along the length of the frontier. Probably no Roman frontier was ever intended to be impermeable, and none would be able to withstand a determined large-scale attack.

37. Hadrian's Wall is probably one of the best-known Roman frontier constructions because there are substantial remains still accessible to visitors. The Wall was built after Hadrian's visit to Britain in AD 122, and stretched from the Solway Firth in the west to the mouth of the Tyne in the east at the appropriately named Wallsend. In the original plan the auxiliary forts were a short distance south of the Wall, like those in Germany, but soon after building had started, forts were added to the Wall itself to become an integral part of it. Like the German frontier there were towers, relabelled turrets in Wall parlance, and small forts every Roman mile, called milecastles, all of these attached to the Wall. The photograph shows the Wall at Walltown Crags in Northumberland, clinging to the slopes of the north-facing cliff called the Whin Sill.

38. Much of the German frontier was manned by auxiliary cohorts and *alae* but on the Odenwald and its later counterpart further east, called the Outer Limes, units called *numeri* were stationed in small forts in territory where undulating hills and small valleys made massed attacks unlikely. Many of these *numeri* were composed of British tribesmen who may have been withdrawn from Britain under Trajan, though the date is uncertain. This inscription dedicated to the goddess Fortuna attests to the presence of the Brittones Trip(utienses) mentioned in the second line, under the command (*sub cura*) of Titus Manius. Several *numeri* were commanded by legionary centurions with the title *praepositus*.

39. This is the reconstructed western gate of the fort at Welzheim Ost, on the Antonine frontier of the province of Upper Germany. The modern gate is rebuilt on the original foundations. An inscription attests that at an unknown date a legionary centurion of *legio VIII Augusta* commanded a *numerus Brittonum et exploratorum* at this small fort.

40. The soldier in the centre of this photograph of Trajan's Column wears trousers and no armour or helmet, and is armed with a club, though he carries a sword on his left side and has a shield for protection. Attempts have been made to recognise these soldiers, of which there are several more examples, as the *numeri*, but the most that can be assumed is that they are intended to portray native levies, of unknown ethnic background, fighting alongside the Romans in the Dacian Wars.

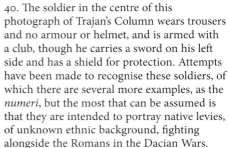

41. A sign of the times in the later third century AD: the city of Rome received walls under the Emperor Aurelian, after centuries of peaceful expansion without the need for protection. This photograph shows the Porta Sao Paolo where the Via Ostiensis from Ostia enters the city. It is virtually impossible to take a photograph in Rome without cars in it, but they give some idea of scale. The circuit of walls covers more than eighteen kilometres with eighteen main gates and several minor ones. The gate in this photograph is similar to the Porta San Sebastiano on the Via Appia, each of which had originally two arches, now reduced to only one passageway, with flanking drum towers. The visible remains of the Aurelian Walls display alterations by the usurper Maxentius in the early fourth century, by the Emperor Honorius in the fifth century and by Belisarius in the sixth.

42. The Arch of Constantine in Rome, dedicated in AD 315 by the Senate and People to commemorate ten years of Constantine's rule and the conclusion of peace after the defeat of Maxentius in 312. It was assembled by using sculptured panels and roundels from monuments of Trajan, Hadrian and Marcus Aurelius. Some of the heads of these previous Emperors were re-carved to represent Constantine as victorious Emperor, described as liberator of the city, and the founder of peace.

43. This frieze is one of the few sculptures of Constantinian date on the Arch of Constantine, documenting the battles in northern Italy on the way to Rome and the final battles at the Milvian Bridge. The sculptures show soldiers of the early fourth century. Body armour was not widely used by this time and some of the men wear felt hats instead of helmets.

44. Late Roman cavalryman from the base of the Arch of Constantine, armed with a spear couched in his right hand. He is shown without helmet or body armour.

45 Consolidated remains of the late Roman bridgehead fort at Köln-Deutz (ancient Divitia), on the Rhine opposite Cologne, are accessible to visitors. The photograph shows the foundations of one of the two towers of the well-defended gateway. This fort was large but claustrophobically compact, with projecting U-shaped towers on all sides, capable of accommodating about 900 men in very closely packed barracks. It was probably built by Constantine after AD 312.

46. The large fourth-century stone fort at Cardiff was the last of a series of forts on the same site that started with a turf and timber version in the first century. The third Marquess of Bute began to restore this late Roman fort from about 1888, building walls on top of the existing remains and insisting that the original Roman work should be outlined in red sandstone, as seen in the photograph. The original height of the walls is not known, nor is it certain that there would have been crenellations or a wall walk and round-headed windows, but the Marquess and his architects researched as thoroughly as possible for all their reconstructions of ancient monuments.

47. The substantial remains of the wall and one of the projecting towers of Burgh Castle, the late third-century Saxon Shore fort near Great Yarmouth. It stood originally on one side of a large estuary and had access to the sea. Like many Roman fortifications in southern England it was built using alternate bands of flint and red tiles, though the tiles do not extend through the entire width of the wall. The projecting round towers were not part of the original plan, but were added later, as evidenced by the fact that the lower portions were not bonded with the circuit walls. Three of the walls of this large fort are still standing but the western wall has collapsed.

the end of Augustus' reign these three had been reduced to one, so the only senatorial armed province was Africa with one legion, *III Augusta*. Even this was soon removed from senatorial control when Gaius Caligula installed an Imperial legate as commander of *III Augusta* with responsibility for the protection of Numidia. The governors of the Imperial provinces were senior to the legionary legates, and could command as many as three legions, or four legions in the larger provinces during the first century AD. Britain initially housed four legions, but the garrison was later reduced to three; Moesia on the Danube had four legions until Domitian split it into two consular provinces with two legions in each; Pannonia likewise started off with four legions until AD 106 when Dacia was annexed by Trajan, and the province was split into Pannonia Inferior with one legion and Pannonia Superior with three. These titles are not value judgements, since a 'Superior' province was usually closer to Rome than an 'Inferior' province. Syria had four legions in the first century, reduced to three by the third century. Each governor, especially of the early four-legion provinces, would therefore have to be thoroughly vetted by the emperor before being let loose with such a formidable force. Most governors of Imperial provinces were ex-consuls, though men of praetorian rank governed the Imperial provinces with only one legion, in which case they commanded the legion as well. All governors of Imperial provinces were given the title of *legatus Augusti pro praetore* even though the majority of them were of consular rank.

The governors of Imperial provinces were distinguished and important men, who owed their promotion to the emperor. Patronage played a part in everyone's career, from the letters of introduction provided by family or friends for a man seeking a post, right up to the favour of the emperors. Promotion in the Roman Empire was often achieved by active canvassing on the part of the individual and by anyone who could be persuaded to recommend him. Conspicuous ability, talent, family background and luck also played their part, but as the saying goes, it was not *what* you knew as much as *who* you knew, and much depended on the character, predilections and prejudices of the ruling emperor. It is customary to write of senatorial and equestrian career patterns, and although this is demonstrated several times over in the career inscriptions of eminent men, there were variations in the general scheme of things, and in neither senatorial nor equestrian careers was there an automatic process that guaranteed advancement from one stage to another. Some men could attain high rank and status as a result of Imperial patronage, omitting certain appointments on the promotional ladder, while others could find their careers blocked, the most famous example perhaps being Gnaeus Julius Agricola, whose son-in-law Tacitus wrote of his achievements in Britain, and of his disappointment at being denied further promotion by Domitian. Tacitus attributes the Imperial snub to jealousy.

In the Imperial Roman army promotion was always a possibility, depending on ability, personal connections, and opportunities. There was a division between senatorial and equestrian posts, but it was not a boundary that could never be crossed, being dependent on wealth. Social mobility for equestrians and for military men increased from Augustus' reign onwards. Equestrian families could assemble sufficient resources for their descendants to qualify for entry to the Senate, and some military men could rise from the ranks to become centurions and eventually achieve equestrian status. Promotion was more rapid in wartime, so if an officer performed well and came to the notice of the emperor, he could be entrusted with special commands and elevated to the Senate as a reward. A few soldiers rose from equestrian beginnings through various appointments to become consul, as demonstrated by the several career inscriptions of Valerius Maximianus, who was originally an equestrian officer. He was made a senator with praetorian rank by Marcus Aurelius, and had a distinguished career with many appointments. He was legate of five different legions, commanded a group of detachments in the Danube wars, and was made legate of *III Augusta* and governor of Numidia.

Senatorial Officers

If all the senators had clamoured for military glory there would not have been enough appointments for them all, so it is perhaps fortunate that not all the senators in the Roman world were equally enthusiastic about following a military career, some of them being content with a part in government, senatorial status, landowning, and a life of leisure. Of the senatorial families who did pursue military commands, their ancestry was supremely important to them, especially if they could count many consulars among their forebears, and it was better still if there were a few much-lauded military heroes. One of the main problems facing Augustus was how to strike the correct balance in his dealings with the senatorial class. If he allowed the military men to pursue glorious careers they might start to imagine that they could direct the affairs of the Empire at least as well, if not better, than he could himself, but on the other hand if he subdued them and made it obvious that they were all to be kept subordinate to his rule, then apathy or rebelliousness could result. One of his first tests came in July 27 BC when Marcus Licinius Crassus, grandson of the wealthy Licinius Crassus who had met defeat in Parthia in 53 BC, returned to Rome from his conquests in Moesia, where he had personally killed an enemy leader. He claimed the title Imperator, a triumph, and also the right to perform the ceremony of *spolia opima* in which a commander who had personally killed an enemy leader dedicated the spoils to Jupiter Feretrius on the Capitol Hill. Augustus allowed the triumph, eventually, but stopped the plans for the dedication of the spoils, and also allegedly took over the title Imperator for himself. The reason given out was that Crassus had not been an independent commander operating under his own auspices as the Republican generals had done, because he was subordinate to Augustus as supreme commander, who was responsible for the auspices for the campaigns. This was bending the truth somewhat because Crassus had been operating in his province since 29 BC, before Octavian had officially become Augustus and before the settlement had been made with the Senate that Augustus should command the Imperial provinces. It set the precedent for Augustus and future emperors to remain as commander-in-chief of the armies, even if they did not lead campaigns in person. Henceforth, military commanders operated under the auspices of the emperors, and however great their victories were, they were not allowed to hold a triumph. Victory titles too were the preserve of the emperors. Claudius received multiple acclamations as Imperator though he did not lead armies in person, and after the conquest of Britain, he claimed the title Britannicus, which in Republican times would have gone to Aulus Plautius, the commander of the invasion forces. The Republic had seen too many commanders elevated to a position of supremacy after important military victories, so Augustus limited the triumph to members of his own family, and awarded *ornamenta triumphalia* to his victorious commanders in place of the parade through the streets. Without some prestigious Imperial and public recognition of outstanding achievements, there would have been little incentive for any senatorial commander to conduct campaigns or defend a territory. Senators eventually came to value their awards and for the most part became accustomed to obtaining promotions from the emperors.

As a class, senators were used to playing a prominent part in public affairs, administering their estates which were worked by hundreds of slaves, and directing the affairs of their clients. Though they may have lacked experience of how an army worked in peacetime and in war, from earliest youth they would be used to making decisions and issuing orders to large numbers of people, in fact the orderly running of their lives depended on their being able to do so. Senators were not known for being shy and retiring or for being afraid of public speaking. Their mindset was utterly different from the average twenty-first-century citizen. Senators did not personally investigate why their rooms were too hot or too cold but gave orders for someone else to attend to it. They did not come home laden with shopping bags and parcels and fumble with their door keys, they would walk home or step out of litters in a suitably authoritative upright position, carrying nothing at all, doors would be opened for them and any luggage would be brought in by slaves. When they were appointed to the command of a legion, their roles would not come as a complete shock to them, nor would they be daunted by the prospect of governing a province after they had gained varied experience in different posts in civil government.

A senator would begin his political and military career in his youth, first serving as a minor official in a group of administrative tasks that became known as the *vigintivirate*, which covered control of the mint and issuing coins, legal duties, or maintenance of the streets. After this first official appointment, the young man, probably in his early twenties, would serve for about a year as a *tribunus laticlavius* or broad stripe tribune, in a legion, possibly stationed in a province where a relative or other patron was governor. Appointments were sought by the young men themselves or by their relatives and friends on their behalf, and no shame attached to the procedure. Patronage at all levels was dispensed and accepted as a matter of course, as demonstrated by the surviving letters of recommendation that were addressed to officials and military commanders. Pliny recommended his friends to a provincial governor, perhaps Javolenus Priscus, with the comment that since the governor had no doubt found places for all his own friends, now it was the turn of Pliny's circle.

Some young men would occasionally serve as military tribune in more than one legion before going on to the next civil appointment, typically as quaestor. In the Republic the quaestors were financial officials, and in the provinces of the Empire they retained these functions, but the more important quaestorships from Augustus onwards were those attached to the emperor and the consuls, who each had two quaestors. The post is usually denoted on career inscriptions as *quaestor Caesaris*. These posts were bestowed on promising young men of distinguished senatorial families, and could be said to lay the foundations of a senatorial career, since the men were now personally known to the emperor.

After serving as quaestor the young senator would seek further posts in Rome, either as aedile, or tribune of the plebs, and then as praetor, the first post where he could hold *imperium* which entitled him to command troops. There were twelve praetors under Augustus, so the number of promotions in each year was limited to a select few, even if appointments as praetor were made for only a short period to clear the way for other candidates in the same year. The duties of the praetors were mainly legal and judicial, but they also supervised the games and shows, which would keep them in the public eye. After this post, there were choices to be made. An ex-praetor could be selected by lot as proconsul of a senatorial province with no troops, or he could command a legion as *legatus Augusti legionis* in an Imperial province, or he could govern an Imperial province with only one legion, where he would also be the legionary legate. Some men would first govern a senatorial province and then go on to command a legion in an Imperial province.

As the title suggests, the military commands as legionary legates were personally bestowed by the emperor. Augustus had initiated the policy of appointing all legionary legates, whose title *legati Augusti legionis* left no doubt about who had bestowed the command on them and to whom they were ultimately answerable, even if they were also subordinate to the authority of the provincial governor. The emperor would hopefully have formed an opinion of the prospective candidates by the time they served as praetors. He might seek advice from his circle of friends as to the character of the ex-praetors, or alternatively he might have to ignore recommendations from overly-keen relatives and friends of the men hoping for promotions. Ultimately, sifting the talented from the not so talented would be the emperor's prerogative. Probably some praetors, who would be about thirty-five years of age by the time they reached the post, would find their careers put on hold because the emperor did not think them suitable, though it would be preferable to weed out unlikely candidates before this stage.

There were between twenty-five and thirty legions in the Imperial period but not all the legates would need to be replaced at once, so there may not have been enough vacancies each year for all praetors who aspired to military commands. Not all of them would necessarily wish to follow a military career. From the middle of the second century, if a senator was more interested in civil administration, he could excuse himself from taking up the post of legionary legate, as demonstrated by the career inscription of Gaius Popilius Carus Pedo, who served Emperor Hadrian in a wide variety of administrative posts, but his military experience was limited to one tour of duty as tribune of *legio III Cyrenaica*. Perhaps this turned him against a military career, leading him to refuse a post as legionary legate. It is generally considered that under Hadrian the first signs of divergence between civil and military careers are discernible, and senators began to specialise in either civilian administrative affairs or military matters in the second century.

Tenure as *legatus legionis* was usually about three or four years, though some men served for longer by going from legion to legion as legate. These were usually career soldiers who served in civilian posts but often came to military prominence in a succession of commands during wars. One such example was Gaius Julius Quadratus Bassus who accompanied Trajan in the Dacian wars and in the east, and who was legate of eight different legions, though it is suggested that these may have been detachments in the various wars and not whole legions.

The next major promotion after serving as legionary legate, or governor of an Imperial province with one legion, would be the consulship. Technically there were only two vacancies per year, but the system was sometimes adopted whereby the eponymous consuls, who gave their names to the year, stepped down after a short time in office to make way for pairs of suffect consuls, who might serve for only a month to gain experience and the necessary rank for appointments as provincial governors, in which they would be in overall command of the legions and auxiliary troops, and responsible for all aspects of civil government.

Most senatorial officers spent only a short time in the armies, as *tribunus laticlavius* for a year, and as legionary legate for three or four years. They had no formal training except by experience. They may have read military manuals, which certainly existed by the first century BC. They may have studied the theory of warfare, strategy and tactics, and learned from other generals, but there was no officer training school and no necessity for recognised qualifications. As Goldsworthy points out, Roman army officers were by no means comparable to the professional officers of the armies of the eighteenth and nineteenth centuries. The first desirable attribute of a senatorial officer was the approval of the emperor, without which no one could hope to advance his career. Other desirable attributes included high social status, wealth, and intelligence.

Equestrian Officers

The government of Egypt did not follow the senatorial pattern, but offered opportunities for equestrians. Augustus installed an equestrian governor as soon as he took control of the country, and forbade any senator or prominent equestrian to visit the province without special Imperial permission. This rule was never relaxed by his successors. The governors of Egypt, *Praefecti Aegypti*, were always equestrian prefects, and the legionary commanders were not senatorial *legati* as was normal in other provinces, but equestrian *praefecti legionis*. There was no senatorial *tribunus laticlavius* in the Egyptian legions.

The career path of the equestrian officers differed from that of the senators. Some equestrians were directly appointed as legionary centurions, but more often they were appointed as commanders of the auxiliary units. During the first century AD a standardised succession of three appointments began to evolve called *tres militiae*. An equestrian usually took up a first post as prefect of a 500-strong auxiliary infantry unit before becoming one of the five equestrian *tribuni angusticlavii* in a legion. An alternative to serving in a legion was to become tribune of a 1,000-strong infantry cohort, but men who chose this route to promotion are not so well attested as the military tribunes. Pliny obtained a post as military tribune for Suetonius, the author of the *Twelve Caesars*, but Suetonius declined and recommended his relative Silvanus instead. The *tribuni angusticlavii* were responsible for administrative duties, for overseeing the security of the camp gates and for some judicial functions. They would probably serve for about three years, but longer service is not unknown; Gaius Fabricius Tuscus was military tribune of *III Cyrenaica* for eight years, and eventually became prefect of a cavalry *ala*, which was the third and most important post of the *tres militiae*. These successive appointments were commonly held for about three or four years, and usually took the officers to different provinces. There was no compulsion to serve in all three posts. A few equestrian officers served in a fourth post, *militia quarta*, as commanders of a milliary *ala*, though there were only a few of these 1,000-strong cavalry *alae* in the Empire, and no province can be shown to have held more than one, so chances of promotion to one of these units would be limited. The troops in Rome offered an alternative career for equestrians. The cohorts of the Praetorian Guard, the Urban Cohorts, and the *Vigiles*, were commanded by equestrian tribunes, and the pinnacle of the equestrian military career was the appointment to one or more of the four prefectures, of the food supply (*Praefectus Annonae*), of the *Vigiles* (*Praefectus Vigilum*), of Egypt (*Praefectus Aegypti*), and of the Praetorian Guard (*Praefectus Praetorio*).

Social mobility in the Roman world allowed some men to move out of their social class into more elevated circles. The boundary line between the equestrian class and the senatorial class was not rigidly fixed for all time, and ordinary soldiers could achieve equestrian status after reaching the higher ranks in the legions. Some equestrians obtained direct entry to the legions as centurions, progressing to the higher ranks as *primus pilus* and camp prefect, which automatically entitled the holder of this post to equestrian status, if these officers had risen from the ranks. This was the slowest and rarest means of entering the equestrian class. It required about fifteen years of service and a progression through the clerical or junior officer posts to arrive at the rank of centurion, as demonstrated by the career of the centurion Petronius Fortunatus. He served successively as *librarius*, *tesserarius*, *optio* and *signifer* before being appointed centurion *ex suffragio legionum* or by vote of the legion. Thereafter he served as centurion in over a dozen legions, in Britain, Lower Germany, on the Danube and in the eastern provinces. There were occasionally alternative methods of becoming a centurion. One soldier started out as a legionary in *legio III Augusta*, then became *duplicarius* (soldier on double pay) in the *ala Pannoniorum*, rose to the rank of decurion, and then returned to *legio III Augusta* as centurion.

For centurions such as these soldiers there was always the possibility of promotion to chief centurion, *primus pilus*. There was only one *primus pilus* post per legion, and it was usually only held for one year. The remaining centurions in each legion had only a limited chance of obtaining this prestigious post. After their year of service the *primi pilares* were eligible for equestrian rank. Some men served for a second term in another legion (*primus pilus bis*). Most commonly a chief centurion moved on to become *praefectus castrorum*, or camp prefect, usually but not always in another legion.

The camp prefect was one of the most senior officers of an Imperial legion, third in command after the legate and the *tribunus laticlavius*, and senior in rank to the five equestrian *tribuni angusticlavii*. The first attested camp prefect dates to the end of Augustus' reign, significantly when more permanent forts were being established. The duties of the camp prefect were concerned with the maintenance of the fortress, ensuring that everything was clean and in working order. The post required extensive experience of military administration and functions. Holders of this important post could obtain promotion to tribune in one or more of the Rome cohorts, or to an appointment as provincial governor of the less militarised provinces. Career inscriptions demonstrate how far soldiers could rise to important posts. Marcus Vettius Valens started as a Praetorian Guardsman, then became clerk to one of the Praetorian Prefects, then served as centurion successively of the *Vigiles*, the Urban Cohorts, and the Praetorians, and then became a legionary centurion. From there he was promoted to *primus pilus*, returned to Rome in a succession of posts as tribune in command of individual cohorts of the Rome units, was admitted to the equestrian order, and became procurator of the province of Lusitania.

The equestrian career began to blossom in the later second century, when there were prolonged wars enabling more professional officers with extensive military experience to gain promotions. Professionalism in the army opened up higher office to several equestrians. In preference to men whose only recommendation was birth and status, Marcus Aurelius began to choose men who had shown great aptitude, promoting several of his officers from the equestrians with long service records. Usually he made them senators, so that technically they were qualified for the positions to which he promoted them, the most famous example being Valerius Maximianus, mentioned above. From then onwards, the equestrians rose in importance in the army. The Emperor Septimius Severus created three new legions and placed equestrian prefects in command of each of them instead of senatorial legates, but this was probably because they were stationed in areas where equestrians and not senators governed the province or commanded the troops, so placing a senatorial officer in a subordinate position to an equestrian was avoided. In the mid-third century, the Emperor Gallienus employed equestrians more frequently as legionary commanders and as provincial governors, without first making them senators as Marcus Aurelius had done. Senatorial commanders and governors were not wiped out all at once and for all time, but it was a significant turning point.

Officers below the Rank of Centurion

In each century there were four ranks below the centurions. The *signifer* who carried the century's standard was responsible for the paperwork of the century. He ranked higher than the *optio*, the deputy who took command if the centurion was absent. These men were *principales* receiving double pay. Below these were the *tesserarius* who gave out the watchword and presumably checked that it was properly administered, and the *custos armorum*, in charge of weapons and equipment.

There were many attested lower-ranking officers in the legions, whose titles do not always convey what their duties would have been, and it is not clear how they all related to each other.

Some titles may be synonyms for the same post, or substitutes that appeared at a later time. The *doctores*, *discentes* and *magistri* were instructors or teachers, for example *doctores ballistarium* are attested, presumably teaching the use of the ballista, but there were probably distinctions between all these posts. *Magistri* were in charge of the workshops, or *fabricae*.

There was a hierarchy among officers sharing the same title, especially those who were attached to the various staffs of high-ranking officers. The equestrian *tribuni angusticlavii*, the camp prefect, the *tribunus laticlavius*, the legionary legate, and the provincial governor, all had offices manned by clerical staff drawn from the legionaries. The most commonly attested are the *cornicularii* and *beneficiarii*, who were ranked according to the status of the officer they served. The *beneficiarii* were specially chosen for a variety of tasks, sometimes far away from legionary or provincial headquarters, where there would be a number of them, usually called *beneficiarii consularis*, since the governors of most of the armed provinces were consulars, despite their official title of *legatus Augusti propraetore*. At Chester, Titinius Felix died aged forty-five, while still in office as *beneficiarius* of the legate of *XX Valeria Victrix*. The *beneficiarii* may have undertaken intelligence gathering and some police work. The *cornicularii* supervised the various administrative offices, the most important being that of the governor, who employed two or three *cornicularii* with a centurion in overall charge, called the *princeps praetorii*. Legionary legates and other officers would make do with one *cornicularius*.

Another title which occurs frequently is the *librarius*. There were several of these junior officers, whose duties were secretarial, including record keeping and financial accounting, for instance the *librarius horreorum* kept a tally of food stores received and distributed to the soldiers, and the *librarius depositorum* kept the savings accounts of the soldiers, who had money deducted from their pay for this purpose. As Vegetius says, soldiers were less likely to desert if they had money on account with their unit. From the end of the second century or the beginning of the third, the *actarius*, or *actuarius*, appeared; he was responsible for keeping the records of the corn supply, and may have superceded the *librarius horreorum*, or the two posts could have existed side by side with slightly different responsibilities. The *actarius* may have kept the daily service records as well as those for the corn supply. An *actarius* of *XX Valeria Victrix*, Gaius Valerius Justus, is commemorated at Chester on a tombstone erected by his wife, Cocceia Irene.

Among the specialists in the army there would be several musicians, who would be on double pay. A fragmentary inscription found at Lambaesis records the various *duplicarii* of *III Augusta* in the early third century, six of whom are trumpeters or horn blowers. Musical instruments are known from Roman military contexts, attested by archaeological finds, from sculptural representations, and from literary references. These sources enable modern craftsmen to reconstruct the instruments, and so the probable range and type of sounds that they made can be ascertained, but it is not known for certain what combinations of notes were played on them in Roman times. In the military context, it is likely that there were standard musical compositions for parades and festivals, but the majority of the meagre information that has come down to us concerns musical instruments used for tactical signals.

The three main instruments commonly used in the Roman army are the *tuba*, the *cornu*, and the *bucina*, played respectively by the *tubicen*, the *cornicen*, and the *bucinator*. The *tuba* was a straight trumpet, while the *cornu* was an almost circular instrument that wrapped right around the player's arm, with a bar across the middle for grip. Very little is known about the *bucina*, but it was probably used in ceremonials, and to give signals in camp.

From literary sources it is known that the Romans used these instruments to sound reveille (cockcrow), and for the changing of the guard when in camps or forts. Tacitus records an occasion when the light of the moon seemed to wane, and to ward off the evil omens, soldiers blew on every kind of trumpet and clattered brass instruments, whereupon the moon obligingly brightened for a short time. The main responsibilities of the *tubicen* were to sound the advance and the retreat, and the signal to leave camp. In Caesar's army at the battle of Thapsus, before the Caesarians engaged, the overenthusiastic *tubicen* on the right wing sounded the charge without orders from Caesar himself, and from then on it was impossible to hold the soldiers back. According to Vegetius each legion had thirty-six horn blowers (*cornicines*), and Arrian says that there were thirty-eight trumpeters (*tubicines*), three for the officers, three in the legionary cavalry, five in the First Cohort, and the rest were assigned to the remaining cohorts.

Certain *tubicines* or trumpet players are recorded on inscriptions. Two gravestones from different parts of the Empire record *tubicines* and include a carved 'portrait' of each soldier carrying his *tuba*. One was found at Cologne, commemorating Caius Vettienus, *tubicen exs* [sic] *leg[ione]* but unfortunately the legion is not named. The other was found in the Chersonese, near Sebastopol, recording Aurelius Salvianus, *tubicen* of *legio XI Claudia*, who served for thirteen years and died aged thirty-six. The *tubicines* of *legio III Augusta* are recorded on an inscription, and from the fort of Brigetio (Szőny, Hungary) on the Danube, the *tubicines* of an unnamed legion, probably *I Adiutrix*, set up a dedication to Minerva. Significantly they called themselves a society or college of trumpet players (*scola tubicinum*), indicating a sense of corporate identity if not an actual college. This sense of cohesion was enhanced by a ceremony called the *tubilustrium*, which was carried out probably every year, to purify the instruments. This was not a purely military observance, since the *tubilustrium* was celebrated in Rome to purify the trumpets used in religious ceremonies.

Promotion

A great deal is known about the career paths of several serving soldiers who were promoted from the ranks, but the information comes from different provinces and different eras. To apply this information indiscriminately to the army of all provinces in all time periods is to run the risk of inadvertently including some anachronisms and anomalies. There is still not enough accumulated evidence to be able to state that there was or was not a structured approach to promotion or to discern whether it was a purely arbitrary process. It may be that soldiers were deliberately given an all-round training to broaden their experience, but this does not seem to be the case if the surviving evidence is taken as representative of normal practice. In general, promotion depended not only on conspicuous ability, but on the recommendation of powerful individuals, so patronage, effort, and self-help were at least as important as ability. In Egypt in the second century AD a soldier called Terentianus, who wanted to transfer from the fleet to a legion, and was ultimately successful, complained that letters of recommendation were of no use unless a man helped himself, and he also said that money was the only thing that really helped, so presumably backhanders were involved in promotion. Self-advertisement was essential. Another soldier in Egypt, the new recruit Julius Apollinarius, wrote home to his father to tell of his progress, congratulating himself on going straight to the top, asking the governor of Egypt, Claudius Severus, for a clerical post on his staff. He was offered instead a clerical post in a legion, avoiding the hard labour that ordinary recruits would have had to perform, and gaining the added bonus of a more or less firm promise of promotion to higher ranks. Timid and reticent recruits or those who could not read and write probably never escaped from back-breaking labours.

It has been estimated that it would probably take twelve to fifteen years for an ordinary legionary to rise to the rank of centurion, often by means of transferring to another unit, as in the case already quoted above, detailing the career of a legionary in *legio III Augusta*, who reached the rank of centurion in the same legion by way of a transfer to an auxiliary cavalry unit as *duplicarius* and then as decurion. A transfer such as this did not always automatically lead to the post of centurion. The career of Tiberius Claudius Maximus shows that he held various appointments, but did not advance to high rank, despite coming to the notice of the Emperor Trajan, who promoted him from *duplicarius* to decurion.

Rank and File

The men who served in the Roman legions and auxiliary troops were of varied ethnic and social backgrounds. Legionaries were all Roman citizens, in theory at least, and in the first century AD they were predominantly Italians. As time passed the number of Italians declined and the number of provincial Roman citizens in the legions increased. As the legions became less mobile and were stationed in permanent forts, the recruitment of replacements was undertaken in the province where the legion was located, often in the vicinity of the fortress. Recruitment of the auxiliary soldiers from among the non-citizens followed roughly the same pattern, in that initially most of them were levied from the tribes on the periphery of the Empire, and then as the years went by the units obtained their recruits less and less often from the original tribes and began to take in non-Romans from the province where they were stationed. Epigraphic evidence from the first century AD attests the presence of ethnic tribesmen in auxiliary units, for instance at Colchester, Longinus, a trooper in the *ala I Thracum*, was described on his tombstone as the son of Sdapezematygus. It has been disputed whether Sdapezematygus is truly a Thracian name in a Romanised form, but Longinus came from the district of Serdica (modern Sofia) which strongly suggests that he was of Thracian origin. An *ala I Thracum* was still in Britain under the Emperor Trajan, named on a diploma found at Malpas in Cheshire, England. By Trajan's reign there may not have been many Thracians in the *ala*. When local recruitment became the norm, the auxiliary units retained their ethnic titles, even though they no longer reflected the nationality of the original soldiers.

More localised recruitment, combined with the more static locations of the legionary fortresses and auxiliary forts, led to a decline in the wholly ethnic composition of the military units, and a corresponding increase in regionalisation, which is not quite the same thing as ethnic origin. Romanisation of soldiers who joined the legions and auxiliary units was more or less inevitable. Indoctrination of recruits and serving soldiers was expressed in the military oath that all soldiers swore when they enlisted. Native names were rendered into acceptable Latin, or on occasion were abandoned altogether and Roman names were substituted for them. Latin was the language of command, administration and record keeping, except for some of the eastern provinces, where Greek was sometimes used in military records and correspondence. However, despite this inevitable Romanisation there were detectable differences between the troops of the different provinces. In the provinces where they served, the soldiers would appear quite normal but when troops were moved around the Empire during major wars, the differences became more apparent. Lawrence Keppie highlights examples from Tacitus' account of the civil wars of 69, when legionaries from the Rhine who were marched into Italy found the climate far too hot, and many of them died of disease. Legionaries of *III Gallica* from Syria took part in the second battle at Cremona in northern Italy, where they all turned to greet the rising sun at dawn, as they would have done in Syria. Soldiers were allowed to worship their own gods and to a large extent follow their own customs, provided that there was no conflict with Roman interests in each province. There may have been differences in physical appearance, military dress, and equipment that would serve to alienate them slightly from the inhabitants of other provinces, and especially from the Italians and the people of Rome. The army was a homogenous entity in that it served the same purpose of defence of the Empire and conquest of new areas, but it was a long way from the armies of the Republic, made up of Romans and Italians of various cities, mostly local youths who did their service and came home again. By the beginning of the Empire the gap between soldiers and civilians was widening, and it would continue to do so. Early Romans admired and honoured their commanders and soldiers, but the ordinary soldiers of Imperial times were looked down upon, sometimes dismissed as a rabble. When Roman soldiers in civil wars were perfectly willing to sack Roman towns and slaughter Roman or Romanised citizens, this low opinion could only be reinforced by such incidents. The short-lived Emperor Vitellius did himself no favours by failing to stop his Rhine legions from running amok in Rome.

Ordinary soldiers were not usually mentioned in the works of the ancient historians unless they had achieved something remarkable or perpetrated some gross infamy. Most of Caesar's accounts of outstanding exploits and personal bravery concern centurions or senior officers. A very small proportion of the vast numbers of soldiers who served Rome throughout her history are known by their names, mostly derived from inscriptions commemorating special occasions or more commonly recording their deaths. Officers were more likely than ordinary soldiers to set up altars to the gods or funerary monuments, which may have been too expensive for some legionaries and auxiliaries. For information about the soldiers who distinguished themselves in Roman military service, historians must rely upon the few sources that record the men and their achievements. The surviving literature and inscriptions can represent only an arbitrary and very limited selection of heroic acts or consistent high achievement; many more must have been forgotten or gone unrecorded.

Contemporary records would have been much more abundant. The army kept records of its personnel from Republican times, with details of when they enlisted and their various duties. It is clear that the officers also noted the characteristics, good and bad, of the men. According to Appian, when Mark Antony wanted to identify the troublemakers in his army, the tribunes produced a list for him from their files. When soldiers had performed particularly well in battles or on campaigns, their names were similarly recorded and written up in reports, from which the commanders could compile lists when rewards were to be handed out. Soldiers appreciated the presence of their generals or the emperor in battles, because then they were more likely to be noticed if they had a chance to excel themselves. In Dacia in 88, Domitian's general Tettius Julianus ordered his men to inscribe their own names and those of their officers on their shields, so that anyone who performed particularly well would be more easily recognised and their exploits recorded.

Imperial recognition and rewards meant a great deal to the recipients, not purely from the point of view of monetary gain or the promotions that often followed a significant act of bravery. Individual awards were not made to auxiliary soldiers, but to the whole unit if it had performed some distinguished act. The standard awards for legionaries consisted of *phalerae*, torques, and *armillae*. The *phalerae* were metal discs which were usually displayed on a leather harness worn over the soldier's armour. Torques were usually made of gold, and came in two forms, one worn round the neck like those of Celtic warriors, and smaller versions which were worn on the leather harness with the *phalerae*, usually near the shoulders. *Armillae* were armbands, or bracelets worn on the wrists.

Great ceremonial attached to the giving of rewards, as evidenced by the special parade organised by Titus for his army in Judaea, reported by Josephus in *The Jewish War*. The names of all men who had performed well during the war were read out, and as each man came forward, Titus himself presented the various decorations appropriate to the deed and the rank of each soldier, accompanied by gifts of silver, gold and clothing.

Some soldiers attached sufficient importance to their decorations to record them on inscriptions, or their heirs recorded the details for them. Titus Camulius Lavenus (the last name is uncertain), a soldier of *III Gallica* who died in Gaul, was awarded torques and armbands by the Emperor Hadrian, but the instigation for these awards had come from his fellow legionaries, as stated on the inscription '*suffragio legionum*' or by vote of the legion. This is the only known example of awards being given in this way, but it could well have been a more frequent occurrence for soldiers who were held in high regard by their colleagues. Some occasions may have gone unrecorded, or perhaps more inscriptions are awaiting discovery. Petronius Fortunatus, mentioned above, was promoted to centurion *ex suffragio legionum* or by vote of the legion.

The fact that these men specifically listed their awards indicates the importance that they attached to them, but with regard to the historical record, it simply proves that the men had performed great exploits in battle, and offers no information with which to reconstruct what they did to earn them. There can be no certainty about which campaign or campaigns they served in, much less the exact location.

Conversely, in at least one incident, the campaign, the location, and the exploit are known, but not the names or ranks of the men who carried it out. Tacitus relates that at the second battle of Cremona in the civil war of 69, the soldiers of Vitellius had mounted their artillery on raised ground and were causing great damage to the troops fighting for the cause of Vespasian under Antonius Primus. The Vitellian operators of one particularly large ballista were hurling huge stones into the Flavian ranks, so two of Antonius Primus' soldiers took shields from the dead men all around them, crept up to the machine and put it out of action by cutting the cords that formed the torsion springs. They were both killed, and no one recorded their names, but at least their joint exploit was recorded.

Rather than relying upon the historians to record their actions, some self-declared heroes set up inscriptions to commemorate them. A soldier serving under Hadrian in Pannonia performed a spectacular feat in peacetime, with the Emperor in attendance. His success is documented on an inscription, which documents what the soldier did, but does not give his name. He belonged to an auxiliary Batavian unit, famous for its expertise in swimming, and while in full armour he swam across the Danube, a considerable achievement in itself, but he also shot two arrows, breaking the first one in two with his second arrow. The inscription states that no one was ever able to compete with him in javelin throwing, and no archer could outdo him in firing arrows. The Emperor would have noticed the soldier, but since this was not conspicuous bravery in battle, and the soldier was an auxiliary, he could not have given an official award.

8

Administration of the Army

Thanks to the discovery of military records from different parts of the Empire, much of the bureaucracy of the army has been revealed. The majority of the extant records come from Egypt and Syria, where papyrus and other documents have been preserved in the hot dry climate. The major collections of papyrus records are those from Oxyrhynchus in Egypt, published in several volumes, and from Syria the records from Dura Europos have been published by the excavators of the fort, edited by C. B. Welles. Some records and letters have been found written on potsherds, called ostraca (ostrakon in the singular form), which were even more durable than papyrus, but these too are mostly found in hot dry countries where the chances of preservation are better than in Europe. In Athens, potsherds were used whenever an ostracism was carried out, the term obviously being derived from ostracon. The voters wrote on the potsherds the name of the man they wished to see exiled for ten years. The writing was incised into the pot in Greece, but written in ink on the Egyptian examples. For the Roman army the most important collections are from Mons Claudianus in the eastern desert of Egypt, where there was a small town which housed Roman troops, and civilians who worked in several Imperial quarries. The records are in Greek and Latin. At the opposite end of the Empire the Vindolanda writing tablets, made of wood which has been preserved in wet conditions, have shown much of the personal details of the commander and soldiers of an auxiliary fort at the edge of the Empire in the late first century AD.

The records listed above concern the day-to-day running of small establishments within a province, or sometimes the administration of the province itself. Ultimately all provincial governors responsible for military and civil administration were answerable to the emperor to whom they would direct their reports and queries. It used to be fashionable in studies of the Roman Empire to write of the central administration or Imperial secretariat, with its departments headed by Imperial freedmen all under central control, which was supposedly organised by Claudius and refined by his successors. More recently the centralisation aspects have been doubted, and it is clear that Claudius did not invent the system, but adapted what was to hand, since Augustus and Tiberius obviously required secretaries to deal with the administration of the Empire. Though there may have been less centralisation than was previously supposed, and less contact between the different sections of the administration, the work was still done under different headings, overseen by men who could be called secretaries for want of a better description, and were often Imperial freedmen, and then later equestrians. Finances were administered by an official called *a rationibus* with a staff of lesser officials; correspondence and several other tasks were the responsibility of the *ab epistulis*. The *a libellis* dealt with appeals, petitions, and complaints and grievances, and the *a cognitionibus* was responsible for legal matters.

Despite their capacity for administrative organisation, the Romans did not develop the equivalent of a war office with its own budget which could organise and finance the various armies and direct their operations in peace and war. The Romans did not operate with overall budgets comprising income and expenditure like modern governments. Various estimates have been made of the total costs of the armies in the Empire, but there are so many variables, such as the size of a single legion and whether all legions contained standard numbers of men at all times; the uncertainty about the pay scales of legionaries and auxiliaries, and whether there were cash pensions for auxiliaries; how many men who would have been eligible for pensions died before they reached retirement, reducing the number who would actually receive pensions; the uncertainty about the pay of officers from centurions upwards; the cost of cavalry horses and draught animals; the amount of money spent on food supplies, weapons and armour, clothing, boots, tents, carts and wagons and artillery engines, and whether the soldiers paid the full costs of their clothing and equipment or only a percentage. It is tempting to say that the army was expensive, and move quickly on. In the reading list for this chapter, Campbell, Herz and Kehne are good starting points for the cost of the army.

It used to be thought that there would be a coterie of distinguished generals, labelled *viri militares*, surrounding the emperor and serving as an advisory and planning body, but this is now discredited, just as the concept of centralisation in the administration has been debunked. There were, of course, always some military men in Rome, perhaps in retirement, or currently in a political appointment, and some of them may have been called in for discussion with the emperor, but there was no official group of *viri militares*, and no organisation co-ordinating the procedure. The emperor alone was in charge of the armed forces and directed where the troops should be deployed. In peacetime the provincial governors, the procurators, the legionary legates and the commanders of auxiliary units would all take care of the various aspects of daily administration of the army, but in planning for a war the emperor would call in various officials of the government in Rome. The *Praefectus Annonae* would deal with all aspects of supplying the army with food while on campaign, and he would liaise with other officials who would deal with transport. The financing of the coming war was the responsibility of the office of the *a rationibus*, and correspondence with provincial governors and allied states was the responsibility of the *ab epistulis*.

Finance

The financial administration of the Imperial provinces with armies, governed by *legati Augusti propraetore*, was the responsibility of the procurators, usually equestrians who had served in the armies as military tribunes and commanders of auxiliary units. They were in charge of the collection of direct and indirect taxes, and the food supply and pay of the troops, all their activities being supervised by the *a rationibus* in Rome, to whom the procurators presumably sent their reports and accounts. At procuratorial headquarters, which need not be in the same location as the offices of the provincial governor, there would be a considerable number of staff, some of whom would be soldiers on secondment, such as the *beneficiarii* who would carry out various different tasks, and the *cornicularii* who supervised the clerical staff. The procurator was entitled to requisition transport and he commanded some troops, presumably acting as bodyguards and law enforcers when he went around the province, tax collectors not being high in the popularity stakes.

At individual forts and fortresses the commander was ultimately responsible for the finance of his own operations, subject to the procurator. There would be day-to-day expenses in running a fort of any size. Letters recovered at Vindolanda concern the purchase of food, some of which may have been for personal consumption, but when the writer of one letter wants twenty chickens and large numbers of apples and eggs, 'if they are sold at a fair price', then it would seem that the purchases are for a number of men in the unit, perhaps for a ceremonial occasion or a festival. Money was probably earmarked for purchases, and accounts would be kept of transactions, usually by the clerical staff called *librarii*. Records of grain and other foodstuffs delivered to, and distributed from, the granaries were kept by the *librarii horreorum*, and the soldiers' savings were recorded by the *librarii depositorum*. The titles of the various headquarters staff of any unit may have differed from province to province and changed over time, so historians are presented with a plethora of titles, some of which may be contemporary synonyms, and others which perhaps went out of use in favour of a new title imposed at a later time, so that at first sight it seems that there were two different types of staff in charge of different tasks, when in fact there was only one task organised by staff with different labels that were current at different times.

There would be cash kept at forts for a variety of purposes. In the headquarters or *principia* of Roman forts there was usually a strongroom underground like a cellar, where it is assumed that money would be kept, probably in chests, and presumably guarded at all times. A famous example of an underground strongroom can be seen at the fort of Chesters on Hadrian's Wall, with a barrel vault roof and steps leading down into the small room. When it was excavated in the nineteenth century, the wooden door was still intact, but the techniques for preserving wood were unknown and it crumbled. At the fort of Housesteads on the Wall, the strongroom was not underground because the fort was built on solid rock.

In the legions, the *aquilifer* who carried the eagle standard was responsible for the pay chest. In auxiliary units the standard-bearers may have had similar duties. When a pay parade was due, this probably involved calculating how much surplus was already in the fort's coffers, and how much extra would be required, and then requesting cash to be sent from the procurator's office to cover the necessary amounts. A collection of letters survives, detailing large amounts of money to be transported to military units in Egypt, 73,000 *denarii* for the soldiers of an *ala*, 65,000 *denarii* for the men of a cohort, and 343,000 *denarii* for legionaries. Military escorts were sent to transport the pay. There is evidence that a convoy of soldiers from Dura Europos in Syria also performed this task in the third century AD.

Flavius Josephus in *The Jewish War* describes a Roman pay parade during the war in Judaea. This particular pomp and ceremony was arranged to impress the Judaeans, but perhaps describes the normal procedure at most pay parades, when the money due to each man was counted out. Certain deductions were made, for food, clothes, weapons, armour, personal savings, and for the burial club. Tacitus lists the grievances of a soldier called Percennius, who complained that out of his salary he had to pay for clothing, weapons, and tents, and also had to find money to bribe the centurions to avoid doing extra fatigues or to obtain leave. The latter payment was taken on by the more kindly emperors after the short-lived Emperor Otho started to pay centurions *vacationes munerum* to cover this little unofficial privilege.

Papyrus records show that while some deductions from military pay such as those for food were standard, other deductions varied. This discrepancy would probably arise because the first deductions for weapons and armour need not be repeated for some considerable time, unless the soldier had lost or damaged some of his equipment, and some deductions would be seasonal, perhaps for special celebrations. The famous papyrus from the double fortress of Nicopolis in Egypt itemises the deductions from the military pay of two Roman citizen soldiers,

Quintus Julius Proculus and Gaius Valerius Germanus. The record covers all three instalments (*stipendia*) for each man in January, May and September 81, shortly before Domitian awarded his 33 per cent pay rise. Unfortunately no unit is named, so it cannot be said that they are legionaries or auxiliaries. The soldiers were Roman citizens, but this does not preclude the possibility that the papyrus concerns auxiliary pay, since it is known that citizens did serve in the *auxilia*, and there were auxiliary soldiers with the legion at Nicopolis. The suggestion that the two soldiers belonged to an auxiliary unit is supported by the fact that the amounts paid to them on each payday, in Greek *drachmae* as was common in the eastern provinces, does not approximate to the seventy-five *denarii* that legionaries would have been paid at each of the three paydays in 81. This bears out the theory that auxiliaries must have been paid less that the legionaries. There are further complications in that it is not clear whether the men were infantry or cavalry.

Taken from a purely administrative point of view, and regardless of the legionary/auxiliary debate, the information in the papyrus is important because it reveals how the records were kept and how deductions were taken from each man's pay. On each of the three paydays the two soldiers were charged eighty *drachmae* for food (*in victum*), twelve *drachmae* for boots and socks or leggings (*caligas fascias*), and ten *drachmae* for hay (*faenaria*). The hay poses no problems if the men were either legionary or auxiliary cavalrymen, but since it has been argued that they were serving in an auxiliary infantry unit, the hay has to be interpreted as bedding, despite the fact that the Romans were perfectly capable of making stuffed mattresses. The men were charged for hay as the first item to be deducted on each of their three paydays, before their own food at eighty *drachmae* so at a pinch it could be said that the two food items, for the horse and for the man, were classified together.

There were other deductions from each of the three instalments, the first one in January being twenty *drachmae* for the camp Saturnalia, possibly a mess bill for the holiday celebrations held in the previous December. From the second instalment, both soldiers paid out four *drachmae* to the standards (*ad signum*), which may have been a contribution to the burial fund which was looked after by the standard-bearers, and on the third payday the two men were charged 145½ *drachmae* for clothing. Since there are no comparable records revealing such minute detail, it is impossible to say whether this was typical of all units in all provinces.

There was a savings bank system where the soldiers could deposit money, though the amounts were probably paper figures rather than actual cash, recorded by the *librarii depositorum*. It is known that Domitian set a limit on the amount of savings in cash that any soldier could keep inside the fort, allegedly not more than 1,000 *sestertii*, so if any soldiers managed to save more than this the balance was probably recorded as a paper figure, and reimbursed in cash when the soldier finally retired. This measure of Domitian's was brought into force after the governor Saturninus attempted to usurp him in 89, gathering together the soldiers from the double legionary fortress of Mogontiacum (modern Mainz), and presumably with their consent, extracting all their combined savings to finance his venture. The unfortunate soldiers who accompanied Saturninus would lose either their lives or their savings, which may have discouraged other legionaries from joining in attempted rebellions.

When the soldiers were due to retire and needed to withdraw their savings, the final totals would be calculated and money to cover the payments would be requested from the procurator who was responsible for military pay. The military records were scrupulously kept by the clerks. At each pay parade the records would show how much money each soldier had already saved, how much he had deposited from his current instalment, and the new total in the regimental savings bank. The Roman clerical assistants would keep at least two sets of financial records, since their accounts were sent to the procurator.

Supply

The Romans of the Republic learned about supply systems empirically, from their experiences in several wars. During the long struggle with Hannibal the Carthaginians constantly raided and destroyed crops, so valuable supplies were denied to the Romans. Until they had secured Sicily and Sardinia, the Romans had to buy grain at tremendously inflated prices from Egypt and then had to guarantee its transport, protecting their sea lanes and above all their ports and the roads leading from them to the interior.

The wars with Carthage placed the Romans on a rapid learning curve with regard to all aspects of war, and in particular about supplies. After the disaster of Cannae and the efforts of Hannibal to seduce or force the Italian cities away from their alliances with Rome, the city of Capua defected, and was besieged from 212 to 211 BC. Livy describes how the Romans secured their supply lines to provide for two consular armies, by establishing a depot for the collection of grain at Casilinum, north of Capua, and building a new fortification at the mouth of the Volturno river, covering the routes from the west. In the south the general Fabius Maximus fortified the port of Puteoli to ensure the delivery of supplies for the armies in Campania.

When the Romans went abroad to fight they fared less well. During the first invasion of Sicily their supply lines were not fully operational, and in Spain, Gnaeus and Publius Scipio complained of the lack of supplies. Special despatches of clothing and provisions were hastily arranged by the Senate, but there was a scandal when the Romans experimented with the use of contractors, who failed to deliver what they had promised. The problem of supplies in Spain had not changed much by the time Pompey the Great arrived there, and he wrote in desperation to the Senate complaining that he had used his own money to buy food and other supplies for his armies. It should be noted that it is particularly difficult to maintain an invading army in Spain; as Henri IV of France pointed out, it is a country where small armies are defeated and large ones starve, so the Spanish experience is perhaps not wholly representative of the problems of supplying Roman armies campaigning abroad.

The Romans obtained all their needs by a variety of means, including food and water for the soldiers and animals, fuel for campfires and cooking, and all the materials that an army needs such as clothing, harness and all kinds of equipment. During peacetime, there was a regular supply system using the well-established roads of the Empire to bring in produce and materials from near and far, though at Vindolanda in northern England a letter survives explaining that delivery of some hides that had been requested was held up because the roads were in very bad condition, and trying to transport anything would probably cause harm to the animals. On campaign the soldiers relied on a combination of foraging, requisitioning (bordering on pillage), and supply lines. The works of Caesar are particularly illuminating with regard to supplies and how they were obtained, transported, and guarded. Appropriation of other people's crops was common while on campaign. In the *Gallic War* Caesar recounts how he captured the stores at Avaricum and later how he captured the stores of the Bituriges. Flavius Josephus refers to sickles carried by the soldiers, and Tacitus says that Corbulo's troops harvested the crops when they reached cultivated land. On the other hand, Domitian ordered that everything should be paid for when he marched against the Chatti in Germany.

There is some debate as to how much the soldiers were expected to carry on the march. Josephus in *The Jewish War* says that the Romans carried food supplies for three days. In later periods this may have increased. In the *Historia Augusta* it is claimed that in the early third century Severus Alexander provided supply dumps for his troops, so that they did not have to carry supplies for the usual period of seventeen days. Ammianus Marcellinus, writing in the fourth century, also says that it was normal practice for soldiers to carry rations (*annona*) to last seventeen days, which is corroborated by a decree of Constantius II when he was preparing for a campaign in the fourth century. Much depends upon the type of food that was carried; it has been suggested that some of it may have been in biscuit form, which weighed less than grain.

With the growth of the Empire the supply system had to evolve in order to provide for thousands of soldiers, horses, and pack animals stationed in permanent forts and fortresses in most of the provinces. The tried and tested methods of supplying an army at war were still relevant, since even when the frontiers were established, the Romans did not abandon offensive or defensive campaigns, where foraging and supply lines were necessary, but for the troops stationed in the provinces foraging was not suitable because apart from upsetting the inhabitants, one expedition would exhaust supplies from the particular area where the foraging was done, so other methods were necessary, combining the transport of food and other supplies over long distances, even from other provinces, requisitioning supplies from the local area, and growing crops and raising animals on military lands.

The Romans were quite capable of long-distance transport of goods. Apart from the shipments of grain to feed the population of Rome, there are documented cases where the produce of one province was shipped or carried to another province. Dio records that the governor of the Spanish province of Baetica was responsible for gathering and transporting grain to Africa across the straits of Gibraltar, and grain from Britain was shipped to the Rhine for the army of the German provinces, a procedure which seems to have lapsed until the Emperor Julian revived it in the fourth century. Conversely, analysis of grain from South Shields in northern England showed that it probably came from the Netherlands. Supplies were carried by ships along the Danube, as attested in the duty roster of *cohors I Hispanorum Veterana equitata*, which records that some soldiers had been sent to the grain ships (*ad naves frumentarias*).

Local provision was probably the most widely used method of supplying the armies with food. The produce to be purchased was estimated by the provincial governor and a fixed price was set for foodstuffs destined for the army. Collection was sometimes carried out by the military authorities, or by the procurator and his staff where relevant, or by the local townsmen or tribal leaders in the areas where the requisitioning was carried out. Transport of goods to the Roman army could involve town councillors in considerable expense, and in the later Empire a case is on record where the unfortunate men who had been delegated to provide and transport supplies for the soldiers simply ran away because of the expense of carrying goods over long distances. Papyrus records show that soldiers were detailed to collect barley, noted in duty rosters and reports as *ad hordeum*, to the barley. This was normally used to feed the horses. Cavalrymen were given a hay allowance in cash for which they signed receipts, which may mean that that they supplemented the horses' feed by buying hay from the civilian population when it was available, but it is also suggested that this cash was given to the men out of the annual allowance for hay when their horses were at grass. It has been claimed that the military presence stimulated provincial agriculture, providing an incentive to grow more crops than would normally have been necessary just to feed the natives. In northern Britain it has been suggested that the highland zones, more notable today for stock-raising than for agriculture, could have produced more grain than hitherto imagined, enabling the army in the hinterland of Hadrian's Wall to provision itself from sources close to home.

It is also known that the army grew some of its own food, and although this would not have been enough to provide food for an entire unit it would help to offset costs of buying food on the open market if the forts were near larger towns, and in remote areas with no organised markets the food grown by the soldiers would be a welcome addition to the diet. Tacitus refers to fields set aside for the use of the soldiers, and at Newstead in southern Scotland sickles were found inside the fort. They had been well used and repaired. An inscription mentions a detachment that was sent to make hay, and a soldier from *cohors I Hispanorum Veterana* was sent across the Danube 'to defend the crops'. The accumulated evidence indicates that the soldiers guarded and harvested crops, but of course there is no proof that all these crops were always grown on lands that belonged to the army, or that the harvest of crops concerned the army's own agricultural efforts.

It is attested that Roman auxiliary forts and legionary fortresses were surrounded by clearly demarcated lands that were owned and administered by the army, usually designated by the terms *prata* and *territorium*. In Spain, two inscribed boundary stones marked the division between the *prata legionis* of *legio IV* and the lands of the civilian settlements of Juliobriga and Segisama, and another inscribed stone from Dalmatia attests to a boundary between a private estate and the *prata legionis* at the settlement of Burnum. The legion had moved from Burnum, but it is probable that the military authorities still regarded the land as theirs. In Britain, an auxiliary cavalry unit claimed the land at Chester-le-Street seemingly after it had been absent for a while, but the term used is *territorium*, not *prata*. There is considerable debate about the exact meanings of *territorium* and *prata*, and how they related to each other. It is probable that *territorium* refers to all the lands administered by the military authorities, and *prata* refers to only a part of the whole. Strictly interpreted, *prata* ought to refer to meadows, perhaps for grazing animals and for producing hay. There were obviously some differences between the two terms as far as the army was concerned, and although these differences are not clear to modern audiences, the main point is that the military authorities owned lands, which they could use as they wished, not necessarily for growing crops. An inscription from Aquincum records building work on the *territorium legionis* of *legio II Adiutrix* in the reign of Severus Alexander.

Food was stored inside the forts in specially constructed granaries, usually sited next to the *principia* or headquarters building. In early forts they would usually be built of wood, leaving only a trace of their post holes, but the stone-built granaries are usually immediately recognisable from their ground plans. The walls were reinforced by evenly spaced buttresses, and the stone-flagged floors were usually raised on pillars, to facilitate the circulation of air, and to prevent rats and mice from reaching the stores. It is not known whether the grain and other produce were stored in bins, or in sacks which could be stacked up on the floor, or laid on shelves. There was probably a particular day when grain rations were given out to each *contubernium*, as both Livy and Caesar refer to distribution days for rations, but this may only concern an army on campaign. In the legions one man from each *contubernium* or tent group would collect the grain for himself and his companions, grind it, and bake the bread in ovens built into the earth backing of the ramparts. One of the best locations where this can be seen is Caerleon in South Wales, where the circular stone bases of ovens in the rampart back have been excavated and consolidated.

In the later Empire, payments to the army were made partly or wholly in rations instead of cash, under a system that is not fully understood, known as the *annona militaris*. Some scholars suggest that this could have begun as early as the reign of Trajan. A large part of the food supply of Rome was levied as a tax in kind administered by an equestrian with the title *Praefectus Annonae*, so it is possible that the system was extended or diverted to feed the army, but this remains hypothetical.

Under the heading of supplies, an ever-present need of any army is for water and for fuel. The water supply of several forts has been studied in Britain and Germany, where storage tanks, extensive lead piping, and sophisticated bathing establishments are well known. On campaign, lack of an adequate water supply could shift the balance between success and failure, especially for cavalry operations. Fuel consumption in a Roman fort or fortress will have been vast. Caesar regarded shortage of wood for campfires as seriously as shortage of food itself, and in the case of the Roman Imperial army huge amounts of timber would be needed for cooking, for central heating in officers' houses and in some headquarters buildings, and most of all for heating the baths that were attached to all forts. The Romans distinguished between timber for building and wood for fuel which was called *lignum*; foraging for fuel was termed *lignari*. The papyrus records of *cohors XX Palmyrenorum* at Dura Europos in Syria show that in the early third century Zebidas son of Barneus, from the century of Nigrinus, had been sent to gather fuel for the baths (*missus lignari balnei*). There is some evidence from Britain that the Romans used coal for fuel, as they certainly did at the temple complex at Bath, where an ancient author says that when burned down the fuel did not go to ash but remained in lumps like rock, by which he most likely meant cinders.

The army made its own roofing tiles and also some of its pottery for cooking and eating and drinking, but pottery studies indicate that the army was one of the largest consumers of pottery manufactured in civilian factories. Some of the pottery on military sites was transported over long distances. In the early days after the conquest of Britain, Italian red pottery dominated, but Italian wares were soon overtaken by the Samian wares produced in southern Gaul, then in central Gaul. The useful habit of stamping the pottery with manufacturers' marks helps to date the vessels and to locate the places where they were made, but even in the absence of these stamps, it is still possible to identify where the pots came from by studying the shapes of the vessels, the decorations, and the type of clay. Though the army operated its own pottery workshops, the presence of a ready market encouraged civilians to set up factories near to the forts where there were accessible sources of clay, and sometimes when the army units moved on, the potteries survived and found civilian markets.

In the age of expansion of the Empire, when the Romans took over a new province they were quick to exploit resources of minerals and metals. Large quantities of lead were required for the plumbing in forts, and for the baths outside forts. The army would require large quantities of iron, which ideally would be mostly worked in the province where the units were stationed and perhaps transported direct to the fort workshops. The greater part of the arms and armour required for the army may have been manufactured and repaired in military workshops (*fabricae*), which are known to exist in some forts and presumed to exist in forts that have not been excavated. Among the specialists in the army designated as *immunes* there are metalworkers, smiths, and other craftsmen who could have performed all the necessary tasks in arms manufacture, at least on a scale to cope with peacetime demands. There were stores in some of the larger forts, called *armentaria* where spares could be kept, and in the military units it is known that there were *custodes armarum* who looked after a unit's arms. Soldiers could and did buy weapons and armour from civilian manufacturers, so that there was considerable variation in the appearance and equipment in the Roman army, much more than in modern armies where uniformity is the norm. The private manufacturers would probably supply large numbers of weapons and armour when campaigns were being prepared, and it is known that on occasion civilian factories were supervised by legionaries.

The army would have used enormous amounts of leather, to make straps for amour, footwear, belts, harness and saddles, and large quantities were used to make military tents. Some of the leather probably came from the livestock belonging to the army. Animals would be kept for food in the lands around the fort, and some would be brought in for sacrifice at various religious festivals, and perhaps the skins were used and the meat was eaten even though the animal had been sacrificed to a god or goddess. The disposal of horses belonging to the army may also have provided skins. A letter mentioned above from Vindolanda concerns the delivery of hides, though it is not clear from which animals. In the correspondence there would be no need to explain where it came from and what it was to be used for. Perhaps the most important source of leather in the western provinces, at least during the early Empire, was from the Frisian tribes, who paid their taxes in ox hides.

The supply of textiles and clothing for the army probably depended on local manufacturers, or at least civilian operatives within the province, although according to a papyrus strength report found in Egypt, but concerning the part-mounted *cohors I Hispanorum Veteranorum* based at Stobi in Macedonia, some soldiers were sent to Gaul to collect clothing. This is not the only example of clothing being obtained from a province for soldiers based in another province. An order for military clothing survives on a papyrus document from Egypt dated to AD 138. The weavers of Philadelphia were to make various items for the soldiers in Cappadocia. Each item was carefully listed with dimensions and weights. Among other items, four white Syrian cloaks were to be made, eight feet eight inches long and five feet eight inches wide, weighing three pounds and six ounces, and a plain white blanket was to be supplied for the hospital in the fort. The advance payments for each item are listed with the instructions detailing the size and weight, and a running total was kept. Then extra instructions follow the list, stating that the clothes were to be made of soft white wool with no stains, woven firmly, and the hems were to be properly finished. The money was to be paid by the state for these items, and when they reached the soldiers in Cappadocia the men would have some of their wages deducted to cover the whole or part of the costs. There may have been standard figures drawn from soldiers' pay for clothing, depending on what was issued, since Quintus Julius Proculus and Gaius Valerius Germanus of an unknown unit at Nicopolis in Egypt were both charged 145 and a half *drachmae* for clothing in the third instalment of their pay in AD 81. On the other hand Germanus had already paid 100 *drachmae* out of his first instalment, so the question of whether soldiers paid the full price is not resolved, nor is it certain how soldiers would request clothing. They probably had to approach their officers, who would collate the lists of required clothing and then pass it on to more senior officers, and then to the office of the procurator, who would authorise the requests and place the orders, but this is speculative.

Transport and Logistics

The military leaders of Imperial Rome could draw on two or three centuries of experience of moving armies from place to place with all their equipment, clothing, tools, artillery, food, horses, draught animals and fodder. Logistical systems developed empirically from Republican times, with a sharp boost during the Punic wars. Early Roman campaigns were mostly annual affairs, and took place not too far from home. Soldiers supplied their own equipment and probably carried most of it, and since they had only to provide food for the summer months and then went home for the harvest, the problems of supplying the army were not as complicated as they later became, when the army had to remain under arms for the winter.

With the growth of Roman influence over a wider and wider extent of territory, wars lengthened in duration and were fought further away from the city and the homes of the allies, eventually extending to Roman armies operating outside Italy. The Romans were forced to develop a more sophisticated supply and transport system in the protracted wars with Hannibal, because their crops and those of their allies were commandeered or destroyed, necessitating the import of food from abroad, for instance from Sardinia. In turn this meant creating fortified harbours, such as Puteoli and Ostia, where grain could be landed safely and then transported under guard into fortified bases.

By the early Empire Roman generals were accustomed to the difficulties of moving armies across seas and establishing themselves in other countries, and of operating in different types of terrain and keeping themselves supplied with food, fuel, equipment, weapons, clothing and tools. Despite their experience in the Punic wars, the later Republican commanders still encountered some problems in supplying their armies, not necessarily from lack of expertise but in faulty administration and application of funds. Roman armies had at their disposal a variety of means of obtaining and transporting food and equipment, using supply lines overland, or by sea from other provinces, and in the war zone itself they obtained supplies of all kinds by foraging, requisition, and pillage, all three shading off almost seamlessly into one another. The Romans did not make regular use of sutlers or merchants as a general means of provision, except perhaps in immediate emergencies. An experiment in using contractors to supply the armies in Spain in the later Republic was quickly abandoned because it did not work. Whenever practical, the Romans made agreements with their allied princes and chieftains to provide food, for instance in Sicily, the natives brought provisions to the Romans in 262 BC when the Carthaginians prevented them from foraging, and Caesar allied with Gallic tribes such as the Aedui and the Remi, who provided his troops with grain and foodstuffs.

The details of the logistical systems of the Empire are not fully elucidated in any source, but Caesar's works furnish one of the best sources, since he took care over his supplies and transport, and mentioned the subject frequently. Since Caesar stands on the cusp of the late Republican and early Imperial armies, some of the information can be used to reconstruct the logistics of the Imperial period. In Caesar's day, while the army was on the move there were opportunities to find food supplies for men and animals by foraging. Food and equipment was carried with the army either by the men themselves, or by pack animals, or in carts and wagons. During the winters, a large campaign army had to disperse to live, so a great deal of the Republican general's time was taken up in finding winter quarters (*hibernae*), and bringing in supplies to see the army through till spring. Sometimes the winter quarters were in towns where stores were already built up, and at other times the army wintered in purpose-built camps. In both of these situations the soldiers could observe the enemy and guard against attacks. Caesar left Marcus Crassus in command at Samarobriva (modern Amiens) with one legion, where he also left the baggage of the army (*impedimenta exercitus*), hostages from various tribes, some of his documents, and the winter supplies (*frumenta*).

With regard to logistics and transport, the main difference between the Republican and Imperial armies is that until the development of the standing army under Augustus and his successors, there were no permanent bases for the troops. As the Empire expanded, the forts and fortresses gradually percolated to the periphery, and finally in the second century the running barriers and frontier roads were established. Military operations thereafter were conducted within the provinces to squash rebellions or to repulse invasions, or expeditions were mounted beyond the frontiers in pre-emptive strikes or punitive campaigns. Only in the latter case did the wars resemble those of Caesar in Gaul or the civil wars of the late Republic, creating the need for temporary bases to house some of the troops through the winter while the bulk of the army probably returned to their frontier forts.

Most of the information about logistics in the Roman army is derived from the supply systems of the peacetime army based in the provinces or on the frontiers, but long-distance transport did not worry the administrators. The supply and transport systems of the provincial armies worked well, but would not be able to support major campaigns mounted by the emperors. Although the soldiers of each unit would have been provided with carts and wagons, and pack animals (*iumenta*) such as mules, donkeys, and (in the eastern provinces) camels, complete with their harness and saddles, many more animals and vehicles would be needed for a campaign. Carts and wagons could be manufactured, purchased, requisitioned with a promise of payment, or simply seized, and pack animals could be assembled from private owners, paid or unpaid. In some cases private ship-owners (*navicularii*) were necessary if transport overseas or along navigable rivers was envisaged. How this vast assembly of supplies and the means of transporting them was achieved is not completely elucidated. The *Praefectus Annonae* would be in charge of organising and transporting supplies of all kinds, but there seems to have been no vast stores of weapons and armour or other equipment kept in readiness for campaigns, so some scholars think that each emperor who planned a campaign beyond the frontiers had to assemble all his needs from scratch. Slightly more surviving information as to what it required and what it carried remains from the time after the army had been assembled there, but the evidence is uncoordinated, derived as it is from a variety of different sources from different periods.

A primary requirement in the study of logistics is to try to establish how much of each commodity would be carried and what it would weigh, but there are divergent estimates of how much food and equipment was required on campaign, and how all these items were obtained and transported. Like other campaigning armies, the Romans carried with them not only their food, fodder, and drink, but also the means of harvesting crops, hunting animals, processing, cooking and eating food, and vessels for drinking water, wine, and beer. They also carried weapons, clothing, and personal effects; then there would be tools for entrenching, for timber felling, and for mending wagons and carts; there were tents made of leather, one for each *contubernium* of eight men, field artillery for each century, and the army siege train consisting of larger artillery if cities and citadels were to be stormed. This list is by no means complete.

The terms used by the ancient authors for food supply are most frequently *frumentum*, commonly found in Caesar's accounts, meaning the grain supply but occasionally applied to food in general, and less commonly *cibaria*, which strictly speaking refers to non-grain food, but can stand in for all food stocks. In working out how much food the soldiers would consume, some facts and figures are available in the literary sources, but only succeed in confusing the issue, because exact equivalents of ancient weights and quantities depend on interpretation. The amounts of wheat that were necessary over a specified period for an entire legion on the one hand, or an individual soldier on the other, have been investigated by several modern scholars. Using Greek measures, Polybius says that the Roman and allied infantrymen received about one third of a *medimnus* of wheat per month, while the Roman cavalry received two *medimni* of wheat, plus seven *medimni* of barley, and the allied cavalry slightly less, receiving only one and a half measures of wheat and five of barley. These amounts have been translated from the Greek into Roman measure, and then into modern equivalents, and consumption of wheat has been estimated in various ways. J. P. Roth has converted Polybius' figures of one third of an Attic *medimnus* per month for a soldier into Roman *modii*, estimating that one legion required 600 *modii* of wheat every day. In terms of modern measures, it is estimated that one legion would require 500 bushels every week. Estimating acreage rather than weight, Le Bohec suggests that one legion would consume the produce of twenty acres in six days, while Goldsworthy rounds down a legion to 5,000 men, and estimates that consumption was probably higher, requiring the produce of ten acres each day.

J. P. Roth assumes that the same ration scales for grain or bread apply equally to legionaries and auxiliaries, and points out that the amount of bread allowed for soldiers did not vary over seven centuries: the ration that Polybius sets for the Republican army is the same as the ration for the Roman army of the sixth century AD. Apart from grain, the archaeological and literary sources reveal that the Roman soldiers ate a large quantity of pork. During the Republic salt pork was exported from Italy to campaign armies overseas. Like other soldiers of all periods the Romans ate any other meat that they could find by requisition or by hunting. Bones from military sites show that beef and mutton formed part of the diet, and Lepidus' army in the campaign against Mithradates ate venison and hare. Lentils and beans are also attested, along with cheese (*caseus*), salt, vinegar and sour wine (*acetum*), which was mixed with water to form a drink known as *posca*. Vintage wine was not unknown, but was usually watered down, and in the Celtic provinces of the west, soldiers also drank beer (*cervesa*). The search for water for soldiers and animals would be a constant need, and in some cases water had to be carried in skins (*utres*). When he was besieging a desert town in Africa in 107 BC Marius transported skins of water by pack trains, and Pompey resorted to the same technique in the Mithradatic war, using pack animals to carry 10,000 skins of water. Where it was possible, liquids were probably transported in barrels. One of the scenes at the base of Trajan's Column shows barrels being unloaded from a ship, but it is not possible to discern what they contained.

Horses and pack animals require different amounts of dry fodder such as barley and oats, and green fodder such as grass, clover and vetch. Horses require the most food, but they are far more fussy about what they will and will not eat compared to mules and donkeys, which can survive on smaller quantities and worse quality foods. Oxen are easier still to feed since their digestive systems allow them to extract more sustenance from the foods they eat. However, many authors have wrestled with the conundrum that the more pack animals the army takes on campaign, the more food the pack animals need, therefore more food has to be carried or found on the march. When they are working hard, horses strictly need increased rations, but on campaign they would not necessarily receive the recommended amounts or even the correct kinds of food; Caesar's troops fed their horses on seaweed in the African campaign, but this was not such an outlandish idea since seaweed supplements are given to horses in modern times.

There are scant references to fodder in the ancient sources. According to Polybius a Roman cavalry soldier of the Republic received seven *medimni* of barley per month for his horse, while an allied cavalryman received only five *medimni*. It has been estimated that since the Republican cavalrymen were expected to maintain three horses, the rations must have been divided, and by translating the Greek measures first into Latin equivalents and then into English, it is estimated that each horse was allowed one and a half kilos or three and a half pounds of barley per day. The only evidence that shows how much barley was actually delivered to an *ala* is found in a papyrus from Egypt, dating to 187, when a *duplicarius* from the *ala Heracliana* received 20,000 *artabai* for the horses of his unit. Walker linked this with a sixth century papyrus showing that each horse was allowed one tenth of an *artaba* per day, so the rations received by the *ala*

Heracliana would feed 548 horses for a year. Horses and pack animals would also need hay. Ann Hyland estimates that each horse would require four and a half kilos or ten pounds of hay per day. In Egypt a receipt has been preserved on papyrus for hay for the *turma* of Donacianus in the *ala Veterana Gallica* in130, and other papyri show that the cavalrymen received hay money to the tune of twenty-five *denarii* for the year. This money was perhaps paid to the men when their horses were put out to pasture, just as the eighteenth century British army allowed 365 days forage ration, but paid the surplus cash to the men when the horses were at grass. During campaigns, foragers would have to find hay, and at Batnae in AD 363 this proved a fatal enterprise, when soldiers started to remove hay from a stack, which fell down and killed about fifty men.

Transportation of all the requirements of a campaign army was a major consideration for Roman generals, who were reliant upon the carrying power of the soldiers and pack animals, and the capacity of vehicles drawn by oxen or mules. The difficulties of transporting the food supplies worried Caesar in the winter of 52 BC, but he was forced to move and take some of the troops out of winter quarters sooner than he would have wished, because he had to protect his allies from attack by other Gauls, in case revolt spread. He asked his allies from the Aedui to take care of the transport of food, but does not say how they accomplished their task. Even if supplies were delivered in ships, the goods had to be carried from the coast or the river banks by the same means, using men, animals, carts and wagons. On campaign, most of the food for men and animals would have to be stored in magazines and transported along supply lines, or alternatively the army carried lesser amounts and when it ran out they foraged and requisitioned supplies at regular intervals. J. P. Roth considers the use of supply lines as routine for the Romans and assembles an impressive array of evidence for them. The general model was to establish an operational base, often in a port, then to gather stores of all kinds, not just food supplies but equipment and clothing. From this base the supplies would be brought to a distribution point in the war zone, usually a fortified camp, and as the army moved forwards so would the fortified camps and stores. In some cases the old bases could still serve as stores and food dumps to relay supplies to the war zone. The forts along the river Lippe in Germany at Holsterhausen, Haltern, Oberaden and Anreppen have been identified as bases used to supply the armies of Drusus and Tiberius as they advanced into Germany in the early first century AD. The use of operational and forward bases was adopted in the Republic and is demonstrated in Caesar's operations, particularly in the Gallic war, and the system was retained without much alteration in the campaigns of the Empire. While campaigning in Britain in the early third century, Severus created supply bases at South Shields on the River Tyne, and other bases on the River Forth and the River Tay so that provisions could be brought in by sea to be stored and distributed from these bases.

How much the soldiers carried has been variously estimated. Vegetius says that the soldier's pack (*sarcina*) weighed sixty Roman pounds, but it is not known precisely what the average soldier carried in the pack. Josephus refers to three days rations carried by each man, but this concerns Vespasian's campaigns, and is not to be taken as a standard procedure applicable to other armies at other times. It is not known how much clothing and personal equipment each soldier would carry himself, but the men probably accrued a surplus and the officers perhaps accrued even more. Generals such as Marius who wanted to move rapidly found it expedient to strip the army of its camp followers and unnecessary baggage, and they probably reduced the personal items that each man was allowed to carry. Scipio Aemilianus decreed that his men should take with them only the barest essentials for cooking and drinking. This probably did not apply to all campaigns. The high-quality finds from the Agricolan base at Elginhaugh in

Scotland show that soldiers and especially officers on campaign did not lead a Spartan existence when it came to personal possessions and equipment.

As well as food and personal baggage the soldiers also carried tools, in particular entrenching tools for making camp. Josephus enumerates the items carried by the men: an axe, a saw, a sickle, a basket, a spade, a rope and a chain. At least some of the men presumably carried these on the march, since Caesar recounts an instance where the soldiers were already entrenching the camp when the baggage train arrived, which implies that the tools were not carried on carts with the baggage but by the men themselves as they marched, unless they had managed to commandeer a wheeled vehicle and an animal to pull it. Those who were assigned to camp building had to get to the site before the rest of the army. It is possible that the tools were issued to the *contubernium* and only certain men were picked for entrenching duty by rota, rather than that the entire force carried their tools at all times.

Some of the items needed by the whole *contubernium* would be included with the baggage train. Surplus tools, the cooking pots, the hand mill for grinding grain, and especially the eight-man tent, would have been carried on a mule or perhaps two mules, but no source states how many mules were allowed per *contubernium*; most likely it varied according to the supply of pack animals and the personal enterprise of the soldiers. The number of pack animals and vehicles required to carry the baggage of an army on campaign was staggering. The animals not only carried goods on their backs but draft animals were needed to pull the carts and wagons of the baggage trains and the siege trains. The baggage train was aptly named by the Romans as *impedimenta*, and would include the food stores over and above the amounts that each soldier carried, and the equipment that was not needed on the march, such as the bridge building materials described by Vegetius, who says that an expeditionary army carried with it hollowed logs, planks, cables and iron nails. Goldsworthy estimates that at least 640 animals would be required for the baggage of one legion, as well as fifty nine carts and ten wagons for the field artillery, which was part of the baggage of each century. Vegetius adds that each cohort had a *ballista*. A full siege train would demand even more animals, for instance Plutarch in his biography of Sulla says that 10,000 pairs of mules were needed for Sulla's siege train alone. The size of the siege train obviously depended upon the nature of the war, and siege equipment would not necessarily be taken on every campaign. It is also possible that not all the field artillery pieces would be carried as a matter of routine, but Roman military planners would sometimes have to cope with the maximum load in the baggage train. Josephus counted 160 artillery engines among Vespasian's three legions in Judaea.

The speed of transport by oxen and mules would have been extremely slow, at an average of two miles or three kilometres an hour for ox carts, and a maximum of four miles or six kilometres per hour for pack animals. The men themselves would not be able to march very much faster unless they divested themselves of much of their equipment, and they would not be able to keep up a rapid march day after day. Movement of a campaign army would be tortuous in the extreme and the troops and baggage would cover several miles of road, with the last men reaching the camp long after the entrenching party and the advance guard had established it.

Examples of the transport ships, carts, wagons and pack animals can be seen on Trajan's Column. The ships carrying barrels have already been mentioned, and other vessels are shown transporting items that look like large sacks. In some scenes mules are shown pulling the artillery pieces (*carroballistae*) on two-wheeled carts. Wagons drawn by mules and oxen are shown delivering supplies in a busy section where the soldiers are building a fort and Dacian envoys are being received by Trajan.

The baggage trains required staff to attend to them, and the Roman army appears to have employed slaves, most commonly referred to as *calones*, but other terms are sometimes found in the sources such as *servi*, *mancipia*, or *pueri* in Latin, and in Greek *therapontes* and *oiketai*. The major problem is that no-one can yet answer the question as to whether the slaves belonged to individual soldiers or were corporately employed by the army. Officers certainly brought their own slaves with them on campaign, and in some cases ordinary soldiers possessed slaves too. Roth suggests that soldiers were discouraged from bringing their slaves on campaigns, but he also says that the ruling did nothing to prevent the occurrence, quoting passages from the ancient authors in which separate figures are given for the numbers of soldiers and the numbers of servants captured or killed in battle. The main purpose of the *calones* was to guard the baggage, and in carrying out these duties it is clear that they were not always seen as non-combatants, since Caesar records an incident where the *calones* joined in the battle against the Belgae in Gaul. This presupposes that they carried arms of some kind, and could be distinguished from another category of unarmed servants, who were sometimes labelled *lixae*. Since the terminology is not precisely defined, it is hazardous to state categorically that the *calones* were light armed and the *lixae* were not armed at all, but it is probably safe to argue that they were all the property of the army, subject to military discipline, and were necessary adjuncts to the soldiers in logistics and transportation when an army went on campaign.

Maps and Itineraries

For the study of Roman military history, it is known that the emperors and generals had access to information about major routes, rivers, mountains and other geographical features across the whole Empire. It is not known whether the military commanders used maps to follow provincial routes and boundaries, or to guide them on expeditions beyond the frontiers of the Empire. The Romans drew up lists of routes, noting the forts, towns, settlements and posting stations along them and the distances between the various named features. One of these lists, probably military in origin, is the *Itinerarium Provinciarum Antonini Augusti*, better known as the Antonine Itinerary. In combination with other sources which also provide the names of certain cities, towns and military features, this itinerary greatly assists archaeologists and historians in establishing routes and tracing Roman roads. Occasionally it has been possible to fill in the gaps in knowledge by applying the place names of the Antonine Itinerary to some of the settlements for which there is no other source, and vice versa scholars have been enabled to speculate as to the likely locations of the towns named on specific routes, but which are hitherto unknown in the archaeological record.

How the Romans controlled and administered their vast Empire without the aid of accurate maps can be baffling to modern historians. The evidence for Roman mapping has been studied by Oswald Dilke but he has been criticised for assuming that Roman cartographers drew up their maps in the same way and for the same purposes as modern map makers. The Romans possessed fairly sophisticated geographical knowledge, but it was practical rather than documentary, and found expression in itineraries or lists of places and their distances from their neighbours. Roman surveyors accurately marked out large tracts of land when making military camps or founding colonies and new towns, together with their attendant territories, but they perhaps thought in terms of regions and provinces rather than the whole of the known world. When laying out plots of land their divisions were straight and regular, and the *agrimensores* made plans (*formae*) to represent the allotments. Some sections of a cadastral plan of the Flavian period survive at Orange (ancient Arausio) in France, and in the reign of Severus, the famous marble plan of Rome was produced (*Forma Urbis Romae*), of which many fragments survive, showing instantly recognisable buildings and monuments of the city of Rome in great detail.

Although the Greeks used maps, the Romans do not seem to have produced any of their own until the reign of Augustus, when Marcus Vipsanius Agrippa drew up a world map with a commentary attached, giving measurements. It was placed on the walls of the Portico Vipsania named after Agrippa, but it has not survived, so it is not known what this map looked like. There were no doubt several other maps that have disappeared, and have not been documented as Agrippa's was by Pliny in his *Natural History*. In the second century AD Claudius Ptolemaeus, better known as Ptolemy, wrote his *Geography* in eight books. His interests were wide, extending from geography to astronomy, and he also wrote several astronomical works, the most famous of which is the *Almagest*, containing the theory of astronomy and his own meticulous observations. Ptolemy was probably the first geographer to use longitudinal and latitudinal co-ordinates to pinpoint the places he mentions in his lists, which are contained in books two to seven of his geographical work. It is not known whether he produced maps to accompany the text, but it is clear that he expected his readers to draw their own maps from his instructions. His co-ordinates for Britain produce a notoriously skewed map of Scotland with the northern areas turned through ninety degrees so that they point east to west instead of north to south, and his Mediterranean is too long from east to west, but considering the date of his work it is an extremely worthy contribution to map making.

Some of Ptolemy's information, especially about Britain, was derived from an earlier work by Marinus of Tyre, who is not otherwise known, but who in turn probably derived much of his knowledge from the military expeditions in Scotland under Agricola, when reconnaissance was carried out on land and by sea. At least one civilian, a Greek scholar called Demetrius, took part in this reconnaissance work, as attested by Plutarch, who met him at Tarsus, just after Demetrius had returned from an expedition to Britain in AD 82, when Agricola was preparing for what would eventually be the final battle in Scotland. It is not known whether Agricola had any maps with him, or created new ones, but some of the information that accrued from his military expeditions survives in Ptolemy's *Geography*.

The known Roman maps and geographical lists date from the later Roman Empire. There are only two pictorial examples. One is the so-called Peutinger Table, a thirteenth-century copy of an ancient road map of the lands around the Mediterranean, and the other is a representation of the Black Sea coast on a shield cover from Dura Europos. Neither of these maps is accurate, but presumably both served their intended purpose. The Peutinger Table shows the Mediterranean much as Ptolemy's co-ordinates would show it, elongated from east to west and much too narrow from north to south. Since much of the surviving geographical information from the Roman word takes the form of itineraries, the Peutinger Table is most likely a graphic representation of a list of places and was never meant to achieve cartographic precision. Apart from itineraries, the Romans documented routes pictorially by means of long strips showing the roads and main places and the distances between them, without regard to orientation, in the same way that John Ogilby documented roads in Britain in the seventeenth century. As well as towns and prominent geographical features, the itineraries listed halting places. Vegetius describes route maps (*itineraria picta*) and recommends that generals should use them, implying that they were common enough in his day. These were presumably devoted to short-range expeditions, but with great detail, and much more practical for the army commanders than an attempt to compile and use a map of the entire province or a group of provinces.

Despite the evidence for Roman expertise in surveying, and for the existence of maps and itineraries, the questions about how the military authorities used them cannot be answered. Within a province, the road systems and the frequency of towns and villages might preclude the use of maps for troop movements, and on the frontiers navigating from one fort to another would have been simple enough, but beyond the frontiers men of expertise would be required who knew the routes. Ammianus Marcellinus emphasises the need for native guides beyond the frontiers of the Rhine and Danube. On the other hand, A. D. Lee points out that in the east, the Romans seemed to know their way about, to the extent that the Emperor Julian could use his knowledge to deceive the Persians about which particular route he intended to take, and also had a withdrawal strategy should he need to retreat. It is possible that at provincial headquarters and also in the archives in Rome there were reports of previous commanders who had campaigned in the regions across the frontiers, for instance the information gained on Agricola's campaigns in Scotland was most likely recorded in some form, perhaps even mapped and used to good effect by the Antonine generals who invaded half a century later and again by Severus in 208, but at 2,000 years' distance it is impossible to be sure.

9

Camps, Forts and Fortresses

At the end of each march the Romans traditionally enclosed their troops in an entrenched camp. This practice was instituted at some unknown point during the Republic, but was fully established by the time that Polybius described the Roman army, and it was standard routine during the Empire. Describing the order of march employed by Vespasian in the first century AD, Josephus says that ten men were drawn from each legionary century, carrying their own kit and tools for marking out the camp. Polybius says that flags and spears were planted on the site chosen for the commander's tent or *praetorium*, which stood at the central point of the lines where the tribunes were to camp, and the streets were marked out in relation to the *praetorium*. The elements of the military camp of Polybius are described in the chapters on the Republican army and it would be somewhat tedious to repeat this here.

The only other source besides Polybius that gives any detail about the location of each section of the army in the marching camp is a work in Latin called *De Munitionibus Castrorum*, or *De Metatione Castrorum*, by Hyginus. In the past it was attributed to Hyginus Gromaticus, since it was thought that the author was probably a military surveyor (*gromaticus*). Unfortunately this theory cannot be substantiated, so the work is usually listed as that of Pseudo-Hyginus. The authorship is not the only unsolved problem. More pertinent to the history of the army is the fact that the date of the work is not established. It concerns the layout of a military camp, and the army on the march, but doubts have been expressed as to whether it concerns a real campaign or a hypothetical one. The army that Hyginus describes includes a contingent of Praetorians, three legions, and auxiliary troops of different kinds, including *dromedarii*. Even if the work has a definite historical context, it is not possible to date it closely, since it concerns a campaign when the emperor was present with the army on the Danube, but Hyginus does not specify which emperor or which campaign he is describing. Candidates include Domitian at the end of the first century AD, Trajan at the beginning of the second century, Marcus Aurelius towards the end of the second century, or even the emperors of the third and fourth centuries who conducted punitive campaigns across the Danube. Arguments have been put forward for all these solutions, but no one has proved any theory conclusively.

The work is incomplete, but for all the inherent problems in using it, there is little else that covers the subject in so much detail. Some of the information seems to corroborate the evidence from archaeological excavations, for instance Hyginus indicates that the number of men in the first cohort of the legion was double that of the other cohorts. It is possible that the double first cohort did not apply to all legions, or to all historical periods, but the excavated barracks at some legionary fortresses, including Inchtuthill in Britain, Nijmegen on the Rhine, and Lambaesis in Africa, show that there was accommodation for a double-strength first cohort. There is mention in Hyginus' text of troops which are distinct from the legions and auxiliaries, such as the *nationes* and *symmachiarii*, about which there is no firm knowledge and only speculation; attempts have been made to recognise these troops in archaeological and historical research, and to relate them to the national *numeri*, formed from tribesmen on or near the frontiers, but without solid proof.

The first area to be marked out, according to Hyginus, was the *praetorium* or commander's tent, as in the camp described by Polybius. This tent at the centre of the camp was also the headquarters, combining what would be two buildings in a fort, the *praetorium* as the commander's house, next to the *principia* as the headquarters. The main streets of the camp were marked out in relation to the commanders' tent, the first running across the front of it called the Via Principalis, connecting the two sides' gates in the ramparts that would be built later. These gates were the *porta principalis sinistra* and *porta principalis dextra*, labelled left and right as seen from the Via Principalis looking towards the commander's tent. The other main road started directly opposite the commander's tent, in the centre of the Via Principalis, and running at right angles to it, connecting the headquarters to the main gate, or *porta praetoria*. The road running behind the commander's tent was the Via Quintana with a road at right angles to it leading to the rear gate, or *porta decumana*.

The streets divided the camp into three main areas of unequal size. The centre range was occupied by the commander's tent or *praetorium*, with two areas called *latera praetorii* flanking it on either side, where the commander's staff, the Praetorians and the first cohort of one of the legions would be accommodated. Behind the *praetorium* was the *retentura*, where the tents for some of the legionaries and auxiliaries would be pitched, on either side of the *quaestorium* of the camp prefect. The area in front of it was the *praetentura*, divided into two parts by the Via Praetoria. This area was slightly larger than the *retentura*, containing the tents of the legionary legates and military tribunes, usually placed opposite the *praetorium* with easy access to the commander. The workshop (*fabrica*), the hospital (*valetudinarium*) and the animal hospital (*veterinarium*) were also located in this part of the camp, with the legionaries and auxiliaries.

All around the camp there was a wide road called the Via Sagularis separating the tents from the ramparts by a wide gap, or intervallum, to render it impossible for missiles that might be hurled into the camp to reach the tents. Outside the camp there would be a ditch, from which the turf and earth would be thrown up to construct the ramparts. At some camps, an annexe may have been erected to shelter the wagons and carts. The layout of the camp described by Hyginus was very similar to the layout of legionary fortresses, with the main difference that the centre range in a fort was usually occupied by the headquarters (*principia*), flanked by the commander's house (*praetorium*) and the granaries (*horrea*).

Marching Camps and Temporary Camps

Camps as opposed to permanent forts have been divided into categories for ease of study, comprising marching camps for an army progressing to and from the war zones, and temporary camps of varied size and length of occupation, including winter quarters (*hiberna*). Any attempts at classification always contain some anomalies which do not fit the pattern, but there are of course some criteria applicable to all camps no matter what their purpose. Vegetius and Hyginus describe the most suitable locations for a camp, including the common-sense advice that higher ground with a good view, near to supplies of water, timber and food is best. Marshy ground and areas liable to flood are to be avoided. Other considerations concerning the location of camps would be dependent upon their purpose; some camps were true marching camps, occupied for only one night, while others may have been intended to shelter the army for a few days while the men rested, repaired weapons and harness, made bread, or foraged for supplies. In some places two or three camps have been discovered side by side, or superimposed one on top of another, implying that an army on campaign made more than one visit, which could have occurred as the army passed through in one direction and then returned, or it may reflect the fluid situation of a campaign when more than one unit occupied the site in succession. Where several camps are found in the vicinity of a later permanent fort, such as those outside the fortresses at Haltern and Neuss in Germany, some of them may be temporary camps reflecting the comings and goings of the army while campaigns were conducted, and one or two camps may be construction camps that housed the builders of the fort when it was decided to establish a more permanent installation. Not all camps can be assigned to an army on the march or on campaign.

During the Republic, some camps served a different purpose than those of the Empire. It was customary for opposing armies, either in civil wars between rival Romans, or between Romans and a non-Roman enemy, to entrench themselves in camps close to each other, and sit there for some time, until battle was offered or the food ran out, but this occurred mostly in the civil wars was not a regular part of the military practice of the Empire. Another type of temporary camp is the siege camp, which by its very nature was generally occupied for a considerable time. These were built during the Republic and the Empire. The best known examples from the Republican era are those at Numantia in Spain, which can still be traced on the ground, and the extended siege lines enclosing the various camps of Pompey and Caesar at Dyrrachium, described in the account of the civil wars. In the Empire the best examples are the siege works and camps at Masada in Judaea. Some famous sieges have left little trace of camps, for instance Hatra in modern Iraq was besieged once by Trajan and twice by Severus, without success. The surrounding siege wall which is still visible may be Persian rather than Roman and no camps have been identified for either Trajan's army or for Severus' troops.

Before the establishment of the standing army, which was housed in permanent forts and backed up by a regular supply system, a large campaign army was forced to disperse in winter to live, especially in northern climates. Winter quarters (*hiberna*) for a campaign army were often located in towns, where negotiations could be made with the inhabitants of the region and supplies could be stockpiled, but in hostile territory the Romans sometimes spent the winter in camps, on occasion *sub pellibus*, in tents. During Caesar's conquest of Gaul, Quintus Cicero, younger brother of the orator, was famously besieged in his winter camp. This camp was an earthwork structure with timber towers, 120 of which were put up in one night, using the timber that had been collected 'for the fortification' (*munitionis causa*).

Several of the temporary camps of the later Republic and the early Empire were irregularly shaped, adapted to the natural terrain, but wherever these camps have been partly or fully excavated, the interior layout is usually more or less regular, with blocks allocated for rows of tents and delineated by straight streets. At Numantia and at Masada the soldiers provided more shelter for themselves by piling up stones around their tents, creating a hybrid hut-cum-tent. This fortunate habit, coupled with the hot dry climates in Spain and Judaea where archaeological remains stand the test of time, enables archaeologists to trace the layout of the camp with more precision.

Britain is the province where by far the greatest numbers of marching camps and temporary camps have come to light. There are several different series of camps, not all of them securely dated, but assigned to various likely campaigns that are attested in the sources. A collection of camps across the Pennines leading towards Carlisle, and possibly into southern Scotland, may belong to the campaigns of Petillius Cerialis in the north of England in the AD 70s. Lines of camps on the eastern side of northern England and southern Scotland have been identified, some of them showing remarkable uniformity of size and shape, and spaced at regular distances from each other. A series of medium sized camps has been assigned to the known campaigns of Agricola in the Flavian period, and the larger ones are thought to belong to the Severan expeditionary army of the early third century. There is rarely any dating material for lines of camps such as these, so archaeologists rely on the literary sources to assign the camps to a particular campaign, It is not usually possible to trace the interior layout in these camps, but there is useful evidence about other features, such as the ditches and gateways.

Temporary camps of the later Imperial period were usually more regular than the early versions. They were shaped like a playing card with rounded corners, like permanent forts. A ditch surrounded the perimeter, and the soil from the ditch was thrown inwards to create the rampart. There may have been a palisade on top of the rampart formed from the stakes that soldiers carried, called *valli* in some sources, or *pila muralia* in others. According to Livy, the soldiers of Scipio Aemilianus' army at Numantia each carried seven *valli*. Both Vegetius and Hyginus refer to stakes as part of the defences. The function of the sharpened stakes labelled *pila muralia*, each with an indented hand grip, is debated. If these stakes were placed individually into the earth of the rampart they would not create much of an obstacle, even if they were bound together, but it is suggested that if they were stacked up against each other in groups of three or more to form a standing structure, they could be used to make large caltrops, somewhat like the anti-tank beach defences of the Second World War. No-one can say if this is how the Roman stakes were used.

Inside the temporary camp the road that ran around the perimeter was usually wide enough to keep the rows of tents out of range of projectiles thrown over the walls, and also this road provided a space in which to form up the army if it had to march out to engage in battle immediately. It has been estimated that it would take two to three hours to erect a typical camp, but there are many imponderables, such as the size of the force to be accommodated, the available manpower for building the camp, and the type of earth that the soldiers were expected to dig. The British Army field manuals of the First World War give different estimates for the time it should take to dig a trench or to construct a specified length of earthwork defences, depending upon the nature of the soils. Another factor that might affect the time taken to erect a camp is whether or not the army was under attack at the time of digging the ditches and building the earth ramparts. Examples are known where this did happen, and part of the army drew up in battle formation to shield the workers. It is suggested that the first two lines of the *triplex acies* battle formation protected the men of the third line, who did all the digging, but in reality this was probably not a prescribed formation to be adopted at all times, and the method of defence was probably much more haphazard and flexible. Vegetius says that all the cavalry and part of the infantry should be drawn up in battle lines to protect those building the camp.

Protection of the entrances would always be a problem without solid wooden gates, and apart from mounting a guard, the Romans usually dug a straight ditch and bank (*titulum*) opposite the opening but unconnected to the rampart, or alternatively they placed a curved ditch and bank (*clavicula*) running directly from the rampart outwards and around the gateway like a protective arm, positioned so that any attackers had to turn and expose their unshielded right side to those on the rampart. Some camps had a double *clavicula*, consisting of the outward projecting arm just described, and also an internal one, curving inwards. Full scale attack was never really envisaged in Roman ideology. Camps were not designed to be defended like castles from the tops of the ramparts, but they were intended to stop unauthorised personnel from entering them, and it has also been suggested that one of their purposes was to keep Roman soldiers inside. In the laws of Ruffus there was a severe penalty for soldiers who crossed the camp or fort wall instead of using the gates, and the law was probably applied in whichever direction the soldiers crossed the ramparts.

The Romans attached great importance to training the soldiers to erect temporary camps, and this is illustrated by the presence in Britain of what can only be termed practice camps, because they are generally too small to be of use, and it seems that emphasis was placed upon digging perfect curved corners with accompanying ditches, and the various forms of gateways, with only short stretches of straight wall. Practice camps have been identified in Wales at Llandrindod Common, Castell Collen, and Tomen-y-Mur, and by aerial photography around the fortress at Chester. Such camps leave little trace on the ground, and it is often difficult for modern visitors to find them without a large scale map and a guide book. It is not in doubt that such practice camps existed in other provinces of the Empire, but most likely they have been obliterated by agricultural work or by the spread of roads and buildings.

Probable siege camps in Britain are represented by the examples at Burnswark, near Ecclefechan in southern Scotland. Two large earthwork camps were placed near a native hill fort, one on the north, which was never properly finished, and one on the south, which has been excavated. This large rectangular camp was preceded by a small fortlet, dating to the middle of the second century, which was enclosed within the north-east corner of the earthworks. *Tituli* guard the entrances on the west, east and south sides of the large camp. On the north side facing the hill fort there are three entrances, not shielded by *tituli*, but by three large mounds which would have been used as artillery platforms. In the excavations at the end of the nineteenth century a quantity of lead sling bullets was found. The purpose of the camp has been variously interpreted. The obvious conclusion in the nineteenth century was that the Romans had attacked the hill fort, perhaps during the Antonine advance into Scotland, when Hadrian's Wall had been partly abandoned and was lightly manned by a caretaker garrison. Then after further excavation at Burnswark in the twentieth century it was thought that the hill fort had gone out of use long before the sling bullets were fired at it, so the theory then evolved that this was a practice camp, not just to give the soldiers experience of digging, but to enable the artillerymen to practice shooting, perhaps to hit targets on the hill. Later still, this theory was overturned in favour of the first conclusion, that this camp and the other unfinished one to the north were in fact siege camps and not practice camps. It was not unknown for the native Britons who opposed the Romans to reoccupy old hill forts that had gone out of use, which may have been the case at Burnswark, the possible contexts being the Antonine advance in the 140s and 150s, or the trouble in Britain at the end of the second and the beginning of the third century, when eventually Severus and his two sons based themselves at York and Severus and Caracalla led an expeditionary force to Scotland in a campaign that lasted from 208 to 211. The Burnswark camps may well represent the army in action, since it would have been perfectly feasible to train and exercise the artillerymen on ranges near their own fortresses and forts, rather than marching them miles to the north with a siege train to batter a hill fort with no one inside it. If it was deemed to be necessary to train artillerymen at an actual British Iron Age site, there were other hill forts in Britain which had gone out of use, besides Burnswark.

A series of earthworks in Yorkshire at Cawthorn demonstrates the difficulty of applying a rigid classification to Roman camps. There are four enclosures, consisting of a small rectangular fort built of earth and timber and surrounded by a ditch, an almost oval irregular camp with three external *claviculae* on the east rampart, and two enclosures joined together, one not quite square with substantial earth ramparts on the north, west and south sides, but very much less impressive ramparts on the east side where another enclosure was tacked on to the camp at a later time, also built with less substantial ramparts. The first of these two joined enclosures started out with double *claviculae* protecting the gates, then in a second phase the ramparts were made much larger with only internal *claviculae* at the entrances. There were also two phases of internal buildings. Any ground plan presenting *claviculae* at the entrances would automatically be classified as a temporary camp, but substantial ramparts, two phases of internal buildings and an enclosure added on the east side all suggest a fort with an annexe, even if it was only intended to occupy it for a short time in each phase. Yet there is also a small fort just to the west, which cuts into the irregularly shaped camp with three entrances, and therefore the small fort post-dates this camp. All this construction work took place between 80 and 120. Trying to classify these structures by type is at best hypothetical, and it is even more difficult to identify their purpose within the historical context of what was happening in Roman Britain at this period.

The existence of camps of whatever type suggests the use of tents inside them. On the march, the eight men of a *contubernium* shared one tent, just as they shared a barrack room in their forts. Different styles of Roman tents are depicted on Trajan's Column, one of them with very low walls, others with higher walls and looking a little more elaborate. The differences may simply be a result of artistic licence, or it could be that it was intended to show different tents for soldiers, officers, and perhaps the general or the emperor; this is a question to which no one can provide a definitive answer. Hyginus gives the dimensions of military tents, but there can be no certainty as to whether his information applied to the army at all periods of its existence.

Tents were usually made of leather, and various pieces of leather panels have been discovered from different parts of the Empire, but it was not possible to make anything other than an informed estimate of the structure and size of tents, until the discoveries of full-sized goatskin panels, with evidence of stitching along the edges, at Vindolanda in northern Britain. Carol van Driel Murray, an expert on ancient leather, concluded that at least in Britain if not in other provinces, the Romans used standard panels of different sizes, the largest seventy-six by fifty-two centimetres, smaller ones fifty-two by thirty-eight centimetres. Miscellaneous narrow strips, pieces used as reinforcements, and attachments for the guy ropes, were also identified. It was possible, from a study of the stitching and stretching of the leather panels, to reconstruct the tent, working out previously unknown factors such as the height of the walls and the pitch of the roof. One of the problems concerned the use of guy ropes to support the tent. Hyginus says that these extended only one Roman foot from the tent walls, implying that they were pegged in at an extremely sharp angle that would not give as much support as would ropes pegged much further apart at a more oblique angle. This led to the conclusion that if Hyginus' figures are correct, the tents were probably framed as well, though it has to be admitted that there is no proof for this. Details such as the arrangements for ventilation of the tent, and how the door flaps were arranged and fastened, remain unclear.

Forts and Fortresses

A typical Roman fort of the Imperial period was shaped like a modern playing card, with two short sides and two long sides, and rounded corners. This is the evolved version of a Roman fort, since the earlier fortified camps of the early Empire were not so regularly shaped and were not generally designed as permanent bases for troops. The fort and supply depot at Rödgen in

Germany was ovoid in shape, and three granaries and traces of post holes for the *principia* were found inside. While the early fortress of Haltern was more regular in plan, it does not compare with the later regularly shaped permanent forts of the Empire.

Typically, early Roman forts were built of earth and turf ramparts (called *murus caespiticus*), topped by a timber breastwork, with access via timber-built gateways, usually with towers on either side, which are represented in the archaeological record by four post holes for each tower. There were usually timber interval towers ranged along the walls, and at each corner. Modern reconstructions of these earth and timber defences can be seen at the Lunt fort at Baginton near Coventry, where there is a section of rampart wall and a timber gate, and at Vindolanda south of Hadrian's Wall, where a turf wall and a timber and a stone tower have been built. Both sites are open to the public, and the Lunt has been described as one of the most instructive military sites of Roman Britain. The walls and the gate were built by the Royal Engineers, using turf blocks for the ramparts and timber for the gate towers and breastworks. The major commanding the soldiers said that he would probably be able to construct a whole auxiliary fort within three days, using pre-shaped timbers.

Vegetius gives the ideal dimensions for the turf blocks for the ramparts, and excavations have shown that they were normally one foot by one foot, and one and a half feet thick, Roman measure being slightly shorter than English measure. Experiments show that if the blocks are too small they will not stack so easily, and larger blocks break up too quickly. The turf blocks are likely to do this anyway depending on the friability of the soil and how dry it is. The blocks were usually laid down turf side to turf side, and soil side to soil side, creating bands of alternate soil and turf, which is possibly what the artist and embroiderers of the Bayeux Tapestry intended to convey by the coloured bands of an earthen motte, which would need to be built with the same care as a Roman rampart, most likely with each layer rammed down hard before the next one was laid on top. The Roman tools for turf cutting look like any modern half-moon-shaped lawn-edger obtainable at garden centres. Before the turves were laid, a corduroy line of logs would be put down lying at right angles to the rampart to provide a firm foundation. As the ramparts were built up, more timbers would be added within the turf wall for strengthening, especially at the corners. Unless a lot of timber had to be used, the turf ramparts were impervious to fire, and would withstand any attempt to batter through them. The ramparts were up to five metres thick, usually constructed with rows of turves on each outer edge, the gap filled with earth from the ditches surrounding the fort, much as walls were built with two rows of squared stones on the outside and rubble and concrete, or on occasion puddled clay, filling the interior. The front of the rampart usually sloped steeply, but not in all cases across the Empire. At Valkenberg there was a box rampart, with earth cased on both sides by upright timbers and horizontal planks, like a garden fence. Graham Webster suggested that this may be the case at Lincoln where a trench was dug to hold such timbers. The rear of the rampart did not slope as steeply as the front and may have had wooden steps placed at intervals to enable soldiers to get up to the wall walk at the top, which was usually strengthened with rammed gravel. The wall walk could be used as a fighting platform, but ideally, attackers would be prevented from getting within close range of the ramparts. Forts were capable of such defence if necessary. On Trajan's Column the Dacians are shown attacking camps or forts defended by Roman soldiers. Some scenes on the column depict building work, and though the blocks that the soldiers carry look like stone they are more probably turf. The timber breastworks on the tops of the ramparts are shown with crenellations, with merlons placed at regular intervals to shield the defenders. These installations, including the ones that are shown under attack, can be classified as temporary camps occupied for longer than a marching camp, or at least hybrids, midway between camps and forts. In the Dacian wars of the early second century, the Romans were invaders and the army was a campaign army, not an occupying force stationed in permanent forts until the country was subdued and annexed.

Forts were usually surrounded by one or more ditches, shaped like a letter V but with an aptly labelled squared off 'ankle-breaker' drainage channel at the bottom. The Romans usually took this drainage feature seriously, judging by the number of excavations showing that the ditch had been cleaned out and the straight sides of the slot re-dug. The usual number of ditches was two, but at some forts there were multiple ditches, possibly revealing how the Romans perceived the degree of danger in those particular areas. In Scotland the fort at Ardoch was occupied in the first century during the campaigns of Agricola and again when Antoninus Pius advanced north of Hadrian's Wall and created the new frontier. It was a heavily used site, with several camps in evidence as well as the forts. On the north and east sides of the existing remains multiple ditches are still visible, five in total, but they belong to two different phases. There were originally three ditches on the north, but the fort was reduced in size with a new northern rampart built further back in the interior of the fort, leaving an unoccupied space where two more ditches were added. The fact that the outer ditches were never filled in when the fort was reduced in size may indicate that the Romans thought that there was a potential threat here. At Whitley Castle in northern England there are three ditches on three sides of the fort, and seven on the south-west side. Significantly there is no evidence of any gate on this side. The fort is overlooked by hills to the south-west, which may have concealed anyone approaching until they were relatively close to the fort, so the elaborate system of ditches would prevent potential attackers from coming right up to the ramparts. The Romans mined lead in this area so part of the garrison's duties may have been to protect the workforce and convoys bringing the lead from the mines.

In the second century from the reign of Trajan onwards the majority of forts had become permanent bases, rather than semi-permanent installations erected while the provinces were still pacified and to some degree Romanised. From this time onwards, forts and fortresses were generally, but not universally, rebuilt in stone. In some cases this meant re-fronting existing forts by cutting back the turf rampart and building the stone walls against the earth. In other forts, such as those of Hadrian's Wall, most of the building work was in stone from the outset. In the north of England stone was more plentiful than timber, so only a short stretch of the eastern section of the Wall was built in earth and turf, replaced in stone at a later date. An anomaly is the earth and timber Hadrianic fort at South Shields which probably predated the Wall, guarding the mouth of the River Tyne, but it was rebuilt in timber, not stone, when the other forts of the frontier were being built. The first stone buildings at South Shields belong to the mid-second century, after Hadrian's Wall was completed. In Germany where timber was more plentiful than stone, the frontier palisade and its accompanying towers were originally built in timber, but the towers were replaced by stone versions in the second century. At the Saalburg fort in Germany the stone fort was preceded by more than one earth and timber fortlet, a pattern repeated at other forts of the frontier.

At Lincoln the legionary fortress was built of earth and timber, occupied by IX *Hispana*, and then by II *Adiutrix* when IX *Hispana* moved north to occupy the new fortress at York, which was built probably in 71. II *Adiutrix* was later moved to Chester, and Lincoln became a colony for veterans in the late 70s. The earth ramparts of the fortress were retained and then re-fronted in stone, with the earth forming the rampart back, so the early colony was to all intents and purposes still a legionary fortress. The first fortress at York was built of clay and turf with timber towers and wooden buildings in the interior. After only two decades or so these were rebuilt in stone, and at least one of the gates was built in stone in AD 108, as attested on a building inscription. In the later second century or at the beginning of the third, there was a complete rebuild in stone, possibly connected with the campaigns of Severus, who used York as his base from 208 to 211. The Chester fortress was originally of earth and timber, founded *c.* 76 on the site of an earlier fort. Stone building began before the end of the first century. The defences and the internal buildings were probably all rebuilt in stone by about 120, and then almost one hundred years later they were rebuilt or extensively repaired. The same building sequence was observed in excavations at Caerleon, founded *c.* 74 and built in earth and timber, replaced quite soon afterwards in stone, though it is thought that the barracks, and possibly some of the other internal buildings, were provided with stone bases and timber superstructures. This may have applied to other forts, since usually the only parts of the barrack blocks to survive are a few courses of stone, with no evidence of how the upper walls were built.

Depending upon the type of unit stationed in them, forts varied in size from 0.6 hectares for the small *numerus* forts in Germany and Dacia, to twenty or twenty-five hectares for a legion. In the first century AD there were a few double legionary fortresses such as Vetera (modern Xanten) and Mogontiacum (modern Mainz) in Germany, until 89 when a military revolt against Domitian was led by Lucius Antonius Saturninus, whose status is uncertain. He may have been the governor of the province of Upper Germany, but this is doubtful because the date when the province was created is uncertain. The areas that that would become Upper and Lower Germany were governed for a while from the province of Gaul. Saturninus probably commanded the military forces of the Rhine rather than a province.

It used to be thought that fort size was a good guide to what sort of unit was stationed in it, and attempts were made to recognise an auxiliary infantry fort or a cavalry fort from little more than its known outline, but more and more excavations have proved that there was no complete uniformity of design and no absolutely standard template for the internal buildings, nor can it be demonstrated that a single unit always occupied a single fort.

The weakest points of any forts were the gates, where the ditch or ditches were interrupted and neatly terminated with rounded ends, to allow for the carriageway to approach the forts. There was no dry or wet moat with a drawbridge across the gap, like the arrangements for a medieval castle, the main purpose of the fort being to house soldiers who marched out to deal with trouble, rather than to defend the fortification itself. The timber gateways and towers of the early forts would have had a limited lifespan, especially in wetter climates, and probably required regular repairs, especially to the four posts that usually supported each of the gate towers. The gateways of stone forts would survive for longer, but the doors would still be of wood, perhaps protected by metal plates on the outside, though there is little evidence for this. Without protection against fire they would be especially vulnerable. The doors were usually double-leaved and equipped with metal pivots at top and bottom, and in some forts in the stonework at floor level the round pivot holes and a carved slot can be seen where the door was slid into place. A cross bar on the inside would hold the doors shut, and if the walls survive to sufficient height the slot can sometimes be seen in the door jambs. There were usually but not always two arches over the entrance road to the fort, possibly with separate carriageways for traffic inwards and outwards, and on each side of the gate there would be a guard room. The whole gateway building would perhaps have three floors, or at least a second storey extending across the road, with small round-headed windows, probably on the outer and inner faces, and above that probably a flat roof surrounded by protective walls with crenellations, for surveillance of the approach road. Flanking towers may have been higher than the section covering the roadway. Several variations of gate design are known. Some gates were recessed with the ramparts projecting beyond them, while others had square or rounded projecting towers on either side of the gates, possibly with pitched roofs covered with tiles, but the details of the upper floors and roofing are not known, so the roofs of some towers may have been flat.

The internal arrangements of fortresses and forts were on the whole standardised, but with regional or local variations. The centre range usually housed the headquarters building (*principia*), flanked by the commander's house (*praetorium*) and the granaries (*horreae*). The four main streets within the fort or fortress were laid out as in the camp described by Hyginus, and the fort orientation was taken from the direction that headquarters faced. In early excavations the name for this building was taken from the descriptions of camps by Polybius and Hyginus, where the commander's house and headquarters were combined and placed in the centre of the camp. The central building in forts and fortresses was accordingly labelled the *praetorium*, until the discovery of a late third-century inscription at Birdoswald on Hadrian's Wall. The text describes the rebuilding of the *praetorium*, and the repair of the *principia*, as well as the *balnea*, or baths. The existence of two distinct buildings makes it clear that the headquarters was called the *principia*, with the Via Principalis running across its facade.

The *principia* would be the busiest area of the fort or fortress. These buildings, especially in legionary fortresses, were impressive, facing anyone who came into the fort from the main gate and along the Via Praetoria. There may have been a colonnade all around the outside of some of the headquarters buildings. The gate in the centre of the facade led into the courtyard, usually paved, which was surrounded by a colonnade on at least three sides, or sometimes on all four sides, as seems to have been the case at the early fortress at Vetera (Xanten) where there was a walkway directly in front of the cross-hall, accessible via entrances at both sides. The courtyard was not large enough to assemble the whole of the garrison, but assemblies were undoubtedly held inside the *principia*, since there was usually a tribunal to one side of the cross-hall, where the commanding officer could stand to address groups of soldiers, raised up to a suitable height so that all the men could see him and he could be heard. Possibly the officers were briefed here, and there may have been occasions when court hearings took place in the enclosed space, most especially in forts in remoter areas where the commander was also in charge of the region and therefore responsible for policing and justice.

Offices were located along the right and left sides of the courtyard, and directly facing the entrance was the cross-hall at the rear of the *principia*, probably with two storeys. In the centre of this there was the shrine or *aedes* of the standards, which housed the eagle in legionary fortresses, with the standards of each century, and in auxiliary forts the standards of the unit and its centuries or *turmae*. This was a sacred place, not simply a store room or sort of large cupboard for keeping the standards, but a religious area which would have been treated with reverence and permanently guarded. At some forts the *aedes* had an apse protruding from the rear wall of the *principia*. At the fortress at Lambaesis there was an apse at the rear of the *aedes*, and there were also extra apses for the offices on either side of it, and at the Nijmegen fortress the projections behind the *aedes* and the flanking offices were square ended, all joined together.

Underneath the *aedes* would be the strongroom where the cash was kept, unless the fort was located on rock, like Housesteads on Hadrian's Wall, in which case the strongroom would be at ground level. All the day-to-day business of running the fort would be recorded in the offices extending on either side of the *aedes* and along the sides of the courtyard. Daily duty rosters would be kept in one of the offices, and copies of all kinds of reports would be filed, for instance the strength reports which were drawn up at least on an annual basis and presumably sent to the governor of the province. Rough totals and explanatory notes were probably compiled each month, or perhaps even more frequently, recording the soldiers who had died, or been killed, or transferred to other units, or even deserted. The names of new recruits that had arrived would be recorded together with the accompanying correspondence from the governor, the number and names of men transferred in from other units would be noted, and details of the century or *turma* to which they had been assigned. Expense accounts for the fortress or fort would be filed in one or more of the offices, and documentation for each soldier, with his pay and deductions on the three annual paydays, arranged by centuries or *turmae* under the names of each centurion or decurion. Disciplinary hearings were no doubt recorded, as well as recommendations for awards. Someone would have to ensure that there were stocks of items to write with and on, as in running any modern office with its stationery stores. Just because papyrus records are not found on many Roman sites in northern Europe it does not mean that the Romans did not use papyrus in their northern provinces, but in damp climates there are few remains because when covered in earth papyrus degenerates to a grey paste. Even in hot dry climates there is another danger: archaeologists joke about insects or larvae which seem to specialise in eating the verbs in documents, leaving names, nouns and numbers but no idea of what was being done. Vellum may have been used for more important transactions, and the wooden writing tablets at Vindolanda served for ordinary correspondence. In the east, ostraca or potsherds were used for compiling records, perhaps for copying up later in more convenient form. The list of activities could continue but perhaps the point has been made that the *principia* in a legionary fortress or an auxiliary fort was a busy place full of clerical staff.

The commander's house in fortresses and forts reflected his status. The buildings were usually courtyard houses of Mediterranean style, with several rooms for the commander, his family and slaves, and probably reception rooms for conducting some of the business of the fort, or for private conversations with officers and for greeting some visitors. In a legionary fortress the *praetorium* would be as impressive in size as the headquarters building, befitting the senatorial rank of the legate. In auxiliary forts the commander's house was roughly the same size as the headquarters building, not as impressive as the legionary legate's houses, but still comfortable, with accommodation for the family and the slaves, and its own kitchens and bath suite.

Next to the *principia* in the central range of the fortress or fort there was usually a granary. In timber forts these storage buildings would be raised off the ground on posts, like the reconstructed version at the Lunt fort at Baginton near Coventry. At least six timber granaries were found at the legionary fortress of Inchtuthil in Scotland, which belonged to the short-lived first-century conquest under Agricola, and five were discovered at Anreppen on the River Lippe in Germany, where supplies for Tiberius' campaign army of AD 4 could be brought in by river and stored in the fortress. If the wooden granaries were raised off the ground, water damage would be restricted to the supporting timber posts, but when fort granaries were rebuilt in stone, the roofs probably projected some distance beyond the walls to keep rainwater, which caused rising damp, away from the foundations. This may be one purpose of the projecting buttresses, to support a projecting roof, as well as strengthening the walls. Several stone granaries, with this distinctive ground plan showing regularly spaced buttresses and stone supports to raise the flagged floor off the ground, were found at South Shields fort on the River Tyne, where a Severan supply base was set up. The second-century stone fort was enlarged, and granaries filled nearly two-thirds of the enlarged fort for much of the third century.

In several forts archaeological evidence shows that there were workshops (*fabricae*) where metalworking, woodworking and repair of equipment and weapons would take place. There was also a hospital (*valetudinarium*). It should be acknowledged that from the ground plans alone, the workshops and the hospitals might have been confused, each consisting of small rooms off a central courtyard, but in a few cases medical instruments have been found, which strongly supports the label 'hospital'. The forts on Hadrian's Wall at Wallsend and Housesteads, and the legionary fortresses at Vetera (modern Xanten) and Novaesium (modern Neuss) are among examples where hospitals have been found.

The majority of the buildings inside the fort would be the barrack blocks. For the infantry in legionary fortresses and auxiliary infantry forts, barracks were normally laid out with ten rooms subdivided into two parts, one for sleeping and eating and one probably for storage, each double room accommodating eight men, and therefore housing one complete century of eighty men. A suite of rooms at the end of each block housed the centurions, and it is suggested that the optio lived in the same house, which usually had several rooms. A verandah ran the full length of the barrack block, with the roof supported on columns. There are exceptions to the rows of ten rooms, some barracks having eleven or twelve cubicles, which may have housed extra men for a unit that was over-strength, or equipment and stores that would have cluttered up the living space of the soldiers. Nothing has as yet come to light that would explain the extra rooms.

Cavalry barracks were different, usually consisting of blocks with a decurion's house at the end and, according to earlier theories, ten barrack blocks. Where it was known that a cavalry unit occupied the fort, but no complete barracks blocks were excavated, plans were usually drawn with this assumption in mind, showing ten cubicles for the cavalrymen. More recently this has been revised, and has already been described in the chapter on cavalry units. From the evidence at the fort at Dormagen on the Rhine, and Wallsend on Hadrian's Wall, it seems that the men and their horses were housed together. In at least three of the Dormagen blocks, there were double cubicles, with soakaway pits in those along one side of the block, and hearths in those on the other side, indicating that men and mounts shared the cubicles. At Wallsend where some of the cavalry barracks were completely excavated in the late 1990s, there were only nine double cubicles, so it was assumed that three men would live with three horses in each one, which gives a total of twenty-seven men, which with two or three officers amounts to about thirty for each *turma*.

The commander's house in each fort usually had its own bath suite, and the family slaves would have looked after the functioning of these establishments. For the soldiers there were larger premises for bathing. Until the late Empire, the military bath houses for the soldiers were situated outside the forts, one reason being to reduce the risk of fire, because the method of heating the rooms depended on lighting fires underneath the floors, usually supported on stone pillars or stacks of tiles, a system called a hypocaust, which was used for heating the rooms of domestic houses as well as baths. Even at forts built of earth and timber, the bath house would be of stone. The Roman method of bathing required rooms of progressively greater heat to induce sweating. Instead of using soap, the body was covered with oil which was scraped off along with the sweat by means of a curved metal *strigil*. In some baths there was a changing room or *apodyterium*, or in the absence of a special room, the cold room or *frigidarium* may have been used, since this is where bathers started off and arrived back at the end of a bathing session in order to cool down. A room of intermediate heat called the *tepidarium* acclimatised the bather ready for the hot room or *caldarium*, where the floors were usually too hot for bare feet, necessitating sandals with wooden soles. The amount of fuel that would have been used on a daily basis in these bath houses must have been staggering. The task of cleaning out the ashes and maintaining the fires under the floors would probably have been done by army slaves.

The roofs of the bath houses would ideally have been constructed as concrete vaults to prevent the steam from warping and damaging the timbers of a pitched roof. At Lambaesis in Algeria the legionary bath house is one of the finest and best-preserved examples of the Roman Empire. At Vindonissa (modern Windisch) there is another fine example of legionary baths. At Exeter, the legionary fortress was not occupied for very long, but the baths were stone-built and were converted into the basilica of the town, which became the capital of the Dumnonii tribe. The best extant remains of a fort bath house are those at Chesters on Hadrian's Wall, where the baths are situated on the sloping ground between the fort and the river. When the fort was abandoned the earth gradually covered the remains, so that the stone walls still exist to a considerable height, and in the apse of the hot bath the lower parts of a window can be seen, a very rare survival in Roman buildings. Glass was found outside it, so it is clear that this window was glazed. The fort baths at Wallsend have been reconstructed, on the same plan as the Chesters example, but in mirror image, and not on the site of the original baths. At Caerleon the fortress baths were excavated from 1964 to 1981, revealing a truly massive structure with a large courtyard and an exercise hall. The baths were built of stone with a concrete vaulted roof, even when the early fortress was a timber and earth construction. Although the complete plan was recovered, not all the remains can now be seen, but there is a modern award-winning roofed structure covering the remains of the rectangular swimming pool that lay to the south-west of the main bath building. The pool was altered and rebuilt in the first and second centuries. In the modern covered building the raised walkway all around the foundations affords views from all directions, complete with sound effects and visual representations of people jumping into the water and talking and yelling to each other: altogether a unique experience on a visit to a Roman site.

Outside nearly all forts and fortresses there were civilian settlements known as *canabae* in the case of legionary sites and *vici* at auxiliary forts. All kinds of people would gravitate towards Roman military establishments because the soldiers formed the only substantial groups of people in the Empire who received regular pay, so profit could be made by selling goods and services to them. The civil settlements at forts are discussed more fully in the chapter on the army and civilians.

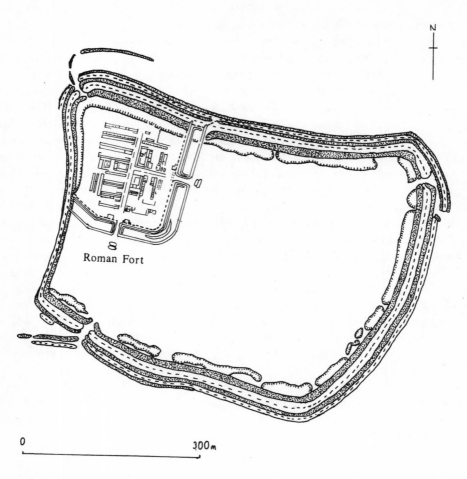

Roman Fort

0   300m

Forts of the late Republic and early Empire were not generally laid out according to a rectangular or square plan, but internally the streets, headquarters and barracks usually conformed to a pattern. The builders of this early fort at Hod Hill took advantage of the ramparts of the British hill fort to form two of the perimeter walls. The different styles of equipment found in this fort led early excavators to conclude that legionaries and auxiliaries were brigaded together, which would have been usual on campaigns, but doubt has been cast on this conclusion. Some evidence of stables was also found here, based on the wear patterns of the floors. Drawn by Jacqui Taylor.

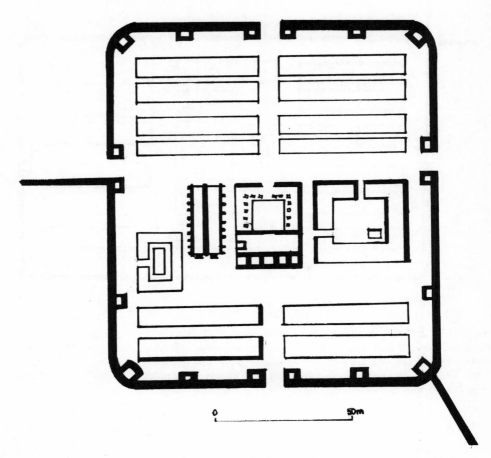

Simplified plan of the fort at Wallsend on Hadrian's Wall. The headquarters building (*principia*) is located in the centre range facing the *via principalis* and is flanked by the commander's house and the granaries, with distinctive buttresses outlining the long walls. Between the granaries and the fort wall there is the hospital (*valetudinarium*). The four sets of barracks behind the centre range are the most important buildings in the fort, consisting of rows of paired rooms, one with a hearth and one with a urine pit that demonstrates that horses and men were housed together, similar to the cavalry barracks at Dormagen in Germany discovered in the late 1970s. A set of baths has been reconstructed at Wallsend, based on the extant remains at Chesters fort, because what remained of the Wallsend baths were destroyed in the nineteenth century. Drawn by Susan Veitch, compiled from different sources.

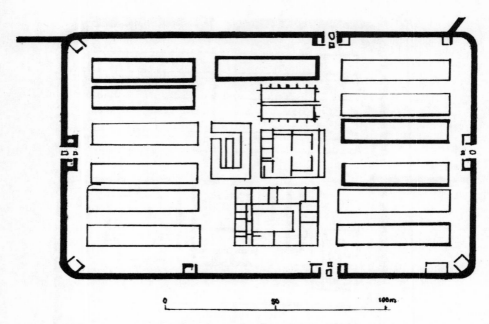

Simplified plan of the fort at Housesteads on Hadrian's Wall, showing how it was laid out in an elongated rectangle according to the lie of the land, on a slope behind a north-facing cliff. The centre range contains the granaries, the headquarters building (*principia*), and the commander's house, and the *valetudinarium* is located behind the headquarters building. Drawn by Susan Veitch, compiled from different sources.

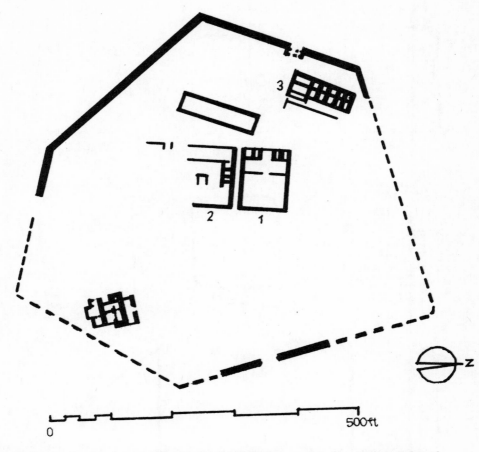

The fort at Bewcastle, an outpost north of Hadrian's Wall, was originally a Hadrianic fort of unknown size and shape and size, but the baths in the south-east corner probably belonged to it. The *principia* and the commander's house, 1 and 2 on the plan, belong to the third century when the fort was rebuilt on an irregular plan that represents the shape of the plateau that it occupies. A ruined castle stands in the north-east corner of the fort, and the route through Bewcastle was frequented by border reivers and raiders in the sixteenth century. Redrawn by Susan Veitch from R. Wilson *Roman Forts*. Bergström and Boyle Books, 1980.

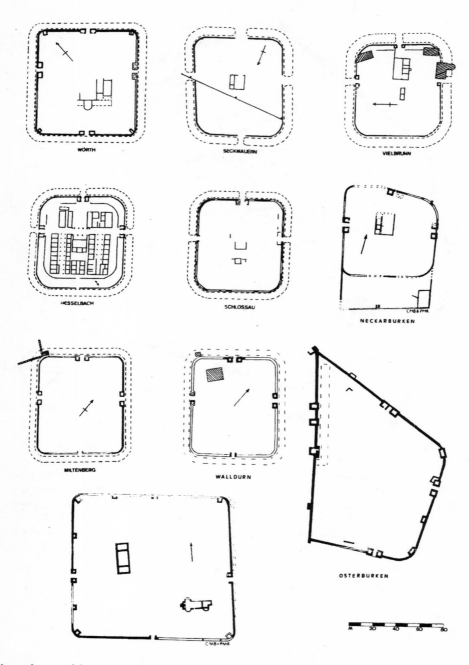

Plans of some of the *numerus* forts of the German frontier drawn to the same scale. The *numeri* were probably originally raised by Trajan. They were smaller than auxiliary units and most often recruited from people on the periphery of the Empire. The small forts of the German frontier of the Odenwald were manned predominantly by British tribesmen. The type site is Hesselbach which was more fully excavated than the others, and revealed that each *numerus* fort possessed a headquarters building, indicating that the *numeri* were not irregulars outside the army organisation, as previously thought. Drawn by Chris and Trish Boyle.

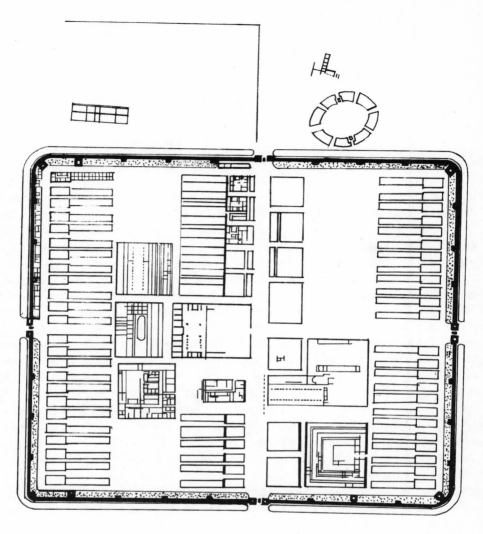

Plan of the legionary fortress at Caerleon, the Welsh version of Latin *Castra Legionis* or camp of
the legion. This was the base for *II Augusta* from about AD 75 until the end of the third century
AD, staring out as a timber and earth fortress, rebuilt in stone *c.* AD 100 and subject to alterations
throughout its life. The whole legion would not be found here all the time, since detachments
were active all over Britain, building or campaigning. Fortresses are instantly recognisable from
their plans with the headquarters buildings in the middle of the central range, but they were not
laid out according to an absolutely standard system. The Caerleon fortress is rectangular, covering
fifty acres or twenty hectares, with four twin-towered gates opposite the principal roads, and the
ramparts are backed with earth and protected by interval and corner towers. Much of the fortress
is occupied by pairs of barrack blocks, with accommodation for the legionaries and a larger house
at one end for the centurion. Notable features at Caerleon are the military baths, situated inside the
fortress, whereas many fort baths are outside the walls. On the plan, locate the amphitheatre and
move down through the unexcavated area, to find the baths, with the long exercise hall with its two
rows of pillars. Parts of the baths are housed in an award-winning museum. Next to the baths is the
hospital (*valetudinarium*). Redrawn by Susan Veitch from R. Wilson *Roman Forts*. Bergström and
Boyle Books, 1980.

10

Artillery and Sieges

In the Imperial Roman army there was no separate artillery corps. The soldiers who operated the artillery were specialists, but were not formed into separate units until the later Empire. The *Notitia Dignitatum*, the list of officials, commanders and units drawn up in the fourth and fifth centuries, lists *ballistarii* units. On the Danube there were units of *ballistarii* stationed in the bridgehead forts. In the early Empire artillery operators were drawn from the legionary centuries to man the machines and presumably to look after them and repair them. Artillerymen (*ballistarii*) are specifically mentioned in Tarrutienus' list of *immunes*, who did not have to perform routine fatigues, but their status was not a rank, and there was no extra pay for their specialist functions. There is little evidence of their numbers or of how they were organised. Vegetius says that there were fifty-five catapults per legion, an odd number which leaves five cohorts without artillery, though he may not have been describing an actual legion but a theoretical version. Vegetius also says that each legion possessed ten stone-throwing engines, which works out satisfactorily at one per cohort. According to Vegetius, eleven men from each century were allocated to the operation of the *carroballista*, which fired large arrows or bolts. Eric Marsden pointed out that in more than one scene on Trajan's Column, only two men are shown working with a bolt-firing machine, but there would be other soldiers who were designated to look after the draught animals, usually mules, and the carriage used for transport, and someone would have to keep the machine furnished with ammunition when it was in operation. By the middle of the first century AD it is probable that each century had one artillery engine, firing arrows or stones. Adrian Goldsworthy estimates that seventy wagons and 160 animals would be needed to carry the artillery of one legion.

The soldiers who formed the artillery teams would have to spend considerable time training and practising, which would be good enough reason for being excused fatigues. They would have to learn how to load and unload their machines on carts as quickly and efficiently as possible, maintain the vehicles, look after the mules, be able to check, service and repair the machines, and most important learn how to shoot them and hit targets. Somewhere there must have been artillery ranges, most likely outside fortresses, though 'must have been' is a dread phrase to archaeologists. Someone would have to make hundreds if not thousands of bolts for practice sessions and for use in battles, though the practice bolts could probably be constantly reused, as could stones unless they had shattered. The training and practice positively demand an instructor, and though instructors are known in the army, it is not certain if there were artillery specialists. Medical teams may have been involved occasionally as well, given that accidents are not entirely out of the question when people associate closely with machines firing projectiles.

The Romans employed various types of artillery, which can be divided into two main categories, double armed like large crossbows, or single armed like the medieval mangonel, though the single-armed stone thrower did not come into general use in the Roman army until the fourth century. The machines are described under several names in the sources, such as *catapultae, scorpiones, ballistae, carroballistae, onagri*. Caesar uses the general description *tormenta* when writing of artillery, without distinguishing between the different types of machines. There is some confusion among ancient and modern works about the terminology applied to Roman artillery. The term *catapulta* appears less frequently in modern works than the term *ballista*, which is often used to describe all types of artillery. Strictly, the *catapulta* fired arrows or bolts, and the *ballista* was used to fire stone projectiles, but it could be adapted to fire bolts. Eric Marsden said that *catapulta* was the main term in use until the fourth century AD and then *ballista* superseded it. A further complication in terminology concerns the use of the slang term *scorpio* or scorpion. It was used in the first century AD by Vitruvius to describe the two-armed wooden framed *catapulta*, but in the later Roman period Ammianus Marcellinus says that *scorpio* was used of the single-armed stone thrower, because in the upright position it resembles the scorpion's upraised sting. This type of machine was also nicknamed *onager* or wild ass, descriptive of its violent kick. These machines would be used in sieges rather than in battles.

The ancient Greeks had already worked out most of the problems of bolt-shooting and stone-throwing artillery, such as how to make efficient torsion springs and how to hold them in place in a frame that would resist the thrust when the machine was fired, how to draw the bow string back, how to hold it in place until ready for firing, and how to make a trigger to release the string easily and quickly with sufficient force to shoot the projectile. Vitruvius, in the tenth chapter of his book *On Architecture*, includes a short section on artillery and siege engines, giving a description of how to construct them. Some of the ancient authors describe artillery in action. Josephus witnessed the use of artillery in the sieges of the Jewish war under Vespasian, and in the later Empire Ammianus Marcellinus gives an account of the siege of Amida. The late Roman author Vegetius discusses the use of artillery in the legions.

The ancient literature provides a great deal of information about artillery machines, but without the archaeological finds the texts by themselves are not sufficient to reconstruct a fully operative version. The study and reconstruction of Roman artillery machines began with German artillery officers such as Erwin Schramm at the end of the First World War. His work has been updated by Professor Dietwulf Baatz as more finds have come to light that elucidate how the machines were constructed and operated.

The practical Romans had only to make one or two refinements to Greek models, and then put the machines to use. Artillery machines came in several different sizes, the determining factor being the size and weight of the bolt to be shot, or the weight of the stone to be thrown. In 1887 at Cremona a metal battle shield for a wood-framed bolt-shooting machine was discovered, minus its top section. It was inscribed with the names of the consuls for 45, and was lost in the battle outside the town in 69. It may have been re-used on one or more new machines, but if attached to its original bolt-shooting engine, it had a working life of twenty-four years. The oblong arched hole in the battle-shield provides evidence for the maximum width of the bolt, with accompanying vanes, that was fired from it. Vitruvius explains how the weight and size of the projectiles affect the proportions in manufacturing *catapultae* and *ballistae*, and for the benefit of men who were not well versed in geometry and mathematical calculation he included a ready-reckoner relating the weight of the projectiles to the proportions of the machine, so that the operators would not have to work it all out painstakingly slowly in times of danger.

In any torsion artillery machine, the springs were the most important parts, providing the energy necessary to fire the bolts or stones. Trajan's troops in the Danube wars took a store of replaceable springs so that the machines would not be out of action for lack of them. The material used to make the torsion springs must be fairly elastic, but not so much that it stretches too easily, and it must be capable of being woven into a rope to hold the ends together. The ancient engineers used hair, perhaps horse hair, but what was especially favoured was human hair, especially women's hair, but this might be less to do with gender than the fact that women frequently had longer hair than men. While hair provided sufficient torsion power, sinew ropes gave the best performance, and increased the range of the projectiles. Vegetius endorses sinew as the best source of power, and Heron of Alexandria, writing in the first century AD, says that sinew from the backs or shoulders of all animals, except pigs, is suitable, the best being from the feet of deer, or from bulls' necks. In connection with a BBC television programme featuring the reconstruction of a Roman artillery piece, Alan Wilkins describes experiments in making sinew rope. The sinews are first dried, then broken up into fibre with a mallet, then the fibre is spun into yarn. Experiments with various kinds of rope for the BBC programme proved that sinew gives by far the best performance. Wilkins also mentions the letter from the Vindolanda collection written by Octavius to Candidus referring to one hundred pounds of sinew (*nervum*) from Marinus, which may have been delivered to the fort, or was still awaiting transport. Its most likely use would be for springs for artillery.

The bundles of ropes of whatever material was used were gathered together like a skein of wool, and a metal rod or bar was inserted into them at each end, then twisted to create the torsion effect. The springs were housed in a wooden frame usually protected by sheets of metal, with the springs protruding from the top and bottom of the frame on either side of the channel which held the projectiles. The springs were threaded through metal washers, and held in place by the bars that had been inserted at either end. Since the metal parts of artillery machines would survive better than the wooden frames, several examples of washers of different sizes and dates have been found, at Ampurias and Azaila in Spain, in a shipwreck off the coast of Tunisia, and one small version in the sacred spring of Sulis Minerva, at Bath, England.

The two arms of the machine were inserted into the springs and joined together at their opposite ends by the bowstring, which Vitruvius says could be drawn back by several means, by winch, block and pulley, or capstan. It was especially important to ensure that the two arms were pulled back equally to give them equal thrust, otherwise the missile would go off course. Vitruvius explains that the remedy for this is to tune the strings, which he says should respond with the same sound on both sides when struck by the hand.

To fire the machine, the bolts or stones were placed in the central channel and the bowstring pulled back on to the trigger. The bow strings for stone-throwing machines approximated to a sling that encompassed the stone ball, with a loop at the back to hook on to the trigger. Examples of iron bolt heads, and stones of different sizes and weights, usually shaped and smoothed like cannon balls, have been found on archaeological sites. In many cases the bolts have been corroded, so it is not possible to guess their weights accurately. The largest stones found at Numantia weighed up to 4 kilos, but at Carthage stones ranged from 2.5 kilos to 40 kilos. Although these probably pre-date the Roman siege of 146 BC, the size of the stones indicates that engines capable of throwing them must have existed in Carthage, and were probably among the 2,000 artillery pieces that were given up to the Romans as part of the terms of capitulation, before the Carthaginians changed their minds and decided to resist.

Bolts from Roman artillery are more commonly found than the parts of the machines that fired them, though the shafts of the bolts have usually perished. The heads hardly varied at all throughout the Roman Empire. The bolts had pyramid-shaped iron heads and timber shafts, with fletchings made not from feathers but from thin pieces of wood. Leather could also fulfil this purpose, and is used by re-enactors who operate reconstructed artillery. The vanes were placed so that one half of the shaft was smooth, allowing it to slot into the groove in the slider of the machine. These bolts could pass straight through armour. During a siege in the later Roman Empire, a Goth was pinned to a tree by a bolt which had passed through his cuirass and his body and had then embedded itself for half its length in the tree trunk. Fully functional modern versions of artillery pieces are now constructed and operated by several re-enactment societies, with frighteningly dangerous results, but unlike re-enactors, the Romans were not restricted by Health and Safety legislation.

Metal frames for catapults were introduced in the later first century AD, an improvement on wood, which does not perform well in hot climates and is subject to warping, and even though the wooden frames were usually clad in metal sheeting, the machine could be set on fire by the enemy. If a wooden frame was damaged the machine would have to be taken to the workshops for repair, but the metal versions came in standardised bronze or iron sections, fitted together by removable pins or wedges, so it could be dismantled and new parts inserted with relative ease. The army probably carried a number of spare parts on campaign, or cannibalised other machines to make one whole one.

The spring frames of the metal versions were further apart than in the wooden-framed artillery pieces, which allowed the arms to be pulled further back by the bowstring. The depictions on Trajan's Column of portable machines of this type seem to indicate that the springs were protected in a cylinder, whereas is the wooden-framed versions they were open to view front and back, and therefore susceptible to damage. Another advantage was that there was greater visibility with the metal-framed catapults. The top strut had a semicircular arch in the centre over the projectile channel, which could be used for siting, whereas the taller wooden-framed machines obscured the view so that the operator had to look over the top of the frame to aim and achieve the correct elevation. The metal fittings of a stone-throwing *ballista* were found at Hatra in Mesopotamia, which was besieged by Septimius Severus, and by the Persians, in the third century AD. The remains of a small fourth-century bolt-shooting machine were found at Orsova in Romania.

The Romans used manually operated torsion crossbows which Vegetius calls *manuballistae*, and the author and mathematician Heron of Alexandria describes and illustrates a *cheiroballistra* (sic), which is generally accepted as a hand-operated machine, equipped with a curving butt so that the weapon could be cocked by pressing down with the stomach on the butt and forcing back the slider for the bolt and the string. However Alan Wilkins has made a case for the *cheiroballistra* as a standard winch-operated catapult. The author Heron states that the catapult developed so much power that the curved stomach bar had to be replaced with a winch. The reconstructed version of this machine mounted on a stand worked just as well as, or even better than, any other catapult.

For evidence as to how the artillery was used in battle, historians have to rely on Arrian's description of his deployment against the Alans, during the reign of Hadrian. Lucius Flavius Arrianus was governor of Cappadocia for six years from 131 to 137, and in 134 he had to counter an incursion by the Alani or Alans, a tribe which frequently tried to cross the Caucasus from their lands in Pontus on the shores of the Black Sea. They were excellent horsemen, armed with spears. Arrian planned to meet the tribesmen with the classic formation of legions in the centre, screened by the foot archers and flanked by auxiliary infantry and cavalry on the higher ground on either side. He placed his catapults on both wings, and also at the rear, where they were to fire over the heads of the troops facing the Alans. Alan Wilkins suggests that some of the catapults on the flanks were the manoeuvrable bolt-shooters, while the rear ones were probably larger like the ones on carts shown on Trajan's Column, consisting of bolt-shooters and stone throwers. Arrian ordered his troops to maintain silence until the Alans were within range, then they were to shout their battle cry as loud as possible, while the archers shot their arrows, the spearmen threw their javelins and spears, and the catapults fired bolts and stones. An estimate of the rate of artillery fire would be about four missiles in one minute, with an effective range of about 250 metres. The phrase withering fire comes to mind.

In the later Empire artillery was used to defend as well as besiege cities, and special platforms were built for machines on the battlements. In 225 the *cohors I Fida Vardullorum* constructed a *ballistarium* at the fort of High Rochester in Northumberland in northern England. Eric Marsden thought that despite the name *ballistarium*, the actual machine would have been an *onager*, since the platform was strong enough to support such a heavy piece, but these machines were more useful in besieging a city or fort, or defending a place that had been invested, and the stones fired from them had the power to damage walls and shatter siege towers. At High Rochester it may not have been necessary to shoot down siege towers, but to aim at humans, and the inscription may mean what it says, that the fort was defended by *ballistae* shooting bolts or stones. It is usually considered that artillery was the preserve of the legions, but in this instance an auxiliary unit was operating the machinery. If the sinew destined for Vindolanda in 122, described above, was to be used for catapults it may be that the auxiliary unit was in charge of them, but legionaries have been attested at the fort at that time, so no firm conclusions can be drawn about which kinds of troops used the artillery. This problem has been discussed by D. B. Campbell with reference to High Rochester fort and the siege of Hatra.

Siege Warfare

On the whole the Romans preferred to decide the outcome of their wars by fighting in the open rather than engaging in sieges, which were time-consuming and expensive, but sometimes a successful siege could bring about a satisfactory conclusion to a war. There were two different ways of besieging a city or stronghold. One way was to blockade the site without storming or attacking the defences, and to wait until lack of food and a decline in enemy morale led to a surrender. Cutting off a city from outside help did not always involve lines of circumvallation, as long as routes and harbours were taken over and watched closely. The siege of Carthage in 146 BC ended when Scipio Aemilianus cut the Carthaginians off from their harbour. Whether or not there were lines of siege works enclosing the besieged city, it would be necessary to build a camp, or more likely a series of camps around the enemy stronghold, to keep watch and to house the soldiers. Caesar made several camps around Alesia, and there were similar camps at Numantia in 133 BC. Eight camps have been detected at the siege works around Masada. In Britain, sieges of hill forts during the conquest, most especially by the future Emperor Vespasian in the South West, may have been brief affairs, not necessitating long-term occupation of camps. Evidence of Roman activity at Maiden Castle in Dorset was found when several skeletons were discovered, one with an artillery bolt embedded in his spine. The Roman camps at the hill fort of Burnswark in Scotland have been labelled as siege camps, then practice camps, and now they are reinstated as siege camps, but the context and the war are not established.

The vital factors in any blockade or active siege would be maintenance of lines of communication, the regular delivery of supplies while denying food and assistance to the enemy, and keeping up morale in the blockading army, which would probably suffer if there was no action and no quick result. If an enemy site was to be invested, ditches and ramparts had to be dug and probably wooden palisades erected, ideally with observation towers, which could also be adapted for artillery to fire into the besieged city. This would involve transport of timber supplies as well as supplies of food for the army. If the blockade was to be conducted in the midst of hostile territory, or where the enemy was likely to attack, two lines of circumvallation would be necessary, one facing inwards, and one facing outwards, like Caesar's siege works at Alesia in the war against Vercingetorix. At Dyrrachium, Caesar hemmed in Pompey's army with two lines of circumvallation, but he did no close off the ends of the two lines on the coast at the southern end, and Pompey very nearly broke through. It was not a successful blockade because Pompey's fleet controlled the sea, so he was not short of supplies, and though his cavalry horses suffered from lack of gazing, the supply problem forced Caesar to move off.

The supply of water was obviously important to both besieged and besiegers. At the siege of Uxellodunum (Puy d'Issolu) in Gaul, Caesar had an embankment constructed so that a mobile siege tower, with no less than ten storeys to accommodate artillery, could be wheeled up to fire on the fresh-water spring where the Gauls obtained their water supplies. This ended the siege. During the war against Jugurtha in Africa, Gaius Marius decided to attack the remote desert city of Capsa in 107 BC. He took cattle with the army for the soldiers to eat, and saved the hides to make water skins to be used on the desert march. When they were within three days march of the city of Capsa, the troops marched by night, lightly equipped and without baggage, to take the city by surprise.

An active siege with regular assaults on the enemy defences required vast organisation. The Romans probably never went to war with the sole intention of besieging a stronghold, but would decide to do so after an initial assault, or several assaults, had failed. At Jerusalem Titus launched several attacks before he erected siege works, though when he did decide to enclose the city he did it very quickly, erecting seven kilometers of siege lines in three days, according to Josephus. Once a Roman siege had begun, only in the direst of circumstances would it be abandoned, especially if it was part of a punitive action. Mark Antony had to abandon the siege of Praaspa (in Iran, exact location not known) in the initial stages of his campaign aimed at Parthia because his siege train was attacked and damaged. Trajan and Severus abandoned their sieges of Hatra in northern Iraq, when it was clear that it was too well defended and it would take a very long time, and consume vast resources, to reduce the city. Otherwise, the Romans would normally pursue the siege to the bitter end.

Lines of communication and food supplies were obviously just as necessary for an active siege as for a blockade, but in addition all kinds of equipment would have to be assembled, not least stocks of weapons, especially projectiles which could not always be gathered up and reused. Even if there were no surrounding lines of siege works, vast quantities of timber would have been necessary for various purposes, especially if any of the siege machinery known to the ancient world was to be employed, such as mobile towers or shelters for approaching the walls.

The main purpose of the siege was to capture and probably destroy the enemy city or stronghold. In order to do this, the besieger had to gain access somehow, through the gates by destroying them with a battering ram or by fire, over the walls by means of ladders or mobile siege towers with drop-down bridges, through the walls by battering them down, or under the walls by mining. There were prestigious awards for the first soldier to cross the enemy ramparts, but in many cases the first soldier would not survive, nor any of his comrades, since entering a town or city was probably the most dangerous activity of any siege.

Reconnaissance could reveal weak spots in enemy defences and dictate where the best place to attack was situated. The historian Sallust records that during the war with Jugurtha, Marius besieged one of Jugurtha's strongholds, situated on an elevated rocky site, seemingly with only one entrance up a steep path. The site gave all the advantages to the defenders, and prevented effective attack by artillery and siege equipment. It was not official reconnaissance that discovered the concealed rear entrance, but a Ligurian auxiliary soldier who had gone to look for snails to cook for his meal. Marius ordered a group of soldiers and centurions accompanied by trumpeters to approach via the back entrance, while he attacked the main access to the fort with his legionaries sheltered by their shields in testudo or tortoise formation, supported by his artillery. When the frontal assault had gained all the attention of Jugurtha's men, the sudden noisy appearance of the soldiers from the rear entrance threw the defenders into disorder and they surrendered.

Apart from direct attack, there was also the chance that none of this strenuous action would be necessary and soldiers could walk in because someone inside the town opened the gates for them. Once the soldiers were inside the besieged city, the commander could rarely if ever control them. There would be no disciplined house-to-house search and an orderly assembly of the enemy in a central place. If the siege had been long and difficult the soldiers were usually angry enough to kill everything that moved and help themselves to loot.

Artillery on the ground or mounted in towers along the siege works was used to keep the defenders off the walls, so that any direct assault had at least some chance of success unless the defenders were as determined as the Gauls witnessed by Caesar, who replaced men on the ramparts one after another as they were killed. Mobile towers being moved close to the walls were vulnerable to being set on fire, and so were the shelters over battering rams, called a ram tortoise, built like a wooden tent covering the frame in which the ram was swung back and forth against a gate or a wall. A covering of hides soaked in vinegar served as protection from fire, or sometimes the wooden structures would be covered with clay to prevent fire from catching hold. The stories of various sieges usually include several references to damage by fire caused by the defenders. At Hatra, the defenders dropped bituminous naphtha on Severus' siege engines to set fire to them, which must have killed many of the soldiers as well as damaging the machines.

Sometimes if mobile towers were to be used to approach the walls, it would be necessary to fill in the ditch surrounding the city walls. For this purpose moveable shelters could be built, covered with hides, sometimes with tightly stuffed leather bags underneath them to protect the roof, absorbing the impact of stones dropped onto it. Underneath the shelters which were arranged in long lines to form the equivalent of tunnels, soldiers could bring brushwood and the equivalent of fascines to throw into the ditch to provide a platform for towers to be brought up to the walls. When he was besieging Aristobulus in Jerusalem, Pompey filled in the defensive ditch to allow his soldiers to approach the walls.

At the siege of Aduatuca in Gaul Caesar built a mobile tower some distance from the defences of the town, which the Gauls found amusing until it was wheeled closer and closer and they could perceive the potential damage it could cause, so they sued for peace. Apollodorus, Trajan's engineer and architect who built the bridge across the Danube, wrote a short manual on the construction of a mobile tower using only short pieces of wood, in case there was a lack of suitable long timbers for this purpose. Vegetius includes a short section on mobile towers, describing how the base of the tower must be in proportion to its height, but he gives no information about where the wheels were placed and how many there would be. The weight of the tower was obviously important too. At the siege of Jerusalem in AD 70 one of the towers collapsed, probably owing to the fact that it was clad like the other towers in iron plating, to guard against fire, and was simply too heavy.

If mobile siege towers were not practicable, or had been used without success, the Romans sometimes built ramps of earth to allow the soldiers to get onto the walls, ideally with a covered passageway to protect the soldiers as they moved along the ramp to approach the besieged city or citadel. Large embankments would require timber shoring at the sides. At Avaricum (Bourges), which was surrounded by marshes except at the entrance on the south, where there was a deep gorge, Caesar spent twenty-five days building an embankment to get across the gorge. In the Jewish war of the 60s and 70s Vespasian besieged the city of Jotapata. The soldiers managed to breach the walls but were driven off. Vespasian built a ramp to get up to the level of the walls, but the Jews hastily built a higher wall on top of the original defences. In response the Romans constructed towers fifteen feet high to defend the men building up the ramp until it did reach the top of the walls. At the Jewish stronghold of Masada besieged by Titus in 74, a very tall tower was built, ninety feet high to elevate the soldiers high enough to fire at the defenders on the plateau, while the soldiers constructed the famous ramp, which can still be seen. Geological investigation has shown that this ramp is not such a feat of Roman engineering as once thought, since it rests on a chalk outcrop at the side of the plateau. Rather than a testimonial to Roman engineering skill, it is a testimonial to Roman common sense.

Mining was not a regular feature of Roman sieges until the fourth century, but it was tried at Marseilles during the civil war between Caesar and Pompey. All other attempts to take the city having failed, the Caesarians started to dig more than thirty mines, according to Vitruvius. The tunnels had to be deep enough to pass underneath the moat outside the walls. The inhabitants dug the moat deeper still, and where the mines were approaching places where the moat could not be dug out, they excavated huge ditches inside the walls and filled them with water from the wells and the harbour. The soldiers were overwhelmed when they opened up the ends of the mines and unwittingly let in the water, which destroyed the mine props, so those who were not drowned were crushed as the mine collapsed. For defenders, it was important to know where the mines were heading. One method of detecting them was described in the fourth century BC by Aineias the Tactician, who wrote a common-sense manual, usually entitled in English *How to Survive under Siege*. The technique for detecting tunnels was to tour around the inside of the city walls, placing the inner side of a bronze shield-plate to the ground, and listening. Where there was no sound, there was no tunnelling, but if a resonance was heard it signified tunnellers at work. Defenders could then dig a tunnel of their own to deal with the menace. It is on record that defenders who detected mines released wasps and bees into the tunnels, or even wild bears in one case.

It was only rarely that Romans found themselves on the receiving end of a siege in the Imperial period, and even then the circumstance was usually a prolonged attack rather than a proper siege. One of the most famous cases is Quintus Cicero's ordeal in his winter camp during Caesar's conquest of Gaul. At Jerusalem in 4 BC, an official called Sabinus was besieged by the Jews after he had been sent to secure the assets of Herod the Great, who had just died. The governor of Syria, Quinctilius Varus, had to rescue Sabinus, bringing two legions and four auxiliary cavalry units, plus some troops from allied states. In most cases the non-Romans who attacked the provinces did not possess the resources or the organisation to attempt a siege, and could never afford to sit down outside a city or fort for very long before being forced to move off for food.

In fighting their enemies the Romans also taught them a lot. In Trajan's Danube wars the

Dacians used Roman artillery that they had captured, probably from the campaign army of Cornelius Fuscus sent into Dacia by Domitian after the first victory. The Jews also captured artillery machines and used Roman prisoners to instruct them in their use. The Goths first appeared in the third century and caused considerable trouble to the Romans who usually managed to defeat them after a struggle. Initially the tribesmen were as disunited and disorganised as many other so-called barbarians, but they soon developed strong leadership and unity in a federation that probably included other tribesmen beside the Goths. Some of them had served in the Roman armies and knew how the Romans fought. It must have been a severe shock to the Romans, who may have been confident that tribesmen could not conduct sieges, when the Gothic King Cniva besieged and captured Philippopolis (Plovdiv) in 250.

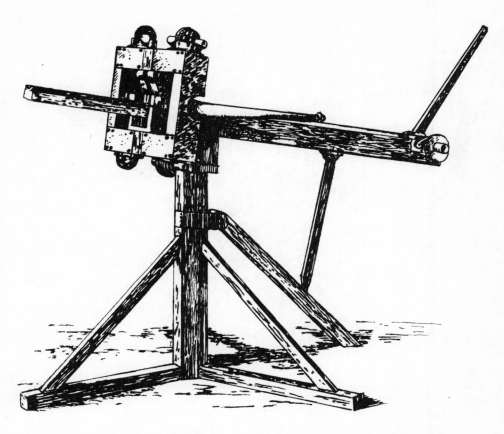

This drawing shows a wooden-framed catapult of the late Republic, reconstructed by German archaeologist E. Schramm, based on finds from Ampurias, alternatively named Emporiae, in Spain. The cord bundles, the most vulnerable parts of any artillery machine, are encased in the wooden frame with their tops protruding above and below on metal washers. Operators had to aim at the target by siting over the top of the frame, and then calculating the elevation. These artillery engines were heavy and unwieldy, and had to be taken apart for transport and reassembled for use. Redrawn by Susan Veitch after M. Feugère *Weapons of the Romans*. Tempus, 2002.

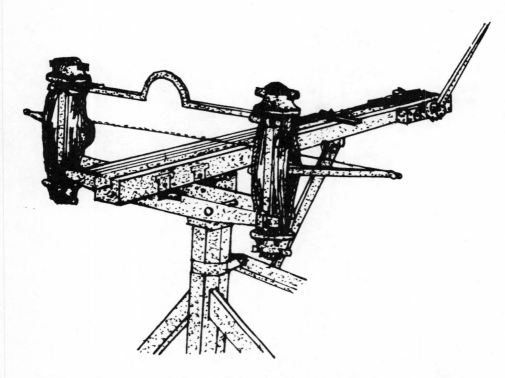

Reconstruction drawing of a metal *manuballista* or *cheiroballistra*, more easily manoeuvred than the wooden versions for use in battle. On Trajan's Column similar machines or *carroballistae* are shown mounted on carts. Aiming the missile was also easier in that operators could site the target along the bolt in the slider, their view assisted by the arch in the top strut. Artillerymen used to take spare parts, especially the cord bundles, so as to be able to make repairs quickly. The cord bundles are visible in this drawing, but would be covered by metal sheets, like the examples shown on Trajan's Column which show metal cylinders around them. Redrawn by Susan Veitch after M. Feugère *Weapons of the Romans*. Tempus, 2002.

11

Frontiers

From Republican times and to a certain extent all through the Empire the concept of Roman rule was one of continual expansion, *imperium sine fine*, power without end, in both the temporal and territorial sense. Borders and boundaries were drawn up with ease, but these were fluid and could be changed by conquest or negotiation, and were not viewed as setting a limit to Roman expansion. There were periods when continual progress and annexations ceased, but it was considered temporary. Conquest was not a feature of Tiberius' reign. Augustus had warned him not to try to advance any further, but this was probably because the disaster of Varus in AD 9 and the consequent loss of three legions in Germany had shaken confidence. The Romans had pulled back from whatever their goals were beyond the Lower Rhine. Tiberius had seen more than enough fighting in Germany and Pannonia and was willing to comply with Augustus' wishes.

Some scholars have suggested that originally Augustus intended to push Roman rule as far as the River Elbe, and then join this new boundary to the Danube. The modern theory that the Elbe was the ultimate goal distorts the view of Roman strategy, since plans that seem eminently logical, with the benefit of atlases and nearly 2,000 years of hindsight, may not have appealed to the Romans, whose own planning was perhaps not motivated by logic, but by opportunism, flexibility and feasibility. *Imperium sine fine* was an amorphous ideology, not an Imperial policy to be pursued in carefully planned stages.

Despite the absence of a consistent policy, the emperors who extended the Empire were usually very popular. Demonstrations of support for their expansionist policies may have been assisted by a little manipulation here and there, by the use of propagandist images in art and architecture, on the coinage, and in the descriptive phrases included in the string of titles adopted by emperors, illustrating their conquests in the name of Rome. One of the prime examples is Severus, who expanded Roman territory in Africa and in the east, and earned the epithet *propagator imperii*, acknowledging that he extended Imperial rule. He advertised his conquests in his titles Adiabenicus, Arabicus, Parthicus, and Britannicus, which last two titles later became Parthicus Maximus and Britannicus Maximus. He was also declared to be *fortissimus* and *felicissimus*, emphasising his great prowess and his good fortune – everything that the Romans could desire their emperor to be, one who could protect them against all evils, whether military or political, and extend Roman authority, bringing wealth to the city and opportunities for the businessmen to expand their trade.

Emperors who were not entirely devoted to constant conquest, or even called a halt to continual expansion, were unpopular. Nero was said to have considered giving up Britain at some unknown point in the history of the province, perhaps just after his accession when the governor Didius Gallus was struggling to pacify the province, or perhaps more likely after the losses incurred during the rebellion of Boudicca. Whatever the context, the idea of abandonment was received with alarm, not least by the upper-class moneylenders who had several eminent Britons firmly in their pockets and would lose a great deal if the province was given up. In the end there was no withdrawal, but after the revolt of Boudicca there was a pause in military activity, and governors were sent out whose expertise was in the political or legal spheres. In Germany, although Domitian had waged a successful war against the tribe of the Chatti, he did not annexe new territory beyond the Rhine. He reaffirmed the boundary line and halted further expansion. Tacitus, who hated Domitian passionately, seemed to think that the halt was a temporary measure. He expressed the view that it was taking an awfully long time to conquer Germany (*tam diu Germania vincitur*) as though complete conquest was always part of the plan. If such was the case, the plan was never fulfilled.

Within a few years of Hadrian's accession, there was a marked change of policy. The concept of *imperium sine fine* was probably still alive and well in the minds of the Romans, but not in the Emperor Hadrian's. By his time, the armies had already moved to the periphery of the Empire, towards the northern parts of Britain, to the Rhine in Germany, and to the Danube in Noricum, Pannonia and Moesia. The eastern border of the Roman Empire was not so clearly defined, and was always potentially troublesome because the next-door neighbours were the Parthians, who controlled an Empire extending over vast territories, and formed the only state with the resources to oppose the Romans on a long-term basis.

Hadrian took a pragmatic view of the Empire. He abandoned part of Trajan's conquests in the east, and redefined the new province of Dacia, which appears as a bulge attached to the north bank of the Danube, leaving the Hungarian plains to the west and large territories to the east outside the Empire. Hadrian decided to consolidate what the Romans had gained so far, retaining only the areas that could be successfully administered, but this was not simply a halt to expansion. The important innovation was the Emperor's decision to enclose the Empire within clearly marked boundaries, some of them consisting of physical barriers, others comprising major rivers or road systems, and all of them manned by soldiers in auxiliary forts and watchtowers, backed up by legionary fortresses. Usually the legions were based at some point in the hinterland of the frontier areas, and the auxiliary forts were either brought right up to the frontier line, as on Hadrian's Wall and the later Antonine Wall in Britain, or placed a kilometre or two behind the line, as on the frontier in Germany. Smaller installations like the milecastles and turrets on Hadrian's Wall and the corresponding small forts (Kleinkastelle) and watchtowers on the German frontier probably served as patrolling bases and guard posts. In the eastern provinces running barriers were not employed, but the borders with the Parthian Empire were monitored by the army. In parts of north Africa, too vast to be enclosed entirely, lines of stone walls of Hadrianic date constitute less of a military frontier and more of a means of controlling the seasonal movements of a pastoral people, to prevent them from straying into the more settled areas with their flocks and herds.

The Rhine and Danube Frontiers

Hadrian was the first Emperor to tour the whole Empire to see for himself what was happening in the provinces. There were no major wars of conquest or retaliation, except for the serious and bloody revolt in Judaea in the 130s, which took a long time to quell, and may have caused the demise and disappearance of *IX Hispana*, last attested at York on a building inscription dated to AD 108, but the legion was probably moved to the Rhine, then to Judaea. In 121 Hadrian was in Germany, and by 122 he was touring Britain. These areas are the ones where Roman frontiers probably made the most impact, and where extensive physical remains can still be traced.

The Roman frontiers of what is now northern Europe extended from the Rhine in the west to the mouth of the Danube in the east, running through the provinces of Lower and Upper Germany, Raetia, Noricum, Pannonia and Moesia. After Trajan's campaigns the province of Dacia was created, approximating to modern Romania north of the Danube. For much of this long frontier, the rivers marked the boundaries, the lower Rhine in the west, and the middle and lower Danube in the east.

The German territories were administered from Gaul until the late AD 80s, when the provinces of Lower and Upper Germany were created. The defences along the lower Rhine, which formed the northern boundary of the province of Lower Germany, were continually developed from Augustan times. At first the river served as the baseline for advances into Germany, then it became the boundary, manned by legionary fortresses, assisted by auxiliary forts spaced about eight miles apart. There were bridges across the Rhine, guarded by forts. It is assumed that the Romans patrolled north of the Rhine, and perhaps from the reign of Claudius the fleet, *Classis Germanica*, patrolled the river. In the early period there were two double legionary fortresses at Cologne and Vetera (Xanten), but in 35 Cologne became a civilian settlement, and its legions were relocated, *legio I* to Bonna (Bonn), and *legio XX* to Noviomagus (Neuss). The double fortress at Vetera was destroyed in the Batavian revolt of 69. A new fortress for a single legion was built close to the old site, and another fortress was constructed at Nijmegen. Some of the troops of Lower Germany were withdrawn for the Dacian wars of Domitian and Trajan, and by the first half of the second century there were only two legions in the province. Xanten was the base of *XXX Ulpia Victrix*, which was probably raised in 101 for the first of Trajan's Dacian wars. The legion raised by Domitian, *I Minervia*, was based at Bonn.

South-east of Bonn, the frontier diverged from the Rhine, going northwards, then turning eastwards, and then back south to skirt round the edge of the Taunus-Wetterau region, defining the peculiar salient projecting northwards, sticking up like a sore thumb. It looks completely illogical to enclose this territory instead of continuing in a straight west–east line, until it is pointed out that the land on the Roman side is fertile, well-drained soil, while on the other side there is clay, not so easily drained even with the aid of modern equipment. This line, guarded by a road and watchtowers, was established probably in the Flavian period, but neither the road nor the towers can be dated with absolute accuracy. The road is considered by some authorities to constitute the first Roman frontier in Germany. The Romans used the term *limes* (plural *limites*) to describe a frontier, and in this connection the archaeological evidence for the Taunus-Wetterau road and watchtowers has been linked with Frontinus' statement in his book *Stratagemata* that in Germany Domitian advanced *limites* over 120 miles during the war against the Chatti in 82–83. The tribe was in the appropriate location, and the Taunus-Wetterau line measures roughly 120 Roman miles. One problem with this ingenious suggestion is that the word *limes* did not always have the connotation of 'limit' as in English, because originally it was applied to the road that led into enemy territory and had nothing to do with boundaries when used in this sense. Frontinus may have been describing Domitian's advance into the Chattan heartland, and not the boundary line.

By the end of the first century auxiliary forts had been established on the Taunus-Wetterau road and there were legionary fortresses to the rear at Mainz, Strasbourg and Windisch. The area east of Mainz and Strasbourg was only lightly defended in Flavian times, but by the end of the first century auxiliary forts had been built beyond the upper Rhine and the upper Danube cutting off the re-entrant angle between the head waters of the two great rivers. Running south-east through the Odenwald a line of several small forts was built which were neither auxiliary forts nor Kleinkastelle. They were all very similar in size and shape and inscriptions showed that they were garrisoned by *numeri*, mostly of Brittones. The date when these units arrived is not established. Some scholars have assigned their origins to Domitian, who may have taken numbers of tribesmen from northern Britain when he abandoned Agricola's conquest of Scotland, but this can also be applied to Trajan when he pulled back even further in Britain and took troops away for the Dacian wars. Yet other scholars assign the British *numeri* to Hadrian. Archaeological investigation of the *numerus* fort at Hesselbach revealed that the *numeri* were complete units with their own headquarters buildings and barracks like auxiliary units, but smaller in size. The terrain of the Odenwald consists of small hills and valleys, rolling countryside not heavily populated and with no clear plains or easy routes of access, so defence could be left to these small units, who probably patrolled regularly beyond the boundary.

Hadrian simply consolidated what had already been established by erecting a wooden palisade in front of the line of forts on the borders of Upper Germany and Raetia, using rivers as the frontier wherever possible. Between the Wetterau and the Odenwald, the River Main formed the frontier, and from the Odenwald to the Raetian frontier the River Neckar served as the boundary line. The palisade continued eastwards through Raetia to Eining on the Danube, and then the river became the frontier all the way to its junction with the Black Sea.

The frontier barrier was constructed entirely of timber, of which there was no lack in Germany. A trench was dug about three feet deep, to take the timber posts, usually of oak. Some of the uprights were held in place with stones packed round their bases, and the finds of Roman nails in some sectors show that the timbers were nailed together, probably by horizontal planks. No one knows how high the palisade would have been, but it is estimated that it was perhaps three metres tall. This was not a frontier that would have withstood a determined attack in strength. It marked the boundary in no uncertain terms, and highlighted the moral ascendancy of the Romans whose considerable military force behind the frontier probably deterred assaults, at least for the first 150 years or so. There were occasional gaps in the palisade, sometimes marked by very large post holes flanking the gap indicating that there were large timbers on either side. These may even have supported a gate, though there is little evidence. The gaps were usually guarded by a watchtower set back from the opening, where perhaps patrols went out beyond the frontier. At Dalkingen in Raetia there was an elaborate timber gateway through the palisade, next to a stone tower. The central passageway of the gateway was flanked by two guard houses. This crossing point was considered important enough to be replaced with an even more elaborate stone version when the Raetian frontier was itself rebuilt in stone

The watchtowers accompanying the Upper German and Raetian palisade had a long history from Flavian times. The earliest towers guarded a road with no running barrier. They were timber built, surrounded by a ditch and bank, most of the ditches being circular, but some ditches are more or less square with rounded corners. Timber towers would have a limited lifespan and some had two timber phases before the palisade was erected. Others were replaced in stone close to the original sites. Some of the rebuilding in stone seems to belong to the reign of Antoninus Pius, in the 140s and 150s.

Between the watchtowers there were small forts, called in German Kleinkastelle, which could not have held an entire auxiliary unit. They correspond to the small forts labelled milecastles on Hadrian's Wall, though the spacing of the German examples is not so regular. The auxiliary forts which provided the soldiers to man these small forts were often some distance behind the palisade. Some were refurbished, probably at the same time as the erection of the palisade and the small forts along its line.

A rationalisation of the eastern end of the Upper German frontier took place under Antoninus Pius, who moved the units of the Odenwald frontier a maximum of twenty-five miles further east. The move is not closely dated, but was probably completed before his death in 161. This does not constitute a conquest of new territory or a military advance involving a campaign. The Romans probably already controlled all this land to the east of the Odenwald frontier, and simply marched into it to construct the new frontier line, which goes by the modern name of the Outer *Limes*. It ran almost due south and more or less dead straight from Miltenberg to Lorch, and was a carbon copy of the Odenwald frontier, with the palisade, the watchtowers and the *numerus* forts. Most of the *numeri* moved forwards to their new bases, built like the old ones. Pius may also have been responsible for the ditch and rampart, called the Pfahlgraben, which was dug behind the palisade around the Taunus-Wetterau frontier, and on the Outer *Limes*. No such bank and ditch has been traced behind the palisade on the Odenwald frontier, so the date of the Pfahlgraben is assumed to be at least post-Hadrianic.

The new Outer *Limes* did not at first join up with the Raetian frontier, though this may have been the intention. The province of Raetia, which incorporates the Tyrol and parts of modern Switzerland and Bavaria, was annexed under Augustus after campaigns by Tiberius and Drusus in 15 BC. It was strategically important for the protection of Italy. The early version of the Hadrianic frontier consisted of a palisade with timber watchtowers, like the German version, but for some time at its western end there was a corridor of about 30 kilometres, guarded only by a road with timber watchtowers, with no running barrier. The gap was finally closed early in the reign of Marcus Aurelius. Timbers of the palisade have been found in the area, dendro-chronologically dated to 165, but it is thought that the new palisade was quickly replaced by a stone wall in the later 160s. Eventually the whole Raetian frontier from Lorch to Eining on the Danube was rebuilt in stone, but accurate dating is elusive. In some places the original palisade may have deteriorated, requiring repairs, which were probably carried out by erecting wattle fencing, traces of which have been found in excavations. The fence is later than the palisade, but the repair work may have been done piecemeal, as and when necessary at different times, which may explain why some sections of the fencing were erected before the stone towers were built, but in other sections the stone towers were already in existence when the wattle fencing was put up. This also suggests that some of the timber towers were replaced by stone versions before the wall replaced the palisade. By the later second century, the stone towers had been integrated with the wall, instead of standing behind it as they had stood behind the palisade. In this respect the Raetian stone wall is similar to Hadrian's Wall in Britain with its turrets, but the Raetian frontier wall is not as wide as the British version, and does not have auxiliary forts attached to it.

East of Eining on the Danube, the river formed the frontier of eastern Raetia, and the provinces of Noricum, Pannonia and Moesia. These Danubian provinces were annexed at different times under Augustus. Noricum guarded the north-eastern approaches to Italy and was incorporated as a province in 16 BC. Originally it was governed by an equestrian in command of auxiliary troops, but when the Marcommanic wars began under Marcus Aurelius the newly raised legion, *II Italica*, was added to the garrison, eventually based at Lauriacum. The legionary legate also governed the province. Pannonia is defined on its northern and eastern sides by the Danube, which flows eastwards and then turns sharply southwards for several miles before resuming its eastward flow to the Black Sea. The area between the Danube and northern Italy was known as Illyricum, fought over several times, and governed by Caesar along with Gaul. It was a senatorial province until 11 BC, but was converted into an Imperial province during

Tiberius' campaigns up to the Danube. In the early first century, the area was split into two provinces, Dalmatia carved out of the southern part, and Pannonia in the north. Pannonia was formally annexed in AD 9, after the revolt that began in AD 6 was finally crushed by Tiberius. It was governed by a consular legate. The legionary fortress at Carnuntum (Deutsch-Altenburg) on the Danube was probably built by Claudius, while another legion was based in the interior at Poetovio (modern Ptuj). At the end of the Dacian wars in 106 Pannonia was divided into two unequal parts. The larger province of Upper Pannonia had a consular governor and three legions, at Vindobona (Vienna) and Carnuntum (Deutsch-Altenburg) in modern Austria, and Brigetio (Szőny) in Hungary. Lower Pannonia had a praetorian governor and one legion at Aquincum (Budapest), and its first governor was the future Emperor Hadrian. The boundaries between the two provinces were adjusted in the early third century by Caracalla, so that both provinces contained two legions and both were governed by consulars.

Moesia, the land of the Moesi, was subdued in 29 BC by Marcus Licinius Crassus, and was at first administered as part of Macedonia. It may have been formally constituted as a province in AD 45, but the date is uncertain. Claudius may have established legions on the Danube at Viminacium (modern Kostolac), Oescus (Gigen) and Novae (Sistov), and there may have been a legion at Singidunum (Belgrade). The river fleet, the *Classis Moesica*, patrolled the lower Danube with harbours at Ratiaria (modern Archer, Bulgaria) and Sexaginta Prisca (Ruse). The province was divided into Upper and Lower Moesia by Domitian in 85 or 86, each with a consular governor. When Trajan annexed Dacia, most of the frontier of Upper Moesia was protected by the new province, and legions were moved into the territory. Under Hadrian and Antoninus Pius, Dacia was split into three provinces for a short time, Upper Dacia in the centre under a praetorian legate, Lower Dacia in the south-east, and Porolissensis in the north-west, both governed by procurators. In 168 the three provinces were amalgamated into the province of Tres Daciae, with a consular governor. The frontier of Dacia was not marked by continuous running barriers, though short stretches of earthwork or stone barriers have been discovered. Around the north-western edge of the province, a line of watchtowers and small forts, called the *limes Porolissensis*, protected the border west of Porolissum, where there were two forts, large enough to hold about 2,500 men. The line of towers and fortlets was backed up by auxiliary forts in the hinterland.

During the reign of Hadrian, when the Rhine and Danube frontiers were consolidated, the legions and auxiliary units arrived at the bases that they were to occupy until the late Empire. The focus of activity in the early first century had been on the Rhine, where eight legions were stationed, while the Danube area was only lightly defended, and gradually, from the Dacian attack on Moesia in 85, the focus shifted to that area, so the Rhine garrison was reduced and that of the Danube provinces was increased. Before the frontiers were established there had been considerable movement of troops from old bases to new ones, so any map showing all the known auxiliary forts and legionary fortresses, taking no account of the successive stages of occupation, gives the impression that the provinces of the Rhine and Danube were more heavily garrisoned than they were in reality. In general, the move towards the Rhine and Danube began under Claudius and was continued until Hadrian called a halt to expansion. In his reign, there were two legions in Lower Germany, *XXX Ulpia Victrix* at Vetera (Xanten) and *I Minervia* at Bonna (Bonn), and two in Upper Germany, *XXII Primigenia* at Moguntiacum (Mainz) and *VIII Augusta* at Argentorate (Strasbourg). Upper Pannonia had three legions: *X Gemina* at Vindobona (Vienna), *XIV Gemina* at Carnuntum (Deutsch-Altenburg) and *I Adiutrix* at Brigetio (Szőny). Lower Pannonia had only one legion, *II Adiutrix* at Aquincum (Budapest). In

Upper Moesia *IIII Flavia Felix* was at Singidunum (Belgrade) and *VII Claudia* at Viminacium (Kostolac), and in Lower Moesia the fortress at Novae (Stiklen/Sistov) was occupied by *I Italica*, and two new fortresses had been built on the lower Danube. Durostorum (Silistra) was established on the site of an auxiliary fort, and was occupied by *XI Claudia*, and *V Macedonica* was at Troesmis (Iglita). In Dacia there were originally three legions later reduced to one at the legionary base at Alba Iulia (Apulum). A frontier which extended over 2,000 miles from the Lower Rhine to the Black Sea was defended by a maximum of fourteen legions and their accompanying auxiliary units. The auxiliary forts were usually placed on routes to and from the frontiers, or at river crossings, their siting dictated by topographical considerations rather than rigid spacing at a day's march apart.

The tribes beyond the frontier were not static, with permanent towns, villages, roads and borders. Their mobility and interchangeable alliances were potentially threatening to the Romans, and also to each other. Not all the pressures on the frontiers came from direct attacks, but sometimes from harassed tribes who wanted to be admitted into the Empire to settle on lands behind the frontiers. Thousands of them were admitted from the reign of Augustus onwards. In the second century, the main tribes opposite the Danube frontiers were the Marcomanni to the north of Noricum and Pannonia, the Quadi directly facing the Pannonian frontier, and the Iazyges in the Hungarian plain. A new element appeared in the later second century, the Sarmatians, driven towards the Roman Empire by tribes beyond them. The tribal names do not always constitute a purely ethnic identity. In the third century a people called the Alamanni appeared beyond the German frontier, but the name simply means 'all men', not a race. Tribesmen from different tribes could amalgamate from time to time and call themselves by another name, and a further complication is that what the Romans called them may not be the names by which the tribes knew each other.

In the reign of Marcus Aurelius, the Marcomanni, Quadi and Sarmatians threatened the Danube frontier and there was fighting for many years. The ancient sources state that Marcus intended to conquer these peoples and create two new provinces beyond the frontiers, called Marcomannia and Sarmatia, but if there was such a plan it never materialised. On his father's death in 180, Commodus made peace, extracting numbers of tribesmen for the Roman army, and built a series of watchtowers called *burgi* to control the Danube river frontier. An inscription from one of these towers in Lower Pannonia states that the whole series of towers along the river was built from the ground up, *per loca opportuna ad clandestinos latrunculorum transitus*, 'at points appropriate for the prevention of clandestine intrusion of petty bandits', *latrunculi* being the diminutive form of *latrones* or robbers.

There were serious attacks on the German frontier in the 230s, concentrated on the Taunus-Wetterau area, where the fertile lands were located, which suggests that as well as engaging in hit and run raids, the tribesmen were coming for food, though no ancient source corroborates this. Traces of destruction which have been found in several forts date to this period, and it seems that not all the forts were rebuilt. About three decades later, worse was to come over the whole Roman world. Every frontier fell, and the Empire split into three separate parts for over a decade.

The African and Eastern Frontiers

Compared to the Rhine and Danube frontiers, the Roman provinces of Africa were very lightly defended. From west to east the provinces in their final form were Mauretania Tingitana, Mauretania Caesariensis, Numidia, Africa Proconsularis, Tripolitania, Cyrenaica and Egypt.

In this enormous extent of territory there were only auxiliary units and never more than three permanent legions, one in Numidia, and two in Egypt, later reduced to only one. The African frontier was never threatened by masses of tribesmen from outside Roman territory, so there were no major wars as there were on the Danube under Domitian, Trajan and Marcus Aurelius. The major tasks of the legionaries and auxiliaries in Egypt and Africa were internal policing, dealing with raids rather than attacks from tribes on the periphery, and guarding the corn supply.

The first Roman province in Africa was a small area taken over by Scipio Aemilianus after the destruction of Carthage in 146 BC. The border between Roman territory and the kingdom of Numidia was clearly marked by a ditch, which the Romans called Fossa Regia, not a frontier as such and not defended by forts. In 46 BC after the battle of Thapsus, Caesar annexed Numidia, because King Juba had fought on the side of the Pompeians. He stationed three legions in the new province, appropriately named Africa Nova, and the old one became Africa Vetus. Augustus combined these two provinces into one, Africa Proconsularis, the name indicating that it was a senatorial province under a proconsul, one of the few proconsular governors who commanded troops. There was one legion, *III Augusta*, which remained in Africa until the late Empire. Mauretania had been annexed but was given to Juba II as a client kingdom. He had been brought up in Rome, and was married to Cleopatra Selene, daughter of Cleopatra VII and Mark Antony.

There was only a low-intensity threat in most of the African provinces. Tripolitania and Cyrenaica were lightly garrisoned. When a revolt broke out under Tacfarinas, a Numidian who had served as an auxiliary soldier, Tiberius had to send *IX Hispana*, or a large vexillation of it, to help *III Augusta* to quell the rebellion, but after peace was restored there was no increase in the number of auxiliary troops, and *IX Hispana* did not remain in the province.

Under Gaius Caligula, Africa was made an Imperial province, and after he had arranged the murder of Juba's son and successor, he annexed Mauretania. The result was a rebellion of the Mauri, or Moors, which was suppressed by Suetonius Paullinus, and Hosidius Geta, who chased the Moors across the Atlas Mountains. Paullinus would later campaign in Snowdonia and Anglesey, and would meet the full onslaught of Boudicca's tribesmen in 60. It may have been Claudius who divided Mauretania into two, Mauretania Tingitana in the west, with a concentration of garrison posts on the Atlantic coast and the Straits of Gibraltar, and Mauretania Caesariensis in the east, mostly restricted to the Mediterranean coastal plain. Under the Flavian Emperors there seems to have been trouble from the tribesmen. Vespasian appointed Sextius Sentius Caecilianus as *legatus Augusti pro praetore ordinandae utriusque Mauretaniae*, to restore order in both provinces, and a short time later Velius Rufus was made leader (*dux*) of the troops of Africa and Mauretania, *ad nationes quae sunt in Mauretania conprimendas*, 'to keep in check the tribes which are in Mauretania'.

In the province of Africa, *III Augusta* was based at Ammaedara in modern Tunisia, until about 75 when it moved to Theveste (Tebessa). This last named base was made into a colony under Trajan, who concentrated on road building, creating municipalities and organising the provinces. *III Augusta* had obviously moved but it is not certain where it was, until it arrived at the base at Lambaesis in modern Algeria, probably under Hadrian, who addressed the troops there in 128. Hadrian began a programme of fort building and established sectors of running barriers, built mostly of mud-brick with a ditch in front, and equipped with gates and towers, collectively known to modern scholars as the *fossatum Africae*. These were not continuous frontiers like the German and Raetian versions, or Hadrian's Wall in England, but were designed for surveillance of routes into and out of the provinces, and to protect water supplies and perhaps crops, and to control the transhumance routes as tribesmen passed through from summer to winter pastures. These barriers run for considerable distances. Around the Hodna Mountains in Mauretania Caesariensis the wall and ditch system has been traced for eighty-seven miles.

There was another Moorish war under Antoninus Pius, necessitating assistance from troops from other provinces. Once the problems were solved the extra troops returned to their provinces. Until the reign of Severus there was no significant advance into the hinterland of the Hadrianic frontier system, which seems to have encouraged prosperity and population growth. Control of the African provinces was exercised by forming alliances with tribal leaders, erecting outpost forts for small detachments of troops, road building in some areas and patrolling, both inside Roman territory and possibly a long way outside it. An inscription found 250 miles beyond the frontier at Agneb was set up in 174 by a group of infantry and cavalry who were most likely on a routine patrol, since no forts are known in the vicinity. In Mauretania Caesariensis Commodus erected watchtowers along the frontier road, probably with the same purpose as his *burgi* on the Danube frontier. Surveillance seems to be the priority, not fighting. When Severus turned his attention to Africa, he detached Numidia, approximating to Algeria, from Africa Proconsularis and made it a province, and he advanced the frontier in Tripolitania by building new forts south of the settled areas. In Mauretania Caesariensis he created a new frontier called the Nova Praetentura, as attested on milestones. New forts and outposts were built, and new roads constructed. G. C. Picard saw this as a zone to control the movement of pastoral tribes heading for the northern pastures in July or August. They could be detained in the zone in the early summer, with plenty of grazing to sustain the animals, while the labourers from the south passed through to work on the harvests. This prevented the pastoralists from moving into the area where crops were growing, and trampling them down before they could be harvested. Frontier control in Africa had little to do with military action, but much to do with policing.

This changed in 235 when the Emperor Severus Alexander was assassinated in Germany, and Maximinus Thrax was declared Emperor in his place. In opposition to Maximinus the two Gordians, father and son, set themselves up as rival candidates, but Capellianus, the governor of Numidia and also commander of *III Augusta*, led his troops against the Gordians at Carthage and defeated them. The elder Gordian committed suicide after his son was killed. *III Augusta* did not profit from the victory, since Maximinus was soon assassinated in his turn, and the grandson of the elder Gordian became Emperor as Gordian III, backed by Timesithius, the Praetorian Prefect. The African legion was disbanded. Valerian and his son Gallienus became joint Emperors in September 253 and reconstituted the legion in the same year, by sending troops from Raetia and Noricum, but little is known of its subsequent history. From this time onwards the whole Empire was affected by unrest and civil war, and the African provinces, hitherto under negligible threat internally and externally, began to be troubled by rebellions of the provincial population and invasions from tribes on the periphery. Commanders were increasingly called upon to campaign against the tribes, and despite their successes the unrest continued until the appointment of an overall commander with authority over the whole frontier. This was Cornelius Octavianus, *dux per Africam Numidiam Mauretaniamque*, who brought order and peace to the provinces for a while in the fateful year of 260.

Egypt became a province in 30 BC, annexed by Octavian after the defeat of Antony and Cleopatra, and governed by an equestrian. This meant that the legions could not be commanded by senators because they would have to answer to a governor of lower rank than themselves, so

Egypt was an anomaly in that equestrians also commanded the legions. There was no frontier or running barrier dividing the province from the tribes to the south, but there was a need to guard the Red Sea coast where the trade ships came in, especially at Myos Hormos where the road network along the coast converged. There were also quarries to be protected inland such as Mons Claudianus, south-east of Myos Hormos. Roman forts and smaller garrison posts were established along the routes, each small post with a cistern for water, and places to tether the animals in lines. The road to Leucos Limen on the Red Sea was equipped with watchtowers, closely spaced, on the high ground overlooking the ravines.

There were originally three legions in Egypt, quickly reduced to two, at Nicopolis, a suburb of Alexandria. These were *XXII Deiotariana* and *III Cyrenaica*. At some unknown date *III Cyrenaica* was removed to the new province of Arabia created by Trajan. It was based at Bostra (Bosra, Syria). There is some evidence that the legion was involved in the initial stages of setting up the province in 106, but if so it was back in Egypt again, probably temporarily, in 119 when its companion legion *XXII Deiotariana* disappeared from the record. No one knows what happened to this legion. By 128 if not earlier *II Traiana Fortis* was at Nicopolis, and remained there until the early third century as the only legion in Egypt. The legionaries and auxiliaries in Egypt were not involved in serious fighting because there were no large-scale invasions. Vexillations were sent to other war zones such as the Parthian campaigns of Lucius Verus and Severus. The main tasks in Egypt were securing the grain supply for Rome, and protecting the quarries and the long-distance trade routes, mostly from the Red Sea, where piracy was a problem. Internal policing probably occupied considerable time. There were riots in Alexandria that required military control, and the tribes on the periphery of Egypt proved troublesome from time to time. The Blemmyes in the east raided Upper Egypt, and in the second half of the third century when unrest erupted almost everywhere they became more adventurous and aggressive. The Nubians in the west also raided on several occasions.

There was an important centre at Coptos on the Nile, where the routes from the Red Sea converged, including the road from the important port of Berenike about 300 kilometres to the south-east. The Romans protected these routes by patrols, in which mounted archers from Palmyra usually escorted the caravans to guard against robbers. There were closely spaced stations with access to water, called appropriately *hydreumata*, with a fortified enclosure surrounding the well and space for men and animals to shelter for the night. Tolls may have been exacted on caravans on the routes to the Nile at Coptos, and it may have been the soldiers who supervised the procedure. An inscription known as the Coptos Tariff lists the charges, two *obols* for anyone travelling with an ass or donkey, four *drachmae* for a covered wagon, and so on, escalating with the size and importance of the vehicles and the goods carried. No one escaped the taxes. Funeral processions had to pay for using the roads, and women travelling along the routes for the purposes of prostitution paid the highest tax of all, 108 *drachmae*. The routes between Coptos and Berenike were important for long-distance trade and were very busy. A Prefect of Berenike was installed at the port, with responsibility for the security of the whole area, and the importance of the post can be gauged by the fact that at least two legionary tribunes held it.

The eastern provinces neighbouring the Parthian Empire include all the territory from the Black Sea to the border with Egypt. The perennial problems in the east concerned the perceived threat from the Parthians, and the consequent struggles over control of Armenia, north of Syria and Mesopotamia, and control of Mesopotamia itself. For most of the time, the best that could be achieved was to install pro-Roman kings in these areas, especially in Armenia, but the Parthians had a vested interest in doing the same, so there was a succession of rulers with sympathies for one Empire or the other. Roman attempts to take over Armenia as a province never succeeded. Trajan annexed it, but only for a short time. Full Roman control may not have solved the problem anyway. Severus created the province of Mesopotamia from the territory that had been overrun by Lucius Verus in the 160s, but it caused more problems than it solved. Wherever the boundary between Rome and Parthia was fixed, there could be no lasting peace. Most of the aggressive moves were made by Rome, sometimes in response to Parthian incursions and sometimes without much provocation. Roman armies penetrated the Parthian Empire several times and sometimes captured the capital at Ctesiphon, but there was never a permanent occupation, and the Romans usually went home again in various states of disrepair. Neither side was ever strong enough to inflict a final decisive defeat on the other. At the end of the second century the Parthians were weakened by internal dissension, and lacked the strong central control that was necessary to govern their Empire. While the king was occupied in the west, dealing with the attacks of Severus and then Caracalla, in the distant eastern parts of the Parthian Empire a Sasanian noble was planning a takeover bid, which resulted in the eradication of the centuries-old Arsacid Royal House, and the establishment of the vigorous and aggressive new dynasty of the Sassanids, led by the first King of Kings Ardashir in 226. From then onwards the Romans were in trouble.

The military installations of the east differed in many respects from those of the northern and African provinces. There were no running barriers marking the frontiers, and though the River Euphrates could be said to form a boundary it was not equipped with closely spaced defence works like the Rhine and Danube. Since it ran north-west to south-east it diverged from the settled areas to the west, separated from them by expanses of desert. The distribution of forts is not well known because some of them have probably been obliterated, either by intensive farming in fertile areas, or by erosion which concealed them with sand in desert conditions. Probably many forts still await discovery. In several cases soldiers were lodged in towns and cities. At the city of Dura Europos on the Euphrates in Syria, legionary vexillations and the auxiliary unit *cohors XX Palmyrenorum*, made famous by the number of papyrus documents that have been found, were accommodated in the northern end of the city where the fortified walls follow an irregular course, not immediately recognisable as a fort from the plan. The internal buildings were laid out on a grid pattern, but what has been excavated so far does not indicate from the shape and size of the buildings that soldiers rather than civilians were living there.

Up to ten legions are known in the eastern provinces, though they were not all in garrison simultaneously. Syria was annexed in the course of Pompey's eastern campaigns, in 64 BC, and had at least three, sometimes four legions. Severus split Syria into two provinces, Syria Phoenice in the south with one legion, *III Gallica* at Raphanea (Rafniye), and Syria Coele in the north with two legions, *IV*, more commonly expressed as *IIII Scythica*, based at Zeugma on the Euphrates, and *XVI Flavia Firma* at Samosata (Samsat). To the north-east of Syria, Cappadocia was annexed in 17 as a procuratorial province until 72 when Vespasian combined it with Galatia under a consular governor. Trajan created a new province combining Cappadocia with Pontus. From Flavian times to the later Empire Cappadocia was part of the frontier system, with two legions at Satala (Sadak) in the north, occupied by *XV Apollinaris*, a much travelled legion which had started out on the Danube at Carnuntum, and taken part in wars in Pannonia, Parthia and Judaea. Further south there was a legionary base at Melitene (Malatya) close to the Euphrates, occupied by *XII Fulminata*. At the southern border of Syria, Judaea was taken over by Pompey after 63 BC and was at first governed from Syria. It became a procuratorial province in AD 6, and then after the defeat of the Jews in AD 70, Judaea was converted into an Imperial province known as Syria Palaestina, with one legion at Jerusalem, occupied by *X Fretensis*. Another legion, *VI Ferrata*, was added probably by Hadrian, and based at Caparcotna (Lejjun, near Megiddo, not to be confused with El Lejjun in Jordan). Trajan took over the kingdom of Nabataea and converted it into the province of Arabia in 106, approximating to modern Jordan and the southern sector of Syria. By about 128 if not earlier, *III Cyrenaica* from Egypt was installed at Bostra (Bosra). Severus raised three new legions *I, II* and *III Parthica* and stationed the second one at Albano near Rome. The other two were placed in the new province of Mesopotamia, in reality only the northern half of the country. Both legions may have been based at Singara (Sinjar, Iraq), and then Nisibis (Nusaybin), though it was once suggested that *III Parthica* was at Rhesaina on the River Khabur.

The legionary bases that have been discovered do not resemble the strictly rectangular fortresses of the northern provinces with rounded corners and four main gates. The fortress at Satala (modern Sadak), south of Trapezus on the Black Sea, has a rectangular plan with two gates identified on the north and east sides, and projecting corner towers. The surviving remains are of the later period but may preserve the outline of the Flavian fort that preceded it. Others are irregular on plan with closely spaced projecting drum towers. Auxiliary units are known from finds and inscriptions, but there is little information about their forts. A large proportion of the auxiliary units were either *alae* or *cohortes equitatae*, demonstrating the importance of cavalry in the eastern provinces.

In the early Empire, greater use was made of the troops of client kings and states in the east than was usual in the western provinces. These kingdoms formed a barrier between the Romans and the Parthians, but were eventually absorbed into the Roman Empire, so the army of the east eventually assumed direct responsibility for defence. One exception is Palmyra, an important trading city in the desert between the Euphrates and the settled areas. The Palmyrenes remained free of direct Roman control for many years, patrolling their territory and providing whole units for the Roman army, which were installed in Dacia and Africa. Accustomed to desert conditions and remote places, their horse archers were well equipped to protect routes. The Palmyrene cohort at Dura was part-mounted. The long-distance trade from India and China came through Palmyra from the Euphrates, and the Palmyrenes had long experience of escorting and protecting the caravans.

The Frontiers of Britain

During the early history of Roman Britain, as the province was being subdued and pacified, there were occasions when the advance halted, and forts and roads were built. Some years ago it was suggested that the Fosse Way, the road running diagonally across the country, linking the early fortress at Exeter to the legionary base at Lincoln, was intended to act as a frontier. At first sight a road with military posts along it seems similar to other early boundaries, but the idea that the Romans had any intention to halt and create a frontier is now dismissed. The other occasion when a frontier might have been planned belongs to Agricola's campaigns in Scotland. In his fourth season he halted his advance, and Tacitus says that he found an ideal place for a *terminus*, building forts (*praesidia*) between the Forth and Clyde. These have proved elusive, and do not seem to have been established on the same sites as the second-century forts of the Antonine Wall running between the same two rivers. If Agricola's *praesidia* were meant to establish a frontier it was only for a short time, since the advance northwards was resumed in the following season. At some point during or after the campaigns, forts were established at the mouths of the glens, and the legionary fortress of Inchtuthil was planted in the Tay valley, but it was never finished. No one can say whether the purpose of these forts was to launch attacks up the glens while still advancing, or to block access to and from the Highlands as part of the consolidation of the country after the final battle. Another line of forts was built running round the western edge of modern Fife, at Camelon, Doune, Ardoch, Strageath and Bertha on the River Tay. One fortlet has been found between Ardoch and Strageath, but there may have been more. The road that linked the forts was equipped with watchtowers, possibly along the entire route, but only attested archaeologically from Ardoch to Strageath and along the Gask Ridge. The towers were all made of wood, supported on four posts, and surrounded by a bank and ditch. The spacing between them is regular, and considered too close for signalling purposes but ideal for surveillance of any unauthorised movement across the line in either direction. The road with watchtowers is similar to the examples in Germany from around the same date, though whether the line qualifies as a frontier is debatable. It was short-lived, since Domitian withdrew all the troops from Scotland, and Trajan completed the process.

When Hadrian visited Britain in 122 he may have surveyed the northern parts of the country, and he perhaps rode or even walked along part or all of the geographical feature known as the Whin Sill, a northward-facing cliff of hard rock that occupies much of the territory between the Solway estuary in the west and the mouth of the Tyne in the east. It may have seemed like a divine gift to anyone intending to create a northward-facing frontier. Geographical considerations overrode existing territorial boundaries. The lands of the Brigantes extended north of the line of the Whin Sill, but the frontier that was eventually built cut across their territory. The narrow gap between the Tyne and the Solway had already been marked as the likely place to form a boundary. When the complete withdrawal from Scotland was organised under Trajan, the most northerly Roman occupation was marked by the Stanegate road running just south of the Whin Sill. The road linked Carlisle with Corbridge, but no trace of it has been found either to the west of Carlisle, or to the east of Corbridge, so it seems that its purpose was to provide communication with the roads heading north–south on either side. Beyond the Stanegate, the Romans would still have patrolled and exercised some influence, but for the first years of the second century the focus was on Dacia and the Danube, and then on the eastern campaigns of Trajan.

When Hadrian decided that a new frontier should be established in Britain, he had perhaps inspected the country to the north, and concluded that there was nothing to be gained by trying to re-conquer the rest of the island, even though Agricola had achieved it about 40 years earlier. There was not much profit potential in administering the northern parts of England and southern Scotland. There was lead in the Pennines in what would become Northumberland, and the Scottish lowlands were fertile enough, but this offered nothing that could not be extracted from the British territory further south. Lead was the last thing that the Romans needed, because there was so much of it in areas further south that according to the elder Pliny, production in Britain had been limited by Imperial decree.

The construction work on the frontier wall probably began straight away after Hadrian left. The governor was Aulus Platorius Nepos, who was in the province by July 122. He probably came as part of Hadrian's entourage. He had been governor of Lower Germany, and it was from this province that *VI Victrix* was brought to the fortress at York. Unlike the frontier of Germany, built in timber, the frontier wall in Britain was to be built in stone. Several quarries are known from which the stone would be supplied. Most of the quarrying and building would be done by the legions, and all three of the British legions are attested on inscriptions from the Wall and the forts, *XX Valeria Victrix* from Chester, *II Augusta* from Caerleon, and *VI Victrix*, newly established at York.

The building of the Wall was probably not unlike the establishment of the first railways, where the whole line would be surveyed in general and the topographical and geological details would be dealt with as work progressed. The first plan was simple, a stone wall ten Roman feet thick, with two outer skins of squared stones filled with rubble and cement, or sometimes puddled clay. There were to be small forts attached to the Wall every Roman mile or where circumstances demanded surveillance. They had two gates, one in the south defences, and one through the Wall itself. In between each one there were to be two towers. In Wall terminology these fortlets and towers are called milecastles and turrets, and they correspond to the Kleinkastelle and watchtowers of the German frontier.

Changes were made to the first plan, probably quite soon after building started. The width of the Wall was reduced from ten feet to eight feet, attested by the fact that foundations are known in some sectors that measure ten Roman feet, but the Wall on top is only eight feet. A more serious change to the plan is labelled by modern scholars the 'fort decision'. The earlier forts on the Stanegate, south of the Wall, such as Vindolanda of writing tablet fame, and Corbridge, were placed like the German auxiliary forts to the rear of the actual frontier, but some of the intended back-up for the frontier would have come from forts further south, which would take time to organise. Perhaps for ease of access through the Wall and better surveillance it was decided to build forts on the Wall itself. This is shown at Housesteads fort, where the Wall and a turret had already been built, but were pulled down and building was started again on the northern wall of the new fort, projecting further north than the original Wall. At other sites similar evidence has been found attesting that original building work was destroyed to allow for the placement of the forts. The final version of the Wall ran from Bowness-on-Solway in the west to Wallsend, aptly named, on the Tyne. An eleven-mile-long sector of the western frontier, starting west of the fort at Birdoswald, was built in earth and turf rather than stone. The turrets in this sector were stone built, but the milecastles were earth and turf like the Wall. Different reasons have been suggested for this anomaly, including a possible shortage of building stone, or a need for haste to erect a defensive line in this area. The first earthen frontier was eventually replaced in stone, on a slightly different alignment. Down the Cumberland coast there was a line of free-standing turrets and milecastles, called milefortlets in this sector. There is evidence of a palisade and ditch system west of Bowness, some sections showing evidence of two phases.

Some of the forts along the Wall had six gates. Part of the fort projected beyond the Wall with three gates to the north and three to the south, allowing soldiers to exit and enter from behind or in front of the Wall. Housesteads is attached to the Wall on its long side, because there is a drop of several feet which would not provide for a northward projection, though there was a ramp in Roman times leading from the north gate. In general, cavalry units were stationed in the flatter areas on the west and east. At Stanwix near Carlisle the only milliary cavalry unit in the whole province was stationed, the grandly titled *ala Augusta Gallorum Petriana bis torquata milliaria civium Romanorum*, indicating that the unit had won battle honours at least three times, and had earned Roman citizenship before discharge for the original men of the unit who had distinguished themselves. In the east, at Chesters fort on the North Tyne, the quingenary *ala II Asturum* was stationed. The central sectors were occupied by infantry units, with a milliary cohort at Housesteads.

Accompanying the wall to the north was a ditch, not continuous because it was not necessary where the forts were perched on the cliff formed by the Whin Sill. To the south there was another ditch, broader and probably deeper, labelled by the Venerable Bede as the Vallum. The Romans used this term to denote the whole system, as in the phrase 'on the line of the Wall', *per lineam valli*, in later documents listing the units occupying the forts. The Vallum causes problems for historians and archaeologists. It is similar to the Pfahlgraben that accompanies parts of the German palisade on the inside, but the Vallum is a much more serious obstacle, with a mound of earth on its northern and southern banks, and only certain designated crossing points where a causeway was built across it, perhaps with gates. The Vallum was a continuous ditch south of the Wall, and was cut through rock where necessary, entailing a lot of hard labour, so it must have been supremely important to the Romans. In some places the Vallum runs close to the Wall and in others it diverges some distance to the south. It would certainly have stopped unauthorised movement and in areas where it runs at some distance from the forts the land enclosed between the Vallum and the Wall may have served as a shelter for sheep, cattle and horses, in place of the annexes at most of the forts on the later Antonine Wall in Scotland. There were causeways across the Vallum, probably guarded by gates, which would allow for troop movements, and there was a gap in the Wall itself, at the Knag Burn east of Housesteads, where civilians may have been allowed to cross going north or south, but under the supervision of the soldiers, and perhaps paying tolls. It may have been comparable in purpose to the crossing at Dalkingen in Raetia, but not nearly so elaborate or impressive.

North of the Wall there were Hadrianic outpost forts at Bewcastle, north-east of Brampton, at Netherby, north of Carlisle overlooking the River Esk, and at Birrens, one and a half miles east of Ecclefechan in Dumfries and Galloway. All are significantly in the west, suggesting that there was a greater threat in this area, and supporting the theory that the eleven-mile-long earth and turf western sector of the Wall had to be built in a hurry to protect the area.

The subsequent history of Hadrian's Wall involved a partial abandonment when Antoninus Pius advanced the frontier to the gap between the rivers Forth and Clyde, and built another Wall of earth and turf, usually on a stone foundation. Most but not all of the accompanying forts were built with earthen ramparts. No ancient source fully elucidates the reason for this advance so soon after the building of Hadrian's Wall. It is similar to the rationalisation of the German frontier, but it involved the establishment of garrisons in forts in the land between the two Walls.

The forts of the Antonine Wall were closely spaced. Originally there were six, then the number was increased by adding eight smaller installations, reducing the spacing to two miles between forts, except in the east where they were placed further apart. The coasts do not seem to have been protected by towers and fortlets as in Cumbria, but there were outpost forts on the eastern side. There was a ditch to the north but no Vallum, but unlike Hadrian's Wall the forts of the Antonine Wall possessed annexes. This frontier lasted for only about two decades. Some years ago it used to be thought that there were two phases on the Antonine Wall, because the available evidence seemed to point to a reoccupation after the abandonment of the 160s, but in 1995 Nick Hodgson reviewed the evidence to conclude that there was only one brief occupation of the Antonine Wall, ending permanently in 163.

Hadrian's Wall was recommissioned, but the units which had occupied the forts in its first phase did not return. As time went on some of the milecastles seem to have been turned over to workshops, and some turrets went out of use. Civilian settlements which had previously been kept away from the forts started to grow up immediately outside the fort gates. A military road parallel to the Wall was added to the system, possibly emulating the road that seems to have been an integral part of the Antonine Wall. The number of outpost forts was increased. Of the three original outpost forts Birrens had been rebuilt in 158 after a fire, and this fort and that at Netherby were garrisoned by milliary part-mounted cohorts. The unit at Bewcastle is not known. On the east side forts at High Rochester and Risingham had been built by the governor Lollius Urbicus around 140, possibly while the Antonine Wall was being constructed. These forts were retained as outposts of Hadrian's Wall when the Antonine Wall was abandoned. Risingham was garrisoned by a cohort of Vangiones, a *numerus exploratorum* and a detachment of *Raeti Gaesati*, and High Rochester held a milliary part mounted unit by the third century, together with a unit of *exploratores*. In the early third century, *numeri* and *exploratores* were brought into the forts on the Wall. The preponderance of cavalry in the outposts, and the presence of *exploratores* on the Wall and beyond it strongly suggest that there was an emphasis on patrolling and surveillance north of Hadrian's Wall in the later second and early third centuries.

When Severus and his sons came to Britain for the campaigns in Scotland, the Emperor established stores bases at Corbridge and South Shields, and he repaired the Wall and its forts so extensively that earlier scholars thought that he actually built the stone frontier. In older history books it is called Severus' Wall. This theory was complicated by a reference in the Historia Augusta, the biographies of the emperors from the second century onwards. In this work it is stated that Hadrian was the first to build a wall, eighty miles long, to separate the Romans from the barbarians. This must definitely concern the frontier in the Tyne-Solway gap, seventy English miles long, so in order to solve the problem a theory was developed that the Vallum constituted Hadrian's frontier. Then inscriptions were found attesting to building work on the Wall and its milecastles and forts under Aulus Platorius Nepos, known to be the governor of Britain under Hadrian. The Wall was therefore renamed.

There are many unanswered questions about Hadrian's Wall. It is not known how high it would have been, whether it had crenellations, or if there was a wall walk at the top. Reconstructions often show it with these features, but they were not present on other frontiers. The German palisade could only have been patrolled on its northern side, not from an elevated walkway, the Raetian stone wall is narrower than the Wall in England, and some stretches of the walls in Africa are simply finished off in a triangular point.

Control on and Beyond the Frontiers

It could be said that the main purpose of establishing frontiers is to avoid having to go to war. The system allowed the Romans to control people outside the Empire by more tranquil means. The forts and fortresses in the vicinity of the frontiers provided bases where troops could be assembled if all other means of control had failed and it was decided that a war was the only solution. The barriers themselves restricted unauthorised small scale movement, channelling it through points where supervision was possible, and customs dues could be paid. The Knag Burn gateway east of Housesteads fort on Hadrian's Wall, and the elaborate gateway through the German Raetian frontier at Dalkingen, may have served these purposes. The question of whether it was intended to allow civilians to cross the frontiers at several points, specifically on Hadrian's Wall through the milecastle gates, was reviewed by Nick Hodgson in 2003. It is usually claimed that Hadrian's Wall was not intended to be an exclusive barrier, and that the gates through the milecastles were probably used by civilians, in the interests of trade and good relations with the natives on both sides of the frontier. However, the causeways across the Vallum do not match up with the milecastles, but only at the forts, and there are no known routes associated with the milecastles leading from or into the lands north of the Wall. It may be relevant to the question of civilian access that the *vici*, or civilian settlements of the forts on Hadrian's Wall, were kept beyond the Vallum until relatively late, and only began to appear round the forts after the withdrawal from the Antonine Wall. By that time, some of the milecastles were out of use, or at least not manned, and some gates had been blocked up. Another factor is that it is easier, and a lot less labour-intensive, to supervise movement of people and to collect tolls and taxes at a few designated places, with soldiers and perhaps provincial officials in attendance all the time.

However the frontiers of the Roman Empire were constructed or manned, they were not designed to withstand a concerted and determined attack, indeed this level of threat was probably not even envisaged, since the Romans were in the ascendancy and simply by a display of overt power they could, for the most part, discourage unified action. The frontiers represented reactions to perceived threat, and the potential enemies that faced Rome on the other side of the barriers could be controlled by various means and prevented from uniting without the necessity for constant military action. River frontiers were just as effective as physical barriers, provided that the territory on the opposite bank was also under Roman control just as the territory beyond the running barriers was watched, not just by means of bridgehead forts and patrols in a narrow area near to the frontier works and riverbanks, but by political, diplomatic and military control extending much deeper into the lands beyond the frontiers.

The whole package besides the erection of the frontiers sometimes included subsidies to the natives beyond the frontiers, paid in cash or in food or both, and cases are on record of complaints if these subsidies were stopped. Other means of control include the bestowal of privileges in the form of alliances with Rome, and the granting of trading rights. In return for privileges and subsidies, tribal rulers undertook to keep their people peaceful and friendly to Rome, and if this failed, another tribal ruler could be elevated instead, or military action could be taken. The mere threat of war could have deterred some tribes from attacking the frontiers. Modern scholars are divided on the importance that the tribesmen placed on trading with Rome, some arguing that it was by no means fundamental to tribal life, while others take the stance that trade was vital to the chieftains if not the tribesmen themselves, because it afforded them the wealth and kudos necessary to remain in their position as leaders. One factor which supports the importance of trade is that the ancient writers suggest that abolition of markets caused genuine hardship to the tribes, and Marcus Aurelius punished recalcitrant tribes by withdrawing their trading rights, or restricting trading to certain guarded locations.

These less bellicose means of control should not imply timidity on the part of the Romans. The ascendancy still rested with them, but Hadrian and his successors chose to demonstrate their ascendancy without constantly dashing about at the head of armies. The only serious fighting under Hadrian was in the Jewish revolt of Bar Kochba in 132–135. Otherwise Hadrian's reign was notable for his rationalisation of the Empire and a total lack of wars of conquest. He had fought in several wars under Trajan, so his reluctance for expansion of the Empire cannot be attributed to an absence of military experience. He had other ideas about how to control the Empire, and how much of it the Romans could administer.

It has to be admitted that we do not know what the Romans wanted to achieve by maintaining their frontiers. There may have been different aims at different times, achieved by adapting the administration, personnel and functioning of the frontiers. The lack of certainty allows for much modern debate. For Edward Luttwak it was all downhill for the Romans after the establishment of rigid frontiers, because their aggressive, energetic expansion up to this point had been successful and the momentum ought to have been maintained. According to Professor John Mann the frontiers marked the places where the Romans simply ran out of energy, and thereafter the retention of the solid barriers and the frontier lines was due to simple inertia. If it was indeed lack of energy that influenced the Romans, an explanation needs to be found for the fact that various emperors from Hadrian onwards nurtured, repaired and reconstituted the frontiers.

Since it is not known what the Romans wanted from their frontiers, it cannot really be said that the static lines were failures from their point of view. If the frontiers were not working properly, or if circumstances had changed so much in later periods that they were outmoded, it is likely that energetic emperors who repaired frontier works would have devoted their time and energies to developing some alternative. Severus repaired and renewed the frontiers of Britain and Germany, and in the fourth century Count Theodosius rebuilt and repaired frontier works in Britain after the destruction of 367. Several strong-minded emperors followed in Hadrian's footsteps and did not tear apart the work that he did in favour of some other radically different plan, so it is just as safe to assume that the frontiers provided whatever the Romans wanted from them as it is to assume that all the emperors from Antoninus Pius to Honorius suffered from a crippling inertia that prevented them from taking stock and applying some thought to the matter.

Modern historians and archaeologists can offer some generalisations about how Roman frontiers worked. It used to be thought that the frontiers were sharply defined barriers where language, culture, and lifestyle were markedly different on each side, but more recently this opinion has been revised. It is clear that frontiers did not mark the limit of civilised *Romanitas* and the beginning of barbarism, nor were they dividing lines between two completely different or inimical cultures. They were not laid out with any regard for tribal boundaries or for the territorial limits of more developed states. In some instances the frontiers divided communities, embracing some of the inhabitants and leaving others outside the boundary. The frontiers were zones rather than lines, where peoples and cultures were already remarkably similar, or gradually melded. Behind the frontier zones lay fully administered Roman territory, and beyond them lay states and tribes that were nominally free but were still controlled by Rome in her own interests. The Roman emperors dealt with peoples beyond their frontiers in different ways, usually fostering the elite groups among city states or tribes, bestowing honours and gifts on them in return for their co-operation in keeping their compatriots under control. On occasion, the Romans discovered that they had backed the wrong group, and then had to mount an expedition to restore order and control, and then choose to cultivate another group. Sometimes they had to go beyond the frontiers to prevent a tribe or a confederation of tribes from obliterating the more peaceful and tractable ones. Marcus Aurelius fought for years to bring stability to the areas beyond the Danube, and there is some suggestion that he intended to annexe the lands and create new provinces called Sarmatia and Marcomannia, but if this is so it never happened, and after the death of Marcus, his son Commodus brought the wars to a speedy end with a treaty that demanded soldiers for the Roman army. This combination of diplomacy and war, or the threat of war, served to extend Roman influence far beyond the frontiers.

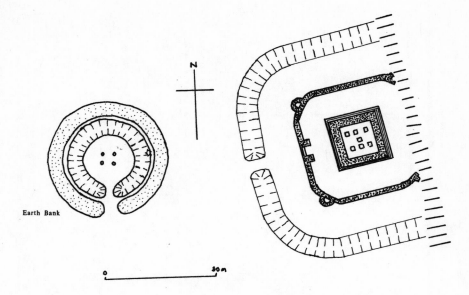

Earth Bank

Before the running barriers were erected to mark the frontiers under the Emperor Hadrian the Romans guarded routes and borders by means of towers of different sizes and designs, variously labelled by modern archaeologists as watchtowers or signal towers. These plans show two of the many kinds of towers discovered all over the Roman Empire. On the left is a plan of a timber tower of the first century AD. It was supported on four posts and surrounded by a ditch, examples of which have been found on the Gask Ridge in Scotland around the northern edge of modern Fife. On the right is the plan of a stone-built tower of the later Empire found on the English east coast at Scarborough. Soldiers from nearby forts probably manned them on a rotational basis. Drawn by Jacqui Taylor.

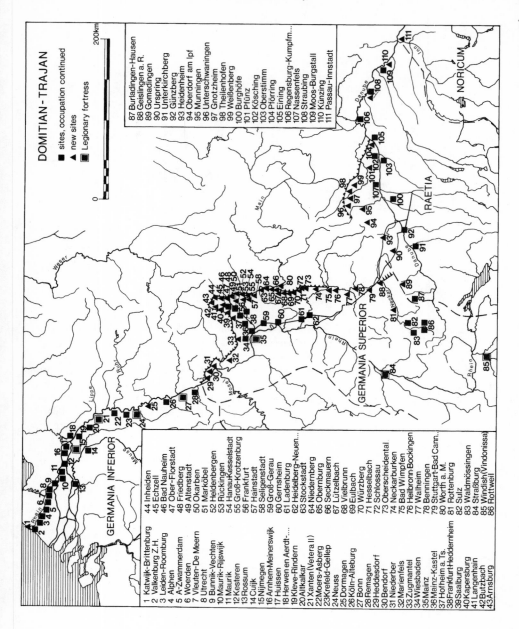

DOMITIAN - TRAJAN

■ sites, occupation continued
▲ new sites
▣ Legionary fortress

0   200km

87 Burladingen-Hausen
88 Geislingen a. R.
89 Gomadingen
90 Urspring
91 Unterkirchberg
92 Günzburg
93 Heidenheim
94 Oberdorf am Ipf
95 Munningen
96 Unterschwaningen
97 Gnotzheim
98 Theilenhofen
99 Weißenberg
100 Burghöfe
101 Pfünz
102 Kösching
103 Oberstimm
104 Pförring
105 Eining
106 Regensburg-Kumpfm...
107 Nassenfels
108 Straubing
109 Moos-Burgstall
110 Künzing
111 Passau-Innstadt

NORICUM

RAETIA

GERMANIA SUPERIOR

GERMANIA INFERIOR

1 Katwijk-Brittenburg
2 Valkenburg Z.H.
3 Leiden-Roomburg
4 Alphen
5 A-Zwammerdam
6 Woerden
7 Vleuten-De Meern
8 Utrecht
9 Bunnik-Vechten
10 Maurik-Rijswijk
11 Maurik
12 Kesteren
13 Rossum
14 Cuijk
15 Nijmegen
16 Arnhem-Meinerswijk
17 Huissen
18 Herwen en Aerdt...
19 Kleve-Rindern
20 Altkalkar
21 Xanten (Vetera II)
22 Moers-Asberg
23 Krefeld-Gellep
24 Neuss
25 Dormagen
26 Köln-Alteburg
27 Bonn
28 Remagen
29 Heddesdorf
30 Bendorf
31 Niederber
32 Marienfels
33 Zugmantel
34 Wiesbaden
35 Mainz
36 Mainz-Kastel
37 Hofheim a. Ts.
38 Frankfurt-Heddernheim
39 Saalburg
40 Kapersburg
41 Langenhain
42 Butzbach
43 Arnsburg
44 Inheiden
45 Echzell
46 Bad Nauheim
47 Ober-Florstadt
48 Friedberg
49 Altenstadt
50 Okarben
51 Marköbel
52 Heldenbergen
53 Rückingen
54 HanauKesselstadt
55 Groß-Krotzenburg
56 Frankfurt
57 Hainstadt
58 Seligenstadt
59 Groß-Gerau
60 Gernsheim
61 Ladenburg
62 Heidelberg-Neuen...
63 Stockstadt
64 Niedernberg
65 Obernburg
66 Seckmauern
67 Lützelbach
68 Vielbrunn
69 Eulbach
70 Würzberg
71 Hesselbach
72 Schlossau
73 Oberscheidental
74 Neckarburken
75 Bad Wimpfen
76 Hellbronn-Bockingen
77 Walheim
78 Benningen
79 Stuttgart-Bad Cann.
80 Worth a. M.
81 Rottenburg
82 Sulz
83 Waldmössingen
84 Straßburg
85 Windish(Vindonissa)
86 Rottweil

This map shows how the long Roman frontier from the Rhine to the Danube utilised the River
Rhine as far as a point south of Remagen, where Hadrian established a frontier comprising a
timber palisade. This frontier took in the line of forts and watchtowers already established by his
predecessors around the Taunus-Wetterau area, forming a northward salient into Free Germany.
As shown on this map, for some years there was an open corridor between Germany and Raetia,
which was eventually closed up, possibly under Antoninus Pius or Marcus Aurelius, when the timber
palisade of the German frontier and the stone wall of the Raetian frontier were joined. Just beyond
Eining the River Danube became the frontier. Redrawn by Graeme Stobbs after H. von Schönberger,
'Die Römische Truppenlager der Frühen und Mittleren Kaiserzeit Zwischen Nordsee und Inn' *Bericht
der Römisch-Germanischen Kommission des Deutschen Archäologischen Instituts* 66, 1985, 321–497.

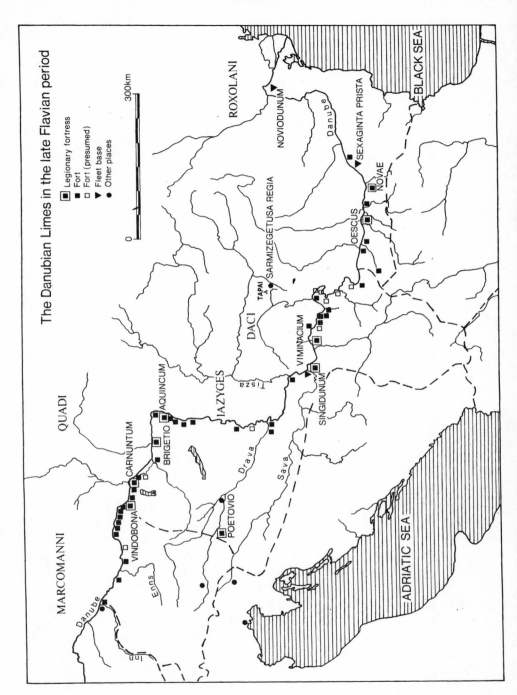

The map includes: The Danubian Limes in the late Flavian period. Legend: Legionary fortress, Fort, Fort (presumed), Fleet base, Other places. 300km scale. Labels include: BLACK SEA, ROXOLANI, NOVIODUNUM, SEXAGINTA PRISTA, NOVAE, OESCUS, SARMIZEGETUSA REGIA, TAPAI, DACI, VIMINACIUM, SINGIDUNUM, IAZYGES, Tisza, AQUINCUM, BRIGETIO, QUADI, CARNUNTUM, Drava, Sava, POETOVIO, VINDOBONA, MARCOMANNI, Enns, Danube, Inn, ADRIATIC SEA.

The middle and lower reaches of the River Danube were manned as the Roman frontier until the province of Dacia was created by Trajan to the north of the river. This province was abandoned by Aurelian, and the Danube became the frontier once again. The map shows the known forts, but since the troop dispositions were altered from time to time it cannot be said that all the bases were occupied continuously or contemporaneously. Drawn by Graeme Stobbs.

12

The Army in Action: Peace and War

Imperial Roman soldiers of the standing army would spend much of their time without fighting in wars. This does not mean that they were all idle, lounging about their forts with nothing to do. There are cases on record where discipline was lax and soldiers were absent from their forts attending to their own business or pleasure activities, and there are recorded examples of a new general arriving, toughening up the men and restoring discipline, like Corbulo when he arrived in the east to prepare for a campaign against Parthia for control of Armenia. The process of reorganising the army, disciplining and retraining the troops, and preparing for the war took him about two years, then he launched the campaign in 58.

What Did the Soldiers Do All Day?

The surviving duty rosters, mostly from the eastern provinces, show that soldiers were kept busy every day, sometimes at some considerable distance from their bases, involved in guard duty, patrolling, administrative tasks at headquarters, police work, bringing food and clothing from various sources, and humble occupations such as gathering wood for the bath furnaces, or hoeing the crops grown outside the forts. The specialists under the heading of *immunes*, such as blacksmiths, armourers, weapons manufacturers, carpenters, stonemasons and the like would probably be found jobs to do every day, and the clerical and medical staff would have no shortage of tasks.

The documentation concerning *cohors XX Palmyrenorum equitata* at Dura Europos in Syria is overworked in all books on the Roman army because so many papyri have been preserved. The working roster of 219 contains some interesting examples of what the soldiers were doing. Several men were absent at different places, such as the town of Appadana on the Euphrates north of Dura, and others were nearly 180 miles to the north at Becchufrayn, probably guarding the route to Antioch. Soldiers were sent to Birtha, Chafer Avira, and Castellum Arabum, but the location of these places is not known. At least fifteen men from the cohort had been sent on scouting missions, denoted by *explorator*, *explorat*, *explor* and other abbreviations. Cavalrymen were sent out *ad man ambul*, which as discussed in the chapter on auxiliary cavalry, may mean that they were sent to exercise the horses. Perhaps the most interesting entry is *ad leones*, to the lions. It is suggested that this is a place name, but it is also possible that several soldiers were out hunting lions for the arena. Lions were not limited to parks in Africa in Roman times.

The papyrus duty rosters of *III Cyrenaica* at Nicopolis near Alexandria are dated, not without some dispute, to some point between 90 and 96. These records cover the first ten days of October in the unknown year in the 90s. The men are listed in no discernible order, but they probably belonged to the same century. In other lists the men of each century are often listed according to date of enlistment. In this case, no centurion is named at the top of the list but a centurion called Helius is mentioned under two different dates, and in one column he has the distinguishing mark, which resembles the figure seven, indicating his rank. Interpretation of the abbreviations denoting the various duties depends on the work of different scholars, who are not always in agreement about what some of the words are, and what they might mean. Despite the problems, the rosters yield fascinating detail.

The lists show that several soldiers were assigned to guard duty in different areas of the fort, such as the headquarters or *principia*, the fort gates and in towers, which may mean the interval towers around the fort perimeter walls, or watchtowers along routes. One man was assigned to rampart duty. On 8 October, three men were down for *vianico*, guarding the roads, generally taken to indicate routes outside the fort. Baths duty features every day in the ten days of the list. The exact task that concerned baths is not explained, but the soldiers assigned to it would hardly need to be told. It could mean that men were sent to collect fuel. Even a small set of baths would consume huge quantities of wood every day, and this record concerns legionary baths catering for about 5,000 personnel. There is an entry in another papyrus, concerning the *cohors XX Palmyrenorum* at Dura Europos in AD 223 to 225, where Zebidas in the century of Nigrinus is listed as *missus lig. balnei*, sent to collect wood for the baths. Whatever baths duty entailed, at Nicopolis a legionary of *III Cyrenaica*, Quintus Fabius, was sent to do it on seven days out of the ten in the list, interrupted only by gate guard. Perhaps he had done something to upset his centurion, since no-one else seems to have been assigned to this duty for such a protracted period. Three soldiers were working in the armoury on separate days. Marcus Arrius Niger was put down for *strigis* every day from 5-10 October. *Strigae* were the smaller streets in the fort, so Niger may have been sweeping or guarding them, or patrolling to keep soldiers out of mischief. His duty was clearly distinct from *vianico*, so he was probably not patrolling roads outside the fort. Gaius Julius Valens may have been digging a ditch on 3 October, though the reading of the abbreviation is uncertain and its meaning is debated, so it is possible that he was sent to the quarries. On 6 October Marcus Longinus was assigned to *stercus*, or cleaning latrines, the only time this appears in the list of duties for the ten days.

Some men were not with their unit during the ten-day period that the lists cover. Gaius Domitius Celer was on leave by the permission of the prefect, which is taken to mean the camp prefect and not the Prefect of Egypt. From 5 to 10 October Lucius Sextilius Germanus was on duty in the century of Decrius, and Gaius Julius Lo... was with the century of Serenus. From 3 October Gaius Julius Longus Amiso (or Auso?) had gone with Asinius for boots, though his destination is not stated. Marcus Antonius Crispus was acting as the tribune's escort on 7–10 October. Marcus Marius Clemens was probably away for the whole ten days, possibly on harbour duty, or alternatively the blank spaces after 5 October might simply indicate that he had returned and was available for duty but had not been assigned to anything. Marcus Domitius was at the granaries at Neapolis, a district of Alexandria, from 3 October, and his task, *ad frumentum*, presumably means that he was organising the legion's food supplies, possibly collecting a delivery of grain. The entry after his name stretches all the way across all the dates in the list, so he was absent for the whole period.

Inscriptions also record soldiers on duty away from *III Cyrenaica*. The centurion Gaius Julius Magnus supervised bridge building at Coptos, and inscriptions found in temples in Nubia show that detachments of soldiers patrolled there, though it was not a Roman province. Detached duties were a regular feature of army service, common enough for lists to be drawn up of personnel who were absent, with the dates of each man's departure and return duly noted. In a fragmentary list concerning four legionaries and their detached duties in the 80s it is clear that the absences did not occur according to any established pattern or at consistent dates. The record is from Nicopolis, but it does not contain any information about which legion it concerns, so it could be *III Cyrenaica* or *XXII Deiotariana* since both legions were stationed there. Several of the absences were concerned with the granaries and the grain supply. Between 80 and 86, Marcus Papirius Rufus had been to the granary at Neapolis for nearly four months, and twice to the granaries in the Mercurium quarter of Alexandria, for unknown periods of time. Titus Flavius Vale… and Titus Flavius Celer also did turns of duty at the Neapolis granaries, and Celer accompanied a grain convoy in 83. Titus Flavius Satur… spent some time dredging harbours for a few months, and Titus Flavius Vale… went to make papyrus in January 81.

Another fragmentary list of an unknown unit records men who were on detachment to other units as replacements. The first entry is the date, followed by the place name and the number of soldiers who had been sent there. No indication is given for the reasons why they were detached for service in another unit. One of the most famous and most disputed documents is a papyrus in the British Museum known as Hunt's *pridianum* or strength report, concerning an auxiliary cohort on the Danube frontier in the reign of Trajan, the *cohors I Hispanorum Veterana equitata*, probably in105. The exact nature of the document and its date are not established, but those details are not as important as the contents, which give the numbers of men in the unit with the number of accessions, and then the numbers of soldiers who were absent. An unknown number of soldiers had been transferred to the *Classis Flavia Moesica*, the feet that patrolled the Danube, by order of the legate, and one man had been transferred to the army of Pannonia. Of the other absentees, two groups of men had gone to Gaul, one to get clothing, and another probably to get grain. Some men, probably infantry and cavalry together, had gone across the Erar, perhaps a river, to get horses. Two cavalrymen had gone to the garrison at Castra, and an unknown number were at the mines in Dardania, both of which places were outside the province. Some men were at the office of the Imperial procurator Latinianus; some were in Dacia, one group at Piroboridava in garrison, and another with a detachment at Buridava; twenty-three cavalrymen and some infantry had gone across the Danube on an expedition, some were on the other side of the Danube guarding crops, and others were across the river on a scouting mission with a centurion. A decurion and some soldiers were at the grain ships, some were at headquarters with the clerks, some were bringing cattle from the Haemus mountains, and some were guarding the draught animals. R. O. Fink, who provides the translation and commentary, suggests that the activities listed in this document signify preparations for war, rather than a wartime situation. Certainly the emphasis on grain and cattle probably indicates that supplies were being gathered.

It is not known if these few documents represent military activity over the entire Empire, but it is likely that other soldiers in auxiliary units and the legions of other provinces were occupied in the same way, kept busy at all times, and sometimes overworked. There would be welcome interruptions to routine by the many religious festivals and ceremonials that punctuated the Roman calendar, when the men would devote their time to the Roman equivalent of spit and polish to present a good turnout.

The Roman War Ethic

From their earliest beginnings to the late Empire the Romans consistently adopted a warlike disposition. This attitude was inbred into the majority of the senatorial class of the Republic, who regarded war as part of life, the primary means of achieving lasting fame and glory for Rome, and for their descendants. The absolute stubbornness of the Romans ensured that even though they were sometimes thoroughly beaten in a battle or a series of battles, in the end they won through sheer staying power. Their advantages in the Republic included their organisation and administration, their discipline, and not least the fact that their manpower was potentially unlimited, at least in the short term, since they could call upon their own citizens and their allies in Italy. The wars of the early Republic could be described, with a little imagination, as mostly defensive, but once the theatre of war extended into other territories and Rome discovered the Mediterranean world, then wars of aggression also entered into the Roman ethic. Not all the wars led immediately to conquest and annexation, at least at first. After the early years of the second century AD, expansion via annexation was rare, but the emperors were no less aggressive than the Republican Senate. The wars with Parthia were most often begun by Rome, as pre-emptive strikes or reactions to perceived threats, but these expeditions did not result in a steady eastward progression of Roman dominion. Elsewhere, wars were more often reactions to internal rebellions or to attacks or incursions by Rome's neighbours.

Each war fought by the Romans was portrayed as a justified action, or *bellum justum*. Whether it was a defensive action, a punitive expedition, a war of conquest, or a war of pure aggression, the politicians of the Republic, and later the Imperial equivalent of modern 'spin doctors' cleverly placed all the blame on the enemy, whatever the circumstances. An example of the tortuous political prelude to wars is provided by Octavian's elimination of Mark Antony, who was the chief rival who stood in Octavian's way, but since he was a Roman and there had been enough civil wars to last for several lifetimes, Octavian exploited Antony's unfortunate if not unwise association with Queen Cleopatra VII of Egypt. Assiduous propaganda ensured that Cleopatra and Egypt were seen as the main enemy, with Antony in thrall to her, bewitched and helpless. It was rumoured that Cleopatra wished to take over the Roman state, and it was said that she often began her musings with 'when I dispense justice from the Capitol'. Whipped up by Octavian, the people were clamouring for him to mobilise against Cleopatra, and he revived an ancient ritual whereby he designated a little plot of land as enemy territory, threw a spear into this symbolic Egypt, and so declared war.

On occasion, Rome fought wars on behalf of another state, kingdom or tribe, after appeals for assistance from a threatened monarch or chieftain. The result was not always annexation of the chieftain's territory, although certain stipulations may be made, such as raising troops for the Roman army, and an understanding that the chief who enjoyed Roman support should keep his own warriors under control and watch his borders to guard against the people who might one day threaten Roman interests. Significantly, when the Romans decided upon annexation, it tended to occur where there was a profit to be made, a concept which embraced political advantages and economic gains. Pompey the Great showed how immensely profitable foreign wars could be, though the eastern territories offered more economic potential than the west, where certain generals like Julius Caesar and Germanicus won great political kudos, but not quite as much wealth.

During the Republic the Senate made corporate decisions about whether or not to go war, who to place in command, how many troops to raise, and the resources that should be voted to the generals. This applied especially when the Romans were operating in Italy, but as the number of provinces increased, governors acted more independently, a situation imposed by the distances involved and the speed of communications. Governors were not given an entirely free hand, but their remit seems to have been broad enough to allow them to make decisions to wage war on a tribe or people, always provided that the relevant reasons could be produced to label the action as a 'just war'. In the early years of the Principate, senators continued to act as their predecessors had done, but Augustus curtailed the degree of independent action for provincial governors. Marcus Licinius Crassus, grandson of the more famous Crassus who met his end in Parthia, successfully conducted a war in Moesia in 29–28 BC, and claimed a triumph, which he was granted. His demands did not end there, however, since he also claimed the title *Imperator*, which until then was customarily voted to a successful general by his troops, and the rare honour of *spolia opima*. This was awarded to a Roman general who had personally killed an enemy leader in battle and it bestowed the right to dedicate the spoils of war in the temple of Jupiter on the Capitol. These last two honours were refused. Henceforth the title *Imperator* belonged exclusively to the emperors, and generals who claimed signal honours were dissuaded from making too much spectacle. The emperors made decisions about going to war, where to wage it and through whom, and the chosen generals were designated appointees or legates of the emperor, subordinate to him in all matters. The award of the triumph, the pinnacle of the Republican military career, ceased for anyone except the immediate family of the emperor, and to demonstrate the point, Augustus' right-hand man, the faithful Marcus Vipsanius Agrippa, was awarded the honour twice but refused it, along with other honours voted to him by the Senate. During the Empire, successful generals had to be content with the lesser award of *ornamenta triumphalia*, the insignia of a triumphant commander, but they did not have the honour of parading in the triumphal chariot through the streets of Rome, displaying the booty and captives that they had won, ending the procession on the Capitol Hill where the trophies were dedicated to the gods.

Emperors sometimes put an end to the exploits of a successful commander in case they ventured too far and embroiled Rome in wars that she did not want, or in case the generals got above themselves and started to think in terms of running the whole Empire. Claudius prevented Domitius Corbulo, legate of Lower Germany, from following up his victory against the Chauci. Corbulo was operating across the Rhine, but the army was brought back to the Roman side of the river. The lessons learned from the disaster of Varus were perhaps still too vivid, but it is also possible that Claudius did not want his generals to eclipse him.

From early in his reign, Augustus quickly made it clear that supreme power and all honours were in his gift and his alone, and his successors saw no reason to relax this unwritten rule. The continual dilemma of the Imperial regime was that the achievements of the military commanders had to be acknowledged in some way, otherwise no one would wish to serve if there were no meaningful distinctions to be earned, but this had to be organised without allowing them more power and influence than the emperors. The Empire had to be defended, so armies had to be stationed at convenient points with commanders in charge of them, with enough ability and power to be able to organise this defence if circumstances demanded it, but on the other hand they must not be encouraged to imagine that they could run the Empire rather better than the reigning emperor. Given the long timespan of Imperial rule, it is perhaps surprising that there were not more attempts at usurpation in the first two centuries. Another Imperial problem was the decentralisation of the armies, which facilitated attempts to usurp the reigning Emperor. The troops in the frontier forts were no longer all Romans or Italians from the core of the Empire, so their ideology of Rome would be based on the concept of a central ruling power, but not of a homeland where they had left their families behind and where they could find repose after their service. They had other loyalties besides their duty to Rome. If the right leader emerged making all the right promises, the provincial armies showed themselves ready to make war on whoever was marked out as the enemy, whether they were Roman, non-Roman or otherwise. The Roman war ethic could just as easily be turned inwards as outwards. The armies were instrumental in creating emperors such as Vespasian and Severus, and if the provincial armies did not create an emperor, other troops such as the Praetorians were just as persuasive.

It is unlikely that there was a strategic plan for the whole Empire at any time in its history, from Gaius Julius Caesar in the first century BC to Justinian in the sixth century AD. It is not always possible to disentangle the reasons for going to war from the literary rhetoric and the personal justification of each emperor who waged war. Neither forward planning, nor a holistic view of the Empire, seems to have applied consistently to Imperial rule. The Roman Empire was after all very large, and it was culturally as well as geographically diverse. The senators of the Republic conceptualised Rome as the centre of the universe with a divine right sanctioned by the gods to extend Roman rule over everyone else, but they did not look at the entire Empire and then clutter up their lives with corporate goals, targets, timescales, mission statements and business plans in order to achieve this vaguely perceived ambition of world rule in logical stages. The emperors perhaps conceptualised the Empire as a collection of regions with different profit potentials, different problems, and different internal and external threats. Their political and military policies tended to be re-active rather than pro-active, piecemeal and tailored to the area and circumstances concerned. This was not simply a concomitant factor of physical geography and the constraints imposed by terrain. It was political geography more than anything else that determined how Rome dealt with the Empire and its neighbours. Physical geography affected the way in which the army operated tactically, but what Rome wished to achieve and how she went about obtaining her aims depended upon the enemy's internal politics. Military and political procedure was generally dictated by the way in which a population or a tribe was organised, whether they were urbanised and centrally governed, or scattered and answerable to a chieftain whose power was always precarious and rapidly became ineffective as soon as he began to lose influence. Strategy to the Romans was basically a matter of going to war if they thought they could win and that there would be some advantage to doing so. At the successful outcome of wars, strategy consisted of staying in control, either by means of moral domination from a distance, or by annexation. The fine details could be worked out empirically on the spot, utilising a combination of military activity and political diplomacy, not to mention cunning and guile. None of the literary sources make any mention of either short-term or long-term strategy, and even the works such as Frontinus' *Stratagems* simply retail anecdotal evidence in roughly classified groupings, without outlining an overall strategy for the Empire.

In the Imperial era when the emperor decided to go to war, there was usually a consultation with the immediate *consilium*, and then with the senators to gain their approval, paying lip service to the old Republican traditions and attempting to eliminate potential trouble at home while the armies fought in distant provinces and sometimes beyond them. The emperors went to war for a variety of reasons, to defend their provinces from outside attack, occasionally to pre-empt attacks, or more often to punish the offenders after raids. Sometimes wars resulted from internal rebellions, which tended to break out while a new province was still being pacified, or roughly twenty years after the conquest, when a new generation had grown up, determined to do better than their parents had done in resisting the Romans. These are the contexts for the German rising against the governor Quinctilius Varus, and the rebellion of Boudicca in Britain. The enemies of the emperors were not always foreigners, threatening the Empire from beyond its boundaries; increasingly often as the Empire progressed into the third and fourth centuries, Roman generals at the head of Roman armies fought each other in civil wars.

Intelligence and Planning

The Romans appreciated the value of good planning, at least in theory, and the literary references extol the virtues of those generals who were renowned for laying careful plans before engaging in active operations. In the *Annals* Tacitus attributed Corbulo's successes to thorough preparation and planning. Much of the initial planning took the form of intelligence gathering and reconnaissance work, for instance the Republican general Scipio Aemilianus thoroughly surveyed the ground in the vicinity of Carthago Nova (New Carthage, modern Cartagena) before he laid siege to the city. Geographical considerations were vitally important to the planning process, but so was an understanding of the enemy's characteristics, and their daily routines. Vegetius recommends that generals should always get to know their enemies well, and Caesar gathered as much information as he could about the inhabitants of southern Britain as well as the terrain before he invaded in 55 and 54 BC.

Republican armies were woefully lacking in intelligence gathering and frequently paid for their neglect with disastrous defeats and the loss of many lives. Painful experiences with Hannibal did very little to foster the art of scouting, reconnoitring, and gathering intelligence, but certain generals such as Scipio Africanus and Caesar managed to remain one step ahead of their adversaries by careful observation and then drawing the right conclusions. Austin and Rankov point out that the interpretation of the knowledge gained by whatever means, and the decisions made thereafter, rested with the general, and some were better than others.

The theory of good intelligence was known to Polybius, who praised Hannibal for reconnoitring not just routes into enemy territory, but the wealth of the lands he was about to enter, the ways of the natives, their political allegiances, and the degree of their affection or disaffection for Rome. Much later, when the Romans had learned a lot, Vegetius stressed the importance of knowing the habits of the enemy, and castigated those generals who entered territory that had not been thoroughly explored. Caesar kept his finger on the pulse of affairs in Gaul as far as possible, and though it could be argued that he presented himself to his public as he wished to be seen, in fairness he also documented occasions when he was taken by surprise. When he invaded Britain Caesar left Labienus behind with three legions and two thousand cavalry, with instructions to guard the ports and the grain supply, to monitor the situation in Gaul, and to make plans to deal with whatever situation arose in the best way he thought fitting. In order to monitor what was happening among the tribesmen, Labienus presumably operated a system of spies and intelligence gatherers, but this is not elucidated. Caesar tells us that he sent out or received news from *exploratores* or less commonly from *speculatores*, though there seems to be no definite distinction between the two. In one passage Caesar says that he received a report from his *speculatores* that was confirmed next day by *exploratores*. There is probably no need to try to attribute radically different functions to the two groups, except in so far as *exploratores* translates best as scouts and *speculatores* as spies. The *exploratores* of Caesar's day were not yet formed into specific units, and it seems that they could be formed arbitrarily from parties of soldiers sent off on missions to find out what lay ahead or what was the general mood of the tribes, or civilians who reported to Caesar about other tribes. He learned from the Ubii (*per Ubios exploratores*) that the Suebi were massing, calling in their warriors.

There are several instances where the Romans actively gathered information while on campaign or in peacetime. For the most part these were short range expeditions, before or after battles. Caesar sent out *exploratores* to observe the tribesmen, and in this way found out that the Gauls were crossing the Loire near Cenabum (modern Orleans), so he attacked them. He also despatched *exploratores* to keep an eye on Afranius and Petreius at Ilerda in the Spanish campaign, before he went to fight Pompey in Greece. After the battle of Mons Graupius in Scotland, Agricola despatched *exploratores* to look for the Britons in case they should be forming up again, but they had been scattered and none were to be found.

Information could reach the ears of the Roman high command in various ways. Embassies sent out from Rome provided useful opportunities for information-gathering, and traders could describe what they had seen on their travels. Soldiers were often designated to supervise meetings and markets, and could listen carefully to what was being said. All these methods could provide useful information, and were among the means that Caesar used to find out all he could about Britain and its inhabitants before he invaded. Pliny the Elder recounts how Aelius Gallus noted useful facts in Arabia about the people, their tribal structure and their agriculture. When Cicero was manoeuvred into going out to govern Cilicia, his correspondence shows how he was aware of what was going on beyond the borders of his province.

The use of spies was well known to the Romans and to their adversaries. During the civil wars between the Caesarians and Pompeians, there were two occasions when the Pompeians sent men pretending to be deserters into Caesar's camp so that they could report back on the state of affairs, but they were discovered and unmasked as *speculatores*. Genuine deserters could provide more meaningful information than civilian observers because they knew what to look for and what were the most salient points in military operations. In Gaul, while he was besieging Gergovia, Caesar learned from deserters what he already knew from his scouts, that there was a weak spot in the defences of the town.

Though the *exploratores* mentioned in the earlier sources were not necessarily permanently appointed to their tasks, by the middle or later second century, whole units called *exploratores* or *numeri exploratorum* had begun to appear on the frontiers, and individual *speculatores* became more common, though not all of these were dedicated to intelligence gathering. The several inscriptions commemorating various *speculatores legionis* do not denote spies but specific ranks in the army, but there were some *speculatores* whose function was to collect and sift information. It is probable that the Marcomannic wars triggered a marked change in intelligence work. Austin and Rankov link the formation of specific *exploratores* units with the appearance on the frontiers of officials on the staffs of the provincial governors called *beneficiarii consularis*, who were probably responsible for intelligence networks both within the provinces and across the frontiers. Though the emperors were at the hub of the Empire, they could not be instantly aware of everything that was happening since the speed of communications prevented them from receiving immediate knowledge of events, and their decisions as to how to respond could not reach the generals on the spot until it was too late. Intelligence therefore became primarily a provincial or regional affair, and the officials reacted on their own initiative, only secondarily reporting to the emperor, and maybe performing a holding action until reinforcements arrived.

Although there was never any central bureau for intelligence, it is possible that the Imperial secretary *ab epistulis* was responsible for monitoring the reports from the provincial *beneficiarii* and other sources. There is no written evidence that states this unequivocally, but a poem dating from the reign of Domitian addressed to the *ab epistulis* Flavius Abascantus indicates that the post was concerned with correspondence flowing into and out of the capital, and to and from the provinces. It has been noted that although the men who filled this post were usually civilians, from the reign of Marcus Aurelius military men were appointed, Titus Varius Clemens being the first, followed by Publius Tarrutienus Paternus, who was a lawyer and also a soldier, and who accompanied Marcus to the wars on the Danube. Austin and Rankov conclude from this that intelligence had become a priority by about AD 160, when the aggressive movements of the northern tribesmen had become a real threat to Rome.

The *stationes* or bases of the *beneficiarii consularis* were not limited to the northern frontiers. They were set up in Egypt in the administrative districts, and in some provinces they were often attached to mining areas. The *beneficiarii* had routinely started out as legionaries and were usually men of long experience; some of them had operated as *frumentarii*, who had first appeared in the early second century AD. These are often labelled as the equivalent of an Imperial secret police, but their functions embraced a wide variety of tasks.

It is likely that the Romans knew much more about the eastern states than they did about the northern tribes, especially since commercial and ambassadorial traffic was more frequent and better established, and the social and political geography of the east was more in tune with Roman ideals, with roads, towns and cities all facilitating an urban way of life. The northern areas, on the other hand, were regarded as trackless wastes without proper roads and cities, and the inhabitants were not urbanised. The Romans relied upon itineraries, or lists of places in their proper order along the route, and their distances from each other, sometimes accompanied by illustrations showing the roads in long strips, naming the major towns and cities. These worked well in the provinces and in the east, but in the northern regions, where settlements could be uprooted and moved on, the natives combined and recombined in different federations, and permanent towns were lacking. In these circumstances the itineraries were not so useful. The relative paucity of knowledge about the northern regions beyond the Rhine and Danube may have been one of the motivating forces behind the institution of military interpreters, who are first attested in the late second and early third centuries, especially in the Danube provinces. On an inscription one soldier called himself *interpres Germanorum officii consularis*, and on another example a soldier was labelled *interprex Sarmatarum(?) ex officio consularis*, his title indicating that he had knowledge of the Sarmatians. Both these men were on the staff of the governor, as were three more interpreters attested on inscriptions, and significantly, all those who are attested were based at or near provincial capitals. The Romans presumably adopted a policy of speaking with the tribesmen in their own languages, and monitoring their opinions. As Austin and Rankov point out, there was a gradual improvement in the quantity and quality of intelligence from Caesar's day to the late Empire, corresponding perhaps to the need for it, and by the fourth century the Roman intelligence systems were extremely good.

A Roman provincial governor was at one and the same time commander of the armed forces and responsible for all civilian matters, and his administrative staff included several army officers, often on secondment, to deal with the paperwork and the transmission of orders in peacetime, not only to the army of the province but also to the judicial staff, the civilian officials, contractors, and businessmen. The *beneficiarii* attached to headquarters played an important part in administration, but it is unfortunately not known if they continued their duties in wartime, or whether the general routinely appointed these officers to his *consilium*. There seems to have been no standard system of official permanent posts on the staff of a general, such as those that evolved in, for instance, Berthier's staff in the army of Napoleon, no-one can say much about Roman staff work, except by extrapolation from the literature, which is not always very helpful.

As part of the planning process generals usually held a meeting of various chosen officers, corporately termed the *consilium*. This term could also refer to a meeting of a private nature in order to arrange household matters, and each senator was accustomed to conferring with their own personal *consilium* at home, so it is even possible that some of the general's trusted civilian retainers would accompany him to command an army and take part in his planning meetings. Since there was no fixed membership of the *consilium*, Roman commanders could ask whoever they liked to attend, so there could be a mixture of the general's personal entourage and army officers. The most senior officers certainly attended and some generals invited centurions to the meetings. Each general would listen to the opinions of his various officers and may have been influenced by their ideas and their knowledge, especially if he had little experience of his own, but total responsibility for the planning procedure lay with him alone and he could override the decisions of his colleagues if he wished. The order of battle would be given at the *consilium* and afterwards the officers would then brief their own sections, each in a smaller *consilium* of their own, so theoretically, even if the troops were not aware of the overall plan, they would know what part they were expected to play once the campaign or the individual battles had started.

One of the desirable aims of good planning on the part of the Romans was to enable the generals to choose their own battle sites, where they could make maximum use of the terrain to protect their flanks, or to keep reserves hidden from the enemy, and then direct the proceedings with enough knowledge to be flexible in dealing with unexpected crises. The supreme example of detailed planning of this sort is Arrian's *Order of March Against the Alans*, where he not only laid down exactly which troops would march under which commanders, but he also included an outline of how he proposed to fight the battle once he had engaged the enemy. His work is designed for a specific set of circumstances in a specific place against a highly mobile enemy; the danger is, as Adrian Goldsworthy points out, that historians interpret Arrian's arrangements as the universal Roman fighting method for the second century all over the Empire, no matter what kind of enemy the Romans were fighting. While there may be a basis of certain broad theoretical concepts to be gleaned from the few close descriptions that we have of the Roman army in action, it is not advisable to extrapolate from them to build up a crystallised static picture of the Romans at war.

In planning how to fight a battle or lay a siege, it was important to form some idea of how to extricate the troops if everything went wrong and it was necessary to retreat. According to Polybius, Scipio planned how to retreat from Carthago Nova (modern Cartagena) in Spain, should the need arise. In this respect detailed local knowledge would help commanders if they were taken by surprise, so they might have a chance to extricate their armies without too much bloodshed. Since nothing is completely predictable in war, and it is not always possible to pre-empt a crisis, there were occasions when the Romans had no opportunity to make leisurely plans, but had to react to unexpected events very quickly, in which case they had to rely upon the experience and training of the soldiers. Onasander, the first century author of a manual on generalship, lays more emphasis on planning how to fight a battle once the enemy is in sight, so that his dispositions can be observed and arrangements made on the spot to deal with them. As Onasander says, the planning process does not stop even when a battle has started, and generals have to think on their feet.

Marching to War

There is a respectable body of information about the order of march at different periods and in different circumstances, and there a wealth of archaeological detail about marching camps, derived chiefly from Britain and Germany, accompanied by literary description of the layout of military camps. Unfortunately the marriage between these two sources is not one of wedded bliss, and it is often difficult to reconcile the words of the ancient authors with the archaeological evidence that emerges from marching camps.

A general commanding an army on the march cannot simply put the soldiers on the road with instructions about the objectives to head for. There has to be proper organisation as to the order in which each section of the army marches out first, and which sections form the centre and the rear. The main literary sources for the order of march are Polybius for the Republican army, Caesar for the late Republic, Josephus for the first century AD in Judaea under Vespasian and Titus, Arrian for the second century AD in Cappadocia in the reign of Hadrian, and Vegetius, who described ideal circumstances and whose account does not concern a specific time or place. While the finer details of the order of march will have depended upon the terrain and the perceived threat from the Roman point of view, there is sufficient similarity between these accounts to draw some general conclusions, mostly related to common sense and good practice. Scouts would head the column, perhaps on all occasions, even when the purely historical accounts neglect to mention them. During the Republic, the allied troops were placed just behind the scouts, with their cavalry contingents preceding the infantry. Auxiliary troops fulfilled this function in the Imperial period, often with the horsemen of the *cohortes equitatae* mixed with those of one or more *alae*. Next came the auxiliary infantry, then the legions, and in the centre the general and his *singulares*, or the emperor and the Praetorians. The baggage could be carried all together, after the legions and commanders, or split up into different sections following the relevant troops. Caesar most often placed the baggage to the rear. In many cases the rearguard mirrored the arrangements at the head of the column, with auxiliary infantry and then cavalry to ward off attacks. Cavalry could be used to guard the flanks, patrolling on either side of the marching column, and if attacks occurred while on the march, cavalry could screen the column while the soldiers formed up from column into battle lines.

An army is in its most disadvantaged and vulnerable position when it moves from place to place, and it is likely that the order of march varied according to circumstances. Polybius indicates the marching order could be adapted. Provided that the ground was open enough, the Romans marched in three parallel columns composed of the *hastati*, the *principes*, and the *triarii*, with the baggage in the spaces between them. With this arrangement, if the army was attacked while moving, the soldiers could turn to the left or the right to face the attack, and form up in advance of the baggage. Polybius admits that on some occasions it might be necessary for the *hastati* to wheel round to get to the front, because if they marched on the left and the attack came from the right, then the troops would turn to the right and the *hastati* would find themselves in the rear. Though it is not specifically mentioned in Polybius' account, the allied troops would presumably precede and follow the legions, and when the column turned into line, they would be on the wings, as usual.

Besides the account of Polybius there are other references to marching in areas of low- or high-intensity threat, and while details are not always included in the ancient sources, if the threat was considered to be low, the position of the various units, the baggage, and the flank guards may have differed from the pattern adopted in areas of high-intensity threat. Some scholars have classified marches into different categories, starting with simply moving the army from one place to another, followed by the arrangements for marching through enemy territory, and concluding with marching purposefully into battle. Others have tried to relate styles of marching order to local conditions and physical geography. All these elements of purpose, threat, and terrain would play a contributory part in a general's decision on his line of march, but not to the exclusion of everything else. There would certainly be greater need for vigilance and keeping close together in enemy territory, and as Polybius demonstrates for the Republican period, it would be important for the order of march to reflect the order of battle so as to reduce the potential chaos if the troops had to turn from column into battle line at short notice. Caesar had this in mind when he wanted to take the Germans by surprise while they were still in their camp. He divided his army into three columns which he describes as the *triplex acies*, and after a rapid march of eight miles he succeeded in taking the enemy unawares and giving battle straight away. When under tremendous threat and the enemy was closing in, the army would adopt the square formation (*agmen quadratum*), where the baggage was placed in the centre and troops marched on all sides. Livy refers several times to this formation, and Onasander also refers to a compact formation with the baggage and the medical equipment in the centre, and the bravest soldiers placed to the front or rear according to the direction of the greatest threat. According to Ammianus Marcellinus, when the Emperor Julian was marching down the Euphrates in the mid-fourth century, he protected the head of the column and the flanks with 1,500 *excursatores*, whose purpose was to ward off unexpected attacks.

The practicalities of marching the Roman armies from one place to another under any circumstances have occupied many scholars, who are at pains to work out how wide and how long any particular column would be. According to Josephus, Vespasian's legions marched six abreast, while Arrian ordered his men to march four abreast, but this should not be interpreted too rigidly as the standard practice of the period when each author described the army, nor should it be taken as evidence that there was a change of policy at some time between the Flavian Emperors and the reign of Hadrian. It seems that there was never any standard formation for the width of the column, which would be decided by the general, after deliberation about the state of the terrain, the needs of the moment, and his plans for the formation of the battle line. The length of the marching column would be quite arbitrary, and it would require vigilance to regulate it. There was great danger in allowing the various units to stretch out too far, since a very long line of march is more vulnerable than a compact one. There are references to centurions going up and down the line to keep everyone together, to round up stragglers and generally sort out any problems.

Order of march according to Polybius:

At this period an army usually consisted one of the consuls in command of two legions and the allied contingents.
The *extraordinarii* at the head of the column
The right wing of the allied troops, cavalry then infantry
Their pack animals with their baggage
The first of the Roman legions
The pack animals with their baggage
The second of the Roman legions
The pack animals with their baggage
The baggage of the remaining allied troops forming the rearguard
The left wing of the allied troops, infantry then cavalry

Polybius adds some further points:

The cavalry sometimes ride behind their sections, or sometimes alongside the baggage animals as guards and to keep them together.

If an attack is expected from the rear, the *extraordinarii* (specially picked soldiers from the allied troops) take up position in the rearguard instead of in the van.

On alternate days the allies and the legions reverse this order, so that the troops have an equal opportunity every second day to be the first to find fresh water and forage for the animals.

Order of march according to Josephus:

In AD 67, the general Flavius Vespasianus, who was not yet Emperor, marched into Galilee in the following order:
Light armed auxiliary troops and archers, to check the terrain ahead to discover ambushes
Heavy armed Roman infantry and cavalry
Ten men from each legionary century, carrying tools for layout of the camp
Engineers to attend to the roads, to clear obstacles and flatten rough ground
Baggage of the general Vespasian and of his senior officers, with a cavalry guard
Vespasian himself with infantry and cavalry guards, as well as his own personal bodyguard
Legionary cavalry
Mules carrying the sections of the siege towers and the siege engines
The officers: the legionary commanders, prefects and tribunes, with guards
The eagles and the standards
Trumpeters
Legionaries, six abreast with a centurion to supervise
Servants and baggage
Auxiliary troops and specially raised allied troops
Rearguard composed of both light armed and heavy armed infantry and cavalry

Order of march in Cappadocia, *c.* AD 135, from Arrian's *Order of March Against the Alans*:

The Alans were a horse people, a branch of the Sarmatians, using heavily armoured cavalry but mobile, and fearsome to the Romans. Most of the units mentioned by Arrian are attested in the archaeological record, except for the unit called *Aplanoi*, who may be Apulians, a unit attested in other sources. Though the list of cohorts, *alae* and legions seems quite explicit, there are still several problems of interpretation when trying to decide upon the fine details of this passage.
Two contingents of mounted scouts, with their own commander
Cohors III Petraeorum sagittariorum milliaria equitata, horse archers commanded by decurions
Ala Auriana
Cavalry of *cohors IV Raetorum*, commanded by Daphne the Corinthian
Ala I Augusta Gemina Colonorum
Cavalry from three part-mounted cohorts: *cohors I Ituraeorum equitata, cohors III Augusta Cyrenaicorum equitata,* and *cohors I Raetorum*, commanded by Demetrius
Cohors I Germanorum equitata, German infantry and cavalry commanded by a centurion, the prefect of the camp
Cohors I Italicorum and 'those present' of *cohors III Augusta Cyrenaicorum*, all auxiliary infantry commanded overall by Pulcher, the commander of *cohors I Italicorum*
Cohors I Bosporanorum milliaria, commanded by their leader Lamprocles
Cohors I Flavia Numidorum under the leader Verus

Equites singulares
Equites legionis
Artillery
Aquila of *legio XV Apollinaris* with the commander Valens, the tribunes and the centurions of the First Cohort.

Battle

On the subject of battle, historians are reliant almost wholly upon literary evidence, which includes the military manuals that have survived, and the eyewitness descriptions of the army in action. The classic arrangement of Roman troops ready for battle was to place the legions in the centre, enclosed on each side by the auxiliary infantry, with the auxiliary cavalry on the wings, but this is by no means a fixed organisation to be rigidly followed in all circumstances. At the battle of Zama, Scipio Africanus reversed this order, placing the legions on the wings. On occasion the main battle was fought by the auxiliary troops, with the legions brought in later if necessary. At the unknown location of Mons Graupius in Scotland, Julius Agricola fought the main battle employing only the auxiliary troops in the front line, with the legions in the rear. In this instance Agricola did not adopt a hastily formed battle plan on the spur of the moment, but he made these arrangements deliberately, with due consideration to the ground where he brought about the battle and the type of enemy he was fighting. Tacitus records that in 29, Lucius Apronius, governor of Lower Germany, was faced with a rebellion of the Frisii and had to gather troops rapidly to combat the threat. He sent in his auxiliary forces against the Frisians, at first not very successfully, but just as the enemy were about to overwhelm the infantry and cavalry units, he placed Cethegus Labeo in command of all the remaining auxiliaries, who rushed forward and saved the day. During another revolt in 71 Petilius Cerialis fought the Batavians using mostly his auxiliaries. Though the exact circumstances of these battles were very different, the enemy shared certain characteristics. Tribal warriors often relied upon the psychological impact of their intimidating war cries, and the initial shock of their massed charge to break the ranks of their enemies, and if this initial attack failed to break the enemy, the tribesmen often lost the battle.

For the legions, the typical *triplex acies* of three ranks was the formation most commonly found in the literary descriptions, usually with four cohorts in the first line and three each in the second and third, but this was not a formula to be rigidly adopted in all circumstances. Some generals employed only two lines, which is how Vegetius describes legionary formation of the 'ancient legion', both of them drawn up with three cohorts at the front and two just behind them, covering the gaps. Four lines were not unknown, for instance at Pharsalus Caesar noticed that Pompey had stationed himself in command of his left wing, with the First and Third legions, together with all his cavalry and his slingers and archers. In response to this, Caesar moved individual cohorts from the third line to create a fourth line, to prevent his right wing from being encircled by the Pompeian horsemen.

Protection of the flanks was always of concern to generals of ancient armies, hence the usual position of the mounted troops on each wing. The Romans, like many other peoples, generally utilised natural features if they were available, such as rivers or streams, hills or woods, which presupposes that these areas had been scouted and found to be free of enemy forces or the potential for ambush. At the battle of Pharsalus Pompey rested his right wing on a river and strengthened his left. In his *Order of March Against the Alans* Arrian describes protection of the flanks by resting them on natural features, to try to prevent the mounted Alani from outflanking or encircling him. Arrian clearly knew where he wished to bring the Alani to battle, which was the optimum circumstance for any general, to pick his own ground and bring about the desired battle on it. Second best was to know the ground well, if forced to fight. During his campaign against the Nervii in Gaul, Caesar was attacked while entrenching the camp site. He hastily gathered his men together, and drew up the army 'according to the character of the ground, the slope of the hill and the exigency of the moment' rather than in a regular tactical formation. Onasander and Vegetius both stress the importance of the terrain, where use of the advantages of the ground could make the difference between defeat and victory. Thorough reconnoitring of the battle ground, or an understanding of the hazards of the potential of a campaign area, were important attributes for all generals. Refusing battle could be just as effective as engaging, if the ground was favourable or unfavourable to the enemy. Fighting the numerically superior Belgae in Gaul, Caesar decided to avoid an engagement if he could, but chose a camp site where he could draw up on a slope, and protect his flanks. Instead of attacking from this direction, the Belgae tried to storm the rear of the camp, across the River Aisne. The Romans received the attacks, but that was all, and the Belgae withdrew since they saw that the soldiers did not advance to unfavourable ground for the sake of fighting a battle. Conversely, in a situation that was unfavourable to the enemy, Caesar was able to use his knowledge of the Spanish terrain to his advantage by forcing the Pompeians to encamp on a hill, where they could certainly protect themselves, but not for very long because there was no accessible water supply. They offered battle but Caesar did not fight them; all he had to do was to wait for the inevitable thirsty surrender.

In the protracted civil wars of the first century BC, Republican armies frequently chased each other back and forth over whole territories, getting to know it well in the process, and then camped near each other, offering battle on a regular basis, but the opposing side did not always commit their troops. The trick was in recognising and seizing the right moment to commit to battle, or to mount an attack. Potentially profitable moments for attack occurred when the enemy army was in the process of drawing up for battle, or breaking camp to move on when the food supplies were exhausted.

In addition to knowledge of the ground, knowledge of the enemy was just as important, and was stressed in the military handbooks. Agricola's true merit in Scotland is the fact that he managed to bring the loosely organised tribal adversaries to battle in the first place, since in utilising their terrain all they had to do was to decamp into the mountains and wait, a technique that their descendants used to good effect against other invaders over the succeeding centuries. In the mountains of Scotland, if the natives utilise their terrain to the best effect, it is the invader who starves. When he did finally bring the Britons to battle, Agricola knew what to expect and dealt with it effectively in his dispositions of his troops.

A full frontal attack using the whole army was not always advisable. Quintus Junius Blaesus did not try to use pitched battle methods when fighting in Africa against Tacfarinas, a mobile enemy whose speciality was hit and run raids, frequently classified under the heading of guerrilla warfare. Blaesus divided his forces into smaller groups combining legionaries and auxiliaries, and constantly chased the enemy, summer and winter, attacking whenever it was feasible. Tacitus says that wherever Tacfarinas' men moved they were confronted by sections of the Roman army, in front of them, on each side and quite often in the rear. Keeping the enemy on the move was also employed successfully in the Danubian wars of Marcus Aurelius, who combined pitched battles with continual harassment. He planted forts in the territory of the Quadi and Marcomanni to watch them and keep them moving, never allowing them to settle in one place, so that they could not pasture their animals or plant crops. When they decided to migrate to another land he hemmed them in and continued the harassment, and in this way he finally exhausted them.

There are some common principles discernible from the literary accounts that illustrate the way in which the Romans used their troops during battle. Cavalry was used to protect flanks, to prevent encirclement by the enemy, or at the right moment to perform an encircling movement themselves. Horsemen were obviously swifter during the pursuit than infantry, and the use of cavalry for chasing the enemy could tip the balance and bring about annihilation instead of a mere defeat. Caesar's troops gained a foothold in Britain after a desperate battle on the shores in 55 BC, but he had no mounted troops with him, so the Britons were able to withdraw, undefeated, and Caesar had to acknowledge that he would have been able to inflict a more serious defeat on the Britons if his cavalry transports had arrived in time.

There are examples of cavalrymen dismounting to fight on foot, for instance in Spain, Caesar's cavalrymen without mounts fought and won an infantry action. Agricola ordered his horsemen to dismount after the main onslaught at Mons Graupius, and Frontinus reports that Domitian did the same in Germany. Normally cavalry would be placed to fight other cavalry and was not necessarily considered to be any match for infantry. There were actions where infantry prevailed over cavalry attacks, whenever the footsoldiers remained in position in a solid mass, but once they had broken up, infantrymen could be picked off by horsemen. During the Danubian wars under Marcus Aurelius, Dio records how the Roman infantry chased the Iazyges on to the frozen river, where the enemy turned on them and their horsemen charged, trying to encircle the Romans to attack them in front, flanks and rear. The Romans formed up all facing outwards, each soldier placing a foot on the bottom of his shield to give him purchase on the ice. The troops then not only received the charge without breaking formation, but pulled the horses and riders into the fight by seizing the bridles or the riders' shields. The horsemen could not stop on the ice because of the momentum of their charge.

A typical pitched battle would probably start with a shower of javelins from the Roman infantry, and then progress to close combat with the sword, the legionary's main fighting weapon. The auxiliaries on the wings would try to close the enemy in and attack the flanks, or even get round the rear. This aim was not always met, of course, depending upon the nature of the enemy and the skill of the opposing leaders. The tribal massed charge depended for its success on noise, confusion and sheer terror but if it did not carry all before it there was scope for the Romans to rally. Other enemies like the Parthians and Persians were formidable because of their armoured mounted warriors, and their archers, whose rapid arrow fire and the famous backward shot as they rode away accounted for several Roman failures. To counteract this menace, Mark Antony took slingers and archers with him when he invaded Parthia via Armenia, but he failed in the end to make any lasting effect and had to withdraw, minus many men and most of his equipment and siege train. Arrian's method of combating a mounted enemy was to draw up his formations with a great number of archers and javelin throwers in the fifth to the eighth ranks firing over the heads of the four front ranks. If his battle was successful, Arrian designated his light armed cavalry for the pursuit of the mounted enemy.

Command

How the army was controlled in battle or on campaign is one of the least illuminated aspects of Roman military history. The main source of information derives from the various literary accounts, which tend to document the extremes but perhaps not the typical or mundane aspects of warfare. The end result is that modern historians have at their disposal accounts of notable successes and notorious failures, in which heroics and disasters feature significantly but not the mechanics of command and control. One of the problems is that many ancient historians elaborated upon events, often utilising their largely fabricated pre-battle speeches to put across to their audiences a political point of view.

Besides the historical literature, there are the military manuals, but although these works offer examples of best practice and outline what *should* happen, they do not help in the quest for what really *did* happen in Roman warfare. Some authors, notably Brian Campbell and Kate Gilliver, have investigated the utility and effectiveness of the manuals, and concluded that they were in fact an important resource in the training of a Roman commander, which in turn implies that the modern historian can place some cautious reliance upon using the manuals as sources of evidence for the Roman army in the field. During the Empire, the overall commander of the armies was of course the emperor himself, who controlled all operations, either from Rome through his subordinates, or directly by his presence in the field. In the first century the emperors were, on the whole, content to leave the conduct of military operations in the hands of their chosen governors. Domitian and Trajan accompanied their armies to the Danube, but after Trajan's victories the succeeding decades of the second century were more peaceful and emperors reverted to directing operations at a distance. In the later second century, and certainly in the third century the presence of the emperor in the field was vital.

Whether the emperor was with them or not, provincial governors and army commanders were his legates and subject to his dictates. Generals who operated at a distance from the emperor, such as Aulus Plautius in Britain, Domitius Corbulo on the Rhine and in the east, and Agricola in Scotland, all had considerable authority within their allotted zones, but were still subject to the emperor's wishes. Corbulo was recalled by Claudius when he seemed ready to progress beyond the Rhine, and he ended badly in the east under Nero, when he was cordially invited to commit suicide. Agricola famously stopped to consolidate his conquest of Lowland Scotland and perhaps to sound out the emperor's opinions on what should be done next. Commanders would work within the broad general framework of the emperor's instructions, but would make their own decisions on the spot as to how to achieve their objectives. As always it was a question of balance; too little power and freedom of action would stultify the generals and risk failure, but too much power and too many troops posed a problem if they should turn into usurpers.

There is a corpus of evidence as to the identity of Roman commanders, and their social and military backgrounds, derived from literary sources and also from their career inscriptions. These sources help to document the various tasks that generals could be asked to perform, but do not inform us how well or how badly they performed them. It is only from this historical record that information can be gleaned as to whether the commanders were ideally suitable for their posts. For the most part commanders of armies were senators, men of education and social standing, and hardly any of them would ever question their military or political abilities. During the Republic, generals were appointed by the assembly and expected to defend Rome or Roman interests and then return to political life, without becoming professional military specialists. Young men such as Scipio Africanus and Pompey the Great rose to power when dangers threatened, and gained commands without too much public disbelief in their aptitude for war. The Imperial system was no longer conducive to the emergence of youthful heroes. While there was never a rigidly prescribed career pattern, aspiring generals followed a broadly similar path. They would gain experience of the legions from their appointments as *tribuni laticlavii* and later as legionary legates, and this, combined with their political experience, formed their training for warfare. There were no staff colleges or training schools, but there were the military manuals and the accounts of the battles of the past, and there were men of experience to talk to and question, all of which are recommended by Polybius as means of becoming a general. Cicero says that Lucullus acquired his expertise by reading manuals while travelling to the east to take up the command that was eventually wrested from him by Pompey the Great. There is no mention in any of the sources of an Imperial archive or an official corpus of military theory and recorded practice.

It has been stated that Roman commanders were amateurs, and the victories that they gained came about almost by accident as a result of the expertise and training of the soldiers and the officers. While the contribution of the centurions and their ability to influence the outcome of a battle should never be doubted, the suggestion that generals were more or less superfluous takes no account of the fact that the responsibility for the conduct of campaigns and individual battles rested with the general. The subordinate officers did not formulate the overall plan for a campaign or a battle, and ultimately they had to obey their commanders even if they did not agree with the planning process. The quality of these subordinate officers was of some concern to conscientious emperors and Roman generals. Vespasian bought off a centurion who had joined the army merely for the pay, so it could be assumed that aptitude for military service played its part in the appointment of officers and commanders. Not all senators pursued their military careers with great vigour up to the rank of provincial governor of an Imperial armed province, and indeed there would not be enough appointments to satisfy them all, so it was perhaps only those men who did have some ability, either self-professed or observed, for command. Catching the eye of men who could advance one's career was an important route to military appointments, and though the emperors did not take a personal interest in the promotion of all the individual centurions, they certainly did take an interest in the appointments and subsequent performances of their higher officers. In the later second century, social rank alone was not always enough to satisfy the emperors when they sought military commanders. Marcus Aurelius chose some of his officers from among the equestrians whose abilities he had noted, admittedly elevating them to senatorial status so that the proper forms were observed.

Roman officers commanding individual units were not necessarily limited to those single units when it came to battle. Before the establishment of a standing army, Caesar chose his legionary commanders from among his associates, without permanently attaching them to these legions, and his officers were expected to take control of collections of troops for specific operations. During the Empire legionary legates kept their posts for longer, but there was still scope for commanders to take charge of vexillations drawn from several units, sometimes simply to bring them safely to the war zone, or in other circumstances to undertake specific tasks during a campaign. Arrian chose to place commanders of other units in charge of a collection of troops, for instance he put the camp prefect of a legion in charge of the *cohors I Germanorum equitata*, and grouped all the mounted elements of three *cohortes equitatae* under one officer called Demetrius. The cohort commander called Pulcher took charge of his own unit and also the men of another auxiliary infantry unit.

Once the command structure had been decided upon for a particular campaign or a specific battle, and the *consilium* had been held, it remained for a general to commit his troops to battle and then control the outcome. The various command positions have been enumerated and discussed in great depth by Adrian Goldsworthy, recounting instances where individual generals led from the front, from among the troops, and from the rear. A general who fought at the front of the army presumably had already outlined what was to happen and then had to leave the soldiers to their own devices, since as Goldsworthy points out it was impossible to observe what was happening on the battlefield, and even if the commander could see what was developing he could not stop to issue orders. Leading from the front could be said to be a last resort, where maybe the soldiers needed the example of personal bravery and the outcome was uncertain. Mingling with the troops is not much better, though there are instances in Caesar's accounts of various wars where he dashed into the midst of the troops to try to stop them from running away or to encourage them to fight harder when threatened with disaster. Once the impending disaster was averted the general would usually take up another position. One of the *topoi* in literary accounts of battles, indeed not confined to the Roman period, is that the general 'seemed to be everywhere at once', but this may not always be a fabrication when it concerns a general who observed closely what was going on and dashed about to the points where he was needed most. The success of these actions would depend largely on the personality of the general, whether he was a charismatic leader in whom the men believed and would follow anywhere, or a routine commander without the necessary spark that fired the exploits of the great generals of history.

Commanding from the rear allowed the general to observe the whole battle, or however much of it he could see from his chosen position, and thus enabled him to make decisions as to how to deal with specific situations and to issue orders to the troops, perhaps sending in each section when it was called for, bringing in the reserves to threatened points, attempting an enveloping manoeuvre, or ordering the pursuit. If the general remained in one place at the rear, messengers could find him more easily to inform him of developments that he may not have been able to see, and he could then make his dispositions accordingly.

Signals and Communications

There is very little evidence as to how Roman generals transmitted their orders during a battle or at any other time. Even those writers who had seen the Roman army in action do not always elucidate the specific details that modern historians would like to know, such as how orders were given, how and in what form messages were sent during a battle, who carried them and what happened when they were received. Caesar's literary works are invaluable for historians trying to document the Roman army in action, but he would never have considered it necessary to give anything more than the barest summary of how he commanded the troops: he simply says laconically 'a message was sent', or 'the signal was given', assuming that his audience would either know how it was done, or would not care. There is only one known instance when a written message was sent during a battle. In his biography of the short-lived Emperor Otho, Plutarch records how a Numidian courier delivered the message and it was left to the officer receiving it to decide what to do. This presupposes that the commander had at his disposal at least one officer or perhaps a scribe with writing implements, and possibly a few riders standing by to deliver instructions to various units, but it is impossible to say whether this was normal procedure. During the Gallic War, Caesar records that he sent a message to Titus Sextius who was in command of the cohorts guarding the camp, to bring them out and post them at the bottom of the hill in case the Romans were driven back down it, so that the cohorts would be able to stop the enemy who might be in pursuit. Caesar does not say whether this was a written or an oral message.

In Julius Frontinus' *Stratagems* the section on sending and receiving messages is devoted to those delivered orally or via written despatches. Caesar's commentaries contain several instances of sending messages by both these methods. Quintus Cicero was besieged in his winter quarters by the tribesmen under Ambiorix, and sent despatches (*litterae*) to Caesar, with the promise of great rewards if the men carried them safely, but the roads were guarded and they were all cut off. On another occasion Cicero sent letters and also messengers (*litterae nuntiisque*) to Caesar, but some of the messengers and those carrying the written despatches were captured and tortured. Caesar always refers to *litterae* in the plural, which may mean that he hedged his bets by sending more than one soldier with the same message to ensure that at least one got through, but there are instances where only one man carried a message. A Gallic slave in Cicero's camp was persuaded to carry a letter to Caesar inside the shaft of a javelin or spear, and Caesar replied to Cicero by means of a message tied to a spear that was thrown into the besieged fort but remained stuck in the side of a tower for two days before it was noticed. This letter was written in Greek in case it was intercepted, which implies that this was a possibility and that Ambiorix and his warriors could read as well as speak Latin. At a later period, campaigning in Germany in the sensitive period after the loss of three legions under Quinctilius Varus in AD 9, Tiberius was aware that the disaster had been caused by lack of caution combined with bad communications. He was particularly anxious that all his orders should be clear, so according to Suetonius he gave all his instructions for the following day in writing, including warning of sudden emergencies, and he insisted that anyone in doubt about an order should consult him, no matter what time of day or night.

Communications by letter or oral delivery were restricted by the state of the roads, the presence of the enemy, the speed of the average man, horse, carriage or ship. The long-distance despatches (*relationes*) to the Senate or to the emperor from the war zone could take several days to reach Rome, even on well-maintained roads. The Imperial post set up by Augustus with relays of fresh horses and posting stations was supposed to be capable of covering seventy-five kilometers per day, depending on terrain. The famous example of Tiberius' journey from Rome to see his injured brother Drusus in Germany is often quoted as the maximum that Roman transport could achieve, at an average of 300 kilometres each day according to Pliny the Elder. Tacitus records how the *aquilifer* of *legio IV Macedonica* travelled from Mainz to Cologne, a distance of 185 kilometres, in twelve hours with the news that the legions of Upper Germany had joined Galba in his bid to take over the Empire from Nero. Other despatches were not so rapid. Austin and Rankov document the number of days that it took for Cicero's correspondence to travel to and from Rome, about a month for letters from his brother Quintus to reach him from Gaul, forty-seven days for a letter from Atticus in Rome to reach Cicero in Cilicia, and seventy-four days for Cicero's despatches from his province to reach the Senate. It is estimated that the optimum speed of communication from the province of Raetia to Rome would be about three days, five to six days for despatches from Germany, nine to ten days from Britain and fourteen days from the eastern provinces. This emphasises the problems of governing the Roman Empire and overseeing its military operations, where the provincial governors and military commanders had to make their own decisions about how to react to a particular set of circumstances, being unable to rely upon receiving instructions from the emperor in time to avert a crisis. For this reason, from the late first century onwards, the emperors ceased to wait at the hub of the Roman world for news of the frontiers and war zones, and took charge themselves.

Much of Caesar's narrative of his wars concerns signals, but these are not usually fully described. Signalling by various means was common in the Roman army, but it is a subject fraught with controversy among scholars. Military communications utilised only a few of the methods familiar to modern armies, being limited to couriers with oral messages, written instructions, or prearranged signals by trumpet, flag, torch, fire, or smoke. Without wireless communication, adequate lighting, or visual aids the Romans must seem greatly hampered to modern observers, but their so-called primitive systems were what they were accustomed to and they worked well within their limitations.

Communications over a short distance could be effected by predetermined visual or auditory signals. When Roman generals of the Republic wished to call the men to arms they usually raised the standard (*vexillum*) outside the commander's tent. Caesar recounts how this was done when he was attacked while still making camp. There are several literary descriptions of raising the alarm or recalling troops by various means, among the most famous examples concerning the siege of Numantia, where Scipio's lines were very extensive and too long to supervise at all times. Appian describes how the soldiers were instructed to raise a red flag if an attack took place in the daytime, or to light a warning fire if they were attacked at night. While investing the stronghold of the Aduatuci, Caesar describes how the tribesmen sallied out and the Roman troops were summoned by fire signals, according to his previous orders, though it is not certain whether these orders applied to the whole army at all times or simply to these specific circumstances. During the civil war where Caesar blockaded Pompey's army at Dyrrachium, Caesar was warned by smoke signals passed from fort to fort that Pompey had attacked the camp of Marcellinus. Smoke and fire signals were often used to recall foragers in times of danger. All these types of signals can only pass on a simple prearranged message, over a relatively short distance.

During battle, signals were given by horn or trumpet, so there were presumably a few combinations of notes that translated into specific manoeuvres, but if so, we do not know what they were. The literary sources detail instances of these types of signal. The overeager *tubicen* who sounded the signal to join battle without orders from Caesar has already been mentioned, and in another battle, during the Gallic War, Caesar ordered the retreat to be sounded but the legions on the opposite side of the valley did not hear it. A more complicated example of orders given during battle comes from the African War, when Caesar was surrounded by Labienus' troops, and ordered every other cohort to turn round so that the Caesarians could fight on two fronts. While it cannot be ruled out that this order was transmitted by word of mouth, it does imply that there was a standard signal for a standard manoeuvre, very simply conveyed, especially in the circumstances that Caesar describes because any confusion or hesitation would have been disastrous.

The emphasis of modern studies has been on long-distance signalling along routes or frontier lines, using fires and torches, for which the evidence has been collected by D. J. Woolliscroft. There is some considerable ancient evidence that beacon fires were used to transmit messages over many miles, but the ancient Greeks and Romans were well aware of the limitations of what types of message could be sent. As Polybius states, beacons work well in warning of attack and summoning help, and can even operate over a distance of two to three days' journey, but they cannot be used to pass on anything more sophisticated, such as a message to say that the occupants of a city have changed sides, or to describe what the enemy is doing at the moment. In these passages, Polybius prepared the ground for an in-depth account of his signalling system using torches to represent each letter of the alphabet. It was invented by the Greeks Cleoxenus and Democleitus, and improved by Polybius himself. The system requires two sets of torches, one on the left and another on the right, to indicate the letters of the alphabet, which are divided into five groups, each containing five letters, except for the last group which contains only four letters. The torches of the left side are raised to indicate which of the five groups of letters are required, one torch for the first group, two for the second group and so on, then the torches of the right side are raised to show which of the five letters are indicated. Polybius gives an example of a message, which starts with the letter K, whose position in the Greek alphabet is the fifth letter in the second group, so the signaller would raise two torches to signify the group, and five torches to signify the letter. With practice it would be perfectly possible to use this system quite quickly, but without telescopic aids its range would be limited. Nevertheless, complicated messages could be transmitted, provided that the sender converted it into the fewest possible letters.

There was a Roman variant on Polybius' scheme documented by Julius Africanus in the third century AD. There were only three torches in total, arranged on the left, in the centre and on the right, so that there would be more letters in each of these three groups than in the Polybian five-group system, but there would be only one torch, raised once for the first letter in the relevant group, twice for the second letter, three times for the third letter, and so on. The comparison with modern text messages will be immediately apparent, and if the speed that small children achieve in using their mobile phones is any guide, then the Romans would have been able to transmit and receive equally well. The major problem is that there is no further evidence of this system in use in the Roman army, and there is no evidence that any soldiers or officers were put in charge of signals and communications, except for the battlefield trumpeters and horn blowers.

Long-distance signalling by whatever means, including smoke, beacon fires, torches or flags, requires many relays with all the errors of transmission and reception, compounded by the number of relays involved. Modern researchers have devoted some considerable time and effort to investigating the feasibility of passing messages along frontier lines, using the series of watchtowers that are known to exist on most frontiers, including frontiers without any physical running barrier. This theory polarises scholars. It could be argued that passing information along the frontier line from tower to tower would have been far less effective than passing it to the forts, so that soldiers could be despatched to deal with the problem. In some cases these forts lay behind the frontier itself, but could receive warning signals from the towers with only one relay. This is just the situation that was revealed on the borders of what had been Roman territory in modern Jordan, where an experiment was conducted by Tom Parker, by lighting fires at night at each of the watchtowers, in the expectation that most of the signals would be intervisible along the various sectors of the line, to pass messages up and down the frontier. In fact the signals were not visible in a sensible linear sequence at all, but every single one of the fires from all sectors was seen at Khirbet el-Fityan, a signal tower on the high ground behind the legionary fortress of Betthorus, which is now modern El Lejjun, and not the same place as Lejjun near Megiddo in Judaea. It is likely that with only one relay to the fortress from this signal tower, legionaries could be turned out to the relevant sector. A thorough knowledge of the terrain would enable an observer to pinpoint where the trouble had arisen.

13

Life in the Army

The Romans obtained their recruits by a combination of conscription and volunteering. Conscription, or the *dilectus*, could be legally carried out at any time in any province, but was usually only applied in times of emergencies or shortages of manpower. The governor of the province was responsible for organising and carrying out conscription, but on occasions high-ranking officials called *dilectatores* could be appointed and sent out to Imperial provinces to gather recruits. In senatorial provinces the title was more usually *legatus ad dilectum*. It was possible to avoid conscription by declaring oneself unfit for service and paying money, or a substitute could be offered, but recruiting officials could be strongly censured for being too lenient, even losing their senatorial rank. A general sweep of provincial manpower would probably include Romans and non-Romans for the legions and the auxiliary units. Another method of recruiting auxiliaries was to demand large numbers by the terms of a treaty after a war, either all at once or by an agreement whereby the tribe or tribes furnished a specified number every year.

There would be several volunteers who would join the army for a variety of reasons, such as poverty or lack of other employment, or family problems. Many soldiers came from military families who lived in the civil settlements outside forts. The would-be legionary and auxiliary soldiers were committing themselves to twenty-five years of continuous service under strict disciplinary conditions, with the possibility of being killed if there was a war. There would be regular meals and issues of clothing, and though soldiers had to pay for these, that would be no different from civilian life. In the army there were expert medical services, comradeship with the members of the tent group of eight men and with the eighty men of the century, or the thirty men of the cavalry *turma*, a roof or a tent overhead for most of the time, and three paydays a year, with a modest amount left for spending after the deductions for food, clothing, weapons, and compulsory savings. If the soldier behaved himself well and survived, there would be honourable discharge and a pension. If he joined at the age of seventeen or even twenty, he would be only about forty-five years old on retirement and hopefully fit enough to engage in some other form of employment, though evidence from tombstones shows that many men died before they reached honourable discharge and retirement.

Joining the Army

An intending recruit would often obtain a letter of introduction from a person of some standing, affirming that he was of good character. It was important for recruiting officers to find out if the potential recruit had ever been a slave, or had a criminal record, both of which were barriers to enlistment. Given the size of the Empire and the slow nature of communications, it would not have been easy to discover this information, and sometimes slaves or criminals slipped through the net. In times when there was an urgent need for manpower, slaves and criminals might be overlooked anyway, but there is an example in the letters of Pliny to Trajan, written when Pliny was governor of Bithynia, where two slaves had nearly managed to join the army before their status was discovered. The case was not straightforward, so Pliny explained that they had taken the oath of loyalty to the Emperor, but had not been enrolled in their designated units. The penalty for slaves who tried to join the army, or succeeded in doing so and were then found out, was usually execution. In this case it is not known what happened to the two men. Trajan's reply to Pliny considered all the possible circumstances. If the slaves had been conscripted, then the fault lay with the examining officer, or if they had been offered as substitutes, the men who presented them to the recruiting officers were to blame. If the slaves had volunteered, without the aid of anyone else, and knowing that they were not freeborn men, the penalty was execution. The slaves were culpable in all circumstances because when they were approved for army service they had obviously lied about their status.

The vetting of potential recruits was called the *probatio*, which embraced not only the moral character but more importantly the physical characteristics of the intending soldiers. There was usually a height qualification, and naturally all soldiers must have sound limbs, not be too fat, and have good eyesight. Ideally they should also be intelligent as well as physically fit. If a recruit passed these tests, he was then put through his paces to see how he performed at certain exercises, and in handling weapons. According to the late Roman author Vegetius this process lasted for four months, at the end of which the recruits should be proficient in using their weapons, marching, swimming and digging ditches and erecting defences. Some men failed at this stage and were rejected. If a soldier passed all the preliminary tests and survived the training, he was accepted into the army.

Before being assigned to a unit, soldiers took the military oath of loyalty to the Emperor, or *sacramentum*. This is probably related to Republican practice, at least in part. Dionysius of Halicarnassus describes how the soldiers of the Republic swore to follow the consuls wherever they commanded, not to desert, and not to break the law. Also writing of Republican practice, Polybius relates how the oath was administered when the legions were assembled for a campaign. One of the soldiers was selected to speak the whole of the oath, and the others simply said '*idem in me*', meaning 'the same for me'. It is not definitely known if this simplified ceremony was adopted during the Empire when recruits were sworn in, but it is very likely. The text of exactly what was pledged has not survived, and it can only be presumed that the oath of loyalty sworn by new recruits was related to the oath that was administered to everyone in the Empire, including soldiers and civilians, when each new emperor succeeded to power. The wording of the military oath may also be linked to the oath which was sworn to Augustus by everyone in the Roman world, on the eve of civil war with Cleopatra and Antony. It was sworn '*sponte sua*' of their own free will, according to Augustus' account of his reign, the *Res Gestae Divi Augusti*. In his biography of Augustus even Suetonius was of the opinion that the whole event must have been carefully engineered. Dio's chronology implies that Octavian declared war on Cleopatra first and then sought the approval of the people in the form of the oath, but this would have been unlike Octavian who moved slowly but surely, exercising the utmost caution in all his projects, and usually made certain that he was within the law. He would need to be even more cautious at this stage, when he was not yet undisputed head of state. The military oath seems to have remained remarkably similar throughout the centuries from the Republic to the late Empire, but of course the purpose behind it was the same, since obedience to the generals and the embargo on desertion would be of paramount importance at all times. In the early fourth century at the council of bishops held at Arles under Constantine I in 314, the ruling was made that allowed Christians to serve in the army in war or in peace, going so far as to threaten any soldiers who laid down their arms in peacetime with excommunication. The military oath changed accordingly and by the time of Vegetius, it had been Christianised, so the recruits swore by God, Christ, and the Holy Spirit, and by the majesty of the emperor, to perform what the emperor commanded, to brave death in the service of the state, and not to desert.

After swearing to obey the emperor, each new recruit was issued with his identification tag (*signaculum*), a leather pouch to hang around his neck, containing an inscribed lead tablet. He could now be sent on his way to join his unit. For this purpose he was given a travel allowance in cash, called the *viaticum*, usually three gold *aurei*, though it is not known for certain whether this was a standard sum applied all over the Empire, or whether it differed for legionaries and auxiliaries. The amount may have been tailored to the particular province, and in some of the eastern provinces it would probably have been issued in *drachmae*. There may also have been some adjustment according to the distance that the recruit would have to travel.

There would probably be a small group of recruits travelling together. They would carry with them a letter of introduction from the governor's office to the unit commander, requesting that they should be entered onto the unit records, and testifying to the fact that the new men had successfully undergone their *probationes*, followed by a list of their names, their ages, and the presence or absence of any distinguishing marks. On 24 February 103 Avidius Arrianus, *cornicularius* or chief clerk of a cohort of Ituraeans in Egypt, filed an original letter of introduction in his fort archives, having made a copy of it. The letter concerned the reception of six recruits who were enrolled on 19 February: Gaius Veturius Gemellus aged twenty-one, with no distinguishing mark; Gaius Longinus Priscus, aged twenty-two, with a scar on his left eyebrow; Gaius Julius Maximus, aged twenty-five, with no distinguishing mark; Gaius Julius Secundus, aged twenty, with no distinguishing mark; Gaius Julius Saturninus, aged twenty-three, with a scar on his left hand; and Marcus Antonius Valens, aged twenty-two, with a scar on the right side of his forehead. All the men were aged between twenty and twenty-five, within the normal range of recruits. In August 156 a strength report was drawn up for *cohors I Augusta Praetoria Lusitanorum equitata*, noting at the end of the document the receipt of nine recruits, all volunteers, approved by the Prefect of Egypt, Sempronius Liberalis. Seven of them were assigned to infantry centuries, one cavalryman was placed in the *turma* of the decurion Artemidorus, and one *dromedarius* (camel rider) was assigned to the *turma* of Salvianus. In this case, the letter or letters of introduction, containing the details of their ages and distinguishing marks, would have been filed by the *cornicularius*, while the strength report was concerned only with numbers of men in the unit, and the centuries and *turmae* to which the men had been assigned.

When the new recruits arrived at their unit headquarters, and their letters of introduction had been received and perused by the commanding officer, they would be assigned to their centuries and entered on the records, described as *in numeros referre*. Only after this was done would the recruits become soldiers, with the obligations, rights and privileges that this conferred on them. One of the privileges was that the soldiers who had been entered on the records would be allowed to make a will. Since most of the men would be quite young, many of the recruits would have fathers still living and in normal circumstances this would mean that the young man would be forbidden to make a will because technically it was his father who owned all his property. As soldiers entered on the records, the men were considered independent, and could bequeath their savings and their property to their families. The existence of a will made it much easier and also legal to dispose of a soldier's property if he died or was killed.

Training

The four-month period of initial training for recruits would not suffice to make them good soldiers unless they practised their skills regularly. Arms drill, route marches, and practice in digging ditches and erecting defences were probably carried out on a regular basis at forts and fortresses and in remote areas, in the same way that modern armies accustom their soldiers to combat conditions. The arms drill was called *armatura*, and was wholeheartedly recommended by Vegetius. This sort of training had lapsed in Vegetius' day, but he says that soldiers with only limited experience of *armatura* were clearly better at fighting than those who had none at all.

The officers who were responsible for training were known by different titles, such as *campidoctor*, or *magister campi*, and sometimes as *exercitator*. It is not known whether there was a subtle difference in these titles, nor can it be shown that there was any attempt at standardisation. Some of the titles may have been used exclusively of each other at different periods or in different parts of the Empire. Many of the trainers were legionary centurions. Titus Aurelius Decimus, centurion of *legio VII Gemina* in Spain, was *praepositus* and *campidoctor* in the reign of Commodus. His titles suggest that he perhaps undertook a special mission combined with training, since *praepositus* was a title bestowed regardless of the recipient's permanent rank, and often denoted an officer in a temporary command. Several of the *campidoctores* and *exercitatores* who are known from inscriptions were associated with the *equites singulares Augusti* or with the Praetorians. Four *centuriones exercitatores*, Ingenuus, Julius Certus, Ulpius Agrippa, and Valerius Bassus, are mentioned in an inscription on a monument erected in AD 139 when forty-nine Thracian *equites singulares* retired after twenty-five years' service. Three more *centuriones exercitatores*, Aelius Flavianus, Aurelius Lupus, and Ulpius Paetus are named on an inscription dating to 205. A legionary centurion from *legio II Adiutrix* from Aquincum calls himself *exercitator*, and may have been assigned to training legionaries. It is not known how the centurions were chosen, or whether they had to apply for the posts, or even if they received a little extra pay.

Military Pay

The soldiers of the early Republic were not paid, but were expected to serve in the army out of a sense of duty, providing their own equipment. When the army was mustered each year for the duration of the campaigning season, and then sent home in time for harvest, the absence of remuneration was not burdensome, but not all wars could be brought to a conclusion within one season. The war with the Etruscan city of Veii involved a long siege, lasting from 406 BC to 396 BC, extending the campaigning season to the full year, so the soldiers were given no opportunity to return home to gather the harvest. Traditionally, in this instance military pay (*stipendium*) was introduced, probably calculated on a daily basis, but nothing is known of the amounts paid or whether officers received more than the men, or if the cavalrymen, who were the wealthiest men of the army, were assisted with feeding their horses.

There is little evidence to show how much the soldiers were paid in succeeding years until the second century, when Polybius says that the rate was two *obols* per day for the soldiers, four *obols* for the centurions and one *drachma* for the cavalry. Since Polybius wrote in Greek, he converted the amounts into Greek equivalents, which now causes problems for scholars who try to estimate equivalent Roman monetary values. There are only a few pieces of evidence that attest to exact figures for legionary pay, so historians must extrapolate backwards and forwards from these fixed points to theorise about earlier and later rates of pay. It is known that under Augustus the legionaries of the standing army received 225 *denarii* per annum, paid to them in three instalments (*stipendia*) in January, May and September. It is not attested that there had been any increase in pay from Julius Caesar's day, and it is known from Suetonius' biography of Caesar that he doubled pay before the civil wars were fought with Pompey, so it follows that the previous rate of pay before Caesar's day was 112.5 *denarii* per annum, pro rata, since technically the soldiers were paid only when they were in service and not all year round.

This does not sit well with the evidence of Polybius, who says that the two *obols* per day were worth one third of a *drachma*. If one *drachma* was equivalent to the Roman *denarius*, the pay works out at a fraction over three *asses* per day, a figure that some scholars find hard to accept. G. R. Watson suggests that the problem hinges on the re-tariffing of the bronze *asses* at some unknown date during the Republic. In the early period there were ten *asses* to the *denarius*, and Watson estimates legionary pay at five *asses* per day, a total of 180 *denarii* per annum. When the *as* was re-tariffed at sixteen to the *denarius*, military pay was reduced to 112.5 *denarii*. This implies a reduction in the standard of living of the legionaries, but since Gaius Gracchus passed a law in 123 BC abolishing the deductions for clothing, this probably compensated for the reduction, at least for a short time until it was reintroduced. The soldiers of the standing army had money deducted from their pay for clothing.

From Caesar to Domitian, a period of over a hundred years, there was no increase in military pay. Probably in 83, Domitian awarded the soldiers a 33 per cent pay rise, increasing the annual sum to 300 *denarii*. He may have increased the three instalments of 75 *denarii* to 100 *denarii*, or as Suetonius implies in his biography of Domitian, he may have added a fourth *stipendium* so that the soldiers were paid on a quarterly basis instead of every four months, either of which methods effectively raised the rate of pay to 300 *denarii* per annum. If Domitian did add a fourth instalment, there was a reversion to the old system of three pay parades per annum later on, which would reduce the amount of paperwork in each unit and at provincial headquarters by 25 per cent.

The rate of pay of the auxiliary soldiers of the standing army is still disputed. The evidence is irritatingly confusing, especially in the case of two Roman citizen soldiers from Nicopolis in Egypt, Quintus Julius Proculus and Gaius Valerius Germanus, who have been discussed above in the chapter on administration of the army, but it is worth going over the salient points again. The two men were Roman citizens, but in each of the three instalments on record, they were paid less than the seventy-five *denarii* that legionaries would have earned. One suggestion is that the men really were legionaries, but they had been charged a small percentage for converting *denarii* into *drachmae*, the currency in use at Nicopolis. Another suggestion is that they were auxiliaries, earning slightly less than legionaries. But even this does not solve the problem, because it is not certain whether they were auxiliary infantry or cavalry, the fact that they were both charged ten *drachmae* for hay in each of the three instalments contributing to the theory that they had horses to feed. The fascinating detail of the pay of these two soldiers cannot be broadly applied to either the legionary or auxiliary forces until it is certain whether they were ordinary legionaries, legionary cavalry, auxiliary infantry, or auxiliary cavalry. Richard Alston has argued more recently that auxiliary pay was on a par with legionary salaries, but it is generally accepted that the cavalrymen would be paid more, as they were responsible for the upkeep of their horses, including at least a contribution to the original purchase of their mounts. One fine day another papyrus may be discovered, detailing pay and deductions like those for Proculus and Germanus, but this time complete with the name of an auxiliary unit.

Inflation would adversely affect soldiers' pay, but in the first two centuries AD the rate of inflation was probably negligible. A series of price rises has been detected beginning in the reign of Marcus Aurelius, which may explain in part the increase in military pay by Severus, but there is no evidence to show exactly what the pay rise was worth. Scholars therefore fall back on estimates for the new annual salaries, which vary from 400 to 500 *denarii* per annum. No one is on sure ground from this point onwards, so when the sources attest that Caracalla granted a further increase worth 50 per cent of the sums arranged by his father, the estimates vary from an annual rate of 600 to 750 *denarii*. After the death of Caracalla, the Emperor Macrinus could not really afford to pay the wages that had been promised to the troops, but at the same time he could not afford to refuse to pay them if he was to remain Emperor, so he had to find the ready cash. In the third century, it is suggested that the Emperor Maximinus doubled pay, but some scholars dispute this, insisting that military pay remained the same until the reign of Diocletian at the end of the fourth century. With or without an increase in the later third century, inflation drastically reduced the buying power of the soldiers' salaries. For a short time, pay in cash was commuted into pay in kind, until the financial problems of the Empire were solved.

The pay of the junior and senior officers is more difficult to establish. According to Polybius the centurions of the Republican armies were paid double the rate of the soldiers. This double rate may have continued into the Empire, but it has been suggested that centurions were paid as much as fifteen times the basic legionary rate, and centurions of the first cohort twice as much again. None of this can be proven beyond doubt. Standardisation across the Empire presumably applied, since as R. O. Fink points out, the centurions who took up successive posts in several legions in different provinces would hardly have done so if there were variations in the pay scales. The only evidence for senior officers' pay derives from an inscription from Thorigny in France, which reveals that the annual salary of a military tribune in the third century AD was 6,250 *denarii*, but there is no evidence on the inscription to show whether he was a senatorial *tribunus laticlavius*, or one of the less senior equestrian tribunes, and it is likely that there was a considerable difference between the rates of pay for senatorial and equestrian tribunes. Yann Le Bohec presents a table of likely rates of pay for officers of the legions and their auxiliary equivalents, basing his figures on work by Brian Dobson.

Junior officers, the *principales*, and some men with specialist functions, such as the *signifer*, the *imaginifer*, and the *aquilifer*, all qualified for extra pay, as did the clerical staff such as the *beneficiarii* and the *commentarienses*. The usual rates of increased pay were one and a half times the rate of basic pay, or double pay, and were called accordingly *sesquiplicarii* and *duplicarii*. Only one instance is known of a *triplicarius*, a soldier on triple pay. The *immunes* who performed special tasks were only paid at the basic rate and received nothing for their special skills.

Supplements to Military Pay

From time to time soldiers could look forward to extra cash from Imperial donatives, from booty, and from their own financial activities such as moneylending, and property transactions. On their accession, emperors usually awarded a donative to the Praetorian Guardsmen, but payments to the rest of the army are only rarely attested. At his death Augustus bequeathed certain sums to all the armed forces, including 125 *denarii* to each Praetorian Guardsman and seventy-five *denarii* to each legionary, which represents one instalment of annual pay for both kinds of troops. Succeeding emperors generally paid out sums to the army whenever an important victory had been won, except that Marcus Aurelius refused to do so when his finances were strained. Other emperors paid unexpected donatives on special occasions, for example it was said that Hadrian paid a total of 75 million *denarii* to the soldiers during his reign, firstly to mark his accession, and then the adoption of his intended heir Aelius Caesar. Antoninus Pius paid out sums on the marriage of his daughter, but the amounts are not known. There may have been more occasions when extra cash was paid to the army, but the sources are lacking. After the reigns of Severus and Caracalla, donatives were paid to the army more regularly.

The value of booty taken in wars is harder to assess, but it was always a possible means of increasing income. Tacitus in the *Histories* says that the spoils from a city taken by storm were usually awarded to the soldiers. During the reign of Gallienus, when the Gallic Empire broke away from Rome, the rival commanders warred among themselves in Gaul. The Gallic Emperor Postumus was murdered by his troops because he refused to allow his armies to sack Moguntiacum (modern Mainz, Germany). Some idea of the amount of booty brought home from foreign wars can be ascertained from the monuments in the Forum in Rome, specifically the reliefs on the Arch of Titus celebrating the conquest of Judaea, and on the Arch of Severus showing the spoils from the Parthian capital.

Extortion was another means of supplementing military pay. This is securely attested in the eastern provinces, where records are better preserved, but presumably the soldiers were no better behaved in the western provinces. The number of times that the Prefect of Egypt issued edicts to try to curb the behaviour of the soldiers only serves to illustrate that the authorities were powerless to eradicate the problem. A papyrus dating to the second century AD records the accounts of a businessman who regularly entered certain sums paid to soldiers for extortion, for which he uses the Greek word *diaseismos*. This may have been a sort of protection racket, perhaps only one example among many.

Soldiers were exempt from direct tax payments and from the reign of Domitian they did not pay the indirect taxes of *portoria* or *vectigalia*. The exemption extended to veterans and to their wives, children, and parents. Military men could run businesses while they were still serving, and many of them probably did so without hindrance or breaking the law, but most of the evidence for soldiers as businessmen and property owners derives from the law codes, concerning cases where there were disputes. A soldier called Cattianus sought justice because a dealer had illegally sold his slaves, and another complained that his brother had sold his share in a vineyard without asking his permission, in order to settle a debt. Typical of Roman realism, tax exemptions were declared invalid on the soldiers' illegal transactions.

Military Law

Roman military law was formulated in the first century BC and the first century AD, and after receiving special attention under Hadrian, its development continued in the second and third centuries AD. Apart from Polybius' description of Roman military discipline and punishments during the Republic, the sources for military law all derive from collections made during the late Empire. These sources incorporate pronouncements and opinions from the second century onwards. The *Codex Theodosianus* of the fifth century is a compilation of civil and military laws and legal decisions, while the sixth-century *Digest of Justinian* lists a wider range of legal opinions, usefully attributing them to their original authors. Another compilation, concerned purely with military law, is found in the work of Ruffus, or Rufius, who may be Sextus Rufius Festus, a provincial governor under Valentinian II, but he is also thought by some scholars to have been an officer on the staff of the Emperor Maurice.

Soldiers enjoyed a privileged legal position. They were exempt from torture and condemnation to the mines, and in the courts, the satirist Juvenal complained that military men were favoured and not subject to the delays and frustrations that ordinary people suffered. The Romans took great pride in military discipline. Anything that jeopardised the security of the unit, the camp, the fort or the army in general was usually classified as a crime. The list of crimes includes treason, conspiring with other soldiers against the commanders, inciting violence, insubordination, striking an officer, fleeing from battle, leaving the ramparts, entering the camp over the walls, feigning illness to avoid battle, betrayal of the camp and giving information to the enemy. Trials of soldiers guilty of these and other crimes were conducted in the camp or fort, and an officer, usually a tribune, was given the task of investigating the matter, while another officer passed judgement.

There is some indication that the Romans were aware of what could be termed shell shock, and were lenient in such cases of battle fatigue. In his account of military law, Ruffus says that any man who had gone AWOL should not be punished until an enquiry had been held about his circumstances, in case he had family problems or other troubles that made him run away for a short time.

Rewards and Punishments

The Romans of the Republic devised rewards and punishments that kept their soldiers under strict discipline and eager to win the recognition of their officers and comrades. Conspicuous bravery on the part of officers and men was always rewarded. The decorations (*dona*) of the Imperial army were rooted in the Republican past, continuing the traditions that had been laid down when Rome had no Empire and no standing army. The ethics behind the awards, and the physical evidence for them, have been intensively studied by Valerie Maxfield. For saving the life of a Roman citizen or an allied soldier, the reward was the civic crown (*corona civica*). The consuls usually presented the hero with gifts and the soldier who had been rescued often gave his saviour an oak leaf crown. The first man to climb over the walls of an enemy city received the *corona muralis*, and likewise the first man across the ramparts of an enemy camp received the *corona vallaris*. Both these crowns were made of gold. For relieving a besieged garrison the reward was traditionally a grass crown (*corona obsidionalis*). Polybius describes how soldiers who had seized an opportunity or used their initiative in a skirmish to wound an enemy or take his weapons were praised and presented with rewards in front of the whole army, which encouraged young soldiers to face danger with bravery. These ceremonials were carried over into the Imperial period, when emperors or victorious generals on campaigns would parade the whole army and present the decorations to named individuals. The honours were always given in the emperor's name, to encourage loyalty to him rather than to the general who recommended the soldiers and officers.

In the Imperial army the crowns mentioned above remained the most prestigious of the decorations awarded to individuals. Different emperors adopted different approaches to the award of decorations, for instance Trajan was considered to be generous with his rewards while other emperors were less so. The award to the *primus pilus* was usually a silver spear (*hasta pura*), while centurions usually received only crowns. Below the centurionate, the decorations consisted of *phalerae*, torques, and *armillae*. Several sculptures are known, the majority of them tombstones, showing these decorations on the soldier's chest, and the accompanying inscriptions specifically mention the awards and sometimes the circumstances in which they were won. The *phalerae* were shaped like discs and were normally displayed on a leather harness over the soldier's armour. The torques were of two kinds, one to be worn round the neck, Celtic warrior fashion, and others smaller and usually hung on the leather harness with the *phalerae*, near the shoulders. *Armillae* were like bracelets, worn on the wrists. Though the decorations were made of precious metal, they were not worth much in terms of cash, but the value to the soldiers was very great. Adrian Goldsworthy quotes the case of a cavalryman of the late Republic who was initially refused the award of *armillae* because he had started his career as an ex-slave. He was offered money instead but refused the offer, clinging firmly to the ideal of military awards, which he eventually received.

Auxiliary soldiers were not personally rewarded for individual exploits, but their contributions were recognised by means of granting honorary titles to the entire unit, such as *torquata* or *armillata*. If there was more than one occasion when the same awards were granted, the unit titles would reflect this, for instance some units were known as *bis torquata*. For exceptional valour, the soldiers of an auxiliary unit could be granted citizenship en bloc, before they had completed their service, and the unit titles again reflected this honour, usually abbreviated to *c.R*. These titles were retained throughout the life of the unit, but the citizen title does not mean that all the new recruits automatically became Roman citizens when they joined the unit.

Polybius stresses the great importance that Republican Romans attached to military honours and obedience, and in the early Roman army any departure from these ideals was brutally punished. Anyone who failed to keep the night watch properly endangered the whole army, so the death penalty was deserved. Those found guilty of this offence were clubbed to death, a process called *fustuarium*. The death penalty could be applied to those who stole from other soldiers, to those who gave false evidence, to men who engaged in homosexual acts, and to anyone who had already been punished three times for lesser offences. A deeply ingrained sense of honour ensured that most of the soldiers stayed at their posts, preferring death to disgrace; if they lost weapons or their shields Polybius recounts that most men fought savagely to get them back or die in the process, rather than suffer the shame that attached to throwing weapons away or running from the battle. If whole units turned and ran, the unit was decimated, which involved selecting one man in every ten to be clubbed to death, while the rest were put on barley rations instead of wheat.

The Imperial army retained many of these Republican procedures, but it seems that the regulations were enforced more rigorously in wartime than in peacetime, and there was always a case for mitigating circumstances. Ruffus recommended that soldiers who committed offences while under the influence of wine should be spared from capital punishment, but should be transferred to a different unit. Tacitus implies in the *Annals* that first offenders and new recruits were treated with leniency by most commanders, depending on the seriousness of their crimes. Much depended on a soldier's rank, his character, and his previous service record, which were well known to the officers. For instance according to Appian, when Mark Antony wanted to find out who were the troublesome elements among his troops, the officers were able to produce a list from their records.

Occasionally whole cohorts or entire units were punished, for instance the legions that survived the battle of Cannae were sent to Sicily, where they lived in tents for several years, until Scipio Africanus took them to Africa, where they redeemed themselves. Some units or parts of units were made to camp outside their forts and were often given barley rations instead of wheat. This is psychological punishment with an inbuilt element of public humiliation, a procedure that Augustus adopted when he made a soldier stand outside his tent clad in only a tunic, and holding a clod of earth. Commanders were at liberty to dream up variations on this theme, and soldiers had few means of making a protest.

Punishments included execution, beating, payment of fines, extra fatigues, demotion or loss of rank, and dishonourable discharge. Though certain punishments were prescribed for certain offences, they were not rigidly applied by commanders, who usually used their discretion. The death penalty was reserved for serious crimes such as inciting mutiny or rebellion, insubordination, going over to the enemy, or striking an officer. On some occasions emperors and commanders could order executions quite arbitrarily, usually when it was necessary to set an example or to restore discipline that had become lax. The stern general Domitius Corbulo treated his eastern troops very severely, allegedly going so far as to execute a man who put his sword down while digging a trench. Loss of armour and weapons could incur the death penalty but more often a flogging, as did the theft of weapons. Ruffus states that the theft of pack animals was treated even more severely, because while the theft of weapons affects only one or two men, the theft of pack animals endangers the whole troop, so the penalty was to cut off the hands of the offender.

Punishments such as loss of rank could mean that a soldier remained in his own unit without his previous rank (*gradus deiectio*), or he could be moved to another less prestigious unit (*militiae mutatio*). A cavalryman could be sent to a part-mounted cohort and legionaries could be transferred to an auxiliary unit, which has implications of a graded status from legionaries downwards. Fines and loss of pay, with or without the imposition of extra fatigues, were probably the most common forms of punishment. A more hard-hitting punishment was dismissal from the service, approximate to cashiering (*missio ignominiosa*), since this stripped the soldiers of all the privileges that would have been their due if they had served their full term and been honourably discharged (*honesta missio*). In the Jewish war, Titus dismissed a soldier who had been captured by the enemy, even though he had managed to escape, because soldiers should not be captured alive. The threat of the loss of pension and privileges, and the prohibition on joining any other unit probably served to keep many soldiers on the side of the law and military discipline.

Desertion

The Romans recognised various types of desertion and dealt with them accordingly. The first duty of captured soldiers was to escape, and if they failed to do so they could be classified as deserters, but the laws recommended that enquiries should be made into the circumstances of desertion, distinguishing between running away on the spur of the moment, being absent without leave, or more seriously, going over to the enemy, which was not unknown. In the *Digest* mitigating circumstances are listed for a man being absent without leave, including illness, family problems, or pursuing a fleeing slave, which were considered legitimate reasons for the soldier's actions. Once again, the man's character and previous record were taken into account.

Ammianus Marcellinus says that the commonest cause of desertion was fear of punishments, implying that the soldier or soldiers concerned had already committed some crime or minor offence. If men returned voluntarily to their units, they were treated more leniently than if they had to be traced and brought back by force, and if a whole group deserted but returned within a specified time, they could avoid corporal punishment, but were often split up and distributed among other units. There would probably be an enquiry into any crimes committed before and during their period of absence, and this could influence the judgement.

Deserting in the face of the enemy, or going over to the enemy, usually incurred the death penalty. Corbulo executed deserters who had been brought back, probably without enquiring into the circumstances. Harsh treatment failed to eradicate the problem, especially during the major wars. Roman soldiers went over to enemy leaders and rendered them valuable service, and from the second century onwards when wars ended and treaties were arranged, there were usually clauses demanding the return of deserters. At the conclusion of the Marcomannic wars, Commodus arranged a treaty demanding among other things the return of deserters and captives, but it is not recorded whether he punished them. Execution or corporal punishment was not always strictly applied in all cases. Soldiers were valuable commodities, and in the mid-fourth century when they were in shorter supply and desertion was rife, the Emperors Valentinian and Valens passed laws to flush out deserters and return them to the ranks, punishing the people who protected and hid them.

Leave and Holidays

Soldiers of the Roman army had no statutory right to a specified number of days' leave of absence during the year, but they could arrange with their officers, usually in the form of cash payments, to be released from fatigues and normal duties. Tacitus indicates that up to a quarter of the men of a military unit could be outside the fort on leave at any one time, or in camp but excused fatigues, having bribed their officers and in some cases having resorted to robbery to obtain the money.

The writing tablets from Vindolanda contain a batch of letters requesting leave (*commeatus*), six of the letters being addressed to the same commander, Cerialis. The majority adopt the same formula, expressing the hope that the commander holds the soldier worthy to be granted leave. These are not simply requests to be relieved of duties, but to go away to another place, which in three cases is actually named in the letter. At the beginning of the second century a soldier called Julius Apollinaris serving in Egypt wrote to his relatives to say that he would try to come home for a visit as soon as his commander started to grant periods of leave. Another letter dated to the third century records a family problem in that a young man who had enlisted in a legion wanted to become a cavalryman in an *ala*, but his relatives could not visit him to discuss his problem, because they were restricted by the leave granted to the boy.

The Romans did not have weekends and statutory periods of annual holiday, but they celebrated a large number of festivals throughout the year. The army celebrated the most important Roman state festivals and ceremonies, probably all over the Empire and at all times, but the most detailed evidence that has come down to us derives from the *Feriale Duranum*, the calendar of events concerning one unit, *cohors XX Palmyrenorum* at Dura Europos in Syria in the early third century AD. It is likely that the ceremonials and holidays celebrated at Dura applied to all units in the Empire, but no one can state categorically that they did, for lack of firm evidence. It is noteworthy, as G. R. Watson pointed out, that the tenor of the Dura calendar is overwhelmingly Roman, even though the unit was formed predominantly from easterners serving in an eastern province, with a variety of local and regional gods and observances to choose from. While worship of local gods was not generally banned, the *Feriale Duranum* makes it clear that as far as the military authorities were concerned the official state festivals were what counted, and the local ones could be left to personal discretion.

The official Roman state festivals observed by the army included the annual sacrifices and ceremonies in honour of the chief gods, Jupiter, Juno and Minerva, on 3 January. It was customary to sacrifice an ox to Jupiter, a cow to Juno and another cow to Minerva. A series of altars from the parade ground of the fort at Maryport in north-west England may be related to this ceremony. Of the several altars found there, seventeen were dedicated 'to Jupiter Best and Greatest' (in Latin, *Iovi Optimo Maximo*, abbreviated to I.O.M.). Two auxiliary units feature on the altars, *cohors I Baetasiorum c.R.* and *cohors I Hispanorum equitata*, so it cannot be said that the practice was limited to only one occupying unit. The dedicators were usually the commanding officers, acting on behalf of their cohorts, signifying that this was a corporate ceremony, and since there are so many altars of this type, it was probably an annual event.

Other Roman gods were honoured by the army, besides Jupiter. On 19 March there was the Quinquatria in honour of Minerva, and on 9 June there was a festival dedicated to Vesta. The anniversary of the foundation of Rome, an important festival that stressed the uniformity of the Empire and focused everyone on the emperor and the central ruling city, was celebrated on 21 April. The reigning emperor's birthday was always celebrated and certain deified emperors were honoured each year, which meant that as time went on the number of observances increased. Among others, Julius Caesar was honoured on 12 July, and Marcus Aurelius on 26 April; there were also celebrations in honour of Germanicus, who never became emperor but was popular with the army.

The purely military observances included elaborate ceremonies on 7 January, the day of *honesta missio*, when the time-served veterans were honourably discharged. If this major event in a soldier's life went unmarked, the incentive to serve what was essentially a hard taskmaster would be considerably diminished, so it was in the army's own interest to make much of this festival. On 10 and 31 May the military standards were decorated in a ceremony called *rosaliae signorum*, and in the legions the anniversary of the eagle standard was observed (*natalis aquilae*), tantamount to the birthday of the legion, which implies that different legions would celebrate this on a different day. All these ceremonies would serve to enhance unit esprit de corps, as well as emphasising *Romanitas* and the sense of belonging to a larger society than the immediate military environment.

It cannot be stated precisely what kind of activities accompanied these various religious and military ceremonies, but it is likely that music was played, and parades in fine armour and military manoeuvres would form a significant part of the celebrations; feasting probably ensued, especially after the ritual sacrifices had taken place.

Food and Clothing

The staple diet of legionaries and auxiliaries was wheat. In the papyrus records, barley is mentioned several times and soldiers were delegated to collect it, usually denoted by an entry saying 'to the barley' (*ad hordeum*) or equivalent abbreviations. Though its main purpose was feed for the horses, the soldiers did eat it on occasion, and it was also used as a punishment ration. According to Vegetius, recruits who did not perform well were issued barley rations until they could demonstrate their proficiency before their senior officers. It used to be thought that cereals formed the main part of the military diet, but the soldiers ate meat whenever they could. Part of the standard military fare was fresh or salted pork, and sausages, ham and bacon were also eaten. Other rations would include peas, beans, lentils, cheese, salt, olive oil, and wine. The legionaries of Vindonissa (modern Windisch in Switzerland) ate peas, beans, and carrots, and a quantity of fruit and nuts. At the legionary fortress of Chester in England there is evidence that soldiers ate a wide variety of meat, including oxen, sheep and goats, and several types of domestic fowl. Not all of the food that reached the forts was necessarily organised by the provincial supply system or by the cultivation of fields on military land. Private enterprise seems to have played a part in the provision of food. The remains of wild birds, hares, boars and deer imply that the legionaries at Chester went on hunting expeditions. An altar to the god Silvanus was set up at Birdoswald fort on Hadrian's Wall by the *venatores Banniesses*, the hunters of Banna, and another more elaborate altar to Silvanus was found on the moors south of Stanhope in County Durham. It was erected by Gaius Tetius Veturius Micianus, prefect of the *ala Sebosiana* in fulfilment of his vow to the god for capturing a boar of exceptional form (*eximia forma*) that no one else had been able to bag. The *ala Sebosiana* was based at Lancaster, so this hunting expedition was perhaps undertaken while Micianus was on a visit to a fort in the vicinity, possibly Binchester, whose officers probably ate well on the day of the capture. Soldiers or their servants probably went fishing for freshwater fish, since fortresses and forts were often located near rivers, and there may have been civilian suppliers of seafood. There is evidence from excavations at forts all over the Empire of freshwater and saltwater fish, and oysters, mussels, and cockles. It is suggested that some units kept chickens for their egg production as well as for eating, and there is a case on record where a man who may have been an army supplier bought a cow in Frisia, now the northern Netherlands, with two centurions from different legions as witnesses. Perhaps some soldiers fancied a bit of fresh cheese.

Greek and Roman authors do not refer to military uniforms in the modern sense, but they do describe 'putting on military dress' in times of crisis. If there was a military dress code as opposed to civilian dress, it must be asked what it was that distinguished soldiers from civilians, apart from the rather obvious items such as armour and weapons. Many funeral reliefs show soldiers without armour, simply dressed in tunics and cloaks, so it was presumably some other attribute of dress that marked an individual as a military man. Most authors agree that it was the leather belt or *cingulum* more than anything else that proclaimed the wearer as a soldier, though the term is not attested before the third century. Variations include *cingulum militare*, or *cingulum militiae*. The belt was both functional and decorative, in that metal plates were attached to it, and various hooks and frogs to which the dagger and initially the sword would be attached, though later on the sword was worn on a baldric over one shoulder. An important feature was that mail armour was usually hitched up over the belt, thus relieving the wearer's shoulders of the full weight. In the early Empire, soldiers are generally depicted on their tombstones wearing two belts crossed at an angle over the hips, but later the fashion was for only one belt, perhaps because this was more practical and comfortable when segmented armour was introduced. The military belt also served to attach the leather thongs or apron, like a sporran, that afforded some protection but probably hindered running. There were most commonly four to six straps in the apron, with metal studs and terminals for decoration and perhaps to weight them.

A great deal is known about what Roman soldiers looked like, in that archaeologists have discovered significant amounts of military equipment, weapons, and armour from several provinces and from several periods, and art historians have studied the various monuments that depict soldiers, but there is still no evidence that there was a standard military uniform at any period over the whole Empire. There were no doubt regional and temporal variations that have escaped the record. Some authors consider that on occasions, Roman soldiers would wear whatever they could lay their hands on, but this probably applies to most armies, especially when soldiers have fought protracted campaigns. It is perhaps significant that in several museums the erstwhile pristine, unsullied portrayals and models of Roman soldiers have been replaced by scruffier versions showing men with two weeks' stubble and wearing patched cloaks. This new attempt at realism reflects the difference between soldiers doing their daily work and soldiers on parade in their best turnout. Decorative parade armour certainly was worn on ceremonial occasions, though it is possible that some this equipment was also used in battle.

Apart from their armour the soldiers obviously required ordinary clothing, such as tunics and cloaks. Tunics may have been dyed in various colours, but there is hardly any evidence for this. White tunics are found on the famous Egyptian funerary portraits, which may represent veteran soldiers, and in a document from Egypt instructions to weavers making clothes for the army it is stipulated that the cloth should be white. It has been suggested that white tunics were worn by ordinary soldiers, and red ones by centurions, and Vegetius describes the blue/green tunics of the marines, together with the blue/green sails that helped to camouflage the operations of the Roman fleets. It is generally agreed that military tunics differed from civilian versions in that they were actually longer but were worn hitched up over the belt and therefore appeared shorter. Augustus punished soldiers for misdemeanours by making them stand outside headquarters clad only in their tunics and without their belts, so they looked rather ridiculous in long tunics and deprived of the one item that marked them as soldiers. Some relief sculptures show the tunics hitched up at both sides, forming a curved skirt at the front and presumably the back. This arrangement perhaps eased the problems of marching or running, freeing the legs just as modern sports shorts are often cut away at the sides. The tunic was made of wool or linen, formed from two squares or rectangles of cloth sewn together, with holes left for the head and arms. Sleeves were mostly worn short, but evidence from some cavalry tombs shows that at least some of the cavalrymen wore long-sleeved tunics, and long sleeves became more common for all soldiers from the third century onwards. Some tunics were worn off one shoulder, with a split down the back and perhaps with the loose material knotted, but this would not be comfortable with armour on top, so it was perhaps just an arrangement that freed up the arms when working, for instance felling trees and chopping wood.

Cloaks of different types are shown on several reliefs, and fall into three main categories. The *sagum* was a simple square draped around the wearer and fastened with a brooch on the right shoulder, leaving the sword arm free. It was probably made of wool, and could be decorated with a fringe. Another type of cloak was the *paenula*, which was more like a poncho, perhaps oval in shape and put on over the head, with a split down the front joined by toggles or buttons, and sometimes equipped with a hood. This would not be a specifically military garment since its practicality would appeal to everyone who had to work in the open air in inclement weather. Similarly the *byrrus* or *birrus* was not necessarily a purely military item, but at least one soldier is on record asking his relatives to send one. In the later third century the *birrus Britannicus* was a valued British export, specifically assigned a maximum price in Diocletian's Edict on Prices in AD 301. Its waterproof qualities perhaps appealed to the soldiers as well as the civilians of the northern provinces, and soldiers were probably allowed to wear clothes that kept them warm and dry even if they were not regulation issue. Military officers wore a more decorative cloak called the *paludamentum*, draped over the left shoulder and wound round the left arm. The portrait of Marcus Favonius Facilis, centurion of *legio XX*, shows this type of cloak quite clearly. The *paludamentum* was associated more and more with the emperors after the first century AD.

Soldiers' boots (*caligae*) are almost as distinctive as military belts, as attested by the terminology of the military records, where the number of soldiers present is often listed as *caligati*. There are fortunately enough extant examples to elucidate all the details of how the boots were made. The uppers looked more like modern sandals, being cut away to form the equivalent of straps which could be laced together at the front to fit most sizes of foot. The uppers, the insoles and the outer soles were nailed together with studs arranged in patterns that prefigure modern training shoes. An army marching along a stone-paved road must have created a considerable clatter, and the studs will have helped to maintain grip in turf and rough terrain, but they did not serve the centurion Julianus very well in Judaea in AD 70, since he slipped on a paved surface, fell heavily and was killed before he could get up. In order to keep warm, the soldiers wore socks (*udones*), which probably had no toes or heels, as shown on a sculpture depicting Praetorians. One of the Vindolanda letters contains a request for *udones*, and from the same source material it is known that underpants (*subligares*) were worn under the tunic. Cavalrymen on some sculptures, especially on Trajan's Column, are shown wearing leggings that come down to the bend of the knee, but it is likely that legionaries and auxiliary infantry wore them as well, as shown on the Adamklissi sculptures.

Soldiers' Wives and Families

By law, soldiers were forbidden to marry while they were serving, until the reign of Severus at the turn of the second and third centuries when marriages were legalised. The original law against soldiers' marriages was passed by Augustus. Until his reign, some Republican soldiers were already married when they enlisted or were conscripted, and the survivors of the campaigns went home to their families, but in the standing army with longer terms of service, families would impede movement if they followed the soldiers around on campaign, and it would exert emotional pressure on the men if families were left behind. In contrast to the Republican army, where married men were enlisted, in the Imperial army if a soldier was married when he joined the army, the marriage was officially ended. Although legal commitment to women was forbidden to serving soldiers, many of them nonetheless formed associations with local women that were tolerated and given tacit recognition by the authorities.

By the second century AD, most legions and auxiliary units were settled in permanent forts and fortresses, and though they could be transferred to other locations they were usually only moved to another post when campaigns were organised, or in emergencies when an area was attacked. In these cases, the unofficial associations with local women could hardly be stamped out, and since a discontented army perhaps posed more of a threat to Imperial rule than an army with families, no emperor chose to enforce the ban on marriages. All that could be achieved was to refuse to recognise the union during the soldiers' service lives, so that the female partner was not officially a wife, and the children were illegitimate. This situation changed when the soldiers were discharged, though all the evidence concerns auxiliary soldiers, who were rewarded with Roman citizenship on completion of twenty-five years in the army, and for those who asked and probably paid a fee, a certificate was issued in the form of a two-leaved bronze tablet called in modern terminology a diploma, recording the official discharge from the army and the grant of citizenship. It is less certain what happened to legionaries who had formed relationships with women while they were still serving soldiers. Certificates of discharge were not issued for legionaries, who were all Roman citizens to start with, so when they were discharged they would have the automatic right to marry a Roman woman. Only a union between a Roman man and a Roman woman constituted a full Roman marriage, so permission was required in the form of a grant of *conubium* for a Roman to marry a non-Roman. Since many of the women in the vicinity of the legionary fortresses would be natives of the particular province, soldiers would have fewer opportunities to form a relationship with a Roman woman. The legionaries who had chosen partners among the local women would require, and were probably granted when they were discharged, the right of *conubium* with a non-Roman, which would legalise any liaison they had formed. There is no proof that this was the normal procedure after legionaries were discharged, nor is it certain what the status of children of such a marriage would have been.

Concerning auxiliary troops, the situation is better documented, thanks to the issue of diplomas naming the individual soldiers and the units that they served in at the time of discharge. The privileges given to auxiliary troops on honourable discharge included citizenship grants to the soldier, his children and their descendants, but not his wife. The careful wording on the diplomas stated that the soldier was granted 'the right of marriage [*conubium*] with the wife he had at the time of his citizenship grant', acknowledging the fact that soldiers had partners while they were serving in the army, and finally making the union legal after twenty-five years of service. If the soldier had no partner, he was given the legal right to marry, 'limited to one wife for each man' as the texts of the diplomas usually state.

Since any children born to a soldier while he was still serving had to wait until their father was discharged before they were given Roman citizenship, in the interim it was important for serving soldiers to recognise them as his own. To this end he could declare unofficially in front of witnesses that he was the father of a child, so that when he was discharged it would be clear that his children were eligible for citizenship. In the reign of Hadrian, Marcus Lucretius Clemens, a cavalryman of *ala I Thracum* in Egypt, declared that he had become the father by Octavia Tamustha of a son called Serenus, born on 25 April AD 127. The text goes on to say that he had made this record so that when he was discharged he would have proof that Serenus was his son. At least six soldiers from different *turmae* of the *ala* are listed as witnesses.

With the passage of time, if the families of auxiliary veterans remained in the vicus, there would be a supply of Roman citizen women, daughters of enfranchised auxiliary veterans. Serving soldiers of the auxiliary units who formed relationships with these women would probably receive but would not necessarily need the grant of *conubium* when they were discharged with citizenship because they would both be Romans. There was a change to the regulations under Antoninus Pius in the 140s, in that the children born before the soldier was discharged remained as non-Romans, and the grant of citizenship was extended only to the soldier himself and any children born after his discharge. This would reduce the number of Roman women, but would ensure a supply of non-Roman young men. If any of these sons of soldiers entertained any military ambitions they would join the auxiliary units, being ineligible for the legions. In 197 Septimius Severus ended the anomaly by allowing all soldiers, legionaries and auxiliaries alike, to enter legal marriages, which merely recognised what had been happening in most provinces, and in 212 or 213 his son Caracalla bestowed Roman citizenship on all freeborn inhabitants of the Empire. This meant that provincials would no longer need to serve in the auxiliary units to obtain their citizenship, and soldiers could marry freeborn women from any province if they chose to do so, without the requirement of a legal grant of *conubium*.

The ban on marriages concerned all ranks up to that of centurion, but equestrian officers who served for only a short time with the army were exempted. The writing tablets from Vindolanda in northern England reveal that wives of commanding officers resided at the forts with their husbands. Senatorial governors and some legionary and auxiliary commanders regularly took their wives to their provinces. At York, Sosia Juncina, wife of the legionary legate Quintus Antonius Isauricus, set up an altar to the goddess Fortuna.

Many soldiers honoured their associations with their chosen women, who were much more than mistresses to them. The majority of the women married to soldiers were non-Romans (*peregrinae*), but on inscriptions there is rarely any distinction between citizens and non-citizens, and understandably there is no mention of legal or illegal unions. Funerary inscriptions set up by veterans for their spouses name the deceased as their *coniugi* or wives. Gaius Aeresius Saenus, veteran of *VI Victrix*, set up a tombstone at York for himself and his family, who all died before him; his wife Flavia Augustina died aged thirty-nine, her son Saenius Augustinus died aged one year and three days, and her daughter lived for only one year nine months and five days. The children specifically named as belonging to the wife were presumably Gaius Aeresius' stepchildren, so perhaps he married Flavia as her second husband. In the first and second centuries soldiers' marriages would be considered illegal until their discharge, but after Severus abolished the ban on marriages, the men could legally acquire wives while still serving, as Gaius Valerius Justus did at Chester. He was an *actarius* of *XX Valeria Victrix* when his wife Cocceia Irene died aged thirty.

The widows of soldiers who set up tombstones for their husbands quite often did not bother to include their own names on the inscriptions. The wife of Marcus Aurelius Nepos, centurion of *XX Valeria Victrix*, paid for an elaborate carved portrait of her husband and herself, but describes herself as *coniux pientissima*, most devoted wife, without giving her name. The wife of Cassius Secundus is not known but the tombstone that she erected for her husband is now broken, so her name may have appeared in the missing section. She informs people that Cassius was aged eighty when he died and had been honourably discharged, though his legion is not named. Aurelia Censorina had a stone coffin made for her husband Aurelius Supero, centurion of *VI Victrix at York*, who died aged only thirty-eight, so they must have been married while Supero was serving in the army.

There may have been many soldiers who chose not to get married. The proportion of soldiers who formed temporary or permanent liaisons with women is not known, but it is likely that even if they were in some kind of relationship many men did not consider themselves as committed to marriage. From various forts and especially from legionary fortresses it seems that there are usually many more funerary inscriptions set up by appointed heirs than there are memorials set up by wives. It could be said that the heirs included wives, but more often than not the heirs give their names, and they are usually male, sometimes friends of the deceased, or their freedmen. In one or two cases the heir is a woman, who set up the tombstone as instructed in the soldier's will, but she is not usually specifically named as a wife. In other instances the text of the inscription mentions that the wife is also the heir, as though it was important to make this distinction. Julia Similina, wife of Titinius Felix, *beneficiarius* of *XX Valeria Victrix* at Chester, describes herself as his wife and his heir on the tombstone she had made for him.

Medical Services

Medicine in the Roman world was derived almost wholly from the Greeks, but in the area of military medicine the Romans developed and improved upon Greek theory and practice. In particular they learned how to treat wounds, but did not neglect the cure of diseases, and they established hospitals in their forts, particularly in the legionary fortresses. The hospitals were staffed by specialist personnel, and medical staff went on campaign with their units. Hyginus in *De Metatione Castrorum* mentions a hospital tent in his work on laying out the camp, recommending that it should be placed where convalescent soldiers could find peace and quiet.

The most common staff are the *medici*, attested in all types of units, including legions, auxiliary cohorts and *alae*, the Urban Cohorts, the Praetorian Guard, the *Vigiles* and the *equites singulares*. It is likely that the title *medicus* covered a range of different ranks and functions. Some of the *medici* were probably ordinary soldiers, included with the *immunes* who were excused fatigues, but others were officers, perhaps of considerable status. On some inscriptions, *medici ordinarii* are named, such as Caius Papirius Aelianus at Lambaesis in North Africa, who incidentally lived for eighty-five years, seven months and fifteen days, in itself a good recommendation for a doctor. In the later Empire at the fort of Niederbieber in Germany a certain Processus set up a dedication to the household of the reigning Emperor, calling himself *medicus hordinarius*, perhaps a guide to the way in which he pronounced the word. It is possible that the *medici ordinarii* held the rank of centurion, but no source confirms this, so it must remain a contested theory. Some scholars suggest that *ordinarius* simply means that the doctor served in the ranks. On a monumental inscription in Rome, listing the officers and men of the fifth cohort of the *Vigiles*, there are four *medici*, Caius Runnius Hilaris, Caius Julius Hermes, Quintus Fabius Pollux and Sextus Lutatius Ecarpus. These men are listed after an enumeration of the centurions and other officers such as the *cornicularii*, but before the soldiers of each century with the centurion's name at the head. The position of their names with the officers lends some support to the theory that the medical men ranked with them. Some or perhaps all of the *medici* in the fleets ranked as *duplicarii* on double pay, as attested on an inscription from Puteoli.

Several of the attested *medici* have Romanised Greek or eastern names, such as Quintus Marcius Artemidorus, of the *equites singulares Augusti* in Rome, Marcus Mucius Hegetor of *cohors XXXII Voluntariorum*, and Marcus Rubrius Zosimus from *cohors IIII Aquitanorum*. Another possible easterner is Marcus Ulpius Telesphorus, *medicus* of the *ala Indiana*, but his name has been reconstructed from only a few surviving legible letters on the inscription. These men may have started out as civilian doctors and then joined the army, but how and where they trained is not known. Teachers or trainers (*discentes*) are known in medical contexts, so in some cases perhaps the army trained its own medical staff, choosing likely candidates from among those who had recently joined or showed some aptitude for the work.

Other medical staff include the *optiones valetudinarii* and the *capsarii*, also attested on inscriptions. The *optiones valetudinarii* were *immunes* according to Tarrutienus' list in the *Digest*, and their function, if their titles are taken literally, was to assist in the hospital, but in what way is not made clear. They may have been clerical assistants rather than surgical or medical staff. Two inscriptions from Lambaesis mention the *optiones valetudinarii* of *legio III Augusta*, naming one of them as Lucius Caecilius Urbanus. The gravestone of Caius Luccius Sabinus from Beneventum in Italy shows that in his varied career he started out as an *optio valetudinarii* and then went on to take up a string of other posts, so either he was not, or did not want to remain, a medical specialist.

The *capsarii* who appear on inscriptions along with *medici* and *optiones valetudinarii* may have been responsible for dressing wounds, since the title *capsarius* is derived from the box (*capsa*) that contained bandages, but some authors say that the box was for scrolls and the *capsarii* may have been clerical assistants. The soldier shown on Trajan's Column bandaging the leg of a wounded man is usually interpreted as a *capsarius*. An inscription from Carnuntum on the Danube mentions the *capsarii* of *legio XIIII Gemina*, and Aelius Munatius is named as *capsarius* of *cohors milliaria Hemesenorum*. Another inscription from the large late Roman fort at Niederbieber in Germany associates the *capsarii* of the *numerus Divitiensium Gordianorum* with the *medicus hordinarius* called Processus.

Hospitals (*valetudinaria*) are archaeologically attested at the legionary fortresses on the Rhine at Vetera (modern Xanten) and Novaesium (modern Neuss), and at Inchtuthil in Scotland. From inscriptions it is clear that a hospital existed at Lambaesis in North Africa. An inscription found at Stojnik in Yugoslavia, dating from AD 179, specifically mentions the *valetudinarium* of *cohors II Aurelia nova milliaria equitata civium Romanorum*. On Hadrian's Wall in Britain, at the forts of Housesteads and Wallsend, the hospitals of auxiliary units have been excavated. A *medicus ordinarius* called Anicius Ingenuus is attested at Housesteads. He died young, aged only twenty-five, and his gravestone is notable for the portrayal of a crouching hare in the arch at the top. The hospital at Wallsend was added to the fort around 180, and it is not known if the timber building that preceded it was dedicated to the same purpose. The hospitals were usually courtyard buildings with small light and airy cubicles opening off the open central area, sometimes with a veranda running all round the interior, though the verandah at Housesteads was removed when the courtyard was flagged. It should be noted that not all the buildings of this type of plan are necessarily hospitals. In some cases, buildings inside forts that look like hospitals may actually be workshops (*fabricae*), which adopted the courtyard plan and small rooms arranged all around it to provide light and air for the metalsmiths and woodworkers who used them.

On campaign, the work of the *medici* would include treating those who had fallen sick, but the treatment of wounds is much better documented. One of the best known manuals is that of Aulus Cornelius Celsus who wrote his *De Medicina* in the early first century AD, relying heavily on Greek works. He writes about diseases, pharmacology, therapy and surgery. Some of his cures for diseases could only have increased the mortality rate, and it is not sure whether the Romans fully understood contagion and the efficacy of isolation of patients. In dealing with wounds, however, Celsus either had valid experience of his own or had gained knowledge from someone who had seen medical service in the wars. He was more of an encyclopaedist than a serving medical officer, but nothing is known of his life. Writing under the Emperor Tiberius, he could just possibly have witnessed the many battles in Germany and Pannonia during Augustus' reign.

Celsus writes in detail about how to remove various types of missile weapons, recommending that if the weapon has not penetrated very far and has not crossed large blood vessels, it should be pulled out through the hole where it had entered, but if the distance that the weapon has to be withdrawn is greater than the distance which remains, then the best way to extract it is to force it right through, cutting the flesh at the opposite side with a scalpel. This is not recommended for broad weapons because it would create two huge wounds instead of only one, so Celsus describes how to use the Dioclean *cyathiscus*, named after its inventor Diocles. This instrument had a curved end with a hole in it, and it had to be inserted next to the weapon lodged in the flesh, until the hole could connect with the point of the weapon, and then the two could be drawn out together. Celsus adds notes about how to stop excessive bleeding of wounds and what to do to prevent inflammation; if all else fails he explains how to amputate limbs. Celsus was aware of the damage that lead sling bullets could cause. If they are simply lodged in the flesh then they can be extracted with forceps, but there are problems if they have embedded themselves in bones or joints. He explains that sometimes it is necessary to cut around the bullet lodged in a bone by making a V-shaped cut, and if the bullet is stuck between joints, then the only means of extraction is to pull the joints slightly apart. Roman medical and surgical instruments, looking startlingly like modern versions, have been found at several sites, especially in the legionary fortresses. From Neuss there are needles, scalpels, probes and spatulas, and from the fortress at Aquincum in Hungary there are scissors and forceps, leg splints and a lancing fork.

Pharmacology consisted mainly of the use of herbs. Medicinal plants have been found on military sites, especially at Neuss where five varieties were discovered. It has been suggested that the courtyards of the military hospitals may have been laid out as gardens where specific herbs could be grown. One of the best ways of securing good health in the army derived from cleanliness. There were elaborate bathing establishments attached to each fort and fortress, and time was clearly allowed for bathing, which probably became a prolonged leisurely affair involving dice games and gambling. Altars to Fortuna are often found in bath houses. Sick and wounded soldiers in the hospitals may have had their own baths, since it is thought that the hospital at Inchtuthil contained a bathroom. There were also kitchens in the hospitals where perhaps special foods were prepared. Celsus stresses the importance of diet in the treatment of the sick, enumerating those foods which were thought to be the most easily digested. In one of the rooms in the hospital at Neuss excavators found remains of eggs, peas, lentils, and shellfish, all of which are on Celsus' list. Sufficient time for convalescence was known to be important in the recovery process, and a papyrus from Egypt shows that some legionaries of *legio XXII Deiotariana* were sent to the seaside for a period of convalescence.

14

The Army and Civilians

Romans of the early Republic made little or no distinction between civilians and soldiers, since it was the duty of all men of a certain property value to serve in the army, and to return to civilian life and their farms after the end of the campaigning season. Even in the later Republic and early Empire, when there was a widening gap between the army as a society and civilians, the career paths of officers still combined military and civilian posts. The provincial governors and even the legionary legates experienced fewer years in the army than they did in civilian government and administrative posts.

The presence of the army had profound effects on the lives of civilians in the provinces, some of it good and some of it not so good. The army helped to establish and maintain internal law and order, and provided protection from external dangers. The presence of hundreds if not thousands of soldiers can be said to have boosted the economy, encouraging agriculture and trading. The other side of the coin is that soldiers were in an almost unassailable position and could bully and exploit civilians with almost total impunity.

Another effect of Roman government was the gradual Romanisation of the provincials. This was never enforced, and it cannot be argued that Romanisation was a proactive mission of the army. The Romans cultivated the local elite wherever they could do so, and ruled via the aristocrats that they associated with. If the local elite and the rest of the provincials expressed an interest in Roman customs and values, they were encouraged; if there was no interest, the ideology of Rome was not enforced. The evidence from Roman Britain serves to illustrate this point. Romanisation made most progress in the south, where the military occupation lasted for only a short time until Wales and the north were conquered. Thereafter the presence of troops in the south was much reduced. Soldiers did not disappear from the scene entirely, since the governor and his entourage, and several officials, would usually be accompanied by soldiers, and the legionary fortress at Caerleon in South Wales was occupied until the later Roman Empire, so it cannot be said that the southern parts of Roman Britain were devoid of soldiers, but compared to the north of Britain it could be said that the south was not occupied and garrisoned. Forts and former legionary fortresses were given up in the south and new ones built further north as the conquest of various tribes progressed. When the troops moved away from their forts, several of the sites developed into towns, some of them becoming populous and successful, one example being Wroxeter, which was a former legionary base taken over by civilians and army veterans. It eventually expanded into one of the largest towns in Roman Britain. Some of the towns established on former military sites had a long and independent civilian life, while others retained their military associations because the old fort sites were converted into colonies for veterans, one at Gloucester, and another at Lincoln, whose modern name, derived from Lindum Colonia, still reflects its origins as a former legionary fortress converted into a colony of veterans.

In the towns of southern Britain, Roman-style houses were built, complete with courtyards and gardens, mosaic floors, and painted walls and ceilings. Several excavations of Roman villas have revealed an unbroken progression from Iron Age round houses and field systems to well-appointed Roman farmhouses, and though it could be argued that on each and every site the natives were ousted and Romans moved in, this is considered unlikely. It seems that aristocratic Britons of the southern lowlands readily converted to living in Roman towns and villas, whereas in the northern uplands, where the majority of the armed forces were permanently stationed in some considerable numbers, Romanisation gained little headway and the natives lived as they had always lived, in clusters of round stone huts, albeit using Roman goods inside them. As pointed out by Martin Millett in *The Romanization of Britain*, if the army was actively engaged in promoting Romanisation, then the northern parts of Britain ought to furnish archaeological evidence of a high degree of Roman culture, but this is not the case even though the Romans were present for nearly four centuries.

The status of civilians all over the Empire differed according to whether they were Roman citizens with valued rights and privileges at law, or ordinary free provincials who lacked Roman citizenship. These non-Romans were called *peregrini*, meaning foreigners. Their legal rights were inferior, and Brunt has argued that probably all non-Roman provincials may have been disarmed. Provincials could rise to eminence via service in their town councils, in which those who had reached the chief magistracy received Roman citizenship.

No matter what was the predominant lifestyle in any province, Roman and non-Roman civilians could scarcely avoid coming into contact with soldiers in some capacity, even in provinces where there was no permanent garrison, largely because the army performed all the functions that modern societies divide into different categories, such as police, customs guards, and tax collectors, as well as road builders, architects and engineers.

Civil Settlements Outside Forts: vici and canabae

During the initial stages of the conquest and annexation of a province, the army was usually divided up into groups, establishing bases wherever necessary, occupying them for a short time and moving on, sometimes coming back to an old base and reoccupying it, sometimes on more than one occasion. Gradually as the provinces were consolidated and pacified the army moved outwards to the boundaries of the Empire, some of which became permanent frontiers, marked in the second century by running barriers or roads guarded by watchtowers and small forts. Where the army units settled down for longer periods as the frontiers were crystallised and forts became permanent, the relationship with civilians developed and expanded. While the Empire was expanding, the prime purpose of the army was fighting battles, and all units had to be mobile and flexible. Once the Empire ceased to expand in the second century the army only occasionally fought in pre-emptive strikes or in reaction to attacks, but did not usually engage in wars of conquest after Trajan's reign, when the Empire reached its greatest extent. The Danube wars of Marcus Aurelius were protracted and involved moving units or parts of units to the war zone, but did not result in expansion of territory and annexation. At the end of the second century Severus fought campaigns against the Parthians, and annexed most of Mesopotamia, which created more problems than it solved. In all these wars soldiers from various provincial garrisons, and sometimes the Praetorians, were uprooted and some of the legions and auxiliary units remained in or near the war zones as part of the new garrison, but in general the army of the second century was much more static than its predecessors.

Whenever army units move about, on campaign or as temporary garrisons, traders and a variety of civilians can usually be found following in their wake. When troops settle for longer periods, in any place and in any era, civilians feature more prominently in their daily transactions. Soldiers begin to form relationships with local women, to trade with local people, and if possible to cultivate the land. Repeated agricultural usage of the land around forts is a certain sign of longer-term occupation or even permanence. Literary and archaeological sources confirm that fields and meadows were laid out within the immediate vicinity of Roman forts, and the soldiers grew crops and grazed their animals. Infantry units would possess riding horses for the officers, baggage animals, and flocks and herds for the food supply and for religious sacrifices. Cavalry units would possess all these and also hundreds of horses which would need grazing lands.

Roman occupation was not simply a matter of placing forts in isolated territory away from towns, and watching routes. Even when there were originally no civilian dwellings, people soon moved in to take advantage of the pay that the soldiers received and wanted to spend. Within a short time, small towns clustered round forts. These would be the locations where the soldiers had the most contact with civilians, interacting with them on a daily basis.

It was the convention in Roman times to label the settlements around auxiliary forts as *vici*, and those around legionary fortresses as *canabae*. The term *vicus* has different meanings. In a military context it refers to a settlement near a fort, but it can also be used to describe a small village not associated with any military installation, a district of a larger town or city, and even a district within the *canabae*. The Romans used plural nouns in some cases where it was logical to suppose that the entity being described consisted of many things, so the word for a camp or fort is *castra*, plural of *castrum* which was rarely used in the singular form, and the civil settlement near a fortress was likewise described in the plural, as *canabae*. The growth of the *canabae* around legionary fortresses and the *vici* around the smaller forts has been demonstrated in many provinces by archaeological finds and by a few inscriptions. Some of the civil settlements were very close to the forts, and others were situated at some distance, for example at Lambaesis in North Africa the *canabae* settlement was situated about a mile from the legionary fortress, while at Carnuntum on the Danube, the civil settlement was wrapped around the fortress on three sides. In the second century another civil settlement was founded to the west of the *canabae* and fortress at Carnuntum. The new town was large enough and its people were influential enough to build their own amphitheatre, even though there was already an amphitheatre at Carnuntum, which was probably used not just by the legionaries but also the civilian population.

The archaeological evidence from the *vici* and *canabae* can show the number of buildings, their extent and orientation, and on occasion archaeology can give hints as to their purpose, but cannot finally prove who lived in them, where they came from, or how they made their livings. A study by Sebastian Sommer tentatively answers these questions, but any investigation of *vici* and *canabae* is restricted by the fact that the people of the civil settlements did not set up as many inscriptions to honour the gods, to commemorate the dead or to celebrate achievements as the soldiers did. Some of the buildings of the settlements around Roman forts are so similar to the internal structures of the forts themselves that it has been postulated that it was the army that built them, and extrapolating from this it is assumed that the fort commander had complete jurisdiction over the inhabitants. In the fourth book of his *Histories* Tacitus relates that during the Batavian revolt in 69, when the legionary commanders at the fortress of Vetera in Germany needed to strengthen their ramparts, they demolished buildings that had been put up in close proximity to the fortress, to prevent them from being of use to the enemy.

The land on which the civil settlements were built was most likely part of the *territorium* of the legions or auxiliary units. Inscriptions and some passages in ancient literature attest to meadows and agricultural lands in the territory belonging to the legionary fortresses, and boundary markers have been found marking the limits of this territory. If the land belonged to the army, it follows that legionary legates had authority over the inhabitants and their buildings in the *canabae* near the fortresses, and commanders of auxiliary units similarly controlled the people of the *vici*. It is reasonable to assume that a civilian trader or would-be tavern keeper could not simply march up to the vicinity of his or her chosen fort and begin to build on an empty patch of land. Graham Webster says that traders of the *canabae* occupied their premises on five-year leases arranged by the *primus pilus* of the legion. The clerks of the Roman army would be perfectly capable of keeping records of such tenancies and their renewal dates, and there were probably worse fates than having the Roman army as a landlord.

A few inscriptions show that the people who dwelt in the *vici* developed a sense of corporate identity, in that they referred to themselves as *vicani*, or 'the *vicus* people', who on occasion acted together to make decisions. The inhabitants of the *canabae* called themselves *canabenses*, and appointed *magistri*, curators and aediles to administer their settlements. A fragmentary inscription from the *vicus* south of Housesteads fort on Hadrian's Wall bears only one name and two surviving abbreviated words, *Jul. S. d. vic* expanded by scholars to read *Julius S... decreto vicanorum* or by decree of the *vicani*, but unfortunately what the people decreed is not known, nor can it be assumed that Julius was a soldier of the unit in the fort. Co-operation between the soldiers and the people of the vicus at Carriden in Scotland may be indicated in the inscription relating to the *vicus*. The inhabitants call themselves *vicani consistentes*, and the inscription states that they repaid their vow to Jupiter under the direction of Aelius Mansuetus, who might be a soldier. At Old Carlisle in north-west England, an altar to the gods Jupiter and Vulcan was set up in the early third century by the *vikanorum magistri* and paid for by contributions from the people of the *vicus*, which implies a form of corporate government. The soldiers may have used the several public buildings that were erected in the *canabae*, and to a lesser extent in the *vici*, such as baths, temples, marketplaces and amphitheatres. At Nijmegen excavations revealed a granary in the *canabae*, dating from the second half of the first century. The size of the *canabae* and their public buildings show that the settlements were a long way from ramshackle shanty towns attached to a military installation. Some of them were attractive enough for Roman citizens to settle in them, and veterans often did so rather than settling in a designated military colony.

In some cases, the *vicus* outside a fort, less prestigious and less populous than the *canabae*, was expanded to the size if not the legal status of a small town, and even if the fort was abandoned and the soldiers moved on to another location, the town sometimes remained in occupation. It cannot be demonstrated whether the same inhabitants remained, or whether new people moved in and the occupants of the old *vicus* followed the army unit to establish another *vicus*, or to join an existing *vicus* near the fort to which the unit had been posted. In some cases the legal status of the legionary *canabae* was upgraded by the reigning emperor, to that of a *municipium*, a chartered town with its own government, or to an even higher status as a *colonia*. Trajan made the civil settlement at Xanten in Germany into a *colonia*. Hadrian made the *canabae* at Carnuntum into a *municipium*, and Severus upgraded the *municipium* to colonial status. It may have been Severus or his son Caracalla who raised the *canabae* at York to colonial status, the only example of a civil colony in Britain, as opposed to the military foundations such as Gloucester and Lincoln which were created when the legions moved out.

Building Work by Soldiers

Relations between the military forces and civilians sometimes extended to soldiers erecting buildings on behalf of civic communities. Military architects were sometimes seconded to civilian projects. Tacitus relates how the governor of Britain, his father-in-law Julius Agricola, encouraged and helped the Britons to build temples, marketplaces (*fora*), and private houses, implying that official sanction for these activities involved the loan of military builders. Inscriptions from other provinces attest the presence of military builders in civilian projects. A veteran, or more correctly a reservist, of *legio III Augusta* called Nonius Datus was sent to help with the reconstruction of a tunnel where the original builders had got into difficulties. It was part of a scheme to bring water to the town of Saldae in the province of Mauretania Caesariensis in North Africa, and no one except Nonius could advise on what to do after the project failed. Another inscription from the province of Dacia (modern Romania) records that in 248, on the order of the Emperor Philip and his wife Marcia Otacilia Severa, a group of soldiers built the walls of their colony of Romula. The legionary surveyors sometimes established boundaries on behalf of civilian communities, as at Ardea in Italy in the reign of Antoninus Pius, and legionaries marked out the boundaries of new towns that were laid out for veteran settlers in Africa and in Pannonia.

This co-operation between army and civilians can sometimes lead to the mistaken conclusion that there was a military presence where none was ever established, for instance finds of bricks and tiles from certain legions may merely represent a building project that had no military purpose, nor do they indicate that any soldiers participated at all in the building work, since bricks and tiles produced by the legions were sometimes sold to private building companies, a procedure that can be traced all through the Imperial period and into the fourth century, so archaeological material that seems to suggest the presence of military buildings must be regarded with caution.

Soldiers as Benefactors and Patrons

The evidence for soldiers and veterans who helped to develop local communities is not abundant until the later second century AD, but since it is mostly derived from inscriptions there may be more examples that have not yet come to light, and for some small communities the habit of recording events on inscriptions was slow to develop, or may never have taken root. Benefactors are more likely to have been officers from centurions upwards, with a majority who had served in several army units, especially the Praetorians, the Urban Cohorts and the *Vigiles* in Rome. Ordinary soldiers would not have been able to afford to give banquets or erect monuments, repair public buildings, and build useful things like bridges. At Tivoli in Italy, Marcus Helvius Rufus Civica, who had served as a legionary and risen to the post of *primus pilus*, and took his name from the award of the civic crown for saving a life, built a set of baths for the residents of the town. In the second century AD, Sextus Aetrius Ferox, a former *cornicularius* of the Prefect of the *Vigiles* in Rome, was made a centurion of *II Traiana* in Egypt, and used his wealth to benefit the inhabitants of Tuficum in Umbria. The townsmen put up a statue to him, and when it was dedicated Ferox gave a banquet and a gift of 4,000 *sestertii* to the people, both men and women. The same man interceded with the Emperor Antoninus Pius to allow the citizens of Tuficum to raise a special tax to pay for the paving of a road. At Capua, an effusive inscription describes a public funeral for Lucius Antistius Campanus, a highly respected veteran who had been honourably discharged and had settled in the colony, where he spent his own money on developing the community, and was offered public offices by the town council. The inscription states that all legal proceedings had been postponed on the day of the funeral to ensure that as many people as possible could attend.

Posts on the local councils were open to veterans who settled in the towns and cities of the Empire. Those who engaged in local politics were more likely to be higher-ranking officers, since town councillors were sometimes expected to pay an entry fee on taking up office, and to embellish their towns and entertain the people out of their own pockets, which would be beyond the capacity of most ordinary legionaries. In the third century, the *primus pilus* Titus Aurelius Flavinus was leader of the council of the colony of Oescus (modern Ghighen) in Lower Moesia, and was also a councillor of five tribal communities around the colony. Gaius Arrius Clemens, who had started out as an ordinary Praetorian Guardsman, earned decorations from Trajan in the Dacian wars, and served as centurion in all the Rome units, was one of the two men (*duumviri*), or leaders of the council of Augusta Taurinorum (Turin) in the first century AD.

Some towns chose a soldier as their patron, who could help them with their projects and intercede with officials or even the emperor on their behalf. Gaius Silius Aviola served as a military *tribunus laticlavius* in *III Augusta*, and must have impressed the natives sufficiently for three small towns in North Africa to ask him to be their patron in the early first century BC. Marcus Vettius Valens, who had a distinguished career as a Praetorian Guardsman, then became centurion in each of the three Rome units, then centurion and *primus pilus* in several legions, was patron of the colony of Ariminum (Rimini). On a lesser scale the *primus pilus* of *II Augusta* at Caerleon paid for a monument, as the inscription states, 'out of his own pocket, and not the public treasury'.

Protection and Defence

The protective role of the Roman army is the least documented aspect of the military presence in any province, though the benefits of the Roman peace are extolled by some ancient authors. The Younger Pliny records that a legionary centurion was sent to Byzantium by Trajan to assist the government in protecting the citizens, in a city which was a vast crossroads with many travellers passing through, but when asked to extend this privilege to another town, Trajan refused because he did not want to set a precedent. There are two famous literary passages which serve to praise the *Pax Romana* in general, one dating from the reign of Antoninus Pius by the Greek rhetorician Aelius Aristides, and another by the Christian author Tertullian, whose works date from the late second and early third centuries AD. Aristides made a speech in the city of Rome called *Romes Encomium*, or *In Praise of Rome*, extolling the virtues of the political institutions and military forces that kept the Empire safe. It is often quoted as proof of Imperial peace and efficiency, but it must be remembered that it outlined the view of the ruling classes. Similarly Tertullian in *de Anima* praises the universal peace, the productivity of the fields, the conquest and taming of the wilderness, rounding off his eulogy with the words 'everywhere there are homes, everywhere people, everywhere order, everywhere life'. He then goes on to destroy this image of peace and prosperity, insisting that the pressures of population are too great and threaten the survival of the Empire. 'Necessities are in short supply,' he says, 'and among everyone there are complaints.'

Between the yin and yang of these extremes lies a modicum of truth, which may be that for the most part Roman provincials lived in relative peace that was ensured for them by the soldiers, who defended the frontiers and also preserved internal law and order as far as possible. The army combined its military role with police work, both of which contributed to stability.

Appian wrote in positive vein about the security of the Empire, but he worked during the reign of Hadrian, when there were no wars except for the serious Jewish rebellion, and the Emperor established frontiers in solid form by means of running barriers. Archaeological evidence from the hinterland of these frontiers in Britain and Germany demonstrates increased civilian development combined with a corresponding growth in prosperity, in a world where invasion from beyond the frontiers was prevented or dealt with in force, at least until the mid-third century, and internal policing helped to keep bandits and criminals under control. Sometimes civilians dealt with bandits by appointing an official in charge of their own police force, but often soldiers were sent to combat groups of lawless men. Commodus had erected large watchtowers called *burgi* along frontiers and roads, and an inscription found in one of them states that they were built to control *latrones* or robbers. In the reign of Severus a famous or infamous bandit named Bulla Felix plagued Italy with his band of 600 men, and although Cassius Dio may have embellished the story, several attempts to capture Bulla were foiled. A centurion and his soldiers were outmanoeuvred, and in the end a cavalry force under a praetorian tribune caught Bulla, because a man whose wife had been seduced by the bandit told the soldiers where he was. Severus advertised himself as the enemy of all bandits, *latronum ubique hostis*. The Emperor Probus sent soldiers to capture runaway gladiators and their followers. In the third century, gangs of brigands proliferated in Italy, and a group known as the Bagaudae caused trouble in Gaul. Soldiers under *praepositi* were sent against the Italian brigands, and soldiers in small road forts and watchtowers helped to control the Bagaudae.

Documents from later Roman Egypt refer to 'the decurion for keeping the peace'. The army commanders of auxiliary units and the legionary centurions spent a lot of their time adjudicating in civilian disputes, and the soldiers could be sent to search for people, to make arrests, and protect individuals if necessary. Suspected criminals were caught and held for trial, sometimes by centurions in a military court. Roads were patrolled, and unsavoury characters could be prevented from travelling or could be arrested, which made travel for civilians safer. Passes for travel could be issued by centurions for civilians to show to the road guards (*stationarii*) in sensitive areas.

Policing, Courts, and Regional Control

In some provinces, the commander of the nearest fort was the only man whom civilians could approach to seek justice, so they would take their problems to the military authorities, as revealed by the correspondence of Flavius Abbinaeus, *praefectus alae* at the fort of Dionysias in Egypt in the third century. Much of the evidence for this civilian and military contact comes from Egypt, because the survival rate of papyrus documents is higher than in damp northern European climates. There are many cases on record, especially but not always in papyrus documents, concerning assault by civilians or sometimes by soldiers, which comprise nearly half the cases, but there are many other problems concerning boundary disputes and landownership, contested wills, theft, and criminal activities of tax collectors and administrative officials. It is likely that legal activities such as these went on in other provinces, but only a fraction of the documentation has been preserved.

It is attested that centurions exercised judicial functions in both military and civilian cases in several provinces, in some instances because the centurion was the highest-ranking official in the vicinity, in other cases because he was the officer sent to arrest people who had been accused of crimes and his judgement was accepted by the civilians. The provincial governor could use soldiers to make arrests and search properties, and tax collectors had the right to search houses and offices, presumably with soldiers in their wake. Soldiers were often asked to act as adjudicators in civil disputes. In the province of Dalmatia in the early first century AD a centurion was sent to adjudicate between two neighbouring tribes and to establish and mark boundaries between them, and in Egypt at around the same period, a civilian sent a letter to a centurion asking for help to stop the depredations of his neighbours on his property. Sometimes a centurion was appointed as a judge by another higher-ranking official, such as a praetor. Civilians may have found that they were handed rough justice by the military men, but simply had to accept it.

Complaints from individuals against soldiers were heard in military courts presided over by a centurion, since soldiers could be tried only by the military authorities. Many civilians would probably not even bother to bring a charge, and even if legal proceedings were started, there was no guarantee of a satisfactory conclusion. Literary sources are unanimous in underlining the difficulties faced by any civilian in bringing a charge against a soldier. The satirist Juvenal sums up the difficulties in Satire XVI, *On the Immunities of the Military*. First of all if a civilian was beaten up by a soldier it was more usual to neglect to bring a charge at all. Juvenal explains that the victim would hide the bruises, the broken teeth and the eye for which the doctor said there was little hope of saving (*oculum medico nil promittente relictum*). But if the case got as far as the military court, Juvenal points out that the whole unit would figuratively speaking close ranks, and any witnesses would be too intimidated to appear, for fear of retribution from the soldiers, which was bound to involve medical attention afterwards. Behind the humour there is a stark reality.

In the more remote areas of some provinces, it is postulated that the fort commanders, usually centurions, were also responsible for the administration of the surrounding areas, sometimes with the title *centurio regionarius*. The title implies that the centurion would be in charge of civilians as well as the unit he commanded, responsible for keeping law and order and probably for judicial functions. If crimes committed by civilians against other civilians were reported the centurion would probably organise the search for culprits and would conduct trials and organise punishments. The earliest indication of such an official comes from one of the writing tablets from Vindolanda where it is attested that a centurion at Carlisle in northern England was responsible for the region at the end of the first century AD. This is further supported by two inscriptions from Bremetenacum (Ribchester), also in northern England, where two different legionary centurions are described as commander of the unit and the region in the third century. Between 225 and 235 a dedication was set up at Ribchester to a deity or deities, whose names have been broken off, for the welfare of the Emperor Severus Alexander and his mother. The text of the inscription describes Titus Floridius Natalis as legionary centurion and *praepositus* of the unit and of the region. In the reign of the Emperor Gordian a few years later, Aelius Antoninus, who came from Melitene on the River Euphrates, is described as centurion of *VI Victrix*, and *praepositus* of the *numerus equitum Sarmatarum*, and also of the region around Ribchester. 5,500 Sarmatian cavalry were originally sent to Britain from the Danube by Marcus Aurelius during the wars against the various tribes at the end of the second century, and some of them were stationed at Ribchester, as attested on other inscriptions. Although this inscription set up by Aelius Antoninus was dedicated to the god Apollo Maponus, it was not an altar, but part of a monument of some kind. On the back there are relief sculptures of two female figures, each in a niche, taken to personify the province of Britannia Inferior, and the *Regio Bremetennacensis*. The term *praepositus* was often used for a commander who was seconded from his own unit to command another body of troops, often on a temporary basis, but the fact that at least two men were appointed to the Ribchester command and the control of the region suggests that the post was not simply a temporary one established to deal with a particular situation, but a continuing function of the officer in command at Ribchester. The nearest legionary bases were at Chester and York, the governor's headquarters is generally agreed to be in London, and though the distances are not great, communications would be slow, and more difficult in winter. There may be valid parallels with the raiders and reivers of the north of England in the fifteenth and sixteenth centuries, when cattle raiding was often carried out in winter, because the cattle were 'in full meat' after grazing during the summer, the long nights helped to conceal activity, and the bogs were frozen and could be ridden over if the raiders were pursued. Similar problems among the British tribesmen may have plagued the *regionarii* of Carlisle and Ribchester.

At the spa town of Bath, Gaius Severius Emeritus restored an area of the bath complex and temple that had been destroyed through vandalism. He is described as centurion at the very end of the inscription and then the letters REG have been added somewhat crudely at the bottom right hand corner of the text, so it is assumed that Emeritus was *centurio regionarius* of the area around Bath. He may have been on detachment from one of the legions, but it is not known where he was based, perhaps in Bath itself, but if so he represents a variation from the known *regionarii*, who were stationed in the more remote militarised zones in Britain.

Similar evidence of a centurion being in command of a region has been found in Egypt, where the title is not given in Latin, but the Greek equivalent refers to the officer as a 'centurion over the places'. Further examples have been found in Noricum, in Pannonia at Brigetio on the frontier, and at Agedincum in Gallia Lugdunensis. An inscription from Antioch in Pisidia set up by grateful civilians praises a *centurio regionarius* for maintaining justice and peace. Fuhrmann suggests that when Pliny wrote to Trajan to ask permission to appoint a *legionarius centurio* and some soldiers at Juliopolis in Bithynia to establish security and keep the peace, this could be a copyist's error for *regionarius centurio*. Pliny was writing at the same time that the earliest recorded officer in this role was operating at Carlisle, but despite the more or less contemporary use of a centurion in Britain, Trajan squashed the suggestion.

Police work on a provincial level was sometimes organised by the *beneficiarii consulares* of the governor. These soldiers were promoted to the post of *beneficiarius* on the basis of their demonstrable skills, and undertook a wide variety of tasks, mostly of an administrative nature. They were not primarily responsible for policing, but could be used for some functions such as ordering arrests, though they did not command groups of soldiers or engage in pursuit of criminals. Civilians could present petitions to the *beneficiarii* as representatives of the Roman government. A wider category of police work organised from Rome involved officials called *frumentarii*, who had probably been initially responsible for the food supply (*frumentum* means grain). In the second century they were organised as police with their headquarters in Rome, or in some sources they acted as secret police, who went about gathering information, especially concerning plots and conspiracies. They were organised on a military basis and were to all intents and purposes a special kind of soldier. Groups of *frumentarii* were attached to provincial headquarters. They could be placed in charge of collecting taxes and supplies for the army. In general, civilians and *frumentarii* did not mix well, but two almost identical inscriptions were set up by the citizens of Aphrodisias in praise of a centurion of the *frumentarii*, or possibly two different centurions. This evidence may be taken to indicate that the *frumentarii* may have exercised peacekeeping functions which, in this case, they carried out to the satisfaction of the civilians.

Requisitioning and Extortion

The most common evidence of the relationship between the army and civilians concerns the arrogance and bullying tactics of the soldiers, so a gloomy picture emerges of the army as corporate villains. There is not much to redress the balance because people do not usually record the good things or kind acts quite as often as they record their grievances, so there is little or no evidence that some Roman soldiers were really quite nice chaps.

As a model governor, Julius Agricola spent his first winter in Britain in correcting abuses that the soldiers and a coterie of administrative officials perpetrated against the natives. The army drew some of its supplies from civilian sources, and one of the schemes that the soldiers employed to make money for themselves was to ask the civilians to transport the requisitioned grain and other produce to a distant objective, then suggest a money payment to transport it themselves, which the provincials most likely paid out of gratitude for not having to make an unnecessary journey. Another abuse may have concerned false measures when the civilians brought their grain to the appointed depot; the corn measure from Carvoran fort near Hadrian's Wall in northern England, dating from the reign of Domitian, actually holds more than the amount stated on the side of the vessel. It is possible that it was never intended to fill the corn measure to the top, but this may be one of several different ways of cheating the natives that Agricola tried to eradicate.

Troops were allowed to requisition goods and animals from civilians, but they were supposed to have a permit from the military authorities, and payment was supposed to be made. Frontinus in his book *Stratagems* describes how Domitian insisted that compensation should be paid to the natives for lands taken for building forts when he set out on his campaign against the Chatti in Germany. This was not the usual practice of all emperors and it was certainly not true of individual soldiers. In describing his adventures after being magically transformed into a donkey, Apuleius relates in *The Golden Ass* how he was taken from his new owner in Greece by a legionary, who used violence to gain him, and then sold him because he was going to Rome and had not needed him in the first place. In many cases soldiers used force to extract goods from civilians, who were powerless at the time of the event and also thereafter if they tried to obtain justice and the return of their goods. In the reign of Hadrian the Prefect of Egypt issued an edict condemning illegal requisitioning because it was giving the army a bad name. Hadrian himself tried to control such abuse in the province of Asia. His pronouncements are recorded on an inscription which divides the abuses into categories. The text states that no cart or wagon should be given to soldiers without a proper document, and the amount of cash that should be paid will be detailed in the document. Since soldiers were supposed to keep to the roads, there ought not to be any need to force local guides to show them the way, unless there was very bad weather and the routes were obliterated. No soldiers should demand food, and if travelling in a private capacity no soldiers were entitled to free board and lodging, which was only to be given to soldiers on public business. Provincial civilians are encouraged at the end of the text to take the names of the soldiers who abuse their privileges, and send the details to the governor or the procurator. The inscription neatly summarises the common abuses by the military, but the number of times this sort of pronouncement had to be made only serves to illustrate how widespread and ineradicable the abuse was.

Sometimes the abuses of the soldiers extended to demands for *hospitium* or what amounted to billeting. It was not illegal, just as requisitioning goods was not illegal, but although the procedure was officially sanctioned, it was supposed to be kept within certain reasonable limits. The inhabitants of the village of Skaptopara in Thrace (modern Bulgaria) complained to the Emperor Gordian in 238 that their village was situated at hot springs and was located between two forts. It was not on the direct route, but soldiers frequently diverted from the main road to demand food and lodging and much else besides, so there was a lot of military traffic coming and going through their settlement. The soldiers who came through were abusing their privileges by taking whatever they wanted free of charge, and were ruining the village: the population was declining because people could not support the depredations of the soldiers. It is revealing that the civilians of this village, and many other towns and villages of the Empire, thought that it was worthwhile to petition the military commanders, the provincial governors, and even the emperor himself. In the case of Skaptopara, the civilians were assisted by one man in their community who had served as a Praetorian, so he would know how to approach the authorities, and this demonstrates the expediency of having a soldier or veteran to give advice. The Emperor Gordian did at least reply to the civilians of Skaptopara, but he referred them to the provincial governor, and it is not known whether the depredations of the soldiers were stopped.

The duties of the provincial governors were outlined by law and included the prevention of illegal requisitions or billeting, but the civilians who should have been protected by the law suffered from a grave disadvantage in that the governor to whom they had to make their complaint was also the commander of the army, with a vested interest in fostering the loyalty of the troops. Groups of soldiers or individuals were in a good position to demand money with menaces from civilians. Protection rackets probably abounded where the soldiers could reach the towns and villages quite easily. The accounts of an unknown businessman in Egypt, listed on a fragmentary papyrus, show his vast outlay to soldiers, the civilian police, and the military road guard (*stationarius*), but the most revealing entry is the 2,200 drachmae expended during only one half of the year for extortion, *diaseismos* in Greek, and though it has to be admitted that the culprits are not actually listed as soldiers, unfortunately for the reputation of the Roman army, soldiers were the most likely people to be able to enforce this kind of thing.

15

Naval Forces

The embryonic Roman navy began life out of sheer necessity during the Republican period, when Rome went to war, perhaps a little unwisely, against the supreme naval power in the Mediterranean, Carthage. The Carthaginians had a long tradition of maritime operations, both for trading purposes and for war. After initial disasters the Romans learned quickly, drawing upon the expertise and manpower of their coastal allies (*socii navales*) who provided ships and crews. The tales of Romans capturing a Carthaginian ship and copying it are probably unfounded, or at best exaggerated in order to enhance the reputation of the Romans struggling successfully against adversity. The naval allies of Rome would be fully cognisant with building warships and would know what Carthaginian vessels looked like; the difficulty would not be in designing and building the ships, but the costs, and the time it would take to organise the assembly of the materials and the workforce to produce ships quickly.

After the first clash with Carthage, in 311 BC the Romans appointed two officials, *duumviri navales*, to take charge of naval affairs, including provision of ships. By 260 BC the Romans had a fleet of 100 quinqueremes and twenty triremes, which enabled them to win the naval battle against the Carthaginians at Mylae.

Polybius documents one of the early operations combining naval and land forces, when Scipio attacked Carthago Nova (modern Cartagena) by land and sea, ordering Gaius Laelius to take command of the fleet to bombard the city with different kinds of missiles, while he brought up 25,000 infantry and 2,500 cavalry to attack from the land, first defeating the Carthaginians sent out from the city to charge his men, and then ordering parties to assault and take the walls by means of sheer manpower and scaling ladders. The battle was hard fought, but Scipio had thoroughly investigated the city and knew that the tide would soon start to ebb, leaving the protective lagoon on the seaward side of the city dry enough for another assault party to gain access to the walls. The city fell soon after this successful attack.

During the later Republic and early Empire the pirates of the Mediterranean threatened Roman merchant shipping to the extent that food supplies to the city were endangered, and there were various efforts using naval forces as well as land forces to eradicate the problem, but insufficient resources were committed to the project, so some expeditions failed. The elder Marcus Antonius, grandfather of Mark Antony, achieved limited success in 102 BC in Cilicia, where the pirates occupied several bases. In 71 BC his son, also called Marcus Antonius, Mark Antony's father, met complete disaster against the pirates, and died in Crete. By the early 60s BC the pirate menace had become endemic. In 67 BC, pirates sailed into the mouth of the Tiber and threatened the port of Ostia, and Romans were outraged. The greatest general of the day, Pompey the Great, angled for the command and was finally granted it, charged with clearing the Mediterranean of pirates. The price of grain fell as soon as his appointment was announced.

The Senate had realised at last that this task required tremendous resources and a commander of wide-ranging powers, and Pompey was voted 500 ships, twenty-four legates (some sources say twenty-five) of his own choosing. Significantly, these legates were responsible to him in the first instance and not answerable directly to the Senate, a dangerous precedent but necessary if Pompey was to co-ordinate the operation without hindrance. Pompey and his legates were given leave to recruit soldiers, sailors and rowers, thus providing significant land forces as well as naval forces for the campaign. Another controversial precedent concerned the extent of Pompey's powers, which were to extend up to fifty miles inland from the entire Mediterranean coast. This gave him temporary command of almost the whole Roman world, but again this dangerous precedent was necessary if he was to eradicate the problem, since the pirates occupied land bases, and if they were flushed out of some of them, they would simply move to other places anywhere around the Mediterranean, either moving off by sea or by retreating further inland.

Pompey divided the Mediterranean into thirteen regions, and placed a legate with a squadron of ships over each. The names of the thirteen legates who commanded the coastal and maritime areas of the Mediterranean have been preserved, which leaves eleven or twelve other commanders who probably directed the land forces, but this must remain an informed guess, since concrete evidence is lacking. The plan was to sweep the seas and the land immediately behind the coasts, except for the rugged inlets of Cilicia, where the main pirate strongholds lay, so that with an open exit they could all be flushed eastwards and bottled up there. In a mere forty days, Pompey had cleared the seas, the hero and saviour of the whole Roman world.

Combined military and naval operations such as this are only rarely documented. Caesar recounts how he used ships and his legions against the Veneti because they had detained some Roman envoys who had been sent to gather food supplies for the winter. The Veneti inhabited the Atlantic seaboard of Gaul, and were excellent seamen and navigators, sailing the turbulent seas to Britain and back as a matter of routine. Caesar had to have warships built on the River Loire and also gather ships from his Gallic allies before he could deal with the rebellious tribesmen, to curb them before the revolt spread to the rest of Gaul. At the beginning of the campaigning season, Caesar placed Decimus Brutus in command of the fleet, while he himself took command of the land forces. The strongholds of the Veneti could not easily be attacked from the seaward side for fear of grounding the Roman ships, and there were few harbours, so at first the Veneti with their flat-bottomed vessels had the advantage, even though the Roman ships were faster. When the strongholds of the Veneti were attacked from the landward side by the legions, the inhabitants simply brought up their ships, loaded their possessions and moved off to another stronghold. The Romans finally won the war in a naval engagement watched by the land forces from the cliffs. They resorted to a new tactic against the ships of the Veneti, using hooks on long poles to snag the halyards that held the yard arm to the mast, then rowing away at full speed until the yards were brought down. Then the Romans boarded the disabled vessels, greatly assisted by a sudden calm that stopped the Veneti from sailing away. According to Caesar, the Veneti had committed the bulk of their manpower to this battle, and from then on could not defend their homes, having lost so many warriors and ships.

In his account of his two expeditions to Britain, Caesar describes different types of vessels, including warships, transports and scout ships (*speculatoria navigia*), all of which he used to support the legions as they fought the Britons on the coast, at first in the sea itself as they struggled to gain a foothold. He ordered the warships to come up on the enemy flanks and use their artillery against them, and later he used the scout ships to support the land troops in the same way.

Naval power was vitally important in the civil wars between the Caesarians and Pompeians. Transport ships ferried the troops to Greece, and warships were used for securing the food supply and for patrolling and guarding the coasts. When he crossed to Greece to follow Pompey, Caesar had only enough ships to transport half his army, and the rest were left behind with Mark Antony as commander, but they were bottled up in Italy by a squadron of the Pompeian fleet under Libo. Watching where Libo came to shore for fresh water, Antony guarded each point until Libo had to withdraw, and then he seized the chance to set sail himself to join Caesar. He avoided as far as possible the Pompeian fleets, but the Mediterranean was dominated by Pompey all though the civil war.

After Pompey was killed in Egypt, the war continued against escaped Pompeians in Africa and Spain, and Caesar used his ships at the battle of Thapsus. He camped opposite the town of Thapsus, which he besieged, but it appeared that he was trapped at the northern end of a corridor between the coast and an inland lake and marshy area running parallel with it. He allowed the enemy to block the escape route at the southern end of this land corridor, and to make a camp at the northern end not far from his own camp. Then he attacked the Pompeians, having ordered the ships to sail round the coast to make a lot of noise as if they were about to land troops behind the enemy, so that they would be caught between the naval force and the Caesarian army. The battle began unexpectedly, because one of Caesar's trumpeters sounded the charge without orders and then soldiers took matters into their own hands. They won the battle and dispersed the Pompeians.

As the Empire was steadily growing out of the declining Republic, Octavian had to fight more than one naval battle against Sextus Pompey, the son of Pompey the Great. Sextus had escaped from the final battle against Caesar in Spain, where his brother Gnaeus Pompey was killed, and being denied anywhere to go because Caesar controlled the Roman world, he took to the seas, using the remnants of the Pompeian fleet as a pirate force to threaten Rome from time to time by interrupting the food supplies. Octavian's ships and crews were nowhere near the same calibre as those of Sextus. In 38 BC Octavian lost the naval battle off Cumae and the following day a storm wrecked most of the ships that had survived the battle. More ships were necessary, so as well as building some new ones, Octavian asked Mark Antony for the loan of 120 ships in 37 BC, promising 20,000 soldiers in return, intended for Antony's Parthian campaign. In the end Octavian kept the ships and delivered only a few men to Antony.

During Octavian's prolonged struggle to eradicate Sextus, the development of what could be called a navy instead of a collection of ships was greatly enhanced by Marcus Vipsanius Agrippa, who built more ships and repaired others, and also constructed an artificial harbour on the Campanian coast near Cumae, where he devoted some time to training the crews for much of 37 BC. He developed a grappling iron known as the *harpax*, which could be catapulted on to enemy ships with a rope attached, and then used to haul the ships closer until they could be boarded. Agrippa improved the original invention by adding a protective wooden shield immediately behind the hooks so that the enemy could not so easily hack away at the ropes and sever them. He also improved the catapults so that they could throw the grappling hooks for a greater distance. In 36 BC Agrippa was ready. The plan was to gain a foothold in Sicily and take the coastal towns in order to deprive Sextus of safe bases, which would force him to take his ships away from Sicily and set up his headquarters elsewhere. For this task Octavian required a fleet and land forces. There was an indecisive naval clash off Mylae, but Octavian managed to establish three legions in Sicily. Then he made the mistake of engaging Sextus at sea, and was not only defeated but nearly killed and had to be rescued. Finally, rather than moving out of

Sicily, Sextus risked everything on another naval battle at Naulochus in September 36 BC, and lost. He fled to Antony in the east, but he had also been negotiating with the Parthians, and he was killed. Octavian was the hero of the hour after the defeat of Sextus, and he had learned the value of naval power.

After the battle of Actium in 31 BC and the fall of Alexandria in the following year, Octavian not only controlled about sixty legions, but also about 700 ships, comprising those of his own forces and those of Antony's. Some of these were destroyed, and most of the rest were sent to Forum Julii (Fréjus) on the Mediterranean coast of Gaul, which had been used as a base in the naval operations against Sextus. Octavian-Augustus could have chosen to disband the fleets that he inherited, in favour of returning to the Republican system of building ships when it was necessary to fight at sea. It would have spared the expense of maintaining a fleet with the crews, and continually having to recruit to keep the numbers up to strength. It has been pointed out that there was no naval action to speak of during the first two centuries AD, largely because there was no pirate threat. Rome now controlled the whole of the lands surrounding the Mediterranean, so there was nowhere for numbers of pirate ships to gather. For the same reason, there was no external naval threat because all states and cities around the Mediterranean were under Roman control and could hardly have furnished a separate fleet. Nonetheless, Augustus thought it necessary to retain the ships and crews. Tacitus says that the system of government, with its provinces, armies and ships, was fully integrated and interrelated. Given that pirates had made life difficult in Rome for many years, the presence of a fleet would have comforted the peoples of the Empire and possibly deterred small-scale piratical activity.

The Imperial Fleets

Early in his reign, Augustus instituted permanent fleets, one based at Misenum and one at Ravenna, on either side of Italy. Misenum (modern Miseno) is on the northern promontory of the bay of Naples, and it was here that the commander of the fleet, Pliny the Elder, was based in AD 79 when Vesuvius erupted and buried Pompeii and Herculaneum. Pliny was killed while sailing to investigate the eruption. There are two harbours at Misenum, the outer one connected to the inner one by a channel. There was eventually a wooden bridge across the channel. The inner harbour at the fleet base of Ravenna was artificially constructed, and a settlement grew up nearby, called Classis, which still survives in the name S. Apollinare in Classe. The Ravenna site was linked to the River Po by a canal called the Fossa Augusta. Octavian had had ships built at Ravenna when he was engaged in the ongoing naval war with Sextus Pompey, and the town remained an important shipbuilding centre.

The Misenum fleet seems to have been larger than that of Ravenna, and contained the Imperial flagship. There was sufficient manpower in the two fleets during the civil wars of 69 to create three legions, and in the Flavian period some men from the Misenum fleet were permanently lodged in Rome, where they operated the awning system of the Colosseum, to protect spectators from the sun. There were 240 wooden masts clamped to the outer walls at the top of the Colosseum, with rigging attached by which the sails could be drawn across the arena on hot days. The men were accommodated in the *Castra Misenatium*, close to the barracks of the gladiators and not far from the Colosseum. Across the Tiber there was the *Castra Ravennatium* for the Ravenna fleet.

There was no unified naval command with the equivalent of high-ranking admirals based at a headquarters in Rome, just as there was no equivalent of a war office to control the armies. To put it another way, there was no Roman army or Roman navy as such, but there were several armies in different provinces, and several fleets based on the coasts of Italy and on major rivers. Co-ordination of their activities would be the prerogative of the emperors.

The fleet commanders were equestrian prefects, though some of them in the early Empire were freedmen. Vespasian made it a rule that prefects had to have gone through the equestrian military career, but this did not exclude freedmen entirely. Although the naval prefects were of fairly low status in the equestrian career path, there were promotion prospects; at least three of them went on to become Praetorian Prefects. Greek terms were used for the officers subordinate to the prefects, the next most senior being the *navarch*, who probably commanded squadrons. There may have been no standard size for a squadron as there was for an army unit. Under the *navarch* the equivalent to a captain of a single ship was the *trierarch*. The order of seniority is supported by the wording on a diploma issued in AD 71 to *navarchis et trierarchis et remigibus* (oarsmen), which appears to be arranged in descending order. What remains uncertain is the relationship between the *trierarchs* and the centurions attested in the fleets. D. B. Saddington points out that legionary centurions were put in charge of ships during Caesar's time and in the early Empire, and they directed operations, so it would seem that they outranked the *trierarchs*, but this is not attested in any written or epigraphic source. By the later first century AD the centurions were not legionaries but were non-Romans, similar to the auxiliary centurions. They appear to have been in command of a single ship, which was sometimes referred to as a century. The sailors described themselves as members of the century of named individuals, just as the auxiliaries and legionaries did.

The crews of the warships of the Misenum and Ravenna fleets, and later fleets, were not slaves, as popular tradition would have it. They were freeborn non-Romans like auxiliary soldiers. Both of the Italian fleets recruited a considerable number of Egyptians, who were denied service in the auxiliary units, though they could sometimes be converted into citizens and be incorporated into the legions. The Misenum fleet also drew a large proportion of its crews from Sardinia, Thrace, and the province of Asia, and the Ravenna fleet recruited largely from Syria, Dalmatia and Pannonia. The naval personnel were organised in centuries commanded by centurions, and were called soldiers (*milites*) not sailors (*nautae*), with no distinction between rowers and the men who operated the sails. The early third-century lawyer Ulpian states that all rowers and sailors were to be regarded as soldiers (*milites*).

The men served for twenty-six years, one year longer than auxiliary soldiers. In the third century the term was raised to twenty-eight years. The men were given Roman citizenship when they completed their service, and were entitled to a diploma, though like the auxiliary soldiers the men probably had to purchase their diplomas. Fleet diplomas are similar to those of auxiliaries in that the citizenship grant is mentioned along with the right of *conubium* with the wives that the men had at the time of *honesta missio*, or with any partners that they chose after discharge, limited to one wife for each man. Some examples of diplomas for men of the Misenum fleet were found in the bay of Naples, and at least five come from Asia Minor, issued to men whose origin was in that area, indicating that the men returned home after their service. The text of some fragmentary diplomas holds clues that the recipient may have served in the fleets, for instance a diploma issued to Gaius Julius Bitho in AD 160 labels him as an ex-soldier, or *ex gregale* which literally refers to herds or flocks, but *gregalis* was another term for 'soldier'. No auxiliary units are named, so it is assumed that Bitho was a member of the fleet, although the portion of the diploma which would have made this certain is lacking. Another diploma issued to Marcus Herennio Pasicrate in AD 214 is more specific, naming the fleet as *classis praetoria Antoniniana Misenensis*. The extra title *praetoria* was probably awarded to the Misenum and

Ravenna fleets by Vespasian, or possibly by Domitian. The title Antoniniana derives from Marcus Aurelius Antoninus, the official name of Caracalla, linking him with the Emperors Marcus Aurelius and Antoninus Pius.

There were other Imperial fleets besides those at Misenum and Ravenna, some of them riverine versions, especially on the Rhine and Danube. These had their origins in the special fleets built to support campaigns. In the German campaigns of Drusus and Tiberius, ships were used for naval operations on the Rhine; Tacitus describes the different ships used by Germanicus in AD16. These naval vessels formed the nucleus of the later German fleet (*Classis Germanica*), which patrolled the Rhine and the coasts while the army operated inland. The *Classis Germanica* was in operation by 69. The first attested mention of it is in Tacitus' *Histories* under that year. It was based south of Cologne at Alteburg.

The same functions of patrolling and supporting the armies were carried out by the Danube fleets. The *Classis Pannonica* may have been based at the mouth of the River Sava where it joins the Danube. Though its base is not known, the *Classis Moesica* patrolled the lower Danube. Both these Danube fleets acquired the title Flavia, so they were operational by the late 60s, but using evidence from diplomas issued to members of the crews, and subtracting twenty-six years' service from the dates of issue, D. B. Saddington suggests that the fleets were probably established under Claudius or possibly Nero. The two fleets supported Trajan's Dacian wars by patrolling the river and helping to transport supplies

The *Classis Britannica* may have been established by Claudius as part of the preparations for the invasion of Britain in 43. Despite its name, the main base of this fleet was in Gaul, at Boulogne (ancient Gesoriacum). The naval base at Dover was created in the second century AD. The use of ships by the army in Britain, not necessarily involving the fleet, is attested at Chester and York. An *optio ad spem ordinis*, whose name is lost along with the top section of his tombstone, perished in a shipwreck (*naufragium*), and whoever put up his tombstone left a space for the letter H in the usual formula H.S.E for *hic situs est*, or 'he lies here'. The absence of the first initial for *hic*, or here, presumably indicates that the body had not been recovered, but that there was hope of finding it, so that the unknown man could be given a proper funeral, and then the letter H could be added to the inscription. Given that the River Dee was navigable until medieval times and that Chester may have been used by ships of the fleet, and also that naval personnel were soldiers rather than sailors with centurions in command, it is not out of the question that this unfortunate *optio* drowned on a naval venture rather than while travelling on a transport ship. At York, Marcus Minucius Audens set up an altar to the Mother Goddesses of Africa, Italy and Gaul, to whom he had made a vow. He describes himself as a soldier of VI *Victrix*, and also *gubernator* of VI *Victrix*, mentioning the legion twice. *Gubernator* is usually translated as pilot, and the title can be associated with warships, though in this instance Minucius Audens was most probably a river pilot guiding ships up and down the Ouse. There may have been legionary river pilots at Chester and Caerleon as well, but there is no evidence for them.

The Roman expeditions to the north of Britain under the Flavian governor Julius Agricola in the later first century, and the northward advance under the Emperor Severus in the early third century, were both supported by naval power. When Agricola was ready to invade Scotland he used the fleet for transport of supplies and for reconnoitring, but also for military purposes. In his biography of Agricola, Tacitus describes how the fleet was sent ahead to spread terror and raid the coastal areas, and refers to the legions and auxiliaries meeting with the fleet in joint camps. Severus followed the same pattern during his Scottish campaigns, using the fleet to supply his troops and to raid the coastal settlements. An inscription from Rome refers to the third century British war as an amphibious expedition, and the coinage supports this description. Severus' coins display a bridge with towers, and coins of Caracalla show a bridge of boats and the legend *Traiectus* – a crossing. The most likely locations for these bridges and crossings are the estuary of the River Forth, where there is a Severan military base at Cramond on the southern shore, and the River Tay, where there is another base at Carpow.

In the late third century the British usurper Carausius made effective use of the *Classis Britannica* to defend his territories, issuing coinage which showed off his galleys. He controlled Boulogne as well as Britain, and was defeated only when the Emperor Diocletian's deputy, Constantius Chlorus, built a rival fleet. By the mid-third century the first of the forts on the south coasts of Britain that would later become part of the series with the collective name 'Forts of the Saxon Shore' had already been built on the standard pattern with rounded corners and four gates. The grandiose title Saxon Shore gives the impression that the whole system was conceived and developed at the same time, but this is not the case. When there was greater need for defence in the fourth century the Romans combined the forts that were already in place with new forts to fill gaps where none existed before, but the new ones were massive and more heavily defended. It is not certain how these coastal forts related to the British fleet, but it is assumed that naval patrols were undertaken around the south and east coasts, and some of the forts with favourable inlets may have been used as naval bases.

There were fleets in the eastern parts of the Empire, the *Classis Pontica* patrolling the Black Sea from Nero's reign, the *Classis Syriaca* probably developed under the Flavian Emperors, and the *Classis Alexandrina* at Alexandria, which can be traced as far back as Gaius Caligula. Ships patrolled the Nile, and it may have been crews of these ships who supervised the collection of customs dues. A single inscription of the second half of the second century attests the *Classis Nova Libyca*, whose title New African Fleet implies either that there had been an old one, or that this was an entirely new fleet created in the second century to patrol the seas off Africa.

The later third century saw a gradual decline of the fleets. Under Diocletian, only three of the former squadrons of the Italian fleets remained. In 323, Constantine gathered 200 warships to fight off his rival Licinius, in what Chester G. Starr calls 'the only real sea battle in the history of the Roman Empire'. Thereafter, Byzantium, not Rome, claimed mastery of the sea.

The Ships

The Romans used a variety of ships for different purposes. Merchant ships called *naves oneraria* were obviously designed for carrying goods in bulk, and transport ships in the fleets went by the same name. In ancient literature there is usually a distinction between transports and warships, and the fleets would need smaller vessels for scouting. Caesar mentions these three kinds of ships in his account of his expeditions to Britain, and on Trajan's Column different sizes of transport ships are depicted carrying barrels and supplies, or being unloaded, and warships appear with banks of oars and *rostra*, which were used for ramming enemy vessels. Warships were quite small compared to transport ships, and were not necessarily used for carrying passengers, much less large numbers of troops. They were equipped with sails, but their main propulsion power derived from their oars, and the names for the types of ships were based on the number of banks of oars. A ship with a single bank of oars was called a monoreme, a ship with two banks of oars was a bireme, and three banks produced the name trireme, the most common and best known Roman warship, which owed its origin to the Athenians who were building them five centuries before Augustus established his navy. There were larger ships, quadriremes and quinqueremes, and the Misenum fleet had a six, called the *Ops*. The arrangement of the oars and rowers in the large ships is not fully explained in any source. It is thought that in a quinquereme there were not five banks of oars as the title suggests, but three banks, with single oarsmen in the lowest tier, and two men to each oar on the middle and top tier, though this remains conjectural.

The Romans had built these larger ships during the Republic to combat adversaries like the Carthaginians, whose quinqueremes they were said to have copied. The smaller ships, especially the triremes and biremes, were faster and more manoeuvrable, and began to predominate in the fleets. Some, but not all, of the ships were decked, and some had towers (*turres*) like the forecastles of medieval ships. Agrippa added *turres* to his ships when he was training the crews in his artificial harbour in 37 BC. The decks and towers would enable the soldiers to hurl missiles at the enemy ships, and provide platforms for the catapults that fired the grappling irons that Agrippa installed, though it is not certain that all ships carried them. There was usually a boarding bridge, called the *corvus*, which could be lowered on to enemy ships. In Roman warships there was no distinction between sailors who managed the ships and marines who did the fighting; as stated above, the crews were all soldiers.

In battle, the best way of dealing with enemy ships was to ram them, by rowing at speed straight at them and allowing the ship's reinforced beak to penetrate the sides of enemy vessels to sink them. Detaching a warship once the ram had engaged would probably have met with varying degrees of difficulty. Another method was to position the ship so that it could be rowed alongside the enemy vessel, then retract the oars and try to sheer off the oars of the enemy to disable the ship. Boarding an enemy ship once contact had been made, and fighting it out with the crews was another option, for which purpose Agrippa developed the grapping irons to haul the ships close enough, or the *corvus* would be lowered to deliver soldiers to the enemy ship.

One of the limiting factors in the operation of any fleet was the need to store food and water, and keep the stores replenished. It is estimated that warships could store enough fresh water to travel for up to 200 miles, then the crews would need to put into shore and find water and supplies. Four days continuously at sea was probably the maximum. Prevention of enemy crews from coming ashore for water features in the accounts of the civil wars in the first century BC. Antony was able to break through the blockade of Brundisium by Pompey's fleet when he prevented the commander Libo from finding water, forcing him to sail away and leave a window of opportunity, as the modern phrase goes, for Antony to sail to join Caesar.

When Augustus established his Italian fleets, naval battles in the Mediterranean were a feature of the past, so although the crews would be trained and prepared for such an eventuality it was not until the middle of the third century that there was any naval threat in the Mediterranean.

Part III

The Army of the Late Empire

Historical Overview, Third to Fifth Centuries AD

In AD 260 the frontiers of the Roman Empire had been breached and for the first time since the days of Marcus Aurelius even Italy had been in danger of invasion. The frontiers had never been designed to withstand determined attacks such as those that the tribesmen from beyond the Rhine and Danube were now capable of mounting. The problems may not have been caused simply because some young tribesmen sought adventure and plunder. There may have been extreme hardship among the tribes, forcing them to move to better territories, either because their farms had been destroyed by the incursions of the sea, as in the north-west, or because other tribes attacked and forced them off their lands. On some occasions, the Romans ceased to pay the subsidies to the tribes, and the result was invasion, and on other occasions tribesmen wanted to settle within the Roman Empire and farm the land. They were accommodated in their thousands during the history of the Empire, and some of the new settlers provided men for the Roman army. Nevertheless there remained large bodies of tribesmen whose purpose seems to have been destruction and pillage. The Empire began to be overwhelmed and had to make political and military changes to enable it to cope.

The Empire Divided

It could be said that the reign of Gallienus laid the foundations for the changes to the political and military organisation of the later Empire, though there was no simple linear development from the middle of the third century to the middle of the fourth. In 260 when his father Valerian was captured by the Persians and the Roman army was defeated, Gallienus was in no position to mount a rescue expedition, much less a major war. He was isolated in the centre of the Empire with a breakaway state in the west known as the Empire of the Gauls (*Imperium Galliarum*), which embraced much more than just the provinces of Gaul, but included the Spanish, British and German provinces, and Raetia, closing off Italy north of the Alps. In the east, the Palmyrene nobleman Odenathus took charge of the defence of the eastern provinces, keeping the Persians at bay.

Gallienus had to adapt everything to the needs of the army. His resources were reduced to what he could gain from Italy, Greece, the Danube provinces, and Egypt and Africa. He had to make the best of the troops that were available to him. On his legionary coinage with which he paid the soldiers, seventeen legions are attested, but they may only have been vexillations from these legions, not whole units. For the Rhine campaigns of the 250s he had assembled some detachments from the legions of Britain, the Rhine and Danube provinces, and he also had the Praetorians, *II Parthica* which Severus had stationed near Rome, and some auxiliary units.

In order to counter the threat to Italy from the Alamanni poised for invasion of Italy in the Alps and beyond, he based himself in the north, around Milan, and concentrated on gathering cavalry of all descriptions to create a rapid response force, not attached to the provincial armies, but quite distinct with its own commander, called Aureolus. He also chose men from different military units and designated them as *Protectores*, but they were not formed into a unit like a bodyguard. The title *Protector* was a mark of distinction, and many of these men went on to higher offices and military appointments. Equestrian officers were appointed by Gallienus to govern provinces and to command troops at the expense of senators, but the theory that the Emperor's policy was to divorce all senators from all appointments is not now accepted. The gradual separation of senatorial and equestrian careers had been going on since Hadrian's reign if not before, but senators were not wiped from the record by Gallienus. They continued to govern the senatorial provinces, and some of the Imperial provinces with two or more legions. The appointment of equestrians was largely to those provinces where there was internal unrest or where invasions across the frontiers were anticipated.

Gallienus spent most of his reign dashing about his reduced Empire to deal with one crisis after another. Near Milan, the Alamanni were defeated and remained peaceful for some time, but there were rebellions in Pannonia and Egypt, and a mutiny in Byzantium. Peace was restored in 262 and lasted for nearly three years, before trouble erupted in the Danube provinces. Moesia, Thrace and Greece were affected by tribal invasions. Gallienus won victories in Illyricum in 267, but was not able to follow them up because the cavalry commander Aureolus raised rebellion at Milan. Gallienus marched there and put the city under siege, but was soon assassinated by his army officers in 268. The Empire passed to one of Gallienus' closest advisers, Marcus Aurelius Claudius, known as Claudius Gothicus because of his victories against the Goths, who had learned to use ships to raid the coastal cities of the Mediterranean. The Prefect of Egypt, Tenagino Probus, used the Egyptian fleet to clear them from the seas, while Claudius defeated the Goths on land at Naissus in Moesia. Claudius was one of the few emperors who died in bed rather than being assassinated. He died of plague in 270 while assembling an army for a Danube campaign against the Juthungi and Vandals. One of his most important officers, Lucius Domitius Aurelianus, hitherto unknown, succeeded him.

Aurelian Reunites the Empire

Aurelian inherited the divided Empire of Gallienus, and managed during his five-year reign from 270 to 275 to bring the Empire back under his control. The western provinces of the Gallic Empire were not necessarily in rebellion against the legitimate emperor, but in 260 when it seemed that the central government could not protect the provinces from invasion by Germanic tribesmen from across the Rhine, the provinces grouped together under a chosen leader who could organise defence. They then set up a duplicate of the Empire, with annually elected consuls and magistrates, and an emperor with tribunician powers and a Praetorian Guard. The first was Marcus Cassianus Latinius Postumus, who ruled for about ten years, based at Cologne, and for all of his reign he was fully occupied in repairing the damage caused by the tribal invasions. It seems that many of the forts had been destroyed and were now abandoned, while city defences were established for the first time, or improved and augmented. Postumus and his successors concentrated on protection of the western provinces, and never tried to march on Rome to take over the government, but Gallienus tried and failed on two occasions to win back control of the breakaway Gallic Empire, probably in AD 261 and 265.

The eastern question was dealt with differently. While Gallienus never officially recognised the Gallic Emperors Postumus and his successors, he seems to have legitimised the claims of Odenathus and the Palmyrenes to govern and protect the eastern provinces. He may have granted the title *dux Romanorum* to Odenathus, but this is not directly attested, except in so far as Odenathus' son Vaballathus adopted it. Gallienus may have been motivated to recognise Odenathus because he needed to ensure that the Palmyrenes did not throw in their lot with the Persians against Rome. It is known that Odenathus conducted two campaigns against the Persians in 262 and 267. He may have been granted the title *corrector totius Orientis*, which would place him in command of the whole of the east with Gallienus' approval, though Odenathus was never given an official appointment as consul or prefect. Odenathus was called to Asia Minor when the Goths overran Roman territory, probably in 268. Before he had restored peace, Odenathus and his eldest son were assassinated, leaving Zenobia, Odenathus' young wife, as successor. There was no opportunity for Gallienus to regain control of the east because he was fully occupied in repelling invasions across the Danube, when he too was assassinated.

Before Aurelian could turn his attention to the western and eastern parts of the Empire he dealt with the Juthungi and Vandals in the Danube provinces. He rounded them up, demanded troops for the army and allowed them to retreat to their homelands, giving food supplies to the Vandals to enable them to journey back without molesting the provinces. Then he went to Rome, where one of his first tasks was to sort out the finances, at least temporarily. When he had more time he reformed the financial systems and also the coinage, but in 271 he had to march north to counter the invasions into Italy by the Juthungi, who had reached Milan, with the Alamanni and Marcomanni following behind. There were several battles as the tribesmen split into groups, were defeated, and then regrouped. When these campaigns were over Aurelian returned to Rome, and suggested something unthinkable for Romans with any sense of history. He was going to build a wall around the city.

The Aurelian Walls took in all Seven Hills of Rome, but not the entire extent of the third-century city. It had not been felt necessary to build walls since the fourth century BC, and the area enclosed by the so-called Servian Walls had been outgrown long ago. Work started on the new circuit in 271 and was still going on under Aurelian's successor, Probus. The walls are eleven miles in length and include 381 towers and eighteen gates. The extensive visible remains in Rome represent Aurelian's original design and also the work of Honorius in the early fifth century, when the height was extended and internal galleries and wall walks were included. The psychological effect of the new walls on contemporary Romans was probably immense. They indicated that the frontiers and the army were no longer capable of guaranteeing the safety of Rome and Italy.

As work on the defences of Rome began, Aurelian marched east to bring the provinces back into the Empire and to deal with the problem of Zenobia and her son Vaballathus, who had taken over Egypt and eventually declared themselves emperors. This may be the occasion when he decided to evacuate Dacia, and to create a new province of the same name south of the Danube in what was Moesia. When the troops were withdrawn along with an unknown number of civilians, the old province of Dacia was opened up to the Goths and Carpi, who may have been bound to Rome by the terms of a treaty which made them responsible for the defence of the abandoned territory.

After spending the winter at Byzantium, Aurelian defeated Zenobia's army near Antioch, and followed when the Palmyrenes moved to Emesa, where he defeated them again. When Zenobia retreated to Palmyra, he blockaded the city, which soon fell to him, which was just as well since the Romans would probably not have been able to supply their army for a long siege.

No one knows what happened to Zenobia and her son. Legend has it that she was captured while trying to flee to the Persians, and was taken to Rome to live in a villa and marry a Roman senator, for which there is not a shred of evidence. The defeat of Zenobia did not end the matter, however. Palmyrenes at home and in Egypt rebelled against Aurelian, resulting in the complete destruction of the desert city, and increased taxes in Egypt. Aurelian issued coins modestly proclaiming himself as *Restitutor Orientis*, restorer of the east.

The Gallic Empire had been having troubles of its own while Aurelian was in the east. Two usurpers, Laelianus and then Marius, rebelled against Postumus, who defeated them both but was killed by his soldiers because he would not allow them to sack Mainz. His successor Victorinus was assassinated within a few months and then the troops declared for Esuvius Tetricus, who was based at Trier, and engaged in trying to stop the Germanic tribesmen who had reached the Loire valley. Aurelian mobilised probably in 274, and defeated Tetricus, probably without even having to fight a battle. A short-lived rebellion was put down at Trier, and Aurelian's kinsman Probus was put in charge of restoring the frontier defences.

Aurelian now called himself *Restitutor Orbis*, restorer of the world. His titles tended towards megalomania, especially when he decided he should be addressed as *Imperator deus et dominus*, signifying that he was lord and god on earth. It was a trend that had been increasing since Severus' day, and would continue under Diocletian, as Roman emperors tried to sanctify and protect their regimes. Aurelian as a god on earth was not spared from the usual fate of rulers of the later Roman Empire when he was assassinated in 275, while he was marching to declare war on the Persians. He did not die by universal consent of the soldiers, who in an unprecedented move sent word to Rome to ask the Senate to choose an emperor. The senators chose Marcus Claudius Tacitus, who was aged seventy-five, but despite his advanced years he spent the six months of his short reign fighting the Goths. When he was assassinated by the troops, the army decaled for his half-brother, the Praetorian Prefect Florian, but the stronger candidate was Probus, whom Aurelian had left in command of the eastern provinces of Syria and Egypt. He met Florian and his army at Tarsus, but the climate decided the issue because Florian's troops could not stand the heat, and killed their leader.

Probus reigned from 275 to 282, and completed Aurelian's work in re-establishing the Rhine and Danube frontiers and repairing the damage. He was the first Emperor for many decades who succeeded in carrying the war across the Rhine into barbarian territory, where nine kings were said to have submitted to him, and he built forts to control the tribes. None of the forts can be located and they probably did not last very long. He settled 100,000 tribesmen within the Empire, in Thrace, and gave some lands to the Franks, probably in the Danube area, but they broke out, seized some ships and started to pillage in Greece, then Sicily and Africa before sailing back to their original homelands of the Rhine. There were various attempts to usurp Probus in different parts of the Empire, but he survived them all and planned a campaign against the Persians, but like Aurelian he was assassinated in 282 before he embarked on it.

The Reign of Diocletian and the Tetrarchy

From 282 to 285 the Empire was ruled by the Praetorian Prefect Carus and his two sons Carinus and Numerianus, who were declared Augusti, and became co-Emperors with Carus. Carinus was in command of the western provinces while Carus and Numerianus went to the east to declare war on the Persians, who were weakened by internal strife in their Empire. Carus waged a successful campaign, but died on the return journey. A short while later, Numerianus also died. The main suspect was the Praetorian Prefect Lucius Aper, whose name Aper means boar.

The commander of Numerianus' guard, Diocles, had been told by a wise woman in Gaul that he would become Emperor after he had killed a boar. And so it turned out. Aper was executed and Diocles took a new name, Gaius Aurelius Valerius Diocletianus.

Although Diocletian was accepted as the new Emperor, Carinus still ruled the west, but he was defeated by Diocletian's army near Belgrade. Recognising that the Empire and its problems were too weighty for one man ruling alone, and that in the absence of any legitimate heirs the succession should be clearly proclaimed, Diocletian took as his colleague Marcus Aurelius Maximianus. They both assumed divine names, Diocletian as Jovius, or Jupiter, and Maximianus as Herculius, or Hercules, and they divided control of the Empire between them, Maximianus in the west where he faced internal problems in Gaul and external problems caused by Saxon and Frankish pirates, and Diocletian in the Danube provinces, continually threatened by tribes from the north.

Events took an unexpected turn in the west. The fleet commander based at Boulogne, Marcus Aurelius Carausius, initially did good service for Maximianus in clearing the pirates from the Channel, but it was suspected that not all the recovered booty had been returned to the owners, so Carausius fled to Britain in 286, where he managed to set himself up as a rival Emperor, but instead of trying to take total control he insisted that he was the equal of Diocletian and Maximianus, even issuing coins depicting all three of them, with the legend declaring them as Carausius and his brothers.

This new British Empire of the late third century is often taken as the context for the establishment of the so-called forts of the Saxon Shore, but the title is not attested until a much later period, and in Carausius' day there was probably no such co-ordinated coastal defence system. The nine forts all date from different periods, and although Carausius had to protect the provinces of Britain from attack by pirates and also from potential invasion by Maximianus, he probably did not envisage the collection of forts as a coherent whole. The Empire of Carausius survived until he was assassinated in 293 by his successor Allectus, who ruled for another three years, but was defeated in 296 by Constantius I, nicknamed Chlorus from his pale appearance.

Constantius, the father of Constantine the Great, had been appointed as Caesar to Maximianus in 293 when Diocletian created the Tetrarchy. Four rulers, two senior Augusti and two junior Caesars, shared power in east and west to combat the many problems that faced the Empire as a whole. There was no intention to establish a hereditary succession for any of the Tetrarchs, but despite this the four men were bound by marriage alliances, in the old Roman fashion. Constantius had divorced his wife Helena to marry Maximianus' stepdaughter Theodora, and the Caesar in the east, Galerius, had married Diocletian's daughter Valeria. All four of the new emperors were soldiers, and all were Illyrians, known to and trusted by Diocletian, who chose his colleagues from among a relatively small circle of friends.

For many years from this time onwards there was almost constant warfare, with pressure from tribesmen on the Rhine and Danube frontiers, a resurgence of Persian activity, revolts in Egypt, trouble in Mauretania, and eventually civil war after the Tetrarchy came to an end, resulting in the supremacy of Constantine. The two Augusti and the two Caesars campaigned in different parts of the Empire, with varying degrees of success against tribesmen and internal bandits. Armies moved over long distances to the most threatened points. Danubian troops fought in the east against the Persians, and troops from Germany were sent to Mauretania. The frontier armies by themselves could not overcome the various threats without these concentrations of extra troops, which was nothing new, but the events were more frequent now, more widespread and more serious. From 298 there was peace. In 296 Galerius had been defeated by the Persian King Narses, but in 299 Diocletian came to terms with Narses, in which he recovered Mesopotamia and was able to install a pro-Roman king on the throne of Armenia. Fighting broke out again on the Danube against the Marcomanni, and on the Rhine against the Franks, but by 303 all was once again peaceful.

Diocletian set in motion reforms in the government of the Empire and in the army, tailored to meet the needs of the situation. The focus was shifting from the western provinces to the Danube and the east, and it was clear that Rome was no longer the hub of the known world. The emperors had to be with the armies wherever the main troubles broke out, and new provincial centres were developed some distance from Rome, which was too far away from the Rhine, Danube and the eastern provinces to be a viable headquarters. Gallienus had based himself at Milan to watch the Alpine passes, Constantius had used Trier as a base to be close to the Rhine, and Carnuntum on the Danube became an important Imperial centre. Aquileia in northern Italy was also used as a base, and Diocletian chose Nicomedia, and Salona (Split) as his headquarters, the latter as his place of retirement.

The constant wars imposed a strain on resources that outstripped income from taxes. Army pay was sometimes in arrears, or was commuted into payments in food and clothing. The tax burden was unfairly distributed so Diocletian tried to reorganise it so that it was more equitable, with all provinces contributing to the cost of defence instead of those closer to the frontiers. He ended the tax exemption enjoyed by Italy since the Republic, and introduced a new method of assessment based on land and agricultural produce. The land unit was the *iugum*, but it did not denote an area of standard size. Instead it was related to the type of soil, the amount of labour required to cultivate it, and the crops produced on it. The labour was taxed per capita, including women, who were mostly taxed at half the rate of a man. There was to be a census every five years to adjust the assessments, and the Praetorian Prefects were responsible for apportioning the amounts to be collected from each province. At local level the magistrates of the cities and towns organised the actual collection.

The attempt to control prices across the Empire, embodied in the edict *de pretiis*, was unsuccessful, but the document is of tremendous interest to historians, since it contains information about the relative prices and values for hundreds of commodities. Better success was achieved in the state control of factories producing arms and armour, textiles and clothing. Production of food was regimented, particularly bread. Mobility of labour ceased and workers were forced to remain in their respective jobs. Farmers facing impoverishment became tenants or *coloni* of the great landowners, in a system not quite equated with serfdom. The *coloni* paid rents, but especially in Africa they had to perform labour on the landlord's farm as well. Diocletian tied the *coloni* to their tenant farms just as he tied most other people to their professions or jobs, and this benefited the landlords, who were sometimes able to defy tax collectors and recruiting agents.

Provincial government changed under Diocletian. The Praetorian Prefects were responsible for overseeing groups of provinces called dioceses, and an extra tier of equestrian officials was inserted, called *vicarii*, one *vicarius* for each diocese, answerable to the Praetorian Prefects. The first attested *vicarius* dates to 298. The provinces themselves were split into smaller units, so the number of provinces almost doubled, and so did the administrative staff to govern them. The administrative systems were organised on military lines. Service in administrative departments, called *scrinia* after the boxes used to carry documents, was known as *militia*, service in the army being distinguished by the term *militia armata*. Civil and military careers were now separated, and many more equestrian officials were appointed, though some senators still governed provinces. The armies were no longer commanded by provincial governors, but were placed under a *dux* (plural *duces*), which literally means leader. Sometimes the *dux* commanded the troops of more than one province, in order to protect stretches of the frontiers that crossed provincial boundaries. The armies themselves underwent reforms, starting under Diocletian and probably completed by Constantine. These reforms are described in the next chapter.

The Tetrarchic system held together while Diocletian guided it. He was ill for some years before he retired in 305, forcing Maximianus to do the same. Constantius and Galerius became the new Augusti, with Severus and Maximinus Daia as their respective Caesars, both of them military men, and both of them Galerius' adherents. In theory the scheme ought to have worked. The succession was established as each Caesar became an Augustus or senior emperor and chose a new Caesar as second in command. As generals already designated as heirs, there was supposedly no danger that one of the Caesars would be declared Augustus by the troops because all he had to do was to wait his turn, and his troops would be rewarded. But the system was defeated by human nature and ambition. Constantius' son Constantine was at Galerius' court in the east when Diocletian retired, but since Constantius was about to begin his campaign in Britain in response to some unknown problems, Constantine sped westwards to join him. In 306 his father died and the troops in Britain proclaimed Constantine Emperor. It would take him nearly two decades to make himself sole Emperor.

In Rome Maximianus' son Maxentius was declared Emperor at more or less the same time as Constantine. Severus, who had been Caesar to Constantius, was killed in 307 by Maxentius and Maximianus, who had no official position. He allied with Constantine, rather than his own son. Civil war was avoided at first. There was a conference between Galerius and Diocletian at Carnuntum in 308, reaffirming the Tetrarchy. Constantine was fobbed off with the title Caesar, Maximianus had to back down, Maxentius was ignored, and Valerius Licinianus Licinius was made Augustus. There were several men between Constantine and supreme power, but in 310 he turned against Maximianus who committed suicide. In 313 Galerius died, and Maximinus Daia was promoted to Augustus in his place. In 312 Constantine defeated and killed Maxentius at the battle of the Milvian Bridge in Rome. In 313 Maximinus Daia died and Licinius took over his provinces, building up a power base in the east.

Eleven years were to elapse before Constantine fought the final battle with Licinius and defeated him. During this time they both consolidated their power over their respective territories. Constantine was in Rome in 315 to celebrate ten years of his reign. Part of the celebrations involved the dedication of the arch named after him close to the Colosseum. At first glance it appears as a homogenous whole, but nearly all the sculptured panels, roundels and figures were taken from other monuments belonging to the reigns of Trajan, Hadrian and Marcus Aurelius. Only the narrow frieze running around the arch near the top is Constantinian in date, celebrating the victory over Maxentius.

Licinius was defeated in battle against Constantine in 316, and ceded Pannonia, part of Moesia and the Balkans. The two emperors appointed their very young sons as Caesars and for six years there was peace, or more realistically an unofficial truce. Then Licinius embarked on a new round of persecution of the Christians, as Diocletian had done. Constantine stood on the side of the Christians, having allegedly seen a cross or some similar Christian sign before the battle at the Milvian Bridge, and heard the words, or seen a written version, 'in this sign you shall conquer'. Matters came to a head in 323 when Constantine pursued a band of Goths into Thrace, which was in Licinius' territory. Licinius thought he intended to invade. Preparations for war escalated, and the two emperors fought it out at Adrianople in July 324. Constantine emerged as sole ruler of the whole Roman Empire. Licinius' adherents were eliminated.

Constantine and His Successors

Constantine's most enduring achievement was his establishment of Christianity as the state religion, which future emperors, with the exception of Julian, endorsed. New churches were built, not in the style of pagan temples but as basilicas, which were originally civil buildings used for administrative and judicial purposes. In 329 St Peter's was completed in Rome, while other churches were on Imperial lands, or outside the city of Rome. The old pagan religion was not deliberately stamped out at this stage, since Constantine himself tried to foster religious freedom, and he never wholly rejected his adherence to Sol Invictus, the unconquered sun.

In his government Constantine did not radically alter the arrangements of Diocletian. He promoted senators and employed them as governors of the consular provinces or as prefects in Rome, but he also fostered equestrians, probably because the Empire with its dioceses and its increased numbers of smaller provinces demanded more personnel. The important change that he made was to move the capital to Byzantium, renamed Constantinople, and today called Istanbul. This city was easier to defend on its peninsula, and it was closer to the Danube and to the eastern provinces where most of the problems of the late Empire arose. It became a duplicate Rome, with seven hills, fourteen administrative regions, and a Senate and annually elected consuls.

After the battle of the Milvian Bridge Constantine had abolished the Praetorian Guard, but the Praetorian Prefects were retained and put in charge of the military supply system, or *annona*. As his bodyguard Constantine adopted the *scholae*, originally established by Diocletian. The armies were finally divided into frontier forces and mobile field armies, with a greater preponderance of cavalry, which rather oversimplified statement is discussed more fully in the next chapter.

There were military campaigns on the Rhine and Danube, against Goths and Sarmatians. A treaty was made with the Goths in 332, but in general tribesmen regarded treaties as personal affairs arranged with an individual not a state, so when all the members of the house of Constantine had died out the treaty would be considered to have run its course. From 334 to 337 when Constantine died there was stability on the frontiers. He designated as his successors his sons, Constantine II, Constans, and Constantius II, who had already been appointed as Caesars, along with another relative, Dalmatius. After Constantine's death the soldiers killed Dalmatius and other more distant members of the family, except for Gallus aged twelve and Julian aged six. The Empire was divided into three zones for the three new Augusti, Constantine II taking the west, Constans ruling Italy, Illyricum and Africa, and Constantius II the eastern provinces. In 340, Constans fought against Constantius II, defeated him and took over the west. Constantius II was not in a position to argue because the Persians under Shapur II were becoming more powerful. Constans survived in the west for ten years, but was defeated and killed by the usurper Magnentius, who was then defeated by Constantius II in 351, but remained free for another two years.

Faced with wars on two fronts, the east and the northern frontiers, Constantius II shared power with Gallus, spared as a child when the soldiers killed most of his relatives, and now aged twenty-eight. He was made Caesar, given responsibility for the eastern frontier, failed, and was executed in 354. His half-brother Julian was made the new Caesar, dragged from his studies at Athens, and without any military experience was made commander in Gaul in 357, where he proved amazingly successful in battling the Alamanni. He defeated them decisively at the battle of Strasbourg, and went on to lead expeditions across the Rhine in 358 and 359. Then Constantius ordered him to bring his troops to the east for the Persian campaign. The troops did not want to go and declared Julian Emperor instead. Both sides prepared for war but Constantius died in Cilicia in 361, so Julian did not have to fight. He inherited the Persian war and decided to march in spring 363. It was a successful campaign, insofar as any Roman campaign against the Persians was ever successful, but Julian was wounded and died the same day. The soldiers chose Jovian, the commander of the Imperial bodyguard, as the next Emperor. After the Tetrarchy and the Constantinian hereditary succession, the Empire was back to the soldier-emperors, chosen by the military establishment, just as it used to be in the later third century.

Jovian extricated the army from the clutches of the Persians by negotiation and by giving up territory. He died of natural causes in 365 after a reign of only eight months, and the army officers chose one of their own companions, Flavius Valentinianus, to succeed Jovian. Valentinian and his brother Valens ruled as joint Augusti, Valentinian in the west and Valens in the east. This does not mean that the Empire was split into two halves, as it was in the fifth century, but the task of governing and protecting such a vast area required more than one man, as Diocletian had recognised. The west was in need of repair and restoration. Valentinian came to terms with the Alamanni and the Franks and began to rebuild the frontiers, repairing and rebuilding a chain of forts to guard Roman territory from the Upper Danube to the Rhine. The British provinces were also in need of assistance, having been damaged by waves of Picts and Scotti from the north and Saxons from the sea. It seemed to the Romans that the barbarians had colluded in these attacks which were grouped under the heading of *conspiratio barbarica*. Valentinian sent his general Flavius Theodosius, usually known as Count Theodosius in modern history books, from his title *comes* (plural *comites*), which originally signified a companion of the emperor, but had acquired official status as a title for important civil administrators and high-ranking army officers. After driving out the tribesmen from the Romanised parts of Britain, Theodosius restored the towns, forts and the northern frontier, where he may have been responsible for the blocking of fort gateways on Hadrian's Wall to reduce access and make them easier to guard. It was not an isolated example in Britain, and forts on the Danube frontier blocked up some gates as well. Theodosius went on to Africa and put down a rebellion, but court intriguers brought him down for some unknown reason and he was executed.

In the east Valens thwarted an attempt at usurpation by a relative of the Emperor Julian, but a greater worry was the continued invasions into Roman territory by the Goths. Valens arranged a treaty in 369 and demanded recruits for the army, but there was further trouble on the Danube in Pannonia, which Valentinian put down after recovering from an illness. He waged several wars against the tribesmen and re-established the frontier and the forts. In 375 he received an embassy from the Quadi, who blamed other tribesmen for the invasions, and then complained about the forts that had been built on the Danube opposite their lands. Valentinian was so angry that he had an apoplectic seizure and died. His teenage son Gratian succeeded him without a hitch, and his other son, aged four, was made Augustus as Valentinian II. The child was placed in charge of Illyricum, with the general Merobaudes as the real commander. Merobaudes was probably a Frankish tribesman in origin, and was a competent general in the Roman army. The Romans made increasing use of Germanic tribesmen in the army, and several of them rose to high rank, serving Rome well.

From 371 to 377 Valens fought the Persians for control of Armenia and Mesopotamia, but was unable to consolidate before a really serious invasion of the Goths occurred in the Danube provinces. They wanted to settle within the Empire because behind them there were the Huns. The Goths were not a single united ethnic people, and one of their groups called the Tervingi were allocated lands, but another group called the Greuthungi joined them. The Romans treated them badly, charging them ridiculously high prices for food when they were starving. The Goths could not go home, and were prevented from moving further into Roman territory to find lands, so they were forced to resort to raiding. The Goths who were serving in the Roman army rebelled when they heard of the treatment of their fellow tribesmen, and Valens rushed to face the rebels and the tribesmen at Adrianople, without waiting for the troops sent from the west by Gratian. The battle of Adrianople in 378 was one of the worst disasters of the Roman army. Valens and large numbers of Roman soldiers were killed and the total defeat meant that the Goths were now free to spread into Thrace and Illyricum.

Theodosius the Great and the Division of the Empire

After the disaster to the eastern army, Gratian and the young Valentinian II needed help in ruling the Empire. Theodosius, son of Count Theodosius who had been executed, was chosen as Augustus in January 379, and given command of the eastern provinces, where his major task would be to remove the Goths from Thrace, Lower Moesia, Macedonia and Thessaly. Gothic disunity favoured the Romans, so for a while Theodosius left the tribesmen alone to fight it out. Two Frankish generals, Arbogast and Bauto, joined him in Constantinople, and gradually forced the Goths into Thrace, but instead of annihilating them, Theodosius made a treaty with them in 382. This was a turning point in Roman relations with the tribes which threatened the Empire. The Goths kept the Thracian lands they had overrun, and were allowed to govern themselves. Theodosius also promised supplies of food, in return for recruits for the Roman army. The unknown factor is whether or not these new soldiers were integrated into Roman auxiliary units, or were allowed to fight as distinct units under their own leaders. Theodosius needed recruits urgently to fill the gaps caused by the losses at Adrianople, and in employing Goths in their thousands he was fortunate that the majority of them performed well for the Romans.

With his hands full in ruling the eastern provinces, Theodosius was powerless to aid Gratian against a usurper from Britain, Magnus Maximus, alias Macsen Wledig of Welsh legend. Maximus stripped the British provinces of troops, invaded Gaul, and executed Gratian in 383. For four years Maximus remained in power, until he moved into the realm of Valentinian II in Italy, and Theodosius marched against him. Maximus' troops put up a good fight at Siscia and again at Pola but were defeated on both occasions. At Aquileia they turned against Maximus and sent him to Theodosius. Valentinian II was sent into Gaul with Arbogast to assist him, and Theodosius married Valentinian's half-sister Galla, with whom Arcadius, Theodosius' son by a previous marriage, was soon at odds.

Gothic raids had begun again in the east. In this case, the Praetorian Prefect Rufinus, and the general Stilicho, originally a Vandal tribesman, were able to exploit the internal strife among the Goths and allow them to destroy each other, so they stopped the raids without engaging their Roman troops in battle. In the west, the Frankish general Arbogast attempted to seize power after Valentinian II was found dead, of unknown causes, in 392. Suspicion would fall on Arbogast whatever the circumstances, so he raised a court official called Eugenius as Emperor, and held power for two years. Civil war began in 394, when Theodosius and Stilicho with an army of Goths defeated Arbogast and Eugenius with an army of Franks, at the battle of the Frigidus. These were Roman armies in name but nothing like the Imperial armies of the previous three centuries.

In the following year Theodosius died at Milan. He had left his elder son Arcadius as Augustus in Constantinople, and had raised his younger son Honorius to Augustus to rule the west. The new emperors were still very young, Arcadius was only about nineteen years old, and Honorius was only ten. The general Stilicho insisted that had promised Theodosius that he would supervise and assist the two boys, a promise that is not proven beyond doubt, but Stilicho took his self-appointed role very seriously. The two halves of the Empire were not yet entirely split into separate entities but the division was not far off. The tribesmen beyond the frontiers were extremely restless and the pressures on the frontiers were increasing to unprecedented levels, and external threats were combined with internal fragmentation. From this time onwards the emperors did not march with their armies to wars, but relied on their generals to fight battles on their behalf, and most of the generals and nearly all the soldiers originated from among the so-called barbarians. Instead of emperors fighting each other for supremacy, the generals did so, while still trying to attend to frontier defence. No one among the military elite or the higher echelons of the civil administration held onto their positions for very long. At the court of Arcadius, the Praetorian Prefect Rufinus wielded tremendous influence, and soon fell out with Stilicho, who considered that he was supreme general in both east and west.

Rufinus was murdered by Gainas, a Gothic soldier. An official of the civil administration called Eutropius took the place of Rufinus, but was not so enamoured of the Goths, so when a new leader of a group of Goths, Alaric, tried to insist that Rufinus had promised him lands and an official military appointment, he achieved nothing in Constantinople and was deflected towards the west. He and his Goths sacked Athens in 396, and it was left to Stilicho to deal with them, by settling them on lands in Epirus, approximating to modern Albania. The Gothic problem in the east was ended bloodily. Eutropius sent two Gothic generals in succession to put down a rebellion in Asia Minor, but they all joined forces and pressurised Arcadius into executing Eutropius. A rising of the populace of Constantinople against the Goths resulted in a massacre, after which the Goths never regained their predominant position. The eastern army had recruited Goths to fill the gaps after the battle of Adrianople in 378, and now the recruitment pattern changed again, restricted to more local regions such as Armenia and the tribal lands of the east.

Alaric and his Goths did not remain in Epirus for long, and began to move into Italy, where Stilicho stopped them at Pollentia and Verona. Alaric got the military command he desired, with the task of recovering the eastern half of Illyricum for Honorius. In 406 another group of Goths under Radagaisus invaded Italy, but Stilicho defeated them, choosing 12,000 of them for the army, and selling the rest as slaves. Then another British usurper, Constantine III, was raised by the troops and invaded Gaul, where he did good service by winning battles against Vandals and Germanic tribes in 407, and he set up his court for the next few years. Roman Britain was effectively at an end. Tradition holds that Honorius wrote to the Britons that they must look after themselves, but some scholars now think that he actually wrote to the Bruttians of southern Italy, a name easily confused with Britons. Instead it seems likely that the British communities broke with Rome voluntarily and expelled their Roman officials, retaining their own forms of government based on Roman principles.

In 408, Arcadius died, and his son Theodosius II succeeded him, but he was only eight years old. At about the same time in the west, a court official called Olympius persuaded Honorius that Stilicho was aiming for Imperial power. Stilicho avoided civil war by giving himself up voluntarily, and was executed. Honorius had removed the one man who would have been able to deal with Alaric, who now had no hope of military appointment in regaining Illyricum, and was soon besieging Honorius at Ravenna, and then marching on Rome in 410. The Goths rampaged through the city for three days, but because they were Christians they spared all those who took refuge in the churches of St Peter and St Paul. When he left Rome, Alaric took Honorius' sister Galla Placidia with him. He died in 411, after failing to cross into Sicily, and was succeeded by Athaulf, his brother-in-law. In 412 the Goths marched into Gaul, and in 414 Athaulf married Galla Placidia. They had a son, Theodosius, who could be considered the legitimate heir of his uncle Honorius, and therefore represented a bargaining tool for Athaulf, but the child died while still very young. In the meantime Flavius Constantius, a soldier of the Roman army, had become supreme general, and in 415 he waged a campaign of attrition against the Goths, by denying them food supplies. This forced them out of Gaul, Athaulf was assassinated, and eventually Wallia took over. The Romans gave the Goths food on condition that Galla Placidia was sent to her brother at Ravenna, and then Constantius employed the Goths to attack the Vandals in Spain. Eventually the Goths were settled in Aquitania.

Constantius achieved great power at the court of Honorius. He married Galla Placidia and they produced a daughter Honoria and a son called Valentinian, and Constantius was made Augustus to share power with Honorius. Within two years both Constantius and Honorius were dead, and a brief power struggle followed among the court officials and the generals, ended in 425 when Placidia brought her son to Italy, where he was proclaimed as Valentinian III. A quarrel between Placidia and the foremost general of the day, Flavius Aetius, was played out against the background of the invasions of the Huns.

The Huns under their leader Attila had first appeared in the eastern Empire, probably in the 430s, but they were successfully bought off with gold. When the demands of the Huns increased they met with opposition, so they retaliated by capturing Margus in Moesia, and the old fortress of Viminacium on the Danube. Then they attacked Naissus, the birthplace of Constantine I. The eastern Empire gave in and paid up. In 445 Attila killed his brother Bleda, and began to move westwards.

The fortunes of the eastern Empire from the fifth century onwards were much better than those of the west. From the death of Arcadius in 408 to almost the end of the fifth century, there were only five emperors in the east, while in the west, threatened from beyond the frontiers and with tribesmen already occupying parts of several provinces, there were sixteen emperors, some of them lasting only for a few weeks. It was indicative of the inability of a supreme ruler to solve the problems of the west, which were compounded by lack of resources. As tribesmen overran territories in the west, the revenues were lost to Rome, whereas in the eastern Empire territories were retained and with them the taxes and agricultural produce. Another factor was the ability of the eastern emperors to persuade one tribe to fight another tribe, or to deflect the threats from various tribes away from their frontiers towards the west, like Alaric and his Goths, and Attila and his Huns. From the fifth century the history of the western Empire is one of slow and gradual decline and fragmentation, while the history of the eastern Empire is one of success against its enemies, a greater degree of unity and stability as it metamorphosed into the Byzantine Empire.

The general Aetius, known as the last of the Romans, had been sent while a young man as a hostage to the Goths, and from them to the Huns, so he was able to use his experience of tribal politics to use the Huns in the service of Rome. He raised 60,000 of them to restore order in the power vacuum caused by the deaths of Constantius and Honorius. The western Empire was fragmenting. The Vandals held the provinces of Mauretania and some of Numidia, Spain was occupied by Germanic tribes, the Goths now called Visigoths, who had been settled in Aquitania by Constantius, wanted independence and home rule, and the Franks, Alamanni and Burgundians were in the Rhineland and the Alps. After fighting the tribes on the Rhine in 428, Aetius lost favour at the court of Placidia, who colluded with the governor of Africa, Bonfacius, to remove him. Aetius lost a battle and retired to his estates, until *c.* 434, when he re-emerged with an army of Huns to restore the frontiers of Gaul and to clear the provinces of the bandits known as the Bagaudae. In the African provinces he had reached an agreement with the Vandals, leaving them in control of Mauretania and some of Numidia, and regaining the rest for the Romans. Trouble broke out again with the Vandals after only a few years, and at the same time the Visigoths seized Carthage and learned how to control a fleet. Aetius and Valentinian III gave them what they wanted, recognition as an independent state in Aquitania, and then started to collect an army to deal with the Vandals. The eastern Empire contributed troops, since tribesmen in control of Africa could threaten the east as well as the west, but the troops were recalled almost immediately because Attila and the Huns were threatening to invade and the Persians had already done so. Aetius had to abandon the campaign against the Vandals, and recognised them as an independent state, like that of the Visigoths. The Roman Empire had now begun to fragment irretrievably.

From now until 451 not much is known of Aetius, until he and his army had to face Attila who had moved into Gaul. The Visigoths under their leader Theoderic joined the Romans, since he would have had to defend the Visigothic state against Attila in any case. Somewhere near Troyes, Aetius defeated Attila, but was unable to stop him from marching into Italy and ravaging several cities. This unhappy episode ended when Attila married a new woman, and on his wedding night died of a massive nasal haemorrhage in 453. The Huns who had been welded together under Attila now dispersed, and the potential threat was removed. Aetius did not enjoy fame and fortune for long. Valentinian III executed him in September 454, and in March 455 Valentinian fell to an assassin who resented the removal of Aetius.

The western Roman Empire had only a few more years to live. The very brief reign of Petronius Maximus in 455 was cut short by an invasion of the Vandals under Gaiseric, who sacked Rome on a more magnificent scale than Alaric had done, and returned to Carthage with Valentinian's widow Eudoxia and her two daughters. The next Emperor, Avitus, survived slightly longer, before being cut down by Ricimer, the grandson of Wallia, leader of the Goths. He had become an army officer but stopped short of declaring himself Emperor, and raised Majorian as Emperor in 457. Ricimer was the de facto ruler despite Majorian's title as Augustus, but he did not lead armies. Majorian campaigned against the Vandals and the Visigoths, but he probably showed too much independence, so Ricimer forced him to abdicate, and the Emperor died soon afterwards in 461. A few months passed with no emperor, then the Senate appointed Libius Severus, who survived until 465.

At this point the eastern Emperor Leo I intervened for a short time. He came to an agreement with Gaiseric and the Vandals, which Ricimer had been unable to accomplish. Eudoxia and her daughter Placidia were sent home from Carthage to Constantinople, while the other daughter Eudocia was married to Gaiseric's son Huneric. When Libius Severus died in 465, Leo I did not intervene for two years, and then appointed Anthemius, a capable general in the eastern army. The power of Ricimer was gradually eroded, and his adherents were replaced with Roman officials, but he was not yet beaten. He raised another Emperor, Olybrius, whose Imperial connections were impressive, being the husband of Placidia and therefore the son-in-law of Eudoxia and the late Valentinian III, but also the brother-in-law of Huneric the Vandal by dint of Huneric's marriage to Placidia's sister Eudocia. It was a perfect power base for Ricimer who was the real ruler behind Olybrius. In July 472 Anthemius was killed. In August Ricimer died, and Olybrius replaced him with Gundobad, whose father was king of the Burgundians in Gaul.

A few months later Olybrius died. In March 473 Gundobad appointed Glycerius as Emperor and went home to assume his role as king of the Burgundians. He had no interest in his Roman titles, which indicates how much Rome had declined in importance compared to honours among the tribesmen.

Glycerius was not recognised by Leo I, who sent his own candidate, Julius Nepos, to depose him, but unusually the deposed Glycerius survived as bishop of Salona. Nepos ruled for about a year, deposed in his turn by his military commander Orestes, a Roman who had once been secretary to Attila. Orestes raised his young son Romulus to the rank of Augustus, but his title was converted to the diminutive Augustulus, little Augustus, by the people of Rome. All went well until Orestes opposed the wishes of some of the Germanic soldiers who had fought for the Romans and wanted to settle on the land. They had a willing leader in Odoacer, who had been a soldier of Anthemius' bodyguard but had joined Ricimer. They called him king, ignoring Roman titles of leadership. Orestes was killed, but Romulus was spared and sent to a country villa, and remained there unmolested.

In 476 Odoacer assumed control of Rome and began to extend his rule over the rest of Italy. He was one of a number of tribal chiefs in command of parts of what had been the western Roman Empire. The Visigoths controlled much of Gaul and had extended into Spain. The Vandal kings of Africa were now in possession of Corsica, Sardinia and the Balearics. The Burgundians had been given parts of Gaul, and their name still survives as the title for a region. Odoacer bridged the two worlds of Romans and the so-called barbarians for two decades. He did not abolish the Senate, and appointed an annual consul from among the Romans. Civilian administrative posts continued to be filled by Romans, and army appointments were reserved for the tribesmen, but this was nothing new by the fifth century. The eastern emperors tried to oust Odoacer by sending other groups of tribesmen against him, but he beat off attacks. The Emperor Zeno persuaded Theoderic, leader of the Ostrogoths, to fight Odoacer, and when Odoacer died in 493, Theoderic was allowed to take his place, with only vague and informal recognition from the eastern emperors. In Italy and Gaul, Roman life continued, Latin and Greek literature was preserved, coinage was issued as before, people continued to live in towns and cities, trade did not die altogether, and administration and law continued on Roman lines. The Roman Empire of the west did not die in a sudden cataclysm, but was slowly, and on occasion painfully, transformed into the kingdoms of medieval Europe.

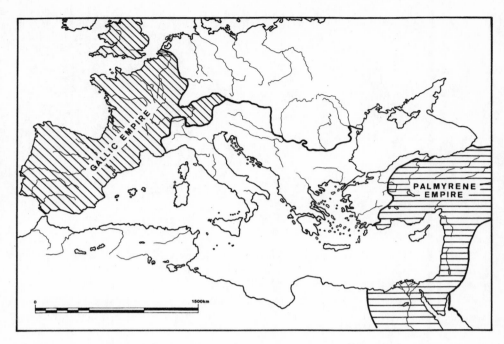

The Empire nearly fragmented in the AD 260s after the capture of Valerian in the east, which was kept together under Palmyrene leadership, while the western provinces were taken over by the so-called Gallic Emperors, confining the legitimate Emperor Gallienus to the central area. Drawn by Graeme Stobbs.

Portrait of the Emperor Gallienus on a gold aureus of AD 267 from the Rome mint. He is shown wearing a lion skin, which identifies him with the god Hercules. During his beleaguered reign Gallienus relied heavily on the army, which he had to assemble from whatever troops and parts of units were available to him. The reverse of this coin bears the legend FIDES MILITUM, proclaiming the loyalty of the soldiers, one of series of coins on the same theme. Drawn by Trish Boyle.

Gold aureus of the Emperor Aurelian, who inherited the problems of the divided Empire. With the help of his armies he reunited it. The reverse shows the goddess Concordia, and the legend proclaims the unity of the army CONCORDIA MIL(ITUM). Drawn by Jacqui Taylor.

2

Army Reorganisation of the Late Third Century AD

Until comparatively recently the later third century AD from the reign of Severus Alexander to the accession of Diocletian was classified as a time of crisis. Books could be confidently produced incorporating the words 'crisis of the third century' in the titles or the chapter headings. French scholars in particular used the phrase, while doing sterling work in unravelling the problems of chronology of the third century, a time when multiple events were playing out simultaneously over many parts of the Empire, for which the source material fails almost entirely. It is currently more fashionable to play down or deny the so-called crisis of the third century, by quibbling about the exact meaning of crisis, by describing the years of turmoil as a transformation, or by casting a different light on the years previously seen as a crisis. In strict definition crisis simply means a time of change, as in an illness where a fever can be seen as the point of crisis and then when it breaks the change occurs, not always for the better.

The problem perhaps boils down to the different slants that scholars put on the events of the third century, and how they interpret the word crisis. It is an unnecessary term for some scholars, who can point out that the Roman Empire emerged on the other side of the so-called crisis and survived for another two centuries. For others it is too sensationalist, because there were many other occasions in Roman history that also qualify for the title, so it could be said that Rome simply lurched from crisis to crisis from 753 BC to the fifth century AD.

Having dealt with the preliminaries and acknowledged in some part the controversies about the difficulties of the third century, it may be worth mentioning that from the assassination of Severus Alexander in 235 to the accession of Diocletian in 284 there were about twenty emperors, plus a host of failed usurpers, in less than fifty years, and not many of them died peacefully in bed. The turnover was too rapid for any single emperor to formulate long-term plans, much less to put them into effect, so all that could be achieved was to react to successive external and internal problems. In the AD 260s the situation was no better. The senior Emperor Valerian had been defeated and imprisoned by the Persians, the eastern provinces and their frontiers were held together by a non-Roman Palmyrene leader, the western provinces were governed by an independent Emperor appointed by the soldiers, the legitimate Emperor Gallienus was in command of Italy and Africa and not much else, the Alamanni were lingering just beyond the Alps, the Franks and other tribes were threatening the Rhine, and also the German land frontiers, several usurpers set themselves up in Illyricum and elsewhere, and Gallienus had to devote time, energy and resources to defeating them. The period may not warrant the description 'crisis' but it does seem that the Empire was in a teensy bit of a mess.

What grew out of the mess, eventually, was the late Roman army, but it was not created overnight or all at once, nor did the organisation of the army suddenly go off on a completely different tack to what had gone before. The late Roman army was a product of cumulative changes that had been going on for some time, because the Romans usually took what they already had, and gradually adapted it to changed circumstances. The fully evolved late Roman army looks somewhat different to the Imperial Roman army, if indeed the evolution ever ceased at any point. Gallienus, and more specifically Diocletian and Constantine, are credited with some of the stages in the organisation of the late Roman army, but it is possible to discern the roots of the late army as far back as the wars of Trajan, and definitely as far back as the wars of Marcus Aurelius and Septimius Severus.

When Gallienus became sole Emperor after the capture of his father Valerian, his resources in cash and manpower were limited. He could not afford to mount an expedition to rescue his father from the Persians, and any negotiations that may have been undertaken did not result in the recovery of the senior Emperor. When Postumus was appointed Emperor of the western provinces, Gallienus was denied access to the taxes and manpower, and though he may have received some of the resources of the eastern provinces, the available manpower was restricted to securing the borders against attacks from the vigorous Persian dynasty of the Sassanids. Gallienus therefore had to make do with the soldiers under his command, probably consisting of vexillations of legions from the Rhine, Noricum and Pannonia, rather than whole units, and an assortment of auxiliary infantry and cavalry. The soldiers from the Rhine were presumably already with him when the Gallic Empire broke away from Rome, so with Postumus now in command of the west there would be no further access to troops from this area, nor from Raetia, which an inscription attests was under Postumus' control.

A Byzantine historian, George Cedrenus, thought that Gallienus was the founder of the first mobile cavalry army. When Cedrenus was writing, the mobile field armies had been the norm from the time of Constantine onwards, so it would seem to Byzantine scholars that the direct forerunner of the mobile mounted armies must have been Gallienus' cavalry army, because it was not like the older auxiliary *alae*, it was not part of any provincial garrison, and although in composition it may have contained different units, it was a unified body formed purely of horsemen and it had its own commander, answerable only to the emperor. This command structure was the important innovation, not the assemblage of horsemen from different units.

Gallienus was far from being the first emperor to notice how useful cavalry could be in wars. The growing importance of cavalry had been demonstrated from the reigns of Domitian and Trajan, if not before. From the late first century onwards emperors on campaign were escorted by mounted escorts and guards formed from different cavalry units in addition to their bodyguards of *equites singulares Augusti*. Gallienus was only emulating established custom in gathering together cavalry of different units, but he was restricted by having to rely on whatever troops he had with him in Italy and the remnants of the Empire still open to him. Entrusting the cavalry army to one permanent commander was just one step further than placing vexillations of different troops under one leader, just as Marcus Aurelius had made Valerius Maximianus commander of legionary vexillations to take them to the war zone. The commander of Gallienus' cavalry was Aureolus, who obviously wielded great power, and could not resist using it to rebel against Gallienus, just after the Emperor had defeated the Heruli at the battle of Nestus. Gallienus hurried back to Italy to besiege Aureolus at Milan, and during the siege he was assassinated. This did not long benefit Aureolus, who was soon killed in his turn and all he had achieved was to clear the path to Imperial rule for Claudius Gothicus.

The cavalry army was made up of different collections of mounted soldiers. A large number of them were Mauri from Mauretania, and Osroeni from the east, who may have represented some of the troops recruited by Severus Alexander for the Rhine campaign, in which Mauri and Osroeni are attested. The problem is that these units are not traceable in the provinces or in Italy after the death of Alexander, and by 260 the original soldiers of Alexander's army would have served for twenty-five years or more. Some of them may have re-enlisted, or perhaps the units had been kept together and had continued recruiting from their homelands. Alternatively, since Gallienus had access to Africa in his own right, and to the eastern provinces through his friendly relations with the Palmyrene ruler Odenathus, he may have recruited horsemen from these two areas with the specific purpose of creating a cavalry army. Another group of horsemen were the *equites Dalmatae*, but it is not certain whether these were Dalmatian tribesmen, or alternatively soldiers from the auxiliary units of the garrison of Dalmatia. Their title does not make it clear which of these two theories is correct. A third group of horsemen in Gallienus' army were the legionary cavalry. It had been customary to detach the mounted sections of the legions to fight as cavalry, so this was not an innovation on the part of the Emperor Gallienus. These *equites legionis* are thought to be the precursors of the *equites promoti* and *equites scutarii* mentioned in the late Roman list of officials and their commands, the *Notitia Dignitatum*.

It is not known how the cavalry army operated, since the soldiers were armed in different ways and fought in different styles. The Mauri fought with javelins and the Osroeni were excellent horse archers. It would seem pointless to waste time in training all the cavalry to fight in a uniform fashion, since Gallienus was not permitted the luxury of spare time until he had fought on several fronts and won some battles. He needed fully operational cavalry immediately, so it was probably decided to use whatever skills they had developed.

The cavalry army was based at Milan, which Gallienus made his headquarters, and he fortified the city. It is a good location for several reasons. Transport facilities are excellent, the surrounding area is fertile and can yield supplies for soldiers and horses, and the routes through the Alps to Gaul, the Rhine and the Danube can be watched from Milan. Coin evidence shows that the cavalry force was called simply *equites*, not as *alae* or distinguished by any other title, such as *vexillatio*, which would imply non-permanence. On the other hand, some modern historians consider that the cavalry was never intended to be a permanent body. The use of Milan as a base need not imply permanent residence there. Depending on the needs of the moment the emperors used other bases in Italy at Verona or Aquileia, and in other wars they occupied Cologne on the Rhine, or Poetovio or Sirmium in the Danube provinces, among other places. Milan may have been just another strategic base, and the cavalry may have been just another vexillation. An inscription dated to 269, the year after the assassination of Gallienus, attests to the presence of *vexillationes adque equites*, as though there was some distinction to be made between two bodies of cavalry, or alternatively the inscription refers to an army made up of infantry and cavalry, which some scholars insist would have been more normal.

The ultimate fate of Gallienus' cavalry is not known. His successors Claudius Gothicus, Aurelian and Probus may have incorporated it into their campaign armies. All that can be said is that it was no longer at Milan after 285, but there would be less need for it to be stationed there after the reunification of the Empire under Aurelian. There is no trace of it thereafter as a complete independent unit with its own commander. The soldiers may have been absorbed into the cavalry which accompanied the emperors on campaign from Claudius Gothicus onwards, and when they had served their time the cavalry as a unit may have disappeared. It may be significant that it was said that Aurelian commanded the cavalry under Claudius, and he had cavalry formed from Mauri and Dalmatae at the battle of Immae in the war against Zenobia of

Palmyra, and they fought together. Aurelian ordered them to feign a retreat when the Palmyrene heavy cavalry or *clibanarii* moved towards them, so as to tempt the heavy armoured horses and men to pursue, then when they showed signs of tiring, the Mauri and Dalmatae were to round on them, which they did, successfully. This may show that some of Gallienus' cavalry was still in existence in 272, but whether it was the precursor of the mobile cavalry field armies is debatable, except that Gallienus had demonstrated the effectiveness of such units and the possibility of creating them, showing how effective a strong cavalry force based at a fortified place could be. This is something which Diocletian and Constantine would have been capable of working out for themselves, but the precedent would have been noted.

Though there is no discernible direct link between Gallienus' cavalry army and the later mobile field armies of the early fourth century, cavalry formations continued to be vital to the emperors, though it should be noted that the infantry of the mobile armies always outnumbered the mounted contingents. Severus may have been responsible for increasing the numbers of the legionary cavalry, which according to early Imperial sources numbered 120 men per legion, but Vegetius, writing in the later Empire, says that there were 726 cavalry associated with each legion. This increase is usually attributed to Gallienus or his successors, but an increase under Severus is consistent with his treatment of other cavalry units. He doubled the size of both the *equites singulares Augusti* and the mounted sections of the Praetorian Guard, and these horsemen survived into the late Empire under different names. The *singulares* became the *protectores Domini nostri*, and the Praetorian horsemen were called *equites promoti Dominici*. The *equites promoti* derived from the legionary cavalry were heavy armoured cavalry, and Diocletian added more heavy cavalry units recruited from the natives of some provinces, especially in the east, and these were given the title *equites promoti indigenae*.

It used to be accepted that it was Gallienus who decisively divorced senators from military commands and government of the provinces by substituting equestrians, but this too was a long drawn-out development. The author Aurelius Victor, who was prejudiced against Gallienus, says that the Emperor issued an edict to exclude senators from military commands because he did not wish to give *imperium* to the upper-class *nobiles*. The existence of such an edict is doubtful, but there is some support for Victor's statements in that senatorial *tribuni laticlavii* and senatorial legionary legates disappear from the record in the later third century. From this starting point it has been assumed that there was a constant struggle between Gallienus and the Senate, but not all scholars accept that there was ever a deliberate policy to exclude senators. Gallienus employed equestrians as army commanders in order to derive the greatest benefit from their experience. Senators generally had less military experience than equestrians, and though their track record as army commanders had not been disastrous, the later third century was a time when experience of military affairs counted for much more than noble status.

However much Gallienus may have wished to rid himself of senatorial influence, the sudden dismissal of senators and the substitution of equestrians could not be accomplished easily even by natural wastage, waiting until each senator's term of office ended and then appointing an equestrian. Senatorial proconsular governors remained in charge of non-threatened provinces, the main differences from previous practice being that senators were now directly appointed by the emperor instead of being chosen by lot, and their terms of office were extended beyond the usual one-year appointment. Senators are still found in provincial government in the late Empire, and the promotion of equestrians has a history starting long before Gallienus' reign, stretching back to the early Empire, from Augustus' arrangements for the government of Egypt. Marcus Aurelius had appointed equestrians of proven ability as military commanders, but he usually elevated them to senatorial status to conform to traditional custom. Severus also paid lip service to senatorial status, by appointing equestrians to command legions with titles indicating that they were acting in place of senators, for example *praefectus agens vice legati legionis*, or prefect acting on behalf of the legionary legate. Equestrian governors were similarly described as *agens vice praesidis*, acting in the place of the *praeses*, by which is meant the senatorial *legatus*, though the title *praeses* eventually indicated an equestrian governor. The praetorian provinces of Numidia, Arabia, Thrace and Cilicia were governed by equestrian *praesides*. The numbers of equestrian provincial governors increased when Diocletian split the provinces into many smaller units.

From Gallienus to Diocletian

Claudius Gothicus was said to have been marked out as the successor to Gallienus, despite the fact that Gallienus had a brother and a son who were his most likely choices of successor. These two were killed soon after the assassination of Gallienus. Claudius Gothicus ruled for too short a time to discern what his policies may have been. He made no sweeping changes to the army, which he used successfully to fight off attacks by the Goths. He had to rely on other commanders to help him to restore order in the Empire. He sent Julius Placidianus, the Prefect of the *Vigiles*, to try to win back the Empire of the Gauls, and ordered the Prefect of Egypt, Tenagino Probus, to collect a fleet and base it off Greece to combat the Goths who were by now threatening the provinces from the sea. Claudius won a victory over the Goths at Naissus, which may have been confused with Gallienus' earlier victory at Nestus, but the main point is that victories over different groups of Goths never solved the problem entirely, since the tribesmen who survived amalgamated with other tribesmen and came back for more. The same could be said of the Alamanni in the Alps, and the Juthungi and Vandals on the Danube. Before he could come to grips with these tribes, Claudius died of plague, and the army proclaimed Aurelian, of obscure origins and social status.

In rounding off Claudius' campaign, Aurelian defeated the tribesmen and demanded 40,000 cavalry and 80,000 infantry from the Juthungi, and 2,000 cavalry from the Vandals. The numbers may have been exaggerated in the sources, but these recruits represent the equivalent of at least thirteen legions or over 200 quingenary cavalry and infantry auxiliary units. Unfortunately it is not known what Aurelian did with them all. He may have used them to fill gaps in his army, in which case the ethnic origins of these troops will have been dissipated, or he may have formed complete units. The Romans never ceased to recruit native troops, and more and more often in the later Empire groups of them fought under their own leaders, as they had done during the Republic.

Aurelian's campaigns against various tribesmen are not clearly documented, and even the tribal names are not necessarily accurate, since later Roman authors tended to label whole groups of tribes as Scythians, and the name Alamanni, meaning 'all men' has perhaps been applied indiscriminately to different groups. What is apparent is that the Roman army under Aurelian's command was involved in a series of rapidly changing scenes of action and wide-ranging movements. The army was probably made up of vexillations of legions and a variety of auxiliary units as in any other campaign army. In the eastern campaigns the army contained troops from Gaul, Moesia and Pannonia, detachments from the eastern troops, Praetorians, and club-wielding Palestinians. Although it was not yet a field army as Constantine would have understood it, Aurelian's army contained high-grade troops and specialists, and would have served very well if Constantine had taken it over half a century later. Unfortunately nothing is known of Aurelian's army except what it did, so there is no archaeological information about marching camps, winter quarters or bases that may have been held, nor is it known whether the army operated in separate groups or whether all the contingents marched and fought together. It is more likely that in combatting the northern tribesmen smaller groups were allotted separate tasks, given the need for speed and mobility in chasing a highly flexible and mobile enemy, who could disperse and regroup with ease.

Aurelian managed to reunite the Empire by 274, fighting first against Zenobia and the Palmyrenes, who had invaded Egypt. Zenobia had declared her young son Augustus, which constituted a direct challenge to the authority of Aurelian. After the first victory in which Zenobia was captured, Aurelian first had to fight against the Carpi on the Danube and then had to return to the war with the Palmyrenes all over again when a revolt broke out, and this time Aurelian took over the entire Palmyrene state. In the meantime the Gallic Empire was becoming increasingly disunited. Postumus was killed and Victorinus was proclaimed in 271, but he was quickly eliminated, leaving what was left of the Gallic Empire to Esuvius Tetricus. Aurelian marched against Tetricus in 273, and after the victory in 274, the army was split up and placed in garrison in Gaul, where the general Marcus Aurelius Probus was given the command, though exactly where the troops were stationed is not clear.

In 275 Aurelian set off with another campaign army for a war with the Persians. He may have used the troops which had formerly garrisoned Dacia, but there are no firm details for the organisation of this army, except that it was assembled in Illyricum. The campaign was never started. On the march, in Thrace, Aurelian was murdered. There are several versions of what happened, but it seems that, unusually, it was not the soldiers who killed the Emperor. In fact the troops were very displeased, and refused to declare for any of the officers of Aurelian's entourage, nor for any of the generals who were in command of troops in other parts of the Empire. They asked the Senate to choose an emperor, and so the elderly Tacitus was appointed, ruling for about six months and spending most of them fighting the Goths. His half-brother Florian was made Praetorian Prefect, and became Emperor for a very short time, but the soldiers declared for Marcus Aurelius Probus, Aurelian's former general.

Probus was a distinguished soldier of obscure origins. As Emperor he was as successful as Aurelian, and his reign lasted for longer, but the source material is merely episodic and anecdotal. Probus campaigned energetically against the Franks and Alamanni in Gaul, and defeated the Burgundians and Vandals in Raetia. While he concentrated on the northern frontiers, Probus came to an agreement with the Persians, who were currently weakened by internal dissensions and in no position to mount a campaign against Rome's eastern borders. Probus may have intended to take up the campaign that Aurelian had planned against the Persians, but was distracted by fighting various tribesmen on different frontiers and also having to suppress banditry in Syria and destructive nomads in Egypt, then by mutinies and attempts at revolt under various generals. After establishing peace for a short while he had offended the army by declaring that there would soon be no need for troops, and he had earned the unwelcome reputation of a strict disciplinarian. Towards the end of 282 he was killed by his own men at Sirmium, and Marcus Aurelius Carus was declared Emperor in Raetia. The chronology is not elucidated, so it cannot be said that Carus had anything to do with the murder of Probus. The soldiers accepted him, and he had the advantage of having two sons, Carinus and Numerianus, who were quickly declared Augusti. The Persian campaign now became a reality, and the Romans once again reached the capital at Ctesiphon. Unfortunately Carus and his son Numerianus both died unexpectedly within a short time, and the Empire passed to Diocles, the commander of the Imperial bodyguard, better known as Diocletian.

There is an almost total lack of information about the constitution of the Roman army of the later third century, until Diocletian's reign, when the changes that he made are better documented. This makes it seem that what Diocletian achieved was innovative and new, but he owed much to his predecessors from Gallienus to Probus. Gallienus fought off tribesmen and usurpers in a series of rapid movements within the confines of the territories still under his command, but since it was Aurelian who finally reconstituted the Empire under his single rule, little credit attaches to Gallienus or his army. Aurelian's work made it possible for Probus to restore the frontiers of the Rhine and Danube, though the details are not documented, except by modern archaeological investigation. The attacks on the Rhine and Taunus-Wetterau frontier in the 230s had been repulsed and many of the forts which have revealed signs of destruction around that time were repaired, but by 260 some of the forts on the Rhine and Danube frontiers had already been given up. After 260 there were only a few forts still in occupation on what had been a strongly manned frontier. The concentration of occupied forts seems to have been around the Rhine mouth and the middle Rhine, though this may reflect where the archaeological work has been carried out as much as it demonstrates which forts were retained. The legionary fortresses of Bonn and Mainz were still occupied but the Taunus-Wetterau line was not manned at all and only a few forts guarded the gap between the Rhine and Danube. Regensburg was the most important post on the middle Danube. The province of Dacia was abandoned by Aurelian, though there is great controversy among even the ancient authors as to whether it was done in stages from the reign of Gallienus onwards and completed by Aurelian, or whether it was his responsibility alone. The new province called Dacia was carved out of the Moesian provinces on the south side of the Danube, and the removal of the troops augmented Aurelian's army. The date is not established but it may have been after the victory over the Carpi on the Danube and before Aurelian fought the second war against the Palmyrenes.

After his campaigns in Gaul, Probus was said to have restored sixty cities, which was inflated to seventy cities in later sources, but very little is known about forts and fortresses of this period except from archaeological investigations. It is stated in literary sources that Probus was victorious against the Vandals and Burgundians, and built Roman forts *in solo barbarico*, on barbarian soil, suggesting that he campaigned beyond the frontiers and established garrisons. It is not certain if this brief notification concerns the outcome of the campaign against the Vandals, in which case it probably means that Probus carried the war beyond the Rhine and Danube gap, but during his Danube wars he may also have campaigned beyond the frontier. No archaeological trace has been found of forts in so-called barbarian territory beyond the two rivers, but the reference to building forts does indicate that the army was successful and Rome was once again in the ascendancy with regard to the containment of the tribesmen, at least for a while. Apart from fighting them, Probus accommodated large numbers of tribesmen within the Empire, as previous emperors had done, notably 100,000 Bastarnae in Thrace, where they were said to have lived 'in the Roman manner'. Probus most likely arranged terms with the tribesmen that included contribution of troops for the army, which was a customary stipulation when settling them within the provinces.

Apart from these few notices in ancient literature, a few generalisations can be made about the army. On campaigns the armies were assembled from provincial troops, as they had always been assembled during the earlier Imperial era, and so presumably contained vexillations of different legions and whole or part auxiliary units, and probably native troops raised in or near the war zones. The Romans usually had no difficulty in persuading tribesmen to fight against other tribesmen. The most important factor is that these campaign armies were successful. No catastrophic defeats are documented on the scale of the defeat of Valerian in the mid-third century, or the battle of Adrianople in the later fourth century. Such events could hardly have been kept secret, and it would be unusual for the literary sources to ignore any newsworthy disasters. The Roman army had fought tribesmen for many years by Probus' day and had learned how to do it. The wars were not full-scale actions dependent on the capture of an important city or a central place, but small scale, localised, and not necessarily decisive, since the tribesmen frequently melted away only to return a short time later. The possibility that some of the tribes simply wanted food and somewhere to settle within the Empire was sporadically acknowledged by different emperors, and the system of subsidies given to native chiefs in return for the guarantee of peace often worked well, but the problem was the way in which this was interpreted by the Roman population, who saw their wealth and food supplies being diverted while the army stood by, apparently doing nothing, according to popular perception. Even some modern authors have viewed the granting of subsidies in money and food as an ignominious method of buying peace, but this was not a new feature just recently instituted in the later Empire. It had been an accepted policy for some time, dating from the first contact between Romans and tribesmen. Some emperors cancelled the subsidies, which always provoked more fighting, but then at least the army could be seen to be active, and this was what mattered to the provincials whose lands, livelihoods and lives were potentially at risk. The army was also successful in suppressing bandits and internal unrest within the provinces. A bandit called Lydius caused much trouble in Pamphylia and eventually took over the city of Cremna, where he held out against a long siege. Another bandit, Palfuerius or Palfurius, is described as a robber (*latro*) who was eventually captured and killed, but he may be the same man as Lydius. The Blemmyes in Egypt raised revolt but were defeated by Probus' generals, as was Saturninus, who attempted to usurp Probus.

From the sparse information about the activities of the armies of Aurelian and Probus, it is clear that they sometimes operated all year round and fought winter campaigns. They were also capable of rapid movements from war zone to war zone. Though there were as yet no field armies as constituted by Constantine in the early fourth century, there were armies almost permanently in the field, just as in the Republic there was no standing army but there were troops almost continually under arms. The later Roman armies which were in the war zones with the emperors or with subordinate generals would have to be kept up to strength and supplied with food and equipment wherever they were, while at the same time whatever garrisons had been left in the frontier forts would continue to be supplied and paid in the usual way. A system would have evolved for gathering and transporting supplies for the more mobile armies, derived from the methods used to supply the campaign armies of the emperors from Domitian's reign, the only difference being that these earlier armies eventually settled in permanent forts in newly won territory, or returned to their bases, whereas there was hardly any time for Aurelian's army to be stationed anywhere for very long, nor was Probus' army allowed much respite in the first years of his reign. Winter quarters are sometimes mentioned or indicated in the sources, for instance Aurelian wintered at Byzantium on his way to Palmyra, but nothing is known of where the soldiers were housed. Billeting in cities was probably already customary wherever there were suitable lodgings. Some troops may have been sent back to their parent forts while fresh soldiers arrived to replace them, but this makes no difference to the need for a more or less parallel administration for troops on the frontiers and troops in the campaign armies. Someone would have to keep track of where the units or part units were, and whether they were static or on the move the soldiers would have to be clothed, fed and paid, though the last two could be combined by means of payments in rations. When the field armies and frontier armies were finally separated, the systems for logistics, transport, supplies, accommodation, and administration would already have been worked out during the previous decades from the mid-third century onwards.

Diocletian's Army

In 284 the Roman world began to change as the last vestiges of the Principate merged into the Dominate. Rome and the provinces were gradually reorganised on a war footing, ready for armed conflict on a permanent basis. Everything was subordinated to the need for arms and armour, food supplies and transport for the army. Factories producing weapons and armour and clothing came under state control. The Empire was divided into four parts under the two Augusti, Diocletian and Maximianus and their two Caesars, known as the Tetrarchy. The Christian author Lactantius was never likely to look favourably on anything that Diocletian did, given that this Emperor persecuted the Christians, but the statement that the army was increased fourfold during the Tetrarchy is probably literary hyperbole. Diocletian did create more legions and he did introduce conscription to keep up numbers, but finding enough recruits to fill gaps was always a potential problem even during the earlier period, and would become even more contentious in the late Empire. Each of the Tetrarchs would be able to draw on the troops already in their provinces, but there was no vast reserve of manpower, because if there had been a central reserve either in the Empire as a whole, or within each quarter of it, then there ought not to have been a need to assemble a campaign army in the old way, by gathering units from different provinces and marching them to the war zone.

Some scholars have interpreted Diocletian's *comitatus* as the closest thing to a reserve, in that it may have been the forerunner of the later *comitatenses*, or Constantinian mobile field armies. This is fraught with several difficulties and it should not be imagined that Diocletian possessed a full-scale mobile army that moved with him at all times. Much depends on what *comitatus* actually meant at the end of the third century. It derives from the *comites* or friends of the earlier emperors and generals, who surrounded themselves with an unofficial body of different advisers, not all of them military. The Imperial entourage would contain a number of such men, who were said to serve *in comitatu principis*. From the reign of Marcus Aurelius and the Danube wars of the later second century, this body became more heavily militarised, and from Severus' reign the *comitatus* was described as *sacra* as the Emperor declared his household divine, distancing himself and his Imperial court from the ordinary populace. By Diocletian's time, the *comitatus* may have become a bodyguard, consisting of cavalry units such as the *equites Dalmatae* and *equites promoti* taken from their parent legions. There may have been an infantry element as well as cavalry. An inscription dating to the Diocletianic period from Lower Moesia records a *lanciarius* of *XI Claudia* described as *lectus in sacro comitatu*. The *lanciarii* were picked from the legions and formed as a specialist force, but still attached to their legions, probably as early as the reign of Severus, and since *lanciarii* were known in Constantine's *comitatus* it is assumed that this means that Diocletian's *comitatus* must have been organised in the same way as Constantine's. But there is still debate as to whether the Diocletian's *comitatus* was a small reserve force, or simply a combined mounted and infantry bodyguard. It is not known if the other three Tetrarchs also possessed a *comitatus*, either as reserves or guards.

Among his measures to strengthen the Empire, Diocletian repaired the frontiers, but the extent of the damage is hard to assess. Probus had already attended to restoration of the frontiers only a few years earlier, but his work is not easily distinguished from Diocletian's, just as

Diocletian's is not always discernible from that of Constantine. There is a brief literary reference in a panegyric by Eumenius mentioning the rebuilding of forts for auxiliary cohorts and *alae* along the Rhine and Danube and in the east along the Euphrates frontier. Archaeologically the sites cannot be securely identified, except in so far as there is evidence of late third-century and early fourth-century rebuilding on the Rhine and Danube and in Africa and the eastern provinces, but Eumenes was a contemporary of Diocletian's, so his statement can possibly be taken at face value, and it attests to the continued existence of auxiliary units in the army. They may have been smaller in size, but this remains a pure speculation, based on archaeological evidence which shows that forts were often smaller than the older auxiliary forts.

The eastern frontier, or a section of it, was studied by van Berchem in the 1950s. About one hundred miles of it are known, consisting of a road labelled the Strata Diocletiana guarded by two legions, one at Palmyra and another at Danaba south of Emesa (Homs), assisted by auxiliary *alae* and cohorts on the actual frontier line with forts about twenty miles apart. There was a preponderance of cavalry simply called *equites* stationed in the rear. Since much of the evidence derives from the *Notitia Dignitatum* which was compiled in the century after Diocletian's reign, the disposition of the troops as enumerated in this document may not necessarily represent the exact late third-century arrangements, but it would seem that the units were based where they could watch the routes and the traffic passing along them as well as any likely approach from beyond the frontier zone.

A new frontier, best known from its reconstruction and repair under Valentinian in the fourth century, may have been Diocletian's work. Much of the territory of the Empire north of the upper Rhine and Danube, consisting of parts of Upper Germany and Raetia, was given up, and a new line was created, running parallel to the Rhine, southwards from Strasbourg, then eastwards from Basle to join the River Iller, to turn northwards to join the middle Danube. Forts and watchtowers guarded the frontier, just as the Hadrianic frontiers were laid out. There is no absolute proof that this was the work of Diocletian or even Constantine, and it could have been initially begun by Probus. The establishment of the frontier so far to the south does not mean that the Romans had abandoned the supervision of the territory, which could have been extensively patrolled, or there could be outpost forts that have not yet been discovered.

Forts began to take on a different appearance from this time onwards. Some gateways were blocked off leaving only one passage open instead of the more usual two, and in some instances the entire gate would be blocked by a projecting drum tower built to enclose it completely. Forts on the Danube received fan-shaped corner towers giving the defenders a view along the walls, which indicates that the army was no longer always on the offensive, going out to meet the enemy in the field, but it was expected that forts would be attacked. The Goths had learned how to conduct sieges in the middle of the third century and had access to ships, so the menace of the mobile tribesmen was much increased. Towns received walls at this period if they had not already built them. On the river frontiers, bridgehead forts on the opposite banks were built, and landing places and harbours were fortified. Roads were guarded by watchtowers, as they had been since at least Flavian times, but now they were more heavily fortified. All this could have been undertaken by Diocletian's successors, but the driving force behind the fortification was his. While the Syrian frontier was strengthened, Diocletian was in Antioch. He campaigned in Raetia, then against the Sarmatians in Pannonia, and probably directed the initial stages of town, river and frontier fortifications of the Danube. A late Roman chronicler records that in 294 Diocletian built forts *in Sarmatia contra Acinco et Bononia*, forts in the land of the Sarmatians opposite Aquincum (Budapest) and Bononia (Vidin, Bulgaria). These have been interpreted as bridgehead forts, but the late Roman document *Notitia Dignitatum* lists two forts answering to this description, one opposite Aquincum *in barbarico*, occupied by an auxiliary unit called *auxilia Vigilum*, and another opposite Bononia, *in barbarico in castello Onagrino*, occupied by an auxiliary unit styled *Augustensia*. It is unlikely that these were bridgehead forts on the north bank of the Danube, since the entries in the *Notitia* concerning the known bridgehead forts do not describe them as being in barbarian territory. Like Probus, it seems that Diocletian campaigned beyond the frontiers and occupied some territory, but as yet no trace of the forts has been found.

A sixth-century author, John Lydus, who was a secretary in the Imperial administration, provides precise figures for Diocletian's army, which he says numbered 389,704 men. Debate about this figure is hampered by lack of accurate knowledge of the number and the size of the legions and auxiliary units. Before AD 305 there was an increase in the number of legions from around thirty-nine to possibly sixty or more. Some scholars suggest there were about thirty-four original legions and Diocletian added another thirty-five. The debatable points are the survival of the old-style legions at full strength or in reduced circumstances, and the size of the new ones. It is likely that the earlier legions remained at *c.* 6,000 men, otherwise they would not have been able to sustain contributions to the *comitatus* or to other provinces, which it is attested that they did. In the fourth century, detachments of soldiers of *III Italica*, originally raised by Marcus Aurelius, were stationed at Regensburg on the Danube and at four other forts, with a sixth detachment in the field army. The size of the detachments is unknown, but if they were all roughly 1,000 strong, then the whole legion would have numbered 6,000. Likewise *II Traiana* in Egypt was split up into detachments at the end of the third century, based at different locations.

Diocletian and Maximianus raised two new legions, each of 6,000 men, with the titles Ioviani and Herculiani, reflecting their divine associations with the two Emperors, but despite this it is suggested that the rest of Diocletian's newly raised legions were only 1,000 strong, in which case the establishment of twenty to thirty new legions would not have strained manpower resources quite so much as the recruitment of so many full-strength units. Vegetius felt obliged to inform his readers that two legions in Illyricum in the late third century were 6,000 strong, implying that in the fourth century when he was writing this was not the norm. This provides some support for the theory that new legions were only 1,000 strong, as does the Tetrarchic fortress at El Lejjun in Jordan, which is only about one-fifth of the size of earlier legionary fortresses. It could accommodate a maximum of 1,500 men, and it was not simply a base for a detachment, since it possessed a headquarters building, which could imply that the fortress contained the whole legion. This is not conclusive, since it is also likely that large numbers of legionaries were permanently outposted along the frontier, so the headquarters served as the administrative base for the whole unit of 5,000 or 6,000 men, but the fortress itself did not need to be large. A complicating factor is that in the late Empire in the eastern provinces, specialist units of legionaries were created, elite infantry called *lanciarii* and cavalry known as *promoti*, and these were eventually permanently split from their parent legions to become independent units commanded by tribunes in the *comitatus*, with a strength of about 1,000 men.

Writing his history of Rome at the very end of the fifth century Zosimus was full of praise for Diocletian's frontier arrangements, which he says secured the Empire and housed the whole army, but he goes on to say that Constantine ruined Diocletian's work by taking troops away for the mobile field armies and leaving the frontiers unprotected. The strong bias of Zosimus towards Diocletian necessitates caution in accepting what he says about Constantine, who did not denude all the frontiers, but repaired and strengthened some frontier posts. Nonetheless it is a testament to Diocletian's energy and determination, and that of his predecessors Aurelian and Probus, that the frontiers were repaired and soldiers were installed to man them, albeit probably stretched a little more thinly than they were in Hadrian's time.

The reconstitution of the frontiers testifies to the continuation of the Imperial concept of frontier control and defence, with some additional fortifications where none had been needed before, for instance harbours were fortified and some forts were placed in the provinces to guard routes, though whether this can be construed as defence in depth in Diocletian's reign is debatable. One of the changes that can be attributed to Diocletian is that the command of the frontier troops was tailored to the needs of the frontiers rather than the provinces. Military command was no longer the preserve of the provincial governors, who were, with some exceptions, confined to civilian administration. In place of provincial commands Diocletian placed high-ranking officers in charge of the armies, with the title *dux* (plural *duces*), meaning literally 'leader', as in Il Duce as adopted by Mussolini. The title is also the origin of the English Duke, but to use this translation for each of the *duces* or the late Roman Empire can be misleading. The title *dux* had originally been used for temporary commands of a single unit or a group of vexillations where the officer was acting in a capacity above his usual rank. Gallienus had appointed officers with this title, one at Dura Europos to command the Euphrates frontier, and another called Marcellinus, who was put in charge of fortifying Verona. Under Diocletian the *duces* became permanent officers whose commands could comprise the soldiers of a single frontier province, or could be extended over zones of the frontiers, comprising the troops of more than one province if necessary. The *duces* were retained and developed by Constantine and succeeding emperors, usually with a territorial designation to clarify the extent and location of the command of the *dux*, sometimes limited to one province as in *dux Africae* or *dux Aegypti*, or extending over a frontier area, in which case they were called *dux limitis*, from *limes*, meaning frontier. In the fourth century one of the commanders in Gaul was called *dux tractus Armoricani et Nervicani*, in command of the territory of the tribes of north-west Gaul, and another was responsible for the river frontier of the new Dacia with the title *dux Daciae ripensis*. There was no rigidity with these commands which could change according to circumstances, much as provincial government changed during the earlier Empire, when Imperial provinces could become demilitarised and governors of lower status could be installed, or more commonly a senatorial province that came under threat could be made into an Imperial province. In the late Empire the rules were flexible, in that there were provincial governors who commanded troops, and *duces* who were responsible for civil government as well as command of troops, but it made more sense to appoint commanders to guard whole frontier areas rather than relying on governors of different provinces to assemble their troops and work together. Since Diocletian divided the provinces into much smaller units there would have been a plethora of governors to be made to act together. An overall military commander would be able to bypass the civil governors and make his own decisions, subject to the emperor.

The reforms to the army and to the government begun by Diocletian were continued and finalised by Constantine, in most cases so seamlessly that it is difficult to distinguish who was responsible for which initial stages of the changes or for later additions and subtractions. It is more convenient to view the period from 284 to 337 in one continuous narrative, insofar as the known chronology will allow, or to deal with topics on a thematic basis. With regard to the army, the origin of the field armies and the frontier armies was an ongoing process, beginning in the later second century, and by the end of Constantine's reign the two were separated in their organisation and deployment. The next chapter covers their history and development.

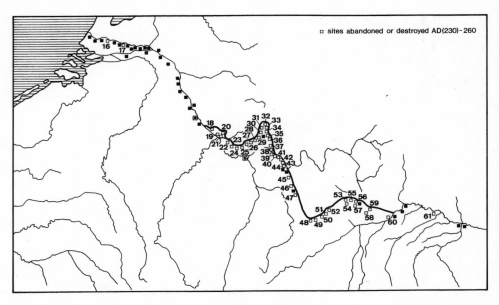

Some of the troubles of the third century started here on the Rhine and Danube frontiers. Many of the forts around the northward-facing salient of the Taunus-Wetterau area of Germany were attacked and damaged in the AD 230s, and though some of the damage was repaired in the next decade, another series of attacks in the AD 260s led to the abandonment of the forts. The lands beyond the Taunus-Wetterau are mostly clay, but the lands within the frontier zone are well drained and fertile for crops, lending support to the theory that the tribesmen may have been forcing their way into the Empire for food as much as for portable booty. Drawn by Graeme Stobbs.
Key to numbered sites: 16. Alphen-Zwammerdam 17. Utrecht 18. Niederbieber 19. Niederberg 20. Arzbach 21. Bad Ems 22. Hunzel 23. Holzhausen 24. Kemel 25. Zugmantel 26. Heftrich 27. Kleine Feldberg 28. Saalburg 29. Kapersburg 30. Langenhain 31. Butzbach 32. Arnsburg 33. Inheiden 34. Echzell 35. Oberflorstadt 36. Altenstadt 37. Ruckingen 38. Gross-Krotzenburg 39. Seligenstadt 40. Stockstadt 41. Niedernberg 42. Obernberg 43. Wörth am Main 44. Trennfurt 45. Walldürn 46. Osterburken 47. Westenbach 48. Schirenhof 49. Böbingen 50. Aalen 51. Rainau-Buch 52. Halheim 53. Gunzenhausen 54. Gnotzheim 55 Theilenhofen 56. Ellingen 57. Weissenburg 58. Pfünz 59. Böhming 60. Pförring 61. Steinkirchen.

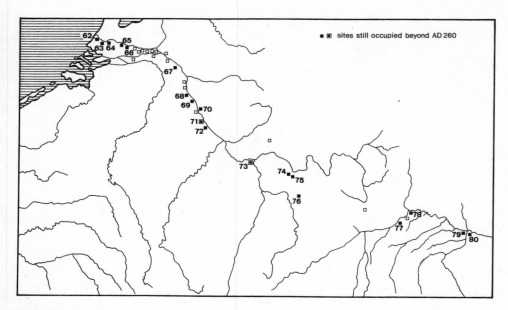

This map shows the state of the frontiers from AD 260 onwards, underlining the potential threat and the need for concerted action that Gallienus could not necessarily provide. This may be one of the main reasons why the Gallic Empire broke away from the control of the sole Emperor Gallienus, probably for self-protection rather than an attempt at usurpation. Drawn by Graham Stobbs.

Key to numbered sites: 62. Valkenberg 63. Leiden-Roomburg 64. Alphen 65. Woerden 66. Vleula De Meern 67. Altkalkar 68. Neuss 69. Dormagen 70. Köln-Deutz 71. Bonn 72. Remagen 73. Mainz 74. Miltenberg-Altstadt 75. Miltenberg Ost 76. Jagsthausen 77. Eining 78. Regensburg 79. Passau 80. Passau-Innstadt

Portrait of Diocletian on a gold coin worth ten aurei, minted at Nicomedia, one of the cities where an Imperial residence was established. Most portraits of emperors from the second half of the third century onwards show them with a determined frown, and many coin portraits lose their realism in favour of stylisation. Drawn by Trish Boyle.

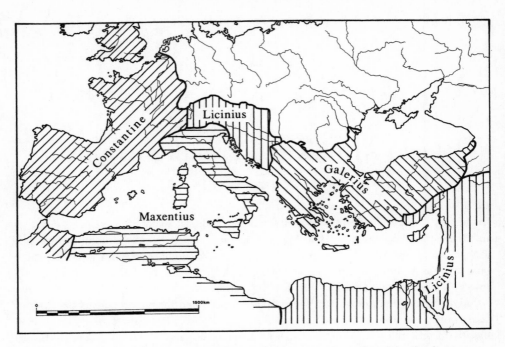

This map shows what became of Diocletian's Tetrarchic government. At first sight, the division into four zones implies that the system was still working, but the relationship between the four main contenders was not harmonious. Constantine I was proclaimed Emperor by the troops in Britain in AD 306, and inherited the domain and armies of his father Constantius in the west. He was recognised as Caesar, not Augustus, and for nearly two decades he had to fight for supremacy against his rivals Maxentius, Galerius and Licinius before he became sole Emperor. Drawn by Graeme Stobbs.

3

Field Armies and Frontier Armies

The Field Armies

The history of the late Roman field armies is derived almost solely from literary sources. A mobile field army leaves less archaeological trace than units in fixed locations on frontiers, and the lack of detectable evidence on the ground is compounded by the dearth of epigraphic data, because in the later third century people did not display the same zeal in setting up inscriptions that their ancestors of the first and second centuries had shown.

The division of the Roman army into frontier troops and mobile forces was the work of Constantine, who was proclaimed Emperor by the troops in Britain just after the death of his father Constantius at York in July 306. He had to wait patiently for his chance to convert his claim into reality. The two senior Augusti, Diocletian and Maximianus, had retired in the previous year, and the two reigning Augusti were Galerius, appointed in May 305, and Severus II, whose accession was dated July 306, after the death of Constantius. Although the army was quite prepared to accept the hereditary principle for the succession, Constantine was not allowed to inherit the political position of his father Constantius, and was not yet in a position to fight for it. He was content with Galerius' offer to make him Caesar, and he went to Gaul to attend to the Rhine frontier. Complications arose when Maximianus' son Maxentius was proclaimed in Rome in October 306, and Maximianus himself, who had only resigned reluctantly in accordance with Diocletian's wishes, reappeared on the scene, offered his daughter in marriage to Constantine and made him Augustus, a title to which Constantine clung with tenacity even though it was not condoned by Galerius and the new Augustus, Licinius.

By 312 Maximianus had been eliminated, Constantine had defeated Maxentius at the battle of the Milvian bridge in Rome, and Galerius had died. Diocletian may have survived until as late as 316, but he had ceased to be a powerful influence. It took another eight years before Constantine defeated Licinius and became sole Emperor.

The armies that Constantine and his rivals commanded through the years from 306 to 324 are not well documented, which is unfortunate since this is the most important formative era for the history of the late Roman army. Significantly Constantine's field army is not attested until 325, the year after his defeat of Licinius. The army is mentioned in a legal document reproduced in the later *Codex Theodosianus*, a compilation of all previous laws which were considered relevant to the circumstances of the fifth century. This particular document makes it clear that the field armies, the *comitatenses*, ranked higher than the frontier armies, called the *ripenses*. Before 325 there had obviously been considerable development of the armies that is not elucidated.

Constantine's field army was probably made up of the troops that he possessed fourteen years earlier after the defeat of Maxentius. He had probably brought soldiers from Britain, Gaul and Germany, which may mean that he took over whole or part units from these areas and also deliberately recruited to augment his forces. In 312 he would have taken over the troops that he had inherited from Maxentius. For the ensuing years virtually nothing is known about the composition of the armies that Constantine and his rivals had assembled. Attempts have been made to extrapolate backwards from later documentation to try to discern how Constantine's field armies were organised, but there are too many problems for this to be a valid method. There was most likely a continual evolution of the field armies and the frontier armies before and after Constantine's reign, but the details of any successive changes have not survived. Any documentation that post-dates the two disasters of Adrianople in 378 and the Frigidus in 394 is thought to be too far removed from the early fourth-century army to be of use in guessing its make-up, because of the major losses and resultant changes to the eastern army in particular.

Nonetheless it is still possible to outline some basic facts about Constantine's military organisation. The Praetorian Guard of Rome was abolished after the battle of the Milvian Bridge in 312, and the Praetorian Prefects eventually lost their military powers and most of their political influence, being assigned to control of the supplies for the armies. Each of the Tetrarchs had a Praetorian Guard, so Licinius retained his until 324 when Constantine defeated him and disbanded his Guard. This would be the most suitable occasion for the creation of a new bodyguard. Diocletian may have been responsible for the establishment of the *scholae palatinae* as a new bodyguard, which Constantine took over and perhaps increased in size, but some scholars think that it was Constantine who created the new bodyguard in the sudden absence of the Praetorians from 312. The *scholae* were answerable to the emperor, and were quite separate from the *comitatenses*, which were the core of the mobile field army, of unknown size. Zosimus says that Constantine's army in the final struggle against Licinius consisted of 120,000 infantry and 10,000 cavalry, but this figure probably applies to an enlarged campaign army, not simply the mobile field army, which would probably always have been supplemented by extra troops when wars were fought.

The strength of the mobile field army was based on cavalry and infantry units, and although the cavalry was supremely important, the footsoldiers outnumbered the mounted troops. The cavalry may have consisted of vexillations from various mounted units including the legionary cavalry and the *alae*, and some of the first infantry units may have been Diocletian's legions of *Lanciarii*, *Ioviani*, and *Herculiani*, the last two named for the Emperors Diocletian himself and Maximianus who adopted the religious titles. These were probably taken over as whole units. The supreme commanders of the *comitatenses*, directly answerable to the emperors, were the *magister peditum* in charge of the infantry, and the *magister equitum* in charge of the cavalry. These two posts were created by Constantine, probably when the Praetorian Prefects lost their military functions, but although the *magistri* are attested at a later period, nothing is known of his original commanding officers, so their military backgrounds and suitability for their commands cannot be estimated. Later on, the title *magister militum*, master of the soldiers, was used, or alternatively *magister utriusque militiae*, but these titles do not seem to mark an evolutionary stage whereby the commanders of the infantry and cavalry were merged into one single command of all the soldiers, since all the titles were used inconsistently and seem to be interchangeable.

A single field army operating close to the emperor would not have been sufficiently strong or rapidly mobile to protect the whole of the Empire, so regional field armies were eventually established in different parts of the Empire which were considered to be under threat, especially in the eastern provinces where the main base was at Antioch. In Illyricum the base was at Sirmium, and in Gaul the main base was at Trier. The regional field armies were usually commanded by *magistri* who ranked lower than the chief *magister militum* and *magister peditum*. The central field army was distinguished from the regional versions by the addition of the title *palatini*, indicating that these *comitatenses* were attached to the emperor, and the *magistri peditum* and *equitum* added extra qualifying titles, *in praesenti*, or *praesentalis*, similarly indicating that they served in the presence of the emperor.

At a later period some of the regional field armies were commanded by *comites*, plural of *comes*, originally meaning companion, and used on an informal basis for the companions of the emperors. Constantine began to use this title on a formal basis for high-ranking officers, and in the later fourth century there were commanders such as the *comes* Theodosius who restored order in Britain after the multiple attacks by different tribes in 367. The title is usually translated as 'Count', and in some instances it seems that the holder of the title ranked higher than the Diocletianic *dux*, no matter how many frontier troops the *dux* commanded. If soldiers from the *comitatenses* were transferred into the frontier armies, the commander was elevated from *dux* to *comes*, but the use of the two titles in some of the documentation indicates that this hierarchy was not so simple. In the mid-fourth century, Valacius, the commander of the military forces in Egypt, was *dux et comes*, but without further information it is not certain what this implies. It may mean that he had military power as *dux* and was also a companion of the emperor, or that he had two official roles, governing the province and commanding the armies.

In the early fourth century new units appeared in the Roman army, distinct from the old-style *alae* and cohorts, and simply called *auxilia*. It is not certain when they were first created. They were made up initially of tribesmen from Gaul and the Rhine, their origin attested by their use of Germanic war cries before they charged into battle. Since they originated from the Rhine they could have been established by Maximianus when he was campaigning in the area, or by Constantius who operated in the same regions. These units are attested in Constantine's field armies, and some scholars credit him with their creation. The *auxilia* were infantry units, but they were not comparable with the old-style auxiliary cohorts, nor were they to be equated with the legions. Some of them may have been formed from existing auxiliary units originally based on the frontiers, such as the *auxilia* called Nervii, Tungri and Batavi, which had been upgraded and incorporated into the field army. Others had names such as Bracchiati, indicating that they wore armlets, or Cornuti, which implies horns, on their helmets rather than a physical description of the men. R. S. O. Tomlin describes the *auxilia* as shock troops, which implies that they were heavily armed and well protected. There is uncertainty about their numerical strength, some evidence suggesting that there were about 600 men in these units, but other evidence suggests that they were twice as large at 1,200 men.

After Constantine's reign the field armies have left only a few traces. Most of the information about them derives from the literary sources such as Ammianus Marcellinus, who had first-hand experience of military matters, having been made a *Protector* and he had served as a staff officer under Ursicinus, who was *magister equitum* from 349 to 359, and *magister peditum* from 359 to 360. Ammianus covers much of the fourth century in great detail until 378, ending with a description of the disastrous battle of Adrianople. From this work it is known what the army did, with some information as to how it was organised. The historian Zosimus wrote a history of Rome at the end of the fifth century or at the beginning of the sixth, incorporating earlier sources of the third century, so he covers a much longer period than Ammianus, but without the details.

Archaeologically the field armies are almost invisible, because while on campaign they would be highly mobile and would leave only a few finds, and while they were not engaged on campaigns they were billeted in towns and cities, rather than in forts. It would have been counter-productive to place a mobile army in specific bases to which the soldiers returned after campaigns. If such forts had existed they would have to be manned when the army went on campaign, either by leaving some of the mobile army behind, or by moving other troops into them. Supplies would have to be delivered to them in peacetime, whereas in cities the soldiers were closer to the centres of production and could tap into the supply systems already in place. The billeting of troops on civilians was not without its problems. The several laws relating to the system have revealed what had been happening. According to the legal codes, the civilian had to give up one-third of the property to the soldier-guest, choosing the best part for himself, while the guest chose the second best, leaving the remaining third to the owner. In principle, only the living space was to be provided, but it is clear from legislation that the soldiers were taking much more than that. Constantine's immediate successors had to try to curb these demands. Constans ruled that no soldiers should take wood, oil and food, but if these were given voluntarily the action would be condoned, which would have made it easy for soldiers to swear that they had not taken anything that was not freely offered. This subterfuge may be one of the reasons why Constantius II passed a law forbidding the free gifts to soldiers. It was not effective, and in 393 Theodosius I had to re-enact the same law, and Theodosius II issued it once again in 416. The officers had a better chance than ordinary soldiers of making demands on civilians with impunity, and laws had to be enacted to prevent them from demanding baths, or the fuel to heat the baths. Many soldiers completely overstepped the mark by ill-treating the civilians, who were robbed of possessions, beaten up, or forced to become virtual slaves to the soldiers. In the early sixth century, even the civilians who were supposed to be exempt from the billeting regulations, such as teachers, doctors, arms manufacturers, Christian clergy and synagogues, were brought into the scheme. Landowners did not escape either, but the government had to declare exactly what the soldiers were entitled to claim from them, which included a fixed quantity of wood and oil, and one bed with its bedding for two men. Scams were operated by the soldiers to make extra cash, for instance the *dux* Cerialis in command in Libya moved the soldiers around from city to city, extracting a money payment with the promise of removing them. He is probably the same Cerialis who sold all the horses of a mounted unit under his command, and converted the men into infantry.

The billeting of soldiers in cities made it impossible to retain the cohesion of various units, and destroyed the feeling of belonging to a corporate entity that fostered esprit de corps. There was no clearly marked military compound in the cities that would have kept the soldiers together, such as there was at Dura Europos. There are questions about organisation for which answers will probably never be found, such as what did the soldiers do all day, how did the staff work function, how was the army administered, was there a building in the city appointed as headquarters where records could be kept, of pay if nothing else, or did record keeping disappear? How were the men mustered ready for a campaign, was there a designated place of assembly, did they muster every day, were they counted and given various tasks as the third-century unit at Dura Europos was, with all details written down to keep track of where the men were at any given time? Where did they put the horses, given that a large part of the mobile army consisted of mounted troops? There is one clue in the laws that helps to answer this, in that workshops were required to provide stabling for one man, but since this would accommodate only a few horses, where did they put the rest?

The track record of the mobile field armies was mostly successful. In the west, the Emperor Julian used the armies to good effect against the Alamanni and the Franks on the Rhine, winning a great victory at the battle of Strasbourg even though his army was greatly outnumbered. He followed up his success with subsequent campaigns from 357 to 359, but in the 360s his Persian campaign went badly wrong, and the army was only extracted successfully because the Persians did not react quickly enough to annihilate it. Valentinian I became Emperor in 364 and appointed his brother Valens as his colleague to take charge of the campaigns against the Goths in the eastern half of the Empire, while he concentrated on the west and the repair of the Rhine frontier. Despite Julian's successes after the battle of Strasbourg, the Alamanni had broken through and were raiding Gaul and Raetia. Valentinian's field army of *comitatenses* was supplemented by legions from Illyricum and Italy under the command of the *comes* Sebastianus, and detachments drawn from the *limitanei* or frontier armies. The units of the *limitanei* that were joined to the field army were given the title *pseudo-comitatenses*, but this was probably not intended to be a value judgement suggesting that they were inferior; the term simply distinguished them from the original *comitatenses*. It has been suggested that because the frontier armies ranked lower than the *comitatenses* they must have been inferior to the field armies in quality and fighting capacity, but there was an interchange of troops on occasion, not only by taking *limitanei* to serve in the field armies, but also in reverse by installing field army troops in frontier forts, suggesting that when it came to performance there was not much difference between field and frontier armies.

In major campaigns, the central mobile army and the regional field armies still required supplementary troops from the provinces, and large-scale movements over long distances were not out of the question. Sometimes an extra recruitment drive would be necessary to fill gaps, even if the new soldiers were enlisted on a temporary basis. Allied troops would be engaged on a similar temporary basis as they had always been when the Romans went to war. At the conclusion of the wars the soldiers were probably not sent back to their original bases, but placed in forts on the frontiers and inside the provinces, so given that the various units were moved around it would be difficult to list the troops in one area at any one time. In the army lists of the eastern provinces in the *Notitia Dignitatum* there are several units called *Galli*, which may have arrived with Julian's army from Gaul, and after the campaign ended they did not return to the west but were stationed in the eastern provinces.

The overall commanders of the field armies until the battle of Adrianople in 378 were the emperors themselves, but Valens was the last emperor to lead his troops into battle and therefore the last to lose his life in a war. After this disaster, the command passed to the *magistri militum* who worked on behalf of the emperors. Theodosius I was the last to accompany the army rather than commanding it in the field, and thereafter the *magistri* directed affairs, sometimes squabbling among themselves in their bids for power. The armies of the east under Theodosius were dispersed, divided into five units each under a *magister militum*, but in the west there was no dispersion and the army command was centralised, especially under Stilicho at the turn of the fourth and fifth centuries. The western field armies can be glimpsed in action from time to time, for instance under Stilicho in 401–402 with the defeat of Alaric and the Goths, and in 406 when Stilicho defeated another group of Goths under Radagaisus. Flavius Constantius became *magister militum* after Stilicho was executed by Honorius in 408, and in 410 he started to force the Goths out of Gaul and into Spain.

Frontier Armies

The division of the Roman military forces into field and frontier armies was achieved under Constantine, and although connections were not completely severed between the two, from his reign onwards the armies evolved into different entities. Diocletian's thorough reconstitution of the frontiers was completed by Constantine, who attended to the Rhine and Danube river frontiers. He established bridgehead forts at Divitia (modern Deutz) opposite Cologne, and Mainz-Kastel opposite Mainz. On the Danube he may have been responsible for the bridgehead fort of Celamantia opposite Brigetio (Szőny, Hungary). After successful campaigns against the Sarmatians, there are hints that a major reorganisation of the Danube frontier took place under Constantine. Diocletian had kept the legions in their bases and installed cavalry units in the forts along the river frontiers, but Constantine may have redistributed the legions in detachments and incorporated the cavalry into the field army. He strengthened the frontier of Pannonia around the Danube bend by a chain of forts and watchtowers, and units called *cunei equitum* appear in place of the *alae* which seem to have disappeared, and the infantry cohorts were moved to the hinterland, with the new-style *auxilia* being put in their place.

The law dated to 325, referred to above, lists the terms of service and privileges of soldiers and veterans, and makes it clear that there were now three classes or grades of troops, starting with the most important, the *comitatenses*, and then the frontier troops or *ripenses* (sometimes called *riparienses*) comprising all the higher-grade frontier troops, the legions, the mounted units simply designated as *equites*, the *cunei equitum* and the *auxilia*. Finally there were the less important *alares* and *cohortales*. The frontier troops were comparable to field army troops in many ways, but they served for longer than the *comitatenses* and did not share the same tax benefits on retirement.

The law of 325 does not mention *limitanei*, a term that may not have been in common usage in the early fourth century, but it eventually comprised all the frontier troops which were based on the *limites*, including the lower-grade *alares* and *cohortales*. By the sixth century, the meaning of the term *limitanei* had changed, signifying a special kind of frontier militia whose soldiers were tied to the land, which they were legally bound to cultivate while at the same time being responsible for the protection of the frontiers and the cities. The literary sources of the fifth and sixth centuries may sometimes have interpreted the *limitanei* of the previous century as a militia, which is not correct. The later meaning of the word may have been responsible for engendering the opinion that the frontier troops of the fourth century were ineffective, but as mentioned above, contingents of the frontier armies were incorporated into the *comitatenses*, which ought to indicate that they were not an ill-organised rabble but were trained soldiers ready to fight on equal terms with the field armies.

The frontier commands of the *duces* were not standardised in terms of number or types of troops, but were tailored to current circumstances, and could change over time. As stated in the previous chapter, their titles were usually quite specific about their sphere of influence, for instance the *dux Aegypti Thebaidos utrarumque Libyarum* commanded Egypt and a part of North Africa. The title, meaning 'leader', had been used for temporary commands such as the *dux* in Macedonia during the reign of Gallienus, who commanded vexillations from two legions. In the mid-third century, the title began to take on a more regular aspect. There was a *dux ripae Mesopotamiae* based at Dura Europos. Some commands were very small, and in these instances the *dux* could be responsible to the provincial governor. When Diocletian began to reorganise the Empire he installed *duces* in command of frontier troops in different areas, but this was not a universal development that took place all at once. If there was a need for a unified frontier command, the *dux* was probably installed quite early, but in other areas where there was no pressing need for defence, the provincial governors remained in command even after the reign of Diocletian. No *dux* is attested in Tripolitania until the end of the fourth century. The simple phrase explaining that 'civil and military commands were separated' conceals a slow and gradual evolution.

When Valentinian I had completed his campaigns on the Rhine principally against the Alamanni, and had also brought peace to the Danube, he began to overhaul the frontiers, repairing older installations, and building watchtowers on threatened sectors of the Danube. On the lower Danube Valens did the same after a victory over the Goths in 369. Valentinian placed sections of the field army in the forts, obviously intending his arrangements to be permanent. This was the last phase of building and repair on the northern frontiers. The Danube was continually attacked, but the Roman garrisons had been reduced. The frontier of Noricum was depleted when Gratian took troops to the east in 378, and the garrison was never built up again. Only the southern part of the province was maintained in the fifth century. On the Pannonian frontier, forts and watchtowers went out of use by the end of the fourth century, and all the inhabitants who could get away migrated to Dalmatia or Italy, leaving the lands open to the Goths and the Alani. Though there were twelve *duces* listed in the *Notitia Dignitatum* for the Rhine and Danube frontiers at the beginning of the fifth century, and the general Aetius won a victory over the Huns in the mid-fifth century, the western Empire was being taken over by different groups of tribes, and the frontiers had ceased to function. The Franks occupied much of Gaul, and the Alamanni overwhelmed the Rhine and areas beyond it, with the results still tangible in modern times, in that the Germans call France Frankreich, and the French call Germany Allemagne.

In Africa the late Roman frontier forces were commanded by the *comes Africae*, who also commanded a field army of about 20,000 men, and was senior to the *dux Tripolitaniae* and the *dux Mauretaniae*. At the beginning of the fifth century, the *Notitia Dignitatum* lists seven *duces* in the African provinces, but eventually the defence of part of this very long frontier was relegated to the *gentiles* who seem to have been natives commanded by their own officers, and the fortified structures associated with them appear more primitive than Roman buildings. They became farmer-soldiers defending their own lands. By the middle of the fifth century the Vandal kingdom had been established in the territory around Carthage, and the frontiers had ceased to exist. The invasions did not come from the south, across the frontiers, but from the sea, and when the Arab conquest took place centuries later, the invasion came through Syria.

The northern frontier of Britain was under the command of the *dux Britanniarum*, the genitive plural indicating that he controlled more than one British province. Britain had been divided into four smaller provinces in the later Roman Empire, with a fifth provincial name attested, but no information as to where exactly it was. The garrison of Hadrian's Wall and other parts of Britain may have been depleted when the usurper Magnus Maximus took troops away in 383 to fight for supremacy in Gaul, and again in 407 when Constantine III left the island taking some troops with him. The outpost forts north of Hadrian's Wall were given up, perhaps in the mid-fourth century, but until the troubles of 367 the areas beyond the frontier were evidently watched by the *arcani*, or *areani*, usually interpreted as scouts, who had proved less than loyal. Archaeological evidence shows that Hadrian's Wall was repaired in the later fourth century, and though the repairs are not closely dated it is hard to resist the temptation to attribute the work to the *comes* Theodosius who restored order after the disasters of 367. At Housesteads the flimsy barracks arranged in lines of small individual buildings, labelled 'chalets' by the archaeologists, may have housed soldiers and their families. It is known that the *vici* were abandoned at some time, and there is some evidence that the population may have moved into the forts, but this could have been after the British provinces had become separated from the central Roman government. Occupation at Birdoswald extended into the sub-Roman era. When Britain was detached from Rome the soldiers in northern Britain, as on the other frontiers, would no longer be able to rely on the infrastructure of the supply system and pay, and perhaps became self-reliant farmers based in the forts until such a way of life became untenable.

The forts of the Saxon Shore on the southern coast of Britain can also be interpreted as a frontier, but less is known about its organisation. The forts date from different periods from the early third century to the later Empire, and were not originally intended to function together until the threat to the coasts from the Saxons and other tribes became endemic, then they were placed under the command of the *comes Litoris Saxonici*, count of the Saxon Shore, whose title provided the name by which modern historians know these forts. The final fate of the Shore forts is not known in detail, but it seems that some of them had gone out of use before Britain parted from Roman government at the beginning of the fifth century. Possibly by the second half of the fourth century military functions had ceased at some of the forts, and what has been termed 'disorderly occupation' into the fifth century may indicate civilian settlement within the defensive walls.

The frontier which survived for the longest period was the eastern one, protected eventually by the Byzantine Empire. Many of the units of the earlier Empire survived into the fifth century, and in the *Notitia Dignitatum* sixteen legions are listed at bases stretching from Armenia to Arabia and the border with Egypt. Diocletian installed cavalry units in each of the eastern provinces, including some mounted archers raised from the native population. The concentration of troops in the east was greater than it had been at the beginning of the third century and the greatest concentration of the late Empire was in Armenia, always the trouble spot in relation to the Persians. The position of Constantinople lent itself to the protection of the city from attacks from the Danube, as successive walls were built across the peninsula. The truncated Byzantine Empire did not fall until the fifteenth century, and the eastern frontier strengthened by Diocletian and Constantine and his successors held out until the seventh century, first overrun by the Persians, won back by the Byzantines, and finally succumbing to the Islamic conquest.

Arms and Armour of the Late Roman Armies

After the disruption of the frontiers in the third century, some forts on the Rhine and Danube were given up, and some of auxiliary units were relocated or disappeared from the record. The legions that garrisoned the bases behind the frontiers were split up into vexillations which did not return to their parent units. Simon James points out that this disruption would have adversely affected the production and repair of arms and armour that was normally carried out at the forts, allowing the army to be as self-sufficient as possible. The army had always utilised civilian production when necessary, and sometimes during wars the allies of Rome were asked to provide armour and equipment. Even in peacetime the soldiers and especially the officers could obtain their equipment from small civilian workshops, but from the end of the third century under Diocletian and his successors this became the normal means of production. Arms factories called *fabricae*, the same description that was used for the workshops in the forts, were established in the provincial cities in the zones relating to the Rhine and Danube and the eastern frontiers. By the fifth century, according to the *Notitia Dignitatum*, there were twenty *fabricae* in the western Empire and fifteen in the east.

Body armour after the mid-third century was mostly *lorica hamata* or mail, *lorica segmentata* having been used up to that time, but not widely attested compared to mail shirts, and possibly disappearing after *c.* 260. Scale armour or *lorica squamata* was used alongside mail, consisting of iron or copper scales sewn on to linen or leather corselets. These types of armour became longer from the beginning of the third century, extending below the knees and hitched up by the belt, and some examples probably had long sleeves, as depicted on a sculpture of the early fourth century that may have come from the vanished arch of Diocletian in Rome. Helmets did not change very much from the types used in the second century, except that the cheek pieces were enlarged to protect all the face but for the eyes, nose and mouth. Until the early fourth century the helmet bowl and neck guard were constructed in one piece, but different styles appeared with the bowl made in two parts, with the neck guard attached as a separate piece like the cheek guards. These helmets usually had a ridged metal strip running from front to back. The most common type of shield in the second half of the third century was oval, as attested on art works and more convincingly from finds from Dura Europos, which enabled archaeologists to reconstruct them. The shields were constructed of wooden planks glued together and covered with hide or linen, and edged with rawhide, which would have been easier to obtain and repair than the earlier metal edging. The Dura shields were up to four feet in length and up to three feet wide, with a hole in the centre to accommodate the metal shield boss, several examples of which were found with the remains of the shields. Preserved in the hot dry conditions, the shields still showed their elaborate decoration in paint on the linen or leather covers, and engraving on the bosses. Finds of fourth- and fifth-century shields are rare, but pictorial evidence such as the ivory portrait of Stilicho shows that oval shields were still in use.

The late Roman author Vegetius says that the Romans ceased to use heavy armour after the reign of Gratian which ended in 383, or in other words after the battle of Adrianople in 378 in which the Emperor Valens was killed. Since a great deal of equipment was probably lost in this battle it is possible that the army of the east had to adapt to the loss for some time, but the west probably did not abandon heavy armour for an instant. Besides, the heavy cavalry still existed in the east, with the *clibanarii* wearing mail armour and possibly segmented armour to protect their arms and legs. The horses may have continued to use the bardings of mail or scale that are attested for the third century.

The *gladius* of the earlier period was supplemented from the third century by the long sword called the *spatha*. Shorter swords did not go out of use entirely, as attested by Vegetius who describes *semi-spathae*, longer than the older types but shorter than the more regular *spathae* which were usually carried on the left side suspended from a wide baldric worn over the right shoulder. The *spathae* had wooden scabbards but hardly any examples have survived except for the metal fittings and chapes that strengthened the tips of the scabbards. In the fourth century the baldric may have been replaced by a waist belt, as shown on the ivory portrait of Stilicho. A variety of spears are known from the third and fourth centuries. The *pilum* survived, renamed the *spiculum* by the fourth century according to Vegetius. It had a triangular head measuring nine inches in Roman measure, slightly shorter than English measure, and a wooden shaft about five Roman feet in length. Socketed iron spearheads can be broadly categorised into long thin versions, elongated triangular versions widest at the base, and leaf-shaped versions widest in the middle. Barbed spearheads with a lead weight attached to the base of the shaft appeared in the fourth century, called *plumbata*, or described by Vegetius as *mattiobarbalus*, which is probably a miscopying for *martiobarbalus* meaning barb of Mars. Vegetius says that each solider was armed with five of them. Composite bows, and arrows of various types were used by the *sagittarii* units in the late armies, and factories producing them are listed in the western sections of the *Notitia Dignitatum*, two in Italy and one in Gaul. Factories producing archery equipment are not listed for the east, but this may be because the archer units mostly drawn from the eastern provinces were already efficiently supplied with equipment from civilian workshops so that there was no need to organise and impose a state-run system. In the late Roman army there were units of Franks who used as their main weapons throwing axes, which could shatter enemy shields, and were therefore used in the initial assault, all at once at a given signal.

The soldiers' clothing consisted of the all-important belt with its metal decorations, and fittings for suspending various items of equipment. The men would wear a linen or wool tunic under their armour, and cloaks. Sculptures on third-century tombstones often show the soldiers wearing their tunics with belts, and their cloaks, but after the third century such sculptured portraits are rare. The mosaics from the villa at Piazza Armerina show men armed with spears and protected by oval shields, wearing long-sleeved, knee-length belted tunics, and no sign of armour. This would seem to support Vegetius' statement that heavy armour was abandoned in the fourth century, but this is far from certain. With the increasing use of Germanic and eastern soldiers, trousers were also worn by some troops.

Although there was great emphasis on cavalry in the late Empire, the infantry troops still formed the backbone of the army, and outnumbered the cavalry. The infantry generally fought in close order, with the men in the front ranks issued with more protective armour, for instance these men may have worn greaves. In the legions, specialists such as the *lanciarii*, archers and artillerymen supported the infantry, and there would be units of archers and spearmen probably on the flanks. Cavalry was divided into light armed and heavy armed units, and would use swords, spears and bows and arrows, so that they could engage at some distance or at close quarters, and could also be used for scouting, patrolling and pursuit after a battle. This brief description sounds very much like the Imperial army of the Principate, but with a different command structure, a preponderance of tribesmen from inside and outside the Empire, and some slightly different equipment and attire.

Problems of Recruitment and the 'Barbarisation' of the Roman Army

In the second half of the fourth century, the two Emperors Valentinian and Valens could not successfully combat all the problems of the Empire. Valentinian had to rely on Count (*comes*) Theodosius to repair the damage in Britain in 367, and had to furnish him with extra troops to take to the island. Three commanders were sent to Africa to subdue the tribesmen of the Mauri who were ravaging the provinces. Wars on several fronts all at the same time stretched manpower resources to the limit and Valentinian and Valens experienced considerable difficulty in recruiting replacements. Diocletian had made it compulsory for sons of soldiers to enlist in the army, but this was not enough to fill all the gaps. Annual conscription had been introduced, with the responsibility for furnishing the stipulated numbers of men resting on the councils of the cities or on the great landowners. During Constantine's reign, there is one case on record where new recruits destined for the *comitatenses* were locked up at nights in case they ran away. Valentinian and Valens passed laws concerning recruitment that became increasingly draconian as time went on. The annual conscription was extended to include workers on Imperial estates. Conscription was resented and the laws demonstrate what had been going on with regard to this enforced recruitment. Some men had been trying to avoid service in the army by masquerading as servants and camp followers, so laws were passed to round them up and enlist them. Desertion had probably always been a problem in the army, but never more so than in the mid-fourth century, when laws were established to seek out deserters and also punish anyone who hid them. The height qualification for recruits was reduced to embrace more manpower, slaves were freed and recruited, and there were severe punishments for men who deliberately mutilated themselves to avoid conscription. Men without a full set of fingers and thumbs were forcibly enlisted and employed in some military capacity, and then later a law was passed condemning self-mutilated men to death by burning, and their masters, if they had any, were also punished for failing to prevent the mutilations. Death by burning was obviously intended as a deterrent, since putting a potential recruit to death somewhat defeated the object of finding men for the army. It is not known if anyone chose this drastic way out of serving in the army. Theodosius I was more realistic, passing a law that made it compulsory to take two mutilated men in place of one undamaged recruit.

The difficulties of recruiting willing candidates for the field armies or the frontier armies, as illustrated by the successively severe laws of the fourth century, directed the Romans to the seemingly inexhaustible manpower of the many tribes and subgroups all around the Empire. Many tribesmen had been settled within the Empire, and given lands to cultivate, in return for which they had to provide men for the army. Many other tribesmen were drafted into the army en masse when wars were ended and treaties were made, so the presence of tribesmen in the armies was nothing new. Groups of barbarians were given different names, such as *laeti*, *gentiles*, and *foederati*, which may indicate subtle differences between them. The *laeti* were settled in Gaul and Italy in the later third century, and groups of them are attested in the late Roman army. Constantius Chlorus settled Franks around Trier, Amiens, and Langres in Gaul after he had defeated them in battle, and Julian allowed another group of Salian Franks to settle around the mouth of the Rhine, where they became partly Romanised, kept the peace for about a hundred years, and gradually extended their territory without raising any objections from the original natives. The Franks remained at ease between the two worlds, as attested by a gravestone of a Frank who died while serving in the Roman army, whose epitaph reads *Francus ego cives, Romanus miles in armis*, 'I am a Frankish citizen and a Roman soldier under arms'.

The settlements of the *laeti* were supervised by military personnel, and a law of 369 refers to a *praepositus* in charge of a group of them, though it is not known what his rank would have been, since the title was given to widely divergent types of officer. By the fourth and fifth centuries, there were about a dozen *praefecti laetorum* in Gaul, which may imply that the appointments of officials in charge of the *laeti* had become more regular. Another law of 399 refers to *terrae laeticae*, lands set aside for the *laeti*. In some documents *laeti* and *gentiles* are mentioned together, with an implication that *gentiles* ranked lower than *laeti* simply because they are always listed in second place. This may be purely incidental, and the origins and status of *gentiles* are not fully understood. Units of *gentiles* served in Diocletian's *scholae* or bodyguard.

The *foederati* are more difficult to define because the term embraced different kinds of troops, the common denominator being that they were raised subject to the terms of a treaty (*foedus*), but the title was also applied to groups of tribesmen who gathered around a leader, such as Alaric the Goth, whose followers comprised many different ethnic groups, so it has been questioned whether he was the leader of a nation or an army. The *foederati* attached to the Roman army were at first commanded by their native leaders, subject to the Roman high command. They were engaged for the duration of a campaign, as in the Republic and early Empire, and then sent home at the end of the wars. By the sixth century the *foederati* of the eastern Empire were regular troops in the army, not just attached to it for campaigns. They were subject to the same discipline and training regimes as the rest of the army and were paid like the other soldiers. More importantly they were not exclusively of tribal origin, and contained many Romans. Caution is therefore required in using literary sources concerning the *foederati*, since the term denotes two distinct types of troops, depending on the date of the sources.

In 382 the Emperor Theodosius I made a treaty with the Goths which seemed to depart from the usual arrangements, in that the units that he raised were commanded by Gothic officers. Modern scholars dispute the exact meaning of this, suggesting that the Goths were only given subordinate commands, and were ultimately responsible to Roman officers. Later authors of the Roman world such as Zosimus deplored this arrangement and blamed Theodosius and the Goths for the ultimate decline of the Roman world. The judgement is unfair to the Goths who were serving in the regular army and the units raised by Theodosius, since they served Rome well, but it was probably hard to dispel the prejudice derived from the devastation that the Goths brought to the Empire from the early third century onwards. At the end of the fourth century and the beginning of the fifth the eastern army purged itself of the Goths. After the battle of Adrianople in 378 sealed orders were sent out to the army commanders to summon the Goths to a pay parade and kill them. Another group was massacred at Tomi in 386, and yet another after a Gothic leader called Gainas raised a revolt at Constantinople which was put down. After this the eastern army recruited locally, chiefly from the Isaurian tribesmen, keeping the numbers small and more easily controlled, and since they were defending their homelands the tribesmen had more interest in serving loyally. For the first years of the fifth century the eastern army struggled to defeat the Huns without the Goths to help them, but they won in the end, came to an understanding with Persia and threw all their energies into defending the Danube.

The western army could not so easily rid itself of tribesmen. Many of its high-ranking officers were drawn from barbarian tribes, such as Valentinian's *magister militum* Arbogast who was a Frank, and Stilicho, the most important commander in the west under Honorius, who was a Vandal. The western Empire never ceased to recruit barbarians into the army, but after the execution of Stilicho, Roman commanders were appointed instead of tribesmen. Almost all the *magistri militum* from 408 onwards were Romans, but when the Roman general Aetius defeated Attila and the Huns in 451 at the battle of the Catalaunian Plains, his army was made up of many different tribal contingents. He used Huns to fight Huns, and had persuaded the Visigoths of Gaul to join him. Aetius was a Roman general but his army was no longer a Roman army. Just over two decades later, Rome was ruled by Odoacer, a Roman citizen but a barbarian by origin, and the western Empire had become a collection of nascent barbarian kingdoms. Long before this the terms *milites*, soldiers, and *barbari*, or tribesmen, had become synonymous, as demonstrated by the lament of a woman in Egypt who complained that her son had gone to join the barbarians, by which she meant that he had joined the army.

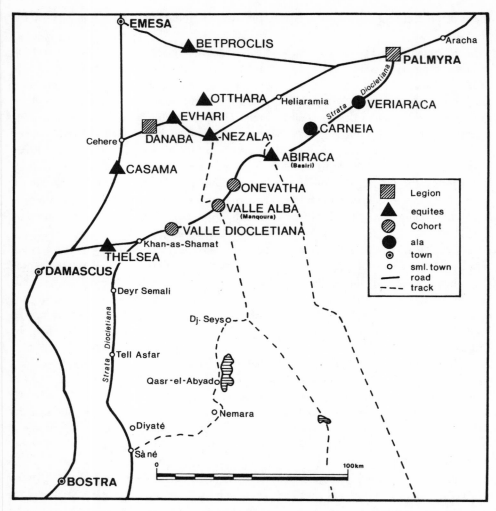

Diocletian repaired the frontiers and established soldiers along them, though they were not all
solid barriers. This map shows the eastern frontier guarded by a road, the Strata Diocletiana,
running from beyond Palmyra to Damascus and Bostra, as reconstructed by D. van Berchem from
archaeological evidence and literary sources. Drawn by Graeme Stobbs.

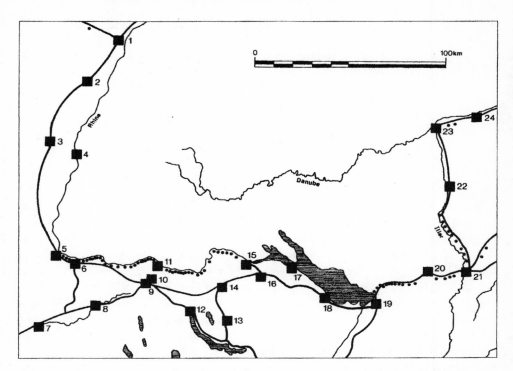

Parts of the old frontiers of the second century were no longer tenable during the late Empire, so the Romans withdrew to the south of the former frontier line joining the Rhine to the Danube, and gradually created a new fortified line known in modern terms as the Danube-Iller-Rhine *limes*. It was manned by forts and watchtowers along the line and supported by forts to the rear. Diocletian and Constantine may have begun the work of fortification or refortification, but this frontier is generally associated with Valentinian I in the mid-fourth century. Redrawn by Graeme Stobbs from W. Drack *Die Spätrömische Grenzwehr am Hochrhein*. Archäologische Führer der Schweiz 13, Zurich, 1980.

Key to numbered sites: 1. Strasbourg (Argentorate) 2. Ebl (Helvetum) 3. Horburg (Argentovaria) 4. Breisach (Brisiacum) 5. Basle (Basilia) 6. Kaiseraugst (Castrum Rauracense) 7. Solothurn (Salodurum) 8. Olten 9. Altenburg 10. Windisch (Vindonissa) 11. Zurzach (Tenedo) 12. Zurich (Turicum) 13. Irgenhausen 14. Winterthur (Vitudurum) 15. Burg (Tasgaetium) 16. Pfyn (Ad Fines) 17. Constance 18. Arbon (Arbor Felix) 19. Bregenz (Brigantium) 20. Bettmauer (Vemania) 21. Kempten (Cambodunum) 22. Kellmünz (Caelius Mons) 23. Uncertain: Febiana? 24. Günzburg (Guntia)

4

Forts and Fortifications

From the later third century fortification extended to cities, towns, villas and farms as well as forts and frontier establishments. New building or rebuilding is found in most provinces because the threat to security was now internal as well as external. The frontiers were not manned in the same strength as they had been in the second century. Several forts of the northern frontiers had been given up, and although different emperors conducted campaigns beyond the frontiers this did not provide a solution to the incursions of the tribesmen, and campaigns against the Persians never resulted in a decisive outcome. Internally the policing by the army no longer eradicated bandits and brigands as it had done from the first century to the end of the second century. Large groups of brigands were formed in some areas in the later third century, such as the Bagaudae in Gaul, who first entered the historical record in 286. Self-reliance and self-help were natural responses to the problems if the government and the army could not provide immediate assistance. Perceived threat is just as compelling as real threat, and the reaction to it is often based on the premise that prevention is at least as effective as a cure, and cheaper in the long run in terms of lives and property.

Under Gallienus the main repairs and new fortification were undertaken in the wake of the invasions of the Goths in the 240s and 250s, which had ravaged Thrace. Cities which had been damaged were repaired, and unprotected cities received new walls. Claudius Gothicus ruled for only a short time and was preoccupied in fighting the Goths, so the Danube frontier probably had to wait until the reigns of Aurelian and Probus before military installations received attention. On the Rhine the Gallic emperors, chiefly Postumus from 260 onwards, tried to fortify the road posts around Cologne by rebuilding earlier earth and timber installations in stone, but the work was done in haste, and was somewhat flimsy, so it had to be strengthened later on. Stephen Johnson dates the reuse of some hill forts and establishment of hilltop refuges in Raetia and Gaul to this period. Some have yielded dated finds, while others show signs of occupation which cannot be closely dated but probably do belong to this period of insecurity, when civilians looked out for their own protection.

After the reign of Gallienus several emperors restored frontier works but there is an imbalance in the sources that results in all the credit being given to Diocletian at the turn of the third and fourth centuries, and to a lesser extent Constantine who continued what Diocletian had begun. In the later fourth century Valentinian was the most active in rebuilding and repairing frontiers and establishing road posts and fortified towers. The work of Aurelian and Probus is submerged in the work of Diocletian, and the gaps in knowledge about who did what, where, and when will probably never be answered even by archaeological investigation, since patterns can only be observed by widespread and long-term excavation producing accurately datable finds. The lack of dating evidence for the later third century makes it difficult to distinguish the work of

Diocletian's predecessors. Aurelian's claim to fame under the heading of fortification concerns the walls of Rome, but according to the *Historia Augusta*, he also repaired forts on the Danube, and Gregory of Tours, writing in the later sixth century, repeats the tradition that Aurelian built the walls of the city of Dijon. If this is so, it is unlikely that Aurelian devoted attention to just one city and ignored other civilian settlements, road posts and forts, but the archaeological or documentary evidence is lacking. Whatever he may have achieved in Gaul, some of his work was probably undone in the raids that occurred in 276. This damage was repaired by Probus. The meagre source material indicates that Probus restored about sixty cities, but it is not certain what 'restored' means. It is not clear whether he built entirely new walls for undefended cities and towns, or repaired sections of existing defensive circuits, gateways and battlements, or even repaired internal buildings which had suffered in the raids. He may have lent soldiers and military architects to help with the work, but there is no evidence to prove this. Two forts were built in the gap between the Rhine and Danube at Isny and Goldberg, and there were probably others that date to Aurelian's and/or Probus' reign, since a couple of isolated forts was hardly likely to plug the gap effectively in this area. In Britain and Gaul, Probus perhaps attended to the defence of the coasts on either side of the Channel against piratical raids.

By Diocletian's time the frontiers looked very different from those of the second century, or even from the frontiers that Septimius Severus had inherited and repaired in the early third century. The damage caused on the German frontiers in the 230s had been repaired, and even in the 240s repair work was still being done, implying that the Romans were confident that their systems would endure, but ten years later reconstitution of the frontiers had slowed to an almost complete halt. In the decades between 250 and 280 huge tracts of territory between the Rhine and Danube were abandoned and left devoid of defences, Dacia was evacuated, parts of Moesia were undefended and Mauretania Tingitana on the western edge of North Africa was lost. In Britain the frontier was still functioning, but at least at one fort on Hadrian's Wall, Birdoswald, an inscription recording rebuilding in the Diocletianic period explains for all and sundry to read that the buildings undergoing repair, such as the headquarters building and the commander's house, had fallen into ruin and been covered with earth. According to one school of thought, declarations such as these on inscriptions are euphemisms for destruction by enemy action, but at least in this instance it probably does mean that Birdoswald had been abandoned and had stood empty for some considerable time. It is not known how far this applied to the other Wall forts.

Under Diocletian rebuilding and new building affected almost the whole Empire. Wars were still fought in various locations, but when the Tetrarchy was established the burden was shared and there was at last some time to devote to long-term planning. Analysis of the problems could be undertaken, and feasible solutions proposed. Though this is largely based on guesswork, Diocletian seemed to have formulated an overall plan for defence, which could be adapted to the needs of different frontiers and provinces. In some cases he may have supervised the siting of new military establishments, especially in the east, in Egypt, Mesopotamia and Syria. The eastern frontier road known as the Strata Diocletiana was a complete system rather than just a line of forts, with surveillance facilities and back-up installations. In the west, Diocletian may have been initially responsible for the Danube-Iller-Rhine frontier between the two great rivers, though some forts probably belonged to Probus, and the predominant building and repair work is that of Valentinian.

On some frontiers small square forts, called *quadriburgia*, began to appear, and similar installations are known in Africa as *centenaria*. The internal buildings in these small forts were arranged all around the inner perimeter. Harbours and landing places on the river frontiers were fortified, along with granaries and food stores. Existing forts were altered and given new external towers, especially on the Danube where projecting fan-shaped corner towers were built to give the occupants of the forts extra supervision of the walls. Despite the accusation of Zosimus that Diocletian strengthened the frontiers and Constantine ruined them by taking the troops away for the field army, Constantine did continue Diocletian's defence work, establishing bridgehead forts on the Rhine at Deutz opposite Cologne and Mainz-Kastel opposite Mainz. Some of the *quadriburgia* and *centenaria* attributed to Diocletian may have been completed or even built by Constantine. The late Roman author Procopius, who recorded Justinian's major rebuilding programme in the eastern Empire in the sixth century, attributes the foundation of three of the eastern forts to Diocletian.

Not much is known of frontier works after Constantine. The civil wars will have distracted attention away from the defence of the Empire, but there were measures against brigands and bandits in the Danube area. In Gaul under Julian some forts were repaired or reoccupied, and repairs were undertaken to city defences. There seems to have been no new building, possibly because by the time of Julian's campaigns against the Alamanni most cities already possessed walls. In the east Constantius II concentrated on fortifying the Euphrates frontier with towers.

The most widespread reconstruction of the frontiers occurred under Valentinian and Valens. According to Ammianus Marcellinus, Valentinian developed an integrated Imperial programme for frontier defence and fortification of cities and towns. Ammianus says that he refortified the entire Rhine frontier. Valentinian established forts across the Rhine and Danube, though he had better success on the Danube frontier, having been driven back at one point when he crossed the Rhine and tried to build a fort. A bridgehead fort was built opposite Basle, and named Robur, meaning strong. Watchtowers or *burgi* proliferated in some sectors of the northern frontiers, complete with lengthy inscriptions recording the fact, and Valentinian wrote to the *dux Daciae ripensis* in very stern terms to encourage him to build his annual quota of towers and keep the existing ones in repair. The towers by themselves could not defend the frontiers, and the numbers of the soldiers who manned them were too small to be effective, but the emphasis was on surveillance of the frontiers and on providing early warning of any attempts to cross them into the Empire. It is not exactly certain how the system worked, but it is reasonable to suppose that forts behind the frontiers received notice of incursions and mustered to combat them.

This was the last great building programme of the western half of the Empire. As the tribesmen grew in strength and numbers the northern frontiers of the late Roman Empire could not contain them, and would perhaps not have been able to do so even if they had been fortified and manned in the same density as they had been in the second century. Given that tribesmen had first broken through in the 230s and caused serious damage to a sector of the Taunus-Wetterau frontier even when it was fully manned, and again in the 260s, the gradual reliance on fortification of military posts and civilian settlements behind the frontier, rather than on the frontier garrisons alone, was perhaps an inevitable consequence, though it evolved slowly over the next hundred years.

The establishment of the central mobile armies, assembled in addition to the frontier armies, made it possible to respond as quickly as possible to attacks without gathering frontier troops and denuding the forts and running barriers while battles were fought, but in the end the pressures were too great and there was simply not enough manpower to keep all the frontier installations fully manned and the field armies functioning. The wastage rate from casualties in war, from disease such as the plague which broke out in 257, and from desertion could not be matched by recruitment unless enormous numbers of tribesmen could be brought in, and without them the western Empire would probably have succumbed to the strain even sooner than it did. The frontiers were gradually eroded despite the attention from the emperors of the later third century and their successors, while the cities and towns and even villas and farms were fortified. The American scholar Edward Luttwak interpreted the system as defence in depth, allowing the tribesmen to penetrate the Empire and then dealing with them from strongholds inside the provinces, where cities were fortified to resist the attacks until the army could disperse the invaders. There was considerable controversy among historians concerning Luttwak's theories, but as Stephen Johnson points out, in the fourth century and beyond, the fortified cities were able to resist and survive attacks, so static defence proved successful when the mobile defence provided by the army was no longer effective.

Military Fortifications

Roman forts and fortresses of the first two and a half centuries AD were equipped with defences such as walls and gates with towers on either side, supplemented by interval and corner towers, and the whole installation was usually surrounded by a ditch or ditches designed to prevent anyone from approaching too close to the walls. It was not envisaged that large-scale attacks would take place, and it was only in the east that sieges could be undertaken by Rome's enemies. The Parthians, succeeded by the Persians, were capable of mounting and maintaining a siege of a Roman fort, but did not do so on a regular basis. In the west, if there was a civil war, a siege by a Roman army was rare but not out of the question, but the tribes who attacked Rome from beyond the Rhine and Danube, and in Africa, did not have the cohesion and organisation for establishing siege works or for sustaining long sieges, mostly because when they had exhausted the food supplies of the immediate area there was no system for supplying their armies.

In the early Empire, Roman forts were bases where the army lived and worked, and kept their stores and records. While territory was being fought over and bases shifted regularly as the army moved, forts might be attacked, but when a province was brought under Roman rule, fighting was generally done outside forts as the army marched to meet its opponents in the open.

In the second half of the third century forts began to change in design and appearance, and a whole range of new fortifications began to be built. The frontiers remained as they had been designed, with cordons of forts and watchtowers to guard them, but more thinly spread out as the third century progressed into the fourth. The Danube-Iller Rhine frontier was built to the south of the old frontier. In concept it remained the same as the earlier frontiers, but the defended line was no longer sufficient to protect the provinces behind the frontiers. In the hinterland communication and supply routes had usually been undefended, but in the third century these routes could not be left as open as they had been, because the invading tribesmen were fast moving and difficult to catch and halt, and could therefore penetrate the interior zones of the provinces. In addition, the insecurity was compounded by roving bands of brigands inside the provinces which became more of a serious menace in the third century, a phenomenon that was probably related to the destruction and the loss of property and livelihoods, and ensuing poverty. It is significant that during the more peaceful prosperous times of the first two centuries of Imperial rule, brigandage was not such a serious problem, and ancient authors were able to comment on the lack of disturbances and lawlessness, describing how the emperors and their armies kept bandits under control.

Late Roman forts are usually much more sturdily built than their predecessors, demonstrating that the Romans perceived the threats as more serious than they had been until the second half of the third century. It became necessary to block access routes into forts, and to watch the whole length of the defensive walls, which seems to indicate that the approach of hostiles to the forts was not ruled out. Access to early Roman forts was obtained via at least four gates, one in each of the two long and two short sides of a rectangular enclosure, but at forts of the old type which were retained in the late third century, access was limited to a reduced number of gates, in most cases to only one gate in the majority of excavated examples. The other gates were blocked off, sometimes by completely enclosing them in outward-projecting towers. This is particularly noticeable in some forts of the Danube frontier of Pannonia, particularly around the Danube bend facing the Hungarian plains. At Ulcisia Castra and Drobeta, only one gate remained accessible, and the smaller flanking towers which hardly projected beyond the line of the walls were augmented at both forts by the addition of strongly built projecting D-shaped towers, which were placed closer together and thus narrowed the original entrance passage. At both forts, projecting fan-shaped towers were built at the corners over the smaller internal square ones, which would have been of little use in surveying the walls or firing missiles along them. From the fan-shaped towers archers or light artillery would have been able to enfilade the walls and eliminate most of the attackers. This is not a concept that would have been endorsed in the earlier Empire. It is usually stated in modern works that frontiers such as Hadrian's Wall and the forts along it were not designed to be defended like castles, from behind crenelated parapets, but by the later Empire a rudimentary castle mentality had begun to enter Roman defensive systems, about six centuries before castles were 'invented'.

Just as the entire complement of a frontier sector had been reduced by giving up some forts on the Rhine and Danube, some forts were retained with a smaller garrison. The classic example of a fort reduced in size was excavated at Eining on the Danube, where a smaller fort was installed in the south-west corner of the original auxiliary fort, using a short stretch of the southern and western walls as it defences, with a ditch forming the eastern and northern perimeters, separating it from the rest of the fort. This ditch cuts into the southern wall of the headquarters building of the earlier fort. On the south wall of the small fort, which represents the western portion of the original fort wall, a rectangular tower was built projecting from the wall over the outer ditch of the earlier fort, probably to protect the access route to the gate by firing missiles.

The small square fort at Eining has been interpreted in two different ways, as a much reduced garrison post, perhaps using the walls of the earlier fort as the enclosure for an annexe, and as a citadel, somewhat like a castle keep. There are some problems with this latter assumption, one being that the original south gate of the earlier fort was retained, giving access directly into the so-called citadel between the new ditch on the right and the stone-built wall of the small square fort on the left. A citadel would function more efficiently if the south gate had been blocked up altogether and equipped with a projecting tower, and access had been arranged via one of the other gates into the larger original fort, similar to the outer bailey of a castle with the keep separated from it by a ditch. At Eining, the ditch surrounding the small fort on two sides appears to run from the eastern tower of the south gate to join the original fort wall on the western side, without a break. If there was access from the small fort into and out of the larger fort it was presumably by means of a wooden bridge over the ditch, which probably rotted and disappeared, though no traces of post holes appear on the plan. Another indication that the small square fort at Eining was meant to operate as an independent fort is its similarity in size and shape to the *quadriburgia* that were established by Diocletian and Constantine. Two rows of buildings were attached to the eastern and northern walls of the Eining fort, reminiscent of the internal buildings of a *quadriburgium* which clustered together all around the internal perimeters of the walls.

Small square forts or *quadriburgia* are found all over the Empire, most probably dating from the Diocletianic period and supplemented under Constantine. These *quadriburgia* vary slightly in design but share common characteristics, being more or less square with enclosing walls of about fifty metres in length, with only one gate with a single passageway, flanked by towers projecting beyond the walls. Interval towers and corner towers also served to protect the walls themselves. Internal buildings consisting of small cubicles are arranged all around the walls, presumably to house the garrison. Other internal buildings have not been as closely investigated as the perimeter cubicles, but at Bourada in Numidia there appears to have been a headquarters building, or at least a large rectangular building that faces the main gate. At Qasr Bshir in Jordan, the four corner towers of the *quadriburgium* are larger than most and each one contains an entrance passage and three separate rooms, probably to house officers of the unit stationed there. Another feature at Qasr Bshir was that the buildings were on two storeys, so if this applied to other forts of the same type, it is possible that the size of the occupying forces, as calculated from the ground plans alone, is incorrect. The *quadriburgia* are not confined to the east and Africa. In Switzerland there are fortifications of similar size and plan at Schaan, and at Irgenhausen, south of the Danube-Iller-Rhine frontier. Both these forts were originally thought to be Diocletianic, largely because of their design, but they are now considered to belong to the reign of Valentinian. The square plan with towers is an eminently useful defensive design, as demonstrated by a very similar fort at Theangela in Caria in south-west Asia Minor, south of the River Maeander, which divides Caria from Lydia. A brief glance at the plan of the Theangela fort immediately brings to mind the *quadriburgia* of Diocletian and Constantine, but this fort is much older than the Roman forts of the later Empire, since it belongs to the Hellenistic era of the fourth to the first centuries BC. This warns against using typology and design of forts as a guide to their foundation dates, unless there is a collection of forts on a frontier line or along a road, all sharing similar shapes, sizes and designs, ideally with at least one of them producing securely dated evidence of its foundation.

Some forts of the later Empire were irregularly shaped, departing from the traditional rectangular or square plan. At Passau the riverside fort at Boiodurum is trapezoidal, like another fort at Alta Ripa (modern Altrip) on the Rhine. Both are comparable with the *quadriburgia* in that the internal perimeters are lined with continuous rows of buildings and they both have only one gate and projecting corner towers. The ground plan of the surrounding walls at Altrip bears a close resemblance to the artillery defences of the seventeenth century, with corner towers shaped like an arrowhead, allowing missile fire to cover all the ground in an arc from the projecting tower, and especially to enfilade the walls on both sides. At the opposite extreme, the late fort at Pevensey in southern England differs from any of its companion forts of the Saxon Shore, which were built at different dates. Pevensey may have been the last fort of this series to be built. It is a large ovoid with projecting D-shaped towers, and only one surviving gate, though there may have been more entrances, in the eroded southern and northern sectors of the walls. The other late Saxon Shore forts such as Portchester, Burgh Castle, and Richborough, which was built over a civilian settlement and the remains of earlier forts, are square or rectangular with projecting towers and more than one gate. The late Roman fort at Cardiff was of similar design and date, and its outline is preserved, having been reconstructed on the same ground plan by the Marquess of Bute in the nineteenth century. These forts are connected with defence against attacks from the sea, but the unknown factor is how they worked. They were massive, and probably housed large numbers of men, but the internal buildings remain largely unknown. This applies to many late forts, where there is rarely any trace of a headquarters building or anything approximating to an administrative centre.

Apart from the frontier forts other posts were fortified in the later Empire. Internal roads required guard posts strung out along them, combining military defence and policing. While it is possible to make a distinction between the two functions, in the Roman world the army performed both tasks, and the existence of lines of fortified posts cannot be said to have been dedicated exclusively to one or the other. In mountainous areas, watching or blocking passes by means of fortified posts would have been vitally important. In Numidia the routes through the Aurès mountains were watched by small forts, and in the Alps some passes could be blocked, as the usurper Magnentius did when fighting against Constantius II. It has been suggested that in the fifth century the Huns could have been stopped if Aetius had blocked the passes. There are traces of walls across passes in the Alps but there is little evidence with which to date them.

Free-standing watchtowers of many designs were used on routes and coasts, proliferating in the fourth century. Four-post timber versions had been erected in Flavian times, by Agricola in Scotland and by Vespasian or Domitian in Germany. Most frontiers were equipped with watchtowers, and in the later Empire so were routes. Commodus had built a series of stone *burgi* to counter the threat from *latrones*, or *latrunculi*, which places the function of the towers and the troops in the category of police work. Diocletian, Constantine and Valentinian made full use of watchtowers on frontiers and routes. The way in which they functioned is not known, and to label them signal towers is probably only part of the answer, though surveillance involves transmitting information to someone so that the situation can be dealt with. There were sophisticated methods of transmitting messages in the Roman world, as described in detail by authors such as Polybius, who gives details of a system for transmitting individual letters by using different combinations of torches, but in a watchtower such sophistication was not possible and perhaps not necessary. Trumpet signals, smoke signals by day and torches at night, and messengers on horseback could all be used as advance warning systems provided that there was a receiving station and available troops to march to the threatened points. The experiment in Jordan with lit torch signals given at night has already been mentioned in a previous chapter. All the signals were visible at a small fort on the heights above the legionary base at El Lejjun, and familiarity with the geography of the area would enable observers to work out precisely where the trouble was. The late Roman towers on the Yorkshire coast in England were very well fortified, consisting of a square tower surrounded by an outer wall with corner towers, and beyond that an external ditch, rendering these towers more like a cross between a watchtower and a fort, which is how an inscription from Ravenscar describes this particular tower. The coastal towers may have served as an early warning system against sea-raiders, perhaps giving time for civilians to seek refuge and for troops to assemble, but where they would come from is debatable. The legion at York, *VI Victrix*, survived long enough to be included in the *Notitia Dignitatum* under the command of the *dux Britanniarum*, but it remains conjectural whether any of the soldiers were detailed to coastal defence to respond to early warnings from the towers. Whatever the functions, capabilities and limitations of watchtowers, the Emperor Valentinian was a devoted advocate of their use, and his instructions to the *dux Daciae ripensis*, mentioned above, indicate that he had instituted an annual programme of building such towers, at least on the Danube.

The fortifications along river frontiers comprised forts, walled towns and cities, bridgehead forts, and harbours and landing places. On the Rhine the bridgehead at Deutz opposite Cologne was constructed in the years 312–315 under Constantine before he became sole Emperor. The fort was strongly built, almost square, with thick walls defended by eighteen projecting towers and two gates. It contained sixteen barrack blocks and was large enough to accommodate 1,000 men, an important site that attests to Roman power at this time. Deutz was occupied until at least the fifth century, and does not seem to have been destroyed by hostile action. There were other important bridgehead forts opposite Mainz and Kaiseraugst, which was like Deutz in plan, but smaller. Another bridgehead was built at Zurzach, and on the Danube it may have been Diocletian who built Contra Aquincum, opposite Budapest. Valentinian's restoration programme for the Rhine included the bridgehead forts, so it is not often possible to date the earlier work precisely.

The fortified landing places on the river frontiers were sometimes labelled *burgi*, but they were more substantial than the towers or blockhouses of the same name. There was usually a central tower set within a rectangular enclosure defined by walls on three sides extending in two arms down to the river, where there would be two terminal towers. Diocletian and Constantine established fortifications of this type, and Valentinian founded new ones on the right bank of the Rhine at Niederlahnstein, Zullestein, and Wiesbaden-Biebrich. In the sixth century Justinian repaired a fortified landing place on the Euphrates, which Procopius says was originally founded by Diocletian, a blockhouse surrounded by a wall on three sides with a tower on each of the two arms reaching to the water, leaving the river itself as the fourth protecting side. Justinian built a new all on the river front, enclosing the installation completely. Procopius' description of the sixth-century fortifications tallies very closely with the design of the fortified landing places that have been discovered on the Danube.

Fortification of Cities and Towns

The inclusion of civilian defences in a book about the Roman army is not out of place, because fortification in the late Empire extended beyond the purely military establishments to towns and cities, and some of the building work was done by soldiers. The army of the first two centuries of the Empire had been able to protect the civilian settlements by guarding the frontiers and keeping the peace internally by policing, but from the third century the pressures increased. The numbers of tribesmen trying to penetrate into the Empire for settlement or for plunder were overwhelming, and the frontiers, which had never been designed as totally impermeable barriers, could not contain them. Even before the army was split into frontier troops and field armies, well-protected cities provided a vital adjunct to overall defence.

The eastern provinces of the Roman Empire such as Syria and Egypt had a much longer tradition of urban living than the provinces of the west, and some of the cities of the east, especially those bordering on the Parthian Empire, were already walled, and could resist sieges, as demonstrated by the ability of Hatra to survive two sieges by Severus. In Augustus' reign new colonies were built complete with defensive walls, and the inhabitants of some cities would provide themselves with walls purely for the prestige value, since for most of the first and early second centuries there was no pressing need for fortification. In the troubled times of the third century, the fortification of cities was probably largely due to the enterprise and initiative of certain individuals, particularly in the west where the city was a relatively recent introduction, but initiative alone would always not be sufficient without some financial help from the emperors. The eastern cities may have been wealthier than those of the west. The same few families are documented in eastern cities time and time again as the magistrates and benefactors, and there is some evidence that there was a spontaneous and voluntary movement towards the establishment of a hereditary ruling class in many cities, long before Diocletian crystallised it and made everyone remain in their hereditary positions. In the east city walls were already established in many cases so the main problems would concern keeping them in good repair.

The decurions who governed cities and towns found that the expenses incurred became increasingly burdensome. Examples of reluctance to serve on city councils can be found as early as the second century, but the phenomenon became much more widespread during the third century. The burdens fell upon the same families and their descendants in some cities, and especially in the east, where there was already a tendency towards hereditary membership of the city councils some time before Diocletian's reforms crystallised the arrangement. Snobbishness precluded anyone from the lower classes or anyone engaged in trade from entering upon office, even when it proved difficult to recruit new councillors. The third century lawyer Callistratus thought that the councils would be degraded if such low class people were admitted to membership. Even if some of the men who were engaged in lowly professions were wealthy, their origins counted for more than their money. The emphasis on land ownership as the qualification for membership of town and city councils was retained, but the dogged adherence to custom resulted in a reduction of the size of holdings as the qualifying figure, so that men with as little as 25 *iugera* could be made councillors; these men could scarcely sustain the costs of office in towns and cities. Inevitably, people began to avoid taking office if they could do so. Some gave up all pretence to property ownership so that they did not qualify, others extricated themselves by renouncing the towns and retiring to their estates, becoming as far as possible self-sufficient magnates, developing unassailable power bases which enabled them to avoid making contributions to the towns and cities. The alternative to withdrawal was to extract wealth from the lower classes, oppressing them in the process. Evidence from the fourth century suggests that this is how some decurions found an answer to their problems.

The complete stagnation of growth and the lack of new building or fresh adornment of cities from the third century has been noted and proclaimed as one of the most compelling pieces of evidence for decline. Instead there was an upsurge in the building of defensive walls, which no doubt absorbed all the attention, effort and expense that would normally have gone into beautifying the interior buildings of the cities. If some of the towns and cities escaped relatively unscathed from invasions of tribesmen and the depredations of roaming robbers, too often the rural areas did not. The effects of the destruction of crops vary according to the region, the type of crop, and the social and economic conditions in which recovery is attempted. Variables such as climate, type of soil, agricultural technique, and collapse or survival of the market also have a bearing on the rate of revival. Recovery of cereal crops can be made within a year, and if enough reserves have been gathered for corporate use, the city could survive until the next harvest; vineyards take longer to revive, and olive groves, with a crop only every second year, require about a decade to re-establish. The relationship between cities and agricultural producers was symbiotic. Cities depended on the countryside to supply them, just as much as the farmers depended on the existence of markets to sell their surplus, thus raising money to pay taxes and to buy other goods. When the local surplus production ceased to be exchanged via urban markets, the economy of the cities began to unravel.

It is easy at a distance of 2,000 years or so to play down the threat posed by brigands, but perceived threat motivates people to pre-empt attacks, and one way of doing so was to fortify rural settlements as well as towns. The people who had experienced loss of property and loss of family members in attacks would be determined not to go through this again. Ramsay

MacMullen points out that under Tiberius and Trajan Roman authors praised these emperors for keeping brigandage under control. There were no records of organised brigandage in the first two centuries of the Empire. One of the first organised gangs to enter the historical record was Bulla, operating in Italy under Severus, and evading all attempts to capture him. The gangs were enlarged in the third century, poverty being the chief contributory factor in uprooting people and forcing them to join the gangs to stay alive. Debt was an oppressive problem, as revealed by the proclamation issued by the Prefect of Egypt, declaring an amnesty for all debtors who had fled their homes to return within a certain period of time, but once the terminal date of the period of grace had expired, all those found wandering and homeless would be arrested. The Bagaudae of Gaul are frequently quoted as an example of large scale brigandage. The members of the gangs may have been made up of the urban and rural poor, deserters from the army, and perhaps some displaced tribesmen. The Bagaudae were powerful enough to take over Armorica, approximating to modern Brittany, and to begin to issue their own coins. From the point of view of ordinary inhabitants of the provinces, there was little to distinguish gangs of brigands from barbarian tribes, in that both were capable of damaging crops and pillaging cities. Another problem was that the soldiers sent to deal with the brigands were not much better behaved, and could and did use their military power to obtain what they wanted from the civilians. Not all the soldiers oppressed the civilians but it would only require a few examples for the bad reputation to gain a foothold. Defensive walls would have seemed very attractive to people living inside the cities and towns and in the countryside around the towns, with barbarians, brigands, and errant soldiers wandering around outside.

Communities already in decline were in no position to recover rapidly from destruction of their surrounding areas, unless there was an injection of ready cash or extra help from the emperors. Imperial permission had to be sought for wall building, and there is no reason to think that this regulation had lapsed in the third and fourth centuries. Those cities where there was a direct Imperial interest, or better still a prolonged Imperial presence with the troops of the field armies billeted inside the cities, were assisted and survived the third-century crisis, and some even prospered in the following century. The soldiers may have caused problems in cities where they were billeted but at least defence was guaranteed. Cities that were on major routes were fortified and the routes themselves were protected by means of watchtowers.

Elsewhere, for cities which were not occupied by the emperors and the field armies, or were not on important routes that it was imperative to guard, the responsibility for building defensive walls would fall on the inhabitants, but the costs cannot have been wholly met by the decurions, even if they instituted extra taxes to pay the bills. When Probus restored cities in Gaul he may have contributed to the costs, and he used troops for building work. Inscriptions show that the soldiers under different emperors helped with building work on the frontiers, but not so frequently in the hinterland. In the fourth century, Julian restored cities in Gaul by using his soldiers to rebuild them. Diocletian allowed the use of funds earmarked for other purposes to be diverted to defence works. Grenoble was given walls by Diocletian and Maximianus, and inscriptions from the main gates show that they were dedicated to Jupiter and Hercules, the gods who protected these two emperors. Stephen Johnson suggests that similar dedications to these gods which have been found in other cities may represent work organised and paid for by Diocletian and Maximianus. Valentinian's programme of fortification embraced cities as well as military establishments.

If the emperors could not spare the manpower to do the building work, they sometimes lent military architects and craftsmen to supervise the civilians. There was no point in allowing inexperienced builders to construct the walls, or to condone jerry-building that could have resulted in collapse of the defences. Proper foundations had to be laid down before any building was done. The town councillors may have been responsible for deciding where the walls were to run, and local knowledge combined with professional building experience would identify weak spots, such as pits and softer ground which would have to be filled in and shored up. Some marshy areas were filled in using timbers driven vertically into the ground. This device was first discovered at the fort on the Rhine bank at Altrip, and in a military context it was interpreted not as a structural underpinning but as a precaution against mining. Opinion had to be revised when more and more such foundations were discovered in civilian contexts as well. The foundations of buildings in Venice, likewise built up from vertical piles, do not represent an innovation of the post-Roman era.

Some of the city walls took a few years to build. The walls of Rome were still being constructed in the years after Aurelian's assassination, and one city in Syria was building walls for a period of at least fifteen years. Although wall building was a more leisurely progress than might be imagined, there are signs of cost cutting and perhaps a need to shorten the length of time it took, by reusing old stone work, statues and inscriptions in the construction of the walls. Sometimes original structures would have to be removed, and the foundations utilized for the defences. On occasion whole buildings were left intact, such as the amphitheatre at Trier which is incorporated into the circuit, using its outer wall as part of the defences, and the *amphitheatrum Castrense* in Rome, near the camp of the *equites singulares Augusti*, can still be seen as a bulge in the Aurelian walls not far from the Lateran palace. Most of the projecting towers of the Aurelian walls are rectangular, but the larger gates were protected by D-shaped towers, sometimes much altered by later emperors. The towers of provincial city walls were predominantly D-shaped, or drum towers projecting beyond the walls. At Senlis in France sixteen of the original twenty-eight towers survive, completely solid up to the level of the rampart walk, and spaced about thirty metres apart. The fortifications of Senlis are very similar to those at Beauvais, Amiens and Soissons, and may be part of the reconstruction undertaken by Probus from 276 to 282. Construction of solid towers up to rampart level was probably the most common method used in city walls, since it prevented any breakthrough. Some towers were open backed. Such features may not have been common in Roman cities, but open-backed towers, even if they have floors, cannot be held by any enemy who has broken in, being subject to missile fire from within the city. It is not certain how such towers were roofed, if at all. They usually had at least two storeys above the rampart walk, and may have had flat open roofs with crenellations. Conical tiled roofs for most towers are not out of the question, like those reconstructed at the medieval city of Carcassonne. A flat roof would facilitate the firing of missiles at attackers, especially using small artillery engines, and though it is not known if city defenders used artillery, the fact that some small windows were enlarged in some towers suggests that the work may have been done to accommodate such weapons. The larger machines would require exceptionally strong towers, and there would have to be a body of experts trained in using them.

The construction methods of most city walls were similar, and have been described by Stephen Johnson. Walls were usually about three to four metres thick, built in similar fashion to Hadrian's Wall, in that two outer skins were built, leaving a gap between them to be filled in with rubble and mortar, each course forming a separate layer. There may have been timber shuttering on each side to prevent the wall from bulging outwards before the mortar had set properly. In some places where walls have fallen down, the joins between each horizontal layer have separated, revealing a weakness in construction, but since it took such an impact to separate them the walls were sturdy enough to defend the cities. Timber scaffolding was used as the walls grew in height, and putlog holes where the supporting beams were inserted were not always filled in, so some of them can still be seen on surviving remains of late Roman walls.

There was still an element of civic pride in the building of city walls. Most walls were faced in stone blocks of various sizes and pointed with hard mortar, or sometimes tiles were used, probably second hand. The tiles could be shaped and arranged in patterns to relieve the monotony of the wall facings. The late Roman tower still standing at Cologne is decorated in this way, though it has been doubted whether the work is Roman. The Roman walls of Le Mans are similarly decorative and much more remains standing than at Cologne.

The expense as well as the considerations of defensibility may have exercised a considerable influence on the extent of the circuits around cities. The walls of western cities usually enclosed a much smaller area than the known city limits of the second century, and there is some argument about what this actually means. Where new defensive walls were built in Gaul, parts of Spain, Raetia and the Upper Danube provinces, enclosing a reduced area, it has been argued that the circuits were built on the most easily defensible ground, containing the area that the citizens could hope to hold, according to their resources and manpower. It is postulated that the majority of the population lived outside the walls, taking refuge inside the city when danger threatened. Evidence from some of the cities in Gaul argues against this theory. In some cases large gardens and open spaces that had made the cities pleasant places to live now disappeared. Buildings encroached upon the streets and public spaces, and in some cases rooms were subdivided, all of which suggests overcrowding and the inclusion within the new walls of most of the population that previously lived on the outskirts. At Tours and Tournai, the lie of the land precludes any settlement outside the walls, so it seems that in these instances at least the cities had in fact shrunk and the population had shrunk with them. Despite the argument that the reconstructed cities were perhaps central citadels or refuges with many of the inhabitants still living outside the perimeter, some authors argue instead for a considerable drop in population in the second half of the third century, with the most serious results being apparent in the countryside.

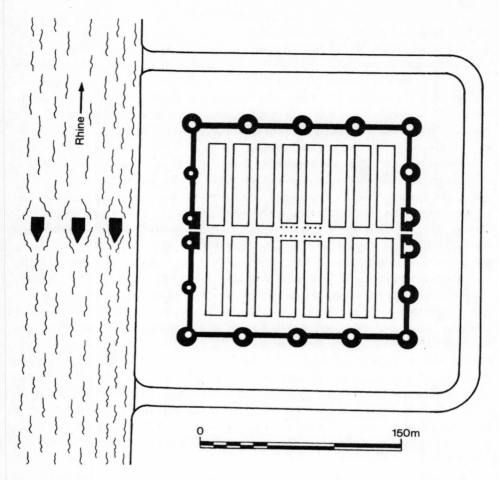

Plan of the bridgehead fort at Divitia (modern Köln-Deutz) on the Rhine, built by Constantine in the early fourth century, showing closely spaced barracks, thick walls, numerous towers and narrow, heavily defended gates. Drawn by Graeme Stobbs.

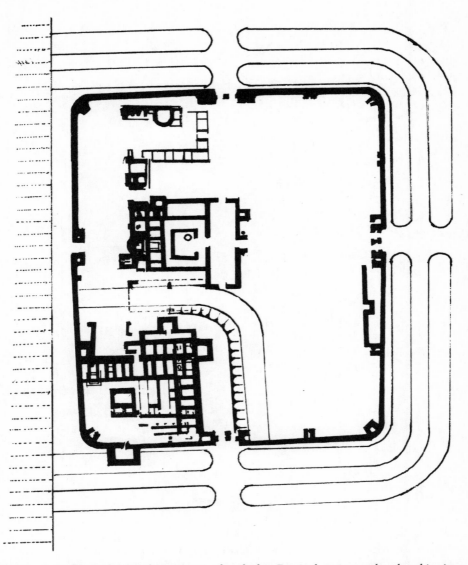

The fort at Eining on the Danube was retained in the late Empire but was much reduced in size, which implies a reduction in manpower. It has been argued that the smaller fort in the corner of the old fort, separated from it by a ditch, is a citadel rather than an independent fort, but the layout of the new small fort resembles others of the late Empire, the new ditch appears to cut an earlier building, and the main entrance is between the fort wall and the ditch, utilising the old south gate of the earlier fort. If it was a citadel inside an occupied fort, it might be expected that three of the gates of the older fort would have been blocked up and the entrance would have been through the remaining one, the fort forming what amounts to an outer bailey of a castle, though castles had not yet been invented. Redrawn by Susan Veitch after T. Fischer and K. Spindler. *Das Römische Grenzkastell Abusina-Eining.* Stuttgart, 1984.

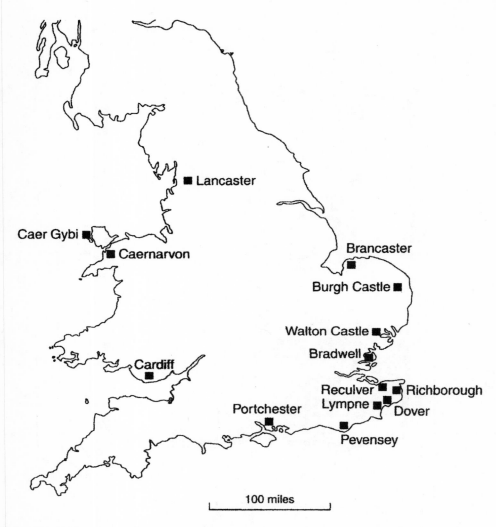

Map showing late Roman forts in Britain, including the so-called forts of the Saxon Shore around the south and east coasts, and forts in the west guarding the rivers and harbours. Raids from the sea by Saxons from across the North Sea, and tribesmen from Ireland, were a feature of late Roman Britain. Drawn by Jacqui Taylor.

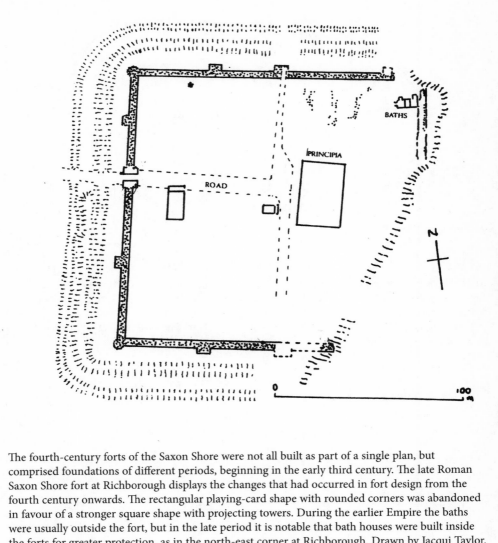

The fourth-century forts of the Saxon Shore were not all built as part of a single plan, but comprised foundations of different periods, beginning in the early third century. The late Roman Saxon Shore fort at Richborough displays the changes that had occurred in fort design from the fourth century onwards. The rectangular playing-card shape with rounded corners was abandoned in favour of a stronger square shape with projecting towers. During the earlier Empire the baths were usually outside the fort, but in the late period it is notable that bath houses were built inside the forts for greater protection, as in the north-east corner at Richborough. Drawn by Jacqui Taylor.

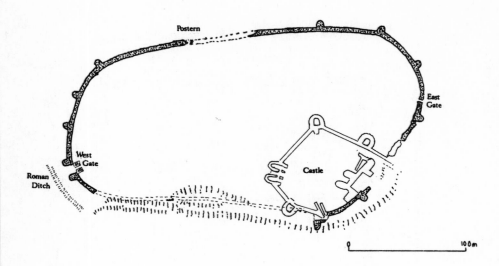

The Saxon Shore fort at Pevensey was the last to be built, and the regular square or rectangular outline was abandoned in favour of an ovoid that suited the terrain, with projecting U-shaped towers that were a common feature of late Roman fortifications. This site was occupied, not necessarily by soldiers, well into the fifth century, and the Normans used the fort as the outer bailey of a castle. Drawn by Jacqui Taylor.

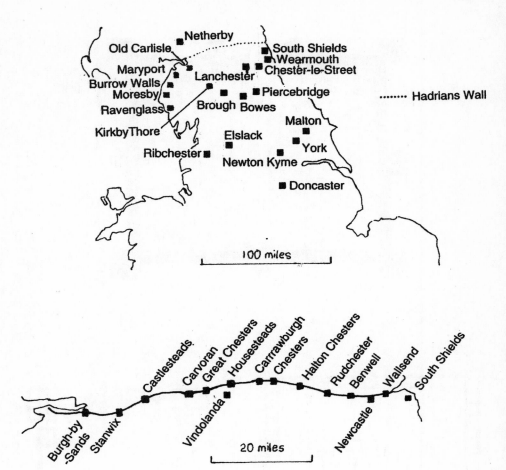

Command of the provincial military forces in the late Empire were entrusted to high-ranking officers called *comites* or *duces*, who could command the troops of one province or of several provinces grouped together. In Britain the *Comes Litoris Saxonicum* controlled the southern parts of the island including the Saxon Shore. This map shows the command of the *Dux Britanniarum* in the north, including Hadrian's Wall. By this time Britain had been divided into smaller provinces. Drawn by Jacqui Taylor.

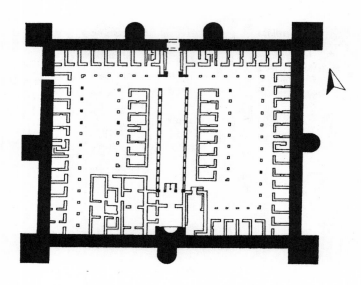

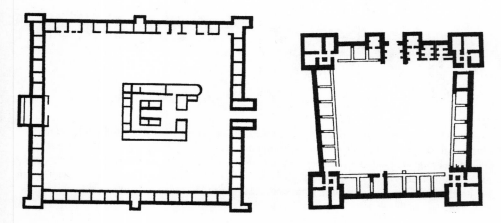

Forts of the later Empire were more compact than their predecessors, measuring just over fifty by fifty metres, with only one gateway, projecting towers all around the thick walls, and buildings clustered around the inner walls. They are sometimes known as *quadriburgia*. These plans show at the top Castra Dionysias, modern Qasr Qarun in Egypt, at bottom left is the early fourth-century fort at Bourada in Numidia, and bottom right is Qasr Bshir in Jordan built between AD 293 and 330. Redrawn by Graeme Stobbs from J. Lander. *Roman Stone Fortifications: Variation and Change from the First Century AD to the Fourth.* Oxford: British Archaeological Reports S206, 1984.

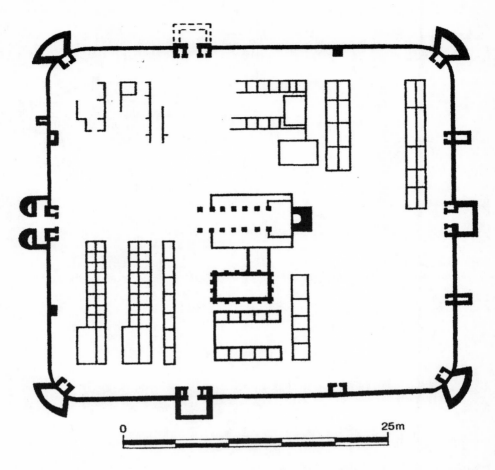

The fort at Drobeta (modern Turnu Severin) was originally a Trajanic bridgehead built during the Dacian wars. It was retained after Aurelian abandoned Dacia, to guard the crossing point of the Danube, and in the late Empire, perhaps under Diocletian or Constantine, fan-shaped towers were added to the rounded corners to allow for a better view along the walls. Three of the gates were blocked up by means of square towers built out from the original flanking towers, and the one gate that remained in use received U-shaped towers projecting far beyond the original entrance. The internal buildings on the plan may date from different periods. Redrawn by Graeme Stobbs from J. Lander. *Roman Stone Fortifications: Variation and Change from the First Century AD to the Fourth.* Oxford: British Archaeological Reports S206, 1984.

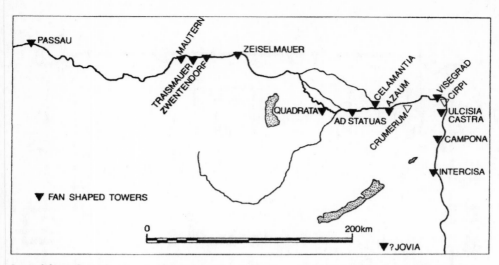

Several forts along the Danube frontier had fan-shaped towers added like those at Drobeta in the late Empire. Redrawn by Graeme Stobbs from S. Johnson. *Late Roman Fortifications*. Batsford, 1983.

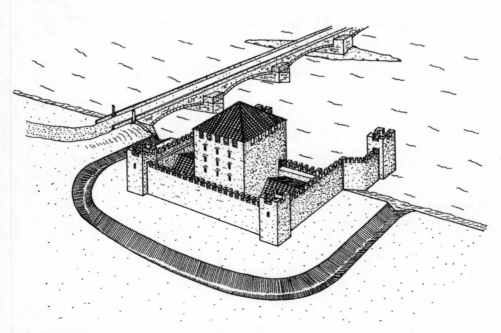

In the late Empire it became necessary to fortify landing places on the Rhine and Danube. This reconstruction drawing shows a typical riverine site with a ditch on three sides, surrounding stone wall with towers reaching down to the riverbank and a central stone tower. Redrawn by Graeme Stobbs from P. Filtzinger et al. (eds.) *Die Römer in Baden-Württemberg*. Theiss, 1986.

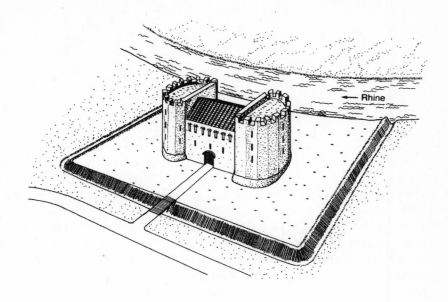

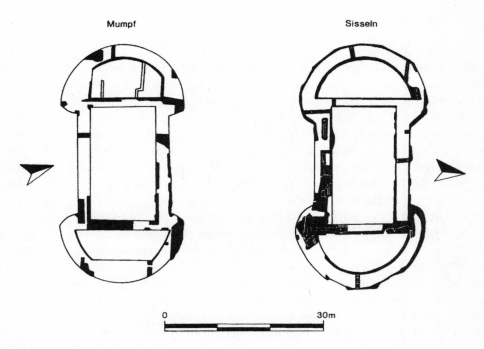

Mumpf   Sisseln

0   30m

Storehouses for food were also fortified in the late Empire, and military commanders had to go through strict protocol to draw rations with the permission of higher-ranking officials. The reconstruction drawing, based on the excavated plans of stores at Mumpf and Sisseln, shows how the fortified stores may have looked. Redrawn by Graeme Stobbs from W. Drack and R. Fellman. *Die Römer in der Schweiz*. Theiss, 1988.

5

Officers and Men

Constantine's remodelled army of the fourth century was subject to major changes in the fifth century, when the army of the western Empire disappeared and the army of the eastern Empire evolved into the Byzantine army. The stages by which this was accomplished are not covered by the major sources. Ammianus described the later fourth century army, and then there is silence until Procopius' description of Justinian's army of the sixth century, when there was a monumental attempt to refortify the frontiers and to reclaim the west. Not knowing the details of the fifth century army it is not always possible to discern how much of Constantine's army survived or how much of the sixth century army is rooted in the fourth. The gap is too wide to be able to use information about the later army to extrapolate backwards to guess the complete evolution from the army of Ammianus Marcellinus.

The High Command

After the abolition of the Praetorian Guard the highest ranking troops under Constantine were the *scholae*, or the new bodyguard that may have been founded by Diocletian and developed by Constantine. The *scholae* were commanded by a civilian official, the *magister officiorum*, and formed the elite troops of the fourth century for as long as the emperors led their armies in person on campaigns, but after Theodosius I, who accompanied the armies rather than commanding them, the Empire split into east and west and the emperors remained in their palaces, while the chief *magistri militum* directed military operations. This gave them enormous power, to the point where some of the emperors were figureheads and the real rulers were the army commanders. Each of the *magistri militum* had a bodyguard and an administrative staff of his own, so the *scholae* diminished in importance in the west, but survived until the fifth century when Theoderic abolished these troops. In the east the *scholae* were retained but became ornamental troops for parade ground spit and polish shows, and no longer saw action in campaigns.

The *protectores* established by Gallienus were retained into the fourth and fifth centuries, by which time there were distinctions between the *protectores domestici* who were closely attached to the emperor, and ordinary *protectores*. There were better promotion prospects for the *protectores domestici*, since most of them had long military experience, but after the mid-third century, young men with no experience of military service were allowed to join the ordinary *protectores*, and were treated as potential officer material. Despite the connotations of the title *protectores*, they were not a bodyguard, but they were treated as a distinct entity, and could be sent on special postings to perform various tasks, such as recording the cargoes of boats heading for barbarian territory via the rivers and seas, or checking the wagons and post-horses at the official *mansiones* or staging posts, to ensure that the goods carried were within the weight restrictions. Some of the tasks were dangerous. Ammianus was one of ten *protectores domestici* sent to serve under the *magister equitum* Ursicinus, when he was ordered to suppress the rebellion of Silvanus against Constantius II, and Ammianus records how frightened he and the other *protectores* were in the dangerous circumstances. Although Ammianus is accused of embroidering or even falsifying the account, it is attested that life expectancy for several of the *protectores* was short.

Service in the *protectores domestici* brought soldiers into the court circle and drew them to the attention of the emperor. Much would depend on each man's existing connections with influential men who could recommend them, subject to the emperor's final verdict. Promotions could follow entry to the *protectores domestici*, but not necessarily rapidly, except in special cases. Promotion to high rank had always depended on acquaintance with influential friends, and being known to the emperors either personally or by reputation, but in the fourth century it was more important than ever before to forge close ties with the court and the emperor, and for many men this entailed having a long, unblemished service record and lots of patience. Flavius Abinnaeus, who was eventually made prefect of the *ala* at Dionysias in Egypt, had served for years in a cavalry vexillation before joining the *protectores domestici* and then obtaining his command in Egypt. On the other hand the future Emperor Jovian served as the senior officer or *primicerius* of the *protectores* at a relatively young age, but his father was the *comes domesticorum*, the commander of the *protectores domestici*. The careers of Abinnaeus and Jovian demonstrate the importance of having the right connections, and a good track record. The optimum situation was to obtain direct connection to the Imperial family. The title *protector* did not denote a military rank, but it did mark out the holder as a person of status, and it was a permanent attribute, to be retained while in command of a military unit.

Among the field armies and the frontier armies there was a hierarchy, not simply to distinguish *comitatenses* from *limitanei*, but a distinction was made between the *comitatenses* of the emperors and those of the regional field armies. The former received the additional title of *palatini*, and were allowed to keep the title even if they were incorporated into the regional *comitatenses*. The frontier troops under the collective term *limitanei* comprised the higher-grade *ripenses* and the *alares* and *cohortales*, but this arrangement did not apply all over the Empire. In Britain, the Danube provinces and Egypt, the cavalry vexillations were called *equites*, and the old-style legions, *alae* and cohorts were retained.

The supreme commanders of all the military forces of the Empire were the emperors themselves, who exercised their control via the *magistri*. Constantine created two commanders, the *magister peditum* and *magister equitum*, possibly on the collegiate principle, emulating the two Praetorian Prefects or the two consuls. These two magistri commanded all the armed forces except for the *scholae*. A separate commander for the infantry and the cavalry was effective, provided that the emperor led the armies and took control during campaigns, but when emperors ceased to command in person, there was a need for an overall senior officer who could direct operations rather than relying on two officers of probably equal rank to co-operate efficiently. There never seems to have been agreement on a consistent title for a commander-in-chief, so compromises were used, such as *magister peditum et equitum*, commander of the infantry and the cavalry, *magister utriusque militiae*, implying command of all the soldiers everywhere, or more economically, *magister militum*, commander of the soldiers. A general could be described in the sources by different versions of these titles, while in exactly the same post.

The *magistri* who commanded the central field armies added *in praesenti* or *praesentalis* to signify their attachment to the emperors. The need to distinguish between *magistri* of infantry and cavalry disappeared, so that the *magistri peditum* combined control of all sections of the military forces, not only the infantry, but the cavalry, the *laeti*, and the fleets. The regional field armies were commanded by lesser *magistri*, with titles indicating the geographical areas under their control, such as *magister equitum per Gallias* in Gaul. From the time of Theodosius I in the east there were two *magistri praesentales* at the court, and three more regional commanders called *magister equitum et peditum per Orientem, per Thracias*, and *per Illyricum*.

The *duces* who commanded the frontier troops were answerable to the *magistri militum* of the *comitatenses* and the *palatini*. The geographical areas commanded by the *magistri* of the regional field armies did not necessarily reflect the areas of the frontier commands of the *duces*. The *duces* could command the troops of a single province or a group of frontier provinces, while the governor of each separate province was a civilian *praeses*, though the split between military commands and civil government was not absolute, and some *duces* combined military and civil commands, and on occasion the *praeses* commanded troops.

Until the reign of Valentinian I the *duces* were usually equestrians, and some of them were tribesmen, such as the Frankish Teutomares, who was *dux Daciae Ripensis*, and is chiefly known to history because he had neglected to build his annual quota of watchtowers. Valentinian upgraded the *duces* to senatorial status.

The *duces* embraced a wide range of responsibilities, some of which would formerly have been allocated to the provincial governors in the earlier Empire. As part of maintaining military discipline, each *dux* had judicial powers, since soldiers who had committed crimes could only be tried in military courts. All aspects of recruitment, some of which were once part of a governor's duties, were supervised by the *dux*, from administration of the whole recruiting procedure to personal inspection of new recruits to weed out those considered unsuitable for military service, just as the provincial governors of the earlier Empire had done before sending recruits to their units. Military administration included control of the food supply, from reception to distribution, and the *dux* and his staff were obliged to send quarterly reports to the Praetorian Prefects who were in overall charge of the supplies.

A list of all the known *duces* of the late Empire would give the impression that there was a large number of them at any one time, but their areas of command changed as circumstances altered, so there was no permanence attached to the post, with continuous chains of successors being appointed to exactly the same region or collections of troops. The separate commands of the *duces* of Moesia Prima, Moesia Secunda, and Scythia were united for a while under a single *dux*. The two posts of *dux tractus Armoricani et Nervicani*, and the *dux Belgicae Secundae* are attested only in the *Notitia Dignitatum*, with no known predecessors, so their commands could have been created in response to a problem, possibly the increase in raiding by pirates from outside the provinces, or by brigands inside them. The *dux Aegypti* was replaced by the *comes rei militaris per Aegyptum*, but on occasion, if troops from the field armies were transferred to the frontier commands, the *dux* himself would be re-titled *comes rei militaris*.

The *comites* were originally companions of the emperors, with no official positions within the Imperial court. Constantine formalized the system, and various posts were created such as the *comes sacrarum largitionum* who had charge of finances, and the *comes domesticorum* who commanded the *protectores*. The *comites* who were given military assignments were distinguished by the unequivocal extra title *rei militaris*. There was no standardisation of such appointments, which could range from a minor command of frontier troops to a major command, such as the *comes* Theodosius was given in Britain after the multiple attacks of 367.

It should be noted that Theodosius' full official title of *comes rei militaris* is not attested, except that Ammianus refers to him as *comes*. In some sections of Ammianus' narrative Theodosius is also called *dux*, but this is in the sense of general, or the literal translation of leader.

Apart from the fact that the *comites* were appointed from within the immediate court circle of the emperors, it seems that there was no sharply defined distinction of rank or importance between the *comites* and *duces* of the frontier commands. The titles *dux limitis* and *comes limitis* are attested. In Britain in the late fourth century, according to the *Notitia Dignitatum*, the northern frontier commander was the *dux Britanniarum*, while the Saxon Shore was under the *comes litoris Saxonici*.

Officers

During the Empire of the first three centuries AD the officers who commanded in the field were distinguishable by their titles from the officers whose duties were mainly administrative, but the information about the various officers of the late army is too patchy to be certain about who did what, and without definite dating evidence for the points when new titles were introduced it is not possible to be categorical about whether different titles are contemporary or successive. There may have been transitory fashions in the use of titles, or possibly some of them could represent different practices in different regions, with no relevance to other parts of the Empire.

Only a few remnants of the command structure of the Imperial armies are found in the later Roman army. Centurions and decurions still existed in the old-style units, but these posts largely disappeared in the fourth century. *Praefecti* in command of legions are attested in the *Notitia Dignitatum* in both the eastern and western Empires, but *praefecti* in command of auxiliary units, specifically cavalry, are attested predominantly in the western armies. Flavius Abinnaeus was appointed *praefectus alae* at Dionysias in Egypt. Another title which had long been used in the army and survived into the fourth century is *praepositus*, which never denoted a specific rank. It was widely used in the late Empire for appointments of varying importance. In its early history the title *praepositus* was usually given to an officer in a temporary or extraordinary command, and the officer kept his original rank, which could be anything from a centurion to a senior officer. In the later Empire the commands of the *praepositi* could be long-term if not permanent. Some *praepositi* were placed in command of whole units, such as the *numeri* stationed on the frontiers. In the late army, there were *praepositi* in the *scholae*, and others in command of legions. Also attested on inscriptions are *praepositi cohortis*, *militum*, *equitum*, and of the *auxilia*, which may not have been permanent commands. The *laeti* in Gaul were also commanded by a *praepositus*.

The order of seniority of officers in the late Roman army was noted by a Christian author who used them to demonstrate the several grades between demons and angels. He started with the recruit (*tiro*), rising through *eques* or trooper (but seems not to mention *miles* or infantryman) *circitor*, *biarchus*, *centenarius*, *ducenarius*, *senator*, *primicerius*, finally arriving at tribune. This list does not mention the *semissalis* which came between the *eques* and the *circitor*. The equation of recruits with demons may have seemed perfectly acceptable to training officers, but the equation of tribunes with angels might not have met with the approval of the soldiers who were obliged to serve under these metaphorical embodiments of ecclesiastical perfection. At least in this list, which omits the *praepositi*, it is clear which officers outranked the others, though next to nothing is known about their duties. One problem is that the same term was used for men of different ranks, depending on their particular commands. The title of tribune embraced widely divergent ranks. The highest ranking tribunes were those of the *scholae*, responsible to the *magister officiorum* and not the *magistri militum*. This is paralleled by the former arrangements in the Praetorian Guard, where tribunes, senior to other tribunes in the Imperial army, commanded the Praetorian cohorts and were answerable to the Prefects. Tribunes were also found in the units of the field armies, in the cavalry vexillations and the new style infantry *auxilia*.

The *primicerius* was the highest ranking officer after the tribunes. In the law codes, the *primicerii* are found in the *scholae*, the *protectores*, and the armies of the *duces* of Africa and Sardinia. Hardly anything is known about the *senators*, used to describe a rank and not a member of the Senate in this case, who ranked just below the *primicerii*, except that they are attested in the law codes in some infantry units and in the *scholae*. Vegetius says that the *ducenarius*, who was next in rank after the *senator*, commanded 200 men. Officers with this title served in the *scholae*, the cavalry and the infantry. Flavius Abinnaeus was a *ducenarius* in a cavalry vexillation, with thirty-three years of military service behind him before he joined the *protectores domestici*. The *centenarius*, on analogy with the *ducenarius*, ought to have commanded 100 men, and this is how the officer is described in the Visigothic laws of the fifth century. *Centenarii* served in the *scholae*, the administrative offices of the *duces*, and in the infantry units and the cavalry, where inscriptions attest them in the *cataphractarii* and in units of mounted archers or *sagittarii*.

The lower-grade officers, the *biarchus* and the *circitor* may have been responsible for the food supply, though the evidence is not conclusive. As early as 327 Flavius Iovianus is attested as the bearer of the dragon standard, *bearchus* [sic] *draconarius*. This may not mean that all the men with the title *biarchus* were standard-bearers, since the *signiferi* still existed, and the less frequently attested *semafori* may have been equivalent to them.

In addition to the officers, there was a collection of clerical staff, probably including civilians and military men. The *magistri militum*, the *duces* and the *comites* all had administrative offices, controlled by a *princeps*, and there may have been a *princeps* in each military unit, where the finances were in the hands of the *numerarii*, usually two to each unit. There was a variety of clerical staff in each *officium*, from the highest-ranking offices attached to the senior officers down to the administration at the level of each military unit, but the origins of some of the posts are not securely dated, so that officials called *a libellis*, *subscribendarius* and *regerendarius* may all have the same functions with successive titles, or they may be regional variations for the same official doing the same work.

The new officer titles found in the late Roman armies illustrate the differences between the military organisation of the fourth century and that of the preceding centuries. There is a well-established comfort zone for students of the armies of the early Empire, with the *optiones*, centurions, *primipili* and legates of the legions, and the centurions and decurions of the auxiliary units, but such a comfort zone with the officers of the late armies is not possible. The word centurion evokes a person, wearing recognisable clothing and armour, with about eighty soldiers under his command, perhaps a wife and a family as shown by various inscriptions, a social life in the civilian settlement outside the fortress or the auxiliary fort where he could spend some of his pay, with promotion prospects and a future to look forward to. A *biarchus* or a *circitor* or even a *centenarius* evokes nothing of this rounded picture; they are words that mean officer of some sort, but are otherwise faceless.

Soldiers

The ratio of volunteers to conscripts in the later Roman Empire is not known. When Diocletian imposed annual conscription as a source of recruits, there were probably still some men who joined the army voluntarily. It is known that some tribesmen were eager to share in the privileges that the army still enjoyed, such as rations or pay, which seemed more attractive than life on the far side of the Roman frontiers, where starvation was a real possibility. Alaric the Goth and Attila the Hun both wanted above all a military command in the Roman army for themselves and supplies for their men. The shortage of willing recruits in the later Empire was often ameliorated by the inclusion of large numbers of tribesmen in the armies, and several so-called barbarians rose to senior commands. When this source failed and men were urgently needed, slaves and convicts, who were normally excluded from service in the army, would be enlisted.

The conscription of soldiers was sometimes burdensome to the provincials. Sons of soldiers were obliged to enlist if they were physically fit, while the rest of the recruits were drawn from the provinces, though sometimes instead of levying men, a tax could be substituted. The largest landowners were responsible for providing one or more recruits according to the size of their holdings, while smaller landowners were sometimes assessed as being responsible for a fraction of a recruit and so were forced to join together to provide a whole recruit by rotation. A law of Valens in the late fourth century made it illegal to produce a landless man who was not a registered tenant, which illustrates one of the avoidance schemes that landowners had tried out. In order to make military service more attractive, there were tax privileges for soldiers. A veteran who had served in the *alae* or cohorts was exempt from the poll tax or *capitatio*, and twenty years' service in the legions or the vexillations earned the same privilege for the soldier's wife.

New recruits were subject to the same *probatio* as the soldiers of the earlier Empire, and Vegetius stresses the importance of a rigorous selection procedure, which probably means that in the fourth century there had been a lapse in standards. The optimum age limits for recruits were twenty to twenty-five years of age, but this was widened to embrace anyone from seventeen to thirty-five years. The height qualification was lowered, but the need for physical fitness was not relaxed. Certain professions were not regarded as suitable for service in the army, such as textile workers and cooks, but anyone who had done strenuous work was welcomed, much like the British and American farm boys converted into soldiers in the Second World War, who were fitter, used to working outside in all weathers, and for whom the wake-up call of reveille meant a nice long lie in bed in the mornings.

After the *probatio* and the initial training period of four months that Vegetius describes, the recruits were given identity discs, like name tags in the modern armies. There is some evidence that this had been commuted to a tattoo in the later Empire, possibly to counteract the problem of desertion, or the fact that new soldiers being taken to their units had to be locked up at nights to stop them from running away. In the late third and early fourth century Christianity was not a universal barrier to service in the army, though there had been documented cases in the past where Christians preferred martyrdom to becoming soldiers. After the council of Arles in 314, ecclesiastical sanction was given for Christians to serve in the army. The recruits were made to swear an oath of loyalty, which by the fourth century placed service for God, Christ and the Holy Spirit above the emperor, and by swearing by the Christian God, the soldier promised to obey the emperor and not to desert. Just as in the earlier Empire, the soldier was not legally a soldier until he had been entered into the records of the unit to which he had been assigned.

Once entered into the records, the soldiers would need clothing, armour, and weapons, and cavalrymen would require a horse. State factories would supply the clothing, armour and weapons, but by the fifth century the factories produced these items for new recruits, and thereafter the enlisted soldiers received cash for their clothes and equipment instead of the actual items. Not much is known about the supply of horses, except that as in all armies animals captured from the enemy constituted a large number of cavalry mounts.

Pay in cash for the soldiers survived into the late fourth century, but since the amounts had not been increased since the third century the purchasing power had been greatly eroded by inflation. Pay was often in arrears, but was supplemented by donatives from the emperors on their accession and various anniversaries. Booty was still an attractive proposition, as it had been from the early days of the Republic, and sometimes cash was offered in civil wars to persuade men to desert to the opposing side.

In the fourth century, payment in kind, especially food rations, but also clothing and equipment, made up a large proportion of the soldiers' pay. In a way, it was a variation on a theme, since until the end of the third century, food, clothing, weapons and armour were supplied to soldiers all through the Empire, but military pay was docked to cover the costs. Supplies in kind and a reduced salary more or less amounted to the same thing. The *annona militaris* was introduced by Diocletian as a tax in kind on land. Just as the units of land to be taxed were variable according to the type of soil and the crops that could be grown, the contributions in foodstuffs for the *annona militaris* were differently assessed in different parts of the Empire, tailored to the needs of the army and the farming systems in use. From Constantine's reign, after the Praetorian Guard was abolished, the Praetorian Prefects were retained, and placed in charge of the whole supply system, which was centrally administered via the *vicarii* of the new dioceses, who were responsible to the Praetorian Prefects, and then via the local mechanisms, down to the level of the individual military units.

On the frontiers the soldiers could grow some food in the lands near their forts, and could be supplied from the local region, but this was not sufficient for all needs, especially since supplies included non-food items. Storehouses had to be set up in the frontier areas, and were usually fortified. Goods were collected by the tax officials called the *susceptores*, then transported to the storehouses, where the nature and quantities of what was received was recorded, probably by an *actarius*, and likewise records were kept of what was issued, how much, and to whom. Warrants had to be issued to troops before they could draw rations and other supplies, and without the proper documentation the officials in charge of the storehouses were not supposed to let anything be taken away. In 357 under Constantius II and Julian the *comes rei militaris* of Africa tried to short-circuit the system, appropriating supplies on his own authority. The two emperors issued a law to the Praetorian Prefects to underline the rules, that the *comes* should first address his request in writing to the *vicarius* of the diocese, stating the number of allowances to be drawn, and to whom they should be issued. The red tape is understandable, if frustrating, because the supplies could not simply be raided by an officer however high up the chain of command he might be and however close to the Imperial court he may have considered himself.

The rations received by different ranks in the army reflected their status. The *semissalis*, one grade above the ordinary cavalrymen or infantrymen, received one and a half *annonae*, the *circitor* and *biarchus* received two *annonae*, the *centenarius* two and a half, the *ducenarius* three and a half, the *senator* four and the *primicerius* five *annonae*. Fraudulent practices were soon set up to try to obtain more than the normal allowances of food and other supplies. The *duces* and *comites* had to send reports to the Praetorian Prefects about the actual strengths of the units under their commands, much as in the earlier Empire strength reports had to be sent to the provincial governors, with details of the new additions of recruits and transfers into the unit, and the various subtractions by transfers out of the units, by deaths and desertions. These reports provided a sensible way of comparing the numbers of soldiers with the number of rations that were issued, but claiming the pay or rations of dead men was by no means an invention of more recent armies. The officers of some units would be willing to co-operate in falsifying the records because they could then share in the extra rations.

In the fifth century, payment in kind gradually ceased and was commuted into money, though the complaints about arrears of pay show that the cash was not always forthcoming. Under Valentinian I soldiers received rations for nine months and money for the remaining three. A law was passed in 409 stating that as soon as the commutation figures had been agreed, then requisitioning in kind should stop. In the west, the commutation figures were standardised, but in the east they varied according to local market prices. Food would still have to be supplied and stored even when the soldiers began to receive money payments, so the duties of the Praetorian Prefects with regard to the *annona militaris* did not diminish.

The diet of late Roman soldiers was basically nutritious, consisting of bread, pork, wine and oil. A papyrus from Egypt dating from the sixth century reveals that each soldier was issued with three pounds of bread, two pounds of meat, two pints of wine, and about one-eighth of a pint of oil. When it was convenient the soldiers could buy extra food, wine and beer on the open market, or go on hunting expeditions. Experienced soldiers usually find ways of supplementing their diets while in camp or on campaign, so the variety of foods that have been found on archaeological sites of the earlier Empire was probably not much different in the fourth and fifth centuries.

Food supplies for the horses in the Roman army did not come under the heading of *annona* or supplies for the men. The term used for equine supplies was *capitus*, which may not have been issued all year round, since horses could probably graze during the spring and summer. All units would possess horses and mules even if they were not cavalry, and officers would probably own more than one horse. In some cases, particularly in the east, the military horses ate up the grasslands of the cities and complaints were addressed to the authorities, who tried to regulate the process.

On campaign the supply system was more seriously stretched. Ideally the routes for the army to follow would be worked out in advance, and places would be designated where supplies were to be collected, some of them requisitioned from the local people who were required to bring supplies to the appointed place, while other supplies would be conveyed over longer distances, with transport organised centrally, most probably by the Praetorian Prefects. A number of officers would be appointed on a temporary basis to oversee the collection and delivery. A decree of Constantius II issued when he was preparing for a campaign in 358 shows that some efforts were made to match the peacetime rations. Every third day the soldiers were to be issued with bread, wine, and salt pork, and on the remaining two days *bucellatum* (biscuit or hardtack) replaced the bread, sour wine (*acetum*) was to be issued instead of good wine, and mutton replaced the salt pork. Constantius also ordered the soldiers to draw rations for twenty days from the storehouses. Roman soldiers of the late Empire did not starve, but they still had to carry everything themselves on the march between stores bases.

The soldiers were subject to the same sort of abuses that were imposed on the soldiers of the early Empire. Officers could extract money in return for granting leave of absence, which strictly ought to have been approved by the military commanders such as the *dux* or the *comes*. Several laws were passed to put an end to the practice, such as a law of Constantine dated to 323, making it illegal for a tribune, a decurion, or a *praepositus* or anyone of lower rank than the *dux* or *comes* to grant leave to any soldier. There was a potential danger to the unit if any fighting occurred and men were not in their ranks, and the penalty for granting leave was graded according to the circumstances. The guilty officer was to be deported or be deprived of his property if there was no fighting, and was to be put to death if there had been any military action and he had allowed men to be absent. Constantius II changed the death penalty to a hefty fine in a law of 352.

The relationship between officers and men was not always harmonious. Soldiers could be deprived of part of their rations which would be shared among the officers, especially in the early fifth century, but it was perfectly legal within certain limits. A law of 406 set the limit at seven days' rations per annum from any soldier, and in 443 another law records that the *limitanei* lost one month's rations to the *dux*, the *princeps* at the head of his *officium*, and the *praepositi*. In turn, the soldiers sometimes abused civilians, as they had done in the earlier Empire, extorting money and food with menaces, and probably operating protection rackets, as seems to have been the case in Egypt in the third century.

Soldiers of the late Empire tended to remain in the army for much longer than their predecessors, not only serving for more years than the legionaries and auxiliaries of the earlier Empire, but also remaining in the same rank without prospects of rapid promotion. R. S. O. Tomlin lists some of the men and their careers from a collection of tombstones at Concordia in north-east Italy, where one of the men who died while still in service had been in the army for twenty-three years without progressing further than the rank of *biarchus*. A *centenarius* had served for twenty-two years, and two *ducenarii* had served for twenty years in one case and twenty-three in another. Compared to the careers of earlier soldiers who progressed from post to post, these men's careers were almost static. Flavius Abinnaeus served for thirty-three years before becoming a *protector*, and inscriptions attest that men were still serving in their sixties. In the earlier Empire there were a few men who remained in the army long after retirement age, but in the late Empire it was more widespread. Soldiers were probably better off in the army with their allocation of rations, companionship, medical attention and a roof over their heads for most of the time. Veterans of the late Empire were not as well off as the veterans of the first two centuries AD. In the late Roman army, the men of the vexillations and legions were legally entitled to discharge or *honesta missio* after serving for twenty years, but were not entitled to the full privileges of veterans until they had served for twenty-four years. When the Empire was ruled by Constantine and Licinius in the early fourth century, conditions of service and privileges awarded to veterans differed slightly in the eastern and western provinces. Licinius wrote a letter to Dalmatius, the military commander in Illyricum in 311 outlining terms of service for his troops. The letter was copied on a bronze tablet which was discovered at Brigetio (Szőny) in Hungary, and is known as the Brigetio table. The text reveals that serving soldiers were allowed exemption from the poll tax for five 'heads' which would include the soldier himself, his wife and his parents and one other person, but none of this is stated in the letter. *Honesta missio* could be granted if a soldier opted to retire after twenty years, but if a soldier chose this option, exemption from the poll tax and taxes in kind would apply only to the man and his wife. If he retired after the full term, probably twenty-four years but not actually stated in the letter, then the soldier would be granted *emerita missio*, and would continue to hold exemption from the poll tax for five people and also from the tax in kind. Any soldier who had been wounded and had to retire before completing twenty years' service was to be granted *causaria missio* and the same privileges as if he had served for twenty years, and would therefore enjoy tax exemptions for himself and his wife.

The letter also states that veteran soldiers were to be given a discharge certificate in their own name, so that they would have verifiable proof that they had served honourably and had been legally discharged. This had been a problem for some veterans since the early Empire, especially legionaries, who did not receive discharge certificates, as illustrated by the case of the Egyptians who had been transferred to a legion from the fleet and who had to put in a request for certificates before they returned home.

The provisions outlined in the Brigetio table of 311 were soon eroded. After the defeat of Licinius in 324, Constantine as sole Emperor was able to impose the same terms of service and privileges for veterans all over the Empire. In 325 Constantine clarified the new terms in a letter to Maximus, *vicarius* of the eastern diocese of Oriens, and the letter was preserved in the law code of Theodosius. Constantine reduced the tax exemptions of all serving soldiers from five people to four, actually naming the people to whom this applied: the soldier, his wife, and his parents. After serving for twenty-four years, the soldier would be awarded *emerita missio* and would retain tax exemption for himself and his wife, but if he retired after twenty years with *honesta missio* the tax exemption applied only to himself. There was a distinction between the field army and the frontier troops with regard to soldiers discharged for medical reasons. The *comitatenses* would receive *emerita missio* whatever their disability and however it had been caused, and retained their tax exemptions, but the *ripenses* or frontier troops who were wounded in action and forced to retire would be awarded *causaria missio* only if they had served for a minimum of sixteen years. If a soldier of the frontier troops had served for only ten years or so, and was then injured in a battle or in an accident, he would receive no privileges if he retired at that point. Another decree of Constantine, issued in 326, or possibly in 320, further clarified privileges for veterans, who were exempted from municipal service, and from taxes if they engaged in trade, being allowed to buy and sell freely. For the veterans who were unemployed, vacant lands were to be given to them and a grant was to be made for farming equipment, or alternatively a much smaller grant was to be issued for the man to set up in business. The money grant had been abolished by the reign of Valentinian I, but the land together with grain and two oxen were supplied. By the sixth century the land grants ceased, perhaps because the vacant lands were on poor soil, and more than likely the perennial problem that had existed since the Republic still pertained, that soldiers did not necessarily make good farmers. Even if a veteran used slaves to run the farm he would have to possess some knowledge and at least a modicum of interest in farming. It was in the soldiers' interests to serve for longer than the legal requirement, to save money if they could from the donatives that they received and to try to engage in trade or business while still serving, otherwise their retirement years would probably have been quite bleak. The need for soldiers to serve for longer and try to save more seems particularly pertinent at the time of writing, when people are faced with the prospect of working for longer and building up pension funds. As the French would say, the more it changes, the more it stays the same.

6

The End of the Roman Army

The traditional date of AD 476 for the fall of the Roman Empire in the west is as artificial as most other dates for the beginnings and endings of historical epochs, which are after all not naturally occurring divisions but invented by historians in order to create manageable sections that are easier to study. Life in what remained of the western Empire continued after 476 in an altered form, and underpinning the law and administrative systems of the kingdoms that emerged, much that was originally Roman survived, except for the army. In the east the Roman army morphed seamlessly into the Byzantine army, and the Roman Empire did not really die until the fall of Constantinople in the fifteenth century. The disappearance of the Roman army in the west was slow and steady, and no traditional date has ever been put forward to pinpoint the time when it vanished, mostly because it did not succumb to a universal collapse that happened simultaneously in all parts of the Empire. It was eroded piece by piece, and there was no single cause for its demise.

The authors of the fourth and fifth centuries noted a decline in the army before the Empire split into two halves. Some historians were certain that the reason behind the decline was the increasing recruitment of tribesmen, and they wrote in derogatory terms about what they saw as barbarisation of the army, which they abhorred and regretted. One of the most vociferous was Synesius, a native of Cyrene who became bishop of Ptolemais in 410. He advocated the complete removal of all barbarians from high office, regardless of the fact that many barbarian commanders had performed excellently for Rome. Snobbery rather than racism motivated Synesius, who thought that tribesmen came from the same stock as slaves, and he would have preferred to see them kept low in the social scale. He hated the idea that the term *senator*, once denoting a dignified upper class member of the government could now be given as a title to an officer in the army, who would most likely be a barbarian.

The treaty that Theodosius I had made with the Goths in 382 probably allowed the tribes to fight under their own leaders and the terms seemed far too lax compared with earlier treaties. Theodosius was blamed for flooding the army with barbarians, though there were some voices raised in his support. In a panegyric addressed to Theodosius, its author Pacatus was full of praise for the Goths, though it cannot be said that a panegyric is the best source for an unbiased view. The Greek orator and philosopher Themistius, who was born in about 317, and Salvian, presbyter at Marseilles from about 439, may not have liked the tribesmen but they were realists who recognised the fact that the barbarians were not going to disappear and the Romans would not be able to defeat them decisively, so they had to be accommodated. Themistius added, with regard to the settlement of barbarians in Thrace, that it was better to fill the land with farmers and soldiers than corpses. An active and continuous policy of assimilation and Romanisation might have solved the problem, as Paulinus of Nola and Orosius suggested, and they thought that Christianisation would help to integrate the barbarians with the Romans.

Several things were lacking in the western Roman Empire that would perhaps have helped to put these ideas into effect. Romanisation was feasible in the long term, especially if the tribesmen could have been distributed in military units which were already trained and accustomed to Roman traditions and customs. But this would take time, and the strong central cadre of trained and Romanised troops was diminished by the end of the fourth century. The soldiers lost at Adrianople in 378 damaged the eastern army, and the battle of the Frigidus in 394 affected the army in the west, and replacements were not as easy to find as they had been. Citizens were less eager to volunteer or to respond to conscription. At the end of the fourth century Theodosius had to reissue and reinforce the laws pertaining to recruitment that had been passed from Diocletian's time and during the reigns of Valentinian and Valens. Sons of veterans were forced to enlist, and anyone producing slaves instead of suitable recruits from their estates were to be punished. By 406 all scruples about slaves were dropped, and the government was calling them to arms.

Manpower shortage for the army is not the same as population shortage. It has been argued that there was not really a serious manpower shortage at all, and that the increasingly savage legislation concerning recruitment was passed only at times of danger when troops had to be raised quickly. But the fact that the laws were passed at all must surely indicate that while there may have been a plentiful population, which is subject to debate, there were problems in finding suitable and willing men, whether or not the need for them was caused by a mini-crisis of some sort. The problem may not have concerned available population but the ability to turn the population into soldiers. There was usually a plentiful supply of tribesmen who could be brought in to fill the gaps in all units. Some tribesmen, like the Goths of Theodosius' treaty, were probably kept together under their own commanders, and fought in their own styles with their own weapons. On campaigns, allied chiefs could be asked to provide troops, as had always been the case from Republican times when allies in or near the war zones contributed troops on a temporary basis. Some tribesmen joined the army voluntarily on the proviso that they would not have to fight at any distance from their homes. For static defence, for mobile defence and for campaigns, manpower could usually be found, moulded into shape, and sent into battle, but this takes time, and the western Empire was too busy fire-fighting, responding to various threats in various different locations, to be able to devote time and attention to training and disciplining their new troops.

The lapse of training is indicated by a law passed in 443 exhorting the *duces* of the frontier armies to supervise the daily training of the soldiers and to restore them to their 'ancient number'. This implies that in the past numbers had been greater and training was undertaken without a law having to be passed to enforce it. The comments of Vegetius are informative. In the dedication his book on the organisation of the army to an emperor, probably Theodosius, Vegetius points out that it was discipline and training that had enabled the Romans to conquer all their enemies in the past, and more significantly he says that a small properly trained force is more effective than an inexperienced and untrained horde. This sounds like an unfavourable comparison of the current situation and the past.

If training had declined, so had morale and discipline. Even Pacatus, who was favourable to the Goths because he wrote in support of Theodosius' arrangements with them, could not avoid acknowledging that these tribesmen were not noted for staying at their posts, and they could not be prevented from pillaging and looting. Ammianus Marcellinus is even more scornful of the abilities of the barbarian troops, referring to them in derogatory terms on more than one occasion, but more pertinently for military purposes he says that the tribesmen could never follow a coherent plan, could not discern the consequences of their actions, and were discouraged by the slightest setback. These are quite different from the tribesmen who had been recruited in former times, who had been Romanized, indoctrinated, and trained, and fought for Rome as Romans. Something had changed in the fourth century that made the barbarians less effective, and it was not the tribesmen, but the military organisation and administration.

According to Zosimus administration and record keeping declined or had been abandoned by the fifth century. Since he was writing with hindsight from a distance of two centuries or more, it is possible that he misinterpreted his sources, or even invented his information, but what he says is damning. The army no longer recorded the names and details of men who had been enrolled in the army, and the deserters that Theodosius had reinstated could go home if they wished to, if they could find a substitute. This flexibility, coupled with the lack of training, shows that the emphasis was on quantity not quality in the late Roman army. As Vegetius said, smaller numbers of trained men are more useful than large numbers of untrained ones.

The problem may have been remediable if there had been a cohesive ideology combined with a strong charismatic leader who could inspire the army as a whole and instil purpose into the soldiers, but the increase of regionalism as opposed to any sense of Rome or Empire only served to compound the issue. The tribesmen would fight on behalf of their leaders, but even if they were Roman leaders, the men were not necessarily fighting for Rome, which they had probably never seen. They would protect the areas that they saw as their homelands, but would not be quite as interested in defending a more distant area, even if it was inhabited by people with the same ethnic background. What had died, before 476, was the concept of the unity of the Roman Empire and a shared purpose. Rome was not in the ascendancy any longer, and could not defend the frontiers or even all the provinces. Regions furthest from Rome were abandoned little by little. Troops were taken out of Britain and the inhabitants declared themselves independent, ejecting the Roman officials probably in 410, though it took some time for them to renounce Rome altogether, since the Britons allegedly wrote to Aetius in the mid-fifth century to ask for help. The Goths had already established a foothold in Spain, and the Roman troops were removed in the early fifth century. In the end, only Italy and Gaul were defended, ultimately by barbarian generals who were Roman citizens but not really Romans, though they tried hard to be more Roman than the Romans, like Odoacer.

Apart from the piecemeal withdrawal from the outlying provinces, there was no official decree from Rome or from Imperial headquarters at Ravenna announcing the disbandment of the Roman army. Soldiers were left to work this out for themselves, and in some cases tried to carry on living in the forts without the infrastructure of the supply system and centralized administration and law. There is evidence from the northern frontier of Britain that people were living inside forts in the post-Roman era, adapting the buildings to their new requirements. When life on these terms became untenable new groupings under different leaders would begin. In Britain the re-emergent Celtic kingdoms revealed just how thin was the veneer of Romanisation after four centuries of Imperial rule.

The demise of the Roman army in the west, not by a cataclysmic event, but by a slow, sad death, is illustrated by the famous story told in the life of St Severin by Eugippius. The tale does not lose any of its emotional impact despite its obligatory retelling in connection with the army. At the junction of the river Inn with the Danube at modern Passau, a fort called Batava, named for the cohort of Batavians which garrisoned it, was still manned in the mid- fifth century. The soldiers had stayed loyally at their posts, probably cultivating the land around the fort, and awaiting the arrival of their pay. When it did not arrive they decided to send a delegation to

Italy to find out what was happening. There was no answer, only the reappearance of the men floating down the river, killed by unknown hands. The end of the Roman army was probably very similar for many of the units that remained on the diminished frontiers. The soldiers would have to decide what to do when they realised that the old order was dead, and they were on their own.

Timeline 753 BC–AD 476

BC

Eighth-century BC Etruscans in central Italy and Greeks colonise southern Italy and Sicily.

753 Traditional date for the foundation of the city of Rome, worked out by Roman historians; other dates were suggested but 753 became the accepted version.

540 Battle of Aleria between Etruscans and Carthaginians.

509 Traditional date for the overthrow of the kings and the establishment of the Republic; first consuls established, according to the Fasti Capitolini; probably the first treaty between Rome and Carthage; first temple built on the Capitol Hill.

497 Battle of Lake Regillus, Rome defeats the Latins.

494 First Secession of the Plebs.

493 Treaty with Latins.

486 Treaty with Hernici.

474 Greeks of Syracuse defeat Etruscans and Carthaginians off Cumae.

471 Creation of tribunes of the plebs.

457 Tribunes of the plebs increased to ten.

451–450 Twelve Tables of law created.

446 Two quaestors elected for financial duties.

444–367 Military tribunes with consular power elected, intermittently replacing consuls.

443/440 Censorship created.

440 Patricians and plebeians equal by law (*Lex Canuleia*).

421 Number of quaestors created in 446 now raised to four.

405 Siege of Veii begins and traditionally lasts until 395.

396/395 Capture of Veii and its destruction; traditional date for introduction of military pay.

390 (or 380s) Romans defeated by Gauls at the battle of the Allia; the Gauls sack Rome.

348 Treaty with Carthage

341 First Samnite war.

340–338 Rebellion of the Latins begins; Rome victorious in 338; end of the so-called Latin League.

338 Colony founded at Antium (Anzio).

335 Ostia founded.

326–304 Second Samnite war.

321 Romans defeated by the Samnites, and the army forced under the yoke at the Caudine Forks.

312 Via Appia established linking Rome with Capua.

309–308 War with the Etruscans.

306 Renewed treaty with Carthage.

298–290 War with Samnites, Etruscans and Gauls.

281–272 War with Pyrrhus King of Epirus.

264–241 First Punic War.

260 Rome wins naval battle with Carthaginians off Mylae.

229–228 First Illyrian war.

227 Rome creates first province of Sicily, followed by Sardinia and Corsica.

225 Battle of Telamon, Rome defeats Gauls.

220 Via Flaminia founded, Rome to Ariminum.

220–219 Second Illyrian war.

218 Second Punic War begins; Hannibal invades Italy; Romans defeated at the battle of the Trebia.

217 Romans defeated at battle of Lake Trasimene. Fabius Cunctator (the Delayer) made Dictator.

216 Romans defeated at battle of Cannae.

215 Hannibal allies with Philip V of Macedon. First Macedonian war begins, 215–205.

213 Tarentum falls to Hannibal.

211 Romans recapture Capua; fall of Syracuse to Marcellus.

210 Publius Cornelius Scipio takes command in Spain; Romans capture Cartagena.

205 Peace with Philip V and end of first Macedonian war.

204 Scipio invades Africa.

202–201 Scipio defeats Hannibal at battle of Zama; end of second Punic War.

200–196 Second Macedonian war; Romans victorious at battle of Cynocephalae.

197 Spain made into two provinces, each under a praetor.

196 Flamininus declares freedom of the Greeks.

192–189 War with Antiochus the Great and the Aetolians.

171 Third Macedonian war begins.

168 Aemilianus defeats Macedonians at battle of Pydna.

167 End of third Macedonian war.

149–148 Fourth Macedonian war.

149–146 Third Punic war; Carthage is destroyed, and the territory annexed as Roman province of Africa.

146 Achaean League rebels against Rome; Romans victorious; Corinth destroyed; province of Macedonia created.

147–139 War in Spain against rebel leader Viriathus/Viriatus.

143–133 War in Spain; Scipio appointed general in 137; siege of Numantia ends 133.

135–132 Slave rebellion in Sicily.

133 Tiberius Gracchus tribune of the plebs; kingdom of Pergamum bequeathed to Rome.

128–126 Creation of the province of Asia.

123–122 Gaius Gracchus tribune of the plebs.

122 City of Aquae Sextiae (Aix-en-Provence) founded.

120 Province of Gallia Narbonensis created.

111–105 War in North Africa against Jugurtha.

108 Marius elected consul and recruits soldiers for the African war from the *capite censi*.

105 Cimbri and Teutones defeat Romans at Arausio (Orange).

105–100 Marius elected consul in successive years, and reforms and trains the army to meet Cimbri and Teutones.

102 Marius defeats Teutones at Aquae Sextiae (Aix-en-Provence)

101 Marius defeats Cimbri at Vercellae.

100 Campaigns against pirates of Cilicia, and creation of province of Cilicia.

90–88 Social War between Rome and Italian allies; rise of Sulla.

89 Roman citizenship offered to Italians.

89–85 First Mithradatic War; Sulla appointed to the command in place of Marius.

87 Marius and Cinna consuls; massacres in Rome.

83 Return of Sulla and rise of Pompey the Great.

82–81 Dictatorship of Sulla.

77–71 Pompey the Great and Metellus command against Sertorius in Spanish war.

74–66 Third Mithradatic war; Lucius Licinius Lucullus in command.

69–67 Caecilius Metellus defeats Cretan pirates; Crete made into a province with Cyrene.

67 Pompey's command against the Mediterranean pirates.

66–63 Pompey takes over Mithradatic war from Lucullus.

63 Province of Bithynia-Pontus organised by Pompey.

59 Julius Caesar elected consul.

58–56 Caesar's campaigns in Gaul.

56 Caesar, Pompey and Crassus form liaison at Lucca.

55–54 Caesar invades Britain.

53 Marcus Licinius Crassus defeated by Parthians at Carrhae.

52–51 Revolt of Vercingetorix in Gaul, which is made a Roman province.

49 Civil war begins between Caesar and Pompey.

48 Pompey defeated at Pharsalus.

48–47 Caesar and the Alexandrian war; Cleopatra VII made Queen of Egypt.

47 Caesar's war against Pharnaces; reports to Rome *veni, vidi, vici*.

46 Pompeians defeated in Africa at Thapsus.

45 Pompeians defeated in Spain at Munda.

Before 44 Caesar doubles army pay.

44 Caesar assassinated.

43 Octavian allies with Antony and Lepidus; the second Triumvirate formed.

42 Antony defeats Brutus and Cassius at Philippi.

36 Final defeat of Sextus Pompey and eradication of his fleet.

31 Battle of Actium; Cleopatra and Antony flee to Alexandria.

30 Alexandria falls to Octavian, who takes over Egypt and instals equestrian governor; commands about sixty legions, gradually reduced to twenty-eight legions. Vast settlement programme begun for veterans.

27 BC to AD 14 Principate of Augustus.

27 Augustus hands over government to Senate; Roman Empire divided into Imperial and senatorial provinces.

25 Galatia made a province; embassy from India arrives in Rome.

20 Augustus negotiates return of military standards from Parthia.

16 Conquest of Noricum.

15 Raetia and Noricum made provinces.

15 Tiberius and Drusus campaign in Alps; Raeti and Vindelici tribes defeated.

14–9 Tiberius conquers Pannonia.

12 Agrippa dies.

12–6 Drusus campaigns in Germany; Tiberius campaigns in Pannonia; Alpine tribes finally subdued.

AD

4 Tiberius adopted as son of Augustus.

6 Augustus forms *aerarium militare* to fund pensions for veterans; *Vigiles* created in Rome; Judaea made a province.

6–9 Tiberius quells Pannonian revolt.

7 Rome divided into fourteen regions.

9 Arminius destroys three legions in Germany; the governor Varus commits suicide.

13 First regular Urban Prefect appointed; Urban Cohorts probably established at the same time under command of Urban Prefect.

14 Augustus dies.

14–37 Tiberius Emperor.

14–17 Germanicus campaigns in Germany.

15 Sejanus appointed Praetorian Prefect.

17 Germanicus in the east; province of Cappadocia annexed.

19 Death of Germanicus.

31 Sejanus eliminated.

37–41 Death of Tiberius in 31; Caligula Emperor.

42 Caligula assassinated.

41–54 Claudius Emperor.

42 Mauretania divided into Caesariensis and Tinigtana.

43 Invasion of Britain; Ostia made into chief port of Rome.

45 Thrace annexed.

54 Claudius dies.

54–68 Nero Emperor.

55–63 War with Parthia for control of Armenia; Corbulo campaigns in the east.

60–61 Rebellion of Boudicca in Britain.

66 Jewish revolt begins.

68 Suicide of Nero; Galba, Otho and Vitellius Emperors.

68–79 Vespasian Emperor.

69 Revolt of Civilis and the Batavians on the Rhine.

70 Capture of Jerusalem.

73–4 Siege of Masada.

79 Vespasian dies and turns into a god; Vesuvius destroys Pompeii and Herculaneum.

79–81 Titus Emperor.

81–96 Domitian Emperor.

82–83 Domitian increases army pay from 225 *denarii* per annum to 300 *denarii*.

83 Domitian campaigns against Chatti in Germany.

83 or 84 Agricola wins battle of Mons Graupius in Scotland and garrisons the country.

85 Germany divided into Upper and Lower provinces, previously administered from Gaul.

85–89 Dacian wars; governor of Moesia killed; army under Praetorian Prefect Fuscus defeated; another army under Tettius Julianus victorious at Tapae; treaty with Dacians.

86 Moesia divided into two provinces.

89 Revolt of Saturninus at Mainz; Domitian puts an end to two-legion fortresses.

89–92 Danube campaigns.

96–97 German campaigns; Trajan as general.

96 Domitian assassinated.

96–98 Nerva Emperor.

98–117 Trajan Emperor.

101–102 First Dacian war of Trajan.

102 Development of port of Ostia begins.

105–106 Second Dacian war of Trajan; annexation of Dacia.

106 Nabataean kingdom annexed and made province of Arabia Petraea.

113–117 Parthian war of Trajan; annexation of northern part of Mesopotamia.

115–117 Jewish revolt.

117 Death of Trajan in the east.

117–138 Hadrian Emperor.

117 Abandonment of Parthian conquests, and parts of Dacian province given up.

122 Building of Hadrian's Wall begins in Britain, using stone except for parts of the eastern sector.

123 Peace arranged with Parthia.

Before 138 German frontier built as timber palisade; stretches of stone wall built in Africa.

132–135 Jewish revolt; possibly the context for disappearance of *IX Hispana*.

138 Death of Hadrian.

138–161 Antoninus Pius Emperor.

140 onwards Construction of Antonine Wall begins in Scotland; German frontier advanced a few kilometres to the east, new line called Outer Limes by archaeologists.

161 Death of Antoninus Pius.

161–180 Marcus Aurelius Emperor with Lucius Verus as colleague 161–169.

162–166 Lucius Verus makes war on Parthia.

167–180 Marcus at war on the Danube against Quadi, Marcommani and Sarmatians.

169 Lucius Verus dies.

176 Commodus made Augustus with Marcus.

180 Death of Marcus on Danube.

180–192 Commodus Emperor; makes peace on Danube, builds watchtowers called *burgi* to control small-scale threats.

192 Commodus assassinated on last day of December.

193 Pertinax Emperor; Didius Julianus Emperor.

193–211 Severus declared Emperor by legions; marches to Rome; disbands Praetorian Guard, creates new Guard; increases number or troops in Rome.

193–197 Civil war between Septimius Severus and Pescennius Niger in the east, then between Severus and Clodius Albinus who brings troops from Britain to Gaul.

195–195 Severus makes war on Parthia.

197–199 Second war on Parthia; part of Mesopotamia reclaimed as Roman province.

197–211 Severus recognises soldiers' marriages and awards first pay rise since reign of Domitian.

198 Caracalla made Augustus with Severus.

208–211 Severan campaigns in northern Britain.

209 Severus' younger son Geta made Augustus.

211 Death of Severus at York.

211–217 Caracalla Emperor.

212 *Constitutio Antoniniana* gives citizenship to all freeborn inhabitants of the Empire; Geta murdered by Caracalla.

213–214 Caracalla campaigns in Germany.

216–217 Parthian war of Caracalla, who is assassinated in 217.

217–222 Civil war; reign of Macrinus 217–218; reign of Elagabalus 218–222; Syrian princesses dominate Empire.

222–235 Severus Alexander Emperor.

224 onwards Rise of Sassanids in Parthia which now becomes Persian Empire.

231–232 Severus Alexander campaigns in the east against Persians.

234–235 Severus Alexander makes war on Rhine frontier, but is assassinated in 235.

235 So-called military anarchy begins, rapid succession of emperors.

235–238 Maximinus Thrax Emperor.

238 Gordian I and Gordian II Emperors.

238–244 Gordian III Emperor.

244–249 Philip the Arab Emperor.

249–251 Decius Emperor; wars with Carpi and Goths on Danube, Franks and Alamanni on Rhine.

251 Goths defeat Decius; plague in Empire.

251–253 Trebonianus Gallus Emperor; civil wars.

253–260 Valerian Emperor with his son Gallienus as colleague.

257 Gallic Empire splits from Rome.

258 Alamanni move from Gaul into northern Italy.

260 Valerian's campaign against the Persians ends with his defeat and capture.

260–268 Gallienus sole Emperor, but with limited access to central area of Empire.

260 Odenathus of Palmyra rules in the east after Valerian's defeat.

267 Goths sack Athens.

268 Aurelian assassinated; Odenathus of Palmyra probably assassinated now, rule in east passes to his wife Zenobia and young son Vaballathus.

268–270 Claudius Gothicus Emperor; victory over the Goths.

270–275 Aurelian Emperor.

271 Aurelian probably evacuates Dacia now and moves population into Moesia.

272 Aurelian reconquers the east and Palmyra; fate of Zenobia and Vaballathus uncertain.

274 Aurelian reconquers Gallic Empire; begins to build walls around Rome; reforms coinage and operation of Rome mint.

275–276 Tacitus Emperor; wars with Goths, Franks, Alamanni.

276–282 Probus Emperor; frontiers restored, cities rebuilt.

282–3 Carus Emperor with his son Numerianus; campaigns against Persians.

282–285 Carinus Emperor in the west.

284 End of Persian campaign; Carus and Numerianus killed; Diocletian made Emperor.

284–305 Diocletian Emperor with Maximianus as colleague from 286; new bodyguard *scholae* created; changes to the army begin, new legions created possibly 1,000 strong; provinces split into smaller units, and grouped into twelve Dioceses, each under the control of a *vicarius*, constituting an extra tier of provincial government.

284 Bagaudae in Gaul.

288–293 Britain breaks away under Carausius.

293 Tetrarchy created, Constantius I Chlorus and Galerius made Caesars.

293–296 Carausius assassinated, Allectus takes command in Britain.

296 Constantius I regains control of Britain and campaigns in the north.

298 Treaty with the Persians made by Diocletian.

305 Diocletian and Maximianus abdicate; Tetrarchy continues with two Augusti and two Caesars.

306 Constantius Chlorus campaigns in Britain and dies in office; Constantine declared Emperor by the troops in Britain.

306–312 Maxentius declared Emperor in Rome; civil war; Constantine defeats Maxentius at the battle of the Milvian Bridge in Rome in 312.

311 Persecution of Christians ends with Edict of Toleration.

313 Edict of Milan establishes Peace of the Church.

317 Constantine II made Caesar.

324 Constantine defeats remaining rival Licinius.

324–337 Constantine sole Emperor.

324 onwards Constantius II appointed Caesar; Constantine abolishes the Praetorian Guard; beginning of division of the army into mobile field armies (*comitatenses*) and frontier armies (*limitanei*). Billeting of troops in cities begins.

325 Council of Nicaea to try to resolve disputes in Christian Church.

326 Execution of Constantine's wife Fausta, and son Crispus.

330 Constantinople becomes the Imperial capital in place of Rome.

333 Constans made Caesar.

337 Baptism and death of Constantine.

337–361 Constantine II, Constantius II and Constans, sons of Constantine, in power.

340 Death of Constantine II.

350 Death of Constans.

350 onwards Huns and Goths appear north of the Black Sea.

355 Julian made Caesar under Constantius II.

357 Julian defeats Alamanni at battle of Strasbourg.

360 Troops proclaim Julian as Augustus at Paris.

361 Death of Constantius II.

363 Julian killed in battle in Persia.

363–364 Jovian Emperor.

364 Valentinian I and his brother Valens made joint Emperors.

367 Gratian, son of Valentinian I, made Augustus.

367 So-called Barbarian Conspiracy and multiple attacks on Britain; Count Theodosius takes command and restores order.

375 Death of Valentinian I; his four-year-old son Valentinian II made Augustus.

377 Goths cross the Danube.

378 Romans defeated at battle of Adrianople against Goths; death of Valens; after the battle, sealed orders sent to eastern army commanders to summon all Goths in the Roman army to a pay parade, and kill them.

379 Theodosius I made Emperor by Gratian; reigns 379–395.

382 Treaty with the Goths on more favourable terms than previous treaties.

383–388 Usurpation of Magnus Maximus, declared Emperor in Britain, enters into Welsh legend as Macsen Wledig.

383 Arcadius, son of Theodosius I, made Augustus with his father.

386 More Goths cross Danube, settled on land in Asia Minor.

387–393 Theodosius I fights Goths and usurpers Maximus and Eugenius, with the help of the Vandal general Stilicho who is made *magister militum* in 391.

393 Honorius, younger son of Theodosius I, made Augustus with his father.

395 Death of Theodosius I; from now on separate Emperors in west and east, but not yet definite split. Alaric emerges as leader of Goths; first attacks by Huns through Caucasus.

Western Empire

395–423 Honorius Emperor in the west.

395 Stilicho takes control of the west in the name of Honorius, and also claims that Theodosius appointed him regent to Arcadius in the east.

401 Alaric invades Italy; driven off by Stilicho.

404–405 General Stilicho makes treaty with Alaric.

405–406 Other Goths under Radagaisus invade Italy; Stilicho defeats them.

406–412 Rhine frontier crossed by Germanic tribes who devastate Gaul and enter Spain, where they create barbarian kingdoms.

407–411 Constantine III declared Emperor in Britain.

408 Alaric bought off with 4,000 pounds of gold; Arcadius dies in the east; Stilicho and Honorius disagree about the rule of the east; execution of general Stilicho.

409–411 Maximus declared Emperor in Spain.

410 Alaric sacks Rome.

410–412 Britain breaks away from the Empire, expels Roman officials; traditionally Honorius writes letter to tell Britons to look to their own defence.

411–413 Jovinus declared Emperor by Burgundians in Gaul.

411–421 Supremacy of Roman general Flavius Constantius.

422–429 Vandals and Alans spread into North Africa; in 427 Gaiseric emerges as leader in Africa; control of Roman provinces lost to Western Empire.

425–455 Valentinian III made Emperor in the west, aged six.

433–454 Rise and supremacy of Roman general Aetius.

436 Aetius defeats Bagaudae in Gaul.

439 Aetius ends three years of war with Visigoths in Gaul and makes treaty.

440 Attila becomes leader of Huns.

451 Attila invades Gaul, defeated by Aetius at battle of Catalaunian Fields.

453 Death of Attila; Huns Empire collapses.

454 Valentinian III executes Aetius.

455 Petronius Maximus murders Valentinian III, and made Emperor in March; killed in May by troops under Gaiseric invading from Africa; Gaiseric takes over Sardinia and Tripolitania.

455–456 Avitus proclaimed Emperor by Visigoths in Gaul; deposed by Ricimer in 456.

457–461 Majorian Emperor; deposed and executed by general Ricimer 461.

461–472 General Ricimer dominates policy of the west, and appoints and removes emperors.

461–465 Severus III Emperor; dies 465.

467–472 Anthemius Emperor; executed by Gundobad the Burgundian, ally of Ricimer.

472 Olybrius declared Emperor before death of Anthemius; rules from April to November; death of Ricimer in August; death of Olybrius in November.

473–474 Glycerius Emperor; deposed by Julius Nepos, and becomes bishop of Salona.

474–475 Julius Nepos Emperor; deposed by Orestes, *magister militum*.

475–476 Romulus Augustulus, young son of Orestes, made Emperor; deposed by Odoacer who executes Orestes but allows Romulus to retire to a Campanian villa.

476 Odoacer King of Italy; traditional date of end of western Roman Empire.

489–493 Theoderic the Amal Goth, supported by Zeno and then Anastasius the Emperor of Byzantium, defeats and kills Odoacer and rules Italy.

Eastern Empire

395–408 Arcadius Emperor.

397–399 Dominance of palace chamberlain Eutropius under Arcadius; treaty with Alaric who is given military command in Illyricum; ends when Eutropius overthrown.

399–400 Gainas the Goth becomes *magister militum praesentalis*; rebels defeated by the Goth Fravitta and killed by Huns; massacre of Goths in Constantinople following the rebellion. In fifth century eastern Empire recruits local tribesmen instead of Goths and other Germanic tribes.

402 Theodosius II, son of Arcadius, made co-Emperor in the east.

408–450 Theodosius II Emperor.

408 (?) Huns invade eastern Empire.

440 onwards Attila leads Huns; invades Balkans in 441 and again in 447.

450–457 Marcian Emperor in the east.

457–474 Leo I Emperor, with grandson Leo II as co-Emperor 473–474.

459 Goths from Danube invade the east; bought off by annual subsidies in gold.

474–491 Zeno, father of Leo II, made Emperor.

476–477 Usurpers Basiliscus and Marcus, executed by Zeno.

484–488 Usurper Leontius, executed by Zeno.

491–518 Anastasius I, first Byzantine Emperor.

Glossary

acetum sour wine.

ad signa deduction from military pay to the burial club.

aedile city magistrate originally responsible for supervision of the *aedes*, or the temples of the plebs. During the Republic there were two aediles subordinate to the tribunes of the plebs, and later two more were elected from the patricians (*aediles curules*). In the Empire the main duties of the aediles were care of the city, including keeping the streets clean, keeping public order, attending to the water supply and markets. They were also in charge of the public games (*ludi*) until Augustus transferred this duty to the praetors. All the municipalities of the Empire employed elected aediles fulfilling the same purposes as they did in Rome.

aerarium militare military treasury set up by Augustus in AD 6 to provide pensions for veterans.

ala milliaria auxiliary cavalry unit with a paper strength of 1,000 men.

ala quingenaria auxiliary cavalry unit of about 500 men.

annona militaris provisions for the army.

aquila eagle standard of a legion, instituted by Marius.

aquilifer standard-bearer carrying the eagle standard of the legion.

armillae decorative armbands awarded for distinguished service.

artaba Egyptian corn measure, equivalent to one-third of a Roman *modius*.

as (plural *asses*) low-denomination Roman coin, made of bronze, and the most common coin used to pay the soldiers; four asses made one *sestertius*; lower denominations than the *as* were the brass *semis* and the bronze *quadrans*, respectively worth half and one-quarter of an *as*.

auctoritas a measure of the reputation and social and political standing of Roman senators and politicians. The literal translation 'authority' does not convey its true meaning. *Auctoritas* could be earned and increased by political or military achievements and lost after disgraceful conduct.

aureus Roman gold coin, worth twenty-five *denarii*.

auxilia literally 'help troops', the term used by the Romans to describe the units recruited from non-Romans, organised as *alae* and *cohortes* during the Empire.

ballista artillery engine firing either arrows or stone projectiles.

beneficiarii usually legionaries with long experience, on the staff of a provincial governor and stationed at important places on the frontiers or within the provinces. They may have undertaken police work and perhaps were responsible for intelligence gathering.

bucellarii literally 'biscuit eaters', used of the private armies formed from the retainers of the powerful landowners of the late Empire.

bucina horn sounded to change the guard and at military ceremonies.

bucinator horn blower.

burgus watchtower or fortified landing place on a river.

campidoctor drill-instructor or trainer; see also *magister campi*.

canabae the civilian settlement outside a legionary fortress; see also *vicus*.

capitatio a poll tax, paid in cash.

capitum fodder; in the later Empire when payments to the soldiers were made partly in kind, *capitum* and *annona* were the terms used for food for the horses and the men.

capsa a box for storing documents, but in a military context it signified a bandage box.

capsarius medical assistant.

carroballista light field artillery *ballista* carried on a cart usually pulled by mules.

cataphractarii heavy armoured cavalry, perhaps armed with lance and shield.

centuria a century, or a division of a cohort, nominally of 100 men, but in practice of eighty men from the late Republic and throughout the Empire.

centurion commander of a century, or *centuria*.

cervesa Celtic beer.

cibarium specifically non-grain foodstuffs, but in the Roman army the term was applied to the food supply in general.

cingulum military belt of leather, with metal attachments for the sword, and other equipment. The use of this name was not common until the third century.

clibanarii slang term for heavy armoured cavalry, derived from *clibanus*, meaning oven. It is not certain whether these troops were the same as *cataphractarii* or whether they were armed and fought in a different way.

clipeus round shield used by soldiers of the early Roman army.

cohors a cohort, which had two meanings, the first a division of a legion containing six centuries, and the second denoting an auxiliary infantry unit, either *quingenaria*, 500 strong, or *milliaria*, 1,000 strong.

cohors equitata part-mounted auxiliary unit, either 500 strong (*quingenaria*) or 1,000 strong (*milliaria*).

colonus tenant of a landowner.

comes the entourage of an Emperor consisted of his friends (*comites*) on an unofficial basis at first, but Constantine gave the title *comes*, usually translated as Count, to his military commanders and provincial governors. There was originally no connotation of rank in the title, but with the passage of time three grades were established, called *ordinis primi*, *secundi*, and *tertii*.

comitatenses collective name for the units of the late Roman field army, comprising cavalry and infantry.

comitatus derived from *comes*, initially describing the entourage of the Emperor; by the fourth century *comitatus* denoted the field army.

commeatus in the Roman army this term was used to describe the food supplies, and also periods of leave.

consul senior magistrates of the Republic, elected annually in pairs, responsible for civil duties and command of the armies. During the Empire the consuls were still elected annually, but with reduced military responsibilities and subordinate to the Emperor.

consul ordinaries during the Empire there were often more than two consuls in the year. The *ordinarii* were the officially elected consuls, who might hold office for a month or two, giving way to the *consules suffecti*. The *ordinarii* were the eponymous consuls, giving their name to the year.

consul suffectus the suffect consuls were those who held office after the *ordinarii*, gaining experience and rank before going on to other appointments.

Constitutio Antoniniana act passed by Caracalla in AD 212, converting all freeborn inhabitants of the Empire into Roman citizens.

contarii cavalry units of the later Roman Empire, carrying the *contus*.

contubernium tent party or the soldiers sharing one barrack block, normally eight men.

contus a long, two-handed lance, used by the *cataphractarii*.

cornicen horn blower playing the *cornu*.

cornu large horn, curved round the horn blower's body and held by a wooden cross piece.

cornicularius clerical assistant, adjutant to a senior officer, or attached to the provincial governor's staff.

cuirass armour protecting the upper body. There were several types used by the Roman army, using mail, plate, or scale; see the various entries under *lorica*.

cuisse armour protecting the thighs, usually employed by cavalrymen.

cuneus wedge shaped battle formation, used in the late Empire to describe cavalry units.

curiales members of the city councils.

custos armarum literally, guard of the arms and armour.

decurio cavalry officer commanding a *turma*.

denarius Roman silver coin worth four *sestertii*; twenty-five *denarii* made one *aureus*.

dilectus the levy, and used of recruitment generally, from the verb *diligere*, meaning to value or favour.

diocese administrative grouping of several provinces, instituted by Diocletian, each governed by a *vicarius*.

diploma literally, in Latin, a letter folded in two; used by modern scholars to describe the pair of bronze tablets issued to discharged auxiliaries and the men of the fleets. Diploma is not the term that the soldiers would have used for the tablets, and it is now thought that soldiers had to apply for these rather than receiving one automatically on discharge.

dona militaria military decorations.

draco dragon standard, perhaps introduced into the army by the Sarmatians. It had a metal dragon's head attached to a fabric tube like a wind sock, and produced a roaring noise when inflated.

draconarius standard-bearer carrying the *draco*.

dromedarius camel rider.

duplicarius soldier on double pay; second in command of a cavalry *turma*.

dux (plural *duces*) literally, leader, and used as such in the earlier Empire; in the later Empire the title was used for equestrian military officers in command of troops in the frontier regions, usually with the title *dux limitis*. Their commands sometimes covered more than one province. *Duces* were raised to senatorial status by Valentinian.

equites legionis cavalry of a legion, initially thought to number 120 men, but increased by the Emperor Gallienus to over 700 men.

equites singulares cavalrymen usually seconded from the *alae*, acting as bodyguards to a provincial governor, usually in units 500 strong. The *equites singulares Augusti* were the cavalrymen guarding the Emperor.

exploratores scouts; initially individuals or small groups of men sent out to reconnoitre, later specific units.

fabrica workshop.

foederati literally those who are allied in war, derived from *foedus*, a treaty, and denoting troops raised according to the terms of a treaty. In the sixth century *foederati* was used of regular troops.

frumentum grain, but often used of the food supply in general.

gentiles non-Romans, applied to free tribes beyond the frontiers, and also tribesmen settled within the Empire.

gladius short thrusting sword, probably originating in Spain. It was used by the Roman army from the third century BC to the third century AD.

greave leg armour, usually of metal, covering the lower limb from knee to ankle.

gyrus circular area used for initial training of horses.

hasta general term for spear, covering a variety of sizes and types, and usually used for thrusting rather than throwing.

hiberna winter quarters.

honesta missio honourable discharge from the Roman army.

hoplon round shield used by Greek hoplites, who fought in a close formation called a phalanx with their shields overlapping.

horrea granary, probably used in forts for storing all types of food rather than just grain.

hippika gymnasia cavalry tournament of the Imperial period in which the men and the horses displayed their expertise, wearing highly decorated clothing and equipment.

imaginifer bearer of the *imago*, or image of the Emperor.

immunes soldiers exempt from fatigues because they had special skills and performed special tasks, but they did not receive extra pay.

impedimenta the baggage train.

in numeros referre phrase used for entering the names of recruits in the military records.

intervallum space between the rampart of a Roman fort or camp and the internal buildings or tents, to distance them from projectiles thrown over the walls.

iugum a unit of land for tax purposes, not always a standard measure since the type of land and the crops grown were taken into consideration by the assessors.

iumenta baggage animals, specifically mules.

laeti tribesmen settled by treaty inside the Empire, with obligations to provide men for the army.

legion the term *legio* originally meant the choosing, or the levy, and was eventually applied to the main unit of the Roman army. Around 5,000 strong, the legion was an infantry unit, but also contained some cavalry. Legions of the late Empire were smaller, newly raised units being probably only about 1,000 strong.

limes (plural *limites*) frontier.

limitanei frontier troops of the late Roman army.

lorica hamata mail armour made from iron rings interlinked.

lorica segmentata armour made from overlapping metal plates and associated with legionaries.

lorica squamata scale armour.

magister campi officer in charge of training.

magister equitum master of horse; in the Republic this title was given to the second in command of a Dictator; in the late Roman army it was an important military post in command of the cavalry units.

magister militum master of the soldiers, i.e.: the whole army in the late Roman period.

magister officiorum late Roman head of the secretarial offices.

magister peditum master of the infantry of the late Roman army.

maniple a unit of the Republican army consisting of two centuries.

medimnus Greek measure for grain used by Polybius; estimates of modern equivalents vary considerably.

medicus doctor.

modius Roman measure for dry goods, the chief measure applied to grain; one *modius* approximated to 2.4 gallons in US measure.

numerus meaning 'unit' in a very general sense, but from the late first or early second century applied to small, so-called ethnic units commonly found on the German and Dacian frontiers and in Africa.

optio second in command to a centurion.

paenula soldier's cloak, something like a duffel coat, with a hood.

paludamentum officer's cloak, worn round the shoulders with the end draped over the left arm.

phalerae military decorations, worn on the breastplate.

pilum missile weapon used by legionaries, frequently consisting of a long thin metal shank with a pyramidal tip, attached to a wooden shaft. There were various different sizes and types of *pila*.

praefectus prefect, a title given to several different officials and military officers; most commonly a commander of an auxiliary *ala* or cohort.

praefectus castrorum camp prefect, third in command of a legion during the Empire.

praeiuratio first stage of the military oath (*sacramentum*) in which the first man repeated the entire oath and the rest declared 'the same for me' (*idem in me*).

praepositus title given to an officer temporarily in command of troops, such as the *numeri* of the German and Dacian frontiers, or vexillations of troops brought together for a war. It is not strictly a rank, and soldiers of different grades could be appointed as *praepositi* for very varied tasks of high or low importance.

praeses (plural *praesides*) provincial governor of equestrian rank, common from Severan times onwards.

praesidium (plural *praesidia*) used in a military context to describe forts and fortified bases.

praetentura part of a Roman fort in front of the headquarters (*principia*), as opposed to the area behind it known as the *retentura*.

praetor the praetorship had a long history. Originally the praetors were the chief magistrates in early Republican Rome, but were eventually superceded by the consuls. When the consuls were absent the praetor was in charge of the courts, acted as president of the Senate, and had the right to command armies.

praetorium commanding officer's tent in the Republican army, also used of the commander's house in a Roman fort, usually with rooms arranged around a courtyard and an en suite bath system, to house his family and servants.

prata literally, meadow, and in the military context probably where the unit's animals were grazed around a fort.

primus pilus the most senior centurion in a legion, commanding the first century of the first cohort.

principia headquarters building of a Roman fort, where the standards were laid up and the administrative offices were situated.

probatio preliminary examination of recruits and also of horses for the army.

protectores a title used by Gallienus for his military entourage, not simply a bodyguard, but perhaps the foundation of a staff college formed from officers loyal to the Emperor.

pseudo-comitatenses late Roman troops taken from the *limitanei* or frontier armies to serve in the field army.

pteruges leather straps attached to armour.

quaestor originally the lowest-ranking magistrates of the Republic appointed to assist the consuls in financial matters. The office was held by young men at the start of their career, before they had entered the Senate. As the Empire expanded more quaestors were created to deal with provincial administration. Quaestors acted as deputies to consular governors, and could hold commands in the army. Sometimes in modern versions of ancient works, quaestor is translated as quartermaster, which is not strictly accurate.

ripenses troops serving on river frontiers in the late Roman army.

sacellum chapel of the standards in the headquarters of a Roman fort.

sacramentum the military oath of obedience and loyalty to the Emperor; during the Republic soldiers swore to obey their commanders, usually the consuls.

sagittarius archer.

sagum cloak worn by soldiers.

schola late Roman cavalry guard unit; *scholae palatinae* were the Emperor's guard.

scutum shield; the term is most commonly used for the rectangular semi-cylindrical version employed by legionaries.

sestertius Roman silver coin; four *sestertii* equalled one *denarius*.

sesquiplicarius soldier earning one and a half times normal pay; third in command of a cavalry *turma*.

signifer standard-bearer carrying the *signum*.

signum military standard of an individual century, consisting of various metal emblems on a pole, frequently topped by a hand with the palm facing forwards.

singulares bodyguards of various Roman officers, chosen from their original units, either cavalry or infantry. *Equites* and *pedites singulares consularis* formed the guard of a provincial governor, chosen from the units in the province, and *equites singulares Augusti* formed the bodyguard of the Emperor, chosen from units all over the Empire.

spatha long sword, used by infantry and cavalry from the second century onwards, and predominantly by the cavalry of the late Roman army.

stipendium military pay, also applied to a period of service, appearing on inscriptions and tombstones in abbreviated form as *stip.*, followed by however many years the soldiers had served.

territorium in the military context, land belonging to the army marked by boundary stones and perhaps used to grow crops.

testudo literally, tortoise or turtle, a formation where soldiers raised their shields above their heads and overlapped them at the front and the sides to advance in almost complete protection.

tiro (plural *tirones*) recruit.

triumph a triumph was granted by the Senate to victorious generals, who valued this opportunity to show off their captives and the spoils of war by processing along the Via Sacra in Rome, to the Temple of Jupiter. The *triumphator* rode in a chariot with his face painted red, and was supposed to approach the Temple on his knees to dedicate the spoils, with a slave at his side constantly reminding him that he was mortal. Augustus recognised the inflammatory nature of the triumph and took steps to limit it to members of the Imperial family. Other generals were denied the procession, and were granted triumphal insignia instead (*ornamenta triumphalia*).

tuba a long straight trumpet.

tubicen soldier who blew the *tuba* to transmit signals.

turma smallest unit of an *ala* or the mounted contingent of a *cohors equitata*, commanded by a *decurio* and probably containing thirty-two men, though this is fraught with debate.

valetudinarium hospital.

velites light armed infantry of the Republican army.

veterinarius veterinarian, used for civilian practitioners as well as soldiers; also listed as *medicus veterinarius*.

vexillum military standard of fringed cloth, usually red or purple, hung from a cross bar on a lance or spear.

vexillarius bearer of the *vexillum*.

vexillatio a detachment of troops, often drawn from different units to fulfil a temporary purpose, usually operating under a *vexillum*.

vexillationes late Roman cavalry units, possibly instituted by Gallienus. Their strength is disputed, perhaps consisting of 500 men, but some scholars argue for *c.* 1,000.

viaticum travelling money, given to new recruits who had passed their *probatio* to help them on the journey to the units to which they had been assigned.

vicarius governor of a diocese, or collection of provinces, from the late third century onwards, in control of civilian affairs and of lesser governors of provinces, and directly answerable to the Praetorian Prefects.

vicus a term that could mean an area within a town, or a rural village, but in the military context it refers to the civilian settlement outside a Roman auxiliary fort; see also *canabae*

Vigiles, the fire brigade of the city of Rome, organised in military fashion by Augustus from the early first century AD.

Bibliography

Ancient Sources
Ammianus Marcellinus. Loeb.
Appian *Roman History*. Loeb.
Caesar *Alexandrian, African and Spanish Wars*. Loeb.
Caesar *Civil War*. Loeb.
Caesar *Gallic War*. Loeb.
Dio *Roman History*. Loeb
Herodian *History of the Empire*. Loeb.
Josephus *Jewish War*. Loeb.
Livy *History of Rome*. Loeb.
Plutarch *Parallel Lives*. Loeb.
Polybius *The Histories*. Loeb.
Scriptores Historiae Augustae. Loeb.
Strabo *Geography*. Loeb.
Suetonius *Twelve Caesars*. Loeb.
Tacitus *Agricola*. Loeb.
Tacitus *Annals*. Loeb.
Tacitus *Germania*. Loeb.
Tacitus *Histories*. Loeb.
Vegetius, Publius *Ars Mulomedicinae*.
Vegetius, Flavius *Epitoma Rei Militaris*. Trans. N. P. Milner, Liverpool University Press, 1993.
Velleius Paterculus *Compendium of Roman History*. Loeb.
Vitruvius *The Ten Books on Architecture*. Translated by M. H. Morgan. New York: Dover Publications
 Inc.

Penguin Editions of Ancient Sources in English Translation
Appian *The Civil Wars*. Penguin Books, 1996.
Livy *The Early History of Rome*. Books I –V of *The History of Rome from Its Foundation*. Penguin
 Books, 1960; reprinted with additions 2002.
Livy *Rome and Italy*. Books VI–X of *The History of Rome from Its Foundation*. Penguin Books, 1982.
Livy *The War with Hannibal*. Books XXI–XXX of *The History of Rome from Its Foundation*. Penguin
 Books, 1965.
Livy *Rome and the Mediterranean*. Books XXXI–XLV of *The History of Rome from Its Foundation*.
 Penguin Books, 1976.
Polybius *The Rise of the Roman Empire*. Penguin Books, 1979.
Tacitus *The Annals of Imperial Rome*. Penguin Books, rev. ed. 1996.

General Works on the Roman Army
Bishop, M. C. and Coulston, J. C. *Roman Military Equipment from the Punic Wars to the Fall of Rome*.
 Batsford, 1993.
Campbell, B. *The Emperor and the Roman Army 31 BC–AD 235*. Clarendon Press, 1984.
Campbell, B. *The Roman Army 31 BC–AD 337: A Sourcebook*. Routledge, 1994.

Campbell, D. B. *The Rise of Imperial Rome AD 14–193*. Osprey Publishing, 2013.

Connolly, P. *Greece and Rome at War*. Greenhill Books, rev. ed. 1998.

D'Amato, R. *Arms and Armour of the Imperial Roman Soldier: From Marius to Commodus*. Frontline Books, 2009.

Erdkamp, P. (ed.) *A Companion to the Roman Army*. Wiley-Blackwell, 2011.

Feugere, M. *Weapons of the Romans*. Tempus, 2002.

Goldsworthy, A. *The Complete Roman Army*. Thames and Hudson, 2003.

Goldsworthy, A. K. *The Roman Army at War 100BC–AD 200*. Clarendon Press, 1996.

Goldsworthy, A. K. *Roman Warfare*. Cassell, 2000.

Keppie, L. *The Making of the Roman Army: From Republic to Empire*. Routledge, 1998.

Le Bohec, Y. *The Imperial Roman Army*. Batsford, 1994; republished by Routledge, 2000.

McNab, C. *Roman Army: The Greatest War Machine in the Ancient World*. Osprey Publishing, 2012.

Pollard, N. and Berry, J. *The Complete Roman Legions*. Thames and Hudson, 2012.

Sabin, P. et al. (eds.), *The Cambridge History of Greek and Roman Warfare Vol. I: Greece, the Hellenistic World and the Rise of Rome*. Cambridge University Press, 2007.

Sabin, P. et al. (eds.), *The Cambridge History of Greek and Roman Warfare Vol. 2: Rome from the Late Republic to the Late Empire*. Cambridge University Press, 2007.

Sabin, P. 'The Face of Roman battle', *Journal of Roman Studies* 90, 2000, 1–17.

Southern, P. *The Roman Army: A Social and Institutional History*. Oxford University Press, 2007; previously published by ABC-Clio.

Travis, H. and Travis, J. *Roman Body Armour*. Amberley, 2011.

Watson, G. R. *The Roman Soldier*. Thames and Hudson, 1969.

Webster, G. *The Roman Imperial Army of the First and Second Centuries AD*. A. and C. Black, 3rd ed. 1985.

Part I The Roman Army of the Kings and the Republic

1 Historical Overview 753–30 BC

Baker, S. *Ancient Rome: The Rise and Fall of an Empire*. BBC Books, 2007. First published in 2006.

Beard, M. and Crawford, M. *Rome in the Late Republic: Problems and Interpretations*. Duckworth, 1985.

Boatwright, M. T. et al. *The Romans: From Village to Empire*. Oxford University Press, 2004.

Brunt, P. A. *Social Conflicts in the Roman Republic*. W. W. Norton and Co., 1971.

Cornell, T. J. *The Beginnings of Rome: Italy and Rome from the Bronze Age to the Punic wars (c. 1000–264 BC)*.

Dillon, M. and Garland, L. *Ancient Rome: From the Early Republic to the Assassination of Julius Caesar*. Routledge, 2005.

Gelzer, M. *Caesar: Politician and Statesman*. Harvard University Press, 1968.

Grandazzi, A. *The Foundation of Rome: Myth and History*. Cornell University Press, 1997. Gruen, E. S. *The Last Generation of the Roman Republic*. University of California Press, 1974.

Heurgon, J. *The Rise of Rome to 264 BC*. University of California Press, 1973.

Le Glay, M et al. *A History of Rome*. Blackwell, 3rd ed. 2005.

Lintott, A. *The Constitution of the Roman Republic*. Oxford University Press, 1999.

Potter, T. W. *Roman Italy*. British Museum Press, 1987.

Ross Holloway, R. *The Archaeology of Early Rome and Latium*. Routledge, 1994.

Salmon, E. T. *The Making of Roman Italy*. Thames and Hudson, 1982.

Scullard, H. H. *The Etruscan Cities and Rome*. Thames and Hudson, 1967.

Shotter, D. *The Fall of the Roman Republic*. Routledge, 1994.

Southern, P. *Ancient Rome: The Rise and Fall of an Empire 753 BC–AD 476*. Amberley, 2009.

2 The Army of the Kings 753–509 BC

Cornell, T. J. *The Beginnings of Rome: Italy and Rome from the Bronze Age to the Punic Wars, c. 1000–264 BC*. Routledge, 1995.

Forsythe, G. 'The Army and Centuriate Organization in Early Rome', in Erdkamp (ed.) *A Companion to the Roman Army*. Wiley-Blackwell, 2011, 24–42.

Fraccaro, P. 'La Storia dellAntichissimo Esercito Romano e l'Eta dell'Ordinamento Centuriata', *Atti II Congresso Nazionale di Studi Romano 3*, 1931, 91–97.

Last, H. 'The Servian Reforms', *Journal of Roman Studies* 35, 1945, 30–48.

Rawson, E. D. 'The Literary Sources for the pre-Marian Army', *Papers of the British School at Rome* 39, 1971, 13–31.

Rich, J. 'Warfare and the Army in Early Rome', in Erdkamp (ed.) *A Companion to the Roman Army*. Wiley-Blackwell, 2011, 7–23.

Snodgrass, A. M. 'The Hoplite Reform and History', *Journal of Hellenic Studies* 85, 1965, 110–122.

Wees, H. van. *Greek Warfare: Myth and Realities*. London, 2004.

3 The Army of the Early Republic 509–400 BC

Cornell, T. J. *The Beginnings of Rome: Italy and Rome from the Bronze Age to the Punic Wars, c. 1000–264 BC*. Routledge, 1995.

Forsythe, G. 'The Army and Centuriate Organization in early Rome', in Erdkamp (ed.) *A Companion to the Roman Army*. Wiley-Blackwell, 2011, 24–42.

Heurgon, J. *The Rise of Rome to 264 BC*. University of California Press, 1973.

Lintott, A. *The Constitution of the Roman Republic*. Oxford University Press, 1999.

Rawson, E. D. 'The Literary Sources for the pre-Marian Army', *Papers of the British School at Rome* 39, 1971, 13–31.

Rich, J. 'Warfare and the Army in Early Rome', in Erdkamp (ed.) *A Companion to the Roman Army*. Wiley-Blackwell, 2011, 7–23.

Snodgrass, A. M. 'The Hoplite Reform and History', *Journal of Hellenic Studies* 85, 1965, 110–122.

Staveley, E. S. 'The Constitution of the Roman Republic', *Historia* 5, 1954, 74–119.

Wees, H. van. *Greek Warfare: Myth and Realities*. London, 2004.

4 The Army of the Fourth Century BC

Bishop, M. C. and Coulston, J. C. *Roman Military Equipment from the Punic Wars to the Fall of Rome*. Batsford, 1993.

Cornell, T. J. *The Beginnings of Rome: Italy and Rome from the Bronze Age to the Punic Wars, c. 1000–264 BC*. Routledge, 1995.

Cowan, R. H. *Roman Conquests: Italy*. Pen and Sword Military, 2009.

de Ligt, L. 'Roman Manpower and Recruitment During the Middle Republic', in Erdkamp, P. (ed.) *A Companion to the Roman Army*. Wiley-Blackwell, 2011, 114–131.

Forsythe, G. 'The Army and Centuriate Organization in Early Rome', in Erdkamp, P. (ed.) *A Companion to the Roman Army*. Wiley-Blackwell, 2011, 24–42.

Keppie, L. *The Making of the Roman Army: From Republic to Empire*. Routledge, 1998.

Picard, G. and Picard C. *The Life and Death of Carthage*. Sidgwick and Jackson, 1968.

Rawlings, L. 'Army and Battle During the Conquest of Italy (350–264 BC)', in Erdkamp, P. (ed.) *A Companion to the Roman Army*. Wiley-Blackwell, 2011, 45–62.

Rawson, E. D. 'The Literary Sources for the pre-Marian Army', *Papers of the British School at Rome* 39, 1971, 13–31.

Rich, J. 'Warfare and the Army in Early Rome', in Erdkamp, P. (ed.) *A Companion to the Roman Army*. Wiley-Blackwell, 2011, 7–23.

Salmon, E. T. *Samnium and the Samnites*. Cambridge, 1967.

Scullard, H. H. *The Etruscan Cities and Rome*. Thames and Hudson. 1967.

Sekunda, N. 'Military Forces: A: Land Forces', in Sabin, P. et al (eds.), *The Cambridge History of Greek and Roman Warfare Vol. I: Greece, the Hellenistic World and the Rise of Rome*. Cambridge University Press, 2007, 325–356.

Snodgrass, A. M. 'The Hoplite Reform and History', *Journal of Hellenic Studies* 85, 1965, 110–122.

Wees, H. van *Greek Warfare: Myth and Realities*. London, 2004.

5 *The Latins and Other Allies*

Badian, E. *Foreign Clientelae 264–70 BC*. Clarendon Press, 1958.

Braund, D. C. *Rome and the Friendly King: The Character of Client Kingship*. Croom Helm, 1984.

Brunt, P. A. *Italian Manpower 225 BC–AD 14*. Oxford, 1971.

Cornell, T. J. *The Beginnings of Rome: Italy and Rome from the Bronze Age to the Punic Wars, c. 1000–264 BC*. Routledge, 1995.

Cornell, T. J. 'The Conquest of Italy', in Walbank, F. W. et al. (eds.) *The Rise of Rome to 220 BC*. Cambridge Ancient History Vol. 7 Part 2, 2nd ed., 1989, 351–419.

Cornell, T. J. 'Rome and Latium to 390 BC' in Walbank, F. W. et al. (eds.) *The Rise of Rome to 220 BC*. Cambridge Ancient History Vol. 7 Part 2, 2nd ed., 1989, 243ff.

Cowan, R. H. *Roman Conquests: Italy*. Pen and Sword Military, 2009.

de Ligt, L. 'Roman Manpower and Recruitment During the Middle Republic', in Erdkamp, P. (ed.) *A Companion to the Roman Army*. Wiley-Blackwell, 2011, 114–131.

Gabba, E. *Republican Rome: The Army and the Allies*. Blackwell, 1976.

Hoyos, D. 'The Age of Overseas Expansion (264–146 BC)', in Erdkamp, P. (ed.) *A Companion to the Roman Army*. Wiley-Blackwell, 2011, 63–79.

Rawlings, L. 'Army and Battle During the Conquest of Italy (350–264 BC)', in Erdkamp, P. (ed.) *A Companion to the Roman Army*. Wiley-Blackwell, 2011, 45–62.

Rawson, E. D. 'The Literary Sources for the pre-Marian Army', *Papers of the British School at Rome* 39, 1971, 13–31.

Ross Holloway, R. *The Archaeology of Early Rome and Latium*. Routledge, 1994.

Salmon, E. T. *Roman Colonization under the Republic*. Thames and Hudson, 1969.

Salmon, E. T. *Samnium and the Samnites*. Cambridge, 1967.

Sekunda, N. 'Military Forces: A: Land Forces', in Sabin, P. et al (eds.), *The Cambridge History of Greek and Roman Warfare Vol. I: Greece, the Hellenistic World and the Rise of Rome*. Cambridge University Press, 2007, 325–356.

Sherwin-White, A. N. *The Roman Citizenship*. Clarendon Press, 2nd ed., 1973.

Suolahti, J. *The Junior Officers of the Roman Army in the Republican Period*. Helsinki, 1955.

6 *The Army of the Middle Republic from the Third to Second Century BC*

Brunt, P. A. *Italian Manpower 225 BC–AD 14*. Oxford, 1971.

Cagniart, 'The Late Republican Army (146–30 BC)', in Erdkamp, P. (ed.) *A Companion to the Roman Army*. Wiley-Blackwell, 2011, 80–95.

Cornell, T. J. *The Beginnings of Rome: Italy and Rome from the Bronze Age to the Punic Wars, c. 1000–264 BC*. Routledge, 1995.

Cornell, T. J. 'The Conquest of Italy', in Walbank, F. W. et al. (eds.) *The Rise of Rome to 220 BC*. Cambridge Ancient History Vol. 7 Part 2, 2nd ed., 1989, 351–419.

de Ligt. L. 'Roman Manpower and Recruitment During the Middle Republic', in Erdkamp, P. (ed.) *A Companion to the Roman Army*. Wiley-Blackwell, 2011, 114–131.

Fields, N. *The Roman Army of the Punic Wars 264–146 BC*. Osprey Publishing, 2007.

Forsythe, G. 'The Army and Centuriate Organization in Early Rome', in Erdkamp, P. (ed.) *A Companion to the Roman Army*. Wiley-Blackwell, 2011, 24–42.

Goldsworthy, A. K. *Cannae: Hannibal's Greatest Victory*. Phoenix, 2007.

Goldsworthy, A. K. *The Fall of Carthage: The Punic Wars 265–246 BC*. Cassell, 2003.

Goldsworthy, A. K. *The Punic Wars*. London, 2000.

Hoyos, D. 'The Age of Overseas Expansion (264–146 BC)', in Erdkamp, P. (ed.) *A Companion to the Roman Army*. Wiley-Blackwell, 2011, 63–79.

Hoyos, D. *Hannibal: Rome's Greatest Enemy*. Liverpool University Press, 2008.

Lancel, S. *Carthage: A History*. Blackwell, 1995.

Lazenby, J. F. *Hannibal's War: A Military History of the Second Punic War*. University of Oklahoma Press, 1988. Reprint of 1978 ed.

Matyszak, P. *Roman Conquests: Macedonia and Greece*. Pen and Sword Military, 2009.

Picard, G. and Picard C. *The Life and Death of Carthage*. Sidgwick and Jackson, 1968.

Rankov, B. and Sabin, P. (eds.) *The Second Punic War: A Reappraisal*. London, 1996.

Rawlings, L. 'Army and Battle During the Conquest of Italy (350–264 BC)', in Erdkamp, P. (ed.) *A Companion to the Roman Army*. Wiley-Blackwell, 2011, 45–62.

Rawson, E. D. 'The Literary Sources for the pre-Marian Army', *Papers of the British School at Rome* 39, 1971, 13-31.

Rosenstein, N. 'Military Command, Political Power and the Republican Elite', in Erdkamp, P. (ed.) *A Companion to the Roman Army*. Wiley-Blackwell, 2011, 132–147.

Roth, J. P. *Logistics of the Roman Army at War (264 BC–AD 235)*. Leiden: Brill (Columbia Studies in the Classical Tradition Vol. XXIII), 1999.

Salmon, E. T. *Samnium and the Samnites*. Cambridge, 1967.

Sekunda, N. 'Military Forces: A: Land Forces', in Sabin, P. et al (eds.), *The Cambridge History of Greek and Roman Warfare Vol. I: Greece, the Hellenistic World and the Rise of Rome*. Cambridge University Press, 2007, 325–356.

7 *The Army of the Second Century BC*

Broadhead, W. 'Colonization, Land Distribution and Veteran Settlement', in Erdkamp, P. (ed.) *A Companion to the Roman Army*. Wiley-Blackwell, 2011, 148–163.

Cagniart, 'The Late Republican Army (146–30 BC)', in Erdkamp, P. (ed.) *A Companion to the Roman Army*. Wiley-Blackwell, 2011, 80–95.

de Ligt, L. 'Roman Manpower and Recruitment During the Middle Republic', in Erdkamp, P. (ed.) *A Companion to the Roman Army*. Wiley-Blackwell, 2011, 114–131.

Gabba, E. *Republican Rome, the Army and the Allies*. Blackwell, 1976.

Hoyos, D. 'The Age of Overseas Expansion (264–146 BC)', in Erdkamp, P. (ed.) *A Companion to the Roman Army*. Wiley-Blackwell, 2011, 63–79.

Lintott, A. 'The Roman Empire and Its Problems in the Late Second Century', in Crook, J. A. et al. (eds.) *The Last Age of the Roman Republic, 146–43 BC*. Cambridge Ancient History Vol. 9, 2nd ed., 1992, 16–39.

Lintott, A. 'Political History, 146–95 BC', in Crook, J. A. et al. (eds.) *The Last Age of the Roman Republic, 146–43 BC*. Cambridge Ancient History Vol. 9, 2nd ed., 1992, 40–103.

Rich, J. 'The Supposed Roman Manpower Shortage in the Later Second Century BC', *Historia* 32, 1983, 287–331.

Rosenstein, N. *Rome at War: Farms, Families and Death in the Middle Republic*. University of North Carolina Press, 2004.

8 *Marius and His Mules: The Emergence of the Professional Roman Army*

Bell, M. J. V. 'Tactical Reform in the Roman Republican Army', *Historia* 14, 1965, 404–422.

Broadhead, W. 'Colonization, Land Distribution and Veteran Settlement', in Erdkamp, P. (ed.) *A Companion to the Roman Army*. Wiley-Blackwell, 2011, 148–163.

Cagniart, 'The Late Republican Army (146–30 BC)', in Erdkamp, P. (ed.) *A Companion to the Roman Army*. Wiley-Blackwell, 2011, 80–95.

de Ligt, L. 'Roman Manpower and Recruitment During the Middle Republic', in Erdkamp, P. (ed.) *A Companion to the Roman Army*. Wiley-Blackwell, 2011, 114–131.

Gabba, E. *Republican Rome, the Army and the Allies*. Blackwell, 1976.

Goldsworthy, A. K. *The Roman Army at War 100 BC–AD 200*. Clarendon Press, 1996.

Hoyos, D. 'The Age of Overseas Expansion (264–146 BC)', in Erdkamp, P. (ed.) *A Companion to the Roman Army*. Wiley-Blackwell, 2011, 63–79.

Lintott, A. 'The Roman Empire and Its Problems in the Late Second Century', in Crook, J. A. et al. (eds.) *The Last Age of the Roman Republic, 146–43 BC*. Cambridge Ancient History Vol. 9, 2nd ed., 1992, 16–39.

Lintott, A. 'Political History, 146–95 BC', in Crook, J. A. et al. (eds.) *The Last Age of the Roman Republic, 146–43 BC*. Cambridge Ancient History Vol. 9, 2nd ed., 1992, 40–103.

Matthew, C. A. *On the Wings of Eagles: The Reforms of Gaius Marius and the Creation of Rome's First Professional Army*. Cambridge Scholars Publishing, 2010.

Rich, J. 'The Supposed Roman Manpower Shortage in the Later Second Century BC', *Historia* 32, 1983, 287–331.

Rosenstein, N. *Rome at War: Farms, Families and Death in the Middle Republic*. University of North Carolina Press, 2004.

Watson, G. R. *The Roman Soldier*. Thames and Hudson, 1969.

9 *The Rise of the Great Generals 100–60 BC*

Baker, G. P. *Sulla the Fortunate*. Cooper Square, 2001.

Cagniart, 'The Late Republican Army (146–30 BC)', in Erdkamp, P. (ed.) *A Companion to the Roman Army*. Wiley-Blackwell, 2011, 80–95.

de Blois, L. 'Army and General in the Late Roman Republic', in Erdkamp, P. (ed.) *A Companion to the Roman Army*. Wiley-Blackwell, 2011, 164–179.

de Souza, P. *Piracy in the Graeco-Roman World*. Cambridge University Press, 1999.

Fields, N. *The Roman Army of the Civil Wars 90–30 BC*. Osprey Publishing, 2008

Gelzer, M. *Caesar: Politician and Statesman*. Harvard University Press, 1968.

Goldsworthy, A. *In the Name of Rome*. Phoenix, 2004.

Greenhalgh, P. *Pompey: The Roman Alexander*. Weidenfeld and Nicolson, 1980.

Greenhalgh, P. *Pompey: Republican Prince*. Weidenfeld and Nicolson, 1981.

Gruen, E. S. *The Last Generation of the Roman Republic*. University of California Press, 1974.

Keaveney, A. *Sulla: The Last Republican*. Routledge, 2005.

Leach, J. *Pompey the Great*. Croom Helm, 1978.

Rosenstein, N. 'Military Command, Political Power and the Republican Elite', in Erdkamp, P. (ed.) *A Companion to the Roman Army*. Wiley-Blackwell, 2011, 132–147.

Seager, R. *Pompey: A Political Biography*. Blackwell, 1979.

Seager, R. 'The Rise of Pompey' in Crook, J. A. et al. (eds) *The Last Age of the Roman Republic, 146–43 BC*, Cambridge Ancient History Vol. 9, 2nd ed., 1992, 208–228.

Seager, R. 'Sulla' in Crook, J. A. et al. (eds.) *The Last Age of the Roman Republic, 146–43 BC*, Cambridge Ancient History Vol. 9, 2nd ed., 1992, 165–207.

Sherwin-White, A. N. 'Lucullus, Pompey and the East' in Crook, J. A. et al. (eds.) *The Last Age of the Roman Republic, 146–43 BC*, Cambridge Ancient History Vol. 9, 2nd ed., 1992, 229–273.

Southern, P. *Pompey the Great: Caesar's Friend and Foe*. Tempus, 2002.

10 *Caesar 58–49 BC*

Bell, M. J. V. 'Tactical Reform in the Roman Republican Army', *Historia* 14, 1965, 404–422.

Bradford, E. *Julius Caesar: The Pursuit of Power*. Hamish Hamilton, 1984.

Canfora, L. *Julius Caesar: The People's Dictator*. Edinburgh University Press, 2007.

de Blois, L. 'Army and General in the Late Roman Republic', in Erdkamp, P. (ed.) *A Companion to the Roman Army*. Wiley-Blackwell, 2011, 164–179.

de Blois, L. *The Roman Army and Politics in the First Century Before Christ*. J. C. Gieben, 1987.

Fields, N. *The Roman Army of the Civil Wars 90–30 BC*. Osprey Publishing, 2008.

Fields, N. *Warlords of Republican Rome: Caesar Versus Pompey*. Pen and Sword Military, 2008.

Fuller, J. F. C. *Julius Caesar: Man, Soldier and Tyrant*. Eyre and Spottiswoode, 1965; reprinted by Wordsworth Editions Ltd, 1998.

Gelzer, M. *Caesar: Politician and Statesman*. Harvard University Press, 1968.

Gilliver, K. et al. *Rome at War: Caesar and His Legacy*. Osprey Publishing, 2005.

Goudineau, C. *César et la Gaule*. Éditions Errance, no date.

Grant, M. *Julius Caesar*. Weidenfeld and Nicolson, 1974.

Gruen, E. S. *The Last Generation of the Roman Republic*. University of California Press, 1974.

Hildinger, E. *Swords Against the Senate: The Rise of the Roman Army and the Fall of the Republic*. Da Capo Press, 2002.

Meier, C. *Caesar*. Harper Collins, 1995.

Shotter, D. *The Fall of the Roman Republic*. Routledge, 1994.

11 The Civil Wars and the End of the Republic 49–30 BC

Cagniart, 'The Late Republican Army (146–30 BC)', in Erdkamp, P. (ed.) *A Companion to the Roman Army*. Wiley-Blackwell, 2011, 80–95.

de Blois, L. 'Army and General in the Late Roman Republic', in Erdkamp, P. (ed.) *A Companion to the Roman Army*. Wiley-Blackwell, 2011, 164-179.

de Blois, L. *The Roman Army and Politics in the First Century Before Christ*. J. C. Gieben, 1987.

Fields, N. *The Roman Army of the Civil Wars 90–30 BC*. Osprey Publishing, 2008.

Gruen, E. S. *The Last Generation of the Roman Republic*. University of California Press, 1974.

Pelling, C. B. R. 'Pharsalus', *Historia* 22, 1973.

Sabin, P. 'The Face of Roman Battle', *Journal of Roman Studies* 90, 2000, 1–17.

Sheppard, S. *Pharsalus 48 BC: Caesar and Pompey – Clash of the Titans*. Osprey Publishing, 2006.

Sheppard, S. *Philippi 42 BC: The Death of the Roman Republic*. Osprey Publishing, 2008.

Southern, P. *Augustus*. Routledge, 2nd ed., 2014.

Southern, P. *Mark Antony: A Life*. Amberley, 2010.

Tarn, W. W. and Charlesworth, M. P. *From Republic to Empire: The Roman Civil War 44 BC–27 BC*. Barnes and Noble, 1996.

Part II The Imperial Roman Army

1 Historical Overview 30 BC–AD 260

Baker, S. *Ancient Rome: The Rise and Fall of an Empire*. BBC Books, 2007.

Barrett, A. A. *Caligula: Corruption of Power*. Routledge, 1990.

Bennett, J. *Trajan: Optimus Princeps*. Routledge, 1997.

Birley, A. R. *Hadrian: The Restless Emperor*. Routledge, 1997.

Birley, A. R. *Marcus Aurelius: A Biography*. Routledge, rev. ed., 1996.

Birley, A. R. *Septimius Severus: The African Emperor*. Routledge, 1997.

Boatwright, M. T. et al. *The Romans: From Village to Empire*. Oxford University Press, 2004.

Campbell, D. B. *The Rise of Imperial Rome AD 14–193*. Osprey Publishing, 2013.

Goodman, M. *The Roman World 44 BC–AD 180*. Routledge, 1997.

Griffin, M. *Nero: End of a Dynasty*. Routledge, 1987.

Icks, M. *Crimes of Elagabalus: The Life and Legacy of Rome's Decadent Boy Emperor*. Tauris, 2013.

Lacey, W. K. *Augustus and the Principate: The Evolution of the System*. Francis Cairns, 1996.

Le Glay, M. et al. *A History of Rome*. Blackwell, 3rd ed., 2005.

Levick, B. *Claudius*. Batsford, 1990.

Levick, B. *Tiberius the Politician*. Routledge, 1999.

Levick, B. *The Government of the Roman Empire: A Sourcebook*. Routledge, 2nd ed., 2000.

Levick, B. *Vespasian*. Routledge, 2005.

Grainger, J. D. *Roman Conquests: Egypt and Judaea*. Pen and Sword, 2013.

Potter, D. S. *The Roman Empire at Bay AD 180–395*. Routledge, 2004.

Sherk, R. K. (ed.) *The Roman Empire from Augustus to Hadrian*. Translated Documents of Greece and Rome Vol. 6, Cambridge University Press, 1988.

Southern, P. *Ancient Rome: The Rise and Fall of an Empire 753 BC–AD 476*. Amberley, 2009.

Southern, P. *Augustus*. Routledge, 2nd ed., 2014.

Southern, P. *Domitian: Tragic Tyrant*. Routledge, 1997.

Southern, P. *The Roman Empire from Severus to Constantine*. Routledge, 2001.

Syme, R. *The Roman Revolution*. Oxford University Press, 1939.

Wacher, J. (ed.). *The Roman World*. Routledge, 2 vols, 1987.

Woolf, G. *Rome: And Empire's Story*. Oxford University Press, 2012.

2 Augustus and the Establishment of the Standing Army

Brunt, P. A. 'The Army and the Land in the Roman Revolution', *Journal of Roman Studies*, 52, 1962, 69–86.

Brunt, P. A. and Moore, J. M. *Res Gestae Divi Augusti: The Achievements of the Divine Augustus*. Oxford University Press, 1967.

Cooley, A. E. *Res Gestae Divi Augusti: Text, Translation and Commentary*. Cambridge University Press, 2009.

Fuhrmann, C. J. *Policing the Roman Empire: Soldiers, Administration and Public Order*. Oxford University Press, 2012.

Gilliver, K. 'The Augustan Reform and the Structure of the Imperial Roman Army', in Erdkamp, P. (ed.) *A Companion to the Roman Army*. Wiley-Blackwell, 2011, 183–200.

Keppie, L. *Colonisation and Veteran Settlement in Italy 47–14BC*. British School at Rome, 1983.

Raaflaub, K. 'The Political Significance of Augustus' Military Reforms', in Hanson, W. S. and Keppie, L. J. F. (eds.) *Roman Frontier Studies 1979*. British Archaeological Reports, 1980, 1005–1026.

Rankov, B. 'Military forces', in Sabin et al. (eds.) *The Cambridge History of Greek and Roman Warfare. Vol II: Rome from the Late Republic to the Late Empire*. Cambridge University Press, 2007, 30–75.

Saddington, D. B. *The Development of the Roman Auxiliary Forces from Caesar to Vespasian*. University of Zimbabwe Press, 1982.

Southern, P. *Augustus*. Routledge, 2nd ed., 2014.

3 The Legions from the First to the Third Century AD

Bishop, M. C. *Handbook to Roman Legionary Fortresses*. Pen and Sword, 2013.

Breeze, D. J. 'Pay Grades and Ranks below the Centurionate'. *Journal of Roman Studies* 61, 1971, 130–135.

Burn, A. R. *The Romans in Britain*. Oxford University Press, 1932.

Campbell, B. *The Emperor and the Roman Army 31 BC–AD 235*. Clarendon Press, 1984.

Goldsworthy, A. K. *The Roman Army at War 100 BC–AD 200*. Clarendon Press, 1996.

Keppie, L. 'Legions in the East from Augustus to Trajan', in Freeman, P. and Kennedy, D. (eds.) *The Defence of the Roman and Byzantine East*. Oxford: British Archaeological Reports, International Series 297 Vol. I, 1986, 411–429.

Le Bohec, Y. *The Imperial Roman Army*. Batsford, 1994; republished by Routledge, 2000.

MacMullen, R. 'How Big Was the Roman Army?' *Klio* 62, 1980, 451–60.

Mann, J. C. *Legionary Recruitment and Veteran Settlement During the Principate*. London: Institute of Archaeology, Occasional Papers 7, 1983.

Parker, H. M. D. *The Roman Legions*. Oxford University Press, 1928; reprinted 1971.

Pollard, N. and Berry, J. *The Complete Roman Legions*. Thames and Hudson, 2012.

Rankov, B. 'Military Forces', in Sabin et al. (eds.) *The Cambridge History of Greek and Roman Warfare. Vol II: Rome from the Late Republic to the Late Empire*. Cambridge University Press, 2007, 30–75.

4 Auxiliary Infantry Cohorts

Alston, R. 'Roman Military Pay from Caesar to Diocletian', *Journal of Roman Studies* 84, 1994, 113–123.

Brunt, P. A. 'Conscription and Volunteering in the Roman Imperial Army', *Scripta Classica Israelica* 1, 90–115.

Cheesman, G. L. *The Auxilia of the Roman Imperial Army*. Clarendon Press, 1914.

Davies, R. W. 'Cohortes Equitatae', *Historia* 20, 1971, 751–763.

Dobson, B. *Die Primipilares*. Cologne and Bonn, 1978.

Gilliver, K. 'The Augustan Reform and the Structure of the Roman Imperial Army', in Erdkamp, P. (ed.) *A Companion to the Roman Army*. Wiley-Blackwell, 2011, 183–200.

Holder, P. *Studies in the Auxilia of the Roman Imperial Army from Caesar to Trajan*. Oxford: British Archaeological Reports 70, 1980.

Mann, J. P. and Roxan, M. M. 'Discharge Certificates of the Roman Army', *Britannia* 19, 341–347.

Phang, S. E. 'Military Documents, Languages and literacy', in Erdkamp, P. (ed.) *A Companion to the Roman Army*. Wiley-Blackwell, 2011, 286–305.

Saddington, D. B. *The Development of the Roman Auxiliary Forces from Caesar to Vespasian*. University of Zimbabwe Press, 1982.

5 Auxiliary Cavalry Alae

Bishop, M. C. 'Cavalry Equipment of the Roman Army in the First Century AD' in Coulston, J.

C. (ed.) *Military Equipment and the Identity of Roman Soldiers*. Oxford: British Archaeological Reports S394, 1988, 67–195.

Bowman, A. K. *The Roman Writing Tablets from Vindolanda*. British Museum, 1983.

Cheesman, G. L. *The Auxilia of the Roman Imperial Army*. Clarendon Press, 1914

Connolly, P. 'A Reconstruction of a Roman saddle', *Britannia* 17, 1986, 353–355.

Coulston, J. C. 'Roman Archery Equipment', in Bishop, M. C. (ed.). *The Production and Distribution of Roman Military Equipment: Proceedings of the Second Roman Military Equipment Seminar*. Oxford: British Archaeological Reports S275, 1985, 220–366.

Davies, R. W. 'The Training Grounds of the Roman Cavalry', *Archaeological Journal*, 125, 1968, 73–100.

Davies, R. W. 'The Supply of Animals to the Roman Army and the Remount System', *Latomus* 28, 1969, 429–459.

Dixon, K. R. and Southern, P. *The Roman Cavalry from the First to the Third Century AD*. Batsford, 1992.

Fields, N. *Roman Auxiliary Cavalryman AD 14–193*. Osprey Publishing, 2006.

Fink, R. O. *Roman Military Records on Papyrus*. American Phililogical Association, Monograph 26, 1971.

Holder, P. *Studies in the Auxilia of the Roman Imperial Army from Caesar to Trajan*. Oxford: British Archaeological Reports 70, 1980.

Holder, P. A. 'Roman Auxiliary Cavalry in the Second Century AD', *History Today* 8:5, June 1987, 12–16.

Hyland, A. *Equus: The Horse in the Roman World*. Batsford, 1990.

Hyland, A. *Training the Roman Cavalry: From Arrian's Ars Tactica*. Alan Sutton, 1993.

Müller, G. *Durnomagus: Das Römische Dormagen*. Cologne: Rheinlandverlag GMBH, 1979.

Pirling, R. 'Die Ausgrabungen in Krefeld-Gellep 1977', *Ausgrabungen in Rheinland* 1977, 136–140.

Saddington, D. B. *The Development of the Roman Auxiliary Forces from Caesar to Vespasian*. University of Zimbabwe Press, 1982.

Van Driel-Murray, C. 'The Vindolanda Chamfrons and Miscellaneous Items of Leather Horse Gear' in Van Driel-Murray, C. (ed.) *Roman Military Equipment: The Sources of Evidence: Proceedings of the Fifth Roman Military Equipment Conference*. Oxford: British Archaeological Reports S476, 1989, 282–318.

War Office. *Manual of Horsemanship, Equitation and Animal Transport*. London: HMSO 1937.

War Office. *Remount Manual (war)*. London: HMSO, 1937.

Wells, C. M. 'Where Did They Put the Horses? Cavalry Stables in the Early Empire', in Fitz, J. (ed.) *Limes: Akten des XI Internationalen Limeskongresses, Szekesfehervar, 1976*. Budapest Akademiai Kiado, 1977, 659–665.

6 Special and Elite Military Units

Baillie Reynolds, P. K. *The Vigiles of Imperial Rome*. Oxford, 1926.

Bingham, S. *The Praetorian Guard: A History of Rome's Elite Special Forces*. Tauris, 2012.

Callies, H. 'Die Fremden Truppen im Römischen Heer des Prinzipats und die Sogenannten Nationalen Numeri', *Bericht der Römisch-Germanischen Kommission des Deutschen Archäologischen Instituts* 45, 1964, 130–227.

Durry, M. *Les Cohortes Prétoriennes*. Paris, 1938.

Freis, H. *Die Cohortes Urbanae*. Epigraphische Studien 2, Cologne, 1967.

Fuhrmann, C. J. *Policing the Roman Empire: Soldiers, Administration and Public Order*. Oxford University Press, 2012.

Nippel, W. *Public Order in Ancient Rome*. Cambridge University Press, 1995.

Passerini, A. *Le Coorti Pretorie*. Rome, 1939.

Rankov, N. B. '*Frumentarii*, the *Castra Peregrina* and the Provincial *officia*', *Zeitschrift für Papyrologie und Epigraphik* 79, 1990, 176–182.

Rankov, N. B. *The Praetorian Guard*. Osprey Publishing, 1994.

Sablayrolles, R. Libertinus Miles: *Les Cohortes de Vigiles*, Rome, 1996

Southern, P. 'The *Numeri* of the Roman Imperial Army'. *Britannia* 20, 1989, 81–140.

Speidel, M. P. *Guards of the Roman Armies: An Essay on the Singulares of the Provinces*, Bonn: Habelt, 1978.

Speidel, M. P. *Riding for Caesar: The Roman Emperors' Horse Guard*. Batsford, 1994.

7 Officers and Men

Alston, R. 'Roman Military Pay from Caesar to Diocletian'. *Journal of Roman Studies* 84, 1994, 113–123.

Breeze, D. J. 'Pay Grades and Ranks below the Centurionate'. *Journal of Roman Studies* 61, 1971, 130–135.

Brunt, P. A. 'Pay and Superannuation in the Roman Army'. *Papers of the British School at Rome* 18, 1950, 50–75.

Brunt, P. A. 'Conscription and Volunteering in the Roman Imperial Army'. *Scripta Classica Israelica* 1, 1974, 90–115.

Cheesman, G. L. *The Auxilia of the Roman Imperial Army*. Oxford: Clarendon Press, 1914.

Develin, R. 'The Army Pay Rises under Severus and Caracalla and the Question of the *annona militaris*'. *Latomus* 30, 1971, 687–695.

Devijver, H. *The Equestrian Officers of the Roman Army*. Vol. 1. Amsterdam: J. Gieben, 1989.

Devijver, H. *The Equestrian Officers of the Roman Army*. Vol. 2. Stuttgart: F. Steiner, 1992.

Dixon, K. R. and Southern, P. *The Roman Cavalry from the First to the Third Century AD*. Batsford, 1992

Dobson, B. 'Legionary Soldier or Equestrian Officer? A Comparison of Pay and Prospects'. *Ancient Society* 3, 1972, 193–208.

Dobson, B. 'The Significance of the Centurion and "Primipilaris" in the Roman Army and Administration'. *Aufstieg und Niedergang der Römischen Welt* II.1, 1974, 392–434.

Fink, R. O. *Roman Military Records on Papyrus*. Case Western Reserve University for the American Philological Society, 1971.

Marsden, E. W. *Greek and Roman Artillery: Historical Development*. Oxford: Clarendon Press, 1969.

Roth, J. P. *Logistics of the Roman Army at War (264 BC–AD 235)*. Leiden: Brill (Columbia Studies in the Classical Tradition Vol. XXIII), 1999.

Saddington, D. B. *The Development of the Roman Auxiliary Forces from Caesar to Vespasian, 49 BC–AD 79*. Harare: University of Zimbabwe Press, 1982.

Southern, P. 'The *Numeri* of the Roman Imperial Army'. *Britannia* 20, 1989, 81–140.

Speidel, M. A. 'Roman Army Pay Scales'. *Journal of Roman Studies* 82, 1992, 87–106.

Speidel, M. P. 'The Captor of Decebalus'. *Journal of Roman Studies* 60, 1970, 142–153.

Speidel. M. P. 'The Pay of the Auxilia'. *Journal of Roman Studies* 63, 1973 141–147.

Speidel, M. P. *Riding for Caesar*. London: Batsford, 1994

8 Administration of the Army

Anderson, J. D. *Roman Military Supply in North East England*. Oxford: British Archaeological Reports, British Series 224, 1992.

Austin, N. J. E. and Rankov, N. B. *Exploratio: Military and Political Intelligence in the Roman World from the Second Punic War to the Battle of Adrianople*. Routledge, 1995.

Campbell, B. *War and Society in Imperial Rome 31 BC–AD 284*. Routledge, 2002.

Davies, R. W. 'The *Medici* of the Roman Armed Forces', *Epigraphische Studien* 8, 1969, 83–99.

Dilke, O. A. W. *Greek and Roman Maps*. Thames and Hudson, 1985.

Dixon, K. R. and Southern, P. *The Roman Cavalry from the First to the Third Century AD*. Batsford, 1992.

Goldsworthy, A. K. *The Roman Army at War 100 BC–AD 200*. Clarendon Press, 1996.

Herz, P. 'Finances and Costs of the Roman Army', in Erdkamp, P. (ed.) *A Companion to the Roman Army*. Wiley-Blackwell, 2011, 306–322.

Kehne, P. 'War and Peacetime Logistics: Supplying Imperial Armies in East and West', in Erdkamp, P. (ed.) *A Companion to the Roman Army*. Wiley-Blackwell, 2011, 307–338.

Le Bohec, Y. *The Imperial Roman Army*. Batsford, 1994; republished by Routledge, 2000.

Lee, A. D. *Information and Frontiers: Roman Foreign Relations in Late Antiquity.* Cambridge University Press, 1993.

Lepper, F. and Frere, S. *Trajan's Column.* Alan Sutton, 1998.

Marsden, E. W. *Greek and Roman Artillery: Historical Development.* Oxford: Clarendon Press, 1969.

Middleton, P. 'The Roman Army and Long-Distance Trade', in Garnsey, P. and Whittaker, C. R. (ed.) *Trade and Famine in Classical Antiquity.* Cambridge University Press, 1983, 75–83.

Rathbone, D. Military Finance and Supply', in Sabin, P. et al (eds.), *The Cambridge History of Greek and Roman Warfare Vol. 2: Rome from the Late Republic to the Late Empire.* Cambridge University Press, 2007, 158–176.

Rogers, H. C. B. *The British Army of the Eighteenth Century.* George Allen and Unwin, 1977.

Roth, J. P. *Logistics of the Roman Army at War (264 BC to AD 235).* Leiden: Brill, (Columbia Studies in the Classical Tradition Vol. XXIII), 1999.

Walker, R. E. 'Roman Veterinary Medicine', in Toynbee, J. M. C. *Animals in Roman Life and Art.* Johns Hopkins University Press, 1973, 303–343.

Welles, C. B. (et al.) (eds.) *Excavations at Dura Europos: Final Report V, Part I: The Parchments and Papyri.* Yale University Press, 1959.

9 Camps, Forts and Fortresses
Bishop, M. C. *Handbook to Roman Legionary Fortresses.* Pen and Sword, 2013.

Breeze, D. *Roman Forts in Britain.* Shire Publications Ltd, 1983.

Brewer, R. J. (ed.). *Roman Fortresses and Their Legions.* Society of Antiquaries of London and National Museums and Galleries of Wales, 2000.

Campbell, D. B. *Roman Legionary Fortresses 27 BC–AD 378.* Osprey Publishing, 2006.

Hodgson, N. and Bidwell, P. T. 'Auxiliary Barracks in a New Light: Recent Discoveries on Hadrian's Wall', *Britannia* 35, 2004, 121–157.

Johnson, A. *Roman Forts of the First and Second Centuries AD in Britain and the German Provinces.* A. and C. Black, 1983.

Lander, J. *Roman Stone Fortifications: Variation and Change from the First Century AD to the Fourth.* British Archaeological Reports S206, 1984.

Welfare, H. and Swan, V. *Roman Camps in England: The Field Archaeology.* HMSO, 1995.

Wilson, R. *Roman Forts.* Constable, 1980.

10 Artillery and Sieges
Aineias the Tactician. *How to Survive under Siege: A Historical Commentary, with Translation and Introduction* by David Whitehead. Bristol Classical Press, 2nd ed. 2001.

Campbell, D. B. 'Auxiliary Artillery Revisited', *Bonner Jahrbücher* 186, 1986, 117–132.

Campbell, D. B. *Greek and Roman Siege Machinery 399 BC–AD 363.* Osprey Publishing, 2003.

Campbell, D. B. 'The Roman Siege of Burnswark', *Britannia* 34, 2003, 19–33.

Campbell, D. B. *Besieged: Siege Warfare in the Ancient World.* Osprey Publishing 2006.

Davies, G. *Roman Siege Works.* Tempus, 2006.

Landels, J. G. *Engineering in the Ancient World.* Constable, 2000; rev. ed. of first edition published by Chatto and Windus, 1978.

Marsden, E. W. *Greek and Roman Artillery: Historical Development.* Clarendon Press, 1969.

Schramm, F. *Die Antiken Geschütze der Saalburg.* Berlin, 1918; new rev. ed. by D. Baatz, 1980.

Wilkins, A. *Roman Artillery.* Shire Publications Ltd, 2003.

11 Frontiers
Breeze, D. J. *The Northern Frontiers of Roman Britain.* Batsford, 1982.

Breeze, D. J. and Dobson, B. *Hadrian's Wall.* Penguin, 4th ed. 2000.

Breeze, D, and Jilek, S. 'Strategy, Tactics, Operation: How Did Frontiers Actually Work?', in Visy, Z. (ed.) *Limes XIX: Proceedings of the XIX International Congress of Roman Frontier Studies Held in Pecs, Hungary, September 2003.* University of Pecs, 2005, 141–146.

Cherry, D. *Frontier and Society in Roman North Africa.* Oxford, 1998.

Daniels, C. M. 'The Frontiers: Africa', in Wacher, J. (ed.) *The Roman World*. Routledge, 1987, 223–265.

Elton, H. *Frontiers of the Roman Empire*. London: Batsford, 1996.

Fields, N. *Hadrian's Wall AD 122–410*. Osprey Publishing Ltd, 2003.

Hanson, W. S. and Keppie, L. J. F. (eds.) *Roman Frontier Studies 1979*. British Archaeological Reports, 3 vols, 1980.

Hodgson, N. 'Were there Two Antonine Occupations of Scotland?', *Britannia* 26, 1995, 24–49.

Hodgson, N. 'Gates and Passage Across the Frontiers: The Use of Openings Through the Barriers of Britain, Germany and Raetia', in Visy, Z. (ed.) *Limes XIX: Proceedings of the XIX International Congress of Roman Frontier Studies Held in Pecs, Hungary, September 2003*. University of Pecs, 2005, 183–188.

Kennedy, D. 'The Frontiers: The East', in Wacher, J. (ed.) *The Roman World*. Routledge, 1987, 266–308.

Lee, A. D. *Information and Frontiers: Roman Foreign Relations in Late Antiquity*. Cambridge University Press, 1993.

Lendering, J. and Bosman, A. *Edge of Empire: Rome's Frontier on the Lower Rhine*. Karwansaray BV, 2013.

Luttwak, E. N. *The Grand Strategy of the Roman Empire*. Johns Hopkins University Press, 1976.

Mann, J. C. 'The Frontiers of the Principate'. *Aufstieg und Niedergang der Römischen Welt* II.1, 1974, 508–531.

Mattingly, D. J. et al (eds.) *Frontiers of the Roman Empire: The African Frontiers*. Society for Libyan Studies, 2013.

Maxfield, V. 'The Frontiers: Mainland Europe', in Wacher, J. (ed.) *The Roman World*. Routledge, 1987, 139–197.

Millar, F. 'Emperors, Frontiers and Foreign Relations', *Britannia* 13, 1982, 1–23.

Parker, P. *The Empire Stops Here: A Journey along the Frontiers of the Roman World*. Jonathan Cape, 2009.

Rankov, B. 'Do Rivers Make Good Frontiers?' in Visy, Z. (ed.) *Limes XIX: Proceedings of the XIX International Congress of Roman Frontier Studies Held in Pecs, Hungary, September 2003*. University of Pecs, 2005, 175–181.

Schönberger, H. von 'Die Römische Truppenlager der Frühen und Mittleren Kaiserzeit Zwischen Nordsee und Inn' *Bericht der Römisch-Germanischen Kommission des Deutschen Archaologischen Instituts* 66, 1985, 321–497.

Shotter, D. *The Roman Frontier in Britain: Hadrian's Wall, the Antonine Wall and Roman Policy in the North*. Carnegie Publishing, 1996.

Southern, P. 'The *Numeri* of the Roman Imperial Army'. *Britannia* 20, 1989, 81–140.

Southern, P. 'Signals Versus Illumination on Roman Frontiers', *Britannia*, 21, 1990, 233–242.

Whittaker, C. R. 1994. *Frontiers of the Roman Empire: A Social and Economic Study*. Baltimore: Johns Hopkins University Press, 1994.

Wilkes, J. 'Frontier History' and 'Frontier Organization' in Bowman et al. (eds) *The Crisis of Empire AD 193–337* Cambridge Ancient History Vol. 12, 2nd ed. 2005, 212–233; 252–268.

Woolliscroft, D. I. *Roman Military Signalling*. Tempus Publishing, 2001.

12 *The Army in Action: Peace and War*

Alston, R. *Soldier and Society in Roman Egypt: A Social History*. London: Routledge, 1995.

Austin, N. J. E. and Rankov, N. B. *Exploratio: Military and Political Intelligence in the Roman World from the Second Punic War to the Battle of Adrianople*. London: Routledge, 1995.

Bell, H. I. (*et al.*; eds.) *The Abbinaeus Archive: Papers of a Roman Officer in the Reign of Constantius II*. Clarendon Press, 1962.

Campbell, J. B. 'Teach Yourself How to Be a General', *Journal of Roman Studies* 77, 1987, 13–29.

Campbell. J. B. *War and Society in Imperial Rome 31 BC to AD 284*. London: Routledge, 2002.

Dixon, K. R. and Southern, P. *The Roman Cavalry from the First to the Third Century AD*. Batsford, 1992.

Fuhrmann, C. J. *Policing the Roman Empire: Soldiers, Administration and Public Order*. Oxford University Press, 2012.

Gilliver, C. M. *The Roman Art of War*. Tempus Publishing, 2000.

Lepper, F. and Frere, S. *Trajan's Column*. Alan Sutton, 1998.

Luttwak, E. N. *The Grand Strategy of the Roman Empire*. Baltimore: Johns Hopkins University Press, 1976.

Woolliscroft, D. I. *Roman Military Signalling*. Tempus Publishing, 2001.

13 Life in the Army

Alston, R. *Soldier and Society in Roman Egypt: A Social History*. London: Routledge, 1995.

Birley, A. R. *Garrison Life at Vindolanda: A Band of Brothers*. Tempus, 2002.

Bowman, A. K. *Life and Letters on the Roman Frontier: Vindolanda and Its People*. British Museum Press, 1994.

Brand, C. E. 1968. *Roman Military Law*. Austin: University of Texas Press, 1968.

Davies, R. 'Joining the Roman Army', *Bonner Jahrbücher* 169, 1969, 208–232.

Davies, R. 'The Roman Military Medical Service', *Saalburg Jahrbuch* 27, 1970, 84–104.

Davies, R. 'The Roman Military Diet', *Britannia* 2, 1971, 122–142.

Davies, R. 'The Daily Life of a Roman Soldier under the Principate', *Aufstieg und Niedergang der Römischen Welt* II.I, 1974, 299–338.

Fink, R. O. *Roman Military Records on Papyrus*. Case Western Reserve University, 1971.

MacMullen, Ramsay. *Soldier and Civilian in the Later Roman Empire*. Cambridge, Mass.: Harvard University Press, 1963.

Maxfield, V. A. *The Military Decorations of the Roman Army*. London: Batsford, 1981.

Roxan, M. *Roman Military Diplomas 1954–1977*. University of London, Institute of Archaeology Occasional Publication No. 2, 1978.

Roxan, M. *Roman Military Diplomas 1978–1984*. University of London, Institute of Archaeology Occasional Publication No. 9, 1985.

Roxan, M. *Roman Military Diplomas 1985–1993*. Occasional Publication University College London Institute of Archaeology No. 14, 1994.

Roxan, M. and Holder, P. 'Roman Military Diplomas', *Bulletin of the Institute of Classical Studies* Supplement 82, 2003.

Whittaker, C. R. 1994. *Frontiers of the Roman Empire: A Social and Economic Study*. Baltimore: Johns Hopkins University Press.

14 The Army and Civilians

Alston, R. *Soldier and Society in Roman Egypt: A Social History*. Routledge, 1995.

Bell, H. I. (*et al.*; eds.) *The Abbinaeus Archive: Papers of a Roman Officer in the Reign of Constantius II*. Clarendon Press, 1962.

Bowman, A. K. and Thomas, J. D. *Vindolanda: The Latin Writing Tablets*. British Museum, 1983.

Brunt, P. A. 'Did Imperial Rome Disarm Her Subjects?', *Phoenix* 29, 1975, 260–270.

Campbell, J. B. *War and Society in Imperial Rome 31 BC–AD 284*. Routledge, 2002.

Cherry, D. *Frontier and Society in Roman North Africa*. Oxford, 1998.

Fuhrmann, C. J. *Policing the Roman Empire: Soldiers, Administration and Public Order*. Oxford University Press, 2012.

Gardner, J. F. *Being a Roman Citizen*. Routledge, 1993.

Hanel, N. 'Military Camps, Canabae and Vici: The Archaeological Evidence', in Erdkamp, P. (ed.) *A Companion to the Roman Army*. Wiley-Blackwell, 2011, 395–416.

Hopkins, K. 'Taxes and Trade in the Roman Empire, 200 BC–AD 400'. *Journal of Roman Studies* 70, 1980, 101–125.

Levick, B. *The Government of the Roman Empire: A Sourcebook*. Routledge, 2nd ed., 2000.

MacMullen, R. *Soldier and Civilian in the Later Roman Empire*. Harvard University Press, 1963.

MacMullen, R. *Roman Social Relations 50 BC to AD 284*. Yale University Press, 1974.

Nippel, W. *Public Order in Ancient Rome*. Cambridge University Press, 1995.

Phang, S. E. *The Marriage of Roman Soldiers (13 BC to AD 235): Law and Family in the Imperial Army*. Leiden: Brill, 2001.

Pollard, N. *Soldiers, Cities and Civilians in Roman Syria*. Ann Arbor: University of Michigan Press, 2000.

Potter, T. *Roman Italy*. British Museum Press, 1987.

Shelton, J. *As the Romans Did: A Sourcebook in Roman Social History*. Oxford University Press 2nd ed., 1998.

Sherwin-White, A. N. *The Roman Citizenship*. Oxford: Clarendon Press, 2nd ed., 1973.

Sommer, C. S. *The Military Vici in Roman Britain*. Oxford: BAR 129, 1984.

Wesch-Klein, G. 'Recruits and veterans', in Erdkamp, P. (ed.) *A Companion to the Roman Army*. Wiley-Blackwell, 2011, 453–450.

15 Naval Forces

Casson, L. *Ships and Seamanship in the Ancient World*. Princeton University Press, 1971.

Mason, D. J. P. *Roman Britain and the Roman Navy*. Tempus Publishing, 2003, reprinted by The History Press, 2009.

Morrison, J. S. and Coates, J. F. *Greek and Roman Oared Warships*. Oxford, 1996.

Rodgers, W. *Greek and Roman Naval Warfare*. Annapolis, 1937, reprinted 1964.

Starr, C. G. *The Roman Imperial Navy 31 BC–AD 324*. Chicago, 3rd ed. 1993.

Starr, C. G. *The Influence of Sea Power on Ancient History*. Oxford University Press, 1989.

Part III The Army of the Late Empire

1 Historical Overview, Third to Fifth Centuries AD

Barnes, T. D. *The New Empire of Diocletian and Constantine*. Harvard University Press, 1982.

Cameron, A. *The Later Roman Empire, AD 284–430*. Fontana Press, 1993.

Cameron, A. *The Mediterranean World in Late Antiquity, AD 395–600*. Routledge, 1993.

Casey, P. J. *Carausius and Allectus: The British Usurpers*. Batsford, 1994.

Corcoran, S. *The Empire of the Tetrarchs: Imperial Pronouncements and Government AD 284–324*. Clarendon Press, 1996.

Drinkwater, J. F. *The Gallic Empire: Separatism and Continuity in the North-West Provinces of the Roman Empire AD 260–274*. Franz Steiner Verlag, 1987.

Esmonde Cleary, A. S. *The Roman West AD 200–500: An Archaeological Study*. Cambridge University Press, 2013.

Garnsey, P. and Humfress, C. *The Evolution of the Late Antique World*. Orchard Academic, 2001.

Grant. M. *The Emperor Constantine*. Weidenfeld and Nicolson, 1993.

Heather, P. *The Fall of the Roman Empire: A New History*. Macmillan, 2005.

Isaac, B. *The Limits of Empire: The Roman Army in the East*. Clarendon Press, 1990.

Jones, A. H. M. *The Later Roman Empire 284–602*. Basil Blackwell, 1964.

Kelly, C. *Ruling the Later Roman Empire*. Belknap Press of Harvard University Press, 2004.

Loriot, X. and Nony, D. *La Crise de l'Empire Romain 235–285*. 1997.

MacMullen, R. *Corruption and the Decline of Rome*. Yale University Press, 1988.

MacMullen, R. *The Roman Government's Response to Crisis AD 235–337*. Yale University Press, 1976.

Mitchell, S. *A History of the Later Roman Empire AD 284–642: The Transformation of the Ancient World*. Blackwell, 2007.

Pohlsander, H. A. *The Emperor Constantine*. Routledge, Lancaster Pamphlets, 1996.

Potter, D. *Constantine the Emperor*. Oxford University Press, 2013.

Southern, P. *Empress Zenobia: Palmyra's Rebel Queen*. Continuum, 2008.

Southern, P. *The Roman Empire from Severus to Constantine*. Routledge, 2001.

Watson, A. *Aurelian and the Third Century*. Routledge, 1999.

Williams, S. *Diocletian and the Roman Recovery*. Routledge, 1997.

2 Army Reorganisation of the Late Third Century AD

Arnheim, M. T. W. *The Senatorial Aristocracy in the Later Roman Empire*. Clarendon Press, 1972.

Barnes, T. *The New Empire of Diocletian and Constantine*. Harvard University Press, 1981.

Campbell, B. 'The Military Reforms of Diocletian and Constantine' in Bowman, K. et al. (eds) *The Crisis of Empire A.D. 193–227*. Cambridge Ancient History Vol. 12, 2nd ed., 2005, 120–130.

Casey, J. *The Legions in the Later Roman Empire*. Fourth Annual Caerleon Lecture, National Museum of Wales, 1991.

de Blois, L. *The Policy of the Emperor Gallienus*. Nederlands Instituut te Rome, 1976.

Duncan-Jones, R. 'Pay and Numbers in Diocletian's Army', *Chiron* 8, 1978, 541–560.

Geiger, M. *Gallienus*. Peter Lang GmbH, 2013.

Lo Cascio, E. 'Gallienus' Reforms: Military Command and the Government of the Provinces', in Bowman, K. et al. (eds.) *The Crisis of Empire A.D. 193–227*. Cambridge Ancient History Vol. 12, 2nd ed., 2005, 158–161.

Nicasie, M. J. *Twilight of Empire: The Roman Army from the Reign of Diocletian until the Battle of Adrianople*. Amsterdam, 1998.

Southern, P. *The Roman Empire from Severus to Constantine*. Routledge, 2001.

Southern, P. and Dixon, K. *The Late Roman Army*. Batsford, 1996.

van Berchem, D. *L'Armée de Dioclétien et la Réforme Constantinienne*. Guethner, 1952.

Williams, S. *Diocletian and the Roman Recovery*. Routledge, 1997.

3 Field Armies and Frontier Armies

Barnes, T. *The New Empire of Diocletian and Constantine*. Harvard University Press, 1981.

Coulston, J. C. N. 'Later Roman Armour, 3rd–6th Centuries', *Journal of Roman Military Equipment Studies* 1, 1990, 139–160.

Crump, G. A. 'Ammianus and the Later Roman Army', *Historia* 22, 1973, 91–103.

Elton, H. 'Military Forces' in in Sabin et al. (eds) *The Cambridge History of Greek and Roman Warfare. Vol II: Rome from the Late Republic to the Late Empire*. Cambridge University Press, 2007, 270–309.

Heather, P. *Goths and Romans 332–489*. Oxford Historical Monographs, 1991.

James, S. 'The Fabricae: State Arms Factories of the Later Roman Empire', in Coulston, J. C. N. (ed.) *Military Equipment and the Identity of Roman Soldiers*. Proceedings of the Fourth Roman Military Equipment Conference. British Archaeological Reports S394, 1987, 257–332.

MacMullen, R. *Soldier and Civilian in the Later Roman Empire*. Harvard University Press, 1963.

Matthews, J. F. *The Roman Empire of Ammianus*. Duckworth, 1989.

Nicasie, M. J. *Twilight of Empire: The Roman Army from the Reign of Diocletian until the Battle of Adrianople*. Amsterdam, 1998.

Southern, P. and Dixon, K. *The Late Roman Army*. Batsford, 1996.

Strobel, K. 'Strategy and Army Structure Between Septimius Severus and Constantine the Great', in Erdkamp, P. (ed.) *A Companion to the Roman Army*. Wiley-Blackwell, 2011, 267–285.

Tomlin, R. S. O. 'The Army of the Late Empire', in Wacher, J. (ed.). *The Roman World*. Routledge, Vol. I, 1987, 107–135.

Watson, A. *Aurelian and the Third Century*. Routledge, 1999.

Wolfram, H. *The History of the Goths*. University of California Press, 1988.

4 Forts and Fortifications

Cotterill. J. 'Saxon Raiding and the Role of the Late Roman Coastal Forts of Britain', *Britannia* 27, 1993, 227–240.

Fields, N. *The Walls of Rome*. Osprey Publishing, 2008.

Johnson, S. *Late Roman Fortifications*. Batsford, 1983.

Johnson, S. *The Roman Forts of the Saxon Shore*. Book Club Associates, 2nd ed. 1979.

Lander, J. *Roman Stone Fortifications: Variation and Change from the First Century AD to the Fourth*. British Archaeological Reports S206, 1984.

Luttwak, E. *The Grand Strategy of the Roman Empire*. Johns Hopkins University Press, 1976.

MacMullen, R. *Enemies of the Roman Order: Treason, Unrest, and Alienation in the Empire*. Harvard University Press, 1966.

MacMullen, R. *The Roman Government's Response to Crisis: AD 235–337*. Yale University Press, 1976.

Pearson, A. *The Roman Shore Forts: Coastal Defences of Southern Britain*. Tempus, 2002.

Petrikovits, H. von. 'Fortifications in the North-Western Roman Empire from the Third to the Fifth centuries AD', *Journal of Roman Studies* 61, 1971, 178–218.

Richmond, I. A. *The City Wall of Imperial Rome: An Account of Its Architectural Development from Aurelian to Narses.* Clarendon Press, 1930.

Todd, M. *The Walls of Rome.* Elek, 1978.

Watson, A. *Aurelian and the Third Century.* Routledge, 1999.

5 Officers and Men

Dauge, Y. A. 'Le Barbare: Recherches sur la Conception Romaine de la Barbarie et de la Civilisation.' *Collection Latomus*, Vol. 176, 1981.

Goffart, W. *Barbarians and Romans AD 418–584: Techniques of Accommodation.* Princeton University Press, 1980.

Heather, P. *Goths and Romans 332–489.* Oxford Historical Monographs, 1991.

James, E. *The Franks.* Basil Blackwell, 1988.

MacMullen, R. *Soldier and Civilian in the Later Roman Empire.* Harvard University Press, 1963.

Minn, H. R. 'Stilicho and the Demise of the Western Empire', *Prudentia* IV, 1972, 23–32.

O'Flynn, J. M. *Generalissimos of the Western Roman Empire.* University of Alberta Press, 1983.

Smith, R. E. 'Dux, Praepositus', *Zeitschrift für Papyrolgie und Epigraphik* 36, 1972, 263–268.

Tomlin, R. S. O. 'The Army of the Late Empire', in Wacher, J. (ed.). *The Roman World.* Routledge, Vol. I, 1987, 107–135.

6 The End of the Roman Army

Collins, R. *Early Medieval Europe 300–1000.* Macmillan, 1991.

Drinkwater, J. and Elton, H. *Fifth Century Gaul: A Crisis of Identity.* Cambridge University Press, 1992.

Ferrill, A. *The Fall of the Roman Empire: The Military Explanation.* Thames and Hudson, 1986.

Lee, A. D. 'The Army', in *The Late Empire, AD 337–425*, Cambridge Ancient History Vol. 13, 1998, 211–237.

Musset, L. *The Germanic Invasions: The Making of Europe AD 400–600.* Elek, 1975.

Whitby, M. 'The Army', in *Late Antiquity: Empire and Successors, AD 425–600*, Cambridge Ancient History Vol. 14, 2nd ed., 2000, 288–314.

Whitby, M. 'Army and Society in the Late Roman World: A Context for Decline?' in Erdkamp, P. (ed.) *A Companion to the Roman Army.* Wiley-Blackwell, 2011, 515–531.

Index

Actium 32, 181, 185
Aedes 326
Aerarium militare 208, 247
Aetius 442–443
Alae sociorum 76–77, 128, 239–240, 241, 249
Alamanni 201, 442, 465, 468
Alaric 441–442
Alesia 155–156
Alexandria 32, 167–168
Ambiorix 151–152
Annona militaris 306–307, 504–505; see also *Praefectus Annonae*
Antiochus the Great 100–101
Antonia 189
Antoninus Pius, Emperor 194
Antony, Mark 143, 158, 163, 164–166, 167, 172–181, 189
Arbogast 440, 473
Arcadius, Emperor 440–441
Arch of Constantine plates 42–44
Arch of Severus plates 7–8
Arch of Titus plates 3–4
Archers (*sagittarii*) 250–251, 266, 266, 470–471
Ariovistus 146–147
Armenia 137, 180, 202
Arms and armour: armies of the kings 34–35; of hoplite armies 36–37; of the five Servian *classes* 41; of the late armies 469–471
Artillery 104, 222, 313, 336–346; plates 23–24; see also sieges
Attila 442–443
Augustus 185–187, 205–213, plate 2
Aurelian, Emperor 432–434, 446
Aurelian Walls, Rome 433, plate 41
Auxilia: native troops of the Republic 117, 144
Auxiliary units of the Empire 211, 239–273

Baggage animals; baggage trains 111, 122, 144, 309, 310, 313–314
Barding, horse armour 268
Beneficiarii 295, 301, 375–376, 418
Blockades, see sieges and blockades
Bows 250–251, 470–471
Britain 149–151, 189, 190–191, 197, 215
Burgi 195–196

Caligula, Emperor 187–189
Camel riders (*dromedarii*) 242

Camp prefect, see *Praefectus castrorum*
Camps 67, 97, 110–112, 117, 317–322
Canabae 329, 411–414; see also *vici*
Caracalla, Emperor 198
Carthage 24, 26–27, 29, 46, 70, 84–86, 87–94, 99, 104, 421; treaties 26, 46, 70
Cataphractarii 267
Catapults, see artillery
Caudine Forks
Cavalry 35, 42–43, 51, 61–62, 110, 113, 144, 210, 239, 241, 254–273, 383, plates 1, 15–20, 44; legionary cavalry 219, 220, 432; Gallienus' cavalry 448–451
Cavalry horses 256–262
Centurio regionarius 417–418
Centurions 34, 39, 143, 145, 147, 155, 210, 213, 218–219, 255, 276, 416–418
Christians 203, 392
City fortifications 476, 483–487
Claudius, Emperor 187–189
Claudius Maximus, Tiberius 255
Cleopatra VII 167, 175, 177–181
Clibanarii 267
Client kings 80, 188
Clipeus 38, 56
Clothing 402–404, 471, 503–504
Cohorts, auxiliary 239–253
Cohorts, legionary 97, 103, 120–121, 143, 210, 219
Coinage 29, 191
Colonies 29, 45, 71–72, 98, 123, 208, 231; 410; see also veteran settlement
Comes; comites 464, 468, 500, 502, 504; *comes litoris Saxonici* 469, 493
Comitatenses 455, 462–466, 467, 471, 499
Comitatus 455, 457
Comitia centuriata 21, 40, 43, 99
Comitia curiata 21, 39, 48
Commodus, Emperor 195–196
Concilium plebis 23
Consilium 288, 373, 376, 385
Constantine, Emperor 437–438, 462–464
Constitutio Antoniniana 198
Consuls; consulship 21–22, 45, 48–49, 81, 89, 96, 100–101, 110, 129, 139–141, 153, 170, 190
Contus 266, 267
Cornelius Scipio Aemilianus 102–103, 104, 121
Cornelius Scipio Africanus, Publius 93–94, 96, 100
Cornelius Sulla, Lucius 29, 124, 125–126, 128–133

Conicularii 295, 301

Dacian wars 192–193
Decebalus 192–193, 255
Decius, Emperor 203
Desertion 397, 399–400
Dictator, Dictatorship 22, 49, 51, 69, 89, 133, 164, 168, 171, 173
Diocletian, Emperor 434–437, 455–458, 460, 476–477
Diplomas 252, 425
Doctors, see medical services
Domitian. Emperor 191–192
Dromedarii, see camel riders
Dux; *duces* 437, 458, 464, 465, 467–468, 500, 502, 505
Dyrrachium 160, 164–166

Elagabalus, Emperor 199–200
Equestrians 27, 186–187; 195; 197; 211; 217; 243; 292–294; 450–451
Equites singulares 275; 283–284; 448
Etruscans 17; 19–21; 25; 33; 36; 46; 82–83
Exercise halls 265, 273
Exploitation 27, 30, 396, 419–420, 465
Exploratores 286, 374–375; see also *speculatores*
Extortion, see exploitation
Extraordinarii 76–77, 97, 110, 111

Flavius Constantius, *magister militum* 442, 466
Fleets, see naval forces
Foederati 472–473
Food supplies 306–307, 310–312, 401, 504–505
Formula togatorum 75
Forts; fortresses 322–335, 453, 456–457, 476–483, 488–497, plates 26–34
Franks 439, 442, 465, 468, 472
Frontiers 193, 194, 201, 248, 347–367, 431, 453, 455–456, 458–460, 467–469, 474–475; plates 35–37
Frumentarii 284–285, 418

Gallic Empire 431, 445, 447
Gallienus, Emperor 204, 217, 431–432, 445, 447–451
Gaul; Gauls 54–55, 63, 82, 87, 105–106, 141, 142–158
Gergovia 154–155, 159
Gladius 97, 110, 226–227, 237, 470
Gordian I and II, Emperors 201
Goths 202–203, 344, 434, 440–442, 451, 466
Gracchus, see Sempronius Gracchus, Gaius; Sempronius Gracchus, Tiberius
Granaries 327, plates 31–32
Guerrilla warfare 103, 382
Gyrus 264, 272, plate 19

Hadrian, Emperor 193–194, plate 6
Hadrian's Wall 358–362, plate 37
Hannibal 88–94
Helmets 34, 60, 110, 113, 114, 144, 227–228, 234–235, 249–250, 266, 268–269, 470
Helvetii 145–146
Hippika gymnasia 268–269
Honorius, Emperor 440–442
Honesta missio 229–231, 399, 401, 506–507; see also veterans
Hoplites 36–38, 42, 56–57, 214
Hoplon 36, 37

Horses, see cavalry horses
Huns 442

Interpreters 376

Jugurtha 118–119
Julian, Emperor 438–439, 465–466

Kings of Rome 18–20

Labienus, Titus 143, 147, 150, 154, 162, 164–165, 166, 169
Laeti 472, 501
Land bills 30, 31, 107–109, 139–140
Latins; Latin League 24, 49, 65–66, 70, 71–72
Leave 400–401, 505–506
Legates, of Republican generals 136, 143; of Emperors 185–186, 189, 289; legionary legates 209, 216, 291–292
Legions: phalanx legion 43–44; reorganisation under Augustus 206, 214–238; under Diocletian 457–458
Licinius, Emperor 437
Limitanei 467, 499
Lorica hamata 228, 266, 469–470
Lorica segmentata 228–229, 232, 233, 250, plates 9–10
Lorica squamata 228, 236, 471
Luca (Lucca) 148
Lucius Verus, Emperor 194

Macrinus, Emperor 198–199
Magister equitum 463–464, 499
Magister militum 463–464, 466, 473, 498–499, 502
Magister peditum 463–464
Mail armour, see *lorica hamata*
Maniples 56–57, 96–97, 103, 121, 214
Maps 314–316
Marcus Aurelius, Emperor 194–195
Marius, Gaius 29, 118–124, 128–130
Marriage of soldiers 197, 230–231, 404–406
Maxentius, Emperor 437
Maximianus, Emperor 435–437
Maximianus, Marcus Valerius, see Valerius Maximianus
Maximinus Thrax, Emperor 200, 201
Medical services 406–409, plate 12
Medicus veterinarius 260
Mithradates VI 128, 130, 137–139
Mulomedicus 260, 270
Munda 171

Naval forces 70, 73, 85–86, 136–137, 170, 195, 421–428, plates 13–14
Nero, Emperor 187–189
Nerva, Emperor 192
Numantia 103–104, 121–122
Numeri 285–287, plates 38–40

Oath, to Octavian 181; military 109, 206, 391
Octavius, Gaius; Octavian 171, 173–174, 185; see also Augustus
Odoacer, king of Italy 444, 473
Optio 110, 218
Order of march 377–381
Ornamenta triumphalia 290, 372

Palmyra 433–434, 445, 447
Parade armour, see sports armour
Parthia; Parthians 137, 172, 177–179, 193, 194, 197, 199, 200, 202; see also Persians
Pay (*stipendium*) 52, 69, 106, 109, 143–144, 209, 247, 302–304, 393–396, 504–505
Pay rises: Caesar 209; Domitian 191; Severus 197
Pensions 208, 231, 247
Persians 204, 434, 452
Pertinax, Emperor 196
Phalanx, see under hoplites
Pharsalus 166–167
Philip V of Macedon 91, 99–102
Philip the Arab, Emperor 202–203
Philippi 175–176
Pilum 60, 68, 97, 110, 116, 121–122, 144, 226, 233, 238, 250
Pirates 31, 136–137, 421–422
Plebs: secession 494 BC, 46–48
Policing 284–285, 416–418
Pompey the Great 31, 131–132, 133–141, 158, 162–167
Praefecti sociorum 76, 110, 128, 239–240
Praefectus Annonae 187, 200, 211, 301
Praefectus castrorum 210, 216, 216, 222
Praefectus Aegypti 211
Praefectus Vigilum 186–187, 211, 213
Praepositus 284, 286, 393, 416, 417, 472, 501, 505, 506
Praetorian Guard 186, 188, 192, 196, 197, 203, 211–212, 274–279, 498
Praetorian Prefects 186, 189, 190, 193, 197, 198, 200, 202, 211, 275, 277–279, 436–437, 441, 452, 504–505
Praetors 22, 27, 78, 96, 103, 170, 209
Primus pilus 143, 210, 213, 229
Probus, Emperor 434, 452–453
Proconsular power of emperors 186
Proconsulship 22–23, 31, 67, 81–82
Protectores 432, 450, 464, 498–499, 502
Provinces 26, 30, 188, 193, 210, 214–215, 289
Punic Wars, see Carthage
Punishments 398–399
Pyrrhus, king of Epirus 26, 81, 83–84, 97

Reconnaissance, or lack of 67, 95, 155
Recruitment; recruits 34, 106–109, 119, 125–126, 145, 195, 200, 223–225, 244–247, 297, 390–392, 471–473, 502–503
Rewards 298–299, 397–398
Roman citizenship 25, 66, 79–80; 109, 126–127, 198
Rufinus 441

Saddles 267–268
Samnites 25, 50, 55, 63–65, 66–68, 70, 81–83
Saxon Shore 435, 469, 490–493, plates 46–47
Scale armour, see *lorica squamata*
Scholae 463, 501–502
Scutum 56, 59–60, 64, 68, 110, 113, 114, 144, 227, 249
Sempronius Gracchus, Gaius, 108–109
Sempronius Gracchus, Tiberius 31, 108
Senate 27, 139, 158, 162, 174, 180, 185, 201
Senators 27–28, 188, 196, 198–199, 209, 217, 290–292, 450–451
Senior centurion, see *primus pilus*
'Servian reforms' 19, 38–44, 55

Severus, Emperor, 196– 198
Severus Alexander, Emperor 200–201
Shapur I, king of Persia 204
Shields, 266–268, 470; see also *clipeus*, *hoplon*, *scutum*
Sieges; blockades 103–104, 121–122, 154–156, 159, 160, 179, 340–344
Signals; signalling 386–389
Slaves 314
Social War 79–80, 126–127
Spain 87–88, 103–104, 107, 134–135, 163–164
Spatha 227, 237, 265, 470
Spears; in hoplite armies 36–37; auxiliary units 250, 265–266; see also *pilum*
Speculatores 375; see also *exploratores*
Sports armour, cavalry 267–268
Stabling 261–262, 271
Standards: eagle (*aquila*; *aquilifer*) 122, 144, 222, 302; *signum*; *signifer* 218, 222, 294; *imaginifer* 222; *vexillarius* 255; see also *aedes*
Stilicho 440, 466, 473
Stratores 258
Subsidies 192, 202, 363, 454
Sulla, see Cornelius Sulla, Lucius
Supplies 304–308, plates 21–22
Swords, see *gladius*; *spatha*

Tetrarchy 434–437, 455
Thapsus 161, 168–169
Theodosius the Great, Emperor 440
Theodosius II, Emperor 441–442
Tiberius, Emperor 187–189, 210
Timesitheus, Praetorian Prefect 202
Titus, Emperor 190–191
Training 95, 120, 164, 200, 262–265, 393
Trajan, Emperor 192–193, plate 5
Trebonianus Gallus, Emperor 203–204
Tribunes, military 49, 68–69, 109, 112, 116, 121, 143, 209–210, 216, 222, 291, 293, 384–385
Tribunes of the plebs 23, 28, 108–109, 123, 133, 135, 148
Tribunician power of emperors 186
Triumph 134, 290, 372; see also *ornamenta triumphalia*
Triumvirate; so-called First, 139; second 174–181

Urban Cohorts 212, 279–281

Valens, Emperor 439–440
Valentinian, Emperor 439
Valerian, Emperor 204
Valerius Maximianus, Marcus 195, 289–290
Veii 25, 35, 52–54, 55
Veneti 149
Vercingetorix 153–157
Vespasian, Emperor 189–191
Veteran settlement 123, 139–140, 170, 177–178, 206–209, 231
Veterans 229–231, 251–252, 506; see also diplomas; *honesta missio*
Veterinarius 260, 270
Vexillum 255
Vici 329, 411–414; see also *canabae*
Vigiles 186, 212–213, 281–282

Zenobia, Queen of Palmyra 433–434, 452